NOISE CONTROL

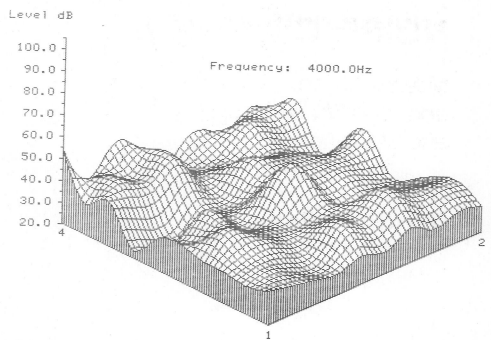

A Sound Intensity Plot (*Source:* Bruel & Kjaer Instruments, Inc.)

NOISE CONTROL

Measurement, Analysis, and Control of Sound and Vibration

Charles E. Wilson

New Jersey Institute of Technology

HARPER & ROW, PUBLISHERS, New York
Cambridge, Philadelphia, St. Louis, San Francisco,
London, Singapore, Sydney, Tokyo

1817

Sponsoring Editor: James Cook
Project Editor: David Nickol
Cover Design: Wanda Lubelska Design
Text Art: RDL Artset Ltd.
Production Manager: Jeanie Berke
Production Assistant: Beth Maglione
Compositor: TAPSCO, Inc.
Printer and Binder: R. R. Donnelley & Sons Company

NOISE CONTROL: Measurement, Analysis, and Control of Sound and Vibration

Copyright © 1989 by Harper & Row, Publishers, Inc.

Library of Congress Cataloging in Publication Data

Wilson, Charles E.
  Noise control: measurement, analysis, and control of sound and
vibration/Charles E. Wilson.
     p.   cm.
  Includes bibliographies and index.
  ISBN 0-06-047155-7
  1. Noise control.   2. Sound.   3. Vibration.   I. Title.
TD892.W55   1989
620.2′3—dc19   88-32135
                                                                      CIP

89   90   91   92   9   8   7   6   5   4   3   2   1

To Liz

CONTENTS

PREFACE

Noise control involves the reduction of energy that a noise source converts to sound power and the interruption of sound transmission paths. Noise control may require measurements and analysis of existing noise environments, prediction and modeling of noise environments, and specification of building elements to reduce noise transmission and reverberation. Vibration analysis, specification of machinery mountings, and redesign of machinery to reduce sound power are often necessary.

This book treats these and other essential topics in noise control, providing a theoretical background in those areas of acoustics that apply directly. Example problems are used throughout to relate basic physical laws to practical applications. Many of the example problems and exercises illustrate the use of personal computers for situations in which several design alternatives may be considered.

The book begins by introducing the terminology used in noise and vibration control and the basic theoretical relationships that describe wave propagation in solids and in air. Frequency bands, frequency weighting, sound pressure level, sound power level, and vector sound intensity are considered in Chapter 1.

Chapter 2 examines modeling of noise sources, room acoustics, and diffraction of sound due to barriers.

Instrument selection and measurement techniques are covered in Chapter 3. Topics include measurements using sound-level meters, real-time analyzers, fast Fourier transform analyzers with sound intensity probes, and other instrumentation for determination of sound level and sound power and for source location. Field and laboratory measurements are discussed, along with problems of calibration, accuracy, and data interpretation.

The hearing mechanism, audiometry, noise-induced hearing loss, and hearing conservation are discussed in Chapter 4. Noise exposure limits based on the Occupational Safety and Health Act and other exposure guidelines are examined.

Chapter 5 considers community noise assessment and control, with emphasis on descriptors and criteria identified by the Environmental Protection Agency. Building-design criteria for control of intrusive noise are treated in Chapter 6. Procedures using sound transmission class and shell isolation rating are used. In addition, the control of interior noise from appliances and mechanical systems is considered.

Industrial noise control is treated in Chapter 7. Impact noise and the noise production of various machine elements are considered in detail. General noise control procedures including mufflers and enclosures as well as specialized case studies are given.

Chapters 8 and 9 cover prediction and control of transportation noise, including control of noise sources by component modification. Procedures are given for formulating environmental impact statements. Aircraft certification measurements, aircraft noise prediction, and noise compatibility planning are covered.

Chapter 10 covers the aspects of vibration analysis and control that relate to noise control. Free and forced vibration are considered, with damping, resonance, transmissibility, and isolation. Applications include response to forces in machines, and the design and specification of shock mounts. Multidegree-of-freedom systems and continuous systems are analyzed. Finite-element analysis, random vibration and shock, and impact loading are among the topics considered. In addition, this chapter covers vibration and shock measurements, modal analysis, machinery monitoring, vibration signature, and human response to vibration.

In practice, noise problems are often multidimensional, involving several sources, transmission paths, and receivers. Considering the general availability of personal computers, computer-aided noise analysis and prediction methods are suggested wherever these methods can be effective. In addition to the multidimensional problems, there are many less complicated problems that may be solved with only a scientific calculator.

Most of this book may be covered in a three-credit-hour course given to engineering and science students in the third or fourth year or at the graduate level. Engineering professors tend to organize course material according to goals they have set for their students. After the basic material in the first two chapters has been covered, changes in the order of presentation and deletion of material should not cause difficulty for students. The problems utilize the mathematical abilities of a typical upper-division engineering or science student. Most professors teaching graduate courses supplement text coverage with topics related to their research or consulting work, and use material from current technical journals. The author has attempted to provide sufficient rigor and advanced topics to challenge graduate students and provide a basis for further study.

In practical disciplines such as noise control, interpretation of results is more important than simply obtaining problem solutions. When modeling physical phenomena in the real world, relationships are developed which have limits of applicability. It is the reader's responsibility to assess methods and formulas to determine their applicability in a particular situation. Although the reviewers, the publisher, and the author have made every attempt to ensure accuracy, errors invariably creep in. Corrections and suggestions are most welcome.

ACKNOWLEDGMENTS

I wish to express my appreciation to all who helped with this book. Many significant changes in the manuscript were incorporated at the urging of the reviewers who included: Yves H. Berthelot of the Georgia Institute of Technology, Malcolm J. Crocker of Auburn University, Thomas H. Hodgson of North Carolina State University, M. G. Prasad of Stevens Institute of Technology, and Rajendra Singh of Ohio State University.

In addition, I wish to thank Elliott H. Berger of the Cabot Corporation who reviewed the sections on hearing conservation; Susan Cuthbert and Jennifer Wilson who proofread portions of the manuscript; my students, friends and colleagues who made helpful suggestions; and the companies and agencies which provided photographs, tables, and other material.

Charles E. Wilson

CONSTANTS AND CONVERSION FACTORS

Common measurement units used in acoustics and noise control are based on the International System of Units (SI). However, plans for buildings, highways, and machinery often utilize customary U.S. units (English units).

Basic SI units include:

> Kilogram (kg)
> meter (m)
> radian (rad)
> second (s)

Derived SI units include:

> hertz (Hz) = cycles/s
> newton (N) = kg · m/s^2
> pascal (Pa) = N/m^2
> watt (W) = N · m/s

SI prefixes include:

> mega (M) = 10^6
> kilo (k) = 10^3
> milli (m) = 10^{-3}
> micro (μ) = 10^{-6}
> pico (p) = 10^{-12}

A detailed list of conversion factors is given by American Society for Testing and Materials, "Standard for metric practice," *Annual Book of ASTM Standards*, Sec. 14, Vol. 14.02, Philadelphia, 1986.

A few constants and conversion factors useful in noise control are given below:

reference intensity (0-dB sound intensity level) $\equiv$ 1 pW/m^2

reference power (0-dB sound power level) $\equiv$ 1 pW
(note: older references may use 10^{-13} W)

reference pressure (0-dB sound pressure level) $\equiv$ 20 μPa

To convert from	to	Multiply by
Atmosphere (standard)	Pa	$1.013\ 250 \times 10^5$
Day (mean solar)	s	$8.640\ 000 \times 10^4$
Degree	rad	$1.745\ 329 \times 10^{-2}$
Foot (ft)	m	$0.304\ 800\ 0$
ft^2	m^2	$9.290\ 304 \times 10^{-2}$
ft^3	m^3	$2.831\ 685 \times 10^{-2}$
Gravity (standard g)	m/s^2	$9.806\ 650$
Horsepower (hp)	W	$745.699\ 9$
Inch (in)	m	$2.540\ 000 \times 10^{-2}$
Mile (international)	km	$1.609\ 344$
Pound avoirdupoise (lb)	kg	$0.4535\ 924$
Pound force (lb or lbf)	N	$4.448\ 222$
lb/in	N/m	$175.126\ 8$
lb/in^2 (psi)	Pa	$6.894\ 757 \times 10^3$
lb/in^3	kg/m^3	$2.767\ 990 \times 10^4$
lb$\cdot$s/in (damping coefficient)	N$\cdot$s/m	$175.126\ 8$
lb$\cdot$s^2/in (mass)	kg	$175.126\ 8$
Slug (mass)	kg	$14.593\ 90$

To convert from	to	Use the equation
Celsius [$T'(°C)$]	kelvin (K)	$T(K) = T'(°C) + 273.15$
Fahrenheit [$t'(°F)$]	kelvin (K)	$T(K) = [t'(°F) + 459.67]/1.8$

NOTATION

(A partial list of the most commonly used symbols).

$$AI = \text{articulation index}$$
$$BW = \text{bandwidth}$$
$$c = \text{wave propagation velocity}$$
$$C = \text{damping coefficient; noise exposure time}$$
$$CL = \text{criterion level}$$
$$C(\tau) = \text{cepstrum}$$
$$dB = \text{decibel}$$
$$dBA = A\text{-weighted decibel}$$
$$DI = \text{directivity index}$$
$$D_\% = \text{noise dose}$$
$$e = \text{base of natural logarithms}$$
$$E = \text{elastic modulus; power of 10}$$
$$EPNL = \text{effective perceived noise level}$$
$$f = \text{frequency; function}$$
$$f^* = \text{critical frequency}$$
$$F = \text{force}$$
$$F_c = \text{crest factor}$$
$$FFT = \text{fast Fourier transform}$$
$$g = \text{acceleration of gravity}$$
$$I = \text{sound intensity}$$
$$\mathbf{I} = \text{vector sound intensity}$$
$$IL = \text{insertion loss}$$
$$j = (-1)^{1/2}$$
$$k = \text{wave number}$$
$$K = \text{a constant; spring rate}$$
$$KE = \text{kinetic energy}$$
$$lg = \text{common (base-ten) logarithm}$$
$$ln = \text{natural logarithm}$$
$$L = A\text{-weighted sound level}$$
$$L_c = C\text{-weighted sound level}$$
$$L_{DN} = \text{day–night sound level}$$
$$L_{eq} = \text{equivalent sound level}$$
$$L_I = \text{sound intensity level}$$
$$L_P = \text{sound pressure level}$$
$$L_W = \text{sound power level}$$
$$L_{10} = \text{sound level exceeded 10\% of a time interval}$$
$$M = \text{mass; mobility}$$

n = rotation speed
N = Fresnel number
NC = noise criteria
NEF = Noise exposure forecast
NIPTS = noise-induced permanent threshold shift
NR = noise rating
NRR = noise reduction rating
p = sound pressure
p_{rms} = root-mean-square sound pressure
PSIL = preferred speech interference level
PTS = permanent threshold shift
Q = directivity factor
r = position; radius
r_d = damping ratio
r_f = frequency ratio
R = room constant, gas constant
Re = real part of complex quantity
$R(\tau)$ = autocorrelation function
S = surface area
$S(\omega)$ = spectral density
SEL = sound exposure level
SIR = shell isolation rating
STC = sound transmission class
t = time, thickness
T = averaging time; allowable exposure time; absolute temperature
TL = transmission loss
TTS = temporary threshold shift
TWA = time-weighted average sound level
T_{60} = reverberation time
u = velocity in a continuous medium
v = velocity
W = sound power
x = location; displacement of a discrete mass
Z = logarithmic decrement; characteristic resistance; impedance
α = absorption coefficient
Δ = dilatation; difference in sound levels
ϵ = strain
ξ = particle displacement
θ = angle of incidence; angular coordinate
λ = wavelength
σ_{rad} = radiation efficiency
ρ = mass density
Σ = summation
τ = period; sound transmission coefficient
ϕ = phase angle, angular coordinate
ω = angular (circular) frequency
∇ = gradient
∇^2 = the Laplacian

NOISE CONTROL

Chapter 1

Basic Principles and Definitions

Sound ordinarily refers to audible pressure fluctuations in air. When a body moves through a medium or vibrates, some energy is transferred to that surrounding medium in the form of sound waves. Sound is also produced by turbulence in air and other fluids, and by fluids moving past stationary bodies. In general, sound may be transmitted by solids, liquids, and gases. The term *ultrasound* is used to refer to high-frequency sounds (frequencies above the audible range). *Infrasound* refers to low-frequency sounds (frequencies below the audible range).

Intentionally generated acoustic signals including speech and music are usually referred to as sound. *Noise* is a term used to identify unwanted sound, including random sound, and sound generated as a byproduct of other activities, including transportation and industrial operations. Intrusive sound, including speech and music unwelcome to the hearer, are also considered noise. Thus, the distinction between noise and sound can be subjective, and the two terms are often used interchangeably. Well-documented effects of noise include hearing damage, interference with communication, sleep interruption, and annoyance. References to noise are even found in myths and epics of 3500 to 4000 years ago. Fragments of one Babylonian tablet (Pritchard, 1969) tell us:

> The land bellowed like wild oxen.
> The god was disturbed by their wild uproar,
> ... heard their clamor ... said to the great gods:
> "oppressive has become the clamor of mankind ...
> by their uproar they prevent sleep ..."

Noise control may involve reduction of noise at the source, control of noise transmission paths, and protection of the receiver. Noise reduction through improved design of machinery is one effective means of noise control. In many instances, both airborne noise and solid-borne noise are significant. Interruption of noise transmission paths by means of vibration isolation and noise barriers is sometimes effective. In some industrial situations, excessive noise is still present after using all feasible controls of noise sources and transmission paths. In such cases, personal hearing protection devices (muff-type and insert-type hearing protectors) are used.

1.1 MECHANICAL VIBRATION

A few concepts common to mechanical vibration and sound are introduced at this point. Due to the important relationship between vibration control and the control of noise, vibration and vibration isolation are treated in detail in another chapter.

A One-Degree-of-Freedom Undamped System in Free Vibration

Consider a one-degree-of-freedom system in free vibration, Figure 1.1.1. This idealized system is made up of a massless spring supporting a rigid mass constrained to move in the x-direction only. Energy loss in the system is neglected. If the mass is displaced a distance x from the equilibrium position, the spring exerts a force of $-kx$. Acceleration of the mass, d^2x/dt^2, results in an inertia force (reversed effective force) of $-M\,d^2x/dt^2$. Equilibrium of forces (including the inertia force) yields

$$M\frac{d^2x}{dt^2} + Kx = 0 \tag{1.1.1}$$

where x = displacement (in or m)
           M = mass (lb s^2/in or kg)
           K = spring rate (lb/in or N/m)
            t = time (s)

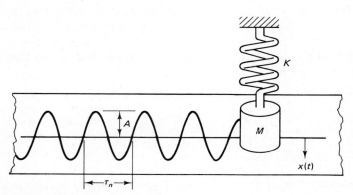

Figure 1.1.1 Vibrating system.

It can be shown by direct substitution that the above differential equation is satisfied by a displacement function in the form

$$x = C_1 \cos(\omega_n t) + C_2 \sin(\omega_n t) \qquad (1.1.2)$$

where C_1 and C_2 are arbitrary constants that depend on initial conditions, and

$$\omega_n = \left(\frac{K}{M}\right)^{1/2} \qquad (1.1.3)$$

the natural angular frequency of vibration (rad/s).

If the initial conditions are given by $x(0) = X_0$, the initial displacement, and $dx/dt(0) = V(0)$, the initial velocity, then the arbitrary constants are $C_1 = X_0$ and $C_2 = V_0/\omega_n$ and the displacement equation becomes

$$x = X_0 \cos(\omega_n t) + \frac{V_0}{\omega_n} \sin(\omega_n t) \qquad (1.1.4)$$

Natural Frequency and Period Imagine a strip chart moving at constant speed to the left as the mass vibrates (Figure 1.1.1). Examining the above equation, we see that a pen attached to the mass would trace a sinusoid on the strip chart. The amplitude of the sinusoidal vibration is

$$A = \left[X_0^2 + \left(\frac{V_0}{\omega_n}\right)^2\right]^{1/2} \qquad (1.1.5)$$

It can be seen that the displacement function repeats itself when

$$\omega_n t = 2\pi, 4\pi, \text{ and so forth}$$

from which the natural period of vibration, τ_n (s) is given by

$$\tau_n = \frac{2\pi}{\omega_n} = 2\pi\left(\frac{M}{K}\right)^{1/2} \qquad (1.1.6)$$

The natural frequency f_n is the reciprocal of the natural period,

$$f_n = 1/\tau_n = \frac{\omega_n}{2\pi} = \frac{(K/M)^{1/2}}{2\pi} \qquad (1.1.7)$$

where f_n is expressed in cycles per second or Hertz (Hz).

Continuous Systems

Displacement of a one-degree-of-freedom system is a function of the single independent variable, time. Sound waves in air and vibrations in a continuous mechanical system are described in terms of two or more independent variables, time and location.

The One-Dimensional Wave Equation Let us consider longitudinal vibration of a slender rod of constant cross-sectional area A (Figure 1.1.2). Let the x-coordinate lie

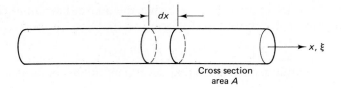

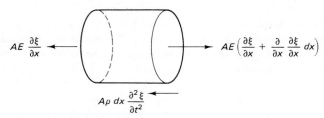

Figure 1.1.2   Wave propagation in a slender rod.

along the rod, and identify displacement along the *x*-axis as $\xi = \xi(x, t)$, a function of location and time. Then, longitudinal strain at any location in the rod is given by

$$\epsilon_x = \frac{\partial \xi}{\partial x} \tag{1.1.8}$$

For small displacements, it is ordinarily assumed that the stress–strain relationship is linear. Then, Hooke's law applies, and the tensile force across the rod cross section is $AE\epsilon_x$ where E is the elastic modulus (Young's modulus).

Consider an infinitesimal element of length dx. Dynamic equilibrium of tensile forces on both ends of the element, and the inertia force (reversed effective force) yields

$$AE\frac{\partial \xi}{\partial x} + \frac{\partial}{\partial x}\left(AE\frac{\partial \xi}{\partial x}\right)dx - AE\frac{\partial \xi}{\partial x} - A\,dx\rho\frac{\partial^2 \xi}{\partial t^2} = 0$$

where ρ = mass density and energy losses are neglected. Since the cross section of the rod is constant, the above equation reduces to

$$\frac{\partial^2 \xi}{\partial t^2} = c^2 \frac{\partial^2 \xi}{\partial x^2} \tag{1.1.9}$$

where

$$c = \left(\frac{E}{\rho}\right)^{1/2} = \text{the wave propagation velocity}$$

Equation 1.1.9 is the one-dimensional wave equation. An equation in similar form describes plane waves in fluids (including airborne sound).

The general solution to the one-dimensional wave equation is

$$\xi = F_1(x - ct) + F_2(x + ct) \tag{1.1.10}$$

where $\xi = \xi(x, t)$ = displacement in the x-direction, and F_1 and F_2 are arbitrary. We see by examination of the form of equation 1.1.10 that two waves or wave systems are represented, each traveling at velocity c. The first term on the right represents a wave or wave system traveling in the $+x$-direction; the second term represents a wave or wave system traveling in the $-x$-direction. This solution, which was published by d'Alembert in 1747 (Lamb, 1925) can be verified by substitution in the wave equation.

Wavelength, Wavenumber, Wave Propagation Velocity and Frequency In the study of forced vibrations, the steady-state response is often of greatest interest. Steady-state response neglects transients which die out quickly in most actual systems. Suppose one end of a semi-infinite slender rod is subject to a steady-state axial harmonic vibratory displacement resulting in a wave traveling to the right (the $+x$-direction) and described by

$$\xi = \xi_0 \cos[k(x - ct)]$$

where
ξ_0 = displacement amplitude (m)
$c = (E/\rho)^{1/2}$ = the propagation velocity of axial waves in the rod (m/s)
$k = \omega/c$ = the wave number (rad/m)
ω = the angular frequency of vibration (rad/s)

For the above case, at a particular instant $t = T_1$, the displacement is described by a sinusoid in x:

$$\xi(x, T_1) = \xi_0 \cos[k(x - cT_1)]$$

If displacements could be measured at this instant, a plot of axial displacement against axial location would appear as in Figure 1.1.3. The function repeats its value whenever kx increases by 2π rad, an increase in x of

$$\lambda = \frac{2\pi}{k} = \frac{2\pi c}{\omega} = \frac{c}{f} \tag{1.1.11}$$

where
λ = wavelength (m)
$f = \omega/2\pi$ = vibration frequency (Hz), the time rate at which the function repeats its value at a given location on the rod

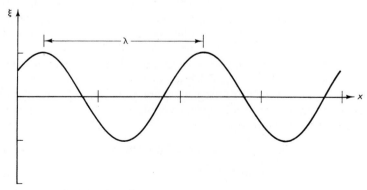

Figure 1.1.3 Wavelength.

EXAMPLE PROBLEM: WAVE PROPAGATION IN A ROD

Find the propagation velocity for axial waves in a steel rod.

Solution. For steel with an elastic modulus $E = 207,000$ MPa and mass density $\rho = 7830$ kg/m^3, the wave propagation velocity is found to be

$$c = \left(\frac{E}{\rho}\right)^{1/2} = \left(\frac{207 \times 10^9}{7830}\right)^{1/2} = 5142 \text{ m/s}$$

The units in the above equation must, of course, be consistent, noting the relationship between force and mass. The result applies only to longitudinal vibration of a slender rod. Transverse waves propagate at a different velocity.

1.2 SOUND WAVES IN AIR

As noted earlier, sound may be produced by mechanical vibration, motion of a body through air or other fluid, motion of a fluid past a stationary body, and fluid turbulence. In general, airborne sound waves may be subject to reflection, diffraction, absorption, dispersion, and other phenomena. Thus, the study of sound utilizes principles of various branches of engineering and science, including solid mechanics, fluid mechanics, thermodynamics, and optics.

Linearity was assumed when deriving the wave equation for longitudinal vibration in Section 1.1. Linearity will also be assumed when describing typical airborne sounds. However, it is sometimes necessary to take nonlinear effects into account when examining high-intensity jet noise, sonic booms, and large amplitude vibrations. Papers discussing problems in nonlinear acoustics and macrosonics appear regularly in the *Journal of the Acoustical Society of America.*

Plane Waves

A plane wave is a special case in which the sound pressure and other acoustic variables are functions of only one spatial coordinate, say the x-coordinate. The behavior of plane sound waves is similar to that of axial vibrations in the slender rod considered above. Sound waves in a straight duct of uniform cross section may resemble plane waves.

Consider a plane pressure wave in air such that the wave propagates in the $+x$-direction and sound pressure and other acoustic variables are constant, at any instant, over any plane perpendicular to the x-axis. Let the following variables refer to a plane of particles (i.e., molecules of nitrogen, oxygen, water vapor, etc., which make up air) whose equilibrium position is x:

ξ = displacement of a particle from the equilibrium position (m)

p_a = absolute pressure (Pa)

ρ = mass density (kg/m^3)

where the values in undisturbed air are

$$p_0 = \text{ambient pressure}$$

$$\rho_0 = \text{ambient mass density}$$

Let us observe a particular set of particles of air, a layer of air that, when in its equilibrium position, has thickness dx and is bounded by planes x and $x + dx$. This same set of particles will be bounded by planes $x + \xi$ and $x + \xi + dx + (\partial\xi/\partial x)dx$ and have thickness $dx + (\partial\xi/\partial x)dx$ at time t in the presence of a plane wave. The ratio of volume change to original volume (called the dilatation) is equal to the ratio of thickness change to original thickness in the plane-wave case. Thus, we have

$$\Delta = \frac{v_s - v_{so}}{v_{so}} = \frac{dx + (\partial\xi/\partial x)dx - dx}{dx} = \frac{\partial\xi}{\partial x} \qquad (1.2.1)$$

where $\quad \Delta$ = the dilatation
$\quad\quad v_s$ = the specific volume (m³/kg)
$\quad\quad v_{so}$ = original specific volume

The ratio of density change to original density (called the condensation) is given by

$$s = \frac{\rho - \rho_0}{\rho_0} \qquad \text{from which} \quad \rho = \rho_0(1 + s) \qquad (1.2.2)$$

where s = the condensation. Noting that specific volume and mass density are reciprocals of one another, we have

$$v_s = v_{so}(1 + \Delta) = \frac{1}{\rho} = \frac{1}{\rho_0(1 + s)}$$

which reduces to

$$s + \Delta + s\Delta = 0$$

Sound waves encountered in everyday life produce relatively small pressure disturbances in air. Thus,

$$|s| \ll 1, \qquad |\Delta| \ll 1$$

and the higher-order term $s\Delta$ may be neglected. Using equation 1.2.1, the result is

$$s = -\Delta = -\frac{\partial\xi}{\partial x} \qquad (1.2.3)$$

The Wave Equation for Airborne Sound

Inertial forces must balance forces resulting from a pressure differential across the layer of air under consideration. Taking a unit area, the result is

$$\rho_0\, dx\, \frac{\partial^2\xi}{\partial t^2} = -\left(\frac{\partial p_a}{\partial x}\right)dx \qquad (1.2.4)$$

Pressure and specific volume are related by

$$p_a v_s^\gamma = \text{constant} = p_0 v_{so}^\gamma \tag{1.2.5}$$

where $\gamma = 1.4$ (approximately) for adiabatic expansion
        = the ratio of the specific heat for air at constant pressure to that at constant
        volume

Using the relationships between specific volume, density, and condensation, we have

$$p_a = p_0 \left(\frac{v_{so}}{v_s}\right)^\gamma = p_0 \left(\frac{\rho}{\rho_0}\right)^\gamma = p_0(1 + s)^\gamma = p_0(1 + \gamma s) \tag{1.2.6}$$

where it is assumed that disturbances are small ($|s| \ll 1$) and only the first two terms
are retained of a binomial expansion of $(1 + s)^\gamma$. Substituting equation 1.2.6 in 1.2.4
and simplifying, the result is

$$\rho_0 \frac{\partial^2 \xi}{\partial t^2} = -p_0 \gamma \frac{\partial s}{\partial x} \tag{1.2.7}$$

Using equation 1.2.3 in the above result, we have the one-dimensional wave equation

$$\frac{\partial^2 \xi}{\partial t^2} = c^2 \frac{\partial^2 \xi}{\partial x^2} \tag{1.2.8}$$

where

$$c = \left(\frac{\gamma p_0}{\rho_0}\right)^{1/2} \tag{1.2.9}$$

the propagation velocity of airborne sound waves. The wave equation can also be
expressed in terms of pressure. In one dimension, the relationship is

$$\frac{\partial^2 p}{\partial t^2} = c^2 \frac{\partial^2 p}{\partial x^2} \tag{1.2.10}$$

and in three dimensions

$$\frac{\partial^2 p}{\partial t^2} = c^2 \nabla^2 p \tag{1.2.11}$$

where $\nabla^2 = \dfrac{\partial^2}{\partial x^2} + \dfrac{\partial^2}{\partial y^2} + \dfrac{\partial^2}{\partial z^2}$, the Laplacian

EXAMPLE PROBLEM: AIRBORNE SOUND PROPAGATION VELOCITY

Find the speed of sound in air as a function of ambient temperature. Base the results
on the properties of dry air at sea level.

Solution. Since air behaves approximately as an ideal gas at ordinary temperatures and pressures, we have

$$p_0 = \rho_0 R T \tag{1.2.12}$$

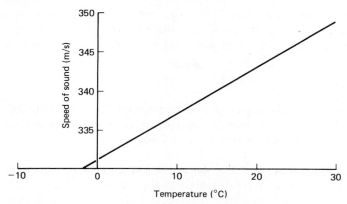

Figure 1.2.1 The speed of sound in dry air versus temperature.

where R is the gas constant and T the absolute temperature. Substituting in equation 1.2.9, the result is

$$c = \sqrt{\gamma R T} \qquad (1.2.13)$$

The gas constant $R = 287 \ \text{N} \cdot \text{m/(kg} \cdot \text{K)}$ for air. The ratio of specific heats, $\gamma = 1.4$ for air, will be considered constant since its value is little affected by temperature changes in the range of interest. Temperature T' in degrees Celsius is added to 273.16 to obtain absolute temperature T in kelvins. Thus, the speed of sound in dry air is given by

$$c = 20.04(T' + 273.16)^{1/2} \qquad (1.2.14)$$

where c = the propagation velocity of sound in dry air at sea level (m/s)
T' = temperature (°C)

A personal computer was used to produce a plot of c versus T' (Figure 1.2.1). The presence of water vapor would cause a slight increase in the speed of sound.

1.3 SOLUTIONS TO THE WAVE EQUATION FOR AIRBORNE SOUND

The general solution to the one-dimensional wave equation for airborne sound is

$$p = F_1(x - ct) + F_2(x + ct) \qquad (1.3.1)$$

where p = sound pressure = instantaneous pressure less ambient pressure (Pa)
F_1 and F_2 = arbitrary functions
x = location (m)
c = wave propagation velocity (m/s)
t = time (s)

The first term on the right of equation 1.3.1 represents a forward-traveling wave, a pressure wave or wave system traveling in the $+x$-direction. The second term on the right represents a pressure wave or wave system traveling in the $-x$-direction.

Pure-Tone Sound Waves

A pure tone is a single-frequency sinusoidal pressure function. Although noise is ordinarily made up of many frequency components, an examination of pure-tone sound waves is useful in the analysis and control of noise.

Wavenumber, Frequency, and Wavelength of Airborne Sound   Consider a forward-traveling pure-tone sound wave described by the following equation:

$$p = P \cos[k(x - ct)] \tag{1.3.2}$$

where p = instantaneous sound pressure (Pa)
P = sound pressure amplitude (Pa)
k = wavenumber (rad/m)

The wavenumber is related to the frequency of the sound wave by

$$k = \frac{\omega}{c} \tag{1.3.3}$$

where ω = angular frequency (rad/s) = $2\pi f$
f = frequency (Hz)

The range of audible frequencies, that is, the range of normal human hearing, is approximately 20 Hz to 20 kHz.

Wavelength is related to frequency by

$$\lambda = \frac{c}{f} \tag{1.3.4}$$

where λ = wavelength (m). An observer at a fixed location would detect the tone or frequency of a sound wave. If the sound pressure of a pure-tone sound wave was plotted against distance at a given instant, then the wave would repeat itself whenever x increased by the wavelength λ. Figure 1.3.1 shows a forward-traveling pure-tone sound wave of the form

$$p = P \cos[k(x - ct)]$$

observed at times $t = 0$ (solid curve), $t = \tau/8$ (short dashes), $t = \tau/4$ (long dashes), where τ = the period (s) = $1/f = 2\pi/\omega$.

At this point, we may examine the assumption that sound waves in air are characterized by adiabatic expansions and contractions. Newton, in 1726, assumed an isothermal process, that is, he assumed $p_a v_s$ = a constant (Lamb, 1925). This assumption resulted in a discrepancy between the calculated speed of sound and the value obtained by measuring the time for the sound of a distant event to reach an observer. The problem was resolved about 80 years later by Laplace and Poisson who assumed an adiabatic relationship. It is known that the speed of a thermal diffusion wave at 1000 Hz is about 0.5 m/s under normal atmospheric conditions (Beranek,

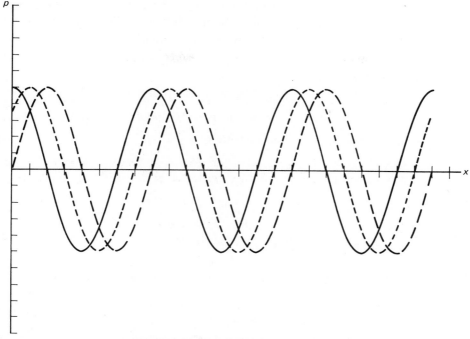

Figure 1.3.1 Forward-traveling pure-tone sound wave.

1954). The time interval between compression and expansion of a 1000-Hz sound wave is one-half period or $(1/1000)/2 = 1/2000$ s, during which time the thermal wave would travel about 0.25 mm. At 20°C, the speed of sound (the wave propagation velocity) is

$$c = 20.04(T' + 273.16)^{1/2} = 343 \text{ m/s}$$

and the wavelength of a 1000-Hz sound wave is

$$\lambda = \frac{c}{f} = \frac{343}{1000} = 0.343 \text{ m} = 343 \text{ mm}$$

Comparing a half-wavelength (about 171 mm) with the thermal wave progress, we can conclude that the heat exchange between compression and expansion is negligible. Thus, the assumption of an adiabatic process is valid.

1.4 ROOT-MEAN-SQUARE SOUND PRESSURE AND SOUND PRESSURE LEVEL

As noted above, sound pressure is the difference between instantaneous absolute pressure and ambient pressure. Mean-square sound pressure is given by

$$p_{\text{rms}}^2 = \frac{1}{T} \int_0^T p^2 \, dt \tag{1.4.1}$$

where $p = p(t)$ = sound pressure (Pa)
p_{rms}^2 = mean-square sound pressure
p_{rms} = root-mean-square sound pressure

If the sound wave is a pure tone, averaging time T may be one period or any integer number of periods.

For a forward-traveling pure-tone sound wave described by

$$p = P \cos[k(x - ct)]$$

the mean-square sound pressure is given by

$$p_{rms}^2 = \frac{P^2}{T} \int_0^\tau \cos^2[k(x - ct)]dt$$

$$= \frac{P^2}{T} \int_0^{2\pi/\omega} \cos^2(kx - \omega t)dt = \frac{P^2}{2}$$

where $\tau = 1/f = 2\pi/\omega$ = one period. Thus,

$$p_{rms} = \frac{P}{2^{1/2}} \tag{1.4.2}$$

where P is the amplitude of the pure-tone sound wave. Note that equation 1.4.2 applies to sinusoidal waveforms. A problem at the end of this chapter illustrates how other waveforms may produce a different relationship.

In typical measurement situations, noise is averaged over a time interval long enough to include several periods of all frequencies of interest. Thus, the contribution of partial periods does not significantly affect the average.

The Decibel Scale

The quietest audible sound, that is, the threshold of human hearing, corresponds to a root-mean-square sound pressure of about 20×10^{-6} Pa (20 μPa). A root-mean-square sound pressure of 200 Pa is the approximate threshold of pain. Because of the wide range of sound pressures of interest, it is customary to report sound measurements in decibels (dB). A decibel level is defined as ten times the base-ten logarithm of a power ratio. It will be demonstrated in a later section that sound power is proportional to mean-square sound pressure. Sound pressure level is defined as follows in terms of mean-square and root-mean-square sound pressure:

$$L_P = 10 \lg\left(\frac{p_{rms}^2}{p_{ref}^2}\right) = 20 \lg\left(\frac{p_{rms}}{p_{ref}}\right) \tag{1.4.3}$$

where L_P = sound pressure level (dB)
lg = common (base-ten) logarithm
$p_{ref} = 20 \times 10^{-6}$ Pa = the reference pressure

It can be seen that the reference pressure (the nominal threshold of hearing) is equivalent to a sound pressure level of 0 dB. A doubling of mean-square sound pressure corresponds to approximately 3-dB increase in sound pressure level. To find sound pressure when sound pressure level is given, we may rewrite equation 1.4.3 to obtain

$$\frac{p_{rms}}{p_{ref}} = 10^{L_P/20} \tag{1.4.4}$$

$$p_{rms} = 20 \times 10^{(L_P/20)-6} = 2 \times 10^{(L_P-100)/20} \tag{1.4.5}$$

EXAMPLE PROBLEM: SOUND PRESSURE

Determine the sound pressure corresponding to a sound pressure level of 90 dB. Compare the sound pressure with atmospheric pressure.

Solution. The root-mean-square sound pressure is given by

$$p_{rms} = 2 \times 10^{(L_P-100)/20} = 2 \times 10^{(90-100)/20} = 0.632 \text{ Pa}$$

In the case of a pure tone,

$$p_{rms} = \frac{P}{2^{1/2}}$$

from which the sound pressure amplitude is given by

$$P = 2^{1/2}p_{rms} = 2^{1/2} \times 0.632 = 0.894 \text{ Pa}$$

The standard atmosphere is defined as an absolute pressure of 101,325 Pa. Thus, the sound pressure corresponding to a pure tone of 90-dB sound pressure level (a relatively loud sound) is less than 1/100,000th of atmospheric pressure.

Audible Sound, Music, and Speech

Figure 1.4.1 shows the approximate envelope of audible sound on a sound pressure level versus frequency plot. Note that the threshold of hearing is frequency dependent; human hearing is most sensitive in the 500-Hz to 5-kHz frequency range. Upper limits of sound levels are sometimes set on the basis of hearing damage risk, the threshold of pain, or the threshold of feeling. In Figure 1.4.1, the upper bound of the audible sound range is arbitrarily shown as the threshold of feeling. A music envelope and a speech envelope are also shown on the sound pressure level versus frequency plot. These ranges represent average conditions. Sound pressure levels and frequencies outside of the given ranges are also possible. The characteristics of human hearing are such that the perception of sound is not proportional to sound pressure. An average individual perceives an increase in sound level of about 10 dB as a doubling in loudness.

1.5 CORRELATED AND UNCORRELATED SOUND

Correlated sound waves have a precise time and frequency relationship. Correlated sound waves can occur as a result of reflections. When two pure-tone sounds occur

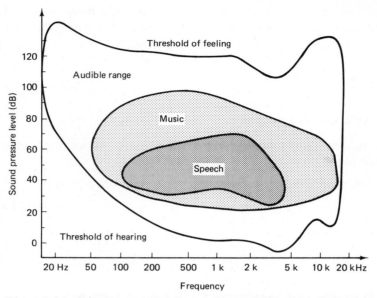

Figure 1.4.1 Sound pressure level versus frequency for the audible range, typical music range, and range of speech. (*Source:* Courtesy of Bruel & Kjaer Instruments, Inc.)

at the same time, the combined effect depends on the phase relationship at the receiver. Consider two sound waves described (at a point in space) by

$$p_1 = P_1 \cos(\omega_1 t + \phi_1) \tag{1.5.1}$$

and

$$p_2 = P_2 \cos(\omega_2 t + \phi_2) \tag{1.5.2}$$

where p = instantaneous sound pressure
        P = sound pressure amplitude
        ω = angular frequency
        ϕ = phase angle

As an alternative, the pure-tone sound waves may be defined in terms of the real part of a complex exponential function as follows:

$$p_1 = \mathrm{Re} P_1 e^{(j)(\omega_1 t + \phi_1)} \tag{1.5.3}$$

$$p_2 = \mathrm{Re} P_2 e^{(j)(\omega_2 t + \phi_2)} \tag{1.5.4}$$

The instantaneous sound pressure due to the two waves is given by the sum of the two instantaneous sound pressures. Mean-square sound pressure of the combined waves is given by

$$p_{\mathrm{rms}}^2 = \frac{1}{T} \int_0^T (p_1 + p_2)^2 \, dt \tag{1.5.5}$$

where T = averaging time = an integer number of periods at both frequencies. In actual measurements, averaging time should include many periods so that any contribution from fractional periods is insignificant. This condition is satisfied if

$$T \gg \frac{1}{f_{min}}$$

where f_{min} is the lower frequency. The form of the two sound waves as given in equations 1.5.1 and 1.5.2 or 1.5.3 and 1.5.4 is substituted in the above equation to obtain the mean square pressure of the combined sound. After integrating (a table of definite integrals may be helpful here), we obtain

$$p_{rms}^2 = \begin{cases} (P_1^2 + P_2^2)/2 = p_{rms1}^2 + p_{rms2}^2 & \text{for} \quad \omega_1 \neq \omega_2 \\ (P_1^2 + P_2^2)/2 + P_1 P_2 \cos(\phi_1 - \phi_2) & \text{for} \quad \omega_1 = \omega_2 \end{cases} \quad (1.5.6)$$

EXAMPLE PROBLEM: COMBINED SOUNDS

(a) Determine the effect of combining two 3-kHz signals that are in phase at the receiver. Each has a sound pressure level of 50 dB.

Solution. Using equation 1.5.6 for sound waves of the same frequency, the mean-square sound pressure is given by

$$p_{rms}^2 = P_1^2 + P_1^2 \cos 0 = 2P_1^2 = 4p_{rms1}^2$$

The increase in sound pressure level due to adding an identical in-phase pure tone is given by

$$L_P - L_{P1} = 10 \lg\left(\frac{p_{rms}^2}{p_{ref}^2}\right) - 10 \lg\left(\frac{p_{rms1}^2}{p_{ref}^2}\right)$$

$$= 10 \lg\left(\frac{4p_{rms1}^2}{p_{rms1}^2}\right) = 10 \lg 4$$

or about 6 dB. The result is a 3-kHz 56-dB signal.

It can be seen from the above example that the root-mean-square sound pressure is doubled by adding two identical pure tones if they are in phase. If the amplitudes and frequencies are equal, but the phase angles differ by 180° (π rad) at the observer, then the sound pressure would theoretically be zero at the observer. The reactive muffler uses this principle in an attempt to cancel sound waves. Design for optimum muffler performance will be considered in a later section.

EXAMPLE PROBLEM (Continued)

(b) Determine the effect of adding a 1000-Hz 50-dB sound wave to a 1100-Hz 50-dB sound wave. Plot pressure versus time for the resulting wave.

Solution. Since the frequencies are unequal, the mean-square sound pressure is double that of one wave. Thus, the sound pressure level is increased by

$$10 \lg\left(\frac{p_{rms}^2}{p_{rms1}^2}\right) = 10 \lg 2 = 3 \text{ (approximately)}$$

The combined sound level is 53 dB. The pressure–time relationship may be examined by visualizing the complex exponentials of equations 1.5.3 and 1.5.4 as rotating vectors (Figure 1.5.1). Arbitrarily, let time $t = 0$ at the instant that both vectors lie along the positive real axis, resulting in maximum sound pressure. The two vectors will be opposed along the real axis when $(\omega_2 - \omega_1)t = \pi$ and again additive along the real axis when $(\omega_2 - \omega_1)t = 2\pi$. Thus, the envelope of the pressure–time curve has a period $\tau_{\text{envelope}} = 2\pi/(\omega_2 - \omega_1) = 1/(f_2 - f_1)$.

The corresponding frequency, $f_2 - f_1$, is called the beat frequency. In this example, the beat frequency is $f_{\text{BEAT}} = f_2 - f_1 = 1100 - 1000 = 100$ Hz. A plot of total sound pressure is generated using a computer (see Figure 1.5.2). Maximum amplitude is 0.0179 Pa and the total length of the plot represents 0.020 s. It can be seen that the sound waves alternately reinforce and cancel at the 100-Hz beat frequency. The relationship between mean-square sound pressure and instantaneous sound pressure is given by equation 1.4.1 where $T = \tau_{\text{envelope}}$. Equation 1.4.2 does not apply since the combined wave is not a pure tone.

EXAMPLE PROBLEM: THE EFFECT OF PHASE ANGLE

A sound source produces a 500-Hz pure tone with 0.0894-Pa peak sound pressure at a receiver 10 m from the source. Another 500-Hz source, in phase with the first, is situated 10.1 m from the receiver and it can also produce 0.0894-Pa peak sound pressure at the receiver. Describe the sound at the receiver when both sources are operating and the air temperature is 21°C. Assume a free field (no reflections) and that no other significant sources are present.

Solution. At 21°C, the approximate speed of sound propagation in air is $c = 344$ m/s. For a 500-Hz tone, the wavelength

$$\lambda = \frac{c}{f} = \frac{344}{500} = 0.688 \text{ m}$$

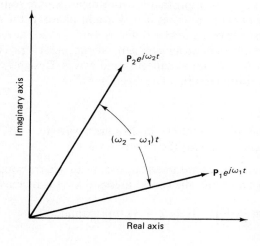

Figure 1.5.1 Complex exponentials represented as rotating vectors.

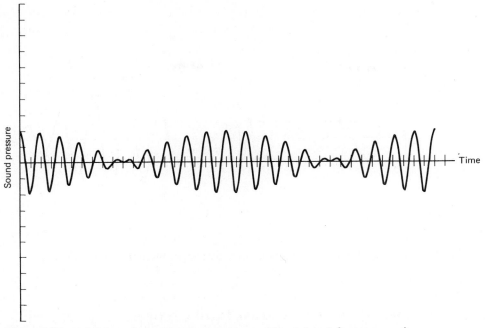

Figure 1.5.2 Addition of pure-tone sound waves with a 1.1 to 1 frequency ratio.

The path of the first sound wave is 0.1 m shorter and it leads the second by 0.1/0.688 = 0.1453 wavelengths. A wavelength represents a complete pressure cycle. Multiplying 0.1453 wavelength by 2π rad, we find the first wave leads the second by a phase angle of 0.9133 rad. The two sound waves combine to produce a 500-Hz sound wave with the mean-square sound pressure at the receiver given by

$$p_{rms}^2 = \frac{P_1^2}{2} + \frac{P_2^2}{2} + P_1 P_2 \cos(\phi_1 - \phi_2)$$

$$= \frac{0.0894^2}{2} + \frac{0.0894^2}{2} + 0.0894 \times 0.0894 \cos(0.9133 \text{ rad})$$

$$= 0.01288 \text{ Pa}^2$$

Most of the community noise and industrial noise problems that we experience represent a combination of many uncorrelated sources. There may be random variations in amplitude and frequency as in Figure 1.5.3. For uncorrelated noise sources, the first of equations 1.5.6 applies. Thus total mean-square sound pressure is simply the sum of the component source mean-square pressures for uncorrelated noise sources. Since most noise sources we will deal with are uncorrelated, we will assume sources to be uncorrelated unless there is reason to believe otherwise.

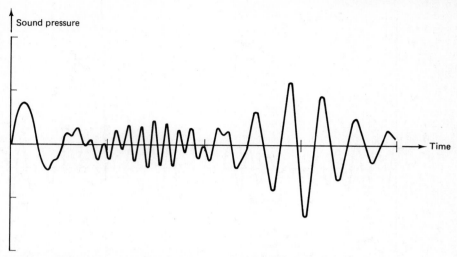

Figure 1.5.3 Noise with random variations in amplitude and frequency.

EXAMPLE PROBLEM: COMBINING NOISE FROM UNCORRELATED SOURCES

Construct a chart for determining total sound pressure level due to contributions from two uncorrelated sources.

Solution. Let the two contributions to total noise be $p_{\text{rms}1}$ and $p_{\text{rms}2}$ corresponding to sound pressure levels L_{P1} and L_{P2} where $L_{P2} = L_{P1} - \Delta$. Total mean-square sound pressure is given by the sum of the individual contributions in the case of uncorrelated sources, and total sound pressure level is given by

$$L_{PT} = 10 \lg[(p_{\text{rms}1}^2 + p_{\text{rms}2}^2)/p_{\text{ref}}^2]$$

$$= 10 \lg(10^{L_{P1}/10} + 10^{L_{P2}/10})$$

$$= 10 \lg(10^{L_{P1}/10} + 10^{(L_{P1}-\Delta)/10})$$

$$= 10 \lg[10^{L_{P1}/10}(1 + 10^{-\Delta/10})]$$

$$= L_{P1} + 10 \lg(1 + 10^{-\Delta/10})$$

where L_{PT} = combined sound pressure level due to both sources
L_{P1} = the greater of the two sound level contributions
Δ = the difference between the two contributions, all in dB

A personal computer was used to plot the quantity $10 \lg(1 + 10^{-\Delta/10})$ against the difference in sound pressure levels Δ (Figure 1.5.4). This quantity is to be added to the higher of the two levels to obtain total sound pressure level. Note that when one of the sound pressure levels is 10 or more decibels below the other, its effect on the total is less than $\frac{1}{2}$ dB.

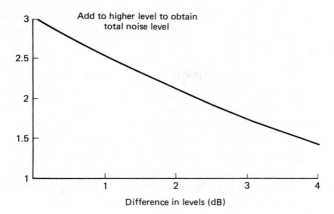

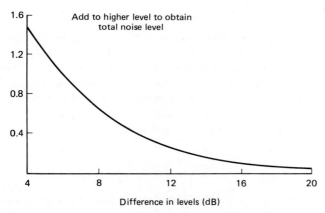

Figure 1.5.4 Combining levels of uncorrelated sound.

1.6 FREQUENCY ANALYSIS

An example in the above section involved combining pure-tone sound waves of different frequencies. Frequency analysis is the reverse process, an attempt to describe sound or vibration in terms of contributions at various frequencies. A known periodic function can be described by a Fourier series in sine–cosine or complex exponential form as follows:

$$F(t) = A_0 + \sum_{i=1}^{\infty} [A_i \cos(i\omega t) + B_i \sin(i\omega t)] \quad \text{or}$$

$$F(t) = \sum_{i=-\infty}^{\infty} C_i e^{ji\omega t} \qquad (1.6.1)$$

Application of Fourier series to vibration problems and determination of the coefficients are described in Chapter 10.

Broadband noise contains sound energy distributed continuously over a wide frequency range. Community noise and industrial noise are made up of contributions from many sources, and may contain sound pressure waves with frequencies across the entire audible range. The sound pressure level of broadband noise can be measured in a series of frequency intervals called frequency bands. Although constant bandwidths are sometimes selected, octave and fractional (percent) octave bands are most common in noise measurement. One reason for this choice is that a one-octave change in frequency anywhere within the audible range has about the same auditory significance. The same could be said of the perception of a one-third octave change in frequency. For example, if the frequency of a sound changed from 40 to 50 Hz, the change could be detected by the human ear about as easily as a change from 4000 to 5000 Hz, whereas a frequency change from 4000 to 4010 Hz would probably be imperceptible. Instrumentation for frequency analysis is discussed in Chapter 3.

Octave Bands

The ten standard octave bands in the audible range have center frequencies f_C = 31.5, 63, 125, 250, and 500 Hz, and 1, 2, 4, 8, and 16 kHz. Some time ago, these octave bands were called the "preferred" octave bands to distinguish them from the "old" octave bands with different center frequencies. Each octave band center frequency is approximately double the preceding one and each bandwidth approximately double the preceding one. The approximate equations relating lower band limit f_L, upper band limit f_U, and center frequency f_C for full octaves are

$$f_L = \frac{f_C}{\sqrt{2}} \quad \text{and} \quad f_U = \sqrt{2}f_C \tag{1.6.2}$$

Thus, the center frequency f_C is the geometric mean of the upper band limit f_U and lower band limit f_L:

$$f_C = \sqrt{f_L f_U} \tag{1.6.3}$$

It can be seen that the ratio of bandwidth (BW) to center frequency is approximately constant. For full octaves, the bandwidth is:

$$\text{BW} = f_U - f_L = f_C\left(\sqrt{2} - \frac{1}{\sqrt{2}}\right) = \frac{f_C}{\sqrt{2}} \tag{1.6.4}$$

based on the above equations.

Rather than specify the bands by irrational numbers, the octave bands have been standardized for acoustic measurements as follows:

Lower band limit, f_L	Center frequency, f_C	Upper band limit, f_U
22.4 Hz	31.5 Hz	45 Hz
45	63	90
90	125	180
180	250	355

Lower band limit, f_L	Center frequency, f_C	Upper band limit, f_U
355	500	710
710	1 kHz	1.4 kHz
1.4 kHz	2	2.8
2.8	4	5.6
5.6	8	11.2
11.2	16	22.4

One-Third Octave Bands

As the name implies, one-third octave bands are formed by dividing each octave band in three parts. Thus, successive center frequencies of one-third octave bands are related by the cube root of 2, and we relate the upper and lower band limits to the center frequency by the sixth root of 2. The approximate relationships for one-third octaves are

$$f_L = \frac{f_C}{2^{1/6}} \tag{1.6.5}$$

$$f_U = 2^{1/6} f_C \tag{1.6.6}$$

$$f_C = (f_L f_U)^{1/2} \tag{1.6.7}$$

Using these approximate relationships, the ratio of bandwidth to center frequency for one-third octave bands is

$$\text{BW} = f_U - f_L = f_C(2^{1/6} - 2^{-1/6}) \tag{1.6.8}$$

The standardized one-third octave-band limits and center frequencies are given in Table 1.6.1. Note that the center frequency of the $n + 10$th band is ten times the center frequency of the nth band. Band limits are similarly related. Frequencies marked with an asterisk correspond to full octave band values.

Although one-third octave bands usually provide adequate information for noise control studies, one-tenth and even one-hundredth octaves are sometimes used. For $1/m$th octaves, successive center frequencies are related approximately by

$$f_{n+1} = 2^{1/m} f_n \tag{1.6.9}$$

Thus, for one-tenth octaves,

$$f_{n+1} = 2^{1/10} f_n \tag{1.6.10}$$

Octave band analysis and fractional octave band analysis are called constant percent bandwidth analysis. Constant bandwidth analysis is an alternative method of noise analysis, which is also used in vibration analysis. Each band could, for example, be 10 Hz in width. In constant bandwidth analysis, the center frequency is defined as the arithmetic mean of the upper and lower band limits:

$$f_C = (f_L - f_U)/2 \tag{1.6.11}$$

TABLE 1.6.1 ONE-THIRD OCTAVE BANDS

Lower band limit, f_L (Hz)	Center frequency, f_C (Hz)	Upper band limit, f_U (Hz)
18.0	20	22.4
22.4*	25	28.0
28.0	31.5*	35.5
35.5	40	45*
45*	50	56
56	63*	71
71	80	90*
90*	100	112
112	125*	140
140	160	180*
180*	200	224
224	250*	280
280	315	355*
355*	400	450
450	500*	560
560	630	710*
710*	800	900
900	1,000*	1,120
1,120	1,250	1,400*
1,400*	1,600	1,800
1,800	2,000*	2,240
2,240	2,500	2,800*
2,800*	3,150	3,550
3,550	4,000*	4,500
4,500	5,000	5,600*
5,600*	6,300	7,100
7,100	8,000*	9,000
9,000	10,000	11,200*
11,200*	12,500	14,000
14,000	16,000*	18,000
18,000	20,000	22,400*

1.7 FREQUENCY WEIGHTING

Human perception of loudness varies, depending on the frequency of a sound. Noise with most of its energy concentrated in the middle frequencies (near 1 kHz, for example) is perceived as louder than noise of equal energy concentrated at low frequencies (say, near 31.5 Hz). Sounds at frequencies near 1 kHz are also perceived as louder than high-frequency sound (near 20 kHz). The effect of frequency is more prominent with soft sounds than it is with loud sounds. The "loudness" control on an audio amplifier takes this frequency-dependent effect into account. When the volume is at a low setting, the loudness control is used to produce a normal effect by giving greater amplification to the high and low frequencies relative to the middle-frequency components.

Frequency weighting takes typical human response into account when all of the audible frequency components of a noise sample are to be described by a single number. Instead of reporting the sound level in each frequency band, the *A*-weighted sound level may be used. The A-weighted sound level is obtained by adjusting the sound level in each frequency band to correspond to the approximate response to soft sounds. The adjustments are given in Table 1.7.1 (ANSI, 1983). The adjusted levels are then combined to produce the overall level in A-weighted decibels (dBA).

Relative response curves for several weighting schemes are shown in Figure 1.7.1. Note that all of the weighting curves show an adjustment of 0 dB for the 1-kHz frequency band. B-weighting and C-weighting correspond, respectively, to human response to moderate and loud sounds. The relative response based on C-weighting is plotted in the figure and tabulated in Table 1.7.1. C-weighting is relatively "flat" in the midrange of frequencies; less than 1 dB is subtracted from levels measured in the frequency bands from 63 Hz through 4 kHz. Subjective measurements made under different conditions have led to additional weighting schemes. D-weighting has been

TABLE 1.7.1 A-WEIGHTING AND C-WEIGHTING

Frequency (Hz)	A-weighting relative response (dB)	C-weighting relative response (dB)
10	−70.4	−14.3
12.5	−63.4	−11.2
16	−56.7	−8.5
20	−50.5	−6.2
25	−44.7	−4.4
31.5	−39.4	−3.0
40	−34.6	−2.0
50	−30.2	−1.3
63	−26.2	−0.8
80	−22.5	−0.5
100	−19.1	−0.3
125	−16.1	−0.2
160	−13.4	−0.1
200	−10.9	0
250	−8.6	0
315	−6.6	0
400	−4.8	0
500	−3.2	0
630	−1.9	0
800	−0.8	0
1,000	0	0
1,250	+0.6	0
1,600	+1.0	−0.1
2,000	+1.2	−0.2
2,500	+1.3	−0.3
3,150	+1.2	−0.5
4,000	+1.0	−0.8
5,000	+0.5	−1.3
6,300	−0.1	−2.0
8,000	−1.1	−3.0
10,000	−2.5	−4.4
12,500	−4.3	−6.2
16,000	−6.6	−8.5
20,000	−9.3	−11.2

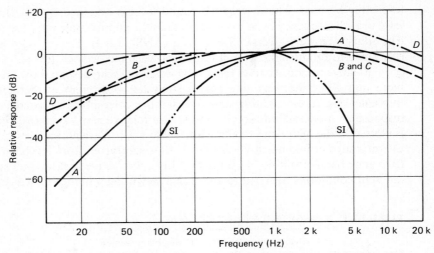

Figure 1.7.1 Relative response curves for *A*-, *B*-, *C*-, *D*-, and SI-weighting.

used to approximate perceived noisiness of aircraft and speech interference (SI) weighting has been used to evaluate noise in terms of speech interference. It can be seen that sounds at frequencies below 100 Hz or above 5 kHz are not considered important with regard to speech interference.

Some representative *A*-weighted noise levels and standards based on *A*-weighting are shown in Figure 1.7.2. Corresponding root-mean-square sound pressures adjusted for *A*-weighting are shown as well.

When sound pressure levels are measured in frequency bands, the levels in each frequency band are usually displayed without weighting, but overall levels are often weighted. Figure 1.7.3, a sound level versus frequency and time plot of truck noise, is an exception. It shows one-third octave-band sound levels measured over 1-s intervals in a computer-generated graph. *A*-weighting of the individual one-third octave-band sound levels was used to aid in identifying the major contributors to overall *A*-weighted sound level.

Overall sound levels may be obtained by combining band levels as uncorrelated sources. Sound level meters incorporate weighting networks so that overall weighted sound levels can be displayed directly.

1.8 EQUIVALENT SOUND LEVEL

Equivalent sound level is an energy average, ordinarily based on *A*-weighted measurements. It is a single-number descriptor of time-varying noise used in noise codes, environmental impact statements, and other documents. Rewriting the definition of sound pressure level, equation 1.4.3, we have

$$\frac{p_{\text{rms}}^2}{p_{\text{ref}}^2} = 10^{L_P/10} \tag{1.8.1}$$

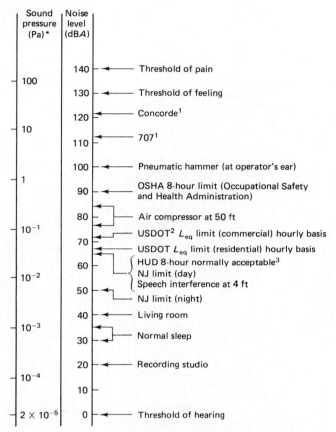

Figure 1.7.2 Typical noise levels and standards. *Notes:*
[1] Aircraft noise measurements 500 ft beyond end of runway,
250 ft to side.
[2] Design noise levels, Federal Highway Admin., U.S. D.O.T.
[3] Dept. of Housing and Urban Development.
* Root-mean-square sound pressure adjusted for *A*-weighting.

Equivalent sound level is obtained by averaging the mean-square sound pressure over the desired time interval and converting back to decibels. Thus,

$$L_{\text{eq}} = 10 \lg\left(\frac{\overline{p_{\text{rms}}^2}}{p_{\text{ref}}^2}\right) = 10 \lg\left(\frac{1}{T}\int_0^T 10^{L/10}\,dt\right) \qquad (1.8.2)$$

where L_{eq} = equivalent sound level (dB*A*)
       $\overline{p_{\text{rms}}^2}$ = the time average of mean-square sound pressure
       T = averaging time (which should be stated)

Common averaging times include one hour, one day, and one year.

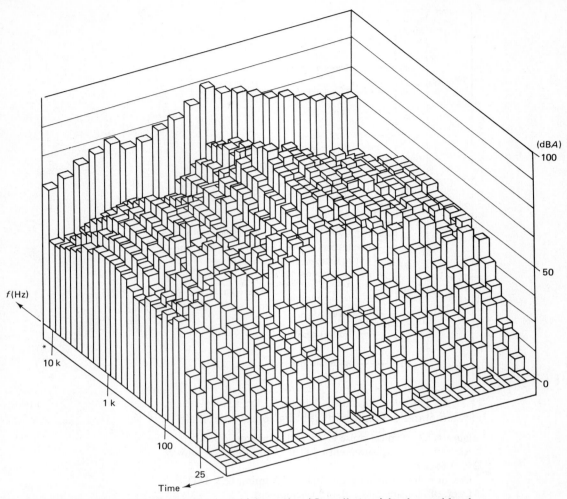

Figure 1.7.3 Traffic noise including heavy vehicle passby. *Overall A-weighted sound level.

EXAMPLE PROBLEM: EQUIVALENT SOUND LEVEL

(a) Write a brief program to determine equivalent sound level from a number of discrete sound level measurements.

Solution. Equation 1.8.2 is rewritten using summation instead of integration:

$$L_{eq} = 10 \lg\left(\frac{1}{N} \sum_{i=1}^{N} 10^{L_i/10}\right) \tag{1.8.3}$$

for N sound level measurements in dBA. The actual program listing depends on the computer or calculator that is available. The flowchart of Figure 1.8.1 outlines the program.

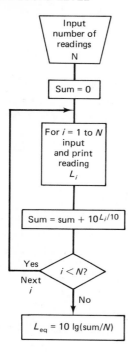

Figure 1.8.1 Equivalent sound level. *Note:* The function lg refers to the base-ten logarithm ($\log_{10}$). Some computers do not include this function. The relationship $\log_{10}(x) = \log_e(x)/\log_e(10)$ may be used.

(b) The highway traffic volume passing location A is relatively steady between 5 and 6 P.M. An observer at location A takes 50 sound level readings at 10-s intervals sometime between 5 and 6 P.M. (an integrating sound level meter is unavailable). The readings (in dB*A*) are as follows: 70, 72, 70, 72, 70, 69, 73, 72, 70, 69, 73, 72, 70, 69, 73, 72, 70, 69, 68, 73, 72, 71, 70, 69, 68, 67, 73, 72, 70, 69, 68, 67, 74, 73, 72, 70, 69, 68, 67, 74, 73, 72, 71, 70, 69, 68, 67, 66, 71, 70. Estimate the equivalent sound level for the 5 to 6 P.M. interval.

Solution. Using the program from part (a), the equivalent sound level is found to be 70.6 dB*A*.

Note that equivalent sound level is an energy average and will, in general, differ from the arithmetic average of the sound levels and the median level. High readings tend to dominate the equivalent sound level. For example, suppose the sound level in a factory is 75, 78, 80, and 100 dB*A* for equal time intervals during an 8-hour workday. The equivalent sound level is 94.1 dB*A* for the workday. Readings 20 dB*A* or more below the peak level make a small contribution to equivalent sound level. If there was no sound at all for the quieter 75% of the workday described above, equivalent sound level would be reduced only about 0.1 dB*A*. Zero sound energy would correspond to an infinite negative sound level. In actual practice, however, a specially constructed acoustical laboratory is usually necessary to obtain sound levels below 10 or 20 dB*A*.

1.9 DAY–NIGHT SOUND LEVEL

Day–night sound level is used as a descriptor when nighttime noise is particularly objectionable, as in residential areas. First, 10 dBA is added to A-weighted sound levels measured between the hours of 10 P.M. and 7 A.M. Day–night sound level is then computed from the adjusted nighttime sound levels along with the (unadjusted) daytime values. Equation 1.8.2 is used with a 24-hour averaging time. The result is

$$L_{DN} = 10 \lg\left[\frac{1}{24}\left(\int_{7\text{A.M.}}^{10\text{P.M.}} 10^{L/10}\, dt + \int_{10\text{P.M.}}^{7\text{A.M.}} 10^{(L+10)/10}\, dt\right)\right] \tag{1.9.1}$$

where L_{DN} = day–night sound level (dBA)
L = measured or predicted sound level (dBA)
t = time (hours)

If representative equivalent sound levels have been determined for the daytime and nighttime periods, the above equation may be rewritten as follows:

$$L_{DN} = 10 \lg\left[\frac{1}{24}\left(15 \times 10^{L_{eqD}/10} + 9 \times 10^{(L_{eqN}+10)/10}\right)\right] \tag{1.9.2}$$

where L_{eqD} = equivalent sound level for the 15-hour period from 7 A.M. to 10 P.M.
L_{eqN} = equivalent sound level for the 9-hour period from 10 P.M. to 7 A.M.

1.10 VECTOR SOUND INTENSITY

Vector sound intensity is the time-averaged energy flux, the net rate of flow of acoustic energy. In a purely active sound field in which particle velocity is in-phase with sound pressure, acoustic intensity in the propagation direction can be determined from a single measurement of sound pressure. In the more general case, particle velocity has an active component (in-phase with sound pressure) and a reactive component (90° out-of-phase with sound pressure). Only the active component contributes to vector sound intensity. A two-microphone sound intensity measurement technique enables us to distinguish between sound produced by a source and reflected sound. These measurements can be used to determine the sound power of a machine, and for source location under field conditions. Theoretical and practical aspects of sound intensity measurement are given by Gade (1982) and by Waser and Crocker (1984).

Instantaneous sound intensity is defined by

$$I_{r(\text{inst})} = \frac{dE_r/dt}{dA} \tag{1.10.1}$$

where $I_{r(\text{inst})}$ = instantaneous vector sound intensity (W/m^2) in the r-direction (the axis of the two-microphone probe)
dE_r = energy passing through an area dA perpendicular to the r-direction during time interval dt (see Figure 1.10.1)

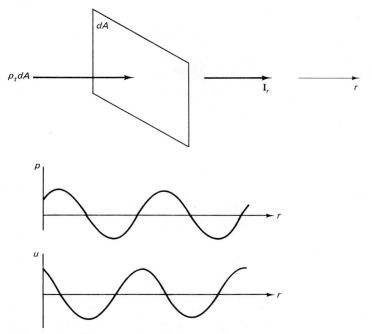

Figure 1.10.1 Vector sound intensity.

Energy can be expressed in terms of pressure and particle displacement as follows:

$$dE_r = p_t \, dA \, d\xi_r \tag{1.10.2}$$

where $p_t = p + p_a$ = total pressure
   p = sound pressure
   p_a = ambient pressure
   $d\xi_r$ = particle displacement in the r-direction

Thus, we have

$$I_{r(\text{inst})} = p_t \frac{d\xi_r}{dt} = (p_a + p)u_r \tag{1.10.3}$$

where $u_r = d\xi_r/dt$ = particle velocity in the r-direction.

   Vector sound intensity is given by the average of instantaneous vector sound intensity over time T:

$$I_r = \overline{pu_r} = \frac{1}{T} \int_0^T pu_r \, dt \tag{1.10.4}$$

where I_r = vector sound intensity (W/m^2) in the r-direction, the bar indicates time averaging, and T = averaging time, which should be sufficiently long to ensure a stable result, considering frequency content and time variation of the sound field. The above result was based on the assumption that particle velocity results from sound waves without net air flow. In that case, no contribution is made by the term containing atmospheric pressure.

Early attempts at vector sound intensity measurement were thwarted by difficulties in measuring particle velocity at acoustic frequencies. However, applying Newton's second law to an elemental volume of air within the sound field, we may relate the rate of change in particle velocity to the pressure gradient:

$$\frac{\rho \partial \mathbf{u}}{\partial t} = -\nabla p \qquad (1.10.5)$$

where ρ = mass density of air (kg/m^3)
          $\mathbf{u}$ = particle velocity (m/s)
          $\nabla p = \mathbf{i}\, \partial p / \partial x + \mathbf{j}\, \partial p / \partial y + \mathbf{k}\, \partial p / \partial z$

Considering the r-direction alone, equation 1.10.5 takes the form

$$\rho \frac{\partial u_r}{\partial t} = -\frac{\partial p}{\partial r} \qquad (1.10.6)$$

The same equations may be obtained by retaining only the significant terms in Euler's equation. Recall that we may neglect changes in air density under ordinary conditions, since sound pressures are small in comparison with atmospheric pressure.

If sound pressure is measured by two closely spaced microphones, the pressure gradient in the r-direction (the axis of the microphone pair) may be replaced by a finite-difference approximation, that is, $\partial p / \partial r$ is replaced by $(p_B - p_A)/\Delta r$ to yield

$$\frac{\partial u_r}{\partial t} = -\frac{1}{\rho\, \Delta r}(p_B - p_A) \qquad (1.10.7)$$

where p_A and p_B = measured pressures
        Δr = the microphone spacing
        $\Delta r \ll \lambda$ for valid results, where
        λ = the wavelength of the highest frequency sound of interest

Particle velocity, obtained by integrating the above equations with respect to time, is given by

$$u_r = -\frac{1}{\rho} \int_{-\infty}^{t} \frac{\partial p}{\partial r}\, dt \qquad (1.10.8)$$

or, using the finite difference approximation,

$$u_r = -\frac{1}{\rho\, \Delta r} \int_{-\infty}^{t} (p_B - p_A)\, dt \qquad (1.10.9)$$

Sound pressure may be taken as the mean value at the two microphone locations:

$$p = (p_B + p_A)/2 \qquad (1.10.10)$$

Finally, we have vector sound intensity in the r-direction given by

$$I_r = \frac{1}{T} \int_0^T pu_r \, dt = \overline{pu_r}$$

$$= -\frac{1}{2\rho \, \Delta r} \overline{(p_B + p_A) \int_{-\infty}^{t} (p_B - p_A) dt} \tag{1.10.11}$$

Vector Sound Intensity Based on the Cross Spectrum

Sound intensity can be expressed in an alternative form by using Fourier transforms. Taking the Fourier transform of equations 1.10.9 and 1.10.10, the results are

$$\tilde{U}_r(\omega) = [j/(\omega\rho \, \Delta r)][\tilde{P}_B(\omega) - \tilde{P}_A(\omega)] \tag{1.10.12}$$

and

$$\tilde{P}(\omega) = [\tilde{P}_B(\omega) + \tilde{P}_A(\omega)]/2 \tag{1.10.13}$$

where equation 1.10.12 has been simplified based on the condition that the sound field in question is sampled for a finite length of time,

$$\tilde{U}_r(\omega) = \text{the Fourier transform of particle velocity } u_r(t)$$

$$\tilde{P}(\omega) = \text{the Fourier transform of sound pressure } p(t)$$

$$\Delta r = \text{the microphone spacing}$$

$$j = (-1)^{1/2}$$

Sound intensity is given in terms of complex quantities as follows:

$$I_r = \tfrac{1}{2} \, \text{Re}\{\tilde{p}\tilde{u}_r^*\} \tag{1.10.14}$$

and

$$I_r(\omega) = \tfrac{1}{2} \, \text{Re}\{\tilde{P}(\omega)\tilde{U}^*(\omega)\} \tag{1.10.15}$$

where $I_r(\omega) = \text{the Fourier transform of vector sound intensity } I_r(t)$
$\text{Re} = \text{the real part of a complex quantity}$
$* = \text{the complex conjugate}$

Substitution of equations 1.10.12 and 1.10.13 in 1.10.15 yields

$$I_r(\omega) = \frac{1}{2} \, \text{Re}\left\{\left[\frac{\tilde{P}_B(\omega) + \tilde{P}_A(\omega)}{2}\right]\left[\frac{j(\tilde{P}_B(\omega) - \tilde{P}_A(\omega))}{\omega\rho \, \Delta r}\right]^*\right\} \tag{1.10.16}$$

After a number of simplifications, the vector sound intensity in the frequency domain is given by

$$I_r(\omega) = \frac{\text{Im}\{\tilde{P}_B(\omega)\tilde{P}_A^*(\omega)\}}{2\omega\rho \, \Delta r}$$

$$= \frac{\text{Im}\{\tilde{G}_{AB}\}}{\omega\rho \, \Delta r} \tag{1.10.17}$$

where ω = circular frequency
       Im = the imaginary part of a complex quantity
       $\tilde{G}_{AB}$ = the one-sided cross spectrum of the two sound pressures

Sound Intensity of Pure-Tone Sound Waves

A sound field may be described at any point in space by its sound pressure p and particle velocity **u**. For a pure-tone sound wave, we may write

$$p = p_1 \cos(\omega t + \phi_P) \tag{1.10.18}$$

and

$$\mathbf{u} = \mathbf{u}_1 \cos(\omega t + \phi_U) \tag{1.10.19}$$

or, using complex form,

$$p = \mathrm{Re}\{p_1 e^{j(\omega t + \phi_P)}\} \tag{1.10.20}$$

and

$$\mathbf{u} = \mathrm{Re}\{\mathbf{u}_1 e^{j(\omega t + \phi_U)}\} \tag{1.10.21}$$

where p_1 = pressure amplitude
             $\mathbf{u}_1$ = velocity amplitude
   ϕ_P and ϕ_U = phase angles

For an averaging time of one period (or an integer number of periods), vector sound intensity is given by

$$\mathbf{I} = \tfrac{1}{2} p_1 \mathbf{u}_1 \cos(\phi_P - \phi_U) = p_{\mathrm{rms}} \mathbf{u}_{\mathrm{rms}} \cos(\phi_P - \phi_U) \tag{1.10.22}$$

The derivation of equation 1.10.22 is given as an exercise.

Sound Intensity Level

Sound intensity measurements are ordinarily expressed as sound intensity level in decibels, defined as follows:

$$L_I = 10 \lg\left(\frac{I}{I_{\mathrm{ref}}}\right) \tag{1.10.23}$$

where L_I = sound intensity level (dB)
         I = sound intensity (W/m^2)
       I_{ref} = 1 pW/m^2 = 10^{-12} W/m^2

Figure 1.10.2 shows a vacuum cleaner with an imaginary measuring surface above it and to one side. Part (b) of the figure is a mesh diagram of the vector sound intensity measured on the imaginary surfaces. In part (c), the same information is given as a contour diagram. Part (d) shows the vector flow diagram. It can be seen that there is a significant sound intensity component running parallel to the top measuring surface.

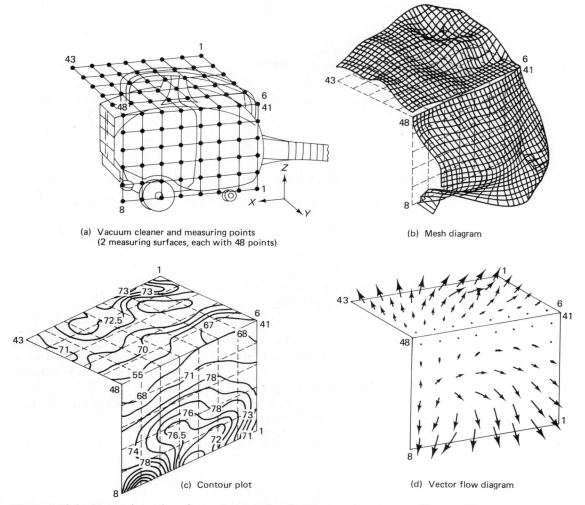

(a) Vacuum cleaner and measuring points
(2 measuring surfaces, each with 48 points)

(b) Mesh diagram

(c) Contour plot

(d) Vector flow diagram

Figure 1.10.2 Vector intensity of sound emanating from a vacuum cleaner. (*Source:* Rion Instruments Div., Mott Associates, Inc.)

EXAMPLE PROBLEM: VECTOR SOUND INTENSITY

Find the vector sound intensity of an ideal standing wave.

Solution. A standing wave results from reflections between parallel walls when the distance between the walls is an integer number of half-wavelengths. The pressure and velocity are 90° out-of-phase. Thus, the cosine of the difference in phase angles is zero and the vector intensity is zero. There is no net energy flow in the ideal case. An actual standing wave must be maintained by a source to make up for sound energy losses. These losses are the portion of sound energy absorbed (converted to heat) as sound propagates through air and as sound is reflected at walls. The vector intensity may be very small, but it cannot actually equal zero.

Specific Acoustic Impedance

Specific acoustic impedance relates sound pressure and particle velocity at a point in space as follows:

$$Z = \frac{p}{u} \qquad (1.10.24)$$

where the terms are in complex form

Z = specific acoustic impedance (rayls, where 1 rayl = 1 N·s/m³)
p = sound pressure (Pa)
u = particle velocity (m/s)

1.11 SOUND INTENSITY WHEN SOUND PRESSURE AND PARTICLE VELOCITY ARE IN-PHASE

Sound pressure and particle velocity are likely to be out-of-phase when measured near a sound source, or near a reflecting wall. In other regions dominated by sound waves propagating directly from a single source, the sound field may be approximated by assuming that sound pressure is in-phase with particle velocity.

Consider a forward-traveling pure-tone plane wave propagating in the *r*-direction in a free field. The wave is described as follows:

$$p = p_1 \cos k(r - ct + \phi) \qquad (1.11.1)$$

and

$$u_r = u_{r1} \cos k(r - ct + \phi) \qquad (1.11.2)$$

where p = sound pressure (Pa)
u_r = particle velocity (m/s), a scalar since we are considering a one-dimensional problem
$k = \omega/c$ = the wavenumber (rad/m)
c = wave propagation speed (m/s)
ϕ = a phase angle (rad)

Substituting these expressions in equation 1.10.6, we have

$$p_1 = \rho c u_{r1} \qquad (1.11.3)$$

from which

$$p = \rho c u_r \qquad (1.11.4)$$

where ρ = the mass density of air (kg/m^3). Using equation 1.10.22 while noting the zero phase difference between pressure and velocity, we have

$$I = p_1 \frac{u_1}{2} = p_{rms}u_{rms} = \frac{p_1^2}{2\rho c} = \frac{p_{rms}^2}{\rho c} \qquad (1.11.5)$$

where I = sound intensity (W/m^2) in the direction of sound propagation.

Sound Intensity Level

Using the above result in the definition of sound intensity level, we find

$$L_I = 10 \lg\left(\frac{I}{I_{ref}}\right) = 10 \lg\left(\frac{p_{rms}^2}{\rho c I_{ref}}\right)$$

$$= 10 \lg\left(\frac{p_{rms}^2}{p_{ref}^2}\right) + 10 \lg\left(\frac{p_{ref}^2}{\rho c I_{ref}}\right)$$

$$= L_P + 10 \lg\left(\frac{p_{ref}^2}{\rho c I_{ref}}\right) \qquad (1.11.6)$$

where L_I = sound intensity level (dB)
      L_P = sound pressure level (dB)

The last term in the above equation vanishes if

$$\frac{p_{ref}^2}{\rho c I_{ref}} = \frac{(20 \times 10^{-6})^2}{\rho c \times 10^{-12}} = 1$$

or

$$\rho c = 400 \text{ rayls.}$$

For airborne sound under common conditions, sound intensity level and sound pressure level are approximately equal if sound pressure and particle velocity are in-phase. For underwater sound transmission, sound transmission through solids, and high altitude sound, sound pressure level may differ significantly from sound intensity level. Also, if there is a phase difference between sound pressure and particle velocity, sound pressure level and sound intensity level may differ significantly.

EXAMPLE PROBLEM: SOUND PRESSURE LEVEL AND SOUND INTENSITY LEVEL

(a) Find the difference between sound intensity level and sound pressure level when sound pressure and particle velocity are in-phase. Base results on atmospheric pressure equal to one standard atmosphere and a temperature of 20°C.

Solution. Combining equations 1.2.9 and 1.2.12, we have

$$\rho c = \rho\left(\frac{\gamma p_0}{\rho}\right)^{1/2} = (\gamma p_0 \rho)^{1/2} = p_0\left(\frac{\gamma}{RT}\right)^{1/2}$$

Using one standard atmosphere = 101,325 Pa, $\gamma = 1.4$, $R = 287$, and $T = 20 + 273.16$, we have

$$\rho c = 101,325\left(\frac{1.4}{287 \times 293.16}\right)^{1/2} = 413.3$$

The difference between the two levels is

$$L_I - L_P = 10 \lg\left(\frac{400}{\rho c}\right) = 10 \lg\left(\frac{400}{413.3}\right) = -0.14 \text{ dB}$$

(b) Find the range of atmospheric pressures and temperatures for which sound intensity level and sound pressure level differ by less than $\frac{1}{2}$ dB.

Solution. Let

$$\Delta = L_I - L_P = 10 \lg\left(\frac{400}{\rho c}\right)$$

from which $400/\rho c = 10^{\Delta/10}$ and $\rho c = 400/10^{\Delta/10}$. For $\Delta = +0.5$,

$$\rho c = \frac{400}{10^{0.5/10}} = 356.5$$

and for $\Delta = -0.5$,

$$\rho c = \frac{400}{10^{-0.5/10}} = 448.4$$

Thus, $356.5 < \rho c < 448.8 \text{ N} \cdot \text{s/m}^3$ (rayls). From the equations in part (a), we write

$$p_0 = \frac{\rho c}{(\gamma/RT)^{1/2}} = \frac{\rho c}{(1.4/287T)^{1/2}}$$

For each of the two limiting values of ρc we may plot atmospheric pressure against temperature. To save time, a personal computer can be used to plot the results. Figure 1.11.1 is a flowchart outlining the major steps for producing one or more curves based on different values of sound level difference. For this example, we would input $L_I - L_P = -0.5$ and $+0.5$. An input of $L_I - L_P = 0$ would produce the curve for $\rho c = 400$.

Characteristic Impedance

When sound pressure and particle velocity are in-phase, then it can be seen from equation 1.11.4 that the ratio of sound pressure to particle velocity is the real quantity ρc, the density of the medium times the speed of sound propagation. Thus, from equation 1.10.24, we have

$$Z = \rho c \qquad\qquad (1.11.7)$$

where Z is now called the characteristic impedance.

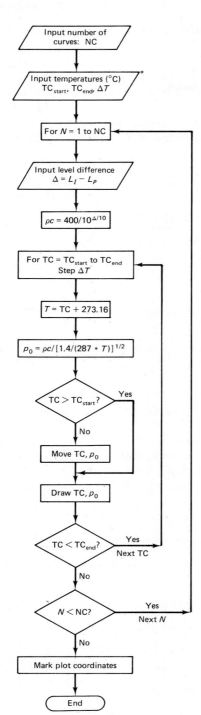

Figure 1.11.1 Atmospheric pressures and temperatures for which sound intensity level and sound pressure level differ by less than Δ.

1.12 SOUND POWER AND SOUND POWER LEVEL

Sound power is the rate at which a machine produces sound energy. Ordinarily, a very small fraction of the energy input to a machine is converted into sound power. In some instances, the resulting sound power of a fraction of a watt to a few watts may result in unacceptable noise levels. Determination of sound power aids in predicting noise levels and evaluating noise reduction attempts.

Sound power level is defined in terms of the ratio of sound power to a reference power as follows:

$$L_W(\text{dB re } 1 \text{ pW}) = 10 \lg\left(\frac{W}{W_{\text{ref}}}\right) = 10 \lg\left(\frac{W}{10^{-12}}\right)$$

$$= 10 \lg W + 120 \qquad (1.12.1)$$

where L_W = sound power level (dB re 1 pW, i.e., dB re 10^{-12} W)
        W = sound power (watts)

EXAMPLE PROBLEM: SOUND POWER

Find the sound power of an aircraft turbojet that has a sound power level of 160 dB re 1 pW.

Solution.   The sound power level equation is rewritten in the form

$$W = 10^{(L_W - 120)/10} \qquad (1.12.2)$$

from which the sound power of the turbojet is

$$W = 10^{(160 - 120)/10} = 10,000 \text{ W}$$

Typical values of sound power and sound power level are given for various noise sources in Table 1.12.1. Sound power levels vary widely, even for similar machines, depending on the age of a machine, the quality of maintenance, and previous noise control efforts. Sound power may be determined from vector

TABLE 1.12.1   TYPICAL VALUES OF SOUND POWER
AND SOUND POWER LEVEL

Sound power (W)	Sound power level (dB re 1 pW)	Sound source
100,000,000	200	— Large rocket
1,000,000	180	— Airliner
10,000	160	
100	140	— Large orchestra
1	120	— Pneumatic hammer
10^{-2}	100	— Automobile └ Loud radio
10^{-4}	80	— Shouting
10^{-6}	60	└ Conversation
10^{-8}	40	— Whisper
10^{-10}	20	
10^{-12}	0	— Reference power

sound intensity measurements, and from measurements of sound pressure under controlled conditions. These relationships will be developed in later chapters.

1.13 ACTIVE AND PASSIVE NOISE CONTROL

Electronic Noise Cancellation

Active noise control involves reduction in noise levels by generation of sound waves out-of-phase with the noise. Early active noise control studies involved reduction of fan noise in ducts. Other applications and potential applications include noise control in aircraft, electric power transformers, diesel engines, electric motors, industrial machinery, pumps, and compressors.

Consider a sound wave described (at a point in space) by

$$p_1 = P_1 \cos(\omega_1 t + \phi_1)$$

Referring to equation 1.5.6, we see that if we generate a second sound wave (anti-phase-noise) described at the same point by

$$p_2 = P_2 \cos(\omega_2 t + \phi_2)$$

where
$$\omega_2 = \omega_1$$
$$P_2 = P_1$$
$$\phi_1 - \phi_2 = 180°$$

then the second wave will cancel the first, resulting in zero root-mean-square sound pressure. However, some of the following practical considerations may limit application of active noise control:

1. Continuous and reliable measurement, signal processing, and sound generation are required.
2. The anti-phase-noise source must be near the noise source or near the receiver.
3. If changes in the relative positions of the noise source, the anti-phase-noise generator, and the observer result in a change in phase difference, the effect could be reinforcement rather than cancellation. This consideration would limit most active-noise-control systems to low-frequency (large wavelength) sounds.

An active-noise-control communications headset system used on the around-the-world flight of the experimental aircraft *Voyager* is described by Gauger and Sapiejewski (1987). Microphones are mounted in the earcups to monitor sound at the ear as shown in Figure 1.13.1. Measured sound is compared with the intended communications signal. The difference is processed to produce the cancellation signal which is reproduced by a speaker in the earcup. Active noise control is effective in this system in the 30-Hz to 1-kHz range. At frequencies above 200 Hz, significant (passive) noise reduction is provided by the earcups, which have sound transmission characteristics similar to hearing protectors discussed in Chapter 4. Performance characteristics of active hearing protection devices are given by Maxwell et al. (1987).

Noise that has a repetitive pattern may be attenuated by active noise control near the source. Chaplin (1987) describes a system for cancellation of exhaust noise of a four-stroke-cycle engine by waveform synthesis. Although the noise waveform is irregular, it is essentially repeated every two crankshaft revolutions. The anti-phase-noise speaker is placed near the exhaust outlet. The synthesized anti-phase-noise waveform is synchronized with engine speed by means of a tachometer sensor mounted at the engine flywheel. A microphone is used to sense the net sound, and its signal is used to improve the synthesized waveform.

Masking

When noise reduces the intelligibility of communications, the effect is called masking. Sometimes, sound is intentionally introduced to produce the effect of privacy by masking intrusive sounds such as conversation in an adjacent office. The masking sound may be broadband noise produced by a small air jet, or recorded instrumental music. The result of masking is an increase in noise level, but the subjective effect may be a reduction in annoyance. Masking should only be used when noise reduction is not feasible.

Passive Noise Control

In most situations, it is not practical to introduce an active noise control system. Thus, most noise control systems are passive, relying principally on absorption and reflection of sound waves. Sound absorption for control of reverberant sound in rooms is discussed in Chapter 2. Noise barrier design is also discussed in that chapter. Selection of construction materials to reduce sound transmission of walls and other building elements is covered in Chapter 6.

Other common methods of controlling noise include noise source reduction, reactive silencing, vibration isolation, and damping. Methods of noise control at the

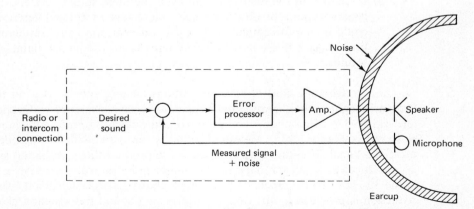

Figure 1.13.1   Active noise control communications headset schematic. (*Source:* Gauger and Sapiejewsk, 1987)

source, that is, reduction in the sound power of the source, are discussed in several chapters, including Chapter 2 (aerodynamic sources), Chapter 6 (home appliances and heating, ventilation, and air conditioning equipment), Chapter 7 (machinery noise), and Chapters 8 and 9 (transportation noise sources). Chapter 10 covers control of noise at the source by vibration isolation and damping. Reactive mufflers and silencers, discussed in Chapter 7, are designed to control noise by destructive interference due to reflected sound waves.

The impact of noise on humans can be reduced by administrative and political controls, which may have the effect of separating the source and receiver. Sound divergence models are discussed in Chapter 2. Chapter 4 considers personal hearing protection devices. Administrative controls are explained in Chapter 7, and noise codes, zoning, and land use planning in Chapters 5, 8, and 9.

1.14 CRITERIA AND STANDARDS

Noise criteria and standards are developed in an attempt to reduce annoyance, sleep interference, communication interference, and hearing damage. Some noise standards and criteria are legally enforceable, while others are used only for guidance in evaluating equipment and noise environments. A few criteria and standards are briefly noted at this point; detailed discussions are found in the applicable chapters.

Noise standards commonly employ A-weighted sound levels. Community noise ordinances limit A-weighted sound level as measured at residential property lines, with lower levels permitted during nighttime hours. Many communities limit fixed-source noise levels at residential boundaries to 55 dBA in the daytime and 50 dBA at night. Some ordinances refer to octave-band sound levels, and include special provisions for pure-tones or sounds with substantial energy concentrated in a single frequency band.

Some noise standards, particularly those based on hearing conservation, consider both noise level and duration. The criterion level for occupational noise is 90 dBA for 8 hours per day exposure in the United States and in many European countries. However, noise dose calculations differ, with the United States halving allowable exposure time with every 5-dBA increase in noise level, while many countries halve allowable exposure with each 3-dBA increase. The U.S. Environmental Protection Agency (EPA) basic hearing conservation criterion is an equivalent sound level $L_{eq24} \leq 70$ dBA (based on 24-hour averaging). The EPA identified criterion for activity interference and annoyance indoors in residential areas is a day–night sound level $L_{DN} \leq 45$ dBA. At this writing, the EPA criteria are not incorporated into any federal law.

Noise criteria (NC) curves were developed as a single-number rating system to identify acceptable noise environments. Various curves are applicable to offices, libraries, homes, and hotels. Octave-band sound pressure level measurements are compared with the applicable NC curve to determine acceptability. The most common use of NC curves is for evaluation of heating, ventilation, and air-conditioning noise.

Statistically based criteria have been used as well, particularly for rating of highway traffic noise impact. These include L_{10}, the A-weighted sound level exceeded 10% of the time during a given time interval; L_{50}, the median sound level; L_{90}, the level exceeded 90% of the time; and other percentage-exceeded values. However, energy averages (L_{eq} and L_{DN}) have largely replaced statistical descriptors due to the availability of more sophisticated instrumentation.

Vibration criteria are related to frequency, amplitude, and exposure time. The human body exhibits whole-body resonances between 4 and 14 Hz, and resonances of various organs between 3 and 90 Hz. Human body vibration in the 2- to 10-Hz frequency range is perceptible at peak accelerations of about 0.001 to 0.01 g, unpleasant at 0.02 to 0.1 g, and intolerable above about 0.1 g for exposures of a few minutes (where 1 g = 9.8 m/s^2 approximately). Where possible, vibration amplitudes should be below perceptible levels.

Vibration measurements are sometimes used for machinery condition monitoring. Machine monitoring often involves a vibration "signature," the typical vibration pattern of the machine. This signature becomes the criterion for the machine; substantial deviation from this pattern is an indication of possible machine malfunction or failure.

BIBLIOGRAPHY

American National Standards Institute, American national standard specification for sound level meters, ANSI S1.4-1983, New York, 1983.

Beranek, L. L., *Acoustics,* McGraw-Hill, New York, 1954.

Chaplin, G. B. B., "The cancellation of repetitive noise and vibration by active methods," Noise Cancellation Technologies, Inc., 1–5, 1987.

Crocker, M. J. (Ed.), *Noise Control,* Van Nostrand Reinhold, New York, 1984.

Crocker, M. J., and A. J. Price, *Noise and Noise Control,* Vol. I, CRC Press, Cleveland, 1975.

Fahy, F. J., "Measurement of acoustic intensity using the cross-spectral density of two microphone signals," *J. Acoust. Soc. Am.* **62**(5), 1057–1059, 1977.

Gade, S., "Sound intensity (Part I: theory)," *Technical Review,* No. 3, Bruel & Kjaer, Marlborough, Mass., 1982.

Gauger, D., and R. Sapiejewski, "Voyager pilots avoid hearing loss on historic flight," *Sound and Vibration* **21**(5), 10–12, 1987.

Kinsler, L. E., A. R. Frey, A. C. Koppens, and J. V. Sanders, *Fundamentals of Acoustics,* 3rd ed., Wiley, New York, 1982.

Lamb, H., *The Dynamical Theory of Sound,* 2nd ed., Edward Arnold Ltd., 1925 (reprinted by Dover, New York, 1960).

Maxwell, D. W., C. E. Williams, R. M. Robertson, and G. B. Thomas, "Performance characteristics of active hearing protection devices," *Sound and Vibration* **21**(5), 14–18, 1987.

Meyer, E., and E-G. Neumann, *Physical and Applied Acoustics* (translated by J. M. Taylor), Academic Press, New York, 1972.

Pierce, A. D., *Acoustics, An Introduction to Its Physical Principles and Applications,* McGraw-Hill, New York, 1981.

Pritchard, J. B. (Ed.), *Ancient Near Eastern Texts Relating to the Old Testament,* 3rd ed., pp. 104–106, Princeton University Press, Princeton, NJ, 1969.

Rayleigh (J. W. Strutt), *The Theory of Sound,* 2nd ed., Vol. 1, 1894, Vol. 2, 1896, Macmillan (reprinted by Dover, New York, 1945).

Reynolds, D. D., *Engineering Principles of Acoustics,* Allyn and Bacon, Reading, MA, 1981.

Waser, M. P., and M. J. Crocker, "Introduction to the two-microphone cross-spectral method of determining sound intensity," *Noise Control Engineering Journal* **22**(3), 76–85, 1984.

The work of Rayleigh (1894, 1896) and Lamb (1925) have significantly influenced modern acoustics. The volume by Crocker (1984) includes papers that have significantly affected the development of noise control; it is part of a series of collections of benchmark papers in acoustics.

Other publications of interest
Acustica
Journal of the Acoustical Society of America
Journal of Sound and Vibration
Noise Control Engineering Journal
Sound and Vibration

The journals listed above contain major papers advancing the theory of acoustics and noise and vibration control. *Sound and Vibration* is a periodical more closely related to the practice of noise and vibration control and to developments in noise and vibration instrumentation.

Abbreviations
The following abbreviations are commonly used in bibliographies.
Acoust. Soc. Am.: Acoustical Society of America
ANSI: American National Standards Institute
ASHRAE: American Society of Heating, Refrigerating, and Air Conditioning Engineers
ASME: American Society of Mechanical Engineers
ASTM: American Society for Testing and Materials
EPA: Environmental Protection Agency
FAA: Federal Aviation Administration
FHWA: Federal Highway Administration
ISO: International Organization for Standardization
J: Journal
NASA: National Aeronautics and Space Administration
NBS: National Bureau of Standards
NIOSH: National Institute for Occupational Safety and Health
OSHA: Occupational Safety and Health Administration
SAE: Society of Automotive Engineers

PROBLEMS

It is suggested that a personal computer be utilized to solve problems requiring substantial calculations or plotting. An electronic spreadsheet (computer worksheet program) and plotting routine may also be helpful.

1.1.1. A 1050-kg mass is supported on mountings with an equivalent spring rate of 150,000 N/m. Find
   (a) the natural frequency of vibration
   (b) the natural period of vibration

1.1.2. Repeat the above problem for a weight of 1400 lb if the mounting system has a spring rate of 1800 lb/in. Use the acceleration of gravity $g = 386$ in/s^2.

1.1.3. A 200-Hz axial wave is propagating in a steel bar. Find
  (a) wavelength
  (b) wavenumber

1.1.4. A 450-Hz axial wave is propagating in an aluminum bar. Find
  (a) propagation speed
  (b) wavelength
  (c) wavenumber
  Use a modulus of elasticity of 10.3×10^6 psi and density of 0.097 lb/in^3.

1.2.1. Describe the effect of altitude on the speed of sound in air.

1.2.2. Derive the one-dimensional wave equation in terms of pressure.

1.2.3. The ratio of specific heats γ is about the same for air, oxygen, nitrogen, and hydrogen. For different gases having the same value of γ, how is the speed of sound related to density, if the comparison is made at the same pressure?

1.3.1. Find the propagation speed, wavenumber, and wavelength of a 25-Hz pure-tone sound wave at 18°C.

1.3.2. Find the wavenumber and wavelength of a 16-kHz pure-tone sound wave at 18°C.

1.3.3. Show that pressure functions in the form $p = F_1(x - ct) + F_2(x + ct)$ satisfy the wave equation.

1.4.1. Plot sound pressure level versus root-mean-square sound pressure for $20 \times 10^{-6} < p_{rms} < 10^{-3}$ Pa.

1.4.2. Plot sound pressure level versus root-mean-square sound pressure for $10^{-3} < p_{rms} < 1.0$ Pa.

1.4.3. Calculate the approximate range of wavelengths for
  (a) audible sound
  (b) music
  (c) speech

1.4.4. Calculate the approximate range of wavenumbers for
  (a) audible sound
  (b) music
  (c) speech

1.4.5. Compare the root-mean-square pressure of a square wave and a triangular wave with that of a sinusoidal pressure wave.

1.5.1. A 70-dB, 630-Hz pure tone is out-of-phase by 0.0002 s with a 73-dB, 630-Hz pure tone. The air temperature is 20°C.
  (a) Find the phase angle.
  (b) Find the root-mean-square sound pressure of each wave.
  (c) Find the root-mean-square sound pressure of the combination, and the sound pressure level.

1.5.2. A 90-dB, 1-kHz pure tone is out-of-phase by 0.0003 s with a 91-dB, 1-kHz pure tone. The air temperature is 20°C.
  (a) Find the phase angle.
  (b) Find the root-mean-square sound pressure of each wave.
  (c) Find the root-mean-square sound pressure of the combination, and the sound pressure level.

1.5.3. A 70-dB, 630-Hz pure tone is out-of-phase by 0.0002 s with a 73-dB, 630-Hz pure tone. The air temperature is 20°C. Plot pressure versus time for the combined wave.

1.5.4. An observer is equidistant from a number of uncorrelated noise sources of equal strength. Write an equation relating the sound pressure level at the observer to the number of sources and the sound pressure level of a single source.

1.5.5. Plot the above result.

1.5.6. An 80-dB, 125-Hz pure tone and an 82-dB, 160-Hz pure tone are combined.
   (a) Find the root-mean-square sound pressure of each wave and of the combined wave.
   (b) Find the beat frequency.
   (c) Make a computer-generated plot of the combined wave. If a computer is not available, simply sketch the envelope.

1.6.1. Pink noise has, by definition, the same sound pressure level in each octave band. Find the overall (unweighted) sound pressure level of pink noise in terms of the sound level measured in a single octave band.

1.6.2. Write a computer program for determining the overall (unweighted) sound pressure level from a series of measurements in each octave band.

1.7.1. Write a computer program for determining the overall A-weighted sound level from a series of unweighted sound pressure level measurements in each octave band.

1.8.1. Write a computer program for determining equivalent sound level from a series of A-weighted sound level measurements.

1.8.2. Find equivalent sound level from the following representative A-weighted sound level readings: 90, 81, 78, 85, 89, 88, 55, 67, 90, 81, 81, 88, 84, 67, 60, 67, 59, 90, 86, 82.

1.8.3. Find equivalent sound level from the following representative A-weighted sound level readings: 47, 57, 49, 51, 52, 54, 55, 59, 57, 45.

1.8.4. **(a)** Find equivalent sound level for an hour during which each of the following levels exists for 15 minutes: 47, 49, 50, and 100 dBA.
   (b) Evaluate the relative contribution of the 100-dBA level.

1.8.5. A worker is exposed to an equivalent sound level of 85 dBA, 40 hours per week, 48 weeks per year. Find the yearly equivalent sound level (based on 365.24 24-hour days) if there is no significant noise exposure outside the workplace.

1.8.6. Find the equivalent sound level for an hour during which sound level increases linearly from 70 to 90 dBA.

1.8.7. Find the equivalent sound level for an hour during which sound level decreases by 0.2 dBA/min, beginning with 85 dBA.

1.9.1. The following sound level versus time pattern is predicted:

Level (dBA)	Time
45	Midnight to 6 A.M.
50	6 A.M. to 8 A.M.
53	8 A.M. to noon
55	Noon to 5 P.M.
51	5 P.M. to midnight

Determine day–night sound level.

1.9.2. The following sound level versus time pattern is predicted:

Level (dBA)	Time
51	Midnight to 5 A.M.
56	5 A.M. to 8 A.M.
60	8 A.M. to noon
64	Noon to 5 P.M.
59	5 P.M. to midnight

Determine day–night sound level.

1.10.1. Derive the equation for vector sound intensity for a sinusoidal wave. Express pressure and velocity as cosine functions.

1.10.2. Derive the vector sound intensity equation for a sinusoidal wave. Express pressure and velocity in complex form.

1.11.1. Find the range of atmospheric pressures and temperatures for which sound intensity level (in the propagation direction) and sound pressure level differ by less than 1 dB. Assume sound pressure and particle velocity are in-phase.

1.11.2. Compare the approximate sound intensity at the threshold of feeling with that at the threshold of hearing for a frequency of 1 kHz. Assume sound pressure and particle velocity are in-phase.

1.12.1. Sources 1 and 2, having sound power levels of 50 and 70 dB re 1 pW, respectively, operate together in a room. It is proposed to eliminate source 1. Find the percentage reduction in total sound power.

1.12.2. Sources 1 and 2, having sound power levels of 85 and 75 dB re 1 pW, respectively, operate together in a room. It is proposed to eliminate source 1. Find the percentage reduction in total sound power.

Chapter 2

Sound Generation and Propagation

The basic elements of a noise problem include the source, the path, and the receiver. Actual noise sources are often represented as idealized point sources or other simple mathematical models. Airborne sound, in traveling to the receiver, may be influenced by reflection, diffraction, and absorption. If the source strength and the noise path are known, it is possible to predict noise levels at various locations and to determine which noise control measures are likely to be effective.

2.1 MODELING OF NOISE SOURCES

When examining a physical problem, we often compromise between the most precise mathematical model and the model that is most useful in obtaining reasonable solutions. In attempting to describe the noise emission of a machine, the directional characteristics could be considered as well as the frequency and time characteristics. Knowledge of directional characteristics is sometimes an aid to designing for minimum operator noise exposure. In many situations, however, the orientation of the source varies relative to the observer, and directional characteristics are not relevant in assessing noise exposure. In such cases, the most simple model may be appropriate. Aerodynamic noise sources are sometimes modeled as monopoles, dipoles, and quadrupoles. One or more of these basic noise sources is usually present in gas flow at subsonic speed.

The Monopole Source, the Spherical Wave Equation

A monopole is an idealization of a noise source as a pulsating sphere generating a spherical sound wave. If the source dimensions are small compared with the wavelength of the sound, the source is considered a *point source.* From equation 1.2.11, we have

$$\frac{\partial^2 p}{\partial t^2} = c^2 \, \nabla^2 p \tag{2.1.1}$$

47

where, for spherical coordinates without angular dependence, the Laplacian reduces to

$$\nabla^2 = \frac{1}{r^2}\frac{\partial}{\partial r}\left(r^2\frac{\partial}{\partial r}\right) = \frac{\partial^2}{\partial r^2} + \frac{2}{r}\frac{\partial}{\partial r}$$

p = sound pressure

r = the radial coordinate

c = the wave propagation speed

t = time

Solutions to the Spherical Wave Equation

Equation 2.1.1, the spherical wave equation, is satisfied by functions of time and location in the form

$$p = \frac{1}{r}\,[F_1(ct - r) + F_2(ct + r)] \tag{2.1.2}$$

which may be verified by direct substitution (a suggested exercise). Note that the term $F_1(ct - r)$ describes waves traveling away from the source. The term $F_2(ct + r)$, which describes waves traveling toward the source, has no physical significance.

A harmonic solution to the spherical wave equation is given by

$$p = \frac{A}{r}\cos[k(ct - r)] \tag{2.1.3}$$

where　　　A = a constant
　　　　　$k = \omega/c$ = the wave number
　　　time $t = 0$ is selected to eliminate a phase angle

Mean-Square Sound Pressure and Root-Mean-Square Sound Pressure for the Spherical Wave

For the harmonic solution, the mean-square sound pressure at a distance r from the source is given by

$$p_{rms}^2 = \frac{1}{T}\int_0^T p^2\,dt = \frac{A^2}{r^2 T}\int_0^T \cos^2[k(ct - r)]dt = \frac{A^2}{2r^2} \tag{2.1.4}$$

and the root-mean-square sound pressure

$$p_{rms} = \frac{A}{2^{1/2}r} \tag{2.1.5}$$

where $T = \tau = 1/f = 2\pi/\omega$ = one period. If many frequencies are present, p_{rms}^2 and p_{rms} can be determined with reasonable accuracy if the integration time is large compared with the period of the lowest frequency sound.

Sound Power

The sound power of a source can be defined in terms of sound intensity as follows:

$$W = \iint_S \mathbf{I} \cdot \mathbf{n} \, dS \qquad (2.1.6)$$

where $\mathbf{I} = \dfrac{1}{T} \displaystyle\int_0^T p\mathbf{u} \, dt$ = vector sound intensity

p = sound pressure
$\mathbf{u}$ = particle velocity vector
S = any closed surface about the source
$\mathbf{n}$ = the unit normal to S
T = averaging time

Although peak values are sometimes of interest when dealing with impulse sounds, intensity and power are usually averaged over some time interval (one or more full periods for a pure tone, or an interval sufficient to produce stable results for random noise).

Sound Power of a Spherical Wave

For a spherical wave, surface S may be specified as a sphere of radius r about the source. Sound power is given by

$$W = \iint_S I_r \, dS \qquad (2.1.7)$$

where I_r = the magnitude of the resultant sound intensity, which is radial, that is parallel to the unit normal $\mathbf{n}$. When the observer is sufficiently distant from the source, sound pressure and particle velocity are in-phase, and equation 1.11.5 yields

$$I_r = p_{\text{rms}} u_{\text{rms}} = \frac{p_{\text{rms}}^2}{\rho c} \qquad (2.1.8)$$

where p_{rms}^2 = mean-square sound pressure
ρ = the mass density of air

Consider an omnidirectional source, and an observer distance r at which particle velocity and sound pressure are in-phase. In this case, intensity has no angular dependence, and integration is over 4π steradians (sr). Sound power is given by

$$W = I_r S = 4\pi r^2 I_r = \frac{4\pi r^2 p_{\text{rms}}^2}{\rho c} \qquad (2.1.9)$$

if sound pressure is measured in full-space. If sound is measured in half-space, that is, if the source lies on a reflective surface, then integration is over 2π sr and

$$W = \frac{2\pi r^2 p_{\text{rms}}^2}{\rho c} \qquad (2.1.10)$$

where W = sound power of the source (W)
I = sound intensity (W/m²) in the wave-propagation direction
r = distance from the center of the source

Thus, for a spherical wave in full-space, mean-square sound pressure and sound intensity in the wave-propagation direction are related to sound power of the source by

$$p_{rms}^2 = \frac{\rho c W}{4\pi r^2}$$ (2.1.11)

and

$$I = \frac{W}{4\pi r^2}$$ (2.1.12)

The intensity versus sound power relationship is called the *inverse-square law*.

Sound Pressure Level and Sound Intensity Level for the Spherical Wave

Using the definition of sound pressure level, we have

$$L_P = 10 \lg\left(\frac{p_{rms}^2}{p_{ref}^2}\right) = 10 \lg\left(\frac{\rho c W}{4\pi r^2 p_{ref}^2}\right)$$

$$= 10 \lg(\rho c W) - 20 \lg r + 83$$ (2.1.13)

where L_P = sound pressure level (dB)
r = distance from the center of the source (m)
$p_{ref} = 20 \times 10^{-6}$ Pa

The sound intensity level is given by

$$L_I = 10 \lg\left(\frac{I}{I_{ref}}\right) = 10 \lg\left(\frac{W}{4\pi r^2 \times 10^{-12}}\right)$$

$$= 10 \lg W - 20 \lg r + 109$$

$$= L_W - 20 \lg r - 11$$ (2.1.14)

where L_I = sound intensity level (dB) in the direction of propagation of the spherical wave
$I_{ref} = 10^{-12}$ W/m²
L_W = sound power level (dB re 1 pW)

Sound Sources Above an Acoustically Hard Surface

If a source of power W is situated above an acoustically hard (reflective) surface, then sound waves expand within a half-space. Sound intensity in the propagation direction is given by

$$I = \frac{W}{2\pi r^2}$$ (2.1.15)

and sound intensity level by

$$L_I = L_W - 20 \lg r - 8 \qquad (2.1.16)$$

for an omnidirectional source with sound pressure and particle velocity in-phase.

Anechoic chambers are constructed with wedges of sound absorbing material on the ceiling and walls and below the (wire mesh) floor to approximate free-field conditions for acoustic measurements. If absorptive wedges are placed on the ceiling and walls, but the floor is acoustically hard, that is, acoustically reflective, the room is called a hemianechoic chamber. Figure 2.1.1 shows a large hemianechoic chamber.

When we are considering free-field conditions, sound intensity level in the propagation direction is approximately equal to sound pressure level for common atmospheric conditions. Recall that the quantities are precisely alike when the product of air density (kg/m^3) and propagation speed (m/s) equals 400.

EXAMPLE PROBLEM: PREDICTION OF SOUND PRESSURE LEVEL

(a) Predict the sound pressure level at an observer situated on an acoustically non-reflective surface, 795 m directly below a turbojet aircraft with a sound power level of 163 dB.

Solution. It is often necessary to make approximations when given limited data. In this problem, we will assume that the spherical wave model applies, as a more precise description of noise sources on the aircraft is not available. Using equation 2.1.14, and assuming that atmospheric conditions are such that sound intensity level and sound pressure level are approximately equal, $L_P = L_W - 20 \lg r - 11 = 163 - 20 \lg 795 - 11 = 94$ dB. For path lengths of several hundred meters, sound waves lose energy due to heat conduction and air viscosity. These effects, called air absorption, could reduce the sound pressure level by several decibels, depending on the relative humidity of the air and the frequency content of the sound. Waveform steepening and shock formation are characteristic of

Figure 2.1.1 Hemianechoic chamber. (*Source:* Eckel Ind. Inc., Cambridge, MA)

jet aircraft and other sources producing high sound pressure levels. Such nonlinear effects, ignored in this example, could affect the accuracy of the prediction.

(b) Relate sound pressure level L_{Pa} at $r = a$ to sound pressure level L_{Pb} at $r = b$ if the spherical wave (point source) model applies.

Solution. Using equation 2.1.13, where both locations are subject to noise from the same source, the difference in sound pressure levels is given by $L_{Pa} - L_{Pb} = -20 \lg a + 20 \lg b = 20 \lg(b/a)$. Figure 2.1.2 is a computer-generated plot of sound pressure level difference versus distance ratio. The result is also applicable if the source is situated on an acoustically hard surface. The result may also be applied when noise levels are given in dBA. Note that the sound pressure level changes by approximately -6 dB per doubling of distance. The result is not applicable near the source (within one or two wavelengths or within one characteristic source dimension), in a sound field subject to reflections, or where background noise becomes significant.

Radiated Sound Power of Aerodynamic Monopole, Dipole, and Quadrupole Sources

When noise sources result from gas flow, the sound power is a function of flow velocity. The power versus velocity relationship depends on the source type.

Aerodynamic Monopoles The radiated sound power of a monopole is given by

$$W = K\rho d^2 v^4/c \qquad (2.1.17)$$

where W = sound power (W)
K = a constant that depends on nozzle configuration
ρ = gas density
d = a characteristic dimension
v = gas flow velocity
c = speed of sound propagation in the gas

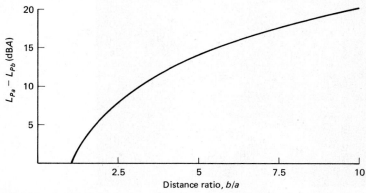

Figure 2.1.2 Difference in sound level between two locations based on the point-source model.

Aerodynamic Dipoles An aerodynamic dipole corresponds to two closely spaced monopoles that are out-of-phase. When gas flows past obstructions and when turbulent flow interacts with rotor blades or stator blades, the resulting noise radiation resembles a dipole pattern. A dipole may also be used to represent the sound generation characteristics of a vibrating beam. The radiated sound power of a dipole resulting from gas flow is given by

$$W = K\rho d^2 v^6/c^3 \qquad (2.1.18)$$

where constant K may differ from the constant in the monopole equation.

Aerodynamic Quadrupoles Four closely spaced monopoles, with adjacent monopoles out-of-phase, form a quadrupole. Turbulent jets at subsonic velocity usually behave as quadrupoles. The radiated sound power of an aerodynamic quadrupole, as given by Lighthill (1952), is

$$W = K\rho d^2 v^8/c^5 \qquad (2.1.19)$$

Line Sources

An ideal line source is equivalent to a continuous line of infinitesimal uncorrelated noise sources producing constant sound power per unit line length. This idealization can be used to approximate the effect of a number of actual sources arranged in a continuous line if the observer is sufficiently distant.

Consider a line source of sound power W' W/m. At a distance r from the source, sound intensity is given by the unit sound power divided by the area of a unit-length cylindrical surface:

$$I = \frac{W'}{2\pi r} \qquad (2.1.20)$$

where I = free-field sound intensity in the sound propagation direction. Thus, the sound intensity of an ideal line source follows an inverse-distance law. Under common temperature and atmospheric pressure conditions, sound pressure level is approximately equal to sound intensity level in the propagation direction, from which

$$L_P = L_I = 10 \lg\left(\frac{I}{I_{\text{ref}}}\right) = 10 \lg\left(\frac{W'}{2\pi r \times 10^{-12}}\right)$$

$$= 10 \lg\left(\frac{W'}{r}\right) + 112 \text{ (approximately)} \qquad (2.1.21)$$

If an ideal line source rests on an acoustically hard surface, then sound intensity in the propagation direction and sound pressure level are given by

$$I = \frac{W'}{\pi r} \qquad (2.1.22)$$

and

$$L_P = 10 \lg\left(\frac{W'}{r}\right) + 115 \text{ (approximately)} \qquad (2.1.23)$$

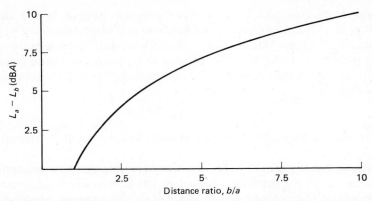

Figure 2.1.3 Difference in sound level between two locations based on the line source model.

Using the last equation to relate sound pressure level at one location $r = a$ to another at $r = b$, we have

$$L_{Pa} - L_{Pb} = -10 \lg a + 10 \lg b = 10 \lg\left(\frac{b}{a}\right) \qquad (2.1.24)$$

The above equation is equivalent to an attenuation of about 3 dB per doubling of distance from the line source, and applies to a line source in full space or on an acoustically hard surface. Figure 2.1.3, which shows the difference in sound level versus distance ratio based on a line source model, was generated with the aid of a personal computer.

Actual Noise Sources

Machines and other actual noise sources have finite dimensions, and may be located in areas where reflections and background noise make significant contributions. The idealized models examined above do not apply close to an actual source, or at distances where other than direct noise contributions dominate. Whenever possible, directional characteristics of noise sources should be determined, and considered when selecting noise control measures.

2.2 DIRECTIVITY

Radiation of noise energy from an ideal point source (a monopole) is independent of direction. Some actual noise sources, however, may radiate substantially more energy in one direction than another.

Directivity index DI is defined as the difference between the sound pressure level in a given azimuth and elevation direction $L_P(\theta, \phi)$ and the space-average sound pressure level L_{PS} at the same radius r from the center of the source. Thus,

$$DI(\theta, \phi) = L_P(\theta, \phi) - L_{PS} \qquad (2.2.1)$$

Space-average sound pressure level is the sound pressure level calculated from the space-average mean-square sound pressure. If the sound power W is known, space-average sound pressure level may be approximated from the ideal point source relationship:

$$L_{PS} = 10 \lg\left(\frac{W}{4\pi r^2}\right) + 120 \qquad (2.2.2)$$

This relationship is valid for airborne sound at most temperature and pressure conditions. If space-average sound pressure level is to be determined experimentally, an integrating sound level meter may be used to scan the field about the source and measure equivalent sound level. Instrumentation and measurement methods will be discussed in a later section.

Usually, the highest directivity index and its direction will be of interest. The lowest value of directivity index and its direction could be useful as well, if we wish to find a location where a machine operator would be subject to the least noise. When the frequency content of noise is measured, it may be found that directivity is a function of frequency as well. If the frequency characteristics of the sound field are required, the directivity index versus direction relationship can be computed for each octave band or each one-third octave band.

Directivity factor $Q(\theta, \phi)$ is a similar indication of directionality defined by

$$Q(\theta, \phi) = \frac{p_{\text{rms}}^2(\theta, \phi)}{p_S^2} \qquad (2.2.3)$$

where p_S^2 is the space-average mean-square sound pressure, and all determinations are made at the same radius measured from the center of the source. Directivity index and directivity factor are related by

$$\text{DI}(\theta, \phi) = 10 \lg Q(\theta, \phi) \qquad (2.2.4)$$

For an ideal (nondirectional) point source in full space, the directivity index and directivity factor are, respectively, $\text{DI}(\theta, \phi) = 0$ and $Q(\theta, \phi) = 1$ for all θ and ϕ. If an ideal point source is located on an acoustically hard surface, then

$$\text{DI}(\theta, \phi) = 3 \quad \text{and} \quad Q(\theta, \phi) = 2$$

for the half-space above the surface.

The sound intensity of a dipole in the direction of sound propagation is given by Crocker and Price (1975) as

$$I = \rho c k^4 (Q l_1)^2 \frac{\cos^2 \theta}{32\pi^2 r^2} \qquad (2.2.5)$$

where Q = source strength
l_1 = separation distance
θ = angular location measured from the dipole axis

The acoustic power of a dipole source, found by integrating the intensity over the area of a sphere of radius r about the source, is

$$W = \int_0^\pi 2\pi I r^2 \sin \theta \, d\theta = \frac{\rho c k^4 (Q l_1)^2}{24\pi} \qquad (2.2.6)$$

The directivity factor equation can be expressed in terms of sound intensity as follows:

$$Q(\theta, \phi) = \frac{I(\theta, \phi)}{I_S} \tag{2.2.7}$$

where $I_S = W/(4\pi r^2)$ = space-average free-field sound intensity in the propagation direction. Thus, for an ideal dipole source, the directivity factor is given by

$$Q_{\text{dipole}} = 3 \cos^2 \theta$$

for a range of values

$$0 \leq Q_{\text{dipole}} \leq 3$$

Actual sources would differ from the ideal source, so that a directivity factor of zero could not be realized. The directivity index is given by

$$\text{DI}_{\text{dipole}} = 10 \lg(3 \cos^2 \theta)$$

EXAMPLE PROBLEM: DIRECTIVITY

A noise source produces a sound field with a maximum directivity index of 11. The A-weighted source power is 0.001 W. Find maximum A-weighted sound level at a radius of 15 m from the source in full space.

Solution. Using equations 2.2.1 and 2.2.2, we have

$$L(\theta, \phi) = L_{PS} + \text{DI}(\theta, \phi)$$

$$= 10 \lg\left(\frac{W}{4\pi r^2}\right) + 120 + \text{DI}(\theta, \phi)$$

from which

$$L_{\max} = 10 \lg\left(\frac{0.001}{4\pi 15^2}\right) + 120 + 11 = 66.5 \text{ dB}A$$

2.3 STANDING WAVES

Sound pressure and particle velocity are in phase for free progressive sound waves. This region where such waves dominate can be called the direct field. Acoustically hard objects in the sound field cause reflections. Under certain conditions, reflections cause sound pressure and particle velocity to be 90° out-of-phase, forming a standing wave. As observed in Chapter 1, the vector sound intensity of a standing wave is (theoretically) zero.

Room Acoustics

This section provides only an introduction into the behavior of sound in enclosed spaces. A comprehensive treatment of room acoustics is given by Kuttruff (1979).

The sound level in a room is affected by reflection and absorption at the walls. If the room has acoustically hard plane walls, and room dimensions are large compared with the wavelength of the sound, the angle of reflection of the sound wave equals the angle of incidence.

The general wave equation is given in Chapter 1 as follows:

$$\frac{\partial^2 p}{\partial t^2} = c^2 \, \nabla^2 p \tag{1.2.11}$$

where

$$
\begin{aligned}
p &= \text{sound pressure}\\
t &= \text{time}\\
c &= \text{speed of sound propagation in air}\\
x, y, \text{and } z &= \text{the coordinates of a point}\\
\nabla^2 &= \partial^2/\partial x^2 + \partial^2/\partial y^2 + \partial^2/\partial z^2 \text{ (the Laplacian)}
\end{aligned}
$$

A plane sinusoidal sound wave may be described in complex form as follows:

$$p = Pe^{j[\omega t(+/-)k_x x(+/-)k_y y(+/-)k_z z]} \tag{2.3.1}$$

where, in this equation, the sound pressure is given by the real part of p, and

$$\omega = 2\pi f$$

is the circular frequency of the sound wave. The minus sign applies before the $k_x x$ term if the wave velocity component along the x-axis is positive, the plus sign applies if the component is negative, and so on. Thus, equation 2.3.1 represents eight equations, depending on the wave propagation direction with respect to the x-, y-, and z-axes.

Substituting equation 2.3.1 in the wave equation, we have

$$\omega^2 = c^2(k_x^2 + k_y^2 + k_z^2) \tag{2.3.2}$$

from which the wavenumber

$$k = \frac{\omega}{c} = \sqrt{k_x^2 + k_y^2 + k_z^2} \tag{2.3.3}$$

The direction cosines formed by the wave propagation direction and the x-, y-, and z-coordinate axes are k_x/k, k_y/k, and k_z/k, respectively.

Particle Motion

The relationship between particle displacement ξ in the x-direction and sound pressure p is given by

$$\frac{\partial p}{\partial x} + \frac{\rho}{}\frac{\partial^2 \xi}{\partial t^2} = 0 \tag{2.3.4}$$

where ρ is the mass density of air. Thus, we have

$$\frac{\partial p}{\partial x} = -\frac{\rho}{}\frac{\partial u_x}{\partial t} \tag{2.3.5}$$

where u_x is the x-component of particle velocity. Substituting the complex form of the particle velocity in the above equation, the result is

$$\frac{\partial p}{\partial x} = -j\omega\rho u_x \tag{2.3.6}$$

from which we obtain

$$u_x = \frac{-\partial p/\partial x}{j\omega\rho} \tag{2.3.7}$$

The other complex particle velocity components, obtained in the same way, are

$$u_y = \frac{-\partial p/\partial y}{j\omega\rho} \tag{2.3.8}$$

and

$$u_z = \frac{-\partial p/\partial z}{j\omega\rho} \tag{2.3.9}$$

where actual velocity components are given by the real parts of the above values.

Boundary Conditions

Consider a rectangular room of dimensions $A \times B \times C$ measured in the x-, y-, and z-directions, respectively, as in Figure 2.3.1. There is a rigid wall at $x = 0$ and another at $x = A$, and so on. The normal component of particle velocity at a wall must be zero, resulting in the following boundary conditions:

$$u_x(0, y, z) = u_x(A, y, z) = 0 \tag{2.3.10}$$

$$u_y(x, 0, z) = u_y(x, B, z) = 0 \tag{2.3.11}$$

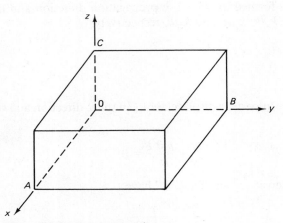

Figure 2.3.1 Room acoustics.

and

$$u_z(x, y, 0) = u_z(x, y, C) = 0 \qquad (2.3.12)$$

Normal Modes, Eigenfrequencies

The normal modes in a room are the sound wave patterns at resonances, the conditions necessary for standing waves to exist as a result of reflections. The discrete frequencies (eigenfrequencies) f_E at which standing waves can occur depend on room dimensions. Assume that sound of frequency

$$f = \frac{\omega}{2\pi}$$

is generated within a room or transmitted through a wall. If the sound frequency corresponds to an eigenfrequency, the presence of standing waves may be objectionable. It can be shown that the eigenfrequencies, the frequencies that satisfy the wave equation, and the boundary conditions for standing waves in a rectangular room are given by

$$f_E = \frac{c}{2}\left[\left(\frac{n_x}{A}\right)^2 + \left(\frac{n_y}{B}\right)^2 + \left(\frac{n_z}{C}\right)^2\right]^{1/2} \qquad (2.3.13)$$

where $n_x = 0, 1, 2, \ldots$
$n_y = 0, 1, 2, \ldots$
$n_z = 0, 1, 2, \ldots$

The number of sound pressure nodes that would be observed in crossing the room in the x-direction is given by n_x, and so on.

Axial Modes   Axial modes are identified by sound waves that move parallel to a coordinate axis. Room modes may be identified in the form $n_x n_y n_z$. Then, axial modes include modes 1 0 0; 0 1 0; 0 0 1; 2 0 0, and so on.

Tangential Modes   When sound waves in a rectangular room move parallel to one pair of surfaces, the mode is tangential. Tangential modes are identified by one zero in the mode number, for example, modes 1 1 0; 0 2 1; and so on.

Oblique Modes   When sound waves impinge on all six walls, the mode is oblique. The mode number is made up of three nonzero components, for example, mode 1 1 1; 2 1 3; and so on.

EXAMPLE PROBLEM: NORMAL MODES AND EIGENFREQUENCIES

Determine some of the eigenfrequencies for a 6-m long by 5-m wide by 3-m high room. Let the temperature be 22°C.

Solution.   Using the equation for the speed of sound propagation from Chapter 1,

$$c = 20.04(T' + 273.16)^{1/2} = 20.04(22 + 273.16)^{1/2}$$

$$= 344.3 \text{ m/s}$$

TABLE 2.3.1 EIGENFREQUENCIES OF A
RECTANGULAR ROOM
Air Temperature = 22°C
Room Dimensions A = 6 m, B = 5 m, C = 3 m
Sound Propagation Velocity = 344.3 m/s

Normal mode:			eigenfrequency (Hz) =	
Normal mode:	1	0	0	eigenfrequency (Hz) = 28.7
Normal mode:	2	0	0	eigenfrequency (Hz) = 57.4
Normal mode:	3	0	0	eigenfrequency (Hz) = 86.1
Normal mode:	0	1	0	eigenfrequency (Hz) = 34.4
Normal mode:	1	1	0	eigenfrequency (Hz) = 44.8
Normal mode:	2	1	0	eigenfrequency (Hz) = 66.9
Normal mode:	3	1	0	eigenfrequency (Hz) = 92.7
Normal mode:	0	2	0	eigenfrequency (Hz) = 68.9
Normal mode:	1	2	0	eigenfrequency (Hz) = 74.6
Normal mode:	2	2	0	eigenfrequency (Hz) = 89.6
Normal mode:	3	2	0	eigenfrequency (Hz) = 110.2
Normal mode:	0	0	1	eigenfrequency (Hz) = 57.4
Normal mode:	1	0	1	eigenfrequency (Hz) = 64.2
Normal mode:	2	0	1	eigenfrequency (Hz) = 81.2
Normal mode:	3	0	1	eigenfrequency (Hz) = 103.4
Normal mode:	0	1	1	eigenfrequency (Hz) = 66.9
Normal mode:	1	1	1	eigenfrequency (Hz) = 72.8
Normal mode:	2	1	1	eigenfrequency (Hz) = 88.2
Normal mode:	3	1	1	eigenfrequency (Hz) = 109
Normal mode:	0	2	1	eigenfrequency (Hz) = 89.6
Normal mode:	1	2	1	eigenfrequency (Hz) = 94.1
Normal mode:	2	2	1	eigenfrequency (Hz) = 106.4
Normal mode:	3	2	1	eigenfrequency (Hz) = 124.3
Normal mode:	0	0	2	eigenfrequency (Hz) = 114.8
Normal mode:	1	0	2	eigenfrequency (Hz) = 118.3
Normal mode:	2	0	2	eigenfrequency (Hz) = 128.3
Normal mode:	3	0	2	eigenfrequency (Hz) = 143.5
Normal mode:	0	1	2	eigenfrequency (Hz) = 119.8
Normal mode:	1	1	2	eigenfrequency (Hz) = 123.2
Normal mode:	2	1	2	eigenfrequency (Hz) = 132.8
Normal mode:	3	1	2	eigenfrequency (Hz) = 147.5
Normal mode:	0	2	2	eigenfrequency (Hz) = 133.8
Normal mode:	1	2	2	eigenfrequency (Hz) = 136.9
Normal mode:	2	2	2	eigenfrequency (Hz) = 145.6
Normal mode:	3	2	2	eigenfrequency (Hz) = 159.1

The axes are oriented so that the x-axis corresponds to the long dimension of the room, the y-axis to the width, and the z-axis is vertical. Thus, $A = 6$, $B = 5$, and $C = 3$. The number of normal modes and eigenfrequencies is infinite, but only the lower eigenfrequencies are of interest. A simple computer program was used to calculate the eigenfrequencies for $n_x = 0$ to 3 and n_y and $n_z = 0$ to 2. The results are given in Table 2.3.1. The lowest eigenfrequency,

$$f_E = 28.7 \text{ Hz}$$

corresponds to a wavelength of

$$\lambda = \frac{c}{f_E} = \frac{344.3}{28.7} = 12 \text{ m}$$

It occurs with $n_x = 1$ and $n_y = n_z = 0$, the 1 0 0 mode, a half-wave in the x-direction. In ascending order the next higher eigenfrequencies are 34.4 and 44.8 Hz, corresponding respectively to axial mode 0 1 0 and tangential mode 1 1 0.

2.4 THE NEAR FIELD, THE FAR FIELD, AND THE REVERBERANT FIELD

The region close to a source was not considered in the sections above. Relationships based on in-phase sound pressure and particle velocity may not be valid in this region called the *near field.* The extent of the near field depends on sound wavelength and source type.

Spherical Sound Waves

Consider a spherical sound wave in which particle velocity is a function of the radial coordinate and time only. Let the sound field be described by

$$u = \frac{\partial \Phi}{\partial r} \tag{2.4.1}$$

where $u = u(r, t) = $ particle velocity
   $\Phi = \Phi(r, t) = $ a velocity potential

In this case, the wave equation may be written in the form

$$\frac{\partial^2 (r\Phi)}{\partial r^2} = \frac{1}{c^2} \frac{\partial^2 (r\Phi)}{\partial t^2} \tag{2.4.2}$$

where $c = $ wave propagation velocity. For a harmonic wave, the velocity potential may be expressed in complex form:

$$\Phi = \Phi_1 e^{jkct} \tag{2.4.3}$$

where $\Phi_1 = \Phi_1(r)$
   $k = $ the wavenumber

Substituting equation 2.4.3 into 2.4.2, the result is

$$\frac{\partial^2 (r\Phi_1)}{\partial r^2} + k^2 (r\Phi_1) = 0 \tag{2.4.4}$$

which is satisfied by

$$r\Phi_1 = C_1 e^{-jkr} + C_2 e^{jkr} \tag{2.4.5}$$

from which

$$\Phi = C_1 r^{-1} e^{jk(ct-r)} + C_2 r^{-1} e^{jk(ct+r)} \tag{2.4.6}$$

Constant $C_2 = 0$ since this term would describe waves traveling toward the source, a meaningless result in this case. Recall a similar situation when the spherical wave equation was solved in terms of pressure.

The Near Field of a Monopole Source

Consider a monopole source represented by a pulsating sphere of radius a. Let particle velocity at the surface of the sphere be given by

$$u(a) = u_1 e^{jkct} \qquad (2.4.7)$$

Using equations 2.4.1, 2.4.6, and 2.4.7, the arbitrary constant is found to be

$$C_1 = -\frac{u_1 e^{jka}}{a^{-2} + jka^{-1}}$$

The velocity potential is

$$\Phi = -u_1(a^{-2} + jka^{-1})^{-1} r^{-1} e^{jk(ct-r+a)} \qquad (2.4.8)$$

and the particle velocity

$$u = \frac{\partial \Phi}{\partial r} = u_1(a^{-2} + jka^{-1})^{-1}(r^{-2} + jkr^{-1}) e^{jk(ct-r+a)} \qquad (2.4.9)$$

Sound pressure is related to the velocity potential by

$$p = -\rho \frac{\partial \Phi}{\partial t} = jk\rho c u_1(a^{-2} + jka^{-1})^{-1} r^{-1} e^{jk(ct-r+a)} \qquad (2.4.10)$$

Actual sound pressure and particle velocity are, of course, the real parts of these complex quantities. The complex representation allows us to observe phase relationships.

Specific Acoustic Impedance   Specific acoustic impedance, the complex ratio of sound pressure to particle velocity, is given by

$$Z = \frac{p}{u} \qquad \textbf{(1.10.24)}$$

For the monopole, using equations 2.4.9 and 2.4.10, we have

$$Z = \frac{jk\rho c r^{-1}}{r^{-2} + jkr^{-1}}$$

$$= \frac{\rho c(k^2 r^2 + jkr)}{1 + k^2 r^2} \qquad (2.4.11)$$

The real part of Z is called the *acoustic resistance* and the imaginary part the *acoustic reactance*. Reynolds (1981) plots these quantities against wavelength ratio kr. The near field of a source is the region in which there is a significant reactive component of specific acoustic impedance.

EXAMPLE PROBLEM: SPECIFIC ACOUSTIC IMPEDANCE;
THE NEAR FIELD OF A MONOPOLE SOURCE

(a) Determine the specific acoustic impedance at a distance of one-quarter wavelength from a monopole source. Interpret the results. (b) Repeat for two wavelengths.

Solution. (a) Wavenumber is given by

$$k = \frac{\omega}{c} = \frac{2\pi}{\lambda}$$

When the distance from the center of an ideal monopole source is one-quarter wavelength, that is, $r = \lambda/4$, we have

$$kr = \frac{\pi}{2}$$

and from equation 2.4.11,

$$Z = \rho c \frac{(\pi/2)^2 + j\pi/2}{1 + (\pi/2)^2} = \rho c(0.712 + j0.453)$$

At this distance, there is a significant imaginary (reactive) component of specific acoustic impedance. This point is within the near field of the ideal monopole.

(b) At two wavelengths, we have $kr = 2k\lambda = 4\pi$ and from equation 2.4.11,

$$Z = \rho c \frac{(4\pi)^2 + j4\pi}{1 + (4\pi)^2}$$

$$= \rho c(0.994 + j0.079) \approx \rho c$$

At this distance, we are no longer in the near field of the ideal monopole source. Sound pressure and particle velocity are approximately in-phase. The specific acoustic impedance is predominantly real (resistive). The near field is commonly identified as the region in which

$$kr < 10$$

where r = field point location
          k = wave number

Figure 2.4.1 shows a noise level versus distance plot for a typical machine. The region beyond the near field is called the *far field.* The *free field* or *direct field* is the region in which progressive sound waves coming directly from the source dominate. Walls and other acoustically hard surfaces result in reflected sound which makes a significant contribution in a region called the *reverberant field.*

A single machine or other actual source may produce noise that spans a wide range of frequencies, and an accurate model of a machine may consist of several sources of various types. Thus, source dimensions may influence the extent of the near field, sometimes overriding the $kr < 10$ criterion. The extent of the reverberant field is also frequency dependent since the absorptive characteristics of walls and other surfaces depend on the wavelength of the incident sound.

When observed in the region between the near field and far field, typical noise sources may approximate point sources, generating spherical waves. This region is often selected when it is necessary to make representative measurements of noise generated by a machine. The sound field in this region commonly follows the inverse-square law with regard to sound intensity, that is, sound pressure level decreases by 6

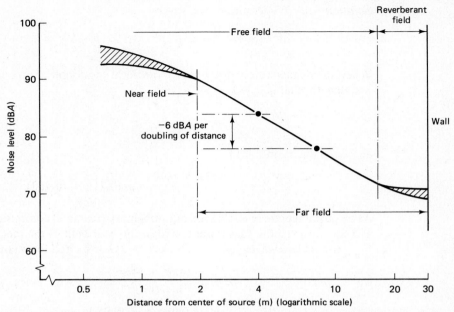

Figure 2.4.1 An illustration of noise level versus distance for a machine approximated by a point source.

dB per doubling of distance from the source. For line sources, the inverse-distance law holds and sound pressure level decreases by 3 dB per doubling of distance from the line source.

Laboratory measurements for determination of sound power of sources and acoustic properties of materials are often made in controlled environments. One such acoustic environment, the anechoic chamber, approximates a free field throughout most of its volume. An alternative, the reverberation room, has acoustically hard walls, floor, and ceiling, and a reverberant field exists throughout most of the volume of the room. A sound field that results from multiple reflections is called a *diffuse field*. In an ideal diffuse field, sound waves travel in all directions with equal probability.

2.5 ABSORPTION AND REVERBERATION TIME

If sound is generated in an initially quiet room, the sound level will grow due to reflections until equilibrium is reached. At that time, the rate of sound energy generation will equal the rate of energy absorption. If the sound generation is stopped, the sound level will decay to the original quiet background level. Growth and decay of sound levels usually occur in a time period of order-of-magnitude of 1 s. By measuring the rate of sound decay, we may determine the amount of absorption in a room, a value that is of practical importance in acoustics and noise control.

Reverberation Time (T_{60})

The reverberation time of a room (T_{60}) is the time in seconds for sound level to decay by 60 dB after a sound source is abruptly turned off. Sixty decibels represents a reduction to one-thousandth of the original sound pressure, or one-millionth of the original sound energy. T_{60} is frequency dependent, and is usually measured for each octave band or one-third octave band. Background noise levels are often too high to permit measurement of the full 60-dB decay. In such cases, T_{60} is determined by extrapolating the experimental decay curve to 60 dB below the original sound level (Figure 2.5.1).

Anechoic chambers are constructed with effective absorptive materials to produce the lowest practical value of T_{60}. Reverberant rooms are constructed with acoustically hard walls to maximize T_{60}. Figure 2.5.2 illustrates the decay of sound in a room, showing a three-dimensional plot of sound level versus frequency and time. A steep level versus time slope indicates a low reverberation time at that frequency. The ideal reverberation time for a room depends on room volume and the intended use of the room. Figure 2.5.3 shows variations in T_{60} with room volume (averaged for the frequencies of interest) for rooms with good acoustical properties.

Absorption Coefficient (α)

Sound absorption is dependent on material properties, angle of incidence, and frequency. The sound absorption coefficient of a material is the ratio of sound energy absorbed by the material to the sound energy that would be absorbed by a perfect absorber of equal area (equivalent to an open window). The tone-burst method of determining absorption coefficient utilizes a speaker that emits a short tone burst at a given angle of incidence. The level of reflected sound energy is measured to determine the reflected and absorbed energy fractions. A different sound absorption coefficient can be determined for each angle of sound incidence on the absorbing material.

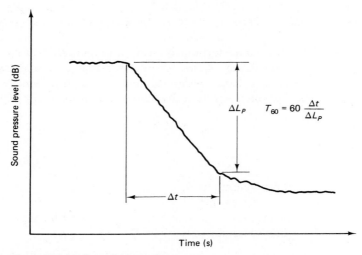

Figure 2.5.1 Sound decay plot.

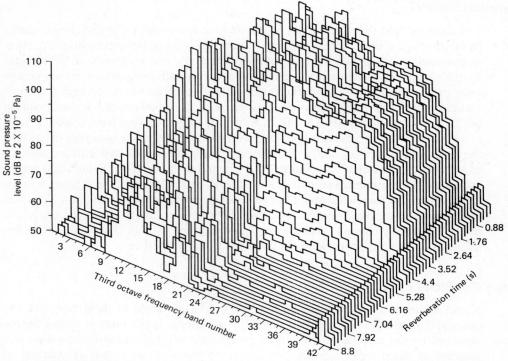

Figure 2.5.2 Representation of reverberation as a three-dimensional landscape where the axes are amplitude, frequency, and time. (*Source:* Bruel & Kjaer Instruments, Inc.)

Statistical sound absorption coefficient ($\alpha_{\text{statistical}}$) is the ratio of absorbed to incident sound energy in a perfectly diffuse field. Values of $\alpha_{\text{statistical}}$ range from about 0.01 for a smooth hard material to about 1.0 for the walls of an anechoic chamber.

The Sabine Formula The Sabine formula is an empirically based relationship between reverberation time, room volume, and total room absorption. It assumes that a uniform, diffuse sound field is approximated within the room. Thus, it provides one means of determining statistical sound absorption coefficient. According to the Sabine formula,

$$T_{60} = \frac{0.16V}{\sum\limits_{i=1}^{n} \alpha_i S_i} \qquad (2.5.1)$$

where
$$V = \text{room volume (m}^3\text{)}$$
$$S_i = \text{surface area (m}^2\text{)}$$
$$\alpha_i = \text{absorption coefficient for each of } n \text{ components}$$
$$\textstyle\sum_{i=1}^{n} \alpha_i S_i = \text{total room absorption (m}^2 \text{ sabins)}$$

One meter squared sabin is the absorption equivalent to 1 m^2 of a perfect absorber.

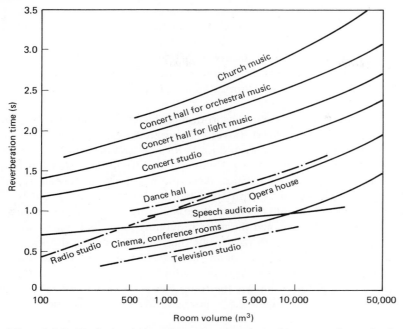

Figure 2.5.3 Typical variation of reverberation time with volume for auditoria considered to have good acoustical properties. (*Source:* Bruel & Kjaer Instruments, Inc.)

Sabine Absorption Coefficient The Sabine absorption coefficient is determined by measuring reverberation time in a reverberant room with and without the presence of a sample of the absorbing material under test. Consider a sample of surface area S and absorption coefficient α which is yet to be determined. Measurements are made in a reverberant room with total wall area S_0 having an average absorption coefficient α_0. The reverberation time is found to be $T_{60(O)}$ without the sample and $T_{60(S)}$ with the sample in the chamber. Using the Sabine formula, we obtain

$$T_{60(O)} = \frac{0.16V}{S_0\alpha_0}$$

and

$$T_{60(S)} = \frac{0.16V}{S\alpha + (S_0 - S)\alpha_0}$$

Combining the above equations, and assuming $\alpha_0 \ll \alpha$, we obtain the absorption coefficient

$$\alpha = 0.16V\frac{1/T_{60(S)} - 1/T_{60(O)}}{S} \qquad (2.5.2)$$

which is sometimes designated as α_{sabine}.

Typical absorption coefficients for construction elements, curtains, and carpeting are given in Table 2.5.1. The sound absorption of clothing is also considered in the design of auditoriums. This is accounted for by the absorption coefficients given in the table based on the sound absorption of one seated person. At the higher frequencies, if path lengths are long, air absorption is sometimes considered. Figure 2.5.4 illustrates the relation between sound absorption, material thickness, and frequency for a porous material.

Most reported values of absorption coefficient are obtained by using the experimental procedure described above. Values of α should theoretically fall between zero for a perfect acoustic reflector and unity for a perfect absorber. Some measurements, however, produce values of $\alpha > 1$, possibly due to diffraction at low frequencies and other test condition irregularities. Absorption coefficient may be reported for each octave band or each one-third octave band. Absorption coefficient is sometimes reported as a single number. The average value based on measurements at 250, 500, 1000, and 2000 Hz is called the noise reduction coefficient α_{NRC}.

A room with smooth hard walls that lacks carpeting, drapes, and an acoustic ceiling is called a "hard room" or an "acoustically hard room." Addition of carpeting, drapes, acoustic paneling, an acoustic ceiling, soft furniture, or other items with high absorption coefficients changes the room characteristics to an acoustically "medium room" or "soft room." Figure 2.5.5 shows average sound absorption coefficients plotted

TABLE 2.5.1 ABSORPTION COEFFICIENTS[a]

Material	Frequency (Hz)					
	125	250	500	1000	2000	4000
Acoustic paneling	0.15	0.3	0.75	0.85	0.75	0.4
Brick	0.05	0.04	0.02	0.04	0.05	0.05
Brick, painted	0.01	0.01	0.02	0.02	0.02	0.03
Concrete block	0.36	0.44	0.31	0.29	0.39	0.25
Curtains	0.05	0.12	0.15	0.27	0.37	0.50
Floor, concrete	0.02	0.02	0.02	0.04	0.05	0.05
Floor, wood	0.15	0.2	0.1	0.1	0.1	0.1
Floor, carpeted	0.1	0.15	0.25	0.3	0.3	0.3
Glass fiber insulation 2 in	0.17	0.55	0.8	0.9	0.85	0.8
Glass, window	0.35	0.25	0.18	0.12	0.07	0.04
Gypsum board on studs	0.29	0.10	0.05	0.04	0.07	0.09
Plaster	0.03	0.03	0.02	0.03	0.04	0.05
Plywood paneling	0.28	0.22	0.17	0.09	0.10	0.11
Water surface	0.008	0.008	0.013	0.015	0.020	0.025
One person[b]	0.18	0.4	0.46	0.46	0.51	0.46
Air[c]	nil	nil	nil	0.003	0.007	0.02

[a] Values vary widely. Sources include: K. B. Ginn, *Architectural Acoustics,* 2nd ed., p. 37, Bruel and Kjaer, Naerum, Denmark, November 1978; *Bulletin of the Acoustical and Insulating Materials Association,* Park Ridge, Il, 1974; H. B. Sabine and R. Moulder, "Sound absorptive materials," *Handbook of Noise Control,* C. Harris, Ed., 2nd ed., pp. 21-11 to 12, McGraw-Hill, New York, 1979.

[b] Total absorption of one seated person (m² basis).

[c] Air absorption per cubic meter.

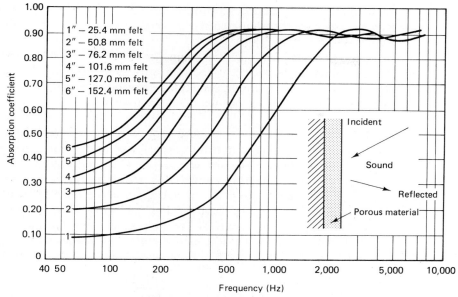

Figure 2.5.4 Dependence of the absorption of a porous material on the thickness of the material. (*Source:* Bruel & Kjaer Instruments, Inc.)

against frequency. These values were computed by Pallett et al. at the National Bureau of Standards (1978) from published data. Room dimensions are 12-ft wide by 8-ft high by 25-ft deep, and no allowance was made for absorption of occupants or furniture. The hard room was assumed to have a floor of vinyl–asbestos tile on concrete, walls of gypsum board on 2 × 4 in (nominal) studs, and a concrete ceiling. The medium room had a carpet and pad substituted for the vinyl–asbestos tile. For the soft room,

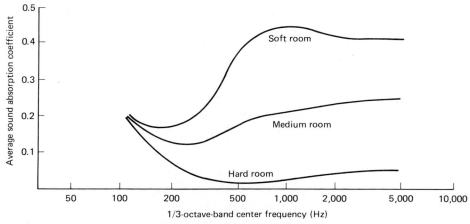

Figure 2.5.5 Average sound absorption coefficients versus frequency for three room configurations. (*Source:* Pallett et al., 1978)

a fissured tile ceiling was also substituted. Occupied rooms with drapes and furniture could have average absorption coefficients higher than the values in the figure.

The Eyring Formula   Although the Sabine formula is reasonably accurate for rooms with low values of absorption, it does not work as well for "dead" rooms. A perfect anechoic chamber, for example, should have a reverberation time of zero, which does not agree with the Sabine formula. This contradiction is avoided in the following analysis.

Consider a sound wave produced in a room by a source that is turned off at time $t = 0$. After one reflection from a typical wall in the room, the sound energy is reduced by the factor $(1 - \alpha_{mean})$ where $\alpha_{mean} = (\sum_{i=1}^{n} \alpha_i S_i)/S_T$ and $S_T =$ total surface area of the empty room. After r reflections, sound energy is reduced by the factor $(1 - \alpha_{mean})^r$. The mean free path, the average distance traveled by the sound wave between reflections, is given by Knudsen (1932) as $4V/S_T$. Thus, at time t, the predicted number of reflections is $r = cS_T t/(4V)$ where c is the speed of sound. At $t = T_{60}$ sound level has fallen by 60 dB, that is, sound energy is 10^{-6} times the original value. The result is $10^{-6} = (1 - \alpha_{mean})^{cS_T T_{60}/(4V)}$ from which we obtain the Eyring formula,

$$T_{60} = -\frac{55.26V}{cS_T \ln(1 - \alpha_{mean})}$$

$$= -\frac{0.16V}{S_T \ln(1 - \alpha_{mean})} \tag{2.5.3}$$

where ln refers to the natural logarithm ($\log_e$).

For small values of absorption ($\alpha_{mean} \ll 1$), the term $\ln(1 - \alpha_{mean})$ may be replaced by $-\alpha_{mean}$, the first term in an infinite series. The result is the Sabine formula. Note that the coefficient 0.16 in the Sabine and Eyring formulas is based on the speed of sound at about 24°C. This coefficient is somewhat higher at lower air temperatures.

The Millington–Sette Formula   Another formula may be used to determine reverberation time when the absorption coefficients of various room components are very different. According to the Millington–Sette formula,

$$T_{60} = \frac{0.16V}{\sum\limits_{i=1}^{n} - S_i \ln(1 - \alpha_i)} \tag{2.5.4}$$

EXAMPLE PROBLEM: ABSORPTION COEFFICIENT

A chamber with dimensions of $20 \times 20 \times 10$ ft has a reverberation time of 4.00 s at 1 kHz. When a 4×4 ft sample of ceiling tile is placed in the room the reverberation time is reduced to 3.15 s. Find the sound absorption coefficient for the ceiling tile.

Solution.   For convenience, the Sabine absorption coefficient equation will be rewritten in English units. Since 1 ft = 0.3048 m, we have

$$\alpha = 0.049V' \frac{1/T_{60(S)} - 1/T_{60(O)}}{S'} \tag{2.5.5}$$

where $\quad V' =$ room volume (ft^3)
$\qquad S' =$ sample surface area (ft^2)

The absorption coefficient is given by

$$\alpha = 0.049 \frac{(20 \times 20 \times 10)(1/3.15 - 1/4.00)}{4 \times 4}$$

$$= 0.83 \text{ (at 1 kHz)}$$

EXAMPLE PROBLEM: REVERBERATION TIME

A $15 \times 12 \times 4$ m room has plaster walls and ceiling and a carpeted floor. One of the 12×4 m walls has acoustical paneling. There are curtains covering the entire opposite wall.

(a) Determine the reverberation time at 500 Hz by the Sabine formula, the Eyring formula, and the Millington–Sette formula.

Solution. Room volume

$$V = 15 \times 12 \times 4 = 720 \text{ m}^3$$

Using the table of absorption coefficients, for sound at 500 Hz, we have

$\alpha_1 = 0.75 \quad$ and $\quad A_1 = 4 \times 12 = 48$ m^2 of acoustical paneling

$\alpha_2 = 0.15 \quad$ and $\quad A_2 = 4 \times 12 = 48$ m^2 of curtained wall

$\alpha_3 = 0.25 \quad$ and $\quad A_3 = 12 \times 15 = 180$ m^2 of carpeted floor

$\alpha_4 = 0.02 \quad$ and $\quad A_4 = 2 \times 15 \times 4 + 12 \times 15 = 300$ m^2 of plaster walls and ceiling

Using the Sabine formula,

$$T_{60} = 0.16V \bigg/ \sum_{i=1}^{n} \alpha_i S_i$$

$$= 0.016 \times 720/(0.75 \times 48 + 0.15 \times 48 + 0.25 \times 180 + 0.02 \times 300)$$

$$= 1.22 \text{ s}$$

Using the Eyring formula

$$\alpha_{\text{mean}} = \frac{\displaystyle\sum_{i=1}^{n} \alpha_i S_i}{\displaystyle\sum_{i=1}^{n} S_i}$$

$$= \frac{0.75 \times 48 + 0.15 \times 48 + 0.25 \times 180 + 0.02 \times 300}{48 + 48 + 180 + 300}$$

$$= 0.163$$

and

$$T_{60} = \frac{0.16V}{-S_T \ln(1 - \alpha_{\text{mean}})}$$

$$= 0.16 \times 720[-(48 + 48 + 180 + 300) \ln(1 - 0.163)]$$

$$= 1.12 \text{ s}$$

Using the Millington–Sette formula

$$T_{60} = \frac{0.16V}{\displaystyle\sum_{i=1}^{n} -S_i \ln(1 - \alpha_i)}$$

$$= \frac{0.16 \times 720}{\begin{array}{l} -48 \ln(1 - 0.75) - 48 \ln(1 - 0.15) \\ \qquad - 180 \ln(1 - 0.25) - 300 \ln(1 - 0.02) \end{array}}$$

$$= 0.87 \text{ s}$$

(b) Recompute reverberation time if 45 people are to be seated in the room.

Solution. The absorption coefficient table indicates that the total absorption of one seated person is 0.46 m² sabins at 500 Hz. That is, each person is equivalent to 1 m² of absorptive material with an absorption coefficient of 0.46 at 500 Hz. Assuming that sound absorption by the floor is not diminished by the presence of people in the room, we simply repeat the calculations with the additional terms $\alpha_5 = 0.46$ and $S_5 = 45$.

At this point, it should be evident that time can be saved by writing a computer program to solve the problem. If T_{60} is to be determined for a range of frequencies and if design alternatives are considered to adjust T_{60}, then hand calculations become very tedious. The reverberation time (in seconds) for the occupied room is

$$T_{60} = 1.00 \text{ (Sabine formula)}$$

$$0.91 \text{ (Eyring formula)}$$

$$0.72 \text{ (Millington–Sette formula)}$$

If the room is constructed and furnished according to the above specifications, actual measurements of T_{60} may be made to determine which of the above predictions is closest to the actual reverberation time.

The results are evaluated according to the intended use of the room. Referring to the plot of typical reverberation time versus room volume, we see that for rooms of this size, a reverberation time of about 0.5 to 0.6 s is desirable for a conference room. A reverberation time of about 0.8 to 0.9 s is desirable for an auditorium or radio studio. Although sound frequency is not considered in the plot, these values may be used as a rough guide for frequencies between 250 Hz and 2 kHz.

If room dimensions are to be expressed in feet instead of meters, the constant 0.16 in each of the equations for T_{60} is replaced by the constant 0.049. Each occupant of a room may be assigned the absorption coefficient from the table and about 10.8 ft^2 of surface area (the equivalent of 1 m^2).

Sound Energy Density

The *sound intensity* I (W/m^2) due to a point source of power W (W) in the direct field (i.e., without reflection) is given by

$$I = \frac{WQ(\theta, \phi)}{4\pi r^2} \qquad (2.5.6)$$

where r = distance from the source (m)
       $Q(\theta, \phi)$ = the directivity factor

The directivity factor

       $Q(\theta, \phi)$ = 1 for an ideal point source in full space

                = 2 for an ideal point source above an acoustically reflective surface

The *sound energy density* is the sound energy contained in 1 m^3 of air at any instant. In the direct field, sound energy density

$$D_D = \frac{I}{c} = \frac{WQ(\theta, \phi)}{4\pi r^2 c} \qquad (2.5.7)$$

where D_D = direct-field sound energy density (W $\cdot$ s/m^3)
       c = the speed of sound propagation (m/s)

Sound Absorption in the Reverberant Field

The rate of sound energy striking a surface area S (m^2), is given by the product IS for sound waves normal to the surface, and by $IS \cos \theta$ for sound waves at an angle of incidence θ. In an ideal reverberant field, with equal probability for all angles of incidence, the average rate of sound energy striking one side of the surface is given by $IS/4$. Thus, for an absorption coefficient α, we have

$$\text{power absorbed} = IS \frac{\alpha}{4} = cD_R S \frac{\alpha}{4}$$

where D_R = reverberant-field sound energy density. The power absorbed is balanced by the power supplied to the reverberant field. This is the portion of the input power W which remains after one reflection:

$$\text{power supplied} = W(1 - \alpha)$$

Thus, the steady-state condition is

$$cD_R S \frac{\alpha}{4} = W(1 - \alpha) \qquad (2.5.8)$$

from which the energy density of the reverberant field is given by

$$D_R = 4W \frac{1 - \alpha}{cS\alpha} = \frac{4W}{cR} \qquad (2.5.9)$$

where $R = S\alpha/(1 - \alpha)$.

Room Constant

In most cases, the walls, ceiling, and other components of an actual enclosure are constructed of several different materials with various sound absorption coefficients. The enclosure is then described in terms of mean properties by

$$R = \frac{S_T \alpha_{\text{mean}}}{1 - \alpha_{\text{mean}}} \qquad (2.5.10)$$

where
$\quad R$ = the room constant (m^2)
$\quad S_T$ = total surface area of the room (m^2)
$\quad \alpha_{\text{mean}}$ = mean sound absorption coefficient of the room

Sound Levels due to Direct and Reverberant Contributions

In this situation, there is an important distinction between scalar sound intensity I and vector sound intensity **I**. Scalar sound intensity and the sound level associated with it are the appropriate measures for assessing noise for hearing damage risk and subjective effects which depend on mean-square sound pressure without regard to direction. Vector sound intensity measurements can be used to determine sound power level of a machine and for other determinations where the directional characteristics of the sound field are of interest. In this section we are concerned with scalar sound intensity.

The contribution of reverberant sound energy to sound intensity is given by

$$I_R = cD_R = 4 \frac{W}{R} \qquad (2.5.11)$$

where
$\quad I_R$ = sound intensity due to reverberant sound energy (W/m^2)
$\quad W$ = source sound power (W)
$\quad R$ = room constant (m^2)

If the direct and reverberant sound contributions are uncorrelated, we may add the two to obtain

$$I = W \left[\frac{Q(\theta, \phi)}{4\pi r^2} + \frac{4}{R} \right] \qquad (2.5.12)$$

where I = total sound intensity (W/m^2). The above analysis assumed that reverberant sound came from many directions, with each direction equally probable. This results in a reasonable approximation of actual conditions in most cases. If room modes are significant, the assumption of uncorrelated sound is not valid, and the above equation will be a poorer model of the actual sound field.

Sound pressure level within the room is approximated by

$$L_P = 10 \lg\left(\frac{I}{I_{ref}}\right)$$

$$= 10 \lg\left[W\left(\frac{1}{4\pi r^2} + \frac{4}{R}\right)\right] + 120$$

$$= L_W + 10 \lg\left(\frac{1}{4\pi r^2} + \frac{4}{R}\right) \tag{2.5.13}$$

for an ideal point source radiating equally in all directions, where the reference sound intensity is

$$I_{ref} = 10^{-12} \text{ W/m}^2$$

and sound power level of the source is defined by

$$L_W = 10 \lg\left(\frac{W}{10^{-12}}\right) \text{ dB re 1 pW}$$

For an ideal point source over an acoustically reflective surface

$$L_P = 10 \lg\left[W\left(\frac{1}{2\pi r^2} + \frac{4}{R}\right)\right] + 120$$

$$= L_W + 10 \lg\left(\frac{1}{2\pi r^2} + \frac{4}{R}\right) \tag{2.5.14}$$

These equations are based on the assumption that the absorptive properties of the room are distributed somewhat uniformly, and that the source is not close to a reflective wall. The equations are not valid in the near field, that is, the results tend to be inaccurate for locations closer to the source than one or two wavelengths or closer than a typical source dimension. If sound power and room absorption characteristics are given for each frequency band, then sound pressure level L_P may be computed for each band in dB/octave, dB/one-third octave, and so on. If A-weighted sound power is given, and if the room constant is based on frequencies in the same range as the frequency content of the source, then sound level L will be in dBA.

EXAMPLE PROBLEM: SOUND LEVELS DUE TO DIRECT AND REVERBERANT CONTRIBUTIONS

(a) Describe the sound field due to a source having a sound power level of 105 dBA re 1 pW in a room with a room constant of 650 m^2 (at the source frequencies). The source lies directly above a hard floor.

Solution. The actual sound field depends on the location of the source in relation to the walls and other reflective and absorptive elements in the room. However, we can estimate the sound field by using the above equation for sound level due to an ideal point source over an acoustically reflective surface. Thus, we have

$$L = L_W + 10 \lg\left(\frac{1}{2\pi r^2} + \frac{4}{R}\right)$$

$$= 105 + 10 \lg\left(\frac{1}{2\pi r^2} + \frac{4}{650}\right)$$

which ranges from 97.2 dBA at $r = 1$ m from the center of the source (which we might estimate to be the extent of the near field) to a minimum value of 82.9 dBA for large values of r.

(b) Plot noise contours at 5-dBA intervals.

Solution. The radius of a given contour is found by the solution of the above equation as follows:

$$L = L_W + 10 \lg\left(\frac{1}{2\pi r^2} + \frac{4}{R}\right)$$

from which

$$\frac{1}{2\pi r^2} = 10^{(L-L_W)/10} - \frac{4}{R}$$

and

$$r = \left[2\pi\left(10^{(L-L_W)/10} - \frac{4}{R}\right)\right]^{-1/2}$$

For $R = 650$, the $L = 85$-dBA contour is given by

$$r = \left[2\pi\left(10^{(85-105)/10} - \frac{4}{650}\right)\right]^{-1/2} = 6.43 \text{ m}$$

A personal computer was used to plot the noise contours shown in Figure 2.5.6. The two contours closest to the source are likely to be inaccurate, since they are probably in the near field.

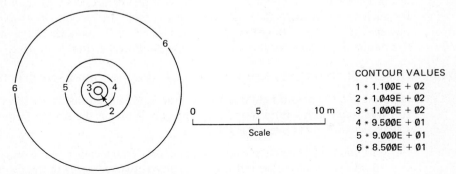

CONTOUR VALUES

1 * 1.100E + 02
2 * 1.049E + 02
3 * 1.000E + 02
4 * 9.500E + 01
5 * 9.000E + 01
6 * 8.500E + 01

Figure 2.5.6 Noise contour plot.

2.6 DIFFRACTION OF SOUND DUE TO BARRIERS

The term "noise barrier" usually refers to an object which interrupts the line of sight between a noise source and observer, but does not completely enclose the source or observer. Noise barriers include walls, fences, earth berms (mounds of earth), dense plantings, and buildings intervening between source and observer. If the barrier is solid (without holes and gaps) and of sufficient mass, noise transmission through the barrier will usually be insignificant compared with refracted noise. Since refraction (bending) of sound waves is dependent on frequency, it is desirable to do a frequency analysis of the noise source. If frequency analysis is impractical, barrier noise attenuation may be approximated by basing the analysis on the average predominant frequency. Traffic noise, for example, is composed of thousands of sources with varying frequency content. To simplify noise predictions when barriers are present, an effective frequency of 550 Hz may be used to represent all vehicles.

Barrier attenuation calculations are based in part on the work of Fresnel who studied diffraction of light waves. When visible light passes through a small hole, there is a distinct shadow zone and a distinct bright zone. When sound reaches a listener by an indirect path through an opening or over a barrier, then the sound level will be less than if the sound had traveled by a direct line-of-sight path. However, the distinction between the bright zone and shadow zone is less significant for audible sound than for visible light, due to the longer wavelengths of audible sound.

The noise attenuation of a barrier may be expressed as a function of the Fresnel number N which is defined as follows:

$$N = \frac{2(A + B - C)}{\lambda} \qquad (2.6.1)$$

where A and B are lengths of the segments of the shortest path over the barrier and C is the length of the line-of-sight path between source and observer as shown in Figure 2.6.1. λ is the wavelength of the sound. Thus, in terms of the speed of sound c and frequency f, the Fresnel number is given by

$$N = \frac{2f(A + B - C)}{c} \qquad (2.6.2)$$

Fresnel number is given a positive sign if the barrier interrupts line-of-sight noise transmission. The region of positive Fresnel number is identified as the shadow zone

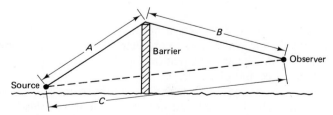

Figure 2.6.1 Barrier geometry for calculation of Fresnel number.

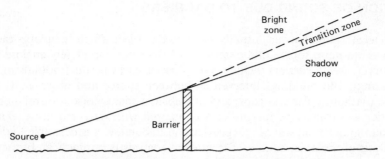

Figure 2.6.2 The bright zone, transition zone, and shadow zone.

in Figure 2.6.2. If a line between the source and observer is not interrupted by the barrier, the Fresnel number is given a negative sign. There is some noise attenuation in the region of negative N if the line between source and receiver passes very close to the edge of the barrier. The extent of this region, identified as the transition zone, depends on the frequency content of the noise. There is no significant barrier effect in the bright zone, the remainder of the region where the barrier does not interrupt line-of-sight noise transmission.

Attenuation other than that resulting from wave divergence due to distance from the source is called excess attenuation. Kurze and Anderson (1971) developed an analytic model for barrier attenuation, which was later verified in the field by Simpson (1976). Applications to highway noise barriers are given by Barry and Reagan (1978). For a point source located behind an infinitely long solid wall or berm, the excess attenuation A' (dB) is given by the following equations, where the arguments of tan and tanh are in radians:

$$A' = 0 \qquad \text{for} \quad N < -0.1916 - 0.0635b' \tag{2.6.3}$$

$$A' = 5(1 + 0.6b') + 20 \lg\left(\frac{\sqrt{-2\pi N}}{\tan \sqrt{-2\pi N}}\right) \qquad \text{for} \quad -0.1916 - 0.0635b' \le N \le 0$$

$$\tag{2.6.4}$$

$$A' = 5(1 + 0.6b') + 20 \lg\left(\frac{\sqrt{2\pi N}}{\tanh \sqrt{2\pi N}}\right) \qquad \text{for} \quad 0 < N < 5.03 \tag{2.6.5}$$

$$A' = 20(1 + 0.15b') \qquad \text{for} \quad N \ge 5.03 \tag{2.6.6}$$

where $b' = 0$ for a wall and $b' = 1$ for a berm. The correction factor b' is used to account for field results showing berms to produce about 3 dB more attenuation than walls of the same height. The above equations apply if the barrier is perpendicular to a line between the source and observer.

Predicted barrier attenuation values will be approximations. A more rigorous analysis is mathematically involved and beyond the scope of this book. A detailed discussion of scattering and diffraction is given by Pierce (1981) who devotes an entire chapter to these topics.

Insertion loss (IL) is commonly defined as the difference in sound levels (measured at the same point in space) before and after a muffler is inserted. The same term may be used to describe the effectiveness of a barrier in terms of sound level at an observer before and after barrier construction:

$$\text{IL} = L(\text{before}) - L(\text{after barrier construction}) \qquad (2.6.7)$$

The value of insertion loss depends on barrier characteristics and location of the source and receiver. If the barrier is finite in length, then the insertion loss will be reduced by flanking (i.e., noise traveling around the ends of the barrier). Insertion loss will also be reduced if reflected sound reaches the observer or if sound is transmitted through a barrier. Noise transmission through a barrier can be significant if the barrier is of low mass per unit area or if the barrier has cracks or holes in it.

EXAMPLE PROBLEM: BARRIER ATTENUATION

A point source with a sound power level of 110 dB re 1 pW is located 0.5 m above level ground. The predominant source frequency is about 2000 Hz and the temperature is 20°C. An observer is located 30 m from the source and 2 m above the ground. It is proposed to construct a long, 3-m-high masonry wall midway between the source and observer.

(a) Find the insertion loss of the proposed wall, assuming free field conditions.

Solution. The path lengths over the barrier are given by

$$A = \sqrt{\left(\frac{30}{2}\right)^2 + (3 - 0.5)^2} = 15.207 \text{ m}$$

$$B = \sqrt{\left(\frac{30}{2}\right)^2 + (3 - 2)^2} = 15.033 \text{ m}$$

and the straight line distance through the barrier is

$$C = \sqrt{30^2 + (2 - 0.5)^2} = 30.037 \text{ m}$$

The speed of sound in air is given by

$$c = 20.04\sqrt{T' + 273.16}$$

from which $c = 343.1$ m/s at 20°C. Using equation 2.6.2, the Frenel number is

$$N = 2 \times 2000(15.207 + 15.033 - 30.037)/343.1 = 2.36$$

N is positive because the observer is in the shadow zone. The barrier may be considered infinite in length. For a masonry wall, noise transmitted through the wall will be insignificant compared with noise that travels over the wall. Thus, the excess attenuation given by equation 2.6.5 will equal the insertion loss:

$$\text{IL} = A' = 5(1 + 0.6 \times 0) + 20 \lg\left(\frac{\sqrt{2\pi 2.36}}{\tanh \sqrt{2\pi 2.36}}\right) = 16.7 \text{ dB}$$

Barrier geometry calculations should be performed with precision so that enough significant figures are retained in the result. Nevertheless, the final value of insertion loss will be only approximate due to the many assumptions necessary in the development of the model. If a computer is used which does not have the hyperbolic tangent available, the following equation may be used:

$$\tanh x = \frac{e^x - e^{-x}}{e^x + e^{-x}} \tag{2.6.8}$$

(b) Predict the sound pressure level at the observer before and after the barrier is constructed.

Solution. Under free-field conditions with absorptive ground, the sound pressure level at the observer, before construction of the barrier, is approximated by

$$L_P = 10 \lg\left(\frac{W}{4\pi r^2}\right) + 120$$

from which

$$L_P = L_W - 10 \lg(4\pi r^2)$$

For the observer at a distance of $r = C = 30.04$ m, the sound pressure level is

$$L_P = 110 - 10 \lg(4\pi 30.04^2) = 69.5 \text{ dB}$$

Subtracting the insertion loss of 16.7 dB, the predicted sound level at the observer will be about 53 dB after the barrier is constructed. If the noise frequency had been lower, then the barrier would not have been as effective. For example, a higher barrier would be required to obtain the same noise reduction in the case of traffic noise with dominant frequencies around 500 to 550 Hz.

(c) Find the maximum insertion loss possible for the barrier described in this example. Find the barrier height necessary to attain it.

Solution. Using equation 2.6.6 the maximum insertion loss is 20 dB and it occurs at a Fresnel number $N = 5.03$. Using equation 2.6.2, we may express path length difference in terms of Fresnel number as follows:

$$A + B - C = \frac{cN}{2f}$$

from which $A + B - C = 343.1 \times 5.03/(2 \times 2000) = 0.431$ m for a 2000-Hz signal.

We may now express A and B in terms of barrier height H and the given dimensions and rewrite the equation as a function of H:

$$\sqrt{15^2 + (H - 0.5)^2} + \sqrt{15^2 + (H - 2)^2} - \sqrt{30^2 + (2 - 0.5)^2} - 0.431 = 0$$

This equation may be solved by successive approximations or by using a calculator with a root finding procedure or by using a packaged computer program. Figure 2.6.3 shows a computer-generated plot of $f(H)$ (the left side of the equation)

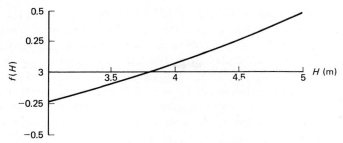

Figure 2.6.3 Determination of maximum practical barrier height. A computer-generated plot of $f(H)$ versus H.

versus H. The program included a root finding routine, determining the root of $f(H) = 0$ to be 3.81. Thus, based on the barrier model we used, it would be ineffective to extend this barrier higher than 3.81 m if the source frequency is 2000 Hz.

A Numerical Procedure

If it is necessary to use a computer or programmable calculator that does not offer the solution to $f(x) = 0$, a simple program may be written. The secant method of determining a root to $f(x) = 0$ can be used as the basis for a brief program that will be applied to the barrier problem.

In order to use the secant method, two values of x are selected, $x1$ and $x2$. Figure 2.6.4 shows points $x1$, $f(x1)$ and $x2$, $f(x2)$ plotted on an $f(x)$ versus x plane. A line drawn through the two points will intersect the x-axis at a third point which we identify as $x3$. Now, if $f(x)$ was a linear function of x, then $x3$ would be the precise root of $f(x) = 0$. Let us assume, however, that we are dealing with a nonlinear function since we would not need a numerical procedure if the function was linear. Then $x3$ will be an approximation of the solution, hopefully a better approximation of the root than either $x1$ or $x2$.

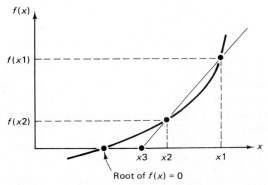

Figure 2.6.4 The secant method, a numerical procedure for solving $f(x) = 0$.

The values of x are now shifted so that $x3$ becomes $x2$, while the previous $x2$ becomes $x1$ and the previous $x1$ is discarded. These new values are used as above to obtain a new approximation of the root (a new intersection point) $x3$. The process is repeated until the root $x3$ differs from the previous value by a predetermined small value.

The procedure is flowcharted in Figure 2.6.5. In solving for the root of $f(x) = 0$, there is no need to actually plot the values of $f(x)$ versus x. The slope of the $f(x)$ versus x curve is approximated by the slope of the line between points $x1, f(x1)$ and $x2, f(x2)$. It is given by

$$f' = \frac{f(x2) - f(x1)}{x2 - x1} \tag{2.6.9}$$

It can be seen from the figure that the approximate slope is also given by

$$f' = \frac{f(x2)}{x2 - x3} \tag{2.6.10}$$

Thus, we can rearrange the second equation to calculate the new approximation of the root

$$x3 = x2 - \frac{f(x2)}{f'} \tag{2.6.11}$$

after having calculated the slope from the first equation.

EXAMPLE PROBLEM: NUMERICAL SOLUTION TO A BARRIER ATTENUATION PROBLEM

Consider the barrier described in the previous example problem. Find maximum practical barrier height if the predominant noise frequency is 550 Hz.

Solution. As was done in the previous problem, we will assume a maximum attenuation of 20 dB corresponding to a Fresnel number of 5.03. Using the speed of sound $c = 343.1$ m/s and the dimensions given in the previous section, the condition for maximum practical height becomes

$$F(H) = \sqrt{15^2 + (H - 0.05)^2} + \sqrt{15^2 + (H - 2)^2}$$
$$- \sqrt{30^2 + (2 - 0.05)^2} - 862.9/f = 0$$

The secant method is more likely to converge on a root if the equation is well behaved in the vicinity of the root and if the initial selections are good guesses. The first criterion is met since $F(H)$ does not fluctuate rapidly or have other troublesome characteristics in the range of interest. We know that higher barriers are needed in the presence of lower frequencies. That is, the root is likely to be larger than $H = 3.81$, the value obtained for $f = 2000$ Hz. Therefore, let us try $H1 = 4$ m and $H2 = 5$ m. Using the simple computer program described in the flowchart, we find the root of $f(x) = 0$ to be 6.17. Thus, a barrier height of 6.17 m should produce a 20-dB attenuation under the given conditions. In actual

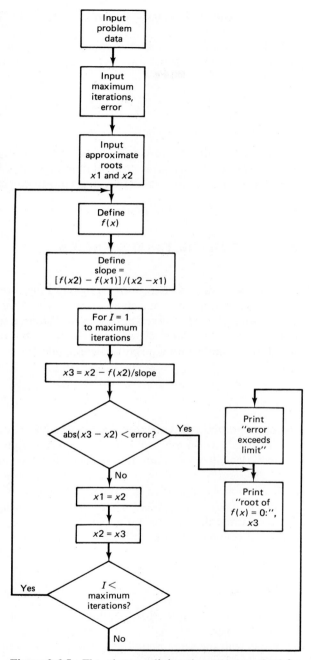

Figure 2.6.5 Flowchart outlining the secant method for solving $f(x) = 0$.

practice, it may not be possible to exceed about 15-dB attenuation of a 550-Hz signal, suggesting a lower barrier.

An alternative numerical method is called Newton's method. With this method, we select only one approximate root, $x1$. The new approximation of the root is given by

$$x2 = x1 - \frac{f(x1)}{f'(x1)} \qquad (2.6.12)$$

where, in this case, f' is the derivative of $f(x)$ with respect to x. The new approximation, $x2$, replaces $x1$ (the old approximation) and the process is continued until $x2$ differs from the previous value by a predetermined small value.

2.7 NOISE CONTOUR MAPPING FOR MULTIPLE SOURCES

It is sometimes necessary to deal with the simultaneous noise contributions from many sources. The sound pressure level at a given location is dependent on the sound power of the relevant sources, sound divergence due to distance, source directivity, air absorption if sound travels for large distances, diffraction due to barriers, sound transmission through walls, and room constant where applicable.

Electronic Spreadsheets

Computer worksheet programs, called electronic spreadsheets, are useful when many sound sources are involved in a noise problem, and where design changes may be necessary. Spreadsheets display information in row and column format. Formulas are written in terms of cells identified by their row and column intersection, but may be replicated automatically for a range of cells. "What if" analysis is convenient since all affected values are immediately updated when one cell is changed. This feature makes it practical to examine the effect of noise control on various machines, or the effect of relocating noise sources or work stations.

Noise Level Contour Plotting

In order to be effective, noise control efforts should be based on the best available information, including the results of predictions or measurements. Mapping of noise contours (joining points with the same noise level) can aid in deciding a cost-effective allocation of resources for noise control. Noise contours can also provide a basis for relocating noise sources, for locating employee workstations, and for determining the need for hearing protection.

A Noise Level Interpolator

In some cases, we may wish to estimate noise levels at various locations where barriers and reverberation have little influence. As determined in Section 2.1, in the direct field of an ideal point source, sound pressure levels are related as follows:

$$L_{Pa} - L_{Pb} = 20 \lg\left(\frac{b}{a}\right)$$

where a and b are distances from the point source. Taking antilogarithms of both sides of the above equation, we obtain the distance ratio in terms of noise level change:

$$\frac{b}{a} = 10^{-\Delta L/20} \qquad (2.7.1)$$

where $\Delta L = L_{Pb} - L_{Pa}$.

Equation 2.7.1 may be used to construct a point-source interpolator by drawing a set of rays as in Figure 2.7.1. For example, if $L_{Pb} - L_{Pa} = 1$ dB, then $b/a = 10^{-1/20} = 0.891$. Thus, measuring perpendicular to the "location of point source" line, the $\Delta L = 1$-dB ray is 0.891 times the distance to the "location 1" ray, and so on. The interpolator may be photocopied on clear plastic, and used with a scale drawing to predict noise levels at various locations.

Consider a point source and two observer locations, all lying on the same line. The noise level at one observer point is known. The interpolator is oriented so that

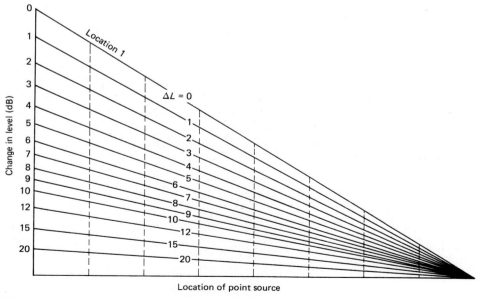

Figure 2.7.1 Point-source noise interpolator.

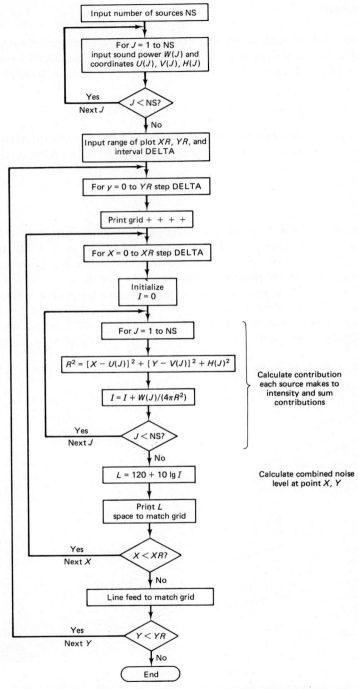

Figure 2.7.2 Computer-aided mapping of noise contours for point sources in full space.

(a) the "location of point source" line lies over the center of the source, (b) the "location 1" line lies over the more-distant observer point, and (c) the line determined by the source and two observer points is perpendicular to the "location of point source" line. The ray nearest the second observer location gives the difference in noise levels. Ob-

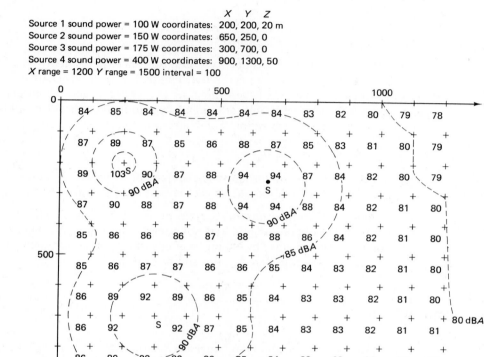

Source 1 sound power = 100 W coordinates: X Y Z 200, 200, 20 m
Source 2 sound power = 150 W coordinates: 650, 250, 0
Source 3 sound power = 175 W coordinates: 300, 700, 0
Source 4 sound power = 400 W coordinates: 900, 1300, 50
X range = 1200 Y range = 1500 interval = 100

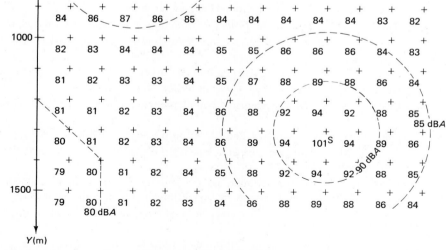

Figure 2.7.3 Computer-aided mapping of noise levels due to sources at various elevations.

viously, the noise level is greater at the nearer point. The results obtained with the interpolator will not be valid in the near field or the reverberant field, or where barriers are present. When contributions due to other sources (including background noise) are within 10 dB or so of the predicted noise level, these contributions must be combined with the predicted level.

Computer-Aided Noise Contour Mapping

A contour map of noise levels due to several sources requires many repetitive calculations, suggesting the use of a computer. Figure 2.7.2 is a flowchart of a simple algorithm which may be used to generate a set of grid points and the noise level values at each point. Where applicable, additional steps to include the effects of barrier diffraction, directivity, reverberation, and background noise can be added.

EXAMPLE PROBLEM: NOISE CONTOURS

Plot a set of noise contours for four noise sources located above an absorptive surface. The sound power and coordinates of each source are given in Figure 2.7.3.

Solution. The algorithm flowcharted in Figure 2.7.2 was coded on a personal computer to obtain the grid and noise level values shown in Figure 2.7.3. The contours were obtained by joining locations with equal noise levels. Only spherical divergence was considered in this simple example.

BIBLIOGRAPHY

Barry, T. M., and J. A. Reagan, FHWA highway noise prediction model, U.S. Dept. of Transportation Rept. FHWA-RD-77-108, December 1978.

Beranek, L. L., *Acoustics,* McGraw-Hill, New York, 1954.

Bulletin of the Acoustical and Insulating Materials Association, Park Ridge, IL, 1974.

Crocker, M. J., and A. J. Price, *Noise and Noise Control,* Vol. I, pp. 18–23, CRC Press, Cleveland, 1975.

Ginn, K. B., *Architectural Acoustics,* 2nd ed., Bruel & Kjaer, Naerum, Denmark, 1978.

Knudsen, V. O., *Architectural Acoustics,* Wiley, New York, 1932.

Kurze, U. J., and G. S. Anderson, "Sound attenuation by barriers," *Applied Acoustics* **4,** 35–53, 1971.

Kuttruff, H., *Room Acoustics,* 2nd ed., Applied Science Publishers, London, 1979.

Lighthill, M. J., "On sound generated aerodynamically. I: General theory," *Proc. Royal Soc. (London)* **A211,** 564–587, 1952.

Pallett, D., R. Wehrli, R. Kilmer, and T. Quindry, Design guide for reducing transportation noise in and around buildings, National Bureau of Standards, April 1978.

Pierce, A. D., *Acoustics, an Introduction to Its Physical Principles and Applications,* McGraw-Hill, New York, 1981.

Reynolds, D. D., *Engineering Principles of Acoustics,* Allyn and Bacon, Reading, MA, 1981.

Sabine, H. B., and R. Moulder, "Sound absorptive materials," in *Handbook of Noise Control,* C. Harris (Ed.), 2nd ed, McGraw-Hill, New York, 1979.

Simpson, M. A., Noise barrier attenuation: field experience, U.S. Dept. of Transportation Rept. FHWA-RD-76-54, February 1976.

PROBLEMS

2.1.1. Verify the general solution to the spherical wave equation.

2.1.2. A spherical wave has a root-mean-square sound pressure of 4.10 N/m^2 at 2 m from the source. Find the root-mean-square pressure at 6 m.

2.1.3. Find the acoustic power of the source in Problem 2.1.2 if the atmospheric pressure is 675 mm Hg and the temperature 22°C.

2.1.4. A small noise source is placed in the center of an anechoic chamber. The sound level is 83 dBA at 2 m. Find the sound intensity and sound level at 2.5 m.

2.1.5. The noise level due to a compressor located outdoors is 87 dBA at 20 m. Find the level at 80 m if there are no intervening structures.

2.1.6. Sound level is determined to be 80 dBA at 20 ft from a line source. Express sound level as a function of distance within the far field.

2.1.7. Write a computer program to generate noise levels (at 1-m intervals) due to line and point sources on an acoustically hard surface.

2.1.8. A work station is to be located 4 m from a conveyor belt generating sound energy of 0.002 W/m, 5 m from a machine with 0.005-W sound power, and 7 m from a machine with 0.008-W sound power. The above values represent A-weighted sound.
   (a) Estimate the noise exposure at the work station if the sources rest on a hard surface but there is no sound reflection from walls or ceiling.
   (b) Find the noise level at a work station 1 m closer to the two machines and 1 m farther from the conveyor.

2.2.1. Find the directivity factor and directivity index for an ideal point source resting at the junction of an acoustically hard paved surface and an acoustically hard wall.

2.2.2. A noise source with 0.005-W A-weighted sound power has a maximum directivity index of 8.0.
   (a) Determine the maximum directivity factor.
   (b) Find the maximum sound level at a radius of 20 m in full space.

2.2.3. Repeat Problem 2.2.2 if the directivity index is 12.0.

2.3.1. Write a program for finding the eigenfrequencies of a rectangular room. Use SI units.

2.3.2. Find the eigenfrequencies of a 12-m-long by 10-m-wide by 3.5-m-high rectangular room at 20°C. Consider up to three half-waves in the length and width directions and two half-waves in the height direction.

2.3.3. Find the eigenfrequencies or a 9 × 8.5 × 2.9 m rectangular room at 18°C.

2.3.4. Write a program for finding the eigenfrequencies of a rectangular room, where data are given in English units.

2.3.5. Find the eigenfrequencies of a 26 × 21 × 16 ft rectangular room at 70°F.

2.3.6. Find the eigenfrequencies of a 30 × 25 × 10 ft rectangular room at 65°F.

2.3.7. Verify that the boundary conditions are met for the 1 0 0 axial mode in the above room.

2.3.8. Repeat Problem 2.3.7 for oblique mode 3 3 2.

2.4.1. A source with 0.005-W sound power and dimensions of $400 \times 500 \times 800$ mm is located on an acoustically hard surface. The background noise level is 65 dBA. Identify the approximate extent of the region in which the inverse-square law will apply if there are no other reflecting surfaces nearby, and the predominant frequencies of the source are above 2 kHz.

2.5.1. Write a program to compute reverberation time. Use SI units.

2.5.2. Repeat the reverberation time example problem for 2 kHz.

2.5.3. Write a program to compute reverberation time using English units.

Room dimensions are given in meters in Problems 2.5.4 and 2.5.5 and in feet in Problems 2.5.6, 2.5.7, and 2.5.8. Compute reverberation time using
(a) the Sabine formula
(b) the Eyring formula
(c) the Millington–Sette formula

2.5.4. Room volume is 600 m^3. The walls and ceiling are made of plaster with an area of 280 m^2. An additional area of 40 m^2 is covered with curtains. The floor is concrete and has an area of 160 m^2. The frequency of interest is 250 Hz.

2.5.5. Reverberation time (dimensions in meters). Room volume = 800.

component 1 area = 50	absorption coefficient = 0.7
component 2 area = 60	absorption coefficient = 0.2
component 3 area = 200	absorption coefficient = 0.25
component 4 area = 350	absorption coefficient = 0.03
component 5 area = 55	absorption coefficient = 0.5

2.5.6. Reverberation time (dimensions in feet). Room volume = 20,000.

component 1 area = 500	absorption coefficient = 0.75
component 2 area = 550	absorption coefficient = 0.38
component 3 area = 2000	absorption coefficient = 0.31
component 4 area = 3000	absorption coefficient = 0.05
component 5 area = 400	absorption coefficient = 0.5

2.5.7. Reverberation time (dimensions in feet). Room volume = 30,000.

component 1 area = 3200	absorption coefficient = 0.1
component 2 area = 3600	absorption coefficient = 0.25
component 3 area = 600	absorption coefficient = 0.55
component 4 area = 650	absorption coefficient = 0.85

2.5.8. Reverberation time (dimensions in feet). Room volume = 11,000.

component 1 area = 250	absorption coefficient = 0.76
component 2 area = 250	absorption coefficient = 0.2
component 3 area = 900	absorption coefficient = 0.25
component 4 area = 1500	absorption coefficient = 0.03
component 5 area = 440	absorption coefficient = 0.45

2.5.9. Verify the Sabine absorption coefficient equation.

2.5.10. Find the sound absorption coefficient of a 1-m² sample of material at 500 Hz. When the sample is placed in a 6 × 6 × 3 m reverberation room, reverberation time is reduced from 3.75 to 3.50 s.

2.5.11. Repeat for a 1-m² sample of a different material which reduces the reverberation time to 3.35 s.

2.5.12. Find the sound absorption coefficient of a 3 × 3 ft sample of material tested at 2 kHz. When the sample is placed in a 4500-ft³ reverberation room, the reverberation time changes from 4.50 to 3.95 s.

2.5.13. Repeat for a 4-kHz test if the reverberation time changes from 4.45 to 3.85 s.

2.6.1. A receiver is in the shadow zone behind a concrete wall. The straight line source-to-receiver distance is 20 m and the distance over the wall 20.5 m. Find the Fresnel number and the excess attenuation if the dominant frequency is 200 Hz.

2.6.2. Repeat the above problem for a dominant frequency of 2000 Hz.

2.6.3. Write a computer program to find the root(s) of $f(x) = 0$. Use the secant method.

2.6.4. Flowchart the solution of $f(x) = 0$. Use Newton's method.

In the four problems that follow (2.6.5–2.6.8), the source-to-barrier and observer-to-barrier distances are given as well as the source and observer heights (m) and source frequency (Hz). Find the barrier height required to obtain the indicated Fresnel number. Assume the speed of sound is 343 m/s.

	Source frequency	Source height	Source distance	Observer height	Observer distance	Fresnel number
2.6.5	500	3	8	1.6	12	2
2.6.6	1200	0	5	1.5	10	3
2.6.7	550	2	20	2	30	2.5
2.6.8	4000	2	20	2	30	2

2.7.1. The following factory layout is proposed. A work station is to be located in the vicinity of seven machines which approximate point sources and a conveyor belt which approximates a line source. The coordinates of the sources and the work station are given in meters. In addition, the A-weighted sound power of the machines and conveyor are given in watts and watts per meter, respectively.

Work station,	$x_0 = 5.5$	$y_0 = 16$					
Point source	B	C	D	E	F	G	H
Power (W)	0.01	0.075	0.065	0.012	0.05	0.055	0.045
x	1	2	3	4.5	2.5	5	7.5
y	2	2	2	2.5	4	4	4.5
Line source	A		$x = $ all x			$y = 1.1$	
Power (W/m)	0.0005						

The sources are to be placed near an acoustically hard floor, but there will be no barriers between the sources and the work station and no nearby reflecting walls. All sources will be at about the same level as the observer at the work station.

(a) Predict the sound level at the work station.

(b) Relocate the work station in the $+y$-direction so that the noise level does not exceed 85 dBA.

2.7.2. Construct a line-source interpolator.

2.7.3. Five machines that behave as point sources and one that behaves as a line source are based on an acoustically hard (reflecting) surface. For convenience, the coordinates are oriented so that the line source is parallel to the x-axis. The sound power in watts for each point source and its x and y coordinates are given below in meters. The line source sound power in watts per meter and its y coordinate are also given. Determine the noise levels at 1-m intervals and plot the noise contours.

Sources on an acoustically hard surface

Source 1 sound power = 0.02 W	coordinates 4, 4
Source 2 sound power = 0.025 W	coordinates 8, 4
Source 3 sound power = 0.03 W	coordinates 6, 6
Source 4 sound power = 0.04 W	coordinates 6, 7
Source 5 sound power = 0.02 W	coordinates 9, 12
Line source power = 1.5×10^{-3} W/m	location $y_L = 14$

2.7.4. Write a computer program to determine noise levels on a plane nonreflective surface due to point sources of noise in full space.

In the next two problems, point sources are located in space over an acoustically non-reflective surface at $z = 0$. Plot noise level in the x–y plane for $x = 0$ to 1200 and $y = 0$ to 1500 m. It is suggested a computer be used to determine values at 100-m intervals.

Point sources:	Sound power (W)	Coordinates (m)
2.7.5	100	300, 300, 20
	200	800, 300, 25
	250	600, 1200, 50
2.7.6	120	250, 250, 0
	250	900, 400, 15
	350	800, 1300, 50

Instrumentation and Measurements

Before beginning any experimental work, the objective should be defined and the data necessary to attain the objective should be specified. The first objective may be simply to determine whether or not a noise problem exists. A survey of sound levels might be adequate in this case. However, if the situation calls for reducing the sound power of a noise source, vector sound intensity measurements would provide more information for reaching the goal.

Noise is considered "steady-state" if the sound level and frequency characteristics are relatively constant during the time interval of interest. The sound level meter is the basic tool for surveying steady-state noise levels and determining compliance with standards that limit overall noise levels. Integrating sound level meters make the characterization of time-varying noise more convenient. Personal noise dosimeters are a special type of integrating meter used to determine individual noise exposure.

Noise control efforts often call for measurement of the frequency content of noise. Filter sets may be used to analyze steady-state noise. Current practice, however, usually includes the use of real-time analyzers and Fast Fourier Transform analyzers, which determine noise levels within each frequency band, even for time-varying noise.

Vector sound intensity measurements can be performed with a sound intensity measurement system that includes a two-microphone probe and Fast Fourier Transform (FFT) analyzer. Such systems permit determination of sound power under field conditions that include the effect of reflected sound. In addition, sound intensity measurement systems are used for noise source location and for the construction of intensity contour maps.

3.1 MEASURING MICROPHONES

The microphone is a critical element in any noise measurement system. It serves as a transducer, sensing sound pressure fluctuations and transmitting an electrical signal to the circuitry that follows.

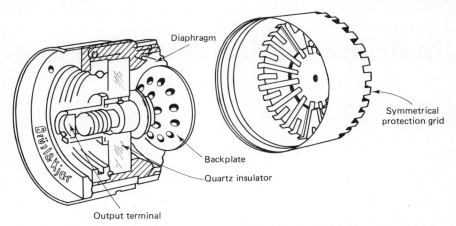

Figure 3.1.1 Sectional view of a condenser microphone cartridge. (*Source:* Courtesy of Bruel & Kjaer Instruments, Inc.)

Piezoelectric materials generate a charge when subject to mechanical strain. In ceramic microphones a piezoelectric ceramic is placed behind a diaphragm. Sound pressure on the diaphragm causes a varying force on the piezoelectric ceramic. Ceramic microphones are comparatively rugged and insensitive to humidity and other environmental effects.

An electret is a polymer film containing an electric charge bonded to the molecules of the polymer. An electret-condenser microphone may be constructed by bonding the electret film to a perforated metal backplate. A thin, metal-coated plastic film is used for the diaphragm. Sound pressure on the diaphragm causes it to move relative to the backplate, varying the capacitance and producing a signal. Electret-condenser microphones do not require an external polarizing voltage as is required with condenser microphones.

Condenser microphones employ two electrically charged plates with an air gap between them. One plate is a light diaphragm which responds to sound pressure, causing the capacitance between the plates to vary. Figure 3.1.1 shows a section view of a condenser microphone cartridge. A capillary tube (an air bleed) is present to ensure ambient pressure equalization. This is because most microphones are designed to sense pressure fluctuations at audible frequencies, while being unaffected by slow changes in atmospheric pressure. Condenser microphones can be designed so that sensitivity is nearly constant over long periods of time, and so that temperature changes have little effect. Because of their stability, they are generally preferred for precision sound measurements. A polarizing voltage must be supplied to the microphone. This makes condenser microphones susceptible to high humidity since electrical leakage is possible. The polarization voltage is supplied via a preamplifier which also presents the correct impedance for connecting the microphone to the rest of the measurement system.

Frequency Response of Microphones

Microphone sizes are identified by the approximate diameter of the microphone cartridge. If the wavelength of a sound wave traveling across the face of a microphone is approximately equal to the microphone size, the instantaneous sound pressures on the microphone diaphragm would tend to cancel. We see that a 13.5-kHz sound wave in air at 20°C would have a propagation velocity of

$$c = 20.04(T' + 273.16)^{1/2} = 343 \text{ m/s}$$

and a wavelength of

$$\lambda = \frac{c}{f} = \frac{343}{13,500} = 0.0254 \text{ m or about 1 in}$$

A typical 1-inch condenser microphone with the appropriate preamplifier is suitable for measurements up to frequencies of about 8 kHz with an accuracy of about ±2 dB (some 1-inch microphones are suitable for higher frequency measurements). A typical $\frac{1}{2}$-inch microphone will measure sounds with frequencies up to about 20 kHz. Quarter-inch and $\frac{1}{8}$-inch microphones are used for sounds above the audible range, for measurement of impulse sounds and for very loud sounds. The sensitivity of a 1-inch condenser microphone–preamplifier combination is typically about 50 millivolts per pascal (mV/Pa). A reduction in microphone size is usually accompanied by a reduction in sensitivity. Some $\frac{1}{2}$-inch microphones have a sensitivity of 12.5 mV/Pa and the sensitivity of $\frac{1}{4}$-inch and $\frac{1}{8}$-inch microphones is still less. The $\frac{1}{2}$-inch microphone is preferred for most noise measurements because it combines adequate sensitivity with a frequency capability over the entire range of audible sound.

Free-Field and Diffuse-Field Measurements

The free field was defined as a region unaffected by reflected waves. The presence of a microphone in the sound field disturbs the field. A microphone designed to compensate for its presence in a free field is called a free-field microphone. Maximum accuracy is obtained if the free-field microphone is pointed toward the noise source (Figure 3.1.2a).

A diffuse sound field is created by multiple reflections. A random-incidence microphone is designed for measuring sound in diffuse fields. It responds uniformly to sounds arriving from all angles simultaneously. A pressure microphone is designed to produce a uniform frequency response to the sound field as it exists, including the disturbance caused by the microphone presence.

Pressure microphones may also be used in diffuse fields. Use of a free-field microphone in a diffuse field will result in reduced accuracy unless the system is equipped with special circuitry to correct the microphone characteristics. When a random-incidence microphone is used to measure sound in a free field, the microphone should be pointed at an angle of 70° to 80° to the source (Figure 3.1.2b). When a pressure microphone is used in a free field, it should be pointed at an angle of 90° from the line between the microphone and source (this is called grazing incidence). Microphone orientation becomes more critical as the sound frequency approaches the upper limit of the microphone accuracy.

The American National Standards Institute (ANSI) calls for microphones with random-incidence response, while the International Electrotechnical Commission (IEC) calls for free-field microphones. Figure 3.1.3 is a flowchart illustrating microphone selection and orientation based on applicable standards and the nature of the sound field.

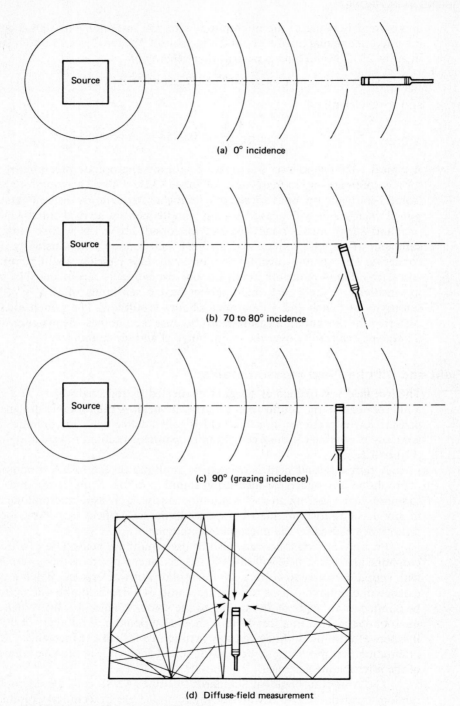

(a) 0° incidence

(b) 70 to 80° incidence

(c) 90° (grazing incidence)

(d) Diffuse-field measurement

Figure 3.1.2 Microphone orientation.

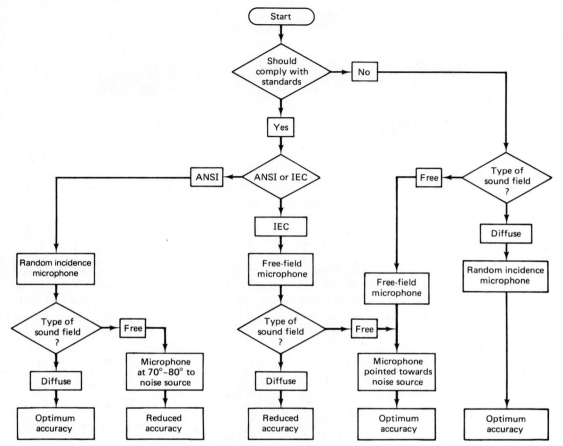

Figure 3.1.3 Microphone selection and orientation. (*Source:* Bruel & Kjaer Instruments, Inc.)

Vector Sound Intensity Probes

A two-microphone probe may be used to measure vector sound intensity. Figure 3.1.4 shows a sound intensity probe with two microphones mounted face to face. Side by side and back to back mounting are possible as well.

The sound intensity probe measures sound pressure at two points simultaneously. Knowing the microphone spacing, sound pressure gradient can be approximated, allowing the calculation of particle velocity in a given direction. Then, the intensity vector component in that direction can be calculated. The approximation of pressure gradient based on a two point measurement of sound pressure is valid only if the microphone spacing is small compared with the wavelength of the sound to be measured. The upper frequency limitation for $\frac{1}{4}$- or $\frac{1}{2}$-inch microphones with 12-mm spacing is about 5 kHz to obtain ± 1 dB accuracy. The corresponding limit for $\frac{1}{4}$-inch microphones with 6-mm spacing is about 10 kHz.

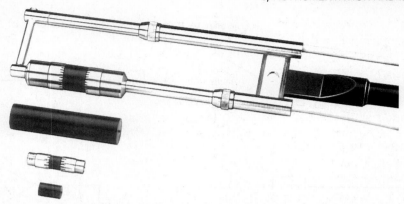

Figure 3.1.4 Sound intensity probe. (*Source:* Bruel & Kjaer Instruments, Inc.)

Windscreens

The presence of a microphone in a moving airstream produces turbulence which causes the microphone diaphragm to deflect. This effect is interpreted as sound by the measurement system, just as blowing air across a microphone is reproduced as sound in a loudspeaker system.

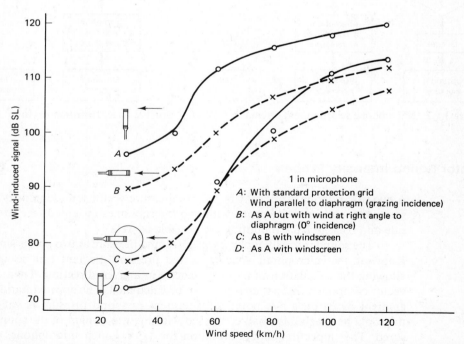

Figure 3.1.5 Wind-induced signal as a function of wind speed. (*Source:* Bruel & Kjaer Instruments, Inc.)

Windscreens made of light foam material are recommended for outdoor measurements to reduce the spurious signal caused by air flow. The windscreens are essentially "transparent" to acoustic signals at frequencies up to 3 kHz. Typical microphone sensitivity loss due to use of a windscreen is about 0.5 dB at 5 kHz and 2 dB at 12 kHz. Figure 3.1.5 shows the wind-induced signal as a function of wind speed. Flat (unweighted) measurements were taken with a 1-inch microphone at 0° incidence and grazing incidence with and without a windscreen.

It can be seen from the figure that noise measurements are greatly influenced by wind effects when wind speed exceeds 40 km/h (about 25 mi/hr), even with a windscreen. Under such conditions, outdoor measurements are usually rescheduled with the hope that the wind will die down.

The energy in a spurious wind-induced signal is greatest near the low-frequency end of the spectrum as shown in Figure 3.1.6, a plot of signal level versus frequency for a 40 km/h wind. *A*-weighting discounts signals at the low-frequency end of the spectrum. Thus, *A*-weighted sound levels are not as significantly affected by "wind noise" as unweighted sound levels. Figure 3.1.7 illustrates the effect of *A*-weighting

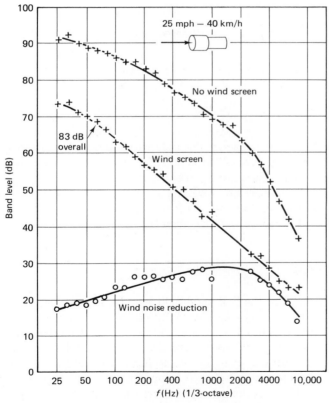

Figure 3.1.6 The "wind noise" spectrum (unweighted) at 40 km/h. (*Source:* GenRad)

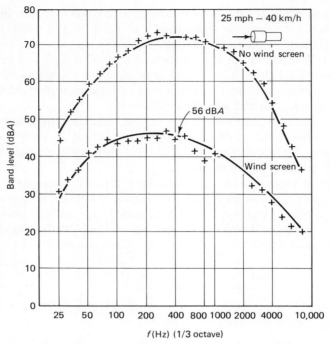

Figure 3.1.7 The *A*-weighted "wind noise" spectrum at 40 km/ h. (*Source:* GenRad)

the signals shown in the plot above. Peterson (1980) states that similar results were obtained with a $\frac{1}{2}$-inch microphone. The plot of "wind noise" versus frequency differs by a few decibels from the plot of "wind noise" versus wind speed at 40 km/h because the measurements were made under different conditions.

Wire framed cloth-covered windscreens, fitted with spikes to discourage birds, are used for long-term outdoor installations. Special nose cones are used instead of windscreens in high-speed air streams when the flow direction is well defined.

3.2 SOUND LEVEL METERS

The basic sound level meter is a hand-held battery-operated instrument that gives direct readings of noise level (see Figure 3.2.1). When we are not interested in the frequency spectrum, a sound level meter is the most convenient instrument for measuring noise that does not vary rapidly with time. It is particularly useful for surveying noise levels in communities and factories to locate problem areas that may require detailed analysis. When surveying noise levels, the investigator will want to measure typical conditions. If he uses large, sophisticated measurement equipment, those responsible for the noise might alter their actions, causing unrepresentative results. This problem could occur when the investigator is measuring truck noise or making pre-

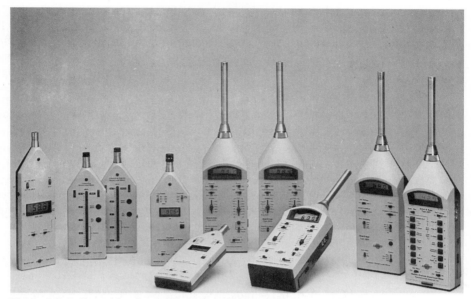

Figure 3.2.1 Sound level meters. (*Source:* Bruel & Kjaer Instruments, Inc.)

liminary surveys of factory noise. In such cases, a lightweight, portable, unobtrusive sound level meter would have an advantage.

A typical sound level meter has a 1-inch or $\frac{1}{2}$-inch microphone, a preamplifier, weighting networks, another amplifier, a root-mean-square (rms) rectifier, and a meter that indicates the noise level in decibels. Figure 3.2.2 shows a block diagram of one possible configuration. The preamplifier (also called a cathode follower) is usually

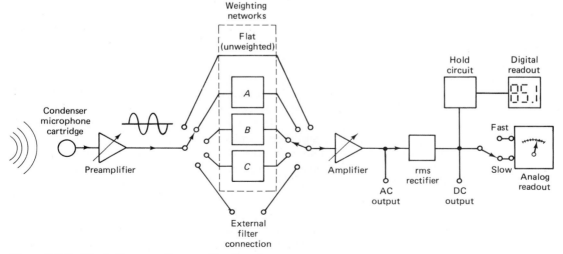

Figure 3.2.2 Block diagram of a sound level meter.

contained in the same housing as the condenser microphone. A switch allows selection of A-, B-, or C-weighting networks, or no weighting at all (see Section 1.7 for A-, B-, and C-weighting curves). After further amplification, the signal is rectified, converted to decibel (logarithmic) form, and fed into an analog or digital readout meter. The sound level meter reading does not change instantaneously with changing sound levels, but averages over a short interval, suppressing old data. When "fast" response is selected, the time constant is about $\frac{1}{8}$ s. If the reading fluctuates rapidly, in the fast response position, "slow" response with a time constant of about 1 s may be used.

Output jacks are available so that AC and DC signals from the sound level meter may be used as an input to other instrumentation including Fast Fourier Transform (FFT) analyzers, graphic level recorders, and printers. Some meters incorporate octave-band filters, or one-third octave filters and some have terminals for filter connection. A maximum-hold circuit may be incorporated on the sound level meter to retain maximum values. Sound level meter configurations vary widely. The features discussed in this section are not common to all models.

Precision of Sound Level Meters

The American National Standards Institute (ANSI) and International Electrotechnical Commission (IEC) specify several types of sound level meters according to their precision. Types 1, 2, and 3 are referred to as "precision," "general-purpose," and "survey" meters, respectively. In addition, IEC specifies a type 0 meter which is intended as a laboratory reference standard. ANSI standards include a suffix S used to designate special-purpose meters, for example, meters with only A-weighting. The actual precision of measurements depends on many factors including meter calibration, measurement methods, and the frequency content of the noise. As a rough guide, however, we may assume most measurements carefully taken with a type 1 sound level meter will have an error not exceeding 1 dB. The corresponding error for a type 2 sound level meter is about 2 dB.

Preparation for Field Measurements
Using Sound Level Meters

Consider a stationary observer subject to steady noise. For example, this case could represent a factory worker at a fixed location. In this case, it might only be necessary to take a limited number of sound level readings in dBA at the worker's ear and compare the readings with established standards.

Most actual measurement problems are more complicated than the example cited above. They often involve moving noise sources and observers, time-varying noise, and poorly defined standards. It is then necessary to design a measurement program. The first step is to determine the intent of the study which may include worker hearing conservation, community noise reduction, elimination of speech interference, or other goals. It is then possible to develop a written plan of action and prepare data sheets to ensure that all relevant data are recorded.

Statistical (Percent Exceeded) Noise Levels

Percent exceeded noise levels are sometimes used as descriptors of noise that varies with time. Levels L_{10} (exceeded 10% of the time) and L_{50} (the median, exceeded 50% of the time) are used as well as L_{90} (exceeded 90% of the time, sometimes called background noise level). It is important to specify the weighting, the measurement location, and the measurement interval. For example, we may wish to determine the level in dBA exceeded 10% of the time during the "worst hour" at a property line. This may be determined with a statistical analyzer, or by sampling, using a sound level meter.

Sampling Procedures

Consider a situation where the noise level varies second by second, but is stationary in a statistical sense over a longer time period. Using highway noise as an example, we might expect statistical descriptors of noise levels over a 5- or 10-minute period to be representative of an entire "rush hour" period. After representative locations have been selected, the following sampling procedure may be used.

1. Prepare data sheets. Figure 3.2.3 shows a typical data sheet. Assemble instrumentation. Select time intervals for representative noise levels or "worst hour" conditions.
2. Calibrate the sound level meter. Measure and record wind speed and relative humidity if applicable.
3. Measure noise level every 10 s for 50 readings. Instantaneous readings should be noted at time = 0 s, 10 s, 20 s, and so on, without regard for peak values that may occur between readings. Record each reading with a mark in the appropriate row of the data sheet.
4. Recheck sound level meter calibration, wind speed, and so on.

Interpretation of Data

If there are 50 readings, 5 readings will be greater than the 10% exceeded level. Thus, L_{10}, the 10% exceeded level, falls between the fifth and sixth highest readings. Readings are ordered from the top of the data sheet; the order in which the readings were taken is, of course, of no consequence. Median noise level, L_{50} falls between the twenty-fifth and twenty-sixth readings and L_{90}, the 90% exceeded level, between the forty-fifth and forty-sixth readings.

Confidence Limits

If noise levels vary over a wide range, it is necessary to take a large number of readings to obtain percent exceeded levels with reasonable precision. For 50 readings, the 95% confidence level error limits for L_{10} are the first and tenth readings. If the error limits are unsatisfactory, more readings may be taken. When 100 readings are taken, then

Location _____ A _____   Wind _5 km/h_ Precipitation _None_

Day _Tue_ Date _Dec 16_   Temperature DB _50_ WB _40°_ R.H. _40%_

Time Begin _4:40_ End _4:50 P.M._   Attached Location Map _____ Map no. _____

Calibration _Begin OK_   Comments _No unusual events_
             End OK

Windscreen _On_   _____

Weighting _A_   _____

Fast/slow _Slow_   Engineer/Technician _Signature_

Noise level ± 0.5 dBA	Occurrences (number of readings at each level)										Cumulative occurrences	
80												
79												
78												
77												
76												
75												
74	X	X									2	2
73	X	X	(X	X)	X	X	X				7	9
72	X	X	X	X	X	X	X	X	X		9	18
71	X	X	X	X							4	22
70	X	X	X	X	X	X	X	X	X	X	10	32
69	X	X	X	X	X	X	X	X			8	40
68	X	X	X	X	X						5	45
67	X	X	X	X							4	49
66	X										1	50
65												
64												
63												
62												
61												
60												

Figure 3.2.3 Data sheet for noise sampling.

L_{10} falls between the tenth and eleventh readings and the 95% confidence level error limits are the fifth and seventeenth readings. Figure 3.2.4 shows the statistical error limits for the 10% exceeded level for various sample sizes, providing confidence limits of about 95%. The effect of instrumentation error is not included in the error limits. In addition, the results are only as meaningful as the sampling period is representative of typical conditions. If, for example, a fire engine siren contributed to the noise level during the measurement period, the readings would be rejected (unless the measurement site was next to a firehouse).

EXAMPLE PROBLEM: STATISTICAL NOISE LEVELS

(a) Find approximate noise levels L_{10}, L_{50}, and L_{90} for conditions recorded on the data sheet in Figure 3.2.3.

Number of samples	Error limits		Confidence coefficient
350	24	46	0.949
350	25	47	0.950
350	26	48	0.944
300	19	40	0.952
300	20	41	0.957
300	21	42	0.955
250	15	34	0.950
250	16	35	0.956
250	17	36	0.952
200	11	28	0.949
200	12	29	0.956
200	13	30	0.952
150	7	22	0.950
150	8	23	0.960
150	9	24	0.955
100	4	16	0.952
100	5	17	0.956
100	6	18	0.932
50	1	10	0.970
50	2	10	0.942

Figure 3.2.4 Error limits for the 10% exceeded level.

Solution. Counting from the top of the data sheet, L_{10} falls between the fifth and sixth readings which are both 73 dBA (circled on the data sheet). Thus, $L_{10} = 73$ dBA, $L_{50} = 70$ dBA, corresponding to the twenty-fifth and twenty-sixth readings. The forty-fifth and forty-sixth readings are, respectively, 68 and 67 dBA. Taking the midpoint, we have $L_{90} = 67.5$ dBA.

(b) Find the limits of L_{10} for a 95% confidence level if the measurements are truly representative.

Solution. The first and tenth readings are 74 (± 0.5) and 72 (± 0.5). Therefore, L_{10} lies between 71.5 and 74.5 dBA, or we may say $L_{10} = 73 \pm 1.5$ dBA with a 95% level of confidence.

3.3 CALIBRATION OF NOISE MEASUREMENT SYSTEMS

A measuring microphone is usually supplied with a calibration chart indicating its sensitivity over its entire frequency range. Bruel (1964 and 1965) describes nine methods of sensitivity calibration of laboratory standard microphones. His results show that the reciprocity method is the most accurate when considering the absolute calibration of condenser microphone cartridges. However, he found that when measuring sound pressure levels, the most accurate results are obtained when a pistonphone is used as a reference.

Pistonphones

The pistonphone is a pressure-response calibrator utilizing a battery-operated motor to drive a pair of pistons. It produces a sound pressure proportional to the ratio of piston displacement to coupler cavity volume. Calibration is performed by simply turning on the pistonphone and placing its coupler over a microphone. Adapters are available to ensure a tight fit for various size microphones. Typical pistonphone specifications call for a 250-Hz signal at 124 (±0.2) dB. If noise levels are to be measured in dB*A,* then the instrument should be calibrated in the *A*-weighted mode. Referring to the table in Chapter 1 showing *A*- and *C*-weighting, we see that the *A*-weighted response to a 250-Hz signal at 124 dB is 124 − 8.6 = 115.4 dB. At 250 Hz, there is no correction applied to *C*-weighted response.

Sound level meters and other noise measurement systems should be calibrated immediately before making noise measurements, and the calibration should be checked when the measurements are completed. If there is a significant change in sensitivity, the instruments should be thoroughly checked and the measurements repeated. When data are tape recorded in the field, the signal from a sound level calibrator should be recorded on the tape. Tape recorder settings should be noted at this time and during measurements since it may be necessary to change attenuator levels.

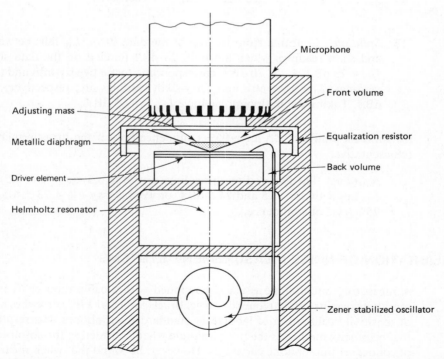

Figure 3.3.1 Oscillator-driven sound level calibrator. (*Source:* Bruel & Kjaer Instruments, Inc.)

Oscillator-Driven Sound Level Calibrators

Pocket size, battery-operated oscillator-driven sound level calibrators are also available. Figure 3.3.1 illustrates the principle of operation of one such calibrator utilizing an oscillator to feed a piezoelectric driver element that vibrates a diaphragm at 1000 Hz ($\pm 1.5\%$). The diaphragm generates a sound pressure level of 94 ± 0.3 dB in the coupler volume. In this calibrator, the cavity behind the diaphragm acts as a Helmholz resonator with a natural frequency of 1000 Hz. The resonant frequency of a Helmholz resonator depends only on the cavity volume and the length and cross section of the constricting neck. Thus, the calibrator is essentially insensitive to changes in ambient pressure. The calibrator sound pressure level of 94 dB corresponds to a root-mean-square sound pressure of 1 Pa (1 N/m^2). The frequency, 1000 Hz, is the reference frequency for the standardized international weighting networks. Thus, no correction is needed when calibrating instrumentation for A-, B-, C-, or D-weighting or for unweighted measurements. Calibrators that operate at several frequencies and sound levels are also available. They allow instrument calibration near the sound levels and frequencies to be measured.

Some sound level meters and other measuring systems generate an internal signal that may be used to check the system electronics. A check of this type cannot replace an acoustic calibration that tests the microphone as well.

3.4 MEASUREMENT ERROR DUE TO THE PRESENCE OF AN OBSERVER

The presence of instrumentation and an observer can cause reflections and distortion in a sound field. If the field is reverberant, sound will impinge on the microphone from all directions and measurement errors will be small, particularly when overall sound levels are measured. When using a sound level meter to make measurements near a source, the observer should stand to the side of a direct path between the source and microphone. The sound level meter may be mounted on a tripod so that the observer can stand at least 0.5 m behind and 0.5 m to the side.

The precision of octave-band measurements and narrow-band measurements is more sensitive to the presence of equipment and personnel. To minimize disturbances in the sound field in such cases, the microphone assembly may be tripod mounted and an extension cable used to position other instrumentation at a distance of at least 1.5 m from the microphone. When measurements are made in specially constructed anechoic chambers or reverberant chambers, the microphone assembly is usually tripod mounted and a long extension cable is used so that the remaining instrumentation can be placed outside of the chamber. As observed earlier, both diffraction and absorption are a function of wavelength.

3.5 BACKGROUND NOISE CORRECTIONS

When we try to measure noise due to a particular source or system, the cumulative effect of all other sources is considered the background. Ideally, we could make our measurements in specially constructed rooms or far from other activity. In practice, however, this may be impossible.

For example, it may be necessary to measure noise due to a truck passby on a highway. If the background noise level is 20 dB or more below the combined (background and truck) noise level, then the background noise contribution is negligible. If the background noise level is 10 to 20 dB below the combined level, there will be a small background noise contribution. If the difference is less than 10 dB, it is necessary to correct for background noise. However, if the difference is less than 5 dB, even the corrected value may be in doubt.

Suppose it is necessary to determine the noise level contribution L due to a particular source when the background noise (measured in the absence of the source in question) is L_B. L_C, the combined noise level (due to the source in question and the background noise), is measured. Since the sources are certain to be uncorrelated, the sound level of the source in question may be expressed in terms of the differences in mean-square sound pressures of the combined noise and the background noise. Using the definition of sound pressure level, we have

$$L = 10 \lg \frac{p^2_{C\text{rms}} - p^2_{B\text{rms}}}{p^2_{\text{ref}}} = 10 \lg(10^{L_C/10} - 10^{L_B/10}) \qquad (3.5.1)$$

Let X be the difference between combined noise level and background noise level. Then, $L_B = L_C - X$ from which

$$L = 10 \lg(10^{L_C/10} - 10^{(L_C-X)/10})$$

$$= 10 \lg[10^{L_C/10}(1 - 10^{-X/10})]$$

$$L = L_C + 10 \lg(1 - 10^{-X/10}) \qquad (3.5.2)$$

The last term in the above equation is used to correct the combined noise level to obtain the noise level contribution of the source in question.

EXAMPLE PROBLEM: BACKGROUND CORRECTION

(a) Determine the correction for background noise if X, the difference between combined noise level and background noise, varies from 1 to 20 dB.

Solution. A simple program is written to determine the background correction

$$10 \lg(1 - 10^{-X/10})$$

for values of X between 1 and 20. As noted above, measurements will be in doubt for $X < 5$. In that range, a change in background noise level during the measurements can cause a significant error in the corrected noise level. The results, which are shown in Table 3.5.1, are rounded off to the nearest 0.1 dB using the integer function $\text{INT}(10*\text{BC} + 0.5)/10$ where

$$\text{BC} = 10 \frac{\log_e(1 - 10^{-X/10})}{\log_e(10)}$$

is the background correction. The correction is applied to combined noise level to obtain the noise level that would result from the source in question alone.

TABLE 3.5.1 Correction applied to combined noise level to obtain level that would result from the source in question

Difference X (dB)	Background correction (dB)
1	−6.9
2	−4.3
3	−3
4	−2.2
5	−1.7
6	−1.3
7	−1
8	−0.7
9	−0.6
10	−0.5
11	−0.4
12	−0.3
13	−0.2
14	−0.2
15	−0.1
16	−0.1
17	−0.1
18	−0.1
19	−0.1
20	0

(b) Plot the background noise correction.

Solution. Figure 3.5.1 shows a computer-generated plot of background noise correction when the difference between combined noise level and background noise level lies between about 4.5 and 12.

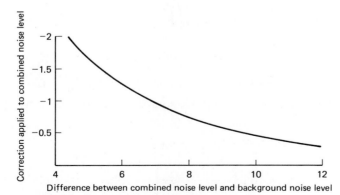

Figure 3.5.1 Background noise correction.

3.6 INTEGRATING SOUND LEVEL METERS

Equivalent Sound Level

Equivalent sound level was defined in Chapter 1 in the integral form

$$L_{\text{eq}} = 10 \lg\left(\frac{1}{T} \int_0^T 10^{L/10} \, dt\right) \tag{3.6.1}$$

and in terms of a set of N sound level measurements

$$L_{\text{eq}} = 10 \lg\left(\frac{1}{N} \sum_{i=1}^N 10^{L_i/10}\right) \tag{3.6.2}$$

An example in that chapter illustrated the computation of L_{eq} from 50 discrete readings taken at 10-s intervals. However, this method may not be feasible if L_{eq} is required over a longer time interval, or if greater precision is necessary. Hence, integrating sound level meters have been developed for automatic calculation of L_{eq}.

One model of integrating sound level meter may be preset for a running time of 1 s up to 600 s in 1-s steps and from 10 minutes to 24 hours in 1-minute steps. A digital display shows L_{eq}, while the instantaneous sound level is shown in an analog display. A pause feature allows the operator to exclude events which are not wanted in the record (e.g., an atypical event such as someone shouting near the microphone).

Sound Exposure Level

An integrating sound level meter may also compute sound exposure level (SEL). SEL may be used to characterize a single event, considering both the level and duration. It is defined as follows:

$$\text{SEL} = 10 \lg\left(\int_0^T \frac{p_{\text{rms}}^2}{p_{\text{ref}}^2} \, dt\right) \tag{3.6.3}$$

or

$$\text{SEL} = 10 \lg\left(\int_0^T 10^{L/10} \, dt\right) \tag{3.6.4}$$

where T is measured in seconds.

EXAMPLE PROBLEM: SOUND EXPOSURE LEVEL

(a) Find the sound exposure level for a 1-s burst of sound with a root-mean-square pressure of 1 Pa.

Solution. Using the first expression for SEL, we have

$$\text{SEL} = 10 \lg\left[\frac{1}{(20 \times 10^{-6})^2}\right] = 93.98 \qquad \text{(say 94 dB)}$$

Note that we might have converted the root-mean-square pressure into a sound level (94 dB) and used the second expression for SEL. Inspecting that equation, we see that SEL equals the sound level in the case of 1-s event at constant level.

(b) Find the sound exposure level for an event lasting 5 s and having an equivalent sound level of 105 dBA.

Solution. Comparing the second expression for SEL with the equation for L, we see that

$$L_{eq} = 10 \lg\left(\frac{1}{T}\right) + SEL$$

from which

$$SEL = L_{eq} + 10 \lg T \qquad (3.6.5)$$

where T is measured in seconds. In this case,

$$SEL = 105 + 10 \lg 5 = 112 \text{ dB}A$$

The above example illustrates a procedure for calculating sound exposure level with an integrating sound level meter which does not offer an automatic SEL mode. For example, we may wish to use SEL as a descriptor of the noise energy caused by a single machine operation. The integrating sound level meter could be used in the L_{eq} mode and integration begun immediately before the event, with the integration time preset to end shortly after the event. Then, the equation relating SEL and L_{eq} could be used, where T is the integration time. If the background noise is low compared with the noise level during the event, the length of integration time T is not critical. For example, if the event takes place over a 3-s interval, selecting $T = 5$ s or $T = 10$ s would produce about the same value of SEL in the absence of other significant noise contributions.

3.7 DOSIMETERS

Personal noise dose meters or dosimeters are special-purpose integrating sound level meters carried by industrial workers and others exposed to high noise levels. Dosimeters measure the accumulated noise exposure of an individual and calculate percent of allowable daily exposure. It is difficult to determine noise dose by other means if noise levels vary and individuals move from place to place during the day.

One model of dosimeter consists of a noise-exposure monitor and an indicator. The indicator has a built-in calibrator to test monitor operation. The monitor is ordinarily carried in the shirt pocket of the exposed individual, with a microphone on an extension cable clipped near the individual's ear. The monitor, which is calibrated and turned on at the start of a workday, automatically computes noise exposure throughout the day. At the end of the workday, the monitor is plugged into the indicator to obtain a digital display of percent of allowable daily exposure. This two-part dosim-

Figure 3.7.1   Microprocessor-based   multifunction
meter. (*Source:* Quest Electronics.)

eter has concealed controls on the monitor portion to discourage tampering. Several
monitors may be serviced by a single indicator.

Figure 3.7.1 shows a microprocessor-based multifunction dosimeter which also
serves as an integrating sound level meter. Functions are displayed digitally, and hard
copy printouts of data for statistical analysis are available. A microcomputer program
is available to read the data stored in the meter, estimate projected noise dose, time-
weighted average level (TWA), and sound exposure level (SEL). The program also
saves records on disks or casettes and reads records from disks or casettes.

3.8 MEASUREMENT OF NOISE IN FREQUENCY BANDS

Frequency analysis allows us to look at the sound levels in each frequency band. This
information is particularly useful when trying to locate the cause of a noise problem.
For example, each time a fan blade passes a particular point, an impulse is generated.
The product of the fan speed (revolutions per second) and the number of blades is
called the *blade frequency.* If a frequency spectrum shows a significant peak at a frequency equal to the blade frequency of a fan, then noise control efforts could be
directed at the fan. The noise contributions of gears, bearings, and many other components can also be identified by frequency analysis.

Real-time analyzers and fast Fourier transform (FFT) analyzers permit continuous or practically continuous measurement of the noise frequency spectrum. They
operate in a parallel fashion in that the input signal passes through many filters simultaneously (or this process is simulated digitally). These instruments, which are
particularly useful in the measurement of time-varying noise, will be discussed in a
later section. Serial analyzers measure the sound level in one frequency band at
a time.

Bandpass Filters

After an acoustic signal is sensed and represented by an electronic signal, it may be further processed by filters. These may be analog filters constructed of electronic circuitry tuned to pass certain frequencies or digital filters designed for the same purpose. An ideal bandpass filter would permit a signal to pass only if the signal frequency fell between the upper and lower frequency limits of the filter (Figure 3.8.1). Signals within that band would be transmitted without change in amplitude. However, filters cannot be designed so precisely.

Characteristics of an actual filter are better described by Figure 3.8.2. Some of the signal from adjacent frequency bands is passed unavoidably due to the "skirts" of a typical filter. Furthermore, signals within the selected band are subject to some change as identified by the "ripple."

The 3-dB bandwidth is the filter bandwidth at half-power or 3-dB attenuation. *Effective noise bandwidth* of a bandpass filter is defined as the bandwidth of an ideal filter which would transmit the same power from a white noise source. *White noise* is a signal consisting of all frequencies and having the same level in all (constant) frequency bands. Effective noise bandwidth can be determined by integrating the area under the amplification factor versus frequency curve. Filter precision is standardized by the American National Standards Institute (ANSI, 1966).

Filter standards are defined in such a way that class III filters are more precise than class II filters, which are more precise than class I filters. This may be confusing when we recall that type 1 sound level meters are more precise than type 2 sound level meters, and so on.

Serial Analysis

Serial analysis consists of measuring the noise level contribution in each frequency band, one band at a time. This may be done by manually switching from one frequency band to the next, or by using an analyzer that sweeps automatically through a range of frequencies.

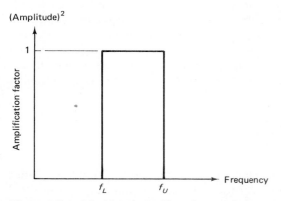

Figure 3.8.1 Ideal bandpass filter characteristics.

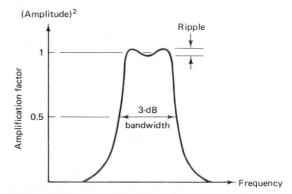

Figure 3.8.2 Actual bandpass filter characteristics.

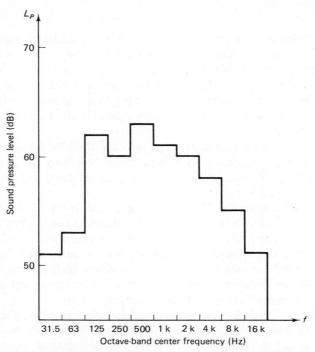

Figure 3.8.3   Fan noise spectrum measured in octave bands.

Octave-band filter sets are sometimes incorporated in sound level meters or attached to sound level meters. If the noise does not vary in level or frequency during the measurement period, serial analysis using an octave-band filter set is possible. Figure 3.8.3 is an example of a spectral analysis of fan noise obtained using a sound level meter with an octave-band filter set. This information could be used to determine if the fan would be acceptable in a particular setting. Noise control efforts directed at the fan might require further analysis using one-third octave or narrower bands.

Time-varying noise, including transient noise, can be analyzed by recording it on magnetic tape and then determining the level of the recorded signal within each frequency band. If a signal is to be analyzed in one-third octave bands with center frequencies ranging from 25 Hz to 20 kHz, then a serial analysis procedure would require that the tape be played 30 times. This time-consuming procedure is no longer common because parallel analysis systems that provide the same results more efficiently are now available.

3.9 REAL-TIME ANALYSIS

Real-time analyzers (RTA's) examine a signal in all of the selected frequency bands simultaneously. This parallel process is illustrated by the schematic of Figure 3.9.1. Most RTA's utilize digital filtering of a sampled time series. Digital filtering is discussed by Oppenheimer and Shafer (1975) and by Rabiner and Gould (1975).

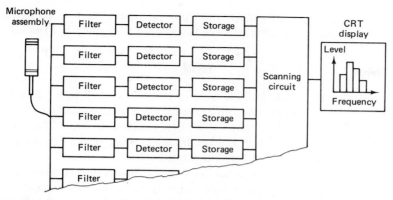

Figure 3.9.1 Simplified schematic illustrating the operating principle of a real-time analyzer.

Consider a varying noise signal converted to an electronic signal by a microphone assembly. In the RTA, the signal is simultaneously presented to a parallel set of filters, detectors, and storage components. The results are then scanned and displayed as a bar graph of sound level versus frequency on a cathode ray tube (CRT) monitor. If desired, the display may be renewed several times per second as the level and frequency content of the signal change. More likely, however, we will be interested in a spectrum averaged over a longer time interval. The time interval could, for example, include an aircraft flyover or truck passby or the time span of a particular machine operation. The RTA output can also be presented to a computer for further processing or to an *xy*-plotter or a printer.

Standard and optional RTA features may include:

1. An alphanumeric display of the level and center frequency of a channel selected by moving a cursor across the bar graph display.
2. Numerical level versus frequency listing.
3. Choice of linear (unweighted) and *A*-, *B*-, *C*-, and *D*-weighted sound levels in each frequency band.
4. Linear and exponential averaging.
5. Selectable averaging time from a fraction of a second to 2 or more minutes, or an integrating time up to 24 hours when using an integrating RTA.
6. Low-frequency channels extending to 1.6 Hz and high-frequency channels extending to 80 or 160 kHz.
7. Fast, slow, and impulse time constants.
8. Spectrum storage for recall and comparison with current data.
9. AC and battery operation.
10. Computer software packages for further analysis of RTA output.

3.10 FAST FOURIER TRANSFORM ANALYSIS

Fourier analysis has many applications in science and engineering. The Fourier series and Fourier transform, for example, are used to study the response of vibrating systems to periodic and impulse forces.

The *Fourier transform* takes us from the time domain to the frequency domain. It relates a function of time $g(t)$ to a function of frequency $F(f)$ as follows:

$$F(f) = \int_{-\infty}^{\infty} g(t)e^{-j2\pi ft}\, dt \qquad (3.10.1)$$

A vibrating system may be described in terms of its complex frequency response, a transfer function that depends on system mass, elasticity, and damping. Assume that the system excitation is a known analytical function of time. The Fourier transform of the response of the system is given by the product of the Fourier transform of the excitation and the complex frequency response.

Noise, however, is not generally deterministic. When measuring noise, a microphone assembly produces a voltage proportional to sound pressure. A *time series* is formed if the voltage is sampled at uniform intervals. Figure 3.10.1 illustrates sampling of a sound pressure wave at discrete points to produce a time series.

A different form of the Fourier transform, the *discrete Fourier transform* (DFT), has been defined to transform a time series to the frequency domain. Using k to represent the kth frequency band f_k, and n to represent the nth sampling time t_n, the discrete Fourier transform is given by

$$F(k) = \frac{1}{N} \sum_{n=0}^{n=N-1} g(n)e^{-j2\pi kn/N} \qquad (3.10.2)$$

or by the matrix equation

$$\mathbf{F} = \frac{1}{N}\,[\mathbf{A}]\mathbf{g} \qquad (3.10.3)$$

where $\mathbf{F}$ is a column array of N complex frequency components, $[\mathbf{A}]$ is a square matrix of unit vectors, and $\mathbf{g}$ a column array of N samples in the time series (Randall, 1977).

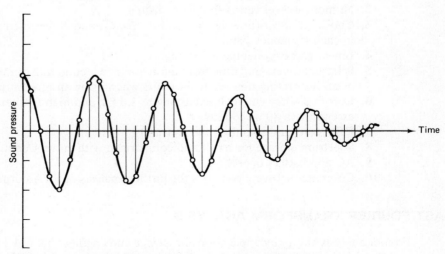

Figure 3.10.1 Sampling of sound pressure at discrete intervals.

For illustration purposes, let each unit vector $e^{-j2\pi kn/N}$ be represented by a directional arrow. Then the matrix equation could be shown in the following form:

$$
\begin{bmatrix} F_0 \\ F_1 \\ F_2 \\ F_3 \\ \cdot \\ \cdot \end{bmatrix} = 1/N
\begin{bmatrix}
\uparrow & \uparrow & \uparrow & \uparrow & \uparrow & \uparrow & \cdot & \cdot \\
\uparrow & \nearrow & \rightarrow & \searrow & \downarrow & \cdot & \cdot & \cdot \\
\uparrow & \rightarrow & \downarrow & \leftarrow & \cdot & \cdot & \cdot & \cdot \\
\uparrow & \searrow & \cdot & \cdot & \cdot & \cdot & \cdot & \cdot \\
& \cdot & \cdot & \cdot & \cdot & \cdot & \cdot &
\end{bmatrix}
\begin{bmatrix} g_0 \\ g_1 \\ g_2 \\ \cdot \\ \cdot \end{bmatrix}
$$

Direct evaluation of the discrete Fourier transform requires a large number of arithmetic operations when a large number of sample readings are taken. Thus, the DFT concept did not have a significant impact on the analysis of noise signals until a more efficient data processing procedure was developed.

The *Fast Fourier Transform (FFT)* algorithm (Cooley and Tukey, 1965) reduces the number of calculations required to obtain a discrete Fourier transform. Although the FFT (or Cooley–Tukey) algorithm was first implemented on large mainframe computers, it is now available principally in dedicated FFT analyzers.

The FFT algorithm rearranges the [A] matrix of equation 3.10.3 by interchanging rows and factoring. The new form of the matrix reduces memory requirements and saves calculation time by permitting calculations to be carried out in place, with results stored in the same memory location as the original data. Further savings in calculation time are realized by tabulating sine and cosine values. Detailed explanations of the process, beyond the scope of this book, are given by Randall (1977) and Herlufsen (1984a and 1984b).

Aliasing

Just as an alias refers to an assumed or false name, *aliasing* is the measurement of an incorrect or false frequency. In Figure 3.10.2, the solid line represents a sound wave with a period of T s and frequency $f = 1/T$ Hz. Let the wave be sampled at intervals of T_S s corresponding to a sampling rate (sampling frequency) of $f_S = 1/T_S$. It can be seen from the figure that the selected sampling rate is too low. The frequency would

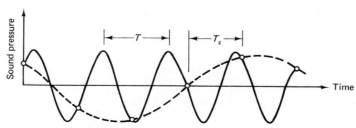

Figure 3.10.2 Aliasing.

be incorrectly identified as that of the dashed line. Aliasing can occur when FFT analyzers and other digital signal processing instrumentation are used.

The *Nyquist frequency* is defined as half the sampling rate. If the noise we wish to measure contains frequency components above the Nyquist frequency, then aliasing may occur. If those high-frequency components are of interest to us, we must increase the sampling rate. In some cases, high-frequency signal components may result from electrical "noise" or other artifacts. Low-pass anti-aliasing filters may be incorporated into FFT and other analyzers to prevent spurious results due to high-frequency signal components that we do not wish to measure.

Dynamic Range

The range of signal amplitude an instrument can handle is called the dynamic range. It is measured from the instrument "noise floor" (spurious signals resulting from electrical noise) to the maximum signal that can be portrayed accurately (Figure 3.10.3). Dynamic range depends on the number of bits used in the calculation and the number of bits with which the input data are represented. FFT analyzers typically have a dynamic range of about 70 dB.

Measurement Error

Most noise is random in that sound pressure cannot be predicted at any instant, but may be described statistically. Noise that is relatively constant in level and frequency content may be considered a stationary random process, one in which statistical measures are invariant with time. For example, the equivalent sound level in an office would be about the same if measured for a 1-hour interval beginning at 9 A.M. or beginning at 10 A.M. Of course, a measurement interval of a few seconds would be

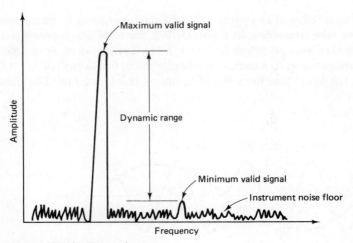

Figure 3.10.3 Dynamic range.

inadequate because conditions at the measurement time might be atypical. If we were interested in frequency analysis of noise levels in a situation of this type, a real-time analyzer or FFT analyzer would save a substantial amount of time over serial analysis.

Consider idealized noise with a Gaussian (normal) amplitude probability distribution. Then, measurement uncertainty is related to filter bandwidth and averaging time. For averaging time T with an ideal filter of bandwidth B, the measurement uncertainty is given by

$$e_{ms} = \frac{1}{(BT)^{1/2}} \qquad (3.10.4)$$

where e_{ms} is uncertainty in the mean-square signal divided by the true (long-term average) mean-square signal. Uncertainty in the root-mean-square signal divided by the true root-mean-square signal is given by

$$e_{rms} = \frac{0.5}{(BT)^{1/2}} \qquad (3.10.5)$$

EXAMPLE PROBLEM: MEASUREMENT UNCERTAINTY

Random noise is to be analyzed in 10-Hz bands. Find the required averaging time if measurement uncertainty is not to exceed 5% of the mean-square signal.

Solution. If the noise amplitude is normally distributed and we assume ideal filter characteristics, then

$$e_{ms} = \frac{1}{(BT)^{1/2}} = \frac{1}{(10T)^{1/2}} \le 0.05$$

from which averaging time $T \ge 40$ s.

Data Windows

Consider a steady pure-tone signal of unknown frequency. If this signal was to be analyzed, it would ordinarily be sampled over a short time interval (called the *window duration*). A *rectangular window* passes a segment of the original signal without adjustment. It might be assumed that the short segment so obtained was representative of the original signal. The assumption would be true if the segment contained an integer number of periods of the original signal. Since the signal frequency is not known, it is likely that the segment would contain a noninteger number of periods as illustrated in Figure 3.10.4. The signal would be analyzed as if the segment were repeated as in the figure. The discontinuities at the ends of the segments would produce a frequency spectrum differing from that of the original signal. Aperiodic signals are also misinterpreted due to the necessity of taking samples of finite length.

The *hanning window* reduces the effect of discontinuity due to finite sampling periods. It is based on a cosine squared function as shown in the figure. Other window functions include the Hamming window and the Gaussian window. Randall (1977) compares various windows in the time and frequency domains.

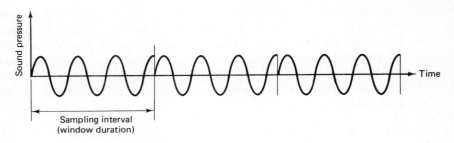

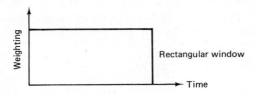

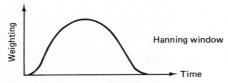

Figure 3.10.4 Data windows.

Resolution

Resolution commonly refers to the smallest increment in a quantity that can be displayed by a measuring system. The resolution in normal FFT analysis is given by

$$\beta = \frac{f_S}{N} = \frac{2f_R}{N} \tag{3.10.6}$$

where β = resolution, the frequency increment between lines in a spectrum
f_S = sampling rate
N = number of samples in the original time series
f_R = frequency range

The frequency range is normally from zero to the Nyquist frequency. FFT analyzers with "zoom" capability utilize a large sample memory, and display selected portions of a spectrum with finer resolution.

3.11 SIGNAL STORAGE

In some cases, a carefully prepared data sheet is adequate for recording noise measurements. When noise varies in level and frequency, other data storage methods may be necessary so that future analysis and comparison are possible.

Real-time analyzers and FFT analyzers often have a memory capability. This permits storage of an analyzed spectrum, or a spectrum entered digitally, which may be later displayed alternately with incoming data for comparison. Analyzers may perform simple calculations relating the stored spectrum and the newly analyzed spectrum. More involved calculations are possible if the data are transmitted from the analyzer to a computer or desk-top calculator via a standard interface (IEEE-488 bus) which also permits computer or calculator control of the analyzer.

Graphic level recorders are often used with frequency analyzers. When level recorders are used with serial frequency analyzers, sound level versus frequency may be plotted automatically with the level plotter controlling the analyzer.

Noise level analyzers accept a microphone input and determine an A-weighted statistical percent-exceeded sound level or equivalent sound level. A noise level analyzer used in combination with an alphanumeric printer will make an automatic hard-copy record of these descriptors at preselected intervals.

Portable instrument tape recorders have long been a preferred method for storing noise signals for further analysis. They are particularly useful for making field measurements that are to be analyzed in the laboratory. Both digital and analog systems are in use, with amplitude modulation and frequency modulation. Usually, signals are recorded directly from a microphone–preamplifier assembly without weighting.

Calibration, important in all measurements, is particularly important when recording data. When using a tape recorder, it is suggested that an acoustical calibrator be used and that the calibration signal be recorded directly on the tape. If the recorder has a cuing channel, the calibration level and frequency should be indicated thereon for future reference. If a graphic level recorder is used, the calibration signal should be recorded somewhere on the chart copy. When adjustments are necessary after the calibration, the adjustments should be in steps (e.g., decades) and should be noted on the cuing channel or on the data sheet. Where possible, some backup measurements should be made with a sound level meter and recorded on the data sheet as a check of system reliability.

3.12 VECTOR SOUND INTENSITY MEASUREMENT

Experimentation in vector sound intensity measurement dates back to the nineteenth century. A patent for a device to measure the energy flow of sound waves was granted in 1932. Other related work includes that of Clapp and Firestone (1941), who describe an acoustic wattmeter, and Hodgson (1977), who determined sound power from measurements of fluctuating pressure and normal surface velocity at radiating surfaces on a machine. Advancements in digital signal processing led to the two-microphone system which is currently used to measure sound intensity. Development and applications of this technique are described by Fahy (1977a and 1977b), Gade (1982), Waser and Crocker (1984), and Nielsen (1986).

Figure 3.12.1 shows a block diagram of a vector sound intensity measuring system utilizing one-third octave digital filters. The system measures the component of vector sound intensity along the probe axis. Vector sound intensity probes are discussed briefly in the section on measuring microphones.

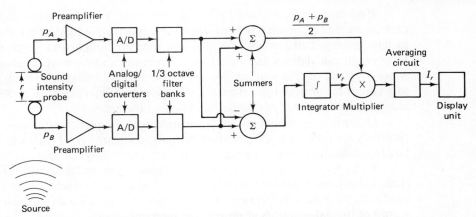

Figure 3.12.1 Block diagram of a vector sound intensity measuring system.

If the acoustic energy flow is not parallel to the probe axis, then the component of vector sound intensity is given by

$$|I_r| = |I| \cos \alpha \qquad (3.12.1)$$

where α is the angle between the energy flow direction and the probe axis. Figure 3.12.2 shows the directivity characteristics of an actual probe, using $\frac{1}{2}$-inch microphones with 12-mm spacing. Polar plots of sensitivity versus angle α are given for sound frequencies of 500 Hz and 8 kHz.

Noise Source Location

When studying the noise emission of a machine or other noise source, it is convenient to define one or more imaginary surfaces near the source. A grid is then defined on each surface and vector sound intensity measurements are taken at each grid element. Space–time averaging is performed by sweeping the probe back and forth over the grid element instead of selecting only one measurement point in the element. Measurements may be taken at each grid element in each of three mutually perpendicular directions to obtain the components to produce a vector flow diagram. In many cases, however, sufficient information is obtained by measuring only the vector sound intensity component normal to a particular surface. The sound intensity measuring system calculates and displays sound intensity level versus frequency for each grid element. This information may be transmitted to a computer for intensity mapping of the most prominent frequency components. An intensity map of the overall unweighted or A-weighted levels may also be of interest.

Figure 3.12.3 is a three-dimensional plot of vector sound intensity measured above the engine cover of a small van. In this case, the probe axis was held normal to the measuring surface for all measurements. Part (a) of the figure shows only positive sound intensity. A region of positive intensity identifies a sound source, a net outward flow of acoustic energy. Part (b) of the figure shows only negative sound intensity. The regions of negative sound intensity identify sound sinks, areas of net inward flow of

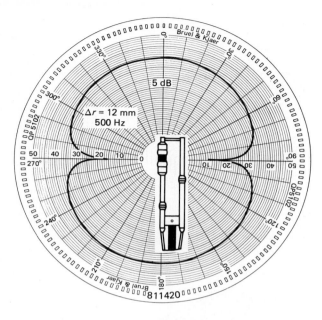

(a) Directivity at 500 Hz

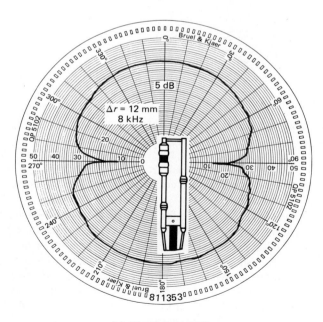

(b) Directivity at 8 kHz

Figure 3.12.2 Directivity of a vector sound intensity probe.
(*Source:* Bruel & Kjaer Instruments, Inc.)

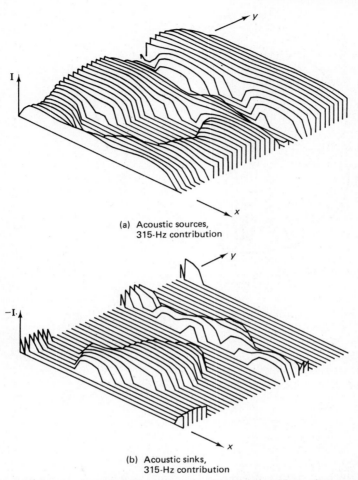

(a) Acoustic sources,
315-Hz contribution

(b) Acoustic sinks,
315-Hz contribution

Figure 3.12.3 The normal component of vector sound intensity measured over an engine cover. (*Source:* Bruel & Kjaer Instruments, Inc.)

acoustic energy. Both plots represent the contribution of the one-third octave band centered at 315 Hz.

Computer software is also available for producing sound intensity maps in the form of mesh line diagrams, contour plots, and vector flow diagrams. Figure 3.12.4 shows the partial results of an experiment involving a source of white noise (broadband noise with constant energy per hertz). The source was placed in a box with cutouts covered with various materials. Measurements were taken at an imaginary surface near the box. A mesh line diagram, a contour plot, and a vector flow diagram are shown for the contribution of the one-third octave band centered at 4 kHz.

The noise produced at various locations within a device may have different frequency components. The results of a noise test on a floppy disk drive are shown in Figure 3.12.5. Part (a) of the figure shows the imaginary surface and measuring grid

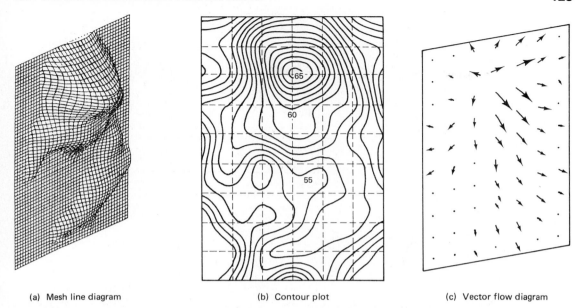

(a) Mesh line diagram   (b) Contour plot   (c) Vector flow diagram

Figure 3.12.4 Noise emitted from a box with cutouts covered with various materials. (*Source:* Rion Instrument Div., Mott Associates, Inc.)

established above the disk drive. Part (b) is a noise spectrum for measuring point 15. Prominent frequencies at this point include 600 and 1200 Hz. Parts (c), (d), (e), and (f) are mesh line diagrams of disk drive noise in various frequency bands.

Validity of Sound Intensity Measurements

Reactivity index L_K is a characteristic of a sound field. It is defined as the difference between vector sound intensity level (measured in a given direction) and sound pressure level. In a pure reactive field, for example, a standing wave, sound pressure is 90° out-of-phase with particle velocity. Thus, there is no net energy flux in a pure reactive field and the vector sound intensity is theoretically zero. One measure of system error is *residual intensity level*, $L_{I,R}$, the intensity level measured in a pure reactive field, or when an identical signal is fed to both channels of a measurement system. The *residual intensity index*, obtained by feeding the same signal into both microphones, is given by

$$L_{K,O} = L_{I,R} - L_{P,R} \qquad (3.12.2)$$

where $L_{K,O}$ = residual intensity index
$L_{P,R}$ = sound pressure level
$L_{I,R}$ = vector sound intensity level

A large negative value of $L_{K,O}$ is an indication of measurement validity.

Approximation Error For a plane free-field sinusoidal sound wave propagating along the axis joining the microphones, the phase difference is $k\,\Delta r$ for microphone spacing

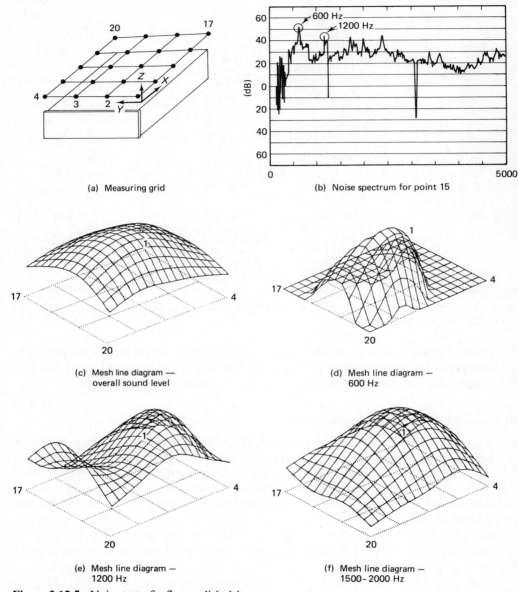

Figure 3.12.5 Noise test of a floppy disk drive.

Δr and wavenumber k. If the probe axis is not aligned with the propagation direction, then the ratio of measured intensity to true intensity is given by

$$\frac{I_{\text{measured}}}{I_{\text{true}}} = \frac{\sin(k \, \Delta r \cos \alpha)}{k \, \Delta r \cos \alpha} \tag{3.12.3}$$

where α = the angle between the probe axis and the propagation direction.

Phase Mismatch Since vector sound intensity measurements depend on measurement of phase differences at the two microphone positions, phase mismatch is critical to accuracy. For free-field conditions,

$$\frac{I_{measured}}{I_{true}} = \frac{\sin(k \ \Delta r \pm \phi)}{k \ \Delta r} \tag{3.12.4}$$

where ϕ = phase mismatch. If free-field conditions do not exist, then

$$\frac{I_{measured}}{I_{true}} = 1/[1 \pm 10^{(L_{K,O}-L_K)/10}] \tag{3.12.5}$$

If $L_K - L_{K,O} > 7$ dB, then phase mismatch error is less than ± 1 dB.

Random Error When measuring sound pressure, the random error is approximated by

$$\epsilon_{random} \approx (BT)^{-1/2} \tag{3.12.6}$$

where ϵ_{random} = 68% confidence interval normalized random error in mean-square sound pressure
B = bandwidth
T = averaging time

The equivalent relationship for random error in vector sound intensity measurements is

$$\epsilon_{random} \approx \left[1 - \frac{(1 - \gamma^2)/(2\gamma^2 \sin^2 \Phi)}{BT} \right]^{1/2} \tag{3.12.7}$$

where
$$\gamma^2 = G_{AB}^2/(G_{AA}G_{BB}) = \text{coherence function}$$
$$\Phi = \arctan(\text{Im } G_{AB}/\text{Re } G_{AB}) = \text{phase angle}$$
$$G_{AA}, G_{BB}, \text{ and } G_{AB} = \text{the auto- and cross spectra.}$$

Gade (1985) derives these relationships and plots BT versus L_K for various values of ϵ_{random}.

High- and Low-Frequency Limits Frequency response of an intensity measurement system is dependent on microphone spacing. For errors of less than ± 1 dB the wavelength of the sound measured should be greater than six times spacer distance. Thus, high-frequency limits are approximately 1.25 kHz for 50-mm spacing, 5 kHz for 12-mm spacing, and 10 kHz for 6-mm spacing. Low-frequency limits are determined by phase mismatch in the system. For errors of less than ± 1 dB, the phase change in a signal should be more than five times the phase mismatch which is typically ± 0.005 rad. Thus, large spacers are needed for low-frequency measurement, and it is necessary to change probes to measure over a wide frequency range. It is expected that future developments in instrumentation design will extend the effective range of sound intensity measurement systems.

3.13 SOUND POWER

Applications of Sound Pressure, Vector Sound Intensity, and Sound Power Measurement

In most cases, our ultimate goal is noise reduction. It might be asked why we consider more than one descriptor to identify and solve a noise problem. Let us consider a few applications where the most useful measurement would be sound pressure, or vector sound intensity, or sound power (or their associated levels).

Sound Pressure   Sound pressure is basic to determination of vector sound intensity and sound power. Sound pressure level (sometimes referred to simply as "sound level") describes the noise exposure of an individual observer. Noise dose or an energy average sound level, such as equivalent sound level at an observer location, permits us to assess the effect of industrial noise exposure or proximity to a highway or aircraft flightpath. Descriptors based on sound pressure are used to determine if an individual will be subject to speech interference, or annoyance, or if there is significant risk of damage to hearing.

Vector Sound Intensity   Vector sound intensity is a useful tool to aid in noise reduction. In earlier sections we considered idealizations such as point sources in free space. Although the point source model is reasonable in many cases, there are other situations where it results in significant errors. A machine may be complicated in that sound energy flows from one point to another point on the machine. Measurements of sound pressure alone (a scalar quantity) may fail to locate the actual machine component that produces the noise. Vector sound intensity measurements may locate the offending component to facilitate redesign of the machine. Vector sound intensity measurements also permit the determination of sound power in the field, where the presence of high levels of background noise or reflections could make other methods inaccurate. Vector sound intensity is not a valid measure for assessing a room in terms of speech interference, annoyance, or hearing damage potential. In a highly reverberant room, for example, the sound pressure and particle velocity would be out-of-phase, producing a low value of vector sound intensity. The sound level, however, could be unacceptably high in terms of hearing damage or nonauditory effects.

Sound Power   A noise source can be described by a sound pressure level measured at a specified distance. For example, some standards relating to truck noise specify a sound level measurement at a distance of 50 ft. In most cases, however, sound power in watts and sound power level in dB re 1 pW are better descriptors of a noise source. These quantities describe the sound energy output of a source, independent of its location. Sound power level may be determined for each frequency band (say, each one-third octave band in the audible range) or it may be expressed as an overall unweighted or A-weighted value. If specifications for the purchase of machinery limit the sound power of each item, it is possible to predict the noise levels that will occur in a room of known characteristics.

Sound Power Determination Using Vector
Sound Intensity Measurements

Recall that vector sound intensity is defined as the net rate of flow of acoustic energy. Therefore, the sound power of a noise source can be determined by integrating the normal component of the vector sound intensity over a surface enclosing the source. The surface may be arbitrarily defined; it need not relate to any dimension on the source. However, the surface should not enclose any sound-absorbing material. The above definition of sound power may be written in the form of an integral over a closed surface S:

$$W = \oint_S \mathbf{I} \cdot d\mathbf{S} = \oint_S I_n \, dS \qquad (3.13.1)$$

where W = sound power
 I_n = the component of the vector sound intensity normal to the surface S

and the outward direction is positive. Sound power calculations based on vector sound intensity using the above integral are theoretically unaffected by sound sources outside the enclosing surface. Background noise should produce no error in sound intensity determinations since sound energy from outside sources entering the enclosing surface is balanced by sound energy leaving. This result is an application of Gauss's theorem. In actual practice, measurement errors have a greater effect when background noise is higher. However, sound power may be calculated with reasonable accuracy from in situ vector sound intensity measurements, even when background noise levels are about equal to noise levels generated by the source in question. Background noise is of much greater consequence when sound power is calculated from sound pressure alone.

For convenience in establishing measuring points, a grid of strings or wires may be set up near the source. The source is often located on an acoustically hard (reflective) surface. The actual calculation of sound power involves a summation of the products of normal intensity measurements and the associated measuring areas:

$$W \, (\mathrm{W}) = \sum_{i=1}^{N} I_{ni} S_i \qquad (3.13.2)$$

Sound power level is given by

$$L_W (\mathrm{dB \ re \ 1 \ pW}) = 10 \, \lg\left(\frac{W}{10^{-12}}\right) \qquad (3.13.3)$$

Both acoustical level calibration and phase calibration are critical when the vector sound intensity method is used. In order to cover a wide range of frequencies, at least two microphone probes with different spacers are required. A large number of measuring points is likely to improve accuracy. Space–time averaging as described above also seems a practical means of improving accuracy.

Sound Power Measured in a Free Field

Test codes written before the availability of vector sound intensity measuring systems may call for free-field measurement of sound power. In a free field, there are no reflections. Sound waves from a point source expand spherically, causing sound intensity to be inversely proportional to the square of the distance from the source. As an alternative, a free field over an acoustically hard (reflecting plane) may be used. A flat open area outdoors over a hard surface approximates a free field over a reflecting plane. Unfortunately, high background noise, wind, and adverse weather often make outdoor tests impractical.

Anechoic Chambers   Anechoic chambers are designed to approximate a free-field environment. They are constructed with wedges or blocks of sound-absorbent material on the walls, floor, and ceiling. A wire mesh floor is installed above the absorbent floor. A semianechoic chamber is similarly constructed, but with an acoustically reflective floor. The lowest frequency at which the chamber simulates a free field is called the cutoff frequency. The cutoff frequency is dependent on the length of the absorbent wedges or blocks. If the chamber is to act as a free field for low-frequency sound, the wedges or blocks must be $\frac{1}{2}$ to 1 m long. For maximum precision, the anechoic chamber volume should be at least 200 times the volume of the source.

Measurement Procedure   When a semianechoic chamber is used, the source may be placed on the center of the floor. Measuring points are located on a hemispherical test surface of radius R which is established about the noise source. Radius R should be at least 1 m and at least twice the largest dimension of the source. The test surface is only conceptual; it does not actually exist. The coordinates of the measurement locations in the table that follows will ensure that each microphone position represents an approximately equal area (see Figure 3.13.1).

Point	z/R	θ (degrees)
1	0.15	0
2	0.15	120
3	0.15	240
4	0.45	60
5	0.45	180
6	0.45	300
7	0.75	0
8	0.75	120
9	0.75	240
10	1	—

The space-energy average sound pressure level over the test surface is given by

$$L_{av} = 10 \lg \left[\frac{1}{N} \sum_{i=1}^{N} 10^{L_{i}/10} \right] \tag{3.13.4}$$

for N measurement points, each representing an equal area of the test surface. In the suggested pattern, $N = 10$. The space-energy average sound level may be converted

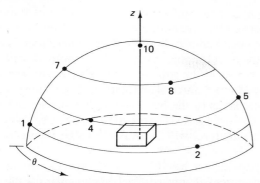

Figure 3.13.1 Suggested measurement points for sound power determination.

into the free-field space-energy average sound intensity level by adjusting for temperature and pressure as determined in Chapter 1:

$$L_I = L_{av} + 10 \lg\left(\frac{400}{\rho c}\right) \qquad (3.13.5)$$

where ρ = medium density (kg/m^3)
  c = speed of sound (m/s)

The space-energy average sound intensity I (W/m^2) is related to source power W (W) by

$$I = \frac{W}{S} \qquad (3.13.6)$$

where S is the area of the test surface in square meters. Sound power level of the source L_W (dB re 1 pW) is defined by

$$L_W = 10 \lg\left(\frac{W}{10^{-12}}\right) \qquad (3.13.7)$$

Thus, we have

$$L_W(\text{dB re 1 pW}) = L_I + 10 \lg S$$
$$= L_{av} + 10 \lg S + C_T \qquad (3.13.8)$$

where

$$C_T = 10 \lg\left(\frac{400}{\rho c}\right) \qquad (3.13.9)$$

is a correction (in decibels) for ambient temperature and pressure. If the test surface is hemispheric, then $S = 2\pi R^2$. For tests in full space, for example, a full anechoic chamber, then the test surface may be a sphere, with area given by $S = 4\pi R^2$.

If it is necessary to determine the sound power of a number of similar products, it may be practical to automate the measurement system. Consider sound power measurement in a semianechoic chamber. In one scheme, the source is rotated on a horizontal turntable, while the microphone, mounted on a boom, describes a circular arc in a vertical plane with center at the source center. As a result, the microphone describes a spiral path relative to the source. The rotation of the boom and the source can be adjusted so that equal areas of the hemispheric test surface are traversed in equal time intervals. If the area–time ratio is constant, then an integrating sound level meter or integrating real-time analyzer will indicate the space-energy average sound pressure level.

An alternative measuring surface has the form of a rectangular parallelepiped. Consider a test object (sound source) of approximately rectangular parallelepiped form placed on the floor of a semianechoic chamber. The measuring surface parallelepiped is formed of planes equidistant from and parallel to the plane surfaces on the test object. Another alternative, a conformal surface, is formed by rounding the corners of the rectangular parallelepiped measuring surface.

In Situ Measurements   Large rooms and some small rooms with sufficient absorption may reasonably approximate free-field conditions. The measurement surface must avoid the near field and the reverberant field. The reverberant contribution is not significant if total room absorption is six or more times the area of the measurement surface. Using the Sabine formula,

$$T_{60} = \frac{0.16V}{\sum\limits_{i=1}^{n} \alpha_i S_i} \tag{2.5.1}$$

we have the total room absorption

$$\sum_{i=1}^{n} \alpha_i S_i = \frac{0.16V}{T_{60}} \geq 6A_{\text{measurement}}$$

where $A_{\text{measurement}}$ = area of measurement surface.

EXAMPLE PROBLEM: FREE-FIELD MEASUREMENT OF SOUND POWER

A prototype impact printer is tested in a semianechoic chamber. A microphone is arranged to traverse a spiral path in a 1.5-m radius test surface (relative to the printer). The relative tangential traverse speed is set so that equal areas of the test surface are "covered" in equal time intervals. When an integrating real-time analyzer is used, the most dominant one-third octave-band contribution is 75 dB (unweighted) at 500 Hz and the equivalent sound level is 81 dBA. The temperature in the chamber is 20°C (68°F) and the absolute pressure is 1.013×10^5 Pa (14.69 psi). Find sound intensity level, sound intensity, sound power, and sound power level. Consider the 500-Hz contribution and the overall A-weighted values.

   Solution.   Using standard data for air, we find that the temperature and pressure correspond to a density

$$\rho = 1.21 \text{ kg/m}^3$$

Referring to Chapter 1, the speed of sound may be found as follows:

$$c = 20.04(T' + 273.16)^{1/2}$$
$$= 20.04(20 + 273.16)^{1/2} = 343 \text{ m/s}$$

Since the area–time ratio was held constant in the test, the integrating real-time analyzer will produce space-energy average sound level, resulting in space-energy average values of sound intensity and sound intensity level.

Converting sound (pressure) levels to sound intensity levels, we obtain

$$L_I = L_{av} + 10 \lg\left(\frac{400}{\rho c}\right)$$
$$= L_{av} + 10 \lg\left(\frac{400}{1.21 \times 343}\right)$$
$$= L_{av} - 0.16$$

The correction

$$C_T = -0.16 \text{ dB}$$

is negligible in acoustic measurements; it will be retained only for purposes of illustration.

Thus, the intensity levels are $L_I = 75 - 0.16 = 74.84$ dB (unweighted) for the 500-Hz contribution, and $81 - 0.16 = 80.84$ dBA overall.

Sound intensity level is also given by

$$L_I = 10 \lg\left(\frac{I}{10^{-12}}\right)$$

from which

$$I = 10^{(L_I - 120)/10}$$
$$= 10^{(74.84 - 120)/10}$$
$$= 3.0479 \times 10^{-5} \text{ W/m}^2 \qquad \text{for the 500-Hz contribution}$$
$$I = 10^{(80.84 - 120)/10}$$
$$= 1.2134 \times 10^{-4} \text{ W/m}^2 \text{ overall } A\text{-weighted sound}$$

For the hemispheric test surface,

$$S = 2\pi R^2 = 2\pi 1.5^2 = 14.137 \text{ m}^2$$

Sound power is given by

$$W = IS$$
$$= 3.0479 \times 10^{-5} \times 14.137$$
$$= 4.309 \times 10^{-4} \text{ W} \qquad \text{for the 500-Hz contribution, and}$$
$$W = 1.2134 \times 10^{-4} \times 14.137$$
$$= 1.715 \times 10^{-3} \text{ W overall } A\text{-weighted sound}$$

Sound power level may be calculated from sound power or sound intensity level, or sound (pressure) level. Using sound pressure level,

$$L_W = L_{av} + 10 \lg S + C_T$$

$$= L_{av} + 10 \lg 14.137 - 0.16$$

$$= L_{av} + 11.3$$

$$= 75 + 11.3 = 86.3 \text{ dB re 1 pW} \qquad \text{for the 500 Hz contribution and}$$

$$L_W = 81 + 11.3 = 92.3 \text{ dB}A \text{ re 1 pW overall sound power level}$$

Sound level meters and analyzers use weighting networks and equivalent digital systems to determine A-weighted sound levels. A-weighting adjusts the 500-Hz one-third octave band by -3.2 dB as indicated in Chapter 1. Thus, the sound (pressure) level in that band is

$$L = 75 - 3.2 = 71.8 \text{ dB}A$$

Similarly, the A-weighted sound power level in the 500-Hz one-third octave band is

$$L_W = 86.3 - 3.2 = 83.1 \text{ dB}A \text{ re 1 pW}$$

which corresponds to an A-weighted sound power of

$$W = 10^{(L_W - 120)/10}$$

$$= 10^{(83.1 - 120)/10}$$

$$= 2.04 \times 10^{-4} \text{ W}$$

Comparing this value with the overall A-weighted sound power, it is seen that the 500-Hz band contributes $2.04 \times 10^{-4}/(1.715 \times 10^{-3}) =$ approximately 12% of the overall A-weighted sound power of the printer.

Directivity

The directivity of a noise source may be examined under free-field conditions, without significant background noise and reflections. This condition is best approximated by an anechoic chamber, if the source is small enough. The measuring points suggested in Figure 3.13.1 and the accompanying table may be used with the noise source in the upright position. Then the noise source must be turned upside down and the procedure repeated.

EXAMPLE PROBLEM: DIRECTIVITY

A disk drive is tested in an anechoic chamber using the procedure suggested above. The space-energy average sound level is 56 dBA based on 20 measuring locations. The greatest contribution is 61 dBA measured near the disk slot at location 1 in the upright position ($\theta = 0°$ and $\phi = +9°$). Find maximum directivity index and directivity factor.

Solution. The maximum directivity index corresponds to position 1. Using equation 2.2.1,

$$DI_{max} = L(0, +9) - L_{PS}$$

$$= 61 - 56 = 5$$

In Chapter 2, directivity index is related to directivity factor Q by

$$DI(\theta, \phi) = 10 \lg Q(\theta, \phi) \tag{2.2.4}$$

from which

$$Q(\theta, \phi) = 10^{DI(\theta,\phi)/10}$$

$$Q_{max} = 10^{5/10} = 3.16$$

Sound Power Measured in a Diffuse Field

Reverberation chambers are specially designed rooms in which the sound field is diffuse except close to the source. They are constructed with acoustically hard (reflective) walls, floor, and ceiling. Moving vanes or diffusers are sometimes installed in reverberation chambers to ensure uniform sound energy distribution. Measurement precision at low frequencies depends on the volume of the chamber. If the 100-Hz one-third octave band is of interest, the recommended minimum chamber volume is 200 m^3. Standing waves are avoided if the chamber is constructed so that opposite walls are not parallel and the floor and ceiling are not parallel. Both anechoic chambers and reverberation chambers provide controlled acoustical testing conditions, but reverberation chambers are ordinarily less expensive than anechoic chambers.

When tests are performed in a reverberation chamber, the steady-state sound level depends on the source sound power and the absorption at the chamber boundaries. Sound power may be determined in a reverberation chamber as follows, where measurements are made for each octave band or each one-third octave band.

1. Determine T_{60}, the reverberation time of the chamber.
2. Measure L_{av}, the space-energy average sound level in the chamber. This may be done by sweeping a boom-mounted microphone within the chamber. An averaging time of at least 10 s is recommended for the 200-Hz frequency band and higher. A 30-s averaging time is recommended for lower frequencies. Measurements in the near field (close to the source) should be avoided as should measurements close to the chamber walls. The microphone traverse should not extend closer to the wall than one-half wavelength of the lowest frequency of interest.
3. Calculate L_W (dB re 1 pW), the contribution of each frequency band to the sound power level of the source using the following equation:

$$L_W = L_{av} - 10 \lg T_{60} + 10 \lg V + 10 \lg\left(1 + \frac{S\lambda}{8V}\right) + 10 \lg\left(\frac{B}{1000}\right) - 14 \text{ dB}$$

$$\tag{3.13.10}$$

where V = chamber volume in cubic meters
         S = total surface area of the room and diffusers
         λ = wavelength in meters at the center of the frequency band
         B = the barometric pressure (mbar).

The fourth term on the right of the above equation compensates for a concentration of energy near the walls of the chamber. The fifth term compensates for barometric pressure, where

$$1 \text{ bar} = 1000 \text{ mbars} = 10^5 \text{ Pa}$$

The standard atmosphere is defined as 1.013250×10^5 Pa.

The sound power contribution W (W) of each frequency band may be calculated from the band sound power level by the following equation:

$$W = 10^{(L_W - 120)/10} \qquad (3.13.11)$$

The total sound power W_{total} of the source is found by simply adding the sound power contributions of all the frequency bands. Then, overall sound power level is given by

$$L_{W(total)} = 10 \lg\left(\frac{W_{total}}{10^{-12}}\right) \qquad (3.13.12)$$

Alternatively, overall sound power level may be calculated from the sound power level contributions as follows:

$$L_{W(total)} = 10 \lg \sum_{i=1}^{N} 10^{L_i/10} \qquad (3.13.13)$$

where L_1 is the sound power level in the first band, and so on, for N bands.

A-weighted sound power (W) and A-weighted sound power level (dBA re 1 pW) may be computed as above if each measured sound pressure level L_{av} is A-weighted. This may be accomplished within the instrumentation or by applying the adjustments given in Chapter 1.

Sound Power Determined by the Comparison Method

The comparison method permits determination of sound power without the necessity of finding the reverberation time of the room. This method is used when neither an anechoic chamber nor a reverberation chamber is available, and for testing of machinery that could not be moved to a laboratory.

The comparison method utilizes a reference source of known characteristics. One commercially available reference source consists of a centrifugal fan designed to produce a steady noise spectrum. The power level L_{Wr} is determined by the manufacturer for each octave band and each one-third octave band, using an anechoic or semianechoic chamber. The procedure for determining sound power of a machine is as follows:

1. Measure L_{av}, the space-energy average sound level of the machine under test for each frequency band.

2. Try to duplicate the conditions in part (1), using a room with similar absorption and reflection characteristics. Operate the reference source in a location comparable to that of the machine under test. Measure reference source space-energy average sound level L_{avr} for each frequency band. Improved accuracy is obtained by a modification of the above procedure called the substitution method. In this case, the machine under test is removed from the test room and replaced by the reference source in the same location. If it is impossible to move the machine under test and a similar test room is not available, the reference source may be placed near the machine. First the sound levels are measured as the machine operates alone; then the levels as the reference source operates alone.

3. Calculate L_W, the contribution of each frequency band to the sound power level of the source using the following equation

$$L_W = L_{Wr} + L_{av} - L_{avr}$$ (3.13.14)

Calculation of total sound power of the source and unweighted and A-weighted overall sound power levels follow the procedure used for other sound power measurements.

Sound Power Determined by the Alternation Method

The alternation method utilizes a reference source with adjustable sound power output. One commercially available source generates wideband pink noise (the same level in each octave band) or octave-band filtered noise. The reference source power output is indicated on a meter. The following procedure is used.

1. The machine under test is operated in a diffuse field. The space-energy average sound level L_{av} is measured in each octave band.
2. The machine under test is replaced by the reference source. The reference source is adjusted until it produces the same sound level as the machine did in the first octave band. The sound power level L_W indicated on the reference source meter is recorded. The procedure is repeated for each octave band.
3. The sound power levels L_W recorded from the reference source meter are the sound power levels for the machine under test for each octave band. Total sound power and overall sound power levels are calculated as described for other procedures.

Sound Power Determined by the Addition Method

The addition method is used when the machine under test cannot be conveniently turned off. This might be the case, for example, if it is necessary to determine the sound power level of a generator in a central power station. The addition method is similar to the alternation method and also utilizes an adjustable reference source. The following procedure is used:

1. Same as for the alternation method.
2. The reference source is placed near the machine under test and both are operated simultaneously. The reference source is adjusted until the sound

level in the first octave band is 3 dB higher than it was when the machine under test operated alone. The reference source will then be producing power in that band equal to that produced by the machine under test. The sound power level indicated on the reference source meter is recorded. The procedure is repeated for each octave band.

3. Same as for the alternation method.

BIBLIOGRAPHY

American National Standards Institute, ANSI standard specification for octave, half-octave and third-octave band filter sets, S1.11-1966.

Bruel, P. V., "The accuracy of condenser microphone calibration methods," *Technical Review,* Parts I and II, Bruel & Kjaer, Naerum, Denmark, Part 4, 1964, and Part 1, 1965.

Bruel & Kjaer, *Measuring Microphones,* Selected reprints from *Technical Review,* Bruel & Kjaer, Naerum, Denmark, 1972.

Clapp, C., and F. A. Firestone, "The acoustic wattmeter—an instrument for measuring sound energy flow," *J. Acoust. Soc. Am.* **13,** 124–136, 1941.

Cooley, J. W., and J. W. Tukey, "An algorithm for the machine calculation of complex Fourier series," *Math. Comp.* **19**(90), 297–301, 1965.

Fahy, F. J., "Measurement of acoustic intensity using the cross-spectral density of two microphone signals," *J. Acoust. Soc. Am.* **62**(5), 1057–1059, 1977(a).

——, "A technique for measuring sound intensity with a sound level meter," *Noise Control Eng. J.* **9**(3), 155–163, 1977(b).

Gade, S., "Sound intensity (Part II: Instrumentation and applications)," *Technical Review,* No. 4, 3–32, Bruel & Kjaer, Marlborough, MA, 1982.

——, "Validity of intensity measurements in partially diffuse sound field," *Technical Review,* No. 4, 3–31, Bruel & Kjaer, Marlborough, MA, 1985.

Hassall, J. R., and K. Zaveri, *Acoustic Noise Measurements,* 4th ed., Bruel & Kjaer, Naerum, Denmark, 1979.

Herlufsen, H., "Dual channel FFT analysis (part I)," *Technical Review,* No. 1, 3–56, Bruel & Kjaer, Marlborough, MA, 1984(a).

——, "Dual channel FFT analysis (part II)," *Technical Review,* No. 2, 3–45, Bruel & Kjaer, Marlborough, MA, 1984(b).

Hodgson, T. H., "Investigation of the surface acoustical intensity method for determining the noise sound power of a large machine in situ," *J. Acoust. Soc. Am.* **61**(2), 487–493, 1977.

Nielsen, T. G., "Field measurements of sound insulation with a battery-operated intensity analyzer," *Technical Review,* No. 4, 3–10, Bruel & Kjaer, Marlborough, MA, 1986.

Oppenheimer, A.V., and R. W. Shafer, *Digital Signal Processing,* Prentice-Hall, Englewood Cliffs, NJ, 1975.

Peterson, A., *Handbook of Noise Measurement,* 9th ed., Gen Rad, Concord, MA, 1980.

Rabiner, L. R., and B. Gould, *Theory and Applications of Digital Signal Processing,* Prentice-Hall, Englewood Cliffs, NJ, 1975.

Randall, R. B., *Application of B & K Equipment to Frequency Analysis,* 2nd ed., Bruel & Kjaer, Naerum, Denmark, 1977.

Rion, *Technical Note, Sound Intensity Technique for Acoustic Measurement,* Rion Co. Ltd., Tokyo, 1984.

Waser, M. P., and M. J. Crocker, "Introduction to the two-microphone cross-spectral method of determining sound intensity," *Noise Control Eng. J.,* **22**(3), May-June, 1984, 76–85.

Wilson, C. E., "Measurement techniques for sound level meters," *Guide for Industrial Noise Control,* Chap. 6, Ann Arbor Science, Ann Arbor, MI, 1982.

Yeager, D. M., "A comparison of intensity and mean square pressure methods for determining sound power using a nine-point microphone array," *Noise Control Eng. J.,* **61**(2), 86–95, 1984.

PROBLEMS

Note: Problems marked with an asterisk (*) involve experimental measurements. All experimental work should be performed under qualified supervision. Unguarded fans, belts, rotating machinery, and other hazards should be avoided. Hearing protection should be worn when noise levels exceed 80 dBA.

If the required instrumentation is not available to make a certain measurement, it is suggested that a data sheet and equipment list be prepared, and that the experimental procedure be outlined. Calculations may be based on assumed values of data.

3.1.1. Noise is to be measured in one-third octave bands in the presence of a 40 km/h (25 mi/hr) wind.
  (a) Find the minimum total sound level in the 1-kHz band for which the wind-induced error will not exceed 1 dB when a windscreen is used. Assume 0° incidence.
  (b) Repeat, assuming a windscreen is not used.

3.1.2. Solve Problem 3.1.1 for the 100-Hz band.

3.1.3. Solve Problem 3.1.1 for the 100-Hz band if the error cannot exceed 0.5 dB.

3.1.4. An unweighted wind noise spectrum is measured in one-third octave bands with and without a windscreen. The wind noise reduction due to the windscreen is plotted. The test is repeated using *A*-weighting.
  (a) Will the one-third octave band plot of wind noise reduction be the same in both cases?
  (b) Will the reduction in overall *A*-weighted sound level be the same as the reduction in overall unweighted sound level?

*3.2.1. Find a location where the sound level varies by several dBA over a 10-minute period. Make 50 or 100 sound level measurements at 10-s intervals. Find the statistical 10%, 50%, and 90% exceeded levels. If a noise level analyzer is available, make simultaneous measurements and compare the results.

3.2.2. Fifty sound level readings are taken at 10-s intervals. They are distributed as follows:

Level (dBA ± 0.5)	Number of readings
87	2
86	6
85	12
84	20
83	3
82	3
81	2
80	2

(a) Determine percent exceeded noise levels L_{10}, L_{50}, and L_{90}.

(b) Determine the 95% confidence limits on L_{10}.

3.5.1. Calculate the correction for background noise if the difference between combined noise level and background noise level ranges from 3 to 12 in 0.5-dB steps.

3.5.2. Plot background noise correction versus difference between combined noise level and background noise level if the difference ranges up to 20 dB.

*3.5.3. Investigate the effect of background noise on measurements as follows:

(a) Measure background noise level in a quiet location, and in a very noisy location.

(b) Measure the noise level of a small machine or other source in the quiet location.

(c) Repeat the measurement at the same distance from the source in the presence of high background noise levels.

(d) Compare the results with theoretical values of background noise correction.

*3.5.4. When background noise levels approach the levels produced by the noise source under test, the test results tend to be invalid, even after correcting for background noise. The minimum allowable difference in levels depends on timewise variation in levels, the instrumentation used, and many other factors. Devise and perform an experiment to determine the relationship between the required minimum allowable difference in levels and the allowable measurement error.

3.6.1. Calculate the equivalent sound level from the data recorded in Figure 3.2.3.

3.6.2. Calculate the equivalent sound level from the data given in Problem 3.2.2.

3.6.3. A noise event is measured over an 8-s interval with an integrating sound level meter. Find the sound exposure level of the event if the reading is 101 dBA.

3.6.4. Repeat Problem 3.6.3 for a 4-s interval and a reading of 97 dBA.

*3.6.5. Make a series of sound level measurements at a location where sound varies substantially with time. Compute equivalent sound level. Compare the results with measurements made with an integrating sound level meter.

*3.7.1. Place a dosimeter in a location where the sound level measures about 100 dBA. Avoid exposure at this level. Check the reading after an hour or two. Compare it with the calculated value of percent allowable exposure.

3.8.1. Find the center frequencies of the 11 one-tenth octave bands beginning with 2 kHz.

3.8.2. Pink noise has a constant level when measured on octave bands or fractional octave bands. Find the overall unweighted sound level of pink noise if the level in each of the ten standard octave bands is 85 dB.

3.8.3. Find the overall A-weighted level in Problem 3.8.2.

3.8.4. White noise has a constant level when measured in frequency bands of constant width. Suppose a noise generator produces white noise over the entire audible frequency range. Find the overall unweighted sound level if a sound level of 92 dB is measured in the 16-kHz octave band.

3.8.5. Find the overall A-weighted level in Problem 3.8.4.

*3.8.6. Measure the frequency spectrum of an automotive engine at slow idle and at fast idle speeds. Compare with the frequency spectrum of an electric fan.

3.9.1. A potential housing site near an airport and a major highway is to be evaluated for noise exposure. It is proposed that measurements be made in one-third octave bands using a real-time analyzer. Will the proposed method produce the required data? Which noise descriptor would you recommend?

3.10.1. A fast Fourier transform analyzer or digital real-time analyzer is to be used to investigate a machine noise problem. Frequencies up to 10 kHz are of interest. What sampling rate would you recommend in order to avoid aliasing?

3.10.2. What sampling rate would you recommend if significant noise levels are likely to be present up to frequencies of 8 kHz?

3.10.3. Random noise is to be analyzed in 100-Hz bands using a fast Fourier transform analyzer. Find the minimum averaging time for 5% measurement uncertainty.

3.10.4. Repeat Problem 3.10.3 for 20-Hz bands.

3.10.5. Discuss the implications of Problem 3.10.4 in terms of selection of a series analyzer (e.g., a swept frequency analyzer) or a parallel analyzer (a real-time analyzer or fast Fourier transform analyzer).

3.10.6. Noise is to be analyzed using a real-time analyzer. Find the measurement uncertainty in the 25-Hz one-third octave band, using a 30-s averaging time. Assume random noise with Gaussian amplitude probability distribution and an ideal filter.

*3.10.7. Measure the 1-kHz octave-band sound level contribution of an electric motor. Measure the level in the 800-Hz, 1-kHz, and 1.25-kHz one-third octave bands. Combine these three levels and compare with the octave-band level.

3.12.1. Describe a procedure that could be used to determine the contribution of fan noise to the one-third octave-band sound levels produced by an automotive engine.

*3.12.2. Make vector sound intensity measurements to determine the contribution of two or more components of a machine to overall sound power. For example, a belt-driven compressor could be examined to determine the contributions of the motor and the compressor to sound power.

3.13.1. Vector sound intensity measurements are made over a test surface enclosing a prototype disk drive. The imaginary (i.e., arbitrarily defined) surface has a total area of 1.9 m^2. Keeping the probe normal to the surface, equal areas are scanned over equal time intervals to produce a space-energy average sound intensity level. The measured levels are 61 dBA overall and 53 dB in the 630-Hz band which is the dominant one-third octave-band contribution. Find the sound power and the sound power level of the drive in terms of:
(a) the overall A-weighted values
(b) the 630-Hz one-third octave-band contributions

3.13.2. Repeat Problem 3.13.1 for an improved prototype drive producing 57 dBA overall and 50 dB at 630 Hz.

3.13.3. A proposed design for a lawnmower is tested in an anechoic chamber with an acoustically reflective floor (a semianechoic chamber). Environmental conditions include an air density of 1.23 kg/m^3 and temperature of 22°C. A microphone traverse at a 2-m radius is designed to keep the traverse area–time ratio constant. An integrating real-time analyzer indicates a space-energy average sound level of 84 dB at 800 Hz, the most prominent one-third octave band, and 91 dBA overall. Find, for the 800-Hz band and for A-weighted overall noise:
(a) space-energy average sound intensity level
(b) space-energy average sound intensity
(c) sound power level
(d) sound power

3.13.4. Repeat Problem 3.13.3 if levels are reduced to 81 dB at 800 Hz and 88 dBA overall.

3.13.5. The space-energy average sound level is 83.5 dB*A* measured over a spherical test surface in an anechoic chamber. The highest reading at any point on the surface is 87 dB*A*. Find maximum directivity index and directivity factor.

3.13.6. Repeat Problem 3.13.5 if the highest reading is 86 dB*A*.

3.13.7. A machine is tested in a reverberation chamber having a volume of 125 m^3 and surface area of 160 m^2 including diffusers. The reverberation time is 1.1 s for a 1-kHz signal. The 1-kHz one-third octave-band sound level is 92 dB measured when the atmospheric pressure is 1013 mbar. Find the sound power level and sound power of the 1-kHz band.

3.13.8. Repeat Problem 3.13.7 if the sound level is reduced to 89 dB in the 1-kHz band.

*3.13.9. Determine the sound power of a machine or other noise source by two different methods and compare results. Possible methods include:
  (a) vector sound intensity measurements, possibly in the presence of significant background noise
  (b) measurement in free-field conditions out of doors
  (c) measurement in an anechoic or semianechoic chamber
  (d) measurement in a reverberation chamber, with known reverberation time
  (e) the comparison method
  (f) the alternation method
  (g) the addition method
  (h) other procedures governed by instrumentation availability and the characteristics of the machine under test

Chapter 4

Hearing Conservation

Helen Keller once said that ". . . blindness cuts people off from things; deafness cuts people off from people." A large segment of the population, however, risks hearing damage due to noise exposure. Although the most significant exposure to damaging noise occurs on the job, entertainment, recreation, and transportation are also part of the problem. And often the excessive noise exposure is unnecessary; in many cases, noise exposure could be substantially reduced at small cost or at no cost at all.

4.1 HEARING

The frequency range of human hearing is compared with that of some other animals in Figure 4.1.1. It can be seen that the human audible range is only a fraction of the hearing range of the bat, which uses hearing for navigation and food location. However, hearing does play a very important part in our lives.

Most individuals do not give as much consideration to the risk of hearing loss as they do to other risks. Possibly this is because hearing damage occurs gradually in most cases, seldom as a result of a single-event accident. Sometimes, noise-induced hearing loss is first observed during audiometric testing. More commonly, the individual first becomes aware of a problem when words are lost in face-to-face conversation and telephone conversation.

Partial deafness does not necessarily mean a uniform loss in loudness sensation at all frequencies. Instead, hearing loss may result in distortion of sounds and garbled understanding of words. This communication problem may, in turn, result in social isolation when friends and business associates find conversation difficult with the hearing-impaired person. Partial deafness also interferes with participation in meetings and other normal activities, and even with radio and television listening.

143

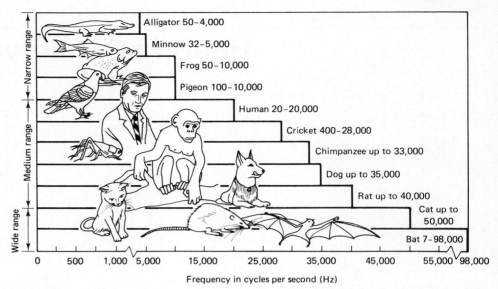

Figure 4.1.1 The frequency range of human hearing compared with that of some other animals. (*Source:* Scarfo Productions, Downingtown, PA)

The Hearing Mechanism

The ear acts as a pressure transducer, converting airborne sound signals to nerve impulses that are transmitted to the brain for decoding. In order to describe the hearing mechanism, we may divide the ear into three parts, the outer ear, the middle ear, and the inner ear, as shown in Figure 4.1.2. Airborne sound is collected by the outer ear (the pinna and the ear canal) and translated into mechanical motion by the ear drum (tympanic membrane), which separates the outer and middle ear. The mechanical vibration of the eardrum is transmitted to the oval window by a chain of small bones, the hammer (malleus), the anvil (incus), and the stirrup (stapes). These three bones form a linkage with a mechanical advantage of about three to one. The middle ear acts as an impedance-matching device between the outer ear and the liquid-filled inner ear.

These elements of the ear are shown in Figure 4.1.3 along with a sketch of the cochlea, shown as if it were straightened out. The cochlea is divided into two canals by the basilar membrane. Motion of the oval window generates a disturbance in the fluid of the cochlea. The fluid waves travel through the scala vestibuli to the scala tympani, finally deflecting the round window. Any disturbance in the cochlea fluid results in motion of the basilar membrane on which are located thousands of cells called "hair cells." These hair cells transform the fluid disturbance to nerve impulses which are transmitted to the brain.

Frequency Discrimination

Frequency sensitivity varies with location along the basilar membrane as shown in the figure. The maximum sensitivity to high-frequency sound (8 to 20 kHz) occurs

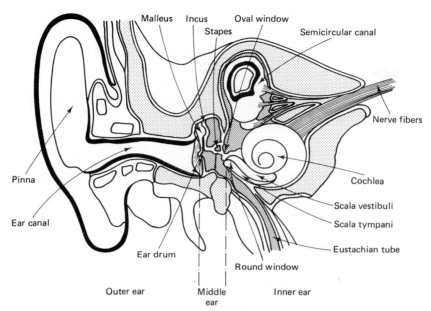

Figure 4.1.2 A cross section showing the main parts of the ear. (*Source:* Bruel & Kjaer Instruments, Inc.)

within about the first 7 mm from the oval window, measured along the basilar membrane. Maximum response to low-frequency sounds (20 to 300 Hz) occurs within about 10 mm from the other end of the basilar membrane.

Thus, the ratio of the highest audible pitch to the lowest audible pitch is 1000 to 1 for undamaged human hearing. However, human perception of frequency changes is not linear. Octave changes in frequency are a better approximation of frequency shifts that are perceived as equal. This subjective response effect was known and incorporated into musical instruments long before the development of sophisticated acoustic measurement instrumentation. Referring to Figure 4.1.4, we see that frequency spacing of the keys on a piano is based on octaves, with some compromise to obtain pleasant sounding ratios. However, the center frequencies selected for musical notes do not correspond to the preferred octave bands used in acoustic measurements. The frequency ranges shown in the figure for the piano and other musical instruments and the human voice are based mostly on fundamental frequencies. Actual frequency ranges are extended if harmonics are included. Musical intervals are discussed in detail by Rayleigh (1894) and Pierce (1981).

Amplitude Perception

A 1-kHz tone at about 0 dB is the threshold of hearing, the softest audible sound. The range from 0 dB to the moderate sound levels of conversation and office work at 60 dBA represents a sound intensity ratio of $10^6/10^0$ or 1 million to 1. The 60-dBA range from moderate sounds at 60 dBA to the threshold of pain at about 120 dBA also represents a sound intensity ratio of 1 million to 1. If we arbitrarily define the range

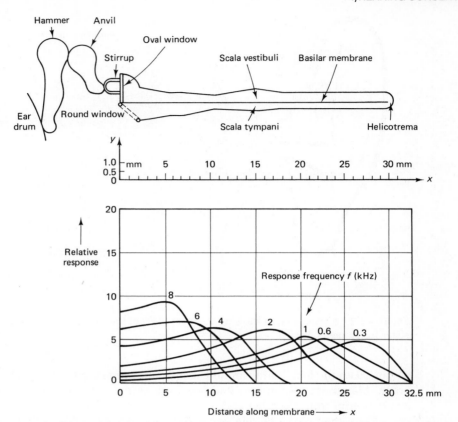

Figure 4.1.3 Longitudinal section of the cochlea showing the positions of response maxima. (*Source:* Bruel & Kjaer Instruments, Inc.)

of human hearing as the 120-dBA range from the threshold of hearing to the threshold of pain, then the range of human hearing spans a sound intensity ratio of 10^{12} to 1. By this definition, human hearing covers a 10^{12} to 1 ratio of mean-square sound pressure and a 1 million to 1 ratio of root-mean-square sound pressure. However long-term exposure to sound levels above 70 dBA results in a risk of hearing damage. Even short-term exposure to uncomfortable and painful sound levels is almost certain to cause hearing loss.

Human perception is nonlinear with regard to sound intensity changes as well as to frequency changes. Jury testing has indicated that a change in sound level of 9 or 10 dB is perceived as a doubling of loudness. A measure of subjective loudness, the sone, is defined on the basis of a 10-dB change constituting a doubling of loudness. One sone is defined as the loudness of a 40-dB, 1-kHz tone, or a tone sounding as loud as a 40-dB, 1-kHz tone. Thus, the loudness of a 50-dB, 1-kHz tone is 2 sones and the loudness of a 60-dB, 1-kHz tone is 4 sones. An extensive discussion of subjective responses to noise is given by Kryter (1970).

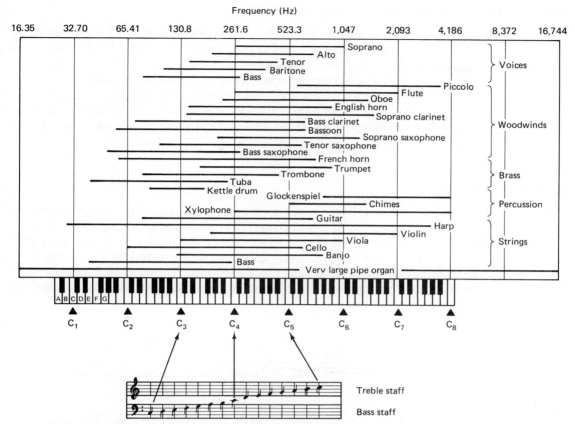

Figure 4.1.4 Musical frequency ranges. (*Source:* Scarfo Productions, Downingtown, PA)

4.2 AUDIOMETRY

Audiometry, the measurement of hearing sensitivity, is an important component of a hearing conservation program. Unfortunately, audiometry is not a timely indication of unsafe noise exposure. Noise surveys and dosimetry serve that purpose. By the time a hearing loss is detected, the damage can be both significant and permanent.

Audiograms

An audiogram is a record of hearing threshold at various frequencies. The "audiometric zero" or hearing level defined as the "no loss" level is based on a set of standardized normal threshold levels for each frequency (ANSI, 1969, ISO, 1975, or subsequent revisions). This convention is more appropriate for hearing evaluation than the 0-dB reference (2×10^{-5} Pa reference pressure) used in noise measurement. Thus, a hearing threshold level of 25 dB at 4 kHz indicates that an individual's hearing is poorer than the standard level by 25 dB at 4 kHz. A negative threshold indicates "better than standard" hearing.

Measurement of Subjective Hearing Threshold

Microprocessor audiometers, automatic audiometers, and manual audiometers are available for air-conduction testing of hearing threshold. Ordinarily, the subject sits in a sound-attenuating testing booth. A continuous or pulsed pure-tone signal is presented via earphones. Tests are made at a series of frequencies, for example, 500 Hz and 1, 2, 3, 4, 6, and 8 kHz. First, the tones are presented to the left ear only, then to the right ear only. The sound level of the tone is adjusted until the subject just hears it. The difference between this sound level and the audiometric zero is recorded as the hearing threshold.

Manual Audiometers

Manual models usually have a lower initial cost and are useful for subjects who cannot operate an automatic machine well enough to produce a valid audiogram. Ordinarily, the subject indicates by hand signals whether or not he hears the tone presented. Models are available with bone-conduction as well as air-conduction testing capability. Some operators believe the greater operator-to-subject contact with manual audiometers makes them preferable for diagnostic use. A sample manually recorded audiogram is shown in Figure 4.2.1.

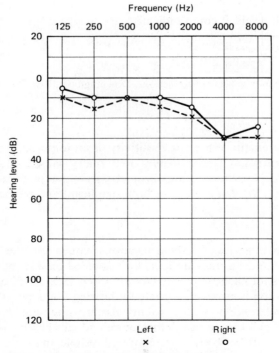

Figure 4.2.1 Manually recorded audiogram.

Automatic Recording Audiometers

Automatic recording audiometers are convenient for monitoring a hearing conservation program and screening a large number of personnel. After a subject is seated in the audiometric booth, the operator adjusts the subject's earphones and sets the audiometer for automatic operation. The subject is instructed as follows:

"First your left ear, then your right ear will be tested with a series of tones. You control loudness with a handswitch. Press it if you hear or think you hear the tone. Release the switch when you no longer hear the tone. Don't let the tone get too loud; press the switch as soon as you hear it. Don't let the tone remain silent; release the switch as soon as the tone is silent."

Control of the test then passes to the subject. In the automatic mode, a pure-tone signal is presented via the left earphone at an increasing sound level (5 dB/s or 10 dB/s). The level increases until the subject presses the handswitch button. The signal level then decreases until the subject releases the button. The sequence is repeated several times at the same frequency to improve test validity. A recording pen traces the hearing threshold levels on an audiogram form throughout the test, as shown on the sample automatically recorded audiogram, Figure 4.2.2. Some audiometers are designed to reduce the rate of change in signal level once the hearing threshold is neared (i.e., after the first subject response at a given frequency). The procedure is repeated until an audiogram is plotted for all of the test frequencies for both ears. The following frequencies form a typical test sequence: 1 kHz, 500 Hz, 1, 2, 3, 4, 6, and 8 kHz. The repetition of the 1-kHz test provides a check of validity. If there is a substantial difference in levels, it could indicate that the subject misunderstands the instructions, or that he is attempting to indicate a false hearing threshold. The test takes about 30 s for each test frequency, or 10 to 12 minutes per subject including time for instructions. The mean value of the zig-zag line at each frequency may be identified as the hearing threshold.

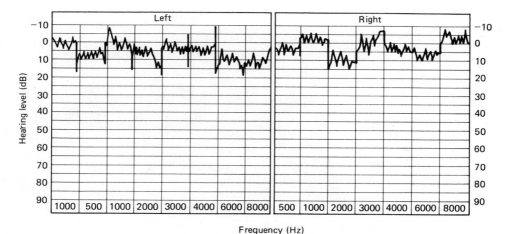

Figure 4.2.2 An automatically recorded audiogram.

Microprocessor Audiometers

Figure 4.2.3a shows a microprocessor audiometer. Systems of this type increase testing and interpretation speed, thereby reducing employee time away from the job. The following description outlines the features of one system.

The subject is fitted with earphones and sits in a booth as with other methods of testing. The operator may choose automatic, semiautomatic, or manual operating modes and pulsed or continuous test tones. In the automatic mode, the test begins with a 1-kHz pretest tone in the left ear. The tone level varies (in 5-dB increments) from -10 to $+90$ dB relative to the audiometric zero. Tones of 1-s duration are presented at random 1- to 3-s intervals to avoid an anticipated response pattern. The subject responds by pressing a handswitch when a tone is heard. The audiometer presents as many tones as necessary (up to 21 tones) at a given frequency until consistent results are obtained. The tone frequency is then changed until a hearing threshold level is determined for each test frequency between 500 Hz and 8 kHz in each ear. The current audiogram, in printed form [part (b) of the figure], includes employee identification, average hearing level at 2, 3, and 4 kHz, and a baseline audiogram if entered from a previous test. The printout also includes threshold shifts, with or without a presbycusis correction, and indicates any values based on manual testing. If the subject fails to release the handswitch or fails to respond at the 90-dB hearing level, then the operator receives an error signal. If the 1-kHz pretest and the 1-kHz main program response do not agree within 5 dB, then the test is interrupted so that the operator can reinstruct the subject. An interface is provided for communication with a cassette recorder or central computer for storage and retrieval of audiometric records.

Audiometric Testing Booths

Poor testing conditions can cause erroneous hearing thresholds to be recorded. Although testing can be done in any reasonably sound-proof room, specially designed audiometric booths are most convenient. The booth usually includes forced ventilation with intake

(a) Microprocessor audiometer

Figure 4.2.3 (*Source:* Tracor Instruments)

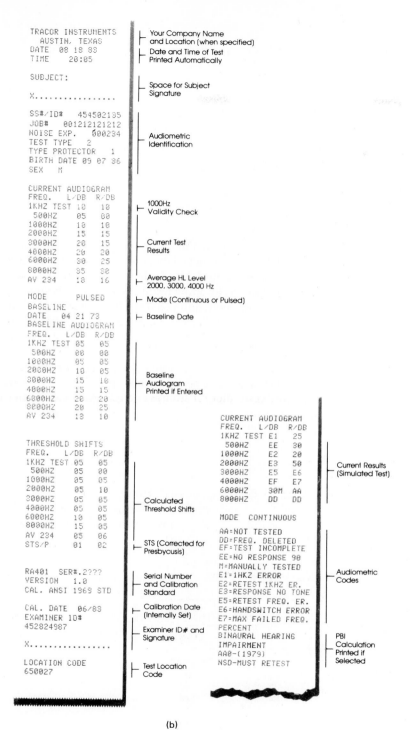

```
TRACOR INSTRUMENTS          ⊢ Your Company Name
    AUSTIN, TEXAS           ⌐ and Location (when specified)
DATE  08 18 83             ⊢ Date and Time of Test
TIME    20:05              ⌐ Printed Automatically

SUBJECT:
                           ⊢ Space for Subject
X................            Signature

SS#/ID#  454502135
JOB#  001212121212
NOISE EXP.   000234        ⊢ Audiometric
TEST TYPE    2               Identification
TYPE PROTECTOR   1
BIRTH DATE 09 07 36
SEX   M

CURRENT AUDIOGRAM
FREQ.   L/DB   R/DB
1KHZ TEST 10    10         ⊢ 1000Hz
  500HZ   05    00           Validity Check
1000HZ    10    10
2000HZ    15    15
3000HZ    20    15         ⊢ Current Test
4000HZ    20    20           Results
6000HZ    30    25
8000HZ    35    30
AV 234    18    16         ⊢ Average HL Level
                             2000, 3000, 4000 Hz
MODE    PULSED             ⊢ Mode (Continuous or Pulsed)
BASELINE
DATE   04 21 73            ⊢ Baseline Date
BASELINE AUDIOGRAM
FREQ.   L/DB   R/DB
1KHZ TEST 05    05
  500HZ   00    00
1000HZ    05    05
2000HZ    10    05
3000HZ    15    10         ⊢ Baseline
4000HZ    15    15           Audiogram
6000HZ    20    20           Printed if Entered
8000HZ    20    25
AV 234    13    10


THRESHOLD SHIFTS
FREQ.   L/DB   R/DB
1KHZ TEST 05    05
  500HZ   05    00
1000HZ    05    05
2000HZ    05    10
3000HZ    05    05         ⊢ Calculated
4000HZ    05    05           Threshold Shifts
6000HZ    10    05
8000HZ    15    05
AV 234    05    06
STS/P     01    02         ⊢ STS (Corrected for
                             Presbycusis)

RA401  SER#.2???
VERSION   1.0              ⊢ Serial Number
CAL. ANSI 1969 STD          and Calibration
                            Standard
CAL. DATE  06/83          ⊢ Calibration Date
EXAMINER ID#                (Internally Set)
452824987                 ⊢ Examiner ID# and
                            Signature
X................

LOCATION CODE             ⊢ Test Location
650027                      Code
```

```
CURRENT AUDIOGRAM
FREQ.   L/DB   R/DB
1KHZ TEST E1    25
  500HZ   EE    30
1000HZ    E2    20
2000HZ    E3    50         ⊢ Current Results
3000HZ    E5    E6           (Simulated Test)
4000HZ    EF    E7
6000HZ    30M   AA
8000HZ    DD    DD

MODE   CONTINUOUS

AA=NOT TESTED
DD=FREQ. DELETED
EF=TEST INCOMPLETE
EE=NO RESPONSE 90
M=MANUALLY TESTED
E1=1HKZ ERROR            ⊢ Audiometric
E2=RETEST 1KHZ ER.         Codes
E3=RESPONSE NO TONE
E5=RETEST FREQ. ER.
E6=HANDSWITCH ERROR
E7=MAX FAILED FREQ.
PERCENT
BINAURAL HEARING
IMPAIRMENT               ⊢ PBI
AA0-(1979)                 Calculation
NSD-MUST RETEST            Printed if
                           Selected
```

(b)

Figure 4.2.3 (*Continued*)

TABLE 4.2.1 SOUND LEVELS IN
AUDIOMETRIC BOOTHS

Test frequency (Hz)	Maximum level (dB)	Desirable level (dB)
500	40	30
1000	40	29.5
2000	47	34.5
3000	52	39
4000	57	42
6000	62	45

and exhaust silencers, and wiring for the earphones and handswitch. ANSI (1971) specifies maximum allowable interior octave-band sound levels for audiometric booths and desirable levels as given in Table 4.2.1. Audiometric booths should be located in quiet areas if possible, and subjects awaiting testing should be discouraged from talking near an ongoing test. The noise reduction provided by an audiometric booth may be evaluated by testing it in a sound field in a reverberation chamber. Typical values of noise reduction (provided by the manufacturers) for two prefabricated audiometric booths are given in Table 4.2.2.

The earphones normally used in audiometric testing provide some attenuation of extraneous noise. If testing cannot be performed in a quiet environment, a noise-excluding headset is available. The attenuation of earphones with and without the noise-excluding headset is shown in Table 4.2.3 as determined by Martin, William, and Lodge (1986).

Calibration

Audiometers are ordinarily factory calibrated. However, frequent recalibration is necessary to ensure the validity of audiograms, and written evidence of recent calibration may be required when claims of hearing loss are involved. Calibration to standard

TABLE 4.2.2 NOISE REDUCTION FOR TWO
MODELS OF AUDIOMETRIC
BOOTHS

Octave-band center frequency (Hz)	Noise reduction (dB)	
	Model 1	Model 2
125	18	Not reported
250	32	35
500	38	40
1000	44	44
2000	51	52
4000	52	53
8000	50	53

TABLE 4.2.3 NOISE ATTENUATION PROPERTIES OF EARPHONES WITH AND WITHOUT A NOISE EXCLUDING HEADSET

| Frequency (Hz) | Noise attenuation of earphones (dB) | |
	Without headset	With headset
500	9	21
1000	12	35
2000	24	42
4000	29	47
8000	24	33

specifications may be performed with a precision sound level meter and a coupler called an artificial ear. A physiological check may be performed daily by making an audiogram of an individual (the usual operator, for example) and comparing it with an audiogram of the same individual which was made immediately after the last calibration.

An instrument called an electroacoustic ear is available to perform the physiological calibration with greater accuracy. The earphones are positioned on the electroacoustic ear and it is connected to the audiometer. If a microprocessor audiometer or automatic recording audiometer is to be tested, the audiometer is set for automatic operation. This test is performed immediately after a full calibration and the resulting baseline audiogram is filed. The test should be repeated each day the audiometer is in use. If threshold readings obtained with the electroacoustic ear vary from the baseline audiogram by more than 5 or 10 dB, the audiometer should be recalibrated.

4.3 HEARING IMPAIRMENT

It is desirable, of course, to avoid any loss in hearing ability. However, threshold shifts of less than 5 dB are difficult to measure. The measurement problem is partly due to instrumentation limitations, but to a greater extent, it is due to day-to-day variations in an individual's ability to detect faint sounds. Thus, small threshold shifts are not considered the same as other injuries for which an individual might receive monetary compensation. This is not to say that a permanent threshold shift (PTS) of less than 5 dB is unimportant. Consider an industry where levels of noise are such that there is a statistical risk that 50% of employees will develop noise-induced permanent threshold shifts (NIPTS) of 4 dB after 5 years of exposure. Cumulative hearing loss over a period of 40 years could represent a significant hearing handicap. In this hypothetical example, it would be a moral, if not legal, responsibility of the management to use all feasible means to eliminate this risk.

Presbycusis

It can be shown statistically that, in adulthood, hearing ability diminishes with age. This effect, called presbycusis, may be part of the normal aging process, or it may be due to the sum of the effects of diseases and other insults to the hearing mechanism. The results of some cross-cultural studies suggest that presbycusis is largely due to accumulated noise exposure.

Ototoxins

Ototoxins cause hearing loss, usually by affecting the cochlea, or cause loss of balance by affecting the vestibular apparatus of the inner ear. Ototoxic drugs include the -mycin type. According to Remington (1980), neomycin destroys the hair cells of the cochlea in such a way that high-frequency hearing loss occurs first. Loss of lower and midrange frequencies occurs later. This sequence is similar to that caused by many industrial noise sources. In both cases, hearing loss may be first detected by audiometry. An individual may be unaware of hearing loss in the early stages because conversational tones are not affected until later. Tinnitus (head noises, ringing in the ears), a common effect of noise exposure, is also known to be a side effect of aspirin and salicylate-based drugs.

4.4 CRITERIA FOR DEFINING HEARING HANDICAP AND HEARING IMPAIRMENT

The American Academy of Otolaryngology (AAO) and the American Council of Otolaryngology (ACO) have given the following definitions for hearing impairment, hearing handicap, and hearing disability (*Sound and Vibration,* 1979).

> Permanent hearing impairment is a hearing loss outside of the normal range. It is not to be evaluated until maximum rehabilitation has been achieved and there is no progression of the impairment. Permanent handicap is defined as an impairment that effects a person's efficiency in daily life. A permanent handicap constitutes a permanent disability if its severity prevents a person from remaining employed at full wages.

Percentage Hearing Impairment

AAO and ACO outline the following procedure for determining percentage hearing impairment.

1. Determine the average hearing threshold in each ear at 500 Hz and 1, 2, and 3 kHz.
2. Calculate percent impairment in each ear separately. Multiply by 1.5 the amount the average hearing threshold exceeds 25 dB. A hearing threshold of 92 dB or greater is considered a 100% impairment. A hearing threshold of 25 dB corresponding to 0% impairment is called the "low fence"; a 92-dB threshold corresponding to 100% impairment is called the "high fence."

3. Multiply the percent impairment of the better ear by 5; add that figure to the percent impairment of the poorer ear. Divide the total by 6 to obtain the individual's percent hearing impairment.

Hearing impairment, as defined by AAO and ACO, implies a significant threshold shift. An individual could be classified as having 0% hearing impairment by the AAO/ACO formula even though that person's hearing loss affected his life, causing difficulty in understanding conversation and failure to experience the full range of music. The AAO/ACO hearing impairment formula differs from an earlier formula of the American Academy of Ophthalmology and Otolaryngology (AAOO, a predecessor to AAO). The earlier formula did not include a 3-kHz threshold measurement in the hearing impairment calculation.

EXAMPLE PROBLEM: HEARING IMPAIRMENT

(a) The following hearing thresholds at 500 Hz and 1, 2, and 3 kHz are recorded on an audiogram. Left ear: 25, 30, 30, and 35 dB, respectively. Right ear: 55, 60, 65, and 75 dB, respectively. Find percent hearing impairment based on the AAO/ACO formula.

Solution. Average hearing threshold levels are

$$(25 + 30 + 30 + 35)/4 = 30 \text{ dB}$$

in the left (better) ear, and

$$(55 + 60 + 65 + 75)/4 = 63.75 \text{ dB}$$

in the right (poorer) ear. Percentage impairment is given by

$$1.5 \,(\text{threshold} - 25) =$$

$$1.5(30 - 25) = 7.5\%$$

in the better ear, and

$$1.5(63.75 - 25) = 58.125\%$$

in the poorer ear. The individual's percent hearing impairment is given by

$$(5 \times \% \text{ in better ear} + \% \text{ in poorer ear})/6 = (5 \times 7.5 + 58.125)/6$$

$$= 16\% \text{ impairment}$$

(b) Consider an individual with a hearing threshold equal to the low fence (0% impairment) at all frequencies in both ears. Describe the impairment on a sound energy and sound pressure basis.

Solution. The low fence corresponds to a 25-dB hearing threshold. This may be compared with normal hearing which we will define as zero threshold (the audiometric zero). Free-field sound intensity (W/m²) is given by

$$I = I_{\text{ref}} \times 10^{L/10}$$

from which we find the ratio of two sound intensities where the sound level differs by ΔL:

$$\frac{I_2}{I_1} = 10^{\Delta L/10} = 10^{25/10} = 316$$

On a sound pressure basis, we have

$$\frac{p_{\text{rms2}}}{p_{\text{rms1}}} = 10^{\Delta L/20} = 10^{25/20} = 17.8$$

To produce the same sensation as would be produced in an individual with normal hearing, the sound intensity would have to be 316 times as great, corresponding to a sound pressure 17.8 times as great.

(c) Describe the impairment in part (b) on a subjective basis.

Solution. If subjective loudness is considered to double with each 10-dB increase in sound level, then the loudness ratio of two tones of the same frequency is given by

$$\text{loudness ratio} = 2^{\Delta L/10}$$

$$= 2^{25/10} = 5.657$$

Sounds in the 500-Hz to 3-kHz frequency range would seem only one-sixth or one-fifth as loud as they would to a person with normal hearing.

4.5 THE SPEECH IMPAIRMENT RISK CRITERION

Kryter (1973) found that methods commonly used for evaluation of hearing impairment and its relation to noise exposure may lead to significant underestimates of the severity of noise-induced hearing impairment and overestimates of tolerable noise exposure limits. At the time the paper was written, the AAOO criterion was in use. The AAOO criterion is based on 500-Hz and 1- and 2-kHz audiometric frequencies with a 25-dB low fence and 92-dB high fence. An individual with a 25-dB hearing level (HL) could understand about 90% of sentences and 50% of phonetically balanced monosyllables (PB words) at normal conversation level at 1-m distance. A number of monosyllabic words divided into phonetically balanced lists is given by ANSI (1960). Tests of this type evaluate the relationship between hearing threshold and the ability to understand individual words, an unexpected message, an unfamiliar name, or a telephone number without contextual clues and redundancy.

The speech impairment risk criterion (SIR) proposed by Kryter has a low fence of 15 dB and a 2%/dB slope based on average hearing levels at the AAOO audiometric frequencies of 500 Hz and 1 and 2 kHz. This is roughly equivalent to a 25-dB low fence based on audiometric frequencies of 1, 2, and 3 kHz. When the AAO/ACO audiometric frequencies of 500 Hz and 1, 2, and 3 kHz are used, the SIR low fence can be expected to fall somewhere between 15 and 25 dB, depending on the relative contribution of each test frequency to hearing loss. An approximate comparison of the AAO/ACA, AAOO, and SIR criteria are shown in Figure 4.5.1.

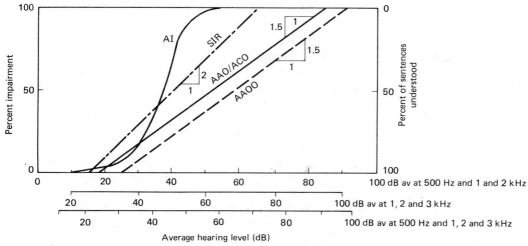

Figure 4.5.1 Comparison of hearing impairment criteria (Kryter, 1973). Key. AI: Percentage of sentences understood at normal conversational level (55 dB) in quiet (articulation index). SIR: Speech impairment risk criterion. AAO/ACO: American Academy of Otolaryngology/American Council of Otolaryngology formula. AAOO: American Academy of Opthalmology and Otolarangology formula.

4.6 THE 4-kHz THRESHOLD SHIFT CRITERION

The U.S. Environmental Protection Agency, in the "levels documents" (1974 and 1978) considers hearing damage from long-term noise exposure. The basic criterion is protection of virtually the whole population against noise-induced permanent threshold shifts (NIPTS) greater than 5 dB at 4 kHz with an adequate margin of safety.

The levels documents use the following basic premises in identifying environmental noise levels requisite to protect the hearing of the general population.

1. Noise-induced permanent threshold shifts (NIPTS) at 4 kHz are the most important signs of irreversible hearing loss, indicating physiological destruction within the hearing mechanism. This frequency is usually the first frequency affected when the ear is damaged by exposure to noise. Furthermore, the protection of hearing acuity at this frequency is critical for the understanding of speech and appreciation of music and other sounds.
2. NIPTS of less than 5 dB are generally not considered noticeable or significant.
3. It is assumed that hearing acuity is not damaged by sounds that cannot be heard. Sensitivity to noise exposure varies among individuals. However, as the most sensitive individuals incur NIPTS, their sensitivity approaches the population mean.
4. If the population is ranked by hearing acuity, from the poorest to the best, the identified levels should protect up to and including the ninety-sixth percentile, or virtually the entire population, against significant hearing loss.

4.7 HEARING DAMAGE RISK RELATED TO NOISE EXPOSURE

Considering the large amount of data available, it would seem a simple matter to relate hearing loss to noise exposure. This is not the case, however. Considerations that complicate the matter include the following:

1. Hearing sensitivity differs throughout the population.
2. Hearing thresholds of adults tend to increase with age. It is difficult to attribute the various contributions to hearing loss between the normal aging process, disease, and exposure to noise.
3. Since noise-induced permanent threshold shifts (NIPTS) ordinarily reach measurable values after years of exposure, most of the available data comes from retrospective studies. As a result, there is often uncertainty about the actual noise levels, exposure-time patterns, frequency content, baseline (pre-employment) audiograms of the subjects, noise exposure that is not job related, and selection of control groups.
4. There is no general agreement on the degree of hearing loss that can be considered significant.

Hearing Handicap Risk

Hearing handicap implies average permanent threshold shifts exceeding 25 dB. Figure 4.7.1 based on data tabulated by Glorig (1971; Glorig et al. 1961) shows the percentage

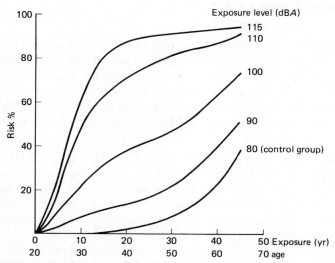

Figure 4.7.1 Percent risk of developing a hearing handicap (PTS exceeding 25 dB) based on the AAOO criterion using 500-Hz and 1- and 2-kHz test frequencies (Glorig, 1971). Note that individuals will experience some noise-induced hearing loss at 80 dB*A*, but it was assumed that only age contributed to AAOO defined handicap at that noise level.

risk of developing a hearing handicap as defined by the AAOO criterion versus exposure level (dB*A*) and time. The AAOO criterion uses the arithmetic average of an individual's hearing thresholds for the 500-Hz and 1- and 2-kHz audiometric frequencies. The percent of individuals developing a hearing handicap due to noise is obtained by subtracting the percent of the control group that developed a handicap.

Risk percentages would be higher if the more recent AAO/ACO criteria (including a 3-kHz measurement) had been used. In addition, as with all such studies, the control group noise exposure is difficult to ascertain. As a result, some of the hearing loss attributed to presbycusis may actually be due to noise exposure. These comments notwithstanding, this and similar studies have been useful predictors of hearing loss for compensation purposes. However, the data must not be misinterpreted. For example, at noise levels of 80 dB*A,* the figure implies no increase in risk of developing a hearing handicap as defined by the AAOO criterion. It is well established, however, that some hearing loss will occur after long-term exposure to noise at 80 dB*A* and even lower levels.

Four-Kilohertz Threshold Shifts

The relationship between noise exposure and hearing threshold shifts at various frequencies was estimated by Tonndorf et al. (1979) based on data from Passchier–Vermeer (1968). They made straight-line approximations of median (inferred) industrial-noise-induced permanent threshold shift (INIPTS) data for ten or more years of broadband noise exposure, 8 hours per day, 5 days per week. INIPTS are obtained by measuring hearing thresholds and correcting for typical hearing loss that would occur from all causes other than industrial noise (presbycusis, disease, ototoxins, and nonindustrial noise exposure). Only median threshold shifts are considered. Some of the population experiences threshold shifts from exposure to industrial noise at lower sound levels. The 4-kHz threshold shift is greater than the shift at other audiometric frequencies for exposure at almost all sound levels. It can be approximated by

$$\text{INIPTS}_{4\text{kHz}} = 2.2(L - 81)$$

where $\text{INIPTS}_{4\text{kHz}}$ = industrial-noise-induced permanent threshold shift (dB) at the 4-kHz audiometric frequency, and

L = broadband noise exposure level (dB*A*)

The importance of hearing at or near 4 kHz is indicated by Figure 4.7.2 which is based on studies of sensation level and frequency content of various sounds in spoken English (Fletcher, 1955). The average speaker pronounces most vowel sounds strongly, and they fall in the 300-Hz to 1-kHz frequency range. O's and a's are usually the strongest. Some sounds have more than one frequency component. These include l, m, and n, which include both high and low sounds. Of the low consonant sounds, v is typically the weakest. Some of the sounds that fall only in the high consonant category include ch, g, h, k, p, s, sh, t, and th as in thin. The last of these is the weakest sound in ordinary speech.

A significant threshold shift at 4 kHz makes it difficult to hear the high consonant sounds. Word identification depends largely on these sounds. Thus, sentence intelligibility can be greatly affected.

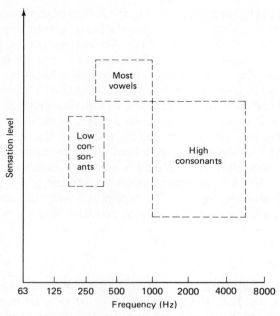

Figure 4.7.2 Sensation level of speech sounds versus frequency.

Temporary and Compound Threshold Shifts

Exposure to moderately high noise levels for a short period of time tends to cause temporary threshold shifts (TTS). In many cases there is recovery to the extent that no measurable permanent shift (NIPTS) remains. Higher noise levels and longer exposure tend to cause compound threshold shifts (CTS), in which there is some recovery and some permanent damage. According to a study by Miller (1974), the following noise level–exposure time combinations will produce 10-dB temporary threshold shifts at the 4-kHz audiometric frequency.

Level (dB)	Exposure time
70	12 hr
75	7 hr
80	2 hr
85	20 min
90	7 min
95	5 min
100	3 min
110	1.5 min
120	50 s

The 10-dB TTS is measured 2 minutes after the noise exposure. It is the average value predicted for a young adult exposed to a band of noise or pure tone centered near 4 kHz.

The precision of audiometric measurements is not adequate to determine whether or not temporary threshold shifts of a few decibels imply some small cumulative permanent damage. However, Miller (1974) assembled data from which hypothetical threshold shift recovery could be predicted. Based on these predictions, 7 days' exposure at 120 dB produces a 102-dB compound threshold shift (at 4 kHz) which, after weeks of recovery, becomes a 50-dB permanent threshold shift. Seven days' exposure at 100 dB produces a 68-dB compound threshold shift (at 4 kHz) which, after days of recovery, becomes an 11-dB permanent threshold shift. The paper identifies noise events causing temporary threshold shifts greater than about 40 dB as a region of possible acoustic trauma. For some people, even a single noise exposure causing a 40-dB TTS may result in a permanent threshold shift.

Threshold Shift due to Impulse Noise

Impulse noises are loud sounds lasting for a short time, usually less than 1 s. The nature of the hearing mechanism is such that sharp impulse noise is more likely to cause acoustic trauma than long-term exposure to steady noise, where both exposures are equivalent on an energy basis. Gunfire and some industrial operations including metal stamping and forging produce impulse noises that result in hearing threshold shifts.

Evidence of impulse noise damage is given in a study by Taylor and Williams (1966), where audiograms of a group of hunters (age 40 to 49) are compared with a control group. Only left ear thresholds are shown, since the left ear of a right-handed hunter is more severely exposed. Significant damage at the higher audiometric frequencies is shown by the following table comparing hearing thresholds averaged for 32 hunters with the average for nine controls:

Audiometric frequency (kHz)	Hearing threshold (dB)	
	Hunters	Controls
2	14	5
3	47	11
4	49	11
6	57	28
8	37	23

Other studies have indicated the need to correct for impulse noise. Passchier-Vermeer (1968) compared audiograms of workers in welding and metal shops who were exposed to significant impulse noise, with audiograms of workers in an industry where steady-state broadband noise was typical. It was found that threshold shifts of workers in welding and metal shops were equivalent to threshold shifts of those exposed to steady broadband noise at levels 10 or 20 dBA higher.

A Possible Hearing Damage Mechanism

An explanation of the mechanism by which impulse noise damages hearing is given by Bruel (1977). Audiometric measurements usually show the first evidence of hearing loss at 4 to 6 kHz. This is true of those exposed to single-event noise such as gunfire and small explosions and those exposed to industrial noise which typically has higher intensities at 250 to 500 Hz. Industrial noises often contain sound impulses in the 2- to 5-kHz frequency range, with peaks 15 to 25 dB above the mean sound level. Maximum duration for a single impulse may be 30 to 200 μs; thus these impulses make little contribution to sound level meter measurements in the slow, fast, or even impulse mode.

The middle ear mechanical transmission system consists of the eardrum, the malleus, incus, and stapes linkage, and the oval window. Stiffness of the membranes impedes low-frequency signal transmission, and inertia impedes high-frequency signal transmission through this system. The best signal transmission is in the 500-Hz to 8-kHz frequency range. The stretching muscle of the eardrum and the stapidius muscle can, by contracting, increase stiffness of the linkage. These muscles begin contracting at sound levels of about 75 dB, and are fully activated at 90 to 95 dB. However, their protection against hearing damage due to impact noise is limited for two reasons. First, since only stiffness is increased, not inertia, only low-frequency sensitivity is decreased, up to 1.5 or 1.8 kHz. The second reason is that the reaction time is too slow to protect against sharp impact sounds, even at low frequencies, and hair cell damage may occur before the brain can signal the muscles to contract.

Another factor influencing the impact noise problem is a quarter-wavelength resonance amplification at about 4 kHz in the ear canal. At 20°C, the speed of sound is about 344 m/s and the wavelength at 4 kHz is

$$\lambda = \frac{c}{f} = \frac{344}{4000} = 0.086 \text{ m}$$

One-quarter wavelength is 21.5 mm, the approximate length of the ear canal. Considering the outer and inner ear together, there is a resonance amplification of 3 to 10 dB at frequencies around 3 to 4 kHz.

Perception of Impulse Noise

In order to detect sounds over the entire audible range, including high-frequency sounds, the inner ear must have an averaging time as short as 50 to 100 μs. The brain, however, has a mean averaging time of about 35 ms. Thus, short impulse noises may not sound loud, even though they are capable of causing damage to hearing. Like the sound level meter in the slow, fast, or impulse mode, the ear fails to warn us of potentially damaging impulse noise.

Crest Factor

The crest factor of a signal is defined by

$$F_C = \frac{p_{\text{peak}}}{p_{\text{rms}}} \tag{4.7.1}$$

For a pure tone (sinusoid),

$$p_{rms} = \frac{p_{peak}}{\sqrt{2}}$$

from which

$$F_C = \sqrt{2}$$

The crest factor in decibels is given by

$$F_{C(dB)} = 10 \lg\left(\frac{p_{peak}^2}{p_{rms}^2}\right) \qquad (4.7.2)$$

Thus, for a sinusoid, we have

$$F_{C(dB)} = 10 \lg 2 = 3 \text{ dB (approximately)}$$

In many industrial situations, loud continuous noise is interspersed with impulse noise. This is a random process, not deterministic as with the sinusoid. However, we may evaluate the impulse noise content by establishing a procedure for approximating the crest factor. For example, a sound level meter with a peak-hold circuit may be used. Peak-hold measurements using a circuit with a 30-μs averaging time may be compared with measurements with a longer averaging time. The impulse mode of a sound level meter has an averaging time of about 35 ms, whereas the fast and slow modes have averaging times of about 125 ms and 1 s, respectively.

A crest factor approximation for a number of noise situations is given by Bruel (1977). In each case, five measurements were taken in impulse-hold mode and five in peak-hold mode. The crest factor approximation is taken as the mean peak-hold minus the mean impulse-hold value. Some of the results are listed below:

Sound source	Crest factor approximation $F_{C'}$ (dB)
1000-Hz pure tone	3
Recorded music	Up to 5
Highway traffic at 15 to 50 m	8
70 km/h train at 10 to 18 m	7 to 8
Training aircraft interior	9
Automobile interior	10 to 14
Lawn mower at 1 m	17
Pneumatic nailing machine (measured near operator's head)	28
Large machine shop	16
400-kN punch press (measured near operator's head)	24
Numerically controlled high-speed drill	9
Vacuum cleaner at 1.2 m	12
Bottling machine	21
Shotgun, 5 m to one side	32

The relatively low crest factor reported for recorded music is probably due to limitations of the sound reproduction system, the (fortunate) inability to transmit sharp peak signals.

Impulse Noise Risk Criterion

The following procedure may be used to evaluate a particular situation:

1. Measure equivalent A-weighted noise level L_{eq}. Determine $F_{C'}$, the difference between the mean of several peak-hold measurements and the mean of several impulse-hold measurements. Use A-weighting for all measurements. If measurements are impractical, $F_{C'}$ may be estimated from the above table.
2. Repeat for a reference environment, an environment of known hearing damage risk.
3. Base risk on an energy criterion, that is, accumulated dose is a function of the sum of the energy contributions during each time interval.

Using the above procedure, one can predict that the risk of hearing damage in a given situation will be equal to the risk in the reference situation if the following equation is satisfied (Bruel, 1977):

$$10 \lg \sum_{i=1}^{N} \left[T_i \times \text{antilog}_{10}\left(\frac{L_{eq1} + F_{C'1}}{10}\right)\right] = (L_{eq} + F_{C'} + 10 \lg T)_{\text{reference}} \qquad (4.7.3)$$

N is the number of different exposure categories and T is the exposure time in each. Many factors influence hearing damage risk, and the above equation makes only an educated guess based on limited data. The results should be used with caution and checked by other methods.

EXAMPLE PROBLEM: IMPULSE NOISE

Suppose it is decided that working in a large machine shop for 40 years at an equivalent sound level of 80 dBA during working hours is an acceptable risk. A job category is proposed in which a worker will operate a large punch press 60% of the time and tend a numerically controlled high-speed drill 40% of the time. The equivalent sound level at the operator location will be $L_{eq} = 95$ dBA at the punch press and 100 dBA at the drill. Assume that measurements have been made to obtain crest factor approximations, and the results agree with the above table.

(a) How long will it take for the worker in the proposed job category to exceed an acceptable risk of hearing damage? Use 48 work weeks per year of 40 hours each in both cases.

Solution. We will make a prediction based on the above equation, where the crest factor approximations are

$$F_{C'} = 16 \text{ dBA for the machine shop}$$

$$24 \text{ dBA for the punch press}$$

$$9 \text{ dBA for the numerically controlled drill}$$

Measuring T in years, we have:

$$10 \lg\left[0.60T \times \text{antilog}_{10}\left(\frac{95 + 24}{10}\right) + 0.40T \right.$$

$$\left. \times \text{antilog}_{10}\left(\frac{100 + 9}{10}\right)\right] = 80 + 16 + 10 \lg 40$$

from which

$$10 \lg(5.0837 \times 10^{11}T) = 112.02$$

and

$$T = \text{antilog}_{10}[11.202 - \lg(5.0837 \times 10^{11})]$$

$$= 0.3132 \text{ years or about 16 weeks}$$

(b) The noise exposure cited in part (a) is obviously unacceptable. Determine the noise reduction required if the exposure time is to be 40 years.

Solution. Noise reduction may be accomplished through the use of hearing protectors, or noise reduction at the source, or enclosures, or a combination of methods. Assume that the noise reduction effect applies equally to noise from the punch press and the drill. Identifying the noise reduction as L_{NR} dBA, and applying the above equation, we have

$$10 \lg\left[0.60 \times 40 \times \text{antilog}_{10}\left(\frac{95 - L_{NR} + 24}{10}\right) + 0.40 \times 40 \right.$$

$$\left. \times \text{antilog}_{10}\left(\frac{100 - L_{NR} + 9}{10}\right)\right] = 80 + 16 + 10 \lg 40$$

from which

$$10 \lg(2.0335 \times 10^{13}) - L_{NR} = 112.02$$

and the required noise reduction is

$$L_{NR} = 21 \text{ dB}A$$

4.8 THE OCCUPATIONAL SAFETY AND HEALTH ACT: NOISE EXPOSURE LIMITS BASED ON HEARING CONSERVATION

The Occupational Safety and Health Administration, the Occupational Safety and Health Act of 1970, and standards developed in response to the act (OSHA, 1978) are all usually referred to as OSHA. Specific references herein to OSHA are intended as examples only. Practical decisions must be based on the latest amendments to the law and the most recent administrative and judicial decisions.

Paragraph 1910.95 of the standard (OSHA, 1978) refers to occupational noise exposure. It states that protection against the effects of noise exposure shall be provided when the *A*-weighted sound level measured with slow response exceeds the values in the following table.

Duration (hr/day)	Sound level (dBA slow)
8	90
6	92
4	95
3	97
2	100
1.5	102
1	105
0.5	110
0.25 or less	115

In addition, exposure to impulsive or impact noise should not exceed 140-dB peak sound pressure level.

In many cases, noise levels vary with time. Dosimeters may be used to determine if individual exposures are within allowable limits. If dosimeters are not available, or if only predicted noise levels are available, allowable exposure is calculated by the equation that follows:

$$\frac{C_1}{T_1} + \frac{C_2}{T_1} + \cdots + \frac{C_n}{T_n} \leq 1 \tag{4.8.1}$$

where C_1 is the actual exposure time at a given noise level for which the allowable time is T_1, and so on. *Noise dose* in percent is defined by

$$D_\% = 100\left(\frac{C_1}{T_1} + \frac{C_2}{T_2} + \cdots + \frac{C_n}{T_n}\right) \tag{4.8.2}$$

When noise levels are determined by octave-band analysis, an alternative procedure for finding *A*-weighted sound levels is given by the standard (OSHA, 1978).

1. Plot octave-band sound levels over the Figure 4.8.1 contours.
2. Define the *A*-weighted sound level at the point of highest penetration into the contours.

In general, this alternative procedure will produce values different from the *A*-weighted sound levels determined by exact calculation using *A*-weighting tables or measured using an *A*-weighting network. Direct measurement of *A*-weighted values is preferable.

When employees are subject to noise levels that exceed the standards, feasible administrative or engineering controls should be utilized. If such controls fail to reduce sound levels to acceptable values, personal protective equipment should be provided and used to reduce noise to within the specified limits. If variations in noise level involve maxima at intervals of 1 s or less, the noise is considered continuous. The last provision of the noise standards, paragraph 1910.95-b3 (OSHA, 1978), requires that in all cases where the sound levels exceed the specified limits, a continuing, effective hearing conservation program shall be administered.

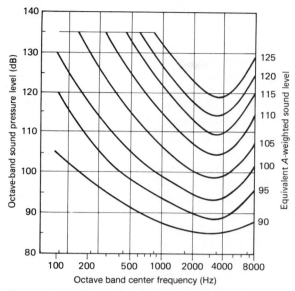

Figure 4.8.1 Sound level contours for an alternative method of determining *A*-weighted sound level. (*Source:* OSHA, 1978) Octave-band sound pressure levels may be converted to the equivalent *A*-weighted sound level by plotting them on this graph and noting the *A*-weighted sound level corresponding to the point of highest penetration into the sound level contours. This equivalent *A*-weighted sound level, which may differ from the actual *A*-weighted sound level of the noise, is used to determine exposure limits.

The Hearing Conservation Amendment (HCA)

The required *hearing conservation program* mentioned in paragraph 1910.95-b3 (OSHA, 1978) is not clearly defined therein. Revisions in the act were promulgated by the Occupational Safety and Health Administration in 1981. Although the revisions were to be effective in April 1983, enforcement was delayed several months by an administrative stay. These revisions, the *Hearing Conservation Amendment (HCA)* may be considered a model regulation or a model program. Some major HCA provisions and definitions are given below. The Occupational Safety and Health Administration should be contacted to determine currently applicable standards and interpretations.

It is estimated that 2.9 million workers in American production industries have an equivalent 8-hour noise exposure greater than 90 dB*A* and an additional 2.3 million have an equivalent noise exposure greater than 85 dB*A* (Berger, 1984b; OSHA-HCA, 1981). HCA targets most of this group of 5.2 million workers. The following definitions apply.

1. *Permissible exposure level (PEL)*. 100% noise dose resulting from exposure to a noise level of 90 dB*A* during an entire 8-hour day, or an equivalent noise exposure.
2. *Time-weighted average sound level (TWA)*. Consider a situation where measured or predicted noise levels vary in time over the workday. The TWA is the continuous sound level which, over an 8-hour period, would produce the same noise dose as the varying sound level. Equation 4.8.2 applies. If the actual sound level is constant for an 8-hour workday, then the actual level is the same as the TWA.
3. *Exchange rate*. The increase in noise level which results in a halving of allowable exposure. OSHA uses a 5-dB*A* exchange rate.
4. *Threshold level*. The level below which no contribution is made to the daily noise dose (not to be confused with hearing threshold). The HCA calls for an 80-dB*A* threshold level.
5. *Criterion level*. Allowable sound level for 8-hour per day exposure. OSHA (1978) and the HCA both use a 90-dB*A* criterion level.
6. *Action level or trigger level*. The level of noise or percent dose that triggers implementation of a continuing effective hearing conservation program. The HCA action level is 85-dB*A* continuous noise or a 50% noise dose. The OSHA (1978) action level is 90-dB*A* continuous noise or a 100% noise dose.
7. *Standard threshold shift (STS)*. A change in hearing threshold (relative to the baseline audiogram) by an average of 10 dB or more at 2, 3, and 4 kHz in either ear. An allowance may be made for presbycusis.

All workers exposed to noise levels at or above the action level should be included in a hearing conservation program with the following components:

1. Exposure monitoring.
2. Audiometric testing.
3. Employee training.
4. Hearing protection.
5. Recordkeeping.

Exposure Monitoring

The monitoring program should accurately identify employees with daily doses at or above the action level. All continuous, intermittent, and impulsive sound levels above the threshold level should be integrated in the computation. Noise dose may be obtained from personal dosimeters or by calculations based on noise level readings in a work area and employee exposure times in the area. As noted in a previous chapter, instrumentation is available which automatically calculates time-weighted average sound level, percent noise dose, and related values. Noise levels should be remeasured whenever a change in machinery or production methods is likely to increase noise exposure. Noise dose calculations should be based on a single workday for each individual employee. That is, an employee with a low noise dose does not balance one with a high noise dose, and a day of low noise exposure does not compensate for a day of high noise exposure.

In both the Hearing Conservation Amendment (OSHA-HCA, 1981) and the original act (OSHA, 1978) exposure to continuous noise levels of 115 dB*A* is limited to 15 minutes per day, and exposure to continuous noise levels above 115 dB*A* is not permitted. Continuous noise is defined as noise that can be measured with a sound level meter in the *slow* mode (about 1-s averaging time). In spite of the 115-dB*A* continuous noise limitation, the HCA provides that all noise levels 80 dB*A* and above be included in noise dose computations. For example, 120-dB*A* noise is treated as if the limit were 7.5 minutes, 125-dB*A* sound as if the limit were 3.75 minutes, and so on.

Audiometric Testing

An audiometric testing program includes baseline audiograms and annual audiograms that are compared with the baseline data. Baseline audiograms should be preceded by 14 hours without occupational noise exposure. A period during which hearing protectors are used is considered a period without occupational noise exposure for this purpose. If a Standard Threshold Shift (STS) is detected, the employee should be notified. The employee exhibiting the STS should be fitted or refitted with hearing protection and referred for clinical evaluation as appropriate, unless it can be shown that the STS is not work related or aggravated by occupational noise.

Hearing Protection

Hearing protectors should be made available to workers exposed to noise at or above the action level. Hearing protection should be required for workers who incur a standard threshold shift (STS) and for those exposed at or above the permissible exposure level (PEL). A variety of hearing protectors, including plug and muff types, should be made available for employee selection.

Training

Employees exposed to noise at or above the action level should be trained in the use of hearing protectors, the effects of noise, and the purpose and procedures of audiometric testing. The time of the audiometric examination might be an appropriate time for training and for attempting to motivate employees to conserve their hearing.

Recordkeeping

Noise exposure records should be retained for 2 years or until new monitoring has been performed, whichever period is longer. Audiometric records should be retained for the duration of an employee's service. It may be prudent to retain all records indefinitely.

Noise Level Versus Allowable Exposure Time

Eight hours of noise exposure is allowed at the criterion level. The allowable exposure time is halved each time the noise level increases by the exchange rate. Thus, for a criterion level CL and exchange rate ER, allowable daily exposure time T (hours) at noise level L (dBA) is given by

$$T = \frac{8}{2^{(L-CL)/ER}} \tag{4.8.3}$$

EXAMPLE PROBLEM: OCCUPATIONAL NOISE EXPOSURE

(a) Write an equation for allowable daily exposure time T (hours) versus noise level L (dBA) if the criterion level is 90 dBA and the exchange rate is 5 dBA.

Solution. Eight hours of noise exposure is allowed at 90 dBA and the exposure time is halved for each 5-dBA increase. Thus,

$$T = \frac{8}{2^{(L-90)/5}} \tag{4.8.4}$$

where L is equal to or greater than the threshold level. Values obtained from the above equation may differ slightly from tabulated values (OSHA, 1978). For example, at 92 dBA, exposure time is calculated to be

$$T = \frac{8}{2^{(92-90)/5}} = 6.06 \text{ hr}$$

which is rounded off to 6 hours in the table.

(b) Plot the result.

Solution. Figure 4.8.2a shows permissible exposure time versus noise level where time is plotted on a linear scale. If time is plotted on a logarithmic scale, the plot is a straight line. Part (b) of the figure shows the relationship for noise levels between 80 and 130 dBA with time plotted on a logarithmic scale. Note that a noise level of 80 dBA is permitted for 32 hours per day. This does not represent an error in the HCA. The 32-hour permissible time may be the denominator of one of the fractions in equation 4.8.2. For example 4-hour exposure at 80 dBA contributes $\frac{4}{32}$ or 12.5% to the total permissible noise dose for the day.

Time-Weighted Average Sound Level (TWA)

The TWA is the steady noise level, which, over 8 hours, will produce the same noise dose as the varying noise. Using the noise dose equation, we obtain

$$D_\% = 100\left(\frac{8}{T_{TWA}}\right) \tag{4.8.5}$$

where T_{TWA} is the allowable exposure time for noise level TWA. Writing the noise level versus allowable exposure time equation in terms of TWA, we obtain

$$T_{TWA} = \frac{8}{2^{(TWA-CL)/ER}} \tag{4.8.6}$$

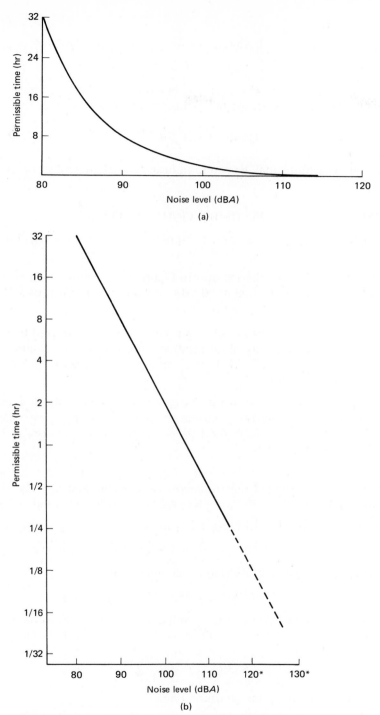

Figure 4.8.2 Example problem: occupational noise exposure. *Continuous noise levels above 115 dB*A* are not permitted. (*Source:* OSHA-HCA, 1981)

171

If the last equation is substituted in the one above it, the result is

$$D_\% = 100(2^{(TWA-CL)/ER})$$ (4.8.7)

Time-weighted average sound level may be expressed in terms of noise dose by rearranging the above equation and taking logarithms of both sides:

$$TWA = CL + ER\left[\frac{\log(D_\%/100)}{\log 2}\right]$$ (4.8.8)

where both logarithms may be common logarithms (base ten) or natural logarithms (base e).

EXAMPLE PROBLEM: NOISE DOSE AND TIME-WEIGHTED AVERAGE

(a) Sketch a flowchart for a computer program to determine noise dose ($D_\%$) and time-weighted average sound level (TWA).

Solution. The flowchart shown in Figure 4.8.3 is based on a criterion level of 90 dBA, a threshold level of 80 dBA, and an exchange rate of 5 dBA.

(b) New machines are to be installed in a work area. It is predicted that an employee will have the following daily noise exposure: 108 dBA for 1.5 hours, 90 dBA for 1 hour, 88 dBA for 4 hours, 80 dBA for 1.5 hours, and 73 dBA for 0.5 hours. Find $D_\%$ and TWA for the employee.

Solution. Instead of writing the program as outlined on the flowchart, the equations were written into an electronic spreadsheet (computer worksheet program). The results given in Table 4.8.1 show individual contributions to $D_\%$ and TWA as well as final values.

(c) How much time could the employee spend at the first task without exceeding allowable exposure during the workday? Assume no change in the other tasks.

Solution. Referring to Table 4.8.1, we see that the other tasks contribute

$$12.50 + 37.89 + 4.69 = 55.08\% \text{ noise dose}$$

Thus, if the first task contributes no more than

$$100 - 55.08 = 44.92\% \text{ noise dose}$$

the allowable noise dose of 100% will not be exceeded. Since allowable exposure time $T = 0.66$ hour for a steady noise level of 108 dBA, we have

$$100\,\frac{C}{T} = 100\,\frac{C}{0.66} = 44.92\%$$

from which maximum exposure time

$$C = 0.66 \times 44.92/100 = 0.296 \text{ hour} \quad \text{(less than 18 minutes)}$$

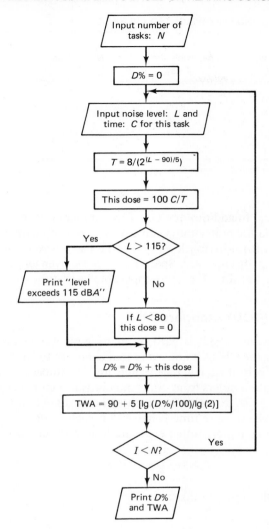

Figure 4.8.3 Noise dose and time-weighted average.

at the first task. The result is checked by changing this entry in the spreadsheet, yielding

$$D_{\%} = 100\% \quad \text{and} \quad \text{TWA} = 90 \text{ dB}A \quad \text{(approximately)}$$

for the workday.

4.9 OTHER NOISE EXPOSURE LIMITS BASED ON HEARING CONSERVATION

The U.S. Department of Defense (DOD), the International Organization for Standards (ISO), and several nations have established standards for hearing conservation which

TABLE 4.8.1   NOISE DOSE ($D_\%$) AND TIME-WEIGHTED AVERAGE (TWA)

Noise level, L (dBA)[a]	Exposure time, C (hr)	Allowable time, T (hr)	Noise dose, $D_\%$	Time-weighted average TWA, (dBA)
108	1.5	.66	227.36	95.92
90	1	8.00	12.50	75.00
88	4	10.56	37.89	83.00
80	1.5	32.00	4.69	67.92
	8		282.44	97.49

[a] If $L > 115$ dBA, note violation. If $L < 80$ dBA, do not enter.

differ from OSHA standards. In addition the U.S. Environmental Protection Agency (EPA) has published criteria for protection against noise-induced hearing loss. Some of the standards use a 90-dBA criterion level and some use a lower criterion level. Exchange rates of 3, 4, and 5 dBA are used. Specific values are given as examples only. Practical decisions must be based on the latest applicable legislation.

The U.S. Department of Defense (DOD) Standard

The DOD standard (Schneider, 1983) is used by many government agencies. The DOD standard is similar to the OSHA standard in that exposure to continuous noise levels above 115 dBA is not permitted, and the absolute limit on impact noise exposure is 140 dBA. The DOD standard differs from other standards in that the criterion level is 84 dBA (i.e., 8 hours of noise exposure is permitted at 84 dBA) and the exchange rate is 4 dBA (the permitted exposure time is halved for each 4-dBA level increase). Thus, for noise level L (dBA), the permitted exposure time T (hours) is given by

$$T = \frac{8}{2^{(L-84)/4}} \qquad (4.9.1)$$

where L must not exceed the upper limits.

U.S. Environmental Protection Agency (EPA) Criteria

As noted in an earlier section, the basic EPA hearing loss criterion is intended to protect virtually the whole population against noise-induced permanent threshold shifts greater than 5 dB at 4 kHz with an adequate margin of safety ("Levels documents," EPA, 1974 and 1978). The Levels documents were published to present information required by the Noise Control Act (1972).

The EPA criteria do not constitute agency regulations or standards, as they do not take into account cost or feasibility. It is assumed that states and localities will use the documents according to their individual needs and situations.

The EPA criterion evaluates an individual's total noise exposure by the equal energy rule. Two noise exposures are assumed to produce equal hearing loss if the products of the noise intensity and exposure time are equal. That is, for exposure time T and (scalar A-weighted) noise intensity I, two noise doses are equivalent if

$$\frac{T_2}{T_1} = \frac{I_1}{I_2} = \frac{10^{L_1/10}}{10^{L_2/10}} \tag{4.9.2}$$

Equivalent sound level L_{eq} is defined on the basis of sound energy. The basic EPA hearing conservation criterion is

$$L_{eq24} \leq 70 \text{ dB}A$$

where the subscript 24 indicates that the energy is averaged over a 24-hour period. If it is impractical to measure noise continuously over a 24-hour period, then L_{eq24} may be calculated from representative samples.

Using the equal energy rule, if the exposure time is halved, then we have

$$\frac{T_2}{T_1} = \frac{1}{2} = \frac{10^{L_1/10}}{10^{L_2/10}} = 10^{(L_1-L_2)/10}$$

from which

$$L_2 - L_1 = 10 \lg 2 = 3 \text{ dB}A \text{ (approximately)}$$

Thus, by the equal energy criterion, equal noise doses are obtained if the exposure time is halved when the noise level is increased by about 3 dBA. In other words, the EPA criterion has a 3-dBA exchange rate.

The approach taken by the EPA in identifying the hearing conservation criterion is indicated by a quotation of E. B. Hill in the forward to the Levels document (EPA, 1974):

> . . . The day of precise quantitative measurement of health and welfare effects has not yet arrived. Until such measurement is possible, action must be based on limited knowledge, guided by the principal of the enhancement of the quality of human life. Such action is based on a philosophy of preventive medicine.

Some of the data and assumptions utilized in determining the hearing conservation criterion are summarized below.

Rationale for the EPA Hearing Conservation Criterion The basic premises used to identify the level used in the criterion are listed in an earlier section. Curve *ABC* of Figure 4.9.1 shows noise exposure level (dBA) plotted against population percentile expected to experience a 5-dB noise-induced permanent threshold shift (NIPTS) at 4 kHz. The curve is based on 40 years of 8-hour-per-day noise exposure. Curve *DBE* shows the hearing level at 4 kHz of non-noise-exposed individuals, plotted against population percentile. The second curve is actually based on a survey of the hearing levels of 60-year-old women who were assumed to have little or no exposure to industrial noise (PHS, 1965).

The EPA criterion is based on the assumption that hearing loss (at 4 kHz) will not be caused by noise that cannot be heard. Suppose the individuals with the greatest

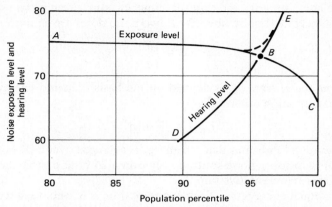

Figure 4.9.1 40-year, 8 hour per day exposure level (dB*A*) for 5-dB NIPTS at 4 kHz, and hearing level at 4 kHz versus population percentile. (*Source:* EPA, 1974)

noise sensitivity are represented by part *BE* of the hearing level curve. Then, exposure level curve *ABC* should not cross hearing level curve *DBE*. Based on the assumptions, the revised 40-year exposure level curve for 5-dB NIPTS at 4 kHz follows segment *AB* and then bends upward near *BE*, possibly along the dashed curve. The exact curve depends on the frequency content of the noise and human sensitivity to hearing damage at frequencies near 4 kHz. This reasoning leads to the conclusion that point *B* on the curves (at about 73 dB*A*) indicates the 40-year 8-hour-per-day exposure level at which the ninety-sixth percentile of the population, and virtually the entire population, will be protected against threshold shifts greater than 5 dB at 4 kHz.

Temporary Threshold Shifts (TTS)   TTS data can be used to predict permanent threshold shifts. According to the TTS hypothesis, a temporary threshold shift (TTS$_2$) measured 2 minutes after cessation of an 8-hour noise exposure approximates the NIPTS that would occur after 10 to 20 years of exposure at the same noise level. TTS$_2$ after 24 hours of exposure are about 5 dB higher than TTS$_2$ after 8 hours of exposure at the same level. This is reasonably consistent with the equal energy criterion since

$$10 \lg\left(\frac{24}{8}\right) = 4.77 \text{ (about 5 dB)}$$

Intermittency   Noise environments are often intermittent. Studies indicate that fluctuating noise, with peaks 5 to 15 dB*A* higher than the background level may be less damaging than steady noise with the same equivalent sound level (NIOSH, 1972; Kryter, 1970). The data suggest a correction of about 5 dB*A* if peak noise levels are 5 to 15 dB*A* above background noise levels, and the noise level falls to a background level below 65 dB*A* for 10% of each hour (i.e., $L_{90} < 65$ dB*A*).

Exposure Time Corrections   As noted above, available data and assumptions lead to the conclusion that steady noise, 8 hours per day for 40 years, at 73 dB*A* will produce no more than 5-dB NIPTS at 4 kHz. It is assumed that the original data are based on significant noise exposure during only 50 five-day work weeks or 250 workdays per year. Based on the equal energy criterion, it would be necessary to reduce noise intensity in proportion to the increased exposure time to calculate an exposure level based on a 365-day year. This leads to a reduction in allowable noise level of

$$10 \lg\left(\frac{365}{250}\right) = 1.58 \text{ (about 1.6 dB}A\text{)}$$

One further adjustment is made by decreasing the criterion levels by 1.4 dBA to provide a small margin of safety.

Protective Exposure Levels: Summary of EPA (1978) Levels Identified for Hearing Conservation   If equivalent sound levels L_{eq8} (energy average for an 8-hour-per-day noise exposure) and L_{eq24} (24-hour-per-day energy average) do not exceed the following values, predicted noise-induced hearing loss will be minimal. Then, protection would extend to the ninety-sixth population percentile, or possibly to almost the entire population.

EXPOSURE LEVELS (dBA) THAT PRODUCE NO MORE THAN 5-dB NIPTS
AT 4 kHz AFTER 40 YEARS' EXPOSURE

Equivalent sound level	Exposure (days/yr)	Without safety margin		With safety margin	
		Steady noise	Intermittent noise	Steady noise	Intermittent noise
L_{eq8}	250	73	78	71.6	76.6
L_{eq8}	365	71.4	76.4	70	75
L_{eq24}	250	68	73	66.6	71.6
L_{eq24}	365	66.4	71.4	65	70

Of these levels, EPA (1978) has identified the yearly equivalent sound level

$$L_{eq24} \leq 70 \text{ dB}A$$

for protection of hearing. In designating "identified levels," the EPA emphasizes that these levels are not to be viewed as official EPA standards, criteria, regulations or goals.

4.10 HEARING PROTECTORS

When noise exposure levels are excessive, an attempt should be made to reduce the noise at the source, possibly by vibration isolation or by redesign of machinery. Consideration should be given to interruption of noise transmission paths by the construction of barriers or enclosures. Administrative controls should also be considered. Such controls include reassignment of personnel to avoid long exposure times in noisy areas. After applying all feasible engineering and administrative controls, some personnel may still be exposed to high noise levels, requiring the use of personal hearing protection devices (HPD's). Earmuff-, earplug-, and semiaural-type hearing protectors are in common use. Earplug–earmuff combinations and communications headsets are sometimes used in areas of very high noise levels. Figure 4.10.1 shows several types of HPD's, including premolded earplugs, earmuffs, hard-hat-mounted earmuffs, semiaural devices, and expanding foam earplugs.

Earmuff-Type Hearing Protectors

Earmuff-type HPD's ordinarily consist of open-cell foam-lined plastic earcups with cushions to seal around the ear, and metal or plastic headbands. This type HPD must fit closely to the head and enclose the external ear in order to be effective. Thus, the most comfortable fit may not produce maximum attenuation. The cushion that makes contact around the ear may be foam filled or liquid filled to improve sealing and comfort. The foam filling has slightly better attenuation at high frequencies and the liquid filling slightly better attenuation at low frequencies. However, overall performance is more dependent on adequate sealing than on filling material. Some HPD models have a universal headband which may be worn over the top of the head, behind the head, or under the chin. When the headband is not worn over the head, a crown strap should be used to ensure a satisfactory fit.

Earmuffs are often chosen when noise exposure is intermittent since they are easier to remove and replace than earplugs. When noise levels exceed acceptable values, management and supervisory personnel have an obligation to provide HPD's and also to ensure that they are used. Compliance is easiest to monitor when earmuff HPD's are used. On construction sites, brightly colored earmuffs may be furnished to aid in monitoring use.

Insert-Type Hearing Protectors

Earplugs, which are inserted in the ear canal to form a seal, are available in premolded, formable, and custom-molded types. Premolded types, made in a number of sizes, are made of vinyls, cured silicones, and other elastomers. Custom-molded earplugs are shaped according to an impression taken for each employee. Formable earplugs are available in a number of materials including spun fiberglass, silicone putty, and slow-recovery foam.

Some wearers find earplugs more comfortable than earmuffs, particularly under warm and humid conditions. Earplug attenuation is not compromised when eyeglasses or safety glasses are worn. The use of earplugs is more difficult to monitor than that of earmuffs, but some earplugs are joined by a cord which makes them more visible. Earplugs are most suitable in steady noise environments where they will not be frequently removed and reinserted.

Semiaural Devices

A typical semiaural device consists of a pair of soft cones attached to a light headband. The cones make a seal directly in the ear canal entrance. They are easily removed and

(a)

(c)

(b)

(e)

(d)

(f)

(g)

(h)

(i)

Figure 4.10.1 Hearing protection devices. (*Source:* Bilsom International, Inc. for (a)–(c); E-A-R Div., Cabot Corp. for (d)–(i))

replaced, they are lighter than earmuffs, and their fit is not affected by the earpieces of eyeglasses or safety glasses. However, the force of the headband makes semiaural HPD's uncomfortable for some wearers, particularly when the noise environment requires their continuous use.

HPD Selection

The cost of HPD's is low when compared to the cost of hearing loss. Thus, the major selection criteria are noise attenuation and comfort. Manufacturers' catalogs can be consulted for noise reduction ratings of particular HPD models. Typical ranges are tabulated later in this chapter. Since comfort is an individual matter, it is desirable to allow the user to choose between different models, including two or more types of HPD. If HPD's are selected without consulting the user, some may find the selected model uncomfortable and avoid wearing it. The names and addresses of manufacturers of hearing protection devices may be found in *Sound and Vibration, Occupational Health and Safety,* and other periodicals concerned with occupational safety and health.

Real Ear Attenuation at Threshold (REAT)

The REAT protocol is a method of determining HPD effectiveness by comparing *occluded threshold* (hearing level wearing HPD) and *open threshold* (hearing level without HPD). The applicable test standard (ANSI, 1984) calls for one-third octave-band test signals in a room with a reverberation time of $T_{60} \leq 1.6$ s. The determination requires a minimum of ten subjects and three tests. Allowable noise levels in the octave bands from 125 Hz to 8 kHz are, respectively, 28, 18, 14, 14, 8, 9, and 20 dB. The experimentor supervises fitting of the HPD on the subject for best attenuation. This procedure results in repeatable tests and provides values that may be used to compare HPD's. However, the results of the test will indicate ideal attenuation which is usually much higher than field attenuation.

Noise Reduction Rating (NRR)

NRR is a single-number rating of personal hearing protection devices (HPD's) (EPA, 1979; Berger, 1979). It is determined as follows.

1. Determine the A-weighted octave-band sound levels L_{OBA}, and C-weighted octave-band sound levels L_{OBC} for a pink noise spectrum. Consider frequencies from 125 Hz through 8 kHz.

2. Determine the overall C-weighted sound level L_C.

3. For each octave band, find mean attenuation A_M (the difference between occluded threshold with the HPD and open threshold) and the attenuation standard deviation A_{SD}.

4. Find protected A-weighted octave-band sound levels L_{POBA} defined as follows:

$$L_{POBA} = L_{OBA} - (A_M - 2A_{SD}) \tag{4.10.1}$$

Assuming a normal distribution, approximately 98% of test subjects should achieve HPD attenuation equal or better than $A_M - 2A_{SD}$ at a given frequency. As noted above, test subjects are instructed in fitting HPD's to produce maximum attenuation. Thus, we must assume less HPD attenuation and higher wearer variability under field conditions; that is, mean attenuation decreases and standard deviation increases.

5. Calculate overall protected A-weighted sound level L_{PA} by combining the octave-band contributions (L_{POBA}).

6. Calculate noise reduction rating in decibels (NRR dB) as follows:

$$NRR = L_C - L_{PA} - 3 \qquad (4.10.2)$$

The 3-dB adjustment is made to correct for possible variations in the spectra of actual industrial noise. By subtracting the noise reduction rating NRR from the C-weighted sound level L_C, we obtain the A-weighted sound exposure level of a subject using an HPD (if correctly fit).

Muff-type hearing protection devices (HPD's) are compared with insert type and with insert and muff type combined in the following table. Typical values of mean attenuation A_M and standard deviation A_{SD} are given for each octave band.

ATTENUATION DATA (dB) FOR SELECTED PERSONAL
HEARING PROTECTION DEVICES

Frequency	Attenuation	Muff type	Insert type	Combined
125 Hz	Mean	12 to 23	10 to 29	25
125	SD	0.9 to 2.8	2.4 to 3.7	4.2
250	Mean	15 to 25	13 to 29	34
250	SD	1 to 2.9	1.6 to 3.8	2.7
500	Mean	21 to 31	16 to 30	45
500	SD	1.6 to 3	1.9 to 3.2	3.1
1 kHz	Mean	30 to 37	20 to 34	45
1	SD	1.7 to 2.8	1.9 to 3.1	3
2	Mean	34 to 40	31 to 37	41
2	SD	1.3 to 3	1.9 to 3	3.4
4	Mean	37 to 47	37 to 46	51
4	SD	1.4 to 3.3	2.4 to 5.1	5.4
8	Mean	32 to 44	34 to 39	46
8	SD	1.4 to 4.8	1.4 to 3.9	4.1
NRR		20 to 28	15 to 26	33

Source: Bilsom International, Inc.

The above table gives the range of attenuation values (mean and standard deviation) for selected HPD's including nine muff-type HPD's, four insert-type HPD's, and one insert combined with a muff-type HPD. Other commercially available HPD's may have attenuation values outside of the ranges listed above.

EXAMPLE PROBLEM: NOISE REDUCTION RATING

Calculate the NRR for the combined insert-muff type HPD listed in the above table.

Solution. The results will be tabulated below. Line 1 is the center frequency (Hz) of each octave in the test range.

Pink noise has a constant level in each octave band. Let the level be L (dB) in each octave band as indicated in line 2. The level we select is immaterial once the attenuation values have been measured.

Line 3 is obtained by applying the C-weighting corrections found in Chapter 1. It gives the C-weighted octave-band sound levels L_{OBC} of pink noise. The overall C-weighted sound level L_C is found by combining these levels in the seven octave bands. We may compute the intensities, add them, and then convert back to decibels. This is done in one step as follows:

$$L_C = 10 \lg\left(\sum_{i=1}^{7} 10^{L_{OBC}/10} \right) \tag{4.10.3}$$

The result is

$$L_C = 10 \lg(2 \times 10^{(L-0.2)/10} + 3 \times 10^{L/10} + 10^{(L-0.8)/10} + 10^{(L-3)/10})$$

$$= 10 \lg[(10^{L/10})(2 \times 10^{-0.2/10} + 3 + 10^{-0.8/10} + 10^{-3/10})]$$

$$= L + 7.95 \text{ dBC}$$

Line 4 is obtained by applying the A-weighting corrections (found in Chapter 1) to pink noise levels L. It gives the A-weighted octave-band sound levels L_{OBA} of pink noise.

The theoretical attenuation level which would be attained by 97.72% of test subjects in a normally distributed sample

$$A_T = A_M - 2A_{SD} \tag{4.10.4}$$

is obtained from the attenuation data given in the table for a combined-type HPD. A_T is listed on line 5.

Line 6 lists protected A-weighted octave-band sound level L_{POBA} calculated from

$$L_{POBA} = L_{OBA} - A_T \tag{4.10.5}$$

TABULATION FOR NRR CALCULATION IN EXAMPLE PROBLEM

		125	250	500	1000	2000	4000	8000
1	f	125	250	500	1000	2000	4000	8000
2	L_P	L	L	L	L	L	L	L
3	L_{OBC}	$L - 0.2$	L	L	L	$L - 0.2$	$L - 0.8$	$L - 3$
4	L_{OBA}	$L - 16.1$	$L - 8.6$	$L - 3.2$	L	$L + 1.2$	$L + 1$	$L - 1.1$
5	A_T	16.6	28.6	38.8	39	34.2	40.2	37.8
6	L_{POBA}	$L - 32.7$	$L - 37.2$	$L - 42$	$L - 39$	$L - 33$	$L - 39.2$	$L - 38.9$

Overall protected A-weighted sound level L_{PA} is found by combining octave-band levels L_{POBA} in the seven octave bands. The following equation may be used:

$$L_{PA} = 10 \lg\left(\sum_{i=1}^{7} 10^{L_{POBA}} \right) \tag{4.10.6}$$

This calculation leads to

$$L_{PA} = 10 \lg(10^{(L-32.7)/10} + 10^{(L-37.2)/10}$$
$$+ 10^{(L-42)/10} + 10^{(L-39)/10} + 10^{(L-33)/10}$$
$$+ 10^{(L-39.2)/10} + 10^{(L-38.9)/10})$$
$$= 10 \lg[(10^{L/10})(10^{-32.7/10} + 10^{-37.2/10}$$
$$+ 10^{-42/10} + 10^{-39/10} + 10^{-33/10}$$
$$+ 10^{-39.2/10} + 10^{-38.9/10})]$$
$$= L - 27.78 \text{ dBA}$$

Finally, we calculate the noise reduction rating:

$$\text{NRR} = L_C - L_{PA} - 3$$
$$= L + 7.95 - (L - 27.78) - 3$$
$$= 32.7 \text{ dB}$$

Bone Conduction and Sound Pathways to the Protected Ear

Sound transmission in the unoccluded ear (i.e., without hearing protectors) involves air conduction and bone conduction. These transmission paths are illustrated in a simplified cross section view, part (a) of Figure 4.10.2 (Berger, 1980). Parts (b) and (c) of the figure show sound transmission paths when the ear is protected with earplugs or earmuffs, respectively. The four pathways shown in the figure are identified as follows.

1. Air leaks. The HPD must make a virtually airtight seal for maximum protection. Air leaks typically reduce HPD effectiveness by 5 to 15 dB over a broad frequency range.

2. HPD vibration. Earplugs can vibrate in a pistonlike manner in the ear canal. Earmuffs can act as a spring-mass system in vibration. As a result, low-frequency performance is limited for both types of HPD. Attenuation at 125 Hz is limited to about 25 dB for earmuffs, 30 dB for premolded inserts, and 40 dB for foam inserts.

3. Transmission through the material of the HPD. Sound transmission through insert-type HPD's is usually small except with cotton or glassdown. Earmuff-type HPD's have much larger surface areas, and transmission through the cup material and the cushion can limit maximum attenuation at some frequencies.

4. Although HPD's effectively reduce air conduction, bone conduction paths remain, limiting maximum possible attenuation.

Field Performance of HPD's

When noise levels are adequately controlled, there is no need to rely on individual employee action for hearing protection. When HPD's are required to reduce exposure levels, individual motivation and skill in HPD use are an important factor. Field

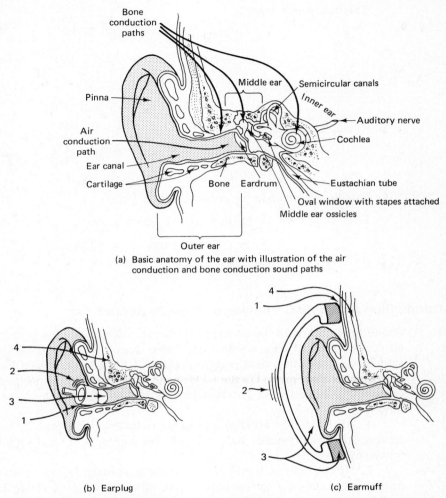

(a) Basic anatomy of the ear with illustration of the air conduction and bone conduction sound paths

(b) Earplug

(c) Earmuff

Figure 4.10.2 Sound transmission in the unoccluded and the occluded ear. (*Source:* E-A-R Div., Cabot Corp (Berger, 1980))

performance of hearing protectors is limited by poor fit, misuse, abuse, and aging of the protectors. A report by Berger (1983b) summarizes the results of a number of studies of "real world" HPD performance compared with NRR ratings.

HPD Usage

Misuse and nonuse of hearing protectors are more significant to hearing conservation than limitations due to HPD design. Studies by Solanky (1981) at construction sites where noise levels exceeded 90 dBA indicated extensive misuse and nonuse of HPD's. Observations of the workers of one utility company showed that 10% of workers used no hearing protection; 60% wore earmuff-type HPD's over their hair, preventing a tight fit; 15% wore earmuff HPD's over hair and glasses; 5% wore earmuff HPD's covering only part of the external ear; and the remaining 10% wore the earmuff HPD's correctly, but without adjustment for maximum attenuation. The utility company had a hearing protection program including annual audiograms, and helmut-muff HPD's were issued to workers. HPD use appears to be poorest among workers for small independent contractors. Based on about 50 observations at outdoor worksites where noise levels exceeded 90 dBA, less than 5% of workers for small independent contractors used HPD's. Some of the nonuser group said they had tried hearing protectors and found them uncomfortable. Others claimed that noise did not affect their hearing. The example problem that follows illustrates the effect of removing HPD's during part of the workday.

EXAMPLE PROBLEM: TIME-CORRECTED NOISE REDUCTION RATING

A hearing protector with an NRR of 25 is required to reduce exposure level to 90 dBA. Most of the noise energy is concentrated in the 1-kHz band. Find the percent noise dose ($D_\%$), time-weighted average noise exposure level (TWA), and time-corrected noise reduction rating (TCNRR) if the protector is removed for 15 minutes during each 8-hour workday. Base results on a 90-dBA criterion level and 5-dBA exchange rate.

Solution. Equations from the Occupational Safety and Health Act section are used. If the HPD is used for the full 8-hour day, the noise dose is $D_\% = 100\%$, and the time-weighted average exposure is TWA = 90 dBA. Since the noise energy is concentrated in the 1-kHz band, it will be assumed that the A-weighted exposure level is $90 + 25 = 115$ dBA when the HPD is removed. If the HPD is removed one-quarter hour per day, the noise dose is given by

$$D_\% = 100\left(\frac{C_1}{T_1} + \frac{C_2}{T_2}\right)$$

where exposure time

$$C_1 = 7.75 \text{ hr at } 90 \text{ dB}A \quad \text{and} \quad C_2 = 0.25 \text{ hr at } 115 \text{ dB}A$$

Allowable exposure time is given by

$$T = \frac{8}{2^{(L-90)/5}}$$

from which

$$T_1 = \frac{8}{2^{(90-90)/5}} = 8 \text{ hr} \quad \text{and} \quad T_2 = \frac{8}{2^{(115-90)/5}} = 0.25 \text{ hr}$$

Thus, noise dose is given by

$$D_\% = 100\left(\frac{7.75}{8} + \frac{0.25}{0.25}\right) = 196.9\%$$

Time-weighted average exposure level is given by

$$TWA = 90 + 5\left[\frac{\log(D_\%/100)}{\log 2}\right]$$

$$= 90 + 5\left[\frac{\log(196.9/100)}{\log 2}\right] = 94.9 \text{ dB}A$$

Thus, the time-weighted exposure level is about 5 dBA higher due to removal of the HPD for 15 minutes per day. This is equivalent to reducing the effectiveness of the HPD by 5 dB, resulting in a time-corrected noise reduction rating of

$$TCNRR = NRR - 5 = 20 \text{ (approximately)}$$

Figure 4.10.3 (Berger, 1980) shows time-corrected noise reduction rating plotted against percent of time worn for various values of noise reduction rating. The results of the above example are shown on the NRR = 25 curve.

Earmuff-Type HPD Effectiveness Under Simulated Field Conditions

In a study of HPD effectiveness under simulated field conditions (Wilson, Solanky, and Gage, 1981), it was determined that when earmuff-type hearing protectors were used, they were usually adjusted for comfort rather than for maximum attenuation. Several conditions of fit were examined. For the *initial fit* condition, subjects were instructed to fit muff-type HPD's for comfort, but the experimentor assured that skin contact existed all around the ear without intervening hair. *Maximum attenuation*

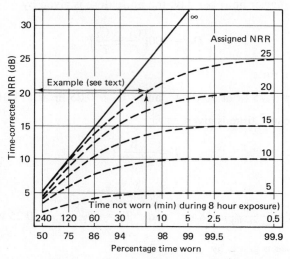

Figure 4.10.3 Time-corrected noise reduction rating for hearing protection devices. (*Source:* E-A-R Div., Cabot Corp. (Berger, 1980))

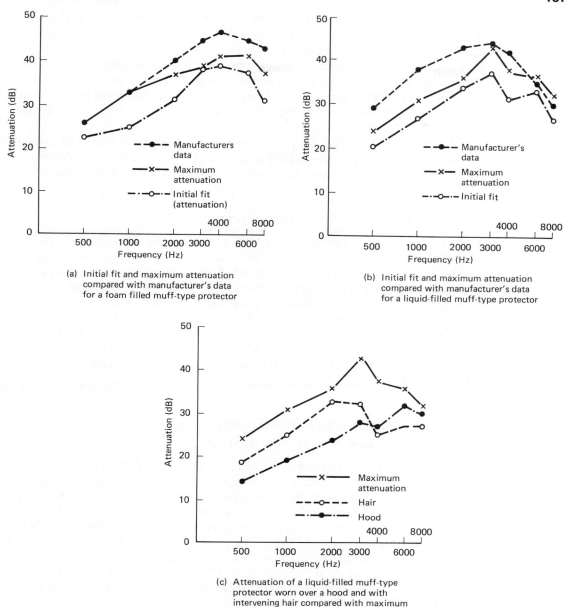

(a) Initial fit and maximum attenuation compared with manufacturer's data for a foam filled muff-type protector

(b) Initial fit and maximum attenuation compared with manufacturer's data for a liquid-filled muff-type protector

(c) Attenuation of a liquid-filled muff-type protector worn over a hood and with intervening hair compared with maximum attenuation

Figure 4.10.4

was defined as the HPD attenuation when fitted by the subject when the subject was instructed to adjust for minimum sound in the presence of white noise at a level of 80 dBA. After adjustment, HPD attenuation was determined by measuring occluded and open thresholds. Some of the results are plotted in Figure 4.10.4. Part (a) of the figure shows attenuation values for foam-filled muff-type HPD's; part (b) shows attenuation values for liquid-filled muff-type HPD's. It is seen that the "maximum attenuation" fit, based on the subject's impression of best noise reduction, yields lower attenuation values than experimenter-supervised fit used in the manufacturer's tests. During cold weather, outdoor workers often wear coat hoods or sweatshirt hoods and wear muff-type HPD's over the hoods. Part (c) of the figure shows the effect of hoods on HPD performance as well as the effect of hair interfering with the seal of muff-type HPD's.

When muff-type HPD's are worn over eyeglasses, sealing is usually inadequate. Nixon and Koblach (1974) showed attenuation losses up to 10 dB at some frequencies due to air leaks at eyeglass earpieces. An attenuation loss of 3 to 7 dB is typical.

Insert-Type HPD Effectiveness Under Field Conditions

An exhaustive field study of insert-type HPD's was made by Edwards et al. (1978). A specially instrumented audiometric van was taken to several industrial sites where 168 workers using insert-type HPD's were tested. The workers were removed from their workplaces without prior knowledge that they would be tested. Occluded and open hearing thresholds were measured. A comparison of results with data reported by HPD manufacturers indicates that half of the workers tested were receiving less than one-third of the potential attenuation of the hearing protectors in terms of noise reduction in dBA. It appears that the poor performance was probably due to workers improperly inserting the HPD's, and in some cases, using the wrong size insert for their ear canals.

Earplugs Worn in Combination with Earmuffs: Attenuation Measured for Various Degrees of Earplug Insertion

Other studies of HPD attenuation (Berger 1983a, 1984a) show the importance of adequate earplug insertion and the advantage of combining earplugs with earmuffs. Figure 4.10.5a compares the mean attenuation and standard deviation of three types of earplugs. The fiber plug was inserted according to the manufacturer's instructions without attempting to pack it tightly. The premolded plug was carefully sized and fitted under experimenter supervision. The vinyl foam plug was tested with partial, standard, and deep insertion. These degrees of insertion represented, respectively, 15 to 20%, 50 to 60%, and 80 to 100% of the length of the plug in the ear canal.

Part (b) of the figure shows the test results for four earmuff types. Types 1 and 2 are small-volume earmuffs (<120 cm^3) with foam- and liquid-filled cushions, respectively. Type 3 is a large muff (355 cm^3) with foam-filled cushions. Type 4 is a damped lead earmuff (>7 lb) constructed specially for the study.

Partially inserted foam plugs are evaluated individually and when combined with an earmuff in part (c) of the figure. The attenuation produced by the combination is better than the attenuation of either HPD alone. However, the attenuation of the combination is less than the sum of the individual attenuations. Maximum attenuation is limited by coupling of the HPD's via body tissues and air trapped between them,

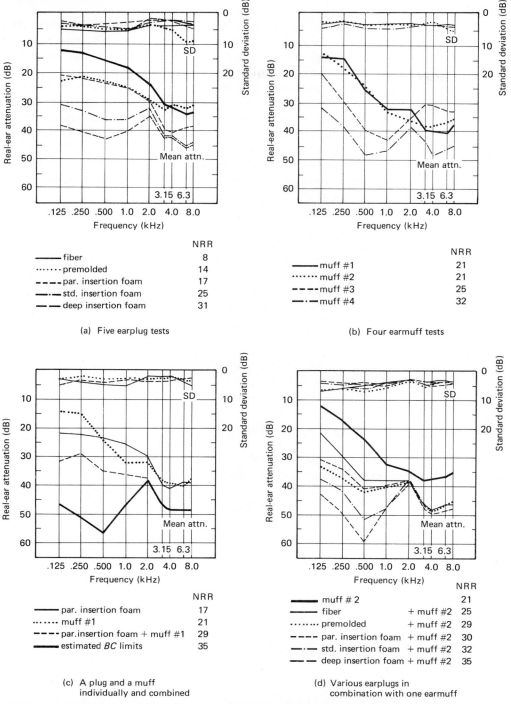

	NRR
—— fiber	8
······ premolded	14
---- par. insertion foam	17
-·-· std. insertion foam	25
- - deep insertion foam	31

(a) Five earplug tests

	NRR
—— muff #1	21
······ muff #2	21
---- muff #3	25
-·-· muff #4	32

(b) Four earmuff tests

	NRR
—— par. insertion foam	17
······ muff #1	21
---- par.insertion foam + muff #1	29
—— estimated *BC* limits	35

(c) A plug and a muff individually and combined

		NRR
—— muff # 2		21
—— fiber	+ muff #2	25
······ premolded	+ muff #2	29
---- par. insertion foam	+ muff #2	30
-·-· std. insertion foam	+ muff #2	32
- - deep insertion foam	+ muff #2	35

(d) Various earplugs in combination with one earmuff

Figure 4.10.5 Earplugs and earmuffs worn separately and in combination. Attenuation measured for various degrees of earplug insertion. (*Source:* E-A-R Div., Cabot Corp. (Berger, 1984))

and by bone conduction. The estimated bone conduction limitation (curve *BC*) is based on flanking paths through the bones and tissue of the skull. Since most of the sound transmitted by bone conduction bypasses the HPD, some sound can still reach the inner ear, even with well-designed and well-fit HPD's.

Fiber-, premolded-, and foam-type earplugs with different degrees of insertion are evaluated in combination with a liquid-filled muff in part (d) of the figure. Parts (c) and (d) of the figure show that when earplug and earmuff combinations are used, that the type and fit of the earplug is important at frequencies below 2 kHz. Another conclusion of this study is that "real world" attenuation of a single HPD is likely to be inadequate at high noise levels, particularly when low frequencies dominate. The author suggests that combined HPD's be considered when 8-hour time-weighted average exposure level exceeds 105 dB*A*.

Risk Estimates When HPD's Are Used

A study by Erdreich (1985) compares risk of hearing loss when workers are exposed to noise levels between 80 and 100 dB*A*. The author concludes that reliance on published NRR values for HPD's when time-weighted sound level TWA falls between 90 and 100 dB*A* may increase the risk of developing noise-induced hearing loss. The use of one insert-type HPD results in a calculated risk of noise-induced hearing loss of 19.8%; another insert-type HPD results in 30.6% risk. Noise-induced hearing loss is defined as the risk of NIPTS exceeding 25 dB (average) for 1, 2, and 3 kHz at age 46 to 54. A reduced noise reduction rating (RNRR) is used, based on a directive of OSHA (1983). The reduced rating that predicts the difference between noise level (dB*A*) and protected exposure level (dB*A*) is defined as follows:

$$\text{RNRR}_A = \frac{\text{NRR} - 7}{2} \qquad (4.10.7)$$

The reduced rating predicting the difference between *C*-weighted noise level and *A*-weighted protected exposure level is defined by

$$\text{RNRR}_{CA} = \frac{\text{NRR}}{2} \qquad (4.10.8)$$

The reduced ratings are used for comparing the benefits of engineering controls against those of HPD's.

BIBLIOGRAPHY

American Academy of Otolaryngology, "AAO hearing impairment formula," *Sound and Vibration* **13**(6), 1, 1979.

American National Standards Institute, American national standard for measuring monosyllabic word intelligibility, ANSI S3.2-1960.

American National Standards Institute, American national standards for specification of audiometers, ANSI S3.6-1969.

American National Standards Institute, Criteria for background noise in audiometric rooms, ANSI 3.1-1960 (rev. 1971).

American National Standards Institute, Method for the measurement of real-ear attenuation of hearing protectors, ANSI S12.6-1984.

Berger, E. H., "EARlog #2—Single number measures of hearing protector noise reduction," *Sound and Vibration* **13**(8), 12–13, 1979.

Berger, E. H., "EARlog #5—Hearing protector performance: how they work—and—what goes wrong in the real world," *Sound and Vibration* **14**(10), 14–17, 1980.

Berger, E. H., "Laboratory attenuation of earplugs both singly and in combination," *Am. Ind. Hyg. Assoc. J.* **44**(5), 321–329, 1983(a).

Berger, E. H., "Using the NRR to estimate the real world performance of hearing protectors," *Sound and Vibration,* **17**(1), 12–18, 1983(b).

Berger, E. H., "EARlog #13—Attenuation of earplugs worn in combination with earmuffs," *Am. Ind. Hyg. Assoc. J.* **45**(5), B36–B37, 1984(a).

Berger, E. H., "The hearing conservation amendment," Parts I and II, *EARlog #11 and 12,* Cabot Corp., Indianapolis, 1984(b).

Bruel, P. V., "Do we measure damaging noise correctly?," *Noise Control Eng. J.* **8**(2), 52–60, 1977.

Edwards, R., W. Hauser, N. Moisseev, A. Broderson, W. Green, and B. Lempert, A field investigation of noise reduction afforded by insert-type hearing protectors, NIOSH Rept. 79-115, November 1978.

Environmental Protection Agency, "Noise labeling requirements for hearing protectors," *Federal Register* **42**(190), 40CFR part 211, 56139–56147, 1979.

Environmental Protection Agency, Protective noise levels, EPA 550/9-79-100, November 1978. This publication is a condensed version of the EPA levels document: Information on levels of environmental noise requisite to protect public health and welfare with an adequate margin of safety, EPA 5500/9-74-004, March 1974.

Erdreich, J., "Alternatives for hearing loss risk assessment," *Sound and Vibration* **19**(5), 22–23, 1985.

Fletcher, H., *Speech and Hearing in Communication,* Van Nostrand, New York, 1955.

Glorig, A., "Damage risk criteria for hearing," in *Noise and Vibration Control,* p. 541, L. L. Beranek (Ed.), McGraw-Hill, New York, 1971.

Glorig, A., W. D. Ward, and J. Nixon, "Damage risk criteria and noise induced hearing loss," *Arch. Otolaryngol.* **74,** 413–432, October 1961.

International Organization for Standards, Acoustics—Standard reference zero for calibration of pure tone audiometers, ISO 389-1975.

Kryter, K. D., "Impairment to hearing from exposure to noise," *J. Acoust. Soc. Am.* **53**(5), 1211–1234, 1973.

Kryter, K. D., *The Effects of Noise on Man,* Academic Press, New York, 1970.

Martin, William, and Lodge, "Noise attenuation of the headset UA 0520," Bruel & Kjaer Electronic Instruments Master Catalog, Marlborough, MA, 1986.

Miller, J. D., "Effects of noise on people," *J. Acoust. Soc. Am.* **56**(3), 729–764, 1974.

National Institute for Occupational Safety and Health, Occupational exposure to noise, criteria for a recommended standard, NIOSH, 1972.

Nixon, C. W., and W. C. Koblach, Hearing protection of earmuffs worn over eyeglasses, Aerospace Medical Research Laboratory Rept. AMRL-TR-74-61, Wright Patterson AFB, June, 1974.

Noise Control Act of 1972, Public Law 92-574, 92nd Congress, HR 11021, October 27, 1972.

Occupational Health and Safety, Stevens Pub. Co., Waco, TX 76710 (periodical).

Occupational Safety and Health Administration, Guidelines for noise enforcement, OSHA Instruction CPL 2-2.35,29 CFR 1910.95(6) (1), 1983.

Occupational Safety and Health Administration, "Occupational noise exposure hearing conservation amendment," *Federal Register* **46**(11), 4078–4181 and **46**(162), 42622–42639, 1981.

Passchier-Vermeer, W., Hearing loss due to exposure to steady-state broadband noise, Rept. 35, Institute for Public Health Engineering, Delft, 1968.

Pierce, A. D., *Acoustics, an Introduction to Its Physical Principles and Applications,* McGraw-Hill, New York, 1981.

Public Health Service National Center for Health Statistics, Hearing levels of adults by age and sex, Vital and health statistics, Public Health Service Publication No. 1000-Ser.11-No. 11, Washington DC, October 1965.

Rayleigh (J. W. Strutt), *The Theory of Sound,* Vol. I, 2nd ed., 1894, reprinted by Dover, New York, 1945.

Remington's Pharmaceutical Sciences, Mack Publishing Co., Easton, PA, 1980.

Schneider, A. J., "An update on noise criteria and noise measurements," *Industrial Hygiene News,* 48–49, July 1983.

Sound and Vibration, Acoustical Publications, Inc., Bay Village, OH 44140 (monthly).

Solanky, H., Hearing protector effectiveness, Masters thesis, N.J. Institute of Technology, Newark, NJ, 1981.

Taylor, G. D., and E. Williams, "Acoustic trauma in the sports hunter," *Laryngoscope* **76,** 863–879, 1966.

Tonndorf, J., H. E. VonGierke, and W. D. Ward, "Criteria for noise and vibration exposure," in *Handbook of Noise Control,* 2nd Ed., C. Harris (Ed.), p. 18-5, McGraw-Hill, New York, 1979.

U.S. Department of Labor, Occupational Safety and Health Administration, General industry standards, OSHA safety and health standards (29 CFR 1910) OSHA 2206, rev Nov. 7, 1978.

Wilson, C., H. Solanky, and H. Gage, "Hearing protector effectiveness," *Professional Safety* **26**(10), ASSE, 1981.

PROBLEMS

4.1.1. Write an equation to determine the number of octaves in a given frequency range in Hertz.

4.1.2. Determine the hearing ranges of various animals in octaves.

4.1.3. Express the frequency range of singers and a few musical instruments in octaves. Consider fundamental frequencies.

4.1.4. Construct a table for converting sound pressure level in decibels to scalar sound intensity, sound pressure, and subjective loudness. Consider the range from the softest audible sound to the threshold of pain.

4.4.1. The following hearing thresholds at 500 Hz and 1, 2, and 3 kHz are recorded on an audiogram. Left ear: 45, 50, 55, and 65 dB, respectively. Right ear: 30, 35, 35, and 40 dB, respectively.
(a) Find percent hearing impairment based on the AAO/ACO formula.
(b) Repeat, using the (earlier) AAOO formula.

4.4.2. Same as Problem 4.4.1, except that hearing thresholds are between 0 and 25 dB in the left ear.

4.4.3. An audiogram indicates a hearing threshold of 35 dB at 1 kHz in both ears. Describe the hearing threshold in terms of:
(a) sound energy
(b) subjective loudness

4.5.1. Determine the speech impairment risk criterion for the audiogram of Problem 4.4.1.

4.7.1. Write an equation to approximately fit the noise level–exposure time combinations that will produce 10-dB temporary threshold shifts at 4 kHz.

4.7.2. A job category is proposed in which a worker will operate a pneumatic nailing machine 1.5 hours per day at 98-dBA equivalent sound level and a large punch press 2 hours per day at 95-dBA equivalent sound level, with 4.5 hours per day essentially noise-free.
(a) How long would it take the worker to exceed the hearing damage risk equivalent to 40 years' exposure in a large machine shop at 75 dBA?
(b) What noise reduction would be required in the proposed job so that it would produce no more hearing loss after 40 years than the machine shop?

4.7.3. Same as Problem 4.7.2 except that the equivalent sound level of the pneumatic nailing machine is 103 dBA.

4.8.1. The following daily exposure pattern is predicted for a machine operator: 103 dBA for 0.5 hours, 99 dBA for 1 hour, 92 dBA for 2 hours, 86 dBA for 2 hours, and 71 dBA for 2.5 hours. Use a criterion level of 90 dBA, a threshold level of 80 dBA, and an exchange rate of 5 dBA.
(a) Find percent noise dose.
(b) Find time-weighted average sound level.

4.8.2. The following daily exposure pattern is predicted for a machine operator: 105 dBA for 0.64 hours, 97 dBA for 2.56 hours, 93 dBA for 1.6 hours, 85 dBA for 2.4 hours, and 72 dBA for 0.5 hours. Use a criterion level of 90 dBA, a threshold level of 80 dBA, and an exchange rate of 5 dBA.
(a) Find percent noise dose.
(b) Find time-weighted average sound level.

4.8.3. The following daily exposure pattern is predicted for a machine operator: 101 dBA for 0.6 hours, 98 dBA for 0.9 hours, 94 dBA for 3.3 hours, 85 dBA for 1.2 hours, and 75 dBA for 1.5 hours. Use a criterion level of 90 dBA, a threshold level of 80 dBA, and an exchange rate of 5 dBA.
(a) Find percent noise dose.
(b) Find time-weighted average sound level.

4.8.4. The following daily exposure pattern is predicted for a machine operator: 106 dBA for 0.25 hours, 91 dBA for 2 hours, 89 dBA for 3 hours, 81 dBA for 2.75 hours, and 79 dBA for 0.5 hours. Use a criterion level of 90 dBA, a threshold level of 80 dBA, and an exchange rate of 5 dBA.
(a) Find percent noise dose.
(b) Find time-weighted average sound level.

4.8.5. (a) Write an equation to calculate allowable noise level L when exposure time T, criterion level CL, and exchange rate ER are given.
(b) Use this equation to calculate L for $T = \frac{1}{4}$ hr, CL = 90 dBA, and ER = 5 dBA.

4.9.1. Plot allowable exposure time versus noise level if the criterion level is 84 dBA, the exchange rate 4 dBA, and the absolute limit 115 dBA.

4.9.2. A worker is exposed to 90 dBA for 3 hours, 96 dBA 1.5 hours, and 98 dBA 1.25 hours per day. Find percent noise dose if the applicable criterion level is 84 dBA and the exchange rate 4 dBA.

4.9.3. Write an equation for permitted exposure time T in terms of exposure level L if the criterion level is 90 dBA and the exchange rate 3 dBA.

4.9.4. Repeat Problem 4.9.2 if a 90-dBA criterion level and 3-dBA exchange rate apply.

4.9.5. Plot permitted exposure time T versus noise level L for a 90-dBA criterion level and 3-dBA exchange rate.

4.9.6. Write an equation for daily exposure time versus noise level based on the EPA protective exposure levels. Assume 250 days-per-year exposure to steady noise.

4.9.7. Repeat Problem 4.9.6 for intermittent noise.

4.9.8. Data from a number of sources indicate that a typical factory worker who lives in the suburbs has the following noise exposure pattern for 250 workdays per year:

7 hours	at	35 dBA
1.5		50
2		55
3		60
1		70
2.5		78
7		92

For the rest of the year, assume the following typical exposure:

7 hours	at	35 dBA
5		50
10		60
2		78

(a) Find L_{eq24} for a typical workday.
(b) Find L_{eq24} based on a 365-day energy average.
(c) Assume the noise is intermittent. Find the reduction in exposure level necessary in order to meet the appropriate EPA (1978) protective exposure level.

4.9.9. Repeat Problem 4.9.8 for an urban factory worker. Use the same data except that noise levels never fall below 53 dBA.

4.10.1. A certain insert-type HPD is tested in the seven octave bands with center frequencies from 125 Hz to 8 kHz. Mean attenuation values are, respectively, 23, 25, 26, 26, 34, 41, and 38. Standard deviations are, respectively, 3.6, 2.8, 2.5, 3, 3, 2.8, and 3.6.
(a) Find noise reduction rating NRR.
(b) Calculate the maximum A-weighted noise level for which this HPD may be used if protected exposure level is not to exceed 90 dBA. Base results on reduced noise reduction rating RNRR.
(c) Calculate the maximum C-weighted noise level on the same basis.

4.10.2. Repeat Problem 4.10.1 except that a muff-type HPD is used with mean attenuations of 15, 19, 24, 33, 39, 39, and 34 dBA. Standard deviations are 2.2, 2.9, 3, 2.2, 2.3, 3.3, and 1.4 dBA.

Chapter 5

Community Noise and Its Effects

Hearing damage is only one of many adverse effects of noise. In this chapter, we are concerned with speech and sleep interference, annoyance, and other nonauditory effects of noise. Community noise descriptors and control strategies are discussed. Surface and air transportation, construction activities, industrial operations, and other sources of community noise are considered. However, the prediction and control of transportation noise and industrial noise are treated in more detail in other chapters. Community noise levels sometimes entail a risk of hearing damage. The Environmental Protection Agency (1978) has identified an exposure level that produces no more than 5-dB noise-induced hearing damage over a 40-year period, with a slight margin of safety. The identified (24 hour per day, 365 day per year average) equivalent sound level L_{eq24} is 70 dBA for intermittent noise. Typical noise exposure patterns are shown for a preschool child, an office worker, and factory worker in Figure 5.0.1 based on data of the EPA (1971a, 1971b, 1971c, 1973, 1974).

Annoyance, sleep interference, and speech interference are more likely to be cited as community noise problems than the long-term risk of hearing damage. Day–night equivalent sound level L_{DN} is a descriptor designed to recognize the greater sensitivity of a community to nighttime noise. L_{DN} is obtained by first weighting nighttime noise (between 10 P.M. and 7 A.M. the next morning) by +10 dBA, and then calculating the equivalent sound level over a 24-hour period.

5.1 ANNOYANCE

It is difficult to establish a quantitative descriptor of annoyance due to its subjective nature. The individual who controls an annoying noise source is often subject to greater noise exposure than the person who is annoyed. A radio volume control may

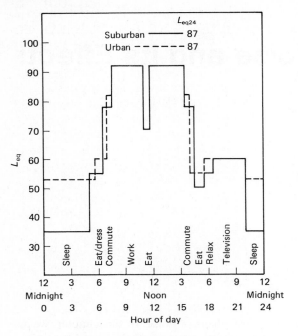

(a) Typical noise exposure pattern of a factory worker

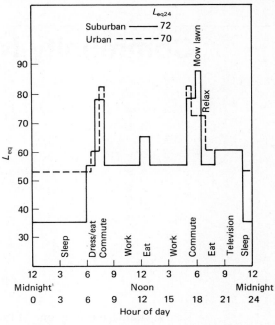

(b) Typical noise exposure pattern of an office worker

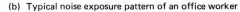

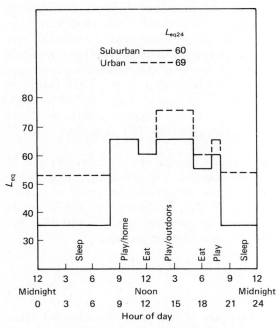

(c) Typical noise exposure pattern of a preschool child

Figure 5.0.1 Typical noise exposure patterns. (*Source:* EPA)

be set so that sound levels are 20 to 30 dB above levels adequate for listening; a special "deep tone" muffler may be installed on an automobile or motorcycle. In both cases, the person responsible finds pleasure in producing the noise, and possibly in making his presence known to others.

Portable radio-cassette players with lightweight stereophonic earphones make some contribution to community noise reduction to the extent that they replace the large "boom box" portable sound systems with external speakers. Unfortunately, both types can produce sound levels that damage hearing. Randomly selected earphone-type players were tested in a study at Tufts-New England Medical Center (Bishop, 1982). For earphone-type players with the volume set at 4, typical sound levels ranged from 93 to 108 dBA and typical levels were over 115 dBA for a volume setting of 8, where volume settings ranged from 1 to 10. The hearing damage potential is illustrated by the 15-minute limit imposed on daily occupational exposure to continuous noise at 115 dBA (see preceding chapter, OSHA 1978, 1981). As an alternative, consider the protective exposure level,

$$L_{eq24} = 70 \text{ dB}A$$

for intermittent noise (EPA, 1978a). By the equal energy criterion, noise doses are equivalent if

$$\frac{T_2}{T_1} = \frac{10^{L_{1/10}}}{10^{L_{2/10}}}$$

from which the daily exposure time to noise levels of 115 dBA would be given by

$$T_2 = \frac{24 \times 10^{70/10}}{10^{115/10}}$$

$$= 7.59 \times 10^{-4} \text{ hr or only 2.7 s}$$

Of course, no prudent user would intentionally expose himself 115-dBA sound levels. The high volume settings on sound systems are sometimes useful for reception of weak radio signals and to compensate for weak batteries. Furthermore, reproduced music may be less damaging than typical industrial noise at the same level since sharp peaks may be "clipped" in the music (as indicated in the preceding chapter). Nevertheless, caution should be exercised in the use of earphone-type players while caution and courtesy should be exercised in the use of other sound systems.

Impulse Noise Penalty

As noted in the preceding chapter, research results indicate that sharp noise peaks result in a greater risk of hearing damage than that predicted on the basis of equivalent sound level alone. Impulse noise is also more annoying. Laboratory tests were conducted by Vos and Smoorenburg (1985) in which subjects rated the annoyance caused by impulse sounds (regular and irregular gunfire noise and metal-construction noise) and by nearby road traffic sounds. Background noise was supplied by a recording of remote traffic noise with small fluctuations. A correction term or penalty was derived from the ratings. The penalty is added to the equivalent sound level of the impulse sounds, to give the level of equally annoying nearby traffic noise. For an indoor background noise level L_{eq} = 35 dBA, the researchers determined that a 10-dBA penalty applies; for background noise level L_{eq} = 55 dBA, the penalty is 5 dBA.

5.2 COMMUNITY RESPONSE

The response to noise pollution is not related to noise level alone, although most people can be expected to react to levels above 90 dBA with complaints and threats of legal action. Noise that contains discernible pure tones is more likely to invoke a response than broadband noise of the same level. Public address systems and other loud speech interfere with concentration and may cause a community response. The reaction to noise depends on the noisemaker, the receiver, and the relationship between the two. If a particular industry or commercial operation causes traffic and parking problems in a community, the community may be more likely to react to noise problems from that operation. The probability of a community reaction also depends on previous noise exposure experience. A significant increase in noise levels is likely to cause a community reaction. When noise levels become objectionable, individuals with more political sophistication are more likely to complain, to threaten legal action, and to organize effectively to bring about relief.

The noise sources that generate the most problems vary from community to community. Transportation noise usually dominates the list of problems. A survey of California residents is typical in that respect (EPA, 1978b). The survey results are summarized in the table that follows.

PERCENT OF RESPONDENTS
IDENTIFYING NOISE PROBLEMS
BY SOURCE

Source	Percent
Aircraft	17
Traffic	17
Motorcycles	14
Dogs barking	11
Loud music	8
Construction	1
Trash pickup	1
Other	1
Source not identified	30
	100

5.3 NONAUDITORY EFFECTS OF NOISE

In addition to the direct pathways in the auditory system which enable us to consciously hear, there are indirect routes by which sounds act as stimuli to the autonomic nervous system. The autonomic nervous system has functions that include production of cardiac and smooth muscle contractions and stimulation of secretion by glands. The human body responds unconsciously to sudden loud sounds, interpreting them as danger signals. Although this response may be inappropriate in many cases, it occurs nevertheless. According to information compiled by the Environmental Protection Agency (1978c), blood pressure rises, heart rate and breathing speed up, muscles tense, perspiration appears, and hormones are released into the bloodstream. These effects even occur during sleep. The changes occur even in people who feel they are accustomed to noise. Although data are inconclusive in some cases, there is some evidence that noise causes stress-related diseases including high blood pressure, asthma, ulcers, headache, and colitis. In addition, noise may aggravate existing diseases by preventing necessary rest and relaxation.

Among the nonauditory effects of noise, cardiovascular effects appear to have the greatest health significance. In addition, there are a number of well-documented epidemiological studies, and animal and human experimental studies relating cardiovascular effects to noise exposure. Some of these studies are evaluated in a survey by DeJoy (1984).

Some studies have indicated that exposure to high levels of noise can produce elevated blood pressure in rats. One study, which failed to demonstrate a relationship between noise exposure and hypertension in rats, did indicate that hypertensive rats were more susceptible to noise-induced hearing loss. Ising and Melchert (1980) exposed rats to random 4-s bursts of noise each night (the time rats are normally active). The noise interval to pause ratio was 1 to 10 and the equivalent sound level was $L_{eq24} = 83$ dB. Instead of using A-weighting which is based on human hearing, the experimenters used a weighting curve based on the hearing level of rats, expressing levels in dB_{rat}. Changes in cardiac structure were observed after periods of noise exposure up to 28 weeks.

Nonhuman primate studies were conducted by Peterson et al. (1975, 1978, 1981), who used catheters for monitoring cardiovascular response to noise in chair-restrained animals. Sustained blood pressure elevations were observed in response to 112-dBA bursts of noise. Although the experimenters observed that acute blood pressure response became smaller with time, there was a progressive increase in blood pressure over the 30-day exposure period of the experiment. Of course, 112-dBA noise bursts are not typical of community noise, but some industrial processes do produce noise levels this high. Noise levels of 78 dBA in another experiment produced elevated blood pressure during a similar 30-day experiment, but blood pressures returned to baseline levels when the noise ceased. As a validity check on these results, the experimenters determined that chair restraint alone has no significant effect on blood pressure for the primates tested. There is some evidence to indicate that typical community noise levels may produce a cumulative elevation of blood pressure, even if noise levels are below those generally associated with hearing damage.

Evidence of the nonauditory effects of noise on humans is usually obtained from epidemiological studies. Most studies attempting to determine a relationship between noise exposure and blood pressure elevation have established a positive correlation. An increase in incidence of hypertension and borderline hypertension with exposure time in the presence of 96-dBA workplace noise was observed by Parvispoor (1976).

In this study, borderline hypertension was defined as systolic pressure > 140 or diastolic > 90, and hypertension as systolic > 160 or diastolic > 95. Unfortunately, studies to date provide insufficient consistent quantitative data to permit prediction of blood pressure rise as a function of noise level.

Experimental studies involving humans are usually limited to an hour or so, and thus, it is difficult to determine from these studies whether or not humans adapt to noise. In a long-term study, Cantrell (1974) exposed human subjects to short 80- to 90-dB bursts of noise for 24 hours per day for 30 days. In this experiment, increases in the stress hormone cortisol and in blood cholesterol level were measured. Measurements were continued for several days after the noise bursts were terminated, and these levels were found to decrease.

5.4 SPEECH INTERFERENCE

When noise interferes with communication, it robs us of one of our most important human attributes. To quote from a report of the Environmental Protection Agency (1978c),

> Interference with speech communication by noise is among the most significant adverse effects of noise on people. Free and easy speech communication is probably essential for full development of individuals and social relations, and freedom of speech is but an empty phrase if one cannot be heard or understood because of noise.

Noise can also be a cause of industrial and transportation accidents when it prevents the hearing of warning signals.

Masking

When one sound is made inaudible by another sound, or when speech is made unintelligible by noise, the process is called masking. Although masking is almost always undesirable, broadband noise is sometimes introduced into an office environment to make conversation from an adjacent office unintelligible. Most of the intelligence in speech is contained in the frequency bands between 200 Hz and 6 kHz, while some speech sounds have frequencies lower than 200 Hz and some are higher than 6 kHz. Thus, noise in the 200-Hz to 6-kHz range is most objectionable in terms of speech masking. However, loud noise in any frequency band can adversely affect speech intelligibility by overloading the auditory system so that it cannot discriminate the speech content from the total signal presented. Consonants are particularly important in carrying information, but many consonants are pronounced softly, so that they are lost in the presence of noise.

Normal voice effort produces an unweighted sound level at 1 m of 55 to 70 dB. Sustained speech at higher voice levels tends to put a strain on the speaker. The average person, shouting with maximum voice effort, produces about 90 dB. In most cases, speech intelligibility in the presence of noise is improved if the speaker and listener are near one another and if the speaker talks louder, increasing the signal-to-noise ratio. The greatest intelligibility is usually obtained if the unweighted sound level of the speech is between 50 or 55 dB and 75 dB at 1 m from the speaker. If vocal effort is increased to produce speech levels above 75 dB, the signal-to-noise ratio will be increased, but the formation of speech sounds may be degraded so that there is little improvement in intelligibility. Intelligibility is improved when the listener is familiar with the words and dialect used. For this reason, certain critical communication including that of air controllers is based on a limited vocabulary. In ordinary communication, the listener may make use of the context in which words appear and redundancies in speech, while observing the speaker's facial expressions and gestures.

Predicting Speech Intelligibility—The Articulation Index (AI)

The articulation index is a predictor of speech intelligibility in the presence of noise (French and Steinberg, 1947; ANSI, 1969; Kryter, 1970; Johnson, 1980). Articulation index may be calculated from the levels of the masking signal and the speech signal in the frequency bands most critical to understanding of speech. The speech intelligibility contribution of each frequency band is defined as 12 dB plus the sound level of the speech minus the masking level. Each frequency band contribution is limited to the range between 0 and 30 dB. The sound level of the speech signal is based on a long-term energy average in each frequency band. Each frequency band contribution is multiplied by a weighting factor. Articulation index is given by the sum of the weighted contributions divided by 10,000.

The table that follows may be used to calculate articulation index. Column 1 gives the center frequency of the one-third octave bands critical to understanding of speech. Column 2 gives the typical male voice long-term average speech level plus 12 dB at 1-m distance. The weighting factor for each one-third octave band is given in column 3.

ARTICULATION INDEX CALCULATION
IN ONE-THIRD OCTAVE BANDS

(1) Frequency (Hz)	(2) Speech level (+12 dB)	(3) Weighting factor
200	67	4
250	68	10
315	69	10
400	70	14
500	68	14
630	66	20
800	65	20
1000	64	24
1250	62	30
1600	60	37
2000	59	37
2500	57	34
3150	55	34
4000	53	24
5000	51	20

If the levels of the masking noise have been measured in full octave bands, the following typical male voice levels (at 1 m) and weighting factors may be used.

(1) Frequency (Hz)	(2) Speech level (+12 dB)	(3) Weighting factor
250	72	18
500	73	50
1000	78	75
2000	63	107
4000	58	83

Tests have shown that articulation index may be used to give a rough estimate of the fraction of nonsense syllables that can be understood in the presence of noise. If the test is made up of phonetically balanced words (PB words), in most cases the average listener will understand a greater fraction than predicted by the articulation index. An even greater fraction of sentences will be understood due to contextual clues.

EXAMPLE PROBLEM: ARTICULATION INDEX

Find the articulation index in the presence of pink noise with a noise level contribution of 45 dB in each octave band. Assume a male speaker at typical voice level, 1 m from the listener.

Solution. The above table for AI calculation in octave bands is used. The 45-dB octave-band noise level is subtracted from the values in column 2, and weighted by the values in column 3. The resulting weighted contributions are added and divided by 10,000, giving the articulation index. The results are as follows:

(1) f	(2) Speech	(3) Weight	(4) Noise	(5)[a] (2)–(4)	(6) (5) × (3)
250	72	18	45	27	486
500	73	50	45	28	1400
1000	78	75	45	30[a]	2250
2000	63	107	45	18	1926
4000	58	83	45	13	1079

[a]Note that this value (12 dB + speech level − noise level) must fall between 0 and 30 dB.

from which

$$AI = (486 + 1400 + 2250 + 1926 + 1079)/10{,}000 = 0.714$$

Speech Interference Level

Speech interference level refers to the noise level at which different degrees of speech interference occur. Originally referred to as SIL, speech interference level was defined as the arithmetic average noise level in the three octave bands having center frequencies at 850, 1700, and 3400 Hz. Current practice uses the arithmetic average noise level in the "preferred" octave bands with center frequencies at 500, 1000, and 2000 Hz. Speech interference level so defined is referred to as PSIL. Beranek (1971) identifies the speech interference level

$$PSIL = 68 \text{ dB}$$

as the level at which reliable speech communication is barely possible in a normal male voice out of doors at 0.3-m (1-ft) distance. If a male speaker uses a raised voice, a very loud voice, or shouts, the speech interference levels become, respectively,

$$PSIL = 74, 80, \text{ and } 86 \text{ dB}$$

Using a point source model (i.e., assuming the speaker is not aided by reverberation), the following table relates PSIL to distance between talker and listener, where M refers to an average male speaker and F to an average female speaker. The table is based on barely reliable (about 60% reliable) communication of numbers and words out of context. Although articulation index cannot be directly related to speech interference level since the latter is based on only three octave bands, it is estimated that 60% reliable communication of numbers and words out of context corresponds to an articulation index of about 0.40.

PSIL (dB) AT WHICH RELIABLE SPEECH COMMUNICATION IS BARELY POSSIBLE

	PSIL (dB)							
	Voice effort							
Distance (m)	Normal		Raised		Very loud		Shouting	
	M	F	M	F	M	F	M	F
0.3	68	63	74	69	80	75	86	81
1	58	53	64	59	70	65	76	71
2	52	47	58	53	64	59	70	65
3	48	43	54	49	60	55	66	61
4	46	41	52	47	58	53	64	59

To obtain a rough approximation of speech masking levels in dBA, 7 dB may be added to the values of PSIL.

EXAMPLE PROBLEM: SPEECH INTERFERENCE LEVEL

Predicted noise levels are 60, 64, and 71 dB, respectively, in the 500-, 1000-, and 2000-Hz octave bands. Describe the implications with regard to speech interference at a distance of 1 m between talker and listener.

Solution. The arithmetic average noise level in the three octave bands is

$$(60 + 64 + 71)/3 = 65 \text{ dB}$$

Using this value in the table relating PSIL to distance and voice effort, we see that reliable speech is barely possible for a male speaker using a raised voice or a female speaker using a very loud voice.

5.5 SLEEP INTERFERENCE

Investigators have divided states of sleep into categories based on eye movement (which can be observed through closed eyelids) and electroencephalographic (EEG) criteria. Rapid eye movement (REM) accounts for about 25% of sleep time, the rest being nonrapid eye movement (NREM) sleep. NREM sleep is divided into four stages based on the frequencies of EEG tracings which range from about 1 to 16 Hz and the EEG voltages. Stage one NREM is observed when sleep begins and after momentary arousals. Sleep then proceeds through the four NREM stages in about 90 minutes and REM cycles then begin to alternate with NREM sleep. It is generally believed that both REM and NREM sleep are essential to well-being, but that NREM sleep is a restful state supporting the recuperative functions.

Certainly, sleep is crucial to health, and noise causes sleep disruption. It is difficult, however, to predict the degree of sleep disruption with accuracy because individuals vary widely in their response. In many cases, individuals are awakened by noise and some people, particularly the elderly, have great difficulty returning to sleep. In other cases, noise causes undesirable changes in sleep stages, interfering with the restorative function of sleep.

A study of apartment residents near major Moscow traffic arteries indicates the influence of noise on sleep patterns (Karagodina, 1974). It was found that the time required to go to sleep increased by as much as one to 1.5 hours at noise levels of 50 to 60 dBA. The research indicated that the depth of sleep decreased by 60%, and that after awakening, people felt tired and had headaches. Sleeping criteria were determined to be normal at noise levels not exceeding 30 to 35 dBA. At the lower noise levels, an average of 15 to 20 minutes was required to fall asleep and the state-of-sleep level criterion was judged to be 85%.

An extensive study of residents living under flightpaths of Heathrow Airport near London included an examination of sleep disturbance (Committee on the problem of noise, 1963; FAA, 1977). The percentage of residents disturbed was determined as a function of noise exposure forecast (NEF) based on the following descriptions of the effect of the noise:

1. Startles.
2. Keeps from going to sleep.
3. Wakes up.
4. Disturbs rest or relaxation.

NEF is a prediction or assessment of outdoor noise based on the number, type, and flight pattern of aircraft overflying the area. Figure 5.5.1 shows the percent of residents disturbed plotted against NEF and day–night sound level L_{DN}. This plot is based on the report data where the following approximate conversion relationship has been used:

$$L_{DN} = NEF + 35 \text{ dB}A \tag{5.5.1}$$

By definition, L_{DN} is determined by calculating equivalent sound level L_{eq} after adding 10 dBA to noise levels between the hours of 10 P.M. and 7 A.M. The NEF to L_{DN} conversion cannot be precise, but will be accurate to within about ±3 dBA in most

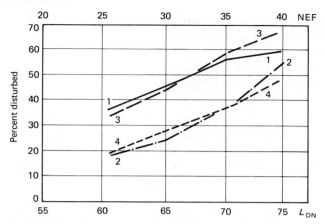

Figure 5.5.1 Percentage of residents disturbed as a function of noise exposure forecast (NEF) and day–night sound level (L_{DN}).
Key:
(1) Startles,
(2) Keeps from going to sleep,
(3) Wakes up, and
(4) Disturbs rest or relaxation.
(*Source:* FAA (1977))

cases. If the plot is used to predict community response to noise sources other than aircraft, prediction validity will be further diminished.

If indoor noise patterns are predicted or measured, then Figure 5.5.2 may be used to estimate awakening response to sounds of brief duration (EPA, 1971d). Variation in the content of the awakening sound and background sound level are among the causes of the wide variation in awakening response. The noise reduction between outdoor sound level and indoor sound level is typically between 10 and 20 dBA.

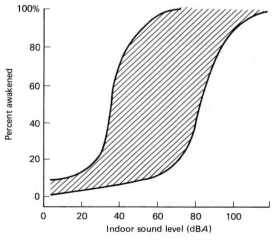

Figure 5.5.2 Awakening response to brief indoor sound levels. (*Source:* EPA (1971))

5.6 ENVIRONMENTAL PROTECTION AGENCY IDENTIFIED VALUES OF EQUIVALENT SOUND LEVEL AND DAY–NIGHT SOUND LEVEL

The Noise Control Act of 1972 established a national policy ". . . to promote an environment for all Americans free from noise that jeopardizes their public health and welfare." The responses to this statuatory mandate included the EPA "levels documents" (1974, 1978a). The principal criteria used in these documents are protection against hearing loss and activity interference. Equivalent sound level and day–night sound level are the principal descriptors used to identify protective levels.

Equivalent Sound Level L_{eq}

Equivalent sound level is the energy average sound level over a given time period. For time period T, equivalent sound level may be computed from

$$L_{eq} = 10 \lg\left(\frac{1}{T} \int_0^T \frac{p^2}{p_{ref}^2} \, dt\right) \tag{5.6.1}$$

where $p^2 = p^2(t)$ is the mean-square (time-varying) sound pressure
$p_{ref} = 20 \times 10^{-6}$ Pa if L_{eq} is to be in dB unweighted

It is usually more convenient to express L_{eq} in terms of sound level $L = L(t)$ using the relationship

$$\frac{p^2}{p_{ref}^2} = 10^{L/10} \tag{5.6.2}$$

from which

$$L_{eq} = 10 \lg\left(\frac{1}{T} \int_0^T 10^{L/10} \, dt\right) \tag{5.6.3}$$

If an integrating sound level meter is used, equivalent sound level may be calculated automatically for a set interval. The EPA levels documents and many other standards call for L_{eq} to be expressed in dBA, in which case all sound level readings are taken using the A-weighting network. When equivalent sound level must be calculated from n equally representative readings, the integral form is replaced by the following summation:

$$L_{eq} = 10 \lg\left(\frac{1}{n} \sum_{i=1}^{n} 10^{L_i/10}\right) \tag{5.6.4}$$

The above summation also applies when an integrating sound level meter or analyzer computes L_{eq} digitally from discrete samples.

One should specify the time period over which L_{eq} is measured or predicted. Thus, we may identify $L_{eq(8hr)}$ for a typical 8-hour workday. EPA identified levels based on hearing conservation and outdoor activity interference are given in terms of annual averages, equivalent to a typical 24-hour day, for which we may use the symbols L_{eq24}.

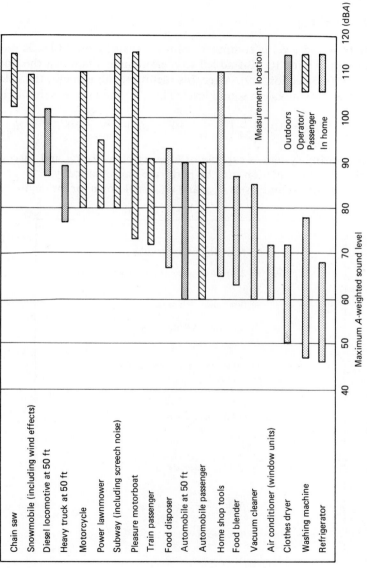

Figure 5.6.1 Typical range of common sounds. (*Source:* EPA (1978))

The ranges of maximum sound level for some common contributors to community noise are shown in Figure 5.6.1. Determination of equivalent sound level requires additional information such as exposure time and source and observer location.

Day–Night Sound Level L_{DN}

Day–night sound level is computed from A-weighted sound levels measured over a 24-hour period with 10 dBA added to measurements between the hours of 10 P.M. and 7 A.M. (see Section 1.9). After this nighttime adjustment, the calculation is the same as that for equivalent sound level. Thus, if time t is measured in hours, we have

$$L_{DN} = 10 \lg\left[\frac{1}{24}\left(\int_{7A.M.}^{10P.M.} 10^{L/10}\, dt + \int_{10P.M.}^{7A.M.} 10^{(L+10)/10}\, dt\right)\right] \quad (5.6.5)$$

If the measuring system is capable of long-term averaging and incorporates a time clock, the above calculation may be performed automatically.

If equivalent sound levels L_{eqD} and L_{eqN} are known for the daytime and nighttime

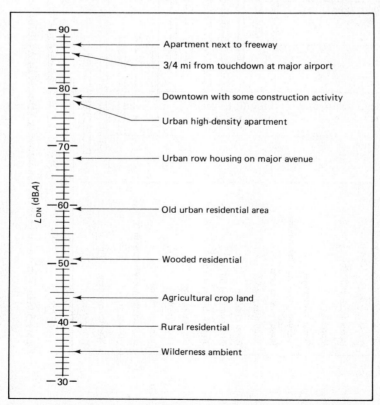

Figure 5.6.2 Examples of outdoor day–night sound levels in dBA measured at various locations. (*Source:* EPA (1978))

periods, respectively, then the following equation may be used to calculate day–night sound level:

$$L_{DN} = 10 \lg\left[\frac{1}{24}(15 \times 10^{L_{eqD}/10} + 9 \times 10^{(L_{eqN}+10)/10}\right] \qquad (5.6.6)$$

This equation may be useful if it is necessary to estimate day–night sound level from representative measurements taken during the 7 A.M. to 10 P.M. and 10 P.M. to 7 A.M. periods. EPA-identified levels relating to activity interference and annoyance indoors and outdoors where quiet is a basis for use utilize L_{DN}. Figure 5.6.2 shows typical outdoor day–night sound levels measured at various locations.

Activity Interference and Annoyance

The Environmental Protection Agency (1978a) includes ". . . personal comfort and well-being, and the absence of mental anguish, disturbances and annoyance as well as the absence of clinical symptoms such as hearing loss or demonstrable physiological injury" in its definition of public health and welfare, identifying noise annoyance as "any negative subjective reaction to noise on the part of an individual or group." Annoyance is not considered an inability to cope with stress, but an indication of transient, or possibly lasting stress beyond the individual's conscious control.

Indoor Noise Level Based on Speech Intelligibility as a Surrogate for Annoyance

Although annoyance is difficult to predict, and even difficult to describe quantitatively, speech interference can be related to noise level with reasonable certainty. The Environmental Protection Agency has selected the criteria of 100% sentence intelligibility inside buildings and 95% outdoor sentence intelligibility at 3 m. The relationship between sentence intelligibility (indoors) and steady A-weighted background noise level is as follows:

SENTENCE INTELLIGIBILITY INDOORS
IN THE PRESENCE OF NOISE

Sentence intelligibility (%)	80	95	99	100
Noise level (dBA)	69	64	54	45

The above table assumes the speaker uses a normal voice, the listener has normal hearing, and the conversation takes place in a typical living room. Due to reverberation, the speech level will be fairly constant throughout the room. Note that sentence intelligibility relies on identifying words in context, and that noise levels are expressed in dBA. For these reasons, the data in the above table are not directly comparable to articulation index and speech interference level data.

The EPA identified level for indoor activity interference and annoyance is 45 dBA, corresponding to 100% sentence intelligibility. This decision was based on the observation that annoyance due to noise often resulted from interruption of listening-

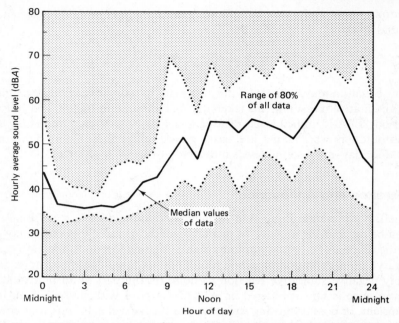

Figure 5.6.3   Time pattern of hourly indoor residential sound levels. (*Source:* EPA (1978))

related activities. The identified levels are based on the energy averages: equivalent sound level and day–night sound level. Considering the importance of sleep during the hours of 10 P.M. and 7 A.M., the identified level for indoor residential areas is

$$L_{DN} \leq 45 \text{ dB}A$$

For other indoor areas with human activities, the identified level is

$$L_{eq24} \leq 45 \text{ dB}A$$

Unfortunately, the identified level is currently exceeded most of the day in most residences. Figure 5.6.3 shows hourly equivalent sound level in residences plotted against time of day (EPA, 1978a). Median, tenth percentile, and ninetieth percentile data are shown. These measurements, however, include noise generated within the residences due to human activities as well as intrusive noise.

Outdoor Levels

The table that follows relates steady noise level in dBA to required voice effort at various distances between talker and listener for 95% sentence intelligibility.

STEADY NOISE LEVELS IN dBA THAT ALLOW
95% SENTENCE INTELLIGIBILITY

Distance (m)	0.5	1	2	3	4	5
Normal voice	72	66	60	56	54	52
Raised voice	78	72	66	62	60	58

Identified levels for outdoor activity interference and annoyance are

$$L_{DN} \leq 55 \text{ dB}A$$

for residential areas and farms where quiet is a basis for use, and

$$L_{eq24} \leq 55 \text{ dB}A$$

for other outdoor areas where people spend limited amounts of time. At these levels, the following effects could be expected:

1. Average outdoor sentence intelligibility of 100% at 0.35 m, 99% at 1 m, and 95% at 3.5 m.
2. A probable 17% annoyance level and 1% complaint level, depending on community attitude and other factors in addition to noise level.
3. A typical indoor intrusive noise level of $L_{DN} \leq 40 \text{ dB}A$.

This value is based on a 15-dBA noise level reduction between outdoor and indoor noise, assuming there are no significant indoor noise sources. This would provide an average sentence intelligibility of 100% indoors with a 5-dBA margin of safety. The approximate national average noise level reduction for buildings with windows open is 15 dBA; it is 25 dBA for closed windows.

The identified outdoor day–night sound level is exceeded in many urban areas. The following table shows estimated percentages of the 135 million urban Americans living in areas subject to various ranges of day–night sound level due to traffic noise.

DAY–NIGHT SOUND LEVEL
DUE TO TRAFFIC VERSUS
PERCENT OF
URBAN POPULATION

L_{DN} (dBA)	Population (%)
Below 48	13
48 to 53	12
53 to 58	21
58 to 63	28
63 to 68	19
Above 68	7

Figure 5.6.4 shows outdoor day–night sound levels plotted against the cumulative number of people in urban areas potentially exposed to these levels. Of course, actual individual noise exposure depends on building design and individual routines including the time spent out of doors.

Summary of Identified Levels

Environmental noise levels identified for protection of public health and welfare are summarized below.

YEARLY VALUES OF EQUIVALENT SOUND LEVEL AND DAY–NIGHT SOUND
LEVEL THAT PROTECT PUBLIC HEALTH AND WELFARE
WITH A MARGIN OF SAFETY

Effect	Level	Area
Hearing	$L_{eq24} \leq 70$ dBA	All areas (at the ear)
Outdoor activity interference and annoyance	$L_{DN} \leq 55$ dBA	Outdoors in residential areas and farms and other areas where quiet is a basis for use
	$L_{eq24} \leq 55$ dBA	Outdoor areas where people spend limited amounts of time, such as school yards, etc.
Indoor activity interference and annoyance	$L_{DN} \leq 45$ dBA	Indoor residential areas
	$L_{eq24} \leq 45$ dBA	Other indoor areas with human activities such as schools, etc.

Source: E.P.A. (1978a).

EXAMPLE PROBLEM: ENVIRONMENTAL EVALUATION BASED ON DAY–NIGHT SOUND LEVEL AND EQUIVALENT SOUND LEVEL

Outdoor noise was measured with an integrating sound level meter at five different
times during the 7 A.M. to 10 P.M. period. In each case, equivalent sound level was
determined for a 15-minute period, and it is assumed that the five values together are

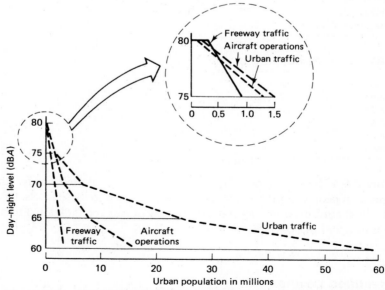

Figure 5.6.4 Cumulative number of people in urban areas exposed to outdoor day–night sound
levels from different sources. (*Source:* EPA (1978))

representative of daytime noise. The following individual daytime values were recorded: L_{eq} = 45, 55, 56, 54, and 50 dBA. Similar representative measurements were made three times during the 10 P.M. to 7 A.M. period. The recorded nighttime values were L_{eq} = 54, 45, and 35 dBA.

Compute:

(a) Outdoor L_{eq24}.

(b) Outdoor L_{DN}.

(c) Estimate indoor values.

(d) Evaluate the results in terms of hearing, speech interference, and indoor and outdoor activity interference and annoyance.

Solution. (a) Since the number of readings in each period is proportional to the period length, we may combine all of the readings in an energy average as follows:

$$L_{eq} = 10 \lg\left(\frac{1}{n} \sum_{i=1}^{n} 10^{L_i/10}\right)$$

$$= 10 \lg\left[\frac{1}{8}(10^{45/10} + 10^{55/10} + \text{etc.})\right]$$

$$= 52.4 \text{ dB}A$$

(b) Using the equation from part (a) for the five daytime measurements, the result is

$$L_{eqD} = 10 \lg\left[\frac{1}{5}(10^{45/10} + 10^{55/10} + \text{etc.})\right]$$

$$= 53.4 \text{ dB}A$$

and for the three nighttime measurements

$$L_{eqN} = 10 \lg\left[\frac{1}{3}(10^{54/10} + 10^{45/10} + 10^{35/10})\right]$$

$$= 49.8 \text{ dB}A$$

If the ratio of the number of nighttime readings to daytime readings had not been equal to 9/15, 24-hour equivalent sound level would have been calculated from the following equation:

$$L_{eq24} = 10 \lg\left[\frac{1}{24}(15 \times 10^{L_{eqD}/10} + 9 \times 10^{L_{eqN}/10})\right]$$

from which

$$L_{eq24} = 10 \lg\left[\frac{1}{24}(15 \times 10^{53.4/10} + 9 \times 10^{49.8/10})\right]$$

$$= 52.4 \text{ dB}A$$

just as in part (a) since the ratio is satisfied. Day–night sound level is calculated in a similar manner, except that nighttime measurements are adjusted by 10 dBA, yielding

$$L_{DN} = 10 \lg\left[\frac{1}{24}\,(15 \times 10^{L_{eqD}/10} + 9 \times 10^{(L_{eqN}+10)/10})\right]$$

$$= 10 \lg\left[\frac{1}{24}\,(15 \times 10^{53.4/10} + 9 \times 10^{(48.9+10)/10})\right]$$

$$= 56.9 \text{ dB}A$$

(c) Intrusive noise levels depend on a number of factors including building construction and whether the windows are open or closed. With closed windows, the typical sound reduction is about 24 dBA in warm climates and 27 dBA in cold climates with a national average of 25 dBA. The additional sound reduction in cold climates is largely due to the use of storm windows or double glazing. When windows are open, the sound energy entering by other sound transmission paths is usually insignificant when compared to the sound energy that enters through the open windows. Typical sound reduction values range from 12 to 17 dBA with open windows, with a national average of 15 dBA. If we use the open-window average value, indoor intrusive noise levels are given by

$$L_{eq24} = 52.4 - 15 = 37.4 \text{ dB}A$$

and

$$L_{DN} = 56.9 - 15 = 41.9 \text{ dB}A$$

Any noise generated indoors would have to be combined with the intrusive noise levels.

(d) Using the criterion:

$$L_{eq24} \le 70 \text{ dB}A$$

we see that there is no problem with regard to hearing conservation.

If indoor-generated noise is not considered, then the identified levels for indoor activity interference and annoyance,

$$L_{DN} \le 45 \text{ dB}A \text{ and } L_{eq24} \le 45 \text{ dB}A$$

are not exceeded by the estimated indoor levels. If the outdoor area is one in which people spend limited amounts of time, then outdoor levels do not exceed the identified level

$$L_{eq24} \le 55 \text{ dB}A$$

However, the calculated day–night sound level

$$L_{DN} = 56.9 \text{ dB}A$$

falls above the range

$$L_{DN} \le 55 \text{ dB}A$$

identified as protective of public health and welfare with a margin of safety for residential and similar areas.

5.7 PREDICTION AND CONTROL OF CONSTRUCTION NOISE

When considering the environmental impact of a proposed project, construction noise is sometimes ignored because it is of a temporary nature. However, construction of a high-rise structure may result in exposure of nearby residents to objectionable noise levels for a year or two. In some areas, urban renewal construction, renovation, and street and utility construction and repair projects may follow one upon the other so that reasonably quiet days are rare.

Construction Equipment

Diesel engines are commonly used to provide motive and/or operating power to construction equipment, but some equipment is powered by spark ignition (gasoline) engines and electric motors. The range of peak or maximum-power noise levels for various models of construction equipment is given in Table 5.7.1 (Reagan and Grant, 1977; EPA, 1974; BBN/EPA, 1971).

The data in Tables 5.7.1 and 5.7.2 may be used to make rough predictions of construction noise. However, other equipment models may produce noise levels outside of the indicated ranges.

Construction Equipment Noise Sources

Engine-powered construction equipment includes mobile earth-moving equipment, partly mobile materials-handling equipment, and stationary equipment. Noise contributions include equipment noise generated by the engine, the transmission, and other components, and process noise (the jackhammer striking the pavement, etc).

Earth-moving Equipment Earth-moving equipment includes excavating machinery (backhoes, dozers shovels, etc.) and specialized highway building equipment (compacters, graders, scrapers, and pavers). Engine noise usually makes the greatest contribution to equipment noise, with exhaust noise most prominent. Other earth-moving equipment noise contributions include inlet noise, structural noise, cooling fan noise, and mechanical and hydraulic transmission noise. When exhaust noise predominates, muffler improvements can make the most significant noise reduction. Process noise is difficult to control, sometimes requiring a change in operating procedures or a complete change in equipment design.

Materials-Handling Equipment Most materials-handling equipment is more or less fixed at a particular work location when operating. If the location is behind a substantial construction fence, this barrier may provide some noise abatement. Engine noise tends to dominate, but power transmissions, working mechanisms, and process noise

TABLE 5.7.1 CONSTRUCTION EQUIPMENT NOISE LEVELS
AT MAXIMUM POWER

Equipment type	Noise level (dBA)	Distance (m)
Earth moving		
Backhoes	74 to 92	15
Front loaders	75 to 96	15
Dozers	70 to 95	15
Graders	72 to 92	15
Scrapers	76 to 98	15
Tractors	76 to 96	15
Pavers	85 to 90	15
Trucks	83 to 95	15
Materials handling		
Concrete mixers	74 to 87	15
Concrete pumps	80 to 85	15
Movable cranes	70 to 84	15
Derrick cranes	85 to 90	15
Stationary		
Pumps	68 to 78	15
Generators	70 to 84	15
Compressors	64 to 87	15
Impact		
Pneumatic wrenches	82 to 88	15
Jackhammers and rock drills	80 to 98	15
Pile drivers (peak noise)	94 to 106	15
Other equipment		
Vibrators	68 to 82	15
Saws	72 to 82	15

sources also contribute. One source of process noise is the aggregate striking the metal parts of a concrete mixer. The most effective noise control measure is likely to be engine noise reduction, particularly improved muffling of engine exhaust.

TABLE 5.7.2 AVERAGE NOISE LEVELS OF AIR COMPRESSORS

Type	Engine	Flow (ft^3/min)	Pressure (psi)	Silenced or standard	Distance (m)	Noise level (dBA)
Reciprocal	Diesel	160 to 330	100 to 105	Standard	7	80 to 84
Reciprocal	Diesel	125 to 170	100 to 850	Silenced	7	70 to 74
Reciprocal	Gasoline	85	100	Silenced	7	76
Rotary-screw	Diesel	750 to 1200	100	Silenced	7	73 to 78
Rotary-screw	Gasoline	185		Silenced	7	77
Rotary-screw	Diesel	750 to 1200	125	Standard	7	88 to 93
Rotary-screw	Gasoline	175	100	Standard	7	88
Vane	Gasoline	85	100	Standard	7	82
Vane	Gasoline	160	100	Silenced	7	74

Stationary Equipment Engine noise is also a major contributor to the total noise output of stationary equipment. Enclosures should be considered as a means of noise control, particularly for small, fixed equipment. Cooling fan selection is important since an enclosure may complicate the problem of engine cooling. It is possible to design very effective reactive (impedance mismatch) mufflers for electric power generators and other equipment that runs at nearly constant speed.

Impact Equipment Process noise is often dominant in impact equipment. Examples of process noise include the impact noise generated by the hammer of a pile driver striking a pile, and the impact of a tool bit striking the work in the case of a rock drill or jackhammer. Engine-driven equipment may produce significant engine noise as well, and high-pressure exhaust noise must be considered when pneumatic equipment is used. Pneumatic hand tools are designed to be small and light, thus limiting the size of air-exhaust mufflers. Since process noise is difficult to control at the source, noise barriers enclosing the work area should be considered. In some cases, other tools may be substituted for impact tools. For example, vibratory (or sonic) pile drivers that vibrate the pile at resonance are practical in some types of soil. The vibration frequency is about 150 Hz and the sound level is well below that of an impact pile driver. Referring to Chapter 1, we see that the A-weighted auditory responses (relative to 1 kHz) for the 125-Hz and 160-Hz one-third octave bands are -16.1 dB and -13.4 dB, respectively. Thus, soft sounds in this frequency range are not perceived as strongly as midrange sounds (800 Hz to 8 kHz).

General Considerations for Prediction and Control of Construction Noise

Noise control should be considered in all construction projects. The following steps may be included in a study.

Predict or Survey Noise Levels The optimum time to consider construction noise is when a project is in the planning stage. Noise predictions can be made on the basis of the type of equipment, the usage factor for the equipment, and the location relative to dwellings and other noise-sensitive activities. If construction is already underway, a noise survey may be made at the construction site and at nearby property lines. Individual equipment noise contributions and hours of use should be identified. In either case, noise exposure of equipment operators and other workers should be considered as well as community noise. The results of a survey will be more representative of actual conditions than the results of a predictive study. However, once construction has begun, noise control options are limited, since it may not be feasible to change equipment and alter construction methods.

Determine Whether or Not a Problem Exists The noise prediction study or survey will indicate whether or not there is a noise problem. Even if community noise levels are acceptable, it is likely that some or all of the construction workers will be at risk of hearing damage. The results of the study or survey may be used to determine the need for personal hearing protection, and the potential benefits of equipment noise reduction.

Identify Major Noise Contributors Assuming a community noise problem exists, the next step is to determine the contribution of various pieces of equipment to equivalent sound level or day–night sound level. Table 5.7.3 shows representative noise data and usage factors for various pieces of construction equipment. As indicated in a preceding table, noise levels of individual pieces of equipment may vary by several dBA from these typical values. The usage factor is the part of the workday that a given piece of

TABLE 5.7.3 IMMEDIATE ABATEMENT POTENTIAL OF
CONSTRUCTION EQUIPMENT

	Noise level (dBA) at 50 ft		Important noise sources[b]					Usage[c]
Equipment	Present	With feasible noise control[a]						
			Earth moving					
Front loader	79	75	E	C	F	I	H	0.4
Backhoes	85	75	E	C	F	I	H	0.16
Dozers	80	75	E	C	F	I	H	0.4
Tractors	80	75	E	C	F	I	W	0.4
Scrapers	88	80	E	C	F	I	W	0.4
Graders	85	75	E	C	F	I	W	0.08
Truck	91	75	E	C	F	I	T	0.4
Paver	89	80	E	C	F	I		0.1
			Materials handling					
Concrete mixer	85	75	E	C	F	W	T	0.4
Concrete pump	82	75	E	C	H			0.4
Crane	83	75	E	C	F	I	T	0.16
Derrick	88	75	E	C	F	I	T	0.16
			Stationary					
Pumps	76	75	E	C				1.0
Generators	78	75	E	C				1.0
Compressors	81	75	E	C	H	I		1.0
			Impact					
Pile drivers	101	95	W	P	E			0.04
Jackhammers	88	75	P	W	E	C		0.1
Rock drills	98	80	W	E	P			0.04
Pneumatic tools	86	80	P	W	E	C		0.16
			Other					
Saws	78	75	W					0.04
Vibrator	76	75	W	E	C			0.4

[a] Estimated levels obtainable by selecting quieter procedures or machines and implementing noise control features requiring no major redesign or extreme cost.

[b] In order of importance:

T	Power transmission system, gearing	F	Cooling fan
C	Engine casing	W	Tool–work interaction
E	Engine exhaust	H	Hydraulics
P	Pneumatic exhaust	I	Engine intake

[c] Proportion of time equipment is operating at noisiest mode in most used phase on site.

Source: EPA (1971b).

equipment is expected to produce the indicated noise level. Pumps, generators, and compressors have a typical use factor of 1.0 since they ordinarily run continuously during the entire workday.

Consider a construction project employing a scraper, a jackhammer, and a saw, producing the noise levels indicated in Table 5.7.3. If each piece of equipment is equidistant from the observer (a residence or other sensitive use), then noise contributions depend on noise level and usage factor. The scraper, producing an estimated 88 dBA at 50 ft (about 15 meters) with a usage factor of 0.4, is obviously the greatest contributor to noise at the receiver, and attempts at noise control should begin with this piece of equipment. In order of importance, typical scraper noise sources are the engine exhaust, engine casing, cooling fan, engine intake, and the work–tool interaction (process noise). The jackhammer with a lower usage factor would be considered next. The saw, with a 10-dBA lower noise level is used only about 4% of the workday. As a result, the saw contributes only 1/100th of the energy contributed by the scraper.

Reduce the Noise Levels to Acceptable Values   Noise reduction will be considered in general terms at this point; details are treated in other sections. Reduction of noise energy at the source, interruption of noise transmission paths, and reduction of noise at the receiver are among the options. The first option would lead to further investigation of the principal noise sources. In the simple example above, the next step would be examination of the possibility of an improved engine exhaust muffler for the scraper, then noise reduction in other components of the scraper and jackhammer. Since the contribution of the saw to total noise energy is small in this example, noise reduction in the saw would not result in a significant improvement in community noise levels. However, design of quieter saws would reduce operator hearing damage risk.

Temporary construction fences are usually required to prevent injury due to unauthorized access to construction sites. If the fence is solid (without holes and gaps) and of sufficient mass, then it serves as a noise barrier, interrupting noise transmission paths to the community. If barrier mass per unit area is about 20 kg/m^2 (about 4 lb/ft^2) noise transmission through the barrier will be small compared with diffracted noise. Barrier design is discussed in Chapter 2. In some instances, workers are protected in noise-reducing enclosures. However, worker mobility makes this solution impractical at most construction sites. Thus, if noise reduction at the source does not result in acceptable operator levels, then noise reduction at the receiver is necessary. Personal hearing protection devices (HPD's) of the insert or earmuff type, or both, are indicated due to the high noise exposure of most construction workers. Obviously, HPD's are not a satisfactory solution to community noise problems.

Changes in work-time patterns can also reduce community noise impact. If day–night noise level is used as a descriptor for community noise, then there is a 10-dBA penalty during the period from 10 P.M. and 7 A.M. Construction activity in residential and other sensitive areas should be avoided during these hours unless it is of an emergency nature such as repair of broken water or sewer lines or other essential utilities.

EXAMPLE PROBLEM: PREDICTION AND CONTROL OF CONSTRUCTION NOISE

A proposed construction project will employ two dozers, three construction trucks, and one each backhoe, tractor, front loader, concrete mixer, generator, and compressor.

The generator and compressor will be located about 75 ft from the nearest residential property lines and the other equipment will be at about 100 ft. The proposal calls for a chain-link security fence which will surround the construction site. It is planned that construction will begin at 6 A.M. daily and end at 6 P.M. with a 1-hour lunch break.

(a) Predict the noise impact on the nearest residential area.

Solution. It would be desirable to have noise data based on tests of a prototype of each piece of equipment. For this example, it will be assumed that the values (for equipment without noise control improvements) given in Table 5.7.3 apply. The usage factors given in that table will be used also. Table 5.7.4 lists the equipment, the number of each type, the distance to the nearest residential property line in feet, the sound level in dBA at 50 ft, and the usage factor. These data are followed by adjustments in dBA for number, distance, and usage. The distances to the nearby property line are large enough to allow use of a point-source approximation. Directivity is not considered since equipment orientation varies.

Sound level adjustments are as follows:

$$L_2 - L_1 = 20 \lg\left(\frac{r_1}{r_2}\right) \qquad \text{(the distance adjustment)}$$

$$10 \lg n \qquad \text{(the number adjustment)}$$

$$10 \lg u \qquad \text{(the usage factor adjustment)}$$

for n pieces of a given equipment type with usage factor u. The algebraic sum of the sound level at the 50-ft test distance and the adjustments produces the contribution of each type of equipment to workday equivalent sound level at the property line.

The sound levels used for this example are based on equipment with standard mufflers, but without any special noise control improvements. Combining the noise contributions of all the equipment, we obtain

$$L_{eq11} = 87.4 \text{ dB}A$$

TABLE 5.7.4 EXAMPLE PROBLEM: PREDICTION AND CONTROL OF CONSTRUCTION NOISE

Source	Dozer	Truck	Backhoe	Tractor	Front loader	Concrete mixer	Generator	Compressor
Number	2	3	1	1	1	1	1	1
Distance	100	100	100	100	100	100	75	75
L, 50 ft	80	91	85	80	79	85	78	81
Usage	0.4	0.4	0.16	0.4	0.4	0.4	1	1
Adjustment								
Number	3	4.8	0	0	0	0	0	0
Distance	−6	−6	−6	−6	−6	−6	−3.5	−3.5
Usage	−4	−4	−8	−4	−4	−4	0	0
L_{eq} contr	73	85.8	71	70	69	75	74.5	77.5
I/I_{ref}	2.00E7*	3.8E8	1.26E7	1.E7	7.94E6	3.16E7	2.82E7	5.62E7
Total	Workday		5.47E8					
L_{eq} (dBA)	Workday		87.4					

*Note: 2.00E7 = 2.00 × 10^7, etc.

for the 11-hour workday. In this problem noise levels are rounded off to 0.1 dBA using the integer function

$$L = \text{int}(10L + 0.5)/10$$

In order to convert the results to 24-hour equivalent sound level, we assume that there is no significant noise generated outside of the work hours. Then, the average scalar sound intensity is 11/24ths of the sound intensity computed above or, in terms of sound level,

$$L_{eq} = 10 \lg\left(\frac{1}{T} \int_0^T 10^{L/10} \, dt\right) \tag{5.6.3}$$

from which

$$L_{eq24} = 10 \lg\left(\frac{1}{24} \times 11 \times 10^{L_{eq11}/10}\right)$$

$$= L_{eq11} + 10 \lg\left(\frac{11}{24}\right)$$

$$= 87.4 - 3.4 = 84 \text{ dB}A$$

Daytime equivalent sound level, the energy average sound level for the 15-hour daytime period beginning at 7 A.M., is defined as follows:

$$L_{eqD} = 10 \lg\left(\frac{1}{15} \int_{7\text{A.M.}}^{10\text{P.M.}} 10^{L/10} \, dt\right)$$

Nighttime equivalent sound level is defined by

$$L_{eqN} = 10 \lg\left(\frac{1}{9} \int_{10\text{P.M.}}^{7\text{A.M.}} 10^{L/10} \, dt\right)$$

Noting that 10 hours of the proposed work day fall in the daytime period and 1 hour in the nighttime period, we have

$$L_{eqD} = L_{eq11} + 10 \lg\left(\frac{10}{15}\right)$$

$$= 87.4 - 1.8 = 85.6 \text{ dB}A$$

and

$$L_{eqN} = L_{eq11} + 10 \lg\left(\frac{1}{9}\right)$$

$$= 87.4 - 9.5 = 77.9 \text{ dB}A$$

Day–night sound level may be found from

$$L_{DN} = 10 \lg\left[\frac{1}{24}\left(15 \times 10^{L_{eqD}/10} + 9 \times 10^{(L_{eqN}+10)/10}\right)\right] \tag{5.6.6}$$

For the equipment without noise control improvements, the day–night sound level is

$$L_{DN} = 10 \lg\left[\frac{1}{24}\,(15 \times 10^{85.6/10} + 9 \times 10^{(77.9+10)/10})\right]$$

$$= 86.6 \text{ dB}A$$

The following alternative calculation would have produced the same result:

$$L_{DN} = 10 \lg\left[\frac{1}{24}\,(10 \times 10^{87.4/10} + 1 \times 10^{(87.4+10)/10})\right]$$

The day–night noise level predicted in this example is unacceptable for a residential area. Furthermore, the construction workers would be exposed to equivalent sound levels much higher than those calculated above, because they would be nearer to the equipment. Even with personal hearing protection devices, construction worker noise exposure might lead to hearing damage.

(b) Recommend changes that would be most effective in reducing predicted sound levels.

Solution. Tabulation of results enables us to determine the greatest contributors to noise level at the property line. If the calculation is done by computer, a spreadsheet program may be written or purchased to aid in the solution. This permits us to say "What if we move the generator and select a truck with a better muffler?" The spreadsheet software immediately recalculates all affected values and updates results to show the effectiveness of the proposed change. Only eight types of equipment are included in this illustrative example. However, spreadsheet programs are available to handle hundreds of columns and rows of data and calculations, reducing the time required to examine situations where many types of equipment are involved.

The tabulated results in this example show that the dozers, trucks, concrete mixer, generator, and compressor make the greatest contributions to equivalent sound level at the residential property line. Table 5.7.3 shows estimates of noise levels that may be attained by implementing noise control procedures and features requiring no major redesign. The engine exhaust, engine casing, and cooling fan are the most important noise sources in dozers, trucks, and concrete mixers. Therefore, it is recommended that the two dozers, the three trucks, and the concrete mixer be modified or replaced with quieter models. In addition, it is recommended that the compressor and generator be moved to 125 ft from the nearest property line.

These changes and their effects are shown in Table 5.7.5. The equivalent sound level for the 11-hour workday will be reduced from 87.4 to 79 dBA if the suggested changes are implemented. Converting to a 24-hour equivalent sound level, we have

$$L_{eq24} = L_{eq11} + 10 \lg\left(\frac{11}{24}\right)$$

$$= 79 - 3.4 = 75.6 \text{ dB}A$$

TABLE 5.7.5　CONSTRUCTION NOISE AFTER EQUIPMENT MODIFICATION

Source	Dozer	Truck	Backhoe	Tractor	Front loader	Concrete mixer	Generator	Compressor
Number	2	3	1	1	1	1	1	1
Distance	100	100	100	100	100	100	125	125
L, 50 ft	75	75	85	80	79	75	78	81
Usage	0.4	0.4	0.16	0.4	0.4	0.4	1	1
Adjustment								
Number	3	4.8	0	0	0	0	0	0
Distance	−6	−6	−6	−6	−6	−6	−8	−8
Usage	−4	−4	−8	−4	−4	−4	0	0
L_{eq} contribution	68	69.8	71	70	69	65	70	73
I/I_{ref}	6.3E6	9.55E6	1.26E7	1.E7	7.94E6	3.16E6	1.E7	2.00E7
Total	Workday		7.95E7					
L_{eq} (dBA)	Workday		79					

For the 15-hour daytime period which includes 10 of the workday hours,

$$L_{eqD} = L_{eq11} + 10 \lg\left(\frac{10}{15}\right)$$

$$= 79 - 1.8 = 77.2 \text{ dB}A$$

For the 9-hour nighttime period which includes 1 hour of construction,

$$L_{eqN} = L_{eq11} + 10 \lg\left(\frac{1}{9}\right)$$

$$= 79 - 9.5 = 69.5 \text{ dB}A$$

Day–night equivalent sound level is given by

$$L_{DN} = 10 \lg\left[\frac{1}{24}\left(15 \times 10^{75.6/10} + 9 \times 10^{(69.5+10)/10}\right)\right]$$

$$= 78.2 \text{ dB}A$$

after implementing feasible noise control procedures on some equipment and moving other equipment.

　　In the solution up to this point, we have considered reduction of noise energy at the source and taken advantage of the effect of distance (the inverse square law). An administrative change should be considered as well. If work is started at 7 A.M. each day instead of 6 A.M., while maintaining the 11-hour workday, there will be no change in total sound energy. Thus, equivalent sound level

$$L_{eq24} = 75.6 \text{ dB}A$$

as above. However, by eliminating the nighttime noise contribution, day–night sound level is reduced to the 24-hour equivalent sound level

$$L_{DN} = L_{eq24} = 75.6 \text{ dB}A$$

Obviously, this change in starting time will have no effect on hearing conservation, but will reduce annoyance due to early morning construction noise.

Another method of noise control involves interruption of sound transmission paths. A solid, continuous construction fence on the sides of the construction site facing the residences would serve as a noise barrier. Although the barrier would not reduce noise exposure of workers at the site, it would substantially reduce community noise. The noise attenuation due to the barrier depends on its mass and the Fresnel number which, in turn, depends on the dominant frequencies of the construction equipment, barrier height and location, and site terrain. The calculation procedure is given in a previous section on noise barriers.

5.8 REGULATORY MEASURES TO CONTROL COMMUNITY NOISE

Regulatory measures and program tools for noise control are exercised by national, state, and local governments, with some additional control measures by consumers, industry, and standards organizations. Some national standards preempt state and local standards. The effectiveness of regulatory measures is sometimes reduced by a lack of coordination between various levels of government. The following are examples of regulatory controls and proposed controls in the United States (EPA, 1977).

Regulatory Measures and Program Tools

A. Federal Government

1. Environmental Protection Agency

Regulations on the operation of interstate motor and rail carriers.

Regulations on new products that are major sources of noise, including such controls as antitampering and warranty provisions.

Labeling requirements for products that produce noise capable of adversely affecting public health or welfare, or products that are marketed for their noise attenuation characteristics.

Providing technical assistance to state and local governments desiring to enforce noise control programs.

Public information dissemination to inform citizens of the hazards of noise to public health and welfare.

Certification of low-noise-emission products.

2. Department of Transportation, Including Federal Highway Administration (FHWA), Federal Aviation Administration (FAA), and Other Agencies

Enforcement of EPA interstate motor carrier and rail carrier emission standards.

Procedures for abatement of highway noise and highway construction noise.

Standards for limitation of in-cab truck and automotive noise.

Standards limiting shipboard crew noise exposure.

Policies for land retention around audible aids to navigation (fog signals).

Noise standards for railroad employee sleeping quarters.

Noise abatement features in airport development and improvement.

Regulations controlling aviation noise.

Grants to airports for noise planning.

Noise specifications and design standards for bus and rail rapid transit systems.

3. Department of Labor, Occupational Safety and Health Administration (OSHA)

Standards for control of occupational noise exposure.

4. Department of Interior

Enforcement of noise standards in mines.

Research, development, and demonstration programs in mining equipment noise control.

5. Housing and Urban Development (HUD)

Limitation of mortgage guarantees and assistance to housing and other noise-sensitive uses in areas with high noise levels, such as near airports and major highways.

Noise requirements in comprehensive planning.

6. Department of Health, Education, and Welfare (HEW), National Institute for Occupational Safety and Health (NIOSH)

Research in noise effects and hearing protector effectiveness.

7. Other Federal Agencies

Development of noise control methodologies and requirements by Department of Defense and Department of Agriculture.

Implement the purchase of low-noise emission products at up to 25% premium.

B. State and Local Regulatory Measures

1. Permit programs (construction sites, manufacturing plants).
2. Controls on purchase and operation of noisy products.
3. Economic incentives including noise-related fees at airports and for motor vehicles.
4. Planning.
5. Zoning.
6. Property line standards.
7. Curfews.
8. Labeling.
9. Regulation of large stationary sources including power plants and cooling towers.

C. Consumers   Purchase of low-noise products.

D. Industry
　　1. Reduction of occupational noise exposure.
　　2. Production of quieter products.
　　3. Provision of noise information to purchasers.

E. Standards Agencies   Establishment and publication of noise instrumentation standards and measurement standards.

Goals of a National Strategy for Noise Control

The Environmental Protection Agency proposed the following tentative goals (EPA, 1977). These support the general goal of promoting an environment free from noise that jeopardizes health and welfare.

　　1. Take all practical steps to eliminate hearing loss as a consequence of noise exposure.

　　2. Reduce environmental noise exposure of the population to

$$L_{DN} \leq 75 \text{ dB}A$$

immediately, utilizing all available tools, except in those isolated cases where this would impose a severe hardship.

　　3. Through vigorous regulatory and planning actions, reduce environmental noise exposure levels to

$$L_{DN} \leq 65 \text{ dB}A$$

and concurrently reduce noise annoyance and related activity interference caused by intrusive noise.

　　4. In planning future programs concerned with or affecting environmental noise exposure, to the extent possible, aim for environmental noise levels of

$$L_{DN} \leq 55 \text{ dB}A$$

　　5. Encourage and assist governmental agencies in the adoption and implementation of long-range noise control policy designed to prevent significant degradation of existing noise levels or exposure in designated areas. Such nondegradation policy could be incorporated into land use and development planning processes to reduce potential increases in noise levels in hospital zones, quiet residential areas, wilderness areas, and other sensitive areas.

Elements of a Community Noise Ordinance

Many communities define noise as a nuisance, but fail to identify prohibited noise levels. The wording of the noise ordinance may have the form: "It shall be unlawful for any person to make, continue, or cause to be made or continued any loud, unnecessary or unusual noise or any noise which annoys, disturbs, injures, or endangers the comfort, repose, health, peace, or safety of others." Some of the ordinances were written before the general availability of noise measuring equipment. In most cases it is preferable to specify limiting noise levels. Although the goals listed above refer to day–night sound level, it may not be practical to specify limitations in terms of that descriptor, since L_{DN} implies measurement over a 24-hour period. Furthermore, several noise sources, including industrial sources, aircraft and highway traffic, may contribute to noise levels at a given location.

Figure 5.8.1 (EPA, 1975) shows fixed source noise levels allowable at residential district boundaries in a number of cities. Daytime and nighttime limits range from 40 to 90 dBA. The median daytime limit for 117 cities is 55 dBA and the average is 56.75 dBA. The median nighttime limit for 118 cities is 50 dBA and the average is 51.76 dBA. The limits indicated usually apply to "continuous noise." In some codes, continuous noise is identified as noise that may be measured using the slow scale on a sound level meter (the slow setting corresponds to an averaging time of about 1 s). Other codes specify a longer measurement period and some do not specify the averaging time. Typically, higher noise levels are allowable at the boundaries of business/commercial and manufacturing/industrial districts. Note that the boundary is defined by the receiving use, not by the location of the noise source. In order to protect individuals whose homes are in commercial or industrial zones, residential district boundaries may be interpreted in terms of land use rather than in terms of zoning.

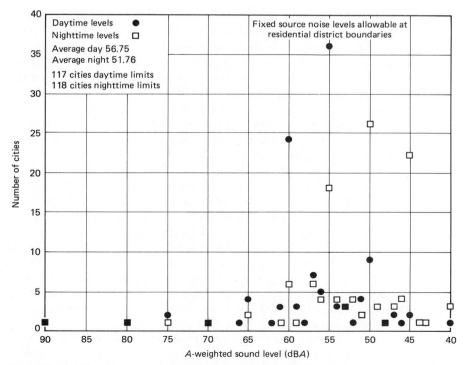

Figure 5.8.1 Fixed source noise levels allowable at residential district boundaries. (*Source:* EPA (September 1975))

A Model Code

The material that follows is based principally on a model community noise ordinance developed by the Environmental Protection Agency (1975) for use by cities and counties in the development of noise control codes tailored to local conditions and goals. Small communities might choose to write a shorter code based on only part of the model. This comprehensive performance-standard model is intended to overcome enforcement problems associated with an outmoded nuisance law approach.

The model code begins by describing excessive sound in terms of health, welfare, safety, and the quality of life. The definitions in a code may include references to community zoning laws and American National Standards Institute (ANSI) instrumentation and measurement standards. In order for a noise code to be effective the powers and duties of an environmental protection officer/noise control office or officer (EPO/NPO) must be specified. The code may also require interdepartmental cooperation in enforcement, in contracts, in purchasing, and in capital improvement programs. Thus, municipal government contracts should require compliance with the noise code, and quiet products may be given preference in purchasing (e.g., up to 25% premium over the least expensive noisier product). Departments responsible for capital improvement programs should submit an environmental impact statement (EIS) which includes noise predictions for the construction period and the postconstruction period where applicable.

Prohibited Acts   Where appropriate, the nuisance paragraphs in older codes may be retained and supplemented with specified limits on noise levels. In most urban and suburban communities, an outright ban on outdoor rifle and pistol ranges and motor vehicle racing and similar high-noise level activities may be the best course. Existing high-noise level activities can be restricted as to time of operation and noise levels at property lines. Restrictions may be justified on the basis of hearing damage to participants as well as community annoyance. Off-road vehicles (ORV's) may be banned from public lands and quasipublic lands (utility rights of way, etc.) for reasons of safety, noise, and other environmental considerations.

A noise code that prohibits outdoor loudspeakers and public address systems will be more effective than one that tries to restrict their noise levels or hours of operation. Exceptions for games and special events can be made on a permit basis. Otherwise, misuse of these systems is likely to cause frequent annoyance within the community, whereas enforcement of loudspeaker sound level limits is usually impractical. One community (West Orange, NJ, 1984) revised its noise control ordinance to allow loudspeakers if they are positioned in "such a way that they are facing away from homes." The directivity of loudspeakers is such that sound levels behind the speaker are only a few decibels less than sound levels in front at the same distance. Thus, code provisions of this type will bring little relief to residents near swim clubs and similar operations.

The code may address other noise-producing activities which cause a noise disturbance across a property line. These include loud radios, television sets, musical instruments, street sales where bells or other sound-producing devices are used to attract customers, loading and unloading, construction, vehicle and motorboat repair and testing, and model vehicles. Some of these activities may be banned outright or banned during certain hours, or subjected to sound level limits at the nearest residential property line.

Power mowers and other powered gardening equipment may be restricted as to hours of operation. However, one community ordinance amendment (Larchmont, NY, 6/4/85) set specific limits for gardening equipment noise for the period between Memorial Day and Labor Day (late May to early September). Noise from lawn mowers and leaf blowers, measured at 60 ft, may not exceed 70 dB from 8 A.M. to 10 P.M. and 62 dB from 10 P.M. to 8 A.M. The law is enforced by the police in answer to complaints.

As noted in a previous section, a large number of noise complaints involve pets. The code of the city and county of Honolulu includes a penalty for keeping a barking dog which is defined as follows:

> "Barking dog" shall mean a dog that barks, bays, cries, howls or makes any other noise continuously and/or incessantly for a period of ten minutes or barks intermittently for a period of 1/2 hour or more to the disturbance of any person at any time of day or night regardless of whether the dog is physically situated in or upon private property . . .

An exception is made if the dog is provoked, or barking at a trespasser. After receiving a warning citation, the owner of a barking dog is required to follow specific instructions for the dog's training. The training method is outlined in a pamphlet by the National League of Cities and Humane Society of the United States.

Noise Originating in Industrial, Commercial, and Service Facilities

The noise level limits that follow are based on a state administrative code (NJAC, 1985). They are listed as a possible model for jurisdictions wishing to limit industrial and commercial noise.

Continuous Airborne Sound Originating in an Industrial, Commercial, Public Service, or Community Service Facility Shall Not Exceed the Following A-Weighted Levels

Receiving property line	Time	Level (dBA)
Residential	7 A.M. to 10 P.M.	65
Residential	10 P.M. to 7 A.M.	50
Commercial	Any	65

Or the Following Octave-Band Levels (dB)

Octave-band center frequency (Hz)	Residential property line 7 A.M. to 10 P.M.	Residential property line 10 P.M. to 7 A.M.	Commercial property line
31.5	96	86	96
63	82	71	82
125	74	61	74
250	67	53	67

Octave-band center frequency (Hz)	Residential property line 7 A.M. to 10 P.M.	Residential property line 10 P.M. to 7 A.M.	Commercial property line
500	63	48	63
1000	60	45	60
2000	57	42	57
4000	55	40	55
8000	53	38	53
Impulse sound in air	80[a]	80[a]	80[a]

[a] Peak sound pressure in decibels for an impulsive sound with a single pressure peak or a single burst with multiple pressure peaks having a duration of less than 1 s.

Continuous airborne sound is that measured by the slow response setting of a sound level meter. Small communities that find it impractical to purchase equipment for frequency analysis and train personnel to operate such equipment may choose to use the A-weighted limits alone.

Additional Noise Code Elements Certain products are manufactured to meet noise emission levels according to federal or state laws. Such products may be identified in the municipal code, specifically or by reference. A tampering provision in the code may prohibit removal or rendering inoperative the noise control elements of the identified products. In addition, the code should require that mufflers on motor vehicles and stationary engines be adequate and in good repair.

Sound levels of amplified music sometimes presents a risk of hearing damage in places of public entertainment. The code may prohibit amplified music that exceeds a certain sound level, 90 dBA for example, unless a conspicuous warning of possible hearing impairment is posted near entrances of the establishment.

Exceptions should be considered carefully, even if a particular activity is not a problem when the code takes effect. For example, auto racing may be permitted in an undeveloped area, but when the area is developed, residents may seek relief from excessive noise.

The environmental protection or noise control office or officer (EPO/NCO) or other agency or official charged with enforcement should be identified by title and responsibilities and penalties and provisions for abatement orders should be stated. The code may contain a provision for citizen suits against any person causing noise that is an immediate threat to health and welfare, or against the EPO/NCO where there is an alleged failure to enforce the code.

Immediate Threats to Health and Welfare The EPO/NCO may be empowered to order an immediate halt to any sound that exposes any person to sound levels in excess of those in the following table.

Sounds that Pose an Immediate Threat to Health and Welfare (Measured at 50 ft or 15 m)

Level (dBA)	Duration (hr)
Continuous sounds	
90	24
93	12

Level (dBA)	Duration (hr)
Continuous sounds	
96	6
99	3
102	1.5
105	0.75

The equal energy principle may be used for other noise levels and for time-varying noise levels.

Level (dB)	Repetitions per 24-hr period
Impulsive sounds	
145	1
135	10
125	100

Again, the equal energy principle may be used for levels that are not listed.

EXAMPLE PROBLEM: NOISE CODES

An example code for limiting noise originating in industrial, commercial, and service facilities was outlined earlier in this section. Consider the case where the receiving property line is residential or commercial. Compare the daytime *A*-weighted limits with those expressed in octave bands.

Solution. The limitations in this example code are the same for a residential receiving zone between 7 A.M. and 10 P.M. and a commercial receiving zone at any time. We will first consider the situation where the sound level in each octave band equals the stated limit. These will be adjusted for *A*-weighting, as given in Chapter 1, and combined to form the overall level in dBA. The adjustments are shown in the following table.

NOISE LEVEL LIMITS IN OCTAVE BANDS

Octave-band center frequency (Hz)	Limit (dB)	Adjustment (dB)	Limit (dBA)
31.5	96	−39.4	56.6
63	82	−26.2	55.8
125	74	−16.1	57.9
250	67	−8.6	58.4
500	63	−3.2	59.8
1000	60	0	60
2000	57	+1.2	58.2
4000	55	+1.0	56
8000	53	−1.1	51.9

The *A*-weighted noise level limits in each octave band are combined by the following equation:

$$L = 10 \lg \sum_{i=1}^{n} 10^{L_i/10} \qquad (5.8.1)$$

to obtain

$$L = 10 \lg(10^{56.6/10} + 10^{55.8/10} + \cdots)$$
$$= 67.3 \text{ dB}A$$

The example code limits *A*-weighted sound levels to 65 dB*A* for commercial receiving zones and residential receiving zones between 7 A.M. and 10 P.M. Thus, if the noise spectrum is the same as the octave-band limits, then the octave-band limits are less restrictive than the *A*-weighted sound level limit. However, industrial noise energy is likely to be concentrated in a few octave bands, and one or more octave-band limits may be exceeded even if the overall *A*-weighted limit of 65 dB*A* is not. For convenience in measurement, community codes should establish a specific limit on *A*-weighted noise levels. Communities with adequate equipment and qualified personnel may wish to supplement these limits with limits expressed in octave bands.

5.9 THE ROLE OF ENVIRONMENTAL COMMISSIONS, PLANNING BOARDS, AND ZONING BOARDS

Environmental commissions, planning boards, and zoning boards are advisory, quasi-judicial, and judicial bodies that serve local governments. They are ordinarily appointed by the governing body.

In many communities, noise is among the foremost environmental problems. An environmental commission may recommend changes in the municipal noise code, and may educate and inform the public on matters related to community noise. The commission may advise and help in setting goals for the health and police departments on matters related to enforcement of the noise code. Guidance in community noise control is available from the Environmental Protection Agency and state departments of environmental protection or offices of noise control.

A natural resources inventory (NRI) should be prepared for the community, identifying noise problem areas and areas that are particularly noise sensitive. Recommendations for land use should take these areas into consideration. The NRI should be submitted to the planning board for adoption as part of the master plan.

The planning board should consider noise impact in its decisions on land use. It should require an environmental impact statement (EIS) including noise predictions as part of any application for a major subdivision.

Requests for variances that come before the zoning board of adjustment should be examined for possible noise impact. This is particularly important where industrial and commercial uses are near residential areas.

EXAMPLE PROBLEM: A ZONING VARIANCE

It is proposed that a go-cart track be constructed on a site previously used for a miniature golf course. Up to ten go-carts will be in operation at one time. Each will use a 4-horsepower 4-stroke-cycle engine. The worst-case distribution about the track will result in the carts being at the following distances from the lot line of a two-story apartment building:

Number of carts	Distance (ft)
1	107
2	114
1	116
2	127
2	131
2	148

The distance to the building facade is about 20 feet greater. Predict the environmental impact of the proposed track.

Solution. It was determined that the proposed go-cart engine with a standard muffler produces a noise level of 80 dBA at 25 ft. The sources will be uncorrelated; thus, we may add scalar sound intensities, from which the adjustment for the number of sources n is given by 10 lg n. Assuming the engines each act as point sources, and following the inverse square law for attenuation with distance r, the distance adjustment is given by

$$L_2 - L_1 = 20 \lg\left(\frac{r_1}{r_2}\right)$$

The results of these calculations are shown in Table 5.9.1. Noise levels and corrections are rounded off to tenths of a dBA. A spreadsheet program was used to speed repetitious calculations. The predicted noise level at the residential lot line is 76.1 dBA; it is 74.8 dBA at the building facade. Using average attenuation values of 15 dBA for open windows and 25 dBA for closed windows, maximum intrusive interior noise levels would be about 50 to 60 dBA when the facility

TABLE 5.9.1 SOLUTION TO EXAMPLE PROBLEM

	Calculations at property line					
Number of sources	1	2	1	2	2	2
L at 25 ft	80	80	80	80	80	80
Distance	107	114	116	127	131	148
Adjustments						
For number	0	3	0	3	3	3
For distance	−12.6	−13.2	−13.3	−14.1	−14.4	−15.4
L at distance	67.4	69.8	66.7	68.9	68.6	67.6
I/I_{ref}	5495420	9549946	4677361	7762487	7244375	5754411
L total	76.1					

was operating. In order to ensure 100% sentence intelligibility, the noise level should not exceed 45 dB*A*. Thus, the predicted values would cause speech interference outdoors and indoors, particularly when the windows were open.

This example is based on an application for a zoning variance in a suburban community. Applicable noise level limits at a residential property line were 65 dB*A* from 7 A.M. to 10 P.M. and 50 dB*A* from 10 P.M. to 7 A.M. It was observed that the predicted noise level at the residential property line would exceed the daytime limit by about 11 dB*A;* thus, the predicted subjective loudness is more than double the allowable value. The board of adjustment denied the variance.

BIBLIOGRAPHY

American National Standards Institute, Methods for calculation of the articulation index, ANSI, S3.5-1969.

Beranek, L. L., *Noise and Vibration Control,* McGraw-Hill, New York, 1971.

Bishop, J. E., "Researchers say portable tape players with earphones can cause hearing loss," *Wall Street Journal,* 14, December 2, 1982.

Cantrell, R., "Prolonged exposure to intermittent noise: audiometric, biochemical, motor, psychological and sleep effects," *The Laryngoscope* **84,** 4–55, 1974.

Committee on the Problem of Noise, Noise final report, H.M. Stationery Office, London, July 1963.

DeJoy, D. M., "A report on the status of research on the cardiovascular effects of noise," *Noise Control Eng. J.* **23**(1), 1984.

Environmental Protection Agency, Community noise, NTID 300.3, December 1971c.

Environmental Protection Agency, Effects of noise on people, NTID 300.7, December 1971d.

Environmental Protection Agency, Transportation noise and noise from equipment powered by internal combustion engines, NTID 300.13, December 1971a.

Environmental Protection Agency, Noise from construction equipment and operations, building equipment, and home appliances, NTID 300.1, December 1971b.

Environmental Protection Agency, Impact characterization of noise including implications of identifying and achieving levels of cumulative noise exposure, NTID 73.4, July 1973.

Environmental Protection Agency, Information on levels of environmental noise requisite to protect public health and welfare with an adequate margin of safety, 550/9-74-004, March 1974.

Environmental Protection Agency, Model community noise control ordinance, EPA 550/9-76-003, September 1975.

Environmental Protection Agency, Toward a national strategy for noise control, U.S. Govt. Printing Office: 1977-720-177/1999, April 1977.

Environmental Protection Agency, Protective noise levels, EPA 550/9-79-100, November 1978a.

Environmental Protection Agency, San Diego, California: Case history of a municipal noise control program, Contract no. EPA-68-01-3845, November 1978b.

Environmental Protection Agency, Noise: a health problem, (not numbered) August 1978c.

Federal Aviation Administration, Impact of noise on people, May 1977.

French, N. R., and J. C. Steinberg, "Factors governing the intelligibility of speech sounds," *J. Acoust. Soc. Am.* **19,** 90–119, 1947.

Johnson, J. A., "A simplified articulation index calculation for open-plan spaces," *Sound and Vibration* **14**(6), 14–16, 1980.

Karagodina, L. L., Hygienic importance of the problem of noise abatement in cities, Soviet noise research literature from the F. F. Erisman Scientific Research Institute for Hygiene, EPA 550/9-74-002, April 1974.

Kryter, K. D., *The Effects of Noise on Man,* Academic Press, New York, 1970.

Ising, H., and H. Melchert, "Endocrine and cardiovascular effects of noise," Proceedings Third International Conference on Noise as a Public Health Hazard, American Speech and Hearing Assn. Washington, D.C. Rept. 10, 1980.

National League of Cities and Humane Society of the US, Washington D.C. "Quiet—Man's Best Friend," undated.

New Jersey Administrative Code, 7:29-1.1 et seq., Noise control, 1/18/74, rev. effective 3/18/85.

Parvispoor, D., "Noise exposure and prevalence of high blood pressure among weavers in Iran," *J. Occupational Medicine* **18,** 730–731, 1976.

Peterson, E. A., et al., "Noise and cardiovascular function in Rhesus monkeys," *J. Aud. Res.* **15,** 234–251, 1975.

Peterson, E. A., J. S. Augenstein, and D. C. Tanis, "Continuing studies in noise and cardiovascular function," *J. Sound Vibration* **59,** 123–129, 1978.

Peterson, E. A., J. S. Augenstein, D. C. Tanis, and D. G. Augenstein, "Noise raises blood pressure without impairing auditory sensitivity," *Science* **211,** 1450–1451, 1981.

Reagan, J., and C. Grant, Highway construction noise: measurement, prediction and mitigation, FHWA/HEV-77-2, 1977.

Vos, J., and G. F. Smoorenburg, "Penalty for impulse noise, derived from annoyance ratings for impulse and road traffic sounds," *J. Acoust. Soc. Am.* **77**(1), 193–201, 1985.

PROBLEMS

5.1.1. Consider the typical noise exposure pattern for a suburban factory worker as given in Figure 5.0.1. Calculate
(a) L_{eq24}
(b) L_{DN} from the plot

5.1.2. Repeat for a suburban office worker.

5.1.3. Repeat for an urban factory worker.

5.1.4. Repeat for an urban office worker.

5.1.5. Repeat for an urban preschool child.

5.1.6. How long could one safely listen to music if the energy average sound level is 93 dB*A?* Base the solution on the protective exposure level $L_{eq24} = 70$ dB*A* and neglect other noise exposure.

5.1.7. Repeat for a sound level of 108 dB*A.*

5.4.1. (a) Find the articulation index (AI) in the presence of band-limited white noise between 180 Hz and 5.6 kHz if the noise level in the 1-kHz octave band is 45 dB. White noise has the same sound level in each band of constant bandwidth. Assume a male speaker at typical voice level 1 m from the listener.

(b) Suppose the white noise spectrum extended across the entire audible frequency range from 20 Hz to 20 kHz. Would the AI change? Would speech intelligibility be affected?

5.4.2. Noise levels are measured in the five octave bands from 250 to 4000 Hz. They are, respectively: 40, 42, 60, 60, and 40 dB. Find the articulation index based on a male voice at 1 m.

5.4.3. Repeat if the noise levels are 55, 58, 45, 35, and 30 dB.

5.4.4. Using the noise spectrum of Problem 5.4.1, determine the distance at which reliable speech communication is barely possible with a normal voice for
(a) a male speaker
(b) a female speaker

5.4.5. Repeat for the spectrum of Problem 5.4.2.

5.4.6. Repeat for the noise spectrum of Problem 5.4.3.

5.5.1. The equivalent sound level is estimated to be 65 dBA during the day (7 A.M. to 10 P.M.) and 60 dBA at night. Predict community impact in terms of sleep disturbance.

5.5.2. Repeat for 68-dBA daytime and 66-dBA nighttime sound levels.

5.6.1. Relate day–night sound level L_{DN} to equivalent sound level L_{eq24} if sound level is constant over the entire 24-hr period.

5.6.2. Estimate indoor day–night sound level with the following sources:

	Duty cycle	
Source	7 A.M. to 10 P.M.	10 P.M. to 7 A.M.
Air conditioner	0.5	0.4
Refrigerator	0.3	0.3
Washing machine	0.1	0

Use average values; assume all sources contribute to sound level at the point in question.

5.6.3. Repeat, using minimum values.

5.6.4. Repeat the example problem "Environmental evaluation based on day–night sound level and equivalent sound level" using the following data. Daytime measurements: 55, 56, 50, 50, and 62 dBA; nighttime measurements: 52, 51, and 40 dBA.

5.6.5. Repeat with daytime measurements of 58, 58, 60, 60, and 62 dBA and nighttime measurements of 45, 45, 47, 48, and 50 dBA.

5.7.1. A proposed construction project will employ various pieces of equipment at the indicated distances from a point on the nearest residential property line. Noise levels measured at 50 ft are as given in dBA.
(a) Determine the contribution of each type equipment at the point on the property line, based on typical usage factors.
(b) Find equivalent sound level for the workday.
(c) Predict L_{eq24} and L_{DN} based on an 8-hour workday beginning at 7:30 A.M.
(d) Evaluate the results.
(e) Identify the most effective noise control procedures that might be considered.
Use the following data:

Source	Dozer	Truck	Backhoe	Tractor	Front loader	Concrete mixer	Generator	Compressor
Number	2	3	1	1	1	1	1	1
Distance	100	100	100	100	100	100	125	125
L, 50 ft	75	75	75	75	75	75	75	75
Usage	0.4	0.4	0.16	0.4	0.4	0.4	1	1

5.7.2. Repeat with the following data:

Source	Dozer	Truck	Backhoe	Tractor	Front loader	Concrete mixer	Generator	Compressor
Number	3	4	2	2	2	1	1	2
Distance	150	125	150	150	150	175	175	155
L, 50 ft	75	75	85	80	79	85	78	81
Usage	0.4	0.4	0.16	0.4	0.4	0.4	1	1

5.7.3. Repeat with the following data:

Source	Dozer	Truck	Backhoe	Jackhammer	Front loader	Concrete mixer	Generator	Compressor
Number	3	2	3	3	2	1	1	3
Distance	300	250	300	275	300	300	300	275
L, 50 ft	75	75	85	88	79	85	78	81
Usage	0.4	0.4	0.16	0.1	0.4	0.4	1	1

5.7.4. Repeat with the following data:

Source	Dozer	Truck	Backhoe	Jackhammer	Front loader	Concrete mixer	Generator	Compressor
Number	4	3	3	3	2	1	1	3
Distance	300	250	300	275	300	300	300	275
L, 50 ft	80	91	85	88	79	85	78	81
Usage	0.4	0.4	0.16	0.1	0.4	0.4	1	1

5.7.5. Repeat with the following data, but let the workday include 13 hours between 7 A.M. and 10 P.M. and 4 hours between 10 P.M. and 7 A.M.

Source	Dozer	Truck	Backhoe	Jackhammer	Front loader	Concrete mixer	Generator	Compressor
Number	4	3	3	3	2	1	1	3
Distance	300	250	300	275	300	300	300	275
L, 50 ft	75	75	75	75	79	85	78	75
Usage	0.4	0.4	0.16	0.1	0.4	0.4	1	1

5.8.1. Select a particular urban jurisdiction. Identify problems, needs, and goals with regard to noise. Outline a noise code, including appropriate noise level limits.

5.8.2. Repeat for a suburban jurisdiction.

5.8.3. Repeat for a rural jurisdiction.

5.9.1. A number of noise sources are located at various distances (in feet) from a point on a residential property line. The measured sound level of each individual source is given in dBA.

(a) Find the noise contribution of each source or group of sources.
(b) Find the combined noise level at the point on the property line.
Data are as follows:

Number of sources	1	2	2	1	2	2
L at 25 ft	80	80	80	80	80	80
Distance	58	62	70	66	69	77

5.9.2. Repeat with the following data:

Number of sources	1	2	2	1	2	2
L at 25 ft	80	80	80	80	80	80
Distance	79	83	91	87	98	98

5.9.3. Repeat with the following data:

Number of sources	3	2	2	4	2	1
L at 25 ft	90	82	80	79	81	84
Distance	100	110	115	125	140	150

5.9.4. Repeat with the following data:

Number of sources	3	2	2	4	2	1
L at 25 ft	84	76	80	79	81	84
Distance	100	110	115	125	140	150

5.9.5. Repeat with the following data, and compute L_{eq24} and L_{DN} if the sources are present continuously from noon until midnight.

Number of sources	3	2	2	4	2	1
L at 25 ft	84	76	80	79	81	84
Distance	200	210	215	225	240	250

Chapter 6

Building Design Criteria for Control of Intrusive Noise

Building design involves a number of considerations related to acoustics and noise control. The building shell controls transmission of noise into the building from transportation sources, industrial sources, and other outside sources. A shell constructed of dense materials tends to be most effective in reducing noise transmission. However, the weakest links severely limit noise control effectiveness. A major portion of the sound energy entering a typical building passes through the windows, even if they are closed. If the windows in a building are open, then other parts of the structure have little effect in reducing intrusive noise.

6.1 SOUND TRANSMISSION THROUGH WALLS AND OTHER BARRIERS

When airborne sound reaches a wall, some of the sound energy is reflected, some energy is absorbed, and some energy is transmitted through the wall. Open windows and doors and cracks around poorly fitted building elements will allow airborne sound to pass directly through. Sound pressure incident on one side of a wall can cause the wall to vibrate and transmit sound energy to the other side. The fraction of incident sound energy transmitted to the wall depends on the impedance of the wall relative to the air. And the fraction of sound energy transmitted to the air on the receiver side of the wall again depends on the impedance of the wall relative to the air. The process is repeated in a double wall with an airspace between. Fortunately, most construction materials transmit only a tiny fraction of the incident sound energy. The major portion of the energy is reflected or converted into heat due to impedance mismatch, absorption, and damping. Masonry walls that have a high mass-per-unit-area allow little sound to pass through. A wall of gypsum board on both sides of a stud frame is an effective sound barrier due to energy losses as sound is transmitted from air to solid and solid to air.

6.2 TRANSMISSION LOSS AND SOUND TRANSMISSION COEFFICIENT

Transmission loss is a measure of the sound insulation provided by a wall or other structural element. It is given by

$$TL = 10 \lg\left(\frac{W_I}{W_T}\right)$$ (6.2.1)

where   TL = transmission loss (dB)
W_I = sound power incident on the wall
W_T = sound power transmitted through the wall

Since transmission loss is dependent on the frequency of the sound, it is usually reported for each octave band or each one-third octave band.

Sound Transmission Coefficient

Sound transmission coefficient is the fraction of sound power transmitted through a wall or other barrier. Thus,

$$\tau = \frac{W_T}{W_I}$$ (6.2.2)

where τ = sound transmission coefficient. Comparing the definitions of transmission loss and sound transmission coefficient, we have

$$TL = 10 \lg\left(\frac{1}{\tau}\right)$$ (6.2.3)

or

$$\tau = 10^{-TL/10}$$ (6.2.4)

Prediction of Sound Transmission Coefficient and Transmission Loss

Consider an infinite panel in the yz-plane, and a plane sound wave approaching it at angle of incidence θ (Figure 6.2.1). The incident wave is identified by subscript I, the reflected wave by subscript R, and the transmitted wave by subscript T. Wave propagation direction (in the xy-plane) is indicated by the arrows. The wave equation

$$\frac{\partial^2 p}{\partial t^2} = c^2 \nabla^2 p$$ (1.2.11)

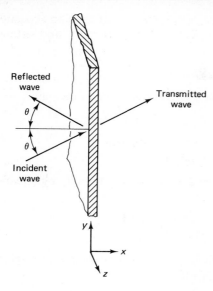

Figure 6.2.1 Transmission loss.

is satisfied by

$$p_I = \mathbf{P}_I \exp[\, jk(ct - x \cos \theta - y \sin \theta)]$$

$$p_R = \mathbf{P}_r \exp[\, jk(ct + x \cos \theta - y \sin \theta)]$$

$$p_T = \mathbf{P}_T \exp[\, jk(ct - x \cos \theta - y \sin \theta)] \qquad (6.2.5)$$

where the real part of p = sound pressure
$\mathbf{P}$ = pressure amplitude (complex, in general)
k = wavenumber

The Mass-Controlled Case If the panel is thin, that is, panel thickness is small compared with one wavelength of sound in air, and if panel stiffness and damping may be neglected, then the following conditions are used to relate the incident, reflected, and transmitted waves:

1. Continuity of velocities normal to the panel.
2. A balance of forces including inertial (reverse effective) force.

Applying the first condition, we obtain

$$u_{\text{panel}} = u_T \cos \theta = u_I \cos \theta - u_R \cos \theta \qquad (6.2.6)$$

where u = particle velocity at the panel surface. When sound pressure and particle velocity are in-phase, then they are related by

$$Z = \frac{p}{u} = \rho c \qquad (1.11.7)$$

where Z = characteristic resistance, a special case of specific acoustic impedance. Using equation 1.11.7 and equations 6.2.5 in equation 6.2.6, and setting $x = 0$ at the panel, we obtain

$$\mathbf{P}_T = \mathbf{P}_I - \mathbf{P}_R \tag{6.2.7}$$

Applying the second condition over a unit surface area of the panel, we obtain

$$p_I + p_R - p_T - ma_{\text{panel}} = 0 \tag{6.2.8}$$

where m = panel mass density per unit surface area
         a = acceleration normal to the surface

Relating panel velocity to transmitted wave particle velocity by equation 6.2.6 and using equation 1.11.7, we obtain

$$u_{\text{panel}} = p_T \frac{\cos \theta}{\rho c} \tag{6.2.9}$$

Substituting the last of equations 6.2.5, and differentiating with respect to time, we obtain

$$a_{\text{panel}} = jkc\mathbf{P}_T \exp[jk(ct - x \cos \theta - y \sin \theta)] \cos \theta/[\rho c]$$

$$= j\omega p_T \cos \theta/[\rho c] \tag{6.2.10}$$

Substituting the result in equation 6.2.8 and using equations 6.2.5 at the panel ($x = 0$), pressure amplitudes are related by

$$\mathbf{P}_I + \mathbf{P}_R - \mathbf{P}_T - j\omega m\mathbf{P}_T \cos \theta/[\rho c] \tag{6.2.11}$$

Equation 6.2.7 may now be used to eliminate $\mathbf{P}_R$. After simplifying, we obtain the ratio of transmitted pressure amplitude to incident pressure amplitude:

$$\frac{\mathbf{P}_T}{\mathbf{P}_I} = \frac{1}{1 + j\omega m \cos \theta/(2\rho c)} \tag{6.2.12}$$

Sound transmission coefficient is given by

$$\tau = \frac{p_{\text{rms}(T)}^2}{p_{\text{rms}(I)}^2} = \frac{|\mathbf{P}_T|^2}{|\mathbf{P}_I|^2}$$

$$= \frac{1}{1 + [\omega m \cos \theta/(2\rho c)]^2} \tag{6.2.13}$$

Finally, we obtain the *mass law transmission loss* equation based on theoretical considerations:

$$\text{TL} = 10 \lg\left(\frac{1}{\tau}\right) = 10 \lg\left[1 + \left(\frac{\omega m \cos \theta}{2\rho c}\right)^2\right] \tag{6.2.14}$$

If the angle of incidence is equal to zero, the above equation becomes

$$\text{TL}_0 = 10 \lg\left[1 + \left(\frac{m\omega}{2\rho c}\right)^2\right] \tag{6.2.15}$$

the *normal incidence mass law* for approximating transmission loss of panels with 0° incident sound in the mass-controlled region of frequencies.

The Field Incidence Mass Law

When examining transmission loss between two rooms, the sound source may produce a reverberant field. Thus, incident sound may strike the wall at all angles between 0 and 90°. For field incidence, it is assumed that the angle of incidence lies between 0 and 72°. This results in a field incidence transmission loss of about

$$TL = TL_0 - 5 \text{ dB}$$

The following additional changes are made in the mass law equation. Converting the frequency of the sound from radians per second to hertz, where

$$\omega \text{ (rad/s)} = 2\pi f \text{ (Hz)}$$

using typical values for the speed of sound in air and air density,

$$\rho c = 400 \text{ (approximately)}$$

and assuming that

$$\frac{m\omega}{2\rho c} \gg 1$$

we obtain the field incidence mass law equation

$$TL = 20 \lg(fm) - 47 \text{ dB} \tag{6.2.16}$$

where m = mass per unit area of the wall (kg/m^2).

Based on the above equation for the mass-controlled frequency region, transmission loss of a panel increases by 6 dB per octave. In addition, a doubling of panel thickness or a doubling of panel density should produce a 6-dB increase in transmission loss at a given frequency. While the above equations are useful for prediction of material behavior, the transmission loss of actual structural elements should be confirmed by laboratory or field testing whenever possible.

The Effect of Panel Bending Stiffness and Damping

Low-frequency sound transmission is governed largely by panel bending stiffness. Transmission of somewhat higher frequency sound is governed by panel resonances. The panel may be considered mass controlled when responding to frequencies above twice the lowest resonant frequency, but below the critical frequency. The critical frequency will be discussed later.

The sound transmission coefficient equation for panels with significant bending stiffness and damping is given by Ver and Holmer (1971) as follows:

$$\tau = \left\{ \left[1 + \eta \left(\frac{\omega m \cos \theta}{2\rho c} \right) \left(\frac{\omega^2 B \sin^4 \theta}{c^4 m} \right) \right]^2 + \left[\left(\frac{\omega m \cos \theta}{2\rho c} \right) \left(1 - \frac{\omega^2 B \sin^4 \theta}{c^4 m} \right) \right]^2 \right\}^{-1} \tag{6.2.17}$$

where it is assumed that the thickness of the panel is small compared with the wavelength of the incident sound,

B = panel bending stiffness (N · m)

m = panel surface density (kg/m^2)

η = composite loss factor (dimensionless)

The Coincidence Effect

Sound in panels and other structural elements can be propagated as bending waves, longitudinal waves, and transverse waves. Bending waves are of particular importance because of the coincidence effect. Figure 6.2.2 shows a panel with an airborne sound wave of wavelength λ incident at angle θ. A bending wave of wavelength λ_B is excited in the panel. The propagation velocity of bending waves is frequency dependent, with higher frequencies corresponding to higher propagation velocities. The coincidence effect occurs when

$$\theta = \theta^* = \arcsin\left(\frac{\lambda}{\lambda_B}\right) \tag{6.2.18}$$

where the asterisk (∗) is used to indicate coincidence and θ^* is called the coincidence angle. When wave coincidence occurs, sound pressure on the surface of the panel is in phase with bending displacement. The result is high-efficiency energy transfer from airborne sound waves in the source room to bending waves in the panel, and thence to airborne sound waves in the receiving room. Efficient sound energy transfer from room to room is obviously undesirable from a noise control standpoint. Figure 6.2.3 is an idealized plot of transmission loss versus frequency, showing the stiffness-controlled, resonance-controlled, mass-controlled, and coincidence-controlled regions for a panel. Note that the transmission loss curve dips substantially at frequencies beyond the critical frequency due to the coincidence effect.

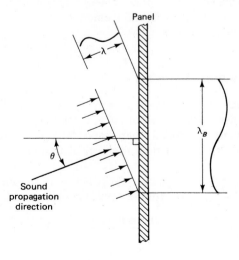

Figure 6.2.2 The coincidence effect.

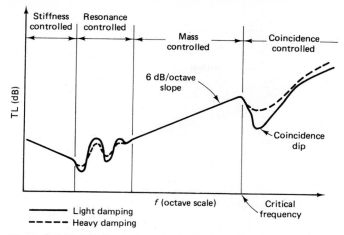

Figure 6.2.3   Idealized plot of transmission loss versus frequency.

Critical Frequency

It can be seen from equation 6.2.18 that the coincidence effect cannot occur if the wavelength of airborne sound λ is greater than λ_B, the bending mode wavelength in the panel. The lowest coincidence frequency, called the critical frequency, occurs at the critical airborne sound wavelength

$$\lambda = \lambda^* = \lambda_B$$

where critical frequency

$$f^* = \frac{c}{\lambda^*}$$

which corresponds to grazing incidence ($\theta = 90°$). For any frequency above the critical frequency, there is a critical angle θ^* at which coincidence will occur.

Critical frequencies are plotted against thickness for a number of materials in Figure 6.2.4 (Bruel & Kjaer, 1980). Unfortunately, the critical frequency often falls within the range of speech frequencies, thereby limiting the effectiveness of some partitions intended to provide privacy and prevent speech interference.

Sound Transmission Coefficient and
Transmission Loss at Coincidence

The coincidence effect depends on characteristics of the plate or panel and on the airborne sound wave. Coincidence occurs when

$$\frac{\omega^2 B \sin^4 \theta^*}{c^4 m} = 1 \qquad (6.2.19)$$

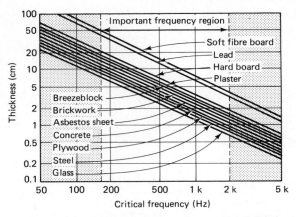

Figure 6.2.4 Critical frequency. (*Source:* Bruel & Kjaer (1980))

Substituting the above condition in the equation for sound transmission coefficient of a plate results in the coincidence condition sound transmission coefficient

$$\tau = \tau^* = \frac{1}{[1 + \eta \omega m \cos \theta^*/(2\rho c)]^2} \qquad (6.2.20)$$

and coincidence condition transmission loss

$$\begin{aligned}
\text{TL} = \text{TL}^* &= 10 \lg\!\left(\frac{1}{\tau^*}\right) \\
&= 10 \lg\!\left(1 + \frac{\eta \omega m \cos \theta^*}{2\rho c}\right)^{\!2} \\
&= 20 \lg\!\left(1 + \frac{\eta \pi f m \cos \theta^*}{\rho c}\right) \qquad (6.2.21)
\end{aligned}$$

Based on the above equations, we would predict

$$\tau^* = 1 \quad \text{and} \quad \text{TL}^* = 0$$

for undamped panels (i.e., if loss factor $\eta = 0$). There is some damping, however, in all construction materials. Note that the above transmission loss equation is based on theoretical behavior of an infinite plate. The actual constraints of windows and walls may produce a different response to sound waves. Once again, it is recommended that the behavior of actual materials be verified by laboratory or field tests.

Resonance in a Double-Panel Partition

The low-frequency resonances of a single-panel wall are ordinarily below the most significant speech frequencies. Walls that are constructed of two panels with an airspace between may exhibit low-frequency resonances in the speech range. Interior partitions, for example, are commonly made of two $\frac{1}{2}$-in or $\frac{3}{4}$-in sheetrock (gypsum-board) panels separated by two-by-four (nominal size) wooden or metal studs. In this case, the actual airspace is about $3\frac{1}{2}$ in.

Consider the wall configuration shown in Figure 6.2.5 where panels of mass per unit area m_1 and m_2 are separated by an airspace h. Since the air between the panels acts as a spring, the spring-mass analogy shown in part (b) of the figure will be used, where K is the spring rate of a uniform spring between two masses. Let the wall breathing mode be represented by the two masses vibrating at the same frequency. There will be a node or motionless point on the spring as indicated in the figure, making the original spring act as two springs with spring rates K_1 and K_2. Thus, the natural frequency of the two-mass system representing a unit area of the wall is given by

$$f_N = \frac{(K_1/m_1)^{1/2}}{2\pi}$$

$$= \frac{(K_2/m_2)^{1/2}}{2\pi} \qquad (6.2.22)$$

The spring rates of the two parts of the original spring are related by the equation for springs in series:

$$\frac{1}{K} = \frac{1}{K_1} + \frac{1}{K_2} \qquad (6.2.23)$$

Eliminating K_2 between the equations, we obtain

$$K_1 = K\frac{m_1 + m_2}{m_2} \qquad (6.2.24)$$

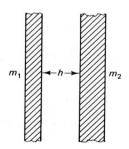

(a) Wall configuration

(b) Spring-mass analogy

Figure 6.2.5 Resonance in a double-panel partition.

Substituting the last result in the first frequency equation, the natural frequency of the system is given by

$$f_N = \frac{[K(m_1 + m_2)/(m_1 m_2)]^{1/2}}{2\pi} \qquad (6.2.25)$$

The effective spring rate of the air between the panels will be calculated on the basis of an adiabatic process. As noted in Chapter 1, pressure changes due to sound waves occur too rapidly to permit an isothermal process. Thus, the relationship between absolute pressure p and specific volume v is given by

$$\frac{p}{p_0} = \left(\frac{v_0}{v}\right)^\gamma \qquad (6.2.26)$$

where γ is the ratio of specific heats, and the subscript 0 refers to ambient conditions. Differentiating, we obtain

$$\frac{dp}{dv} = -\gamma p_0 v_0^\gamma v^{-\gamma-1} \qquad (6.2.27)$$

Typically, sound waves cause the absolute pressure and specific volume of air to vary only slightly from ambient values. Thus, the subscripts may now be dropped, and the above equation becomes

$$\frac{dp}{dv} = -\frac{\gamma p}{v} \qquad (6.2.28)$$

Since the mass of air between the panels remains constant, the ratio of panel displacement dh to original spacing h_0 equals the ratio of specific volume change to the ambient value:

$$\frac{dh}{h_0} = \frac{dv}{v_0} \qquad (6.2.29)$$

Spring rate K is the force per unit displacement, or for a unit surface area of the wall,

$$K = -\frac{dp}{dh} \qquad (6.2.30)$$

Combining the last two equations and again dropping the subscripts, we obtain

$$K = \frac{\gamma p}{h} \qquad (6.2.31)$$

Substituting the spring rate equation into the natural frequency equation, we have the low-frequency resonance equation for the wall in terms of panel mass and spacing, and atmospheric pressure:

$$f_N = \frac{[\gamma p(m_1 + m_2)/(h m_1 m_2)]^{1/2}}{2\pi} \qquad (6.2.32)$$

Using the standard atmosphere,

$$p = 1.01325 \times 10^5 \text{ Pa} \quad \text{and} \quad \gamma = 1.4$$

the double-panel wall low-frequency resonance f_N (Hz) is given by

$$f_N = 60\left(\frac{m_1 + m_2}{m_1 m_2 h}\right)^{1/2} \tag{6.2.33}$$

for surface masses m_1 and m_2 in kg/m² and panel spacing h in meters.

EXAMPLE PROBLEM: PREDICTION OF TRANSMISSION LOSS OF A WALL FOR THE MASS-CONTROLLED FREQUENCY REGION

Assume sound transmission of a wall is mass controlled. (a) Plot transmission loss against the product of frequency and mass per unit area.

Solution. Using the field incidence mass law under typical conditions, we have

$$\text{TL} = 20 \lg(fm) - 47$$

and using the normal incidence mass law,

$$\text{TL}_0 = 20 \lg(fm) - 42$$

Both relationships are shown by straight lines plotted on semilog paper, Figure 6.2.6. Note that these values are likely to be much higher than transmission loss values measured in actual tests.

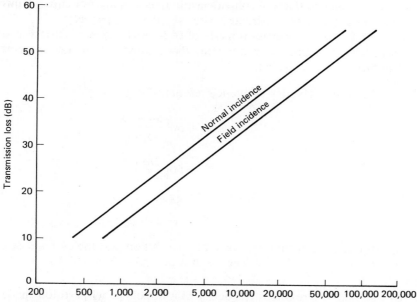

Figure 6.2.6 Transmission loss versus the product of frequency and surface mass (Hz·kg/m²).

(b) Estimate the transmission loss for a 6-in- (152-mm-) thick concrete wall at 500 Hz.

Solution. Poured concrete walls have a density of about 145 lb/ft^3 (2323 kg/m^3). The surface density is

$$m = 0.152 \times 2323 = 353 \text{ kg/m}^2$$

Using the field incidence mass law, we obtain

$$TL = 20 \lg(fm) - 47$$
$$= 20 \lg(500 \times 353) - 47$$
$$= 58 \text{ dB}$$

The measured transmission loss for the same thickness of concrete is about 47 dB at 500 Hz based on laboratory tests. Comparison of the theoretical and laboratory values indicates that the mass law provides only a rough approximation of transmission loss in this case. In situ measurements of apparent transmission loss are even lower, principally because of flanking noise transmission paths in actual construction.

EXAMPLE PROBLEM: RESONANCE IN A DOUBLE-PANEL PARTITION

Double-panel walls are sometimes erected with different panel thicknesses on either side of the wall so that the coincidence frequencies are not equal. However, interior partitions are usually constructed with two identical panels.

(a) Consider a partition made of two panels, each of surface mass m (kg/m^2) separated by an airspace of width h (m). Plot the resonant frequency against the product of surface mass and spacing.

Solution. The low-frequency resonance is given by

$$f_N = 60\left(\frac{m_1 + m_2}{m_1 m_2 h}\right)^{1/2}$$
$$= 60\left(\frac{2m}{m^2 h}\right)^{1/2}$$
$$= \frac{84.85}{\sqrt{mh}}$$

It can be seen from the form of the solution that the plot will be a straight line on logarithmic paper. The result is plotted in Figure 6.2.7.

(b) Estimate the resonant frequency of a double-panel partition made of a 3 lb/ft^2 and 4 lb/ft^2 gypsum-board with a 3.5-in airspace.

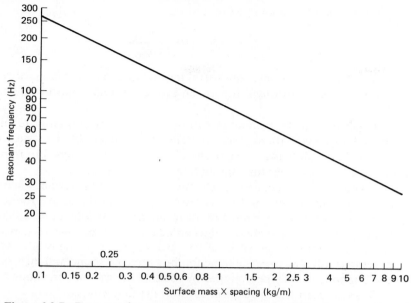

Figure 6.2.7 Resonant frequency of a double-panel partition plotted against surface mass of a single panel times spacing.

Solution. 1 lb/ft^2 = 4.882 kg/m^2 and 1 in = 0.0254 m. For surface weight w (lb/ft^2) and spacing h' (in), the natural frequency is given by

$$f_N = 60\left(\frac{m_1 + m_2}{m_1 m_2 h}\right)^{1/2}$$

$$= 170.4\left(\frac{w_1 + w_2}{w_1 w_2 h'}\right)^{1/2}$$

$$= 170.4\left(\frac{3 + 4}{3 \times 4 \times 3.5}\right)^{1/2} = 70 \text{ Hz}$$

Measurement of Transmission Loss

Expressing transmission loss in terms of vector sound intensity, we have

$$\text{TL} = 10 \lg\left(\frac{\mathbf{I}_I}{\mathbf{I}_T}\right) \tag{6.2.34}$$

where $\mathbf{I}_I$ = incident vector sound intensity
$\mathbf{I}_T$ = transmitted vector sound intensity

When sound pressure and particle velocity are in-phase, we have

$$I = \frac{p_{\text{rms}}^2}{\rho c}$$

and transmission loss could be expressed as

$$TL = 10 \lg\left(\frac{p^2_{rms(I)}}{p^2_{rms(T)}}\right)$$

However, the last equation is not useful for measurement purposes, since sound pressure alone does not distinguish between incident sound, transmitted sound, and reflected sound.

Experimental determination of transmission loss ordinarily requires a source room and a receiving room. A panel made of the material to be tested is installed in a window in a wall between the rooms. The rooms are designed to minimize sound transmission paths other than through the test specimen.

Figure 6.2.8 shows one possible measurement configuration, where a noise generator, filter, and power amplifier control a speaker in the source room. Sound level is measured in the source room and the receiving room with a microphone assembly, measuring amplifier, and filter, and recorded on a level recorder. The measured sound is filtered to minimize the effect of background noise on the results. Of course, the filter settings will always be the same for the generated sound and the measured sound filters. Sound level may be averaged by rotating the microphone boom.

Transmission loss is determined from the following equation:

$$TL = L_S - L_R + 10 \lg\left(\frac{A_W}{A_R}\right) \qquad (6.2.35)$$

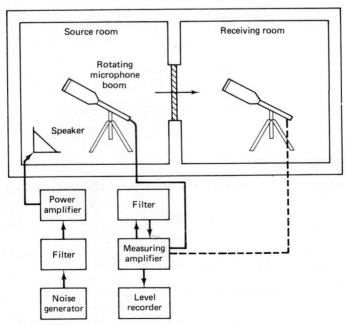

Figure 6.2.8   Transmission loss measurement.

where L_S = average sound level in the source room
        L_R = average sound level in the receiving room
        A_W = area of the material under test
        A_R = equivalent absorption area of the receiving room

An alternative arrangement is shown in Figure 6.2.9. This configuration includes a sound source which combines a pink-noise generator, filters, power amplifier, and speaker. The microprocessor-based serial analyzer includes a random noise generator and automatic controller for the microphone boom for spatial and temporal averaging. One such analyzer measures the following quantities in one-third octave bands: source room level, receiving room background level, receiving room level, and receiving room reverberation time.

Field Measurements

It is sometimes necessary to find the transmission loss of a wall or partition that is already installed. The procedure may be modeled after the laboratory methods described above, or modified to use available equipment such as a sound level meter with an octave band or one-third octave filter set. If a noise generator is not available, another source may be used. In a factory, for example, a piece of production machinery will serve as a sound source if it produces broadband noise without dominant pure tones. The noise output of the source should be stationary. That is, if each reading represents an average over a few seconds, the average noise output of the source during that period should be typical. When transmission loss measurements are made in situ, accuracy may be affected by background noise. To reduce this problem, generated sound levels should be relatively high, exceeding background noise levels by at least 6 to 10 dB.

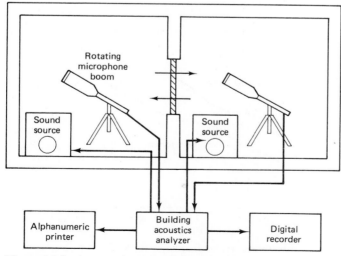

Figure 6.2.9 Automatic transmission loss test.

Figure 6.2.10 (Ginn, 1978) compares laboratory and in situ measurements of transmission loss in a concrete wall. Although measured transmission loss is substantially below theoretical values, the experimental values do approximate a 6 dB per octave slope, which is consistent with the mass law.

Flanking

Consider a noise source in one room and observer in an adjacent room. Noise transmission from source to observer will involve several paths in addition to transmission directly through the wall between the rooms. There may be acoustic leaks through cracks around doors and through electrical outlets or medicine cabinets mounted back to back. In addition there will be flanking paths that may be through adjacent rooms, or through hollow walls other than the common wall. When partitions are designed to end at a suspended ceiling, sound energy may penetrate the ceiling and be reflected to an adjacent room. Figure 6.2.11 illustrates flanking paths. Flanking and acoustic leaks reduce transmission loss measurement accuracy as well as limiting the effectiveness of sound insulation in buildings.

Combined Sound Transmission Coefficient

An actual wall may include several elements such as doors, windows, and cracks around doors. The combined sound transmission coefficient then depends on the τ of the individual elements and their areas. If the incident sound is approximately equal on all elements, then combined sound transmission coefficient is predicted from

$$\tau_{\text{combined}} = \frac{\sum_{i=1}^{n} (A\tau)_i}{\sum_{i=1}^{n} (A_i)} \tag{6.2.36}$$

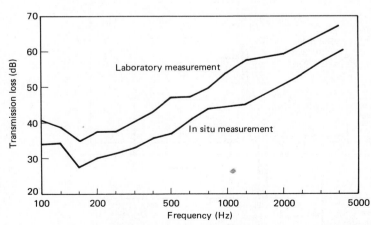

Figure 6.2.10 Transmission loss versus frequency for a 150-mm-thick concrete wall. (*Source:* K. B. Ginn, Bruel & Kjaer Instruments, Inc.)

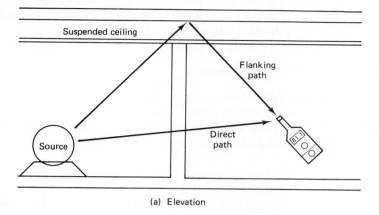

(a) Elevation

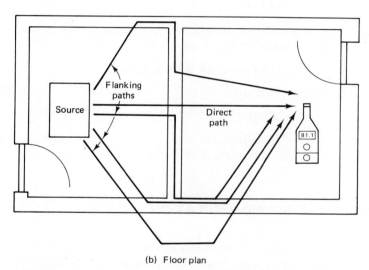

(b) Floor plan

Figure 6.2.11 Noise transmission by direct and flanking paths.

for n elements of area A_1, A_2, and so on. It is assumed that $\tau = 1$ for cracks and open areas. The transmission loss of the actual wall is then given by

$$\text{TL}_{\text{combined}} = 10 \lg\left(\frac{1}{\tau_{\text{combined}}}\right)$$

$$= 10 \lg\left[\frac{\sum\limits_{i=1}^{n}(A_i)}{\sum\limits_{i=1}^{n}(A10^{-\text{TL}/10})_i}\right] \qquad (6.2.37)$$

Although it would appear that transmission loss values could be doubled by using a double wall, this is not actually the case. In practical structural elements, sound leakage and flanking tend to dominate sound transmission, thus limiting the advantages of double walls and double-glazed windows.

EXAMPLE PROBLEM: TRANSMISSION LOSS

(a) A wall is made up of 4-in dense poured concrete with a transmission loss of 45 dB and a wood door with a transmission loss of 25 dB at a 500 Hz. The solid wall makes up 80% of the exposed area, the door 19%, and cracks around the door 1%. Estimate the effective transmission loss of the composite wall for sound with a dominant frequency of 500 Hz.

Solution. Let the total wall area be A. Then

$$TL_{combined} = 10 \lg[A/(0.80A10^{-45/10} + 0.19A10^{-25/10} + 0.01A10^{0/10})]$$

$$= 19.7 \text{ dB}$$

(b) Suppose a redesign calls for a thicker wall with a transmission loss of 55 dB and door with a 45-dB transmission loss. Evaluate the change.

Solution. If the area of the crack is unchanged,

$$TL_{combined} = 10 \lg[A/(0.80A10^{-55/10} + 0.19A10^{-45/10} + 0.01A10^{0/10})]$$

$$= 20 \text{ dB}$$

The improvement is insignificant because the crack governs noise transmission. A properly installed acoustical door would seal this area.

6.3 DESIGN FOR IMPROVED SOUND INSULATION

It can be seen that increased wall mass will increase transmission loss in the frequency region where the mass law applies. Sound insulation can also be improved by damping, by the use of double-panel walls, by reduction of flanking transmission paths, and by reduction of acoustic leaks.

Damping

Damping refers to the energy dissipation properties of a material. All materials have inherent damping characteristics. For materials with low internal damping, a thick coating of viscoelastic material may be added to the surface to improve damping. Energy dissipation occurs when the damping material flexes. Thus, additional damping is effective in the resonance and coincidence frequency ranges. Damping has little effect in the mass-controlled frequency range, except for the added mass of the damping material. Viscoelastic coatings are used to improve transmission loss of thin steel partitions, but would not be effective if used on heavy masonry walls.

Double-Panel Walls

Within the range of application of the mass law, a doubling of surface mass of a wall increases transmission loss by 6 dB. This is reasonably close to experimental results, as shown in the plot of transmission loss versus frequency for a concrete wall. It would seem that transmission loss could be doubled by constructing a second wall. As pointed out earlier, this is not the case due to flanking paths and sound transmission paths through studs and other members joining the two walls. However, the transmission loss for a double-panel wall of total surface mass M usually exceeds that of a single panel with surface mass M. Double-panel walls are most effective if the panels on one side are supported by studs that are isolated from the studs supporting the panels on the other side. For double-panel walls made of thin panels, sound transmission at resonance may be reduced by fiberglass insulation within the cavity.

Control of Air Leaks and Flanking Paths

If there are significant cracks around doors or if there are other air leaks, then most of the sound energy may be transmitted by such paths. In such cases, improvements in transmission loss of the wall will not be effective. Air leaks around doors can be reduced by close-fitting doorstop molding and by felt or rubber gaskets.

A hallway may provide access to two adjacent rooms. If there is no door in the wall common to the two rooms, more noise energy may be transmitted by the flanking path (through the hallway) than by the direct path. In this case, noise control may be improved by use of close-fitting hallway doors.

Suspended ceilings are sometimes installed when buildings are remodeled. If partitions extend only to a suspended ceiling, the space above the suspended ceiling can be an important flanking path. Flanking noise transmission can be reduced by extending the partitions to the original ceiling.

Doors and Windows

Doors and windows are often "weak links" with regard to protection against intrusive noise. Specially designed and installed acoustic doors have sound transmission class (STC) ratings of 45 to 65. The STC rating scheme, based on transmission loss at a set of frequencies, is discussed in a later section. A $1\frac{3}{4}$-in-thick solid wood door weighing 3.6 lb/ft^2 has an approximate STC 26 rating if weatherstripped with plastic or spring metal seals at four edges. A weatherstripped steel-faced door of the same thickness weighing 3.2 lb/ft^2 will also have an approximate STC 26 rating. A typical poorly fit entrance door may have an effective STC rating of only about 12, largely due to air leakage.

Noise transmission through doorways can be reduced by using two well-sealed doors separated by a short passageway. Careful installation is required in every case to meet the somewhat conflicting requirements of close tolerances for noise control and free operation for utility and safety.

Window transmission loss can be improved by double glazing, which improves thermal insulation as well. If we assume that windows behave in the same manner as wall panels, then the low-frequency resonance may be estimated on the basis of a mass-spring model. A small airspace is represented by a stiff spring, and a large airspace by a soft spring. The resonant frequency is inversely proportional to the square root of surface mass times spacing, as determined in the preceding section. For typical panes spaced a few millimeters apart, the low-frequency resonance may be in the range of road traffic noise frequencies and the speech frequency range. Spacing of 75 to 100 mm (about 3 to 4 in) between panes reduces the low-frequency resonance, usually improving the performance of the window as a sound barrier. Thermal insulation may be improved by the wider spacing as well.

Fixed windows usually provide higher transmission loss values than windows which can be opened. However, a mechanical ventilation system is usually required when fixed windows are used. Thus, improved performance with regard to exterior noise may be balanced by noise of the mechanical ventilation system, a lack of fresh air, and a perception of being "closed in."

Roofs, Floors, and Ceilings

Concrete and other heavy roofing materials provide high transmission loss values. If there is an unoccupied attic, sound transmitted through the roof must then pass through a second barrier to reach the highest occupied floor. Thus, in most situations, more noise energy is transmitted to a building interior via the walls and windows than through the roof.

When floors are made of concrete or other heavy materials, they provide an effective barrier to transmission of airborne sound. However, concrete floors are not as effective for impact noise. Carpeting and other resilient floor coverings, which absorb impact energy rather than transmitting it to the floor, are recommended to reduce noise transmission.

Floating floor construction, in which a floating floor is separated from a structural floor by a resilient support, is described by Ginn (1978). A damped spring-mass model applies in this case. The natural frequency of the system should be below the audible range if the system is to be effective. This condition is met if the floating mass is large and the support has a low spring rate. Rigid mechanical connections between the floating floor and the structural floor should be avoided since any such connections would make the system ineffective.

6.4 SOUND TRANSMISSION CLASS (STC)

Sound transmission class (STC) is a single-number descriptor of noise insulation effectiveness of a structural element. It is commonly used to describe the characteristics of interior walls with regard to noise in the speech-frequency range (e.g. speech, music, television, and radio). STC is calculated from transmission loss values measured in one-third octave bands in the 125-Hz to 4-kHz range.

The standard STC contour is shown in Figure 6.4.1. Beginning at 125 Hz, the contour slopes upward at 3 dB per one-third octave (9 dB per octave) to 400 Hz, where the slope changes to 1 dB per one-third octave (3 dB per octave) up to 1.25

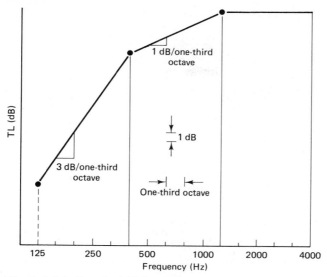

Figure 6.4.1 Standard STC contour.

kHz. The slope is zero from 1.25 to 4 kHz. The STC contour is identified by its level at 500 Hz.

The STC rating of a structural element is determined by comparing measured transmission loss values with standard STC contours. Where the contour lies above the measured transmission loss, the difference in decibels for each one-third octave band is called a deficiency. The STC rating is given by the highest STC contour for which no deficiency exceeds 8 dB and the total deficiencies do not exceed 32 dB.

EXAMPLE PROBLEM: SOUND TRANSMISSION CLASS

(a) Construct an overlay for determining STC from measured values of transmission loss.

Solution. Using a clear plastic sheet, and using the same scale as the transmission loss values, plot nine standard STC contours at 1-dB intervals. The contours may be numbered 0 through 8 as in Figure 6.4.2. The overlay is aligned with a plot of measured transmission loss versus frequency so that each measured value falls on or above contour 8. It is then adjusted to the highest integer STC value for which the sum of the deficiencies (given by the sum of the contour numbers) does not exceed 32, with no deficiency exceeding 8. The STC rating is given by the ordinate of contour 0 at 500 Hz.

(b) Find the STC rating of a wall based on the following values of transmission loss measured in the 16 one-third octave bands with center frequencies beginning at 125 Hz: 22, 23, 28, 31, 34, 36, 38, 39, 36, 41, 41, 43, 44, 45, 45, and 47 dB.

Solution. If the overlay is not used, we may estimate the STC value. Let the first approximation be STC 42. The STC 42 contour has a transmission loss of

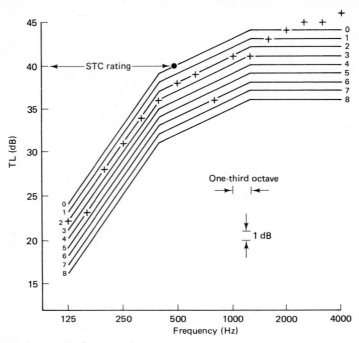

Figure 6.4.2 STC overlay.

42 dB at 500 Hz. Other transmission loss values for the STC 42 contour are determined from the slopes of the standard STC contour. It can be seen that the standard contour transmission loss at 125 Hz is 16 dB less than the transmission loss at 500 Hz. Thus, the STC 42 contour begins at

$$TL = 42 - 16 = 26 \text{ dB at } 125 \text{ Hz}$$

and increases by 3 dB per one-third octave to 41 dB at 400 Hz. The STC 42 contour then increases by 1 dB per one-third octave to 46 dB at 1.25 kHz, remaining at that level to 4 kHz. These relationships were incorporated into a spreadsheet program which generated Table 6.4.1a. It shows the measured transmission loss values for each one-third octave band, the transmission loss values for the STC 42 contour, and the differences or deficiencies. Although the largest deficiency is 8 dB, total deficiencies for the STC 42 contour exceed 32 dB. Thus, the actual STC is lower than 42.

Let the second approximation be STC 40. The spreadsheet table is automatically adjusted when the sound transmission class value is changed from 42 to 40. Table 6.4.1b shows the new results. The largest deficiency for the STC 40 contour is 6 dB and the sum of the deficiencies is 31 dB. Thus, the wall has an STC 40 rating. Figure 6.4.3, showing the transmission loss values and the STC 40 contour, was plotted by the spreadsheet program. A solution utilizing the overlay is illustrated in Figure 6.4.2.

TABLE 6.4.1(a) SOUND TRANSMISSION CLASS CONTOUR: STC 42

1/3 octave band	Frequency (Hz)	Contour level − STC	Contour level (dB)	TL (dB)	Deficiency CL − TL (dB)	1 = pass 0 = fail
1	125	−16	26	22	4	1
2	160	−13	29	23	6	1
3	200	−10	32	28	4	1
4	250	−7	35	31	4	1
5	315	−4	38	34	4	1
6	400	−1	41	36	5	1
7	500	0	42	38	4	1
8	630	1	43	39	4	1
9	800	2	44	36	8	1
10	1000	3	45	41	4	1
11	1250	4	46	41	5	1
12	1600	4	46	43	3	1
13	2000	4	46	44	2	1
14	2500	4	46	45	1	1
15	3150	4	46	45	1	1
16	4000	4	46	47	0	1
			Sum of deficiencies (dB) =		59	0

Typical STC Ratings for Common Structural Elements

STC ratings for structural elements are available from manufacturer's catalogs. However, noise transmission through a wall or other structural element depends on many factors including the materials used in construction, air leakage, and flanking noise

TABLE 6.4.1(b) SOUND TRANSMISSION CLASS CONTOUR: STC 40

1/3 octave band	Frequency (Hz)	Contour level − STC	Contour level (dB)	TL (dB)	Deficiency CL − TL (dB)	1 = pass 0 = fail
1	125	−16	24	22	2	1
2	160	−13	27	23	4	1
3	200	−10	30	28	2	1
4	250	−7	33	31	2	1
5	315	−4	36	34	2	1
6	400	−1	39	36	3	1
7	500	0	40	38	2	1
8	630	1	41	39	2	1
9	800	2	42	36	6	1
10	1000	3	43	41	2	1
11	1250	4	44	41	3	1
12	1600	4	44	43	1	1
13	2000	4	44	44	0	1
14	2500	4	44	45	0	1
15	3150	4	44	45	0	1
16	4000	4	44	47	0	1
			Sum of deficiencies (dB) =		31	1

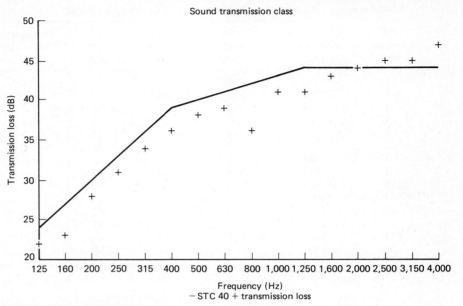

Figure 6.4.3   STC 40 contour.

transmission through adjacent elements. Typical ranges of STC are listed below. Actual values may fall outside of these ranges due to variations in construction.

Description	STC
4-in- (100-mm-) thick brick wall with airtight joints	40
4-in- (100-mm-) thick brick wall with gypsum-board on one side	45 to 50
8-in- (200-mm-) thick brick wall with gypsum-board on one side	50 to 60
4-in- (100-mm-) thick hollow concrete block with airtight joints	36 to 41
4-in- (100-mm-) thick hollow concrete block with gypsum-board on one side	42 to 48
8-in- (200-mm-) thick hollow concrete block with airtight joints	46 to 50
8-in- (200-mm-) thick hollow concrete block with gypsum-board on both sides	50 to 55
2 × 4-in (nominal) wood or metal stud wall with gypsum-board on both sides, spackled at joints, floor, and ceiling	33 to 43
Single-glazed window	20 to 30
Double-glazed window	26 to 44
Hollow core wood or steel door	20 to 27
Specially mounted acoustical door	38 to 55
Double-walled soundproof room, 12-in- (300-mm-) thick walls including airspace	70
Quilted fiberglass mounted on vinyl or lead (limp mass) barrier septum	21 to 29

6.5 SHELL ISOLATION RATING (SIR)

The SIR method is the result of a study at the U.S. National Bureau of Standards (Pallett et al., 1978). The objective of the study was to derive a simple system to predict the attenuation of *A*-weighted transportation noise by building shells. Spectral data were obtained from the literature for 11 examples of highway noise, 11 examples of railway noise, and 5 examples of aircraft noise. The 27 noise spectra were analyzed with 507 partitions for an acoustically hard room, a medium room, and a soft room. A sound transmission class (STC) contour, a flat contour, and a +3 dB per octave contour were considered. Based on the results of a statistical study, the +3 dB per octave contour was selected for the standard SIR contour. STC is generally favored for describing the noise reduction effectiveness of building partitions in the presence of the sounds of speech, radio, and television. The authors of the study indicate that shell isolation rating (SIR) is a better descriptor for noise reduction of building shells subject to transportation sounds.

Determination of SIR from Transmission Loss Data

An element-SIR or member-SIR is an estimate of the difference in A-weighted sound levels if the member is placed between a transportation noise source and observer, assuming that all noise transmission is through the member. A room-SIR or composite-SIR estimates the A-weighted sound level difference, considering all members that act as noise transmission paths between the source and receiver. If the meaning is clear in the context, member-SIR and composite-SIR may both be identified simply as SIR.

Member-SIR may be determined from a set of transmission loss measurements in octave bands or one-third octave bands as follows:

1. Plot transmission loss versus frequency.
2. Plot the +3 dB per octave SIR reference contour on a transparent overlay sheet.
3. Shift the overlay vertically over the transmission loss data to the highest position at which the sum of the deficiencies is less than twice the number of test frequencies. A deficiency is the number of decibels by which the SIR reference value exceeds the measured transmission loss of the member.
4. The SIR of the member is given by the transmission loss value corresponding to the 500-Hz coordinate of the SIR reference curve.

The predictive value of SIR is improved by increasing the number of transmission loss measurements. One-third octave measurements will generally give better results than octave-band measurements. Manufacturers of building materials often report the one-third octave-band transmission loss measurements used to determine STC; these transmission loss values may be used to determine SIR.

EXAMPLE PROBLEM: DETERMINATION OF SIR FOR A MEMBER

Consider the wall examined in the sound transmission class example problem above. Determine the SIR.

Solution. If an overlay is not used, we may estimate the SIR value. Let the first approximation be SIR 40 based on the value of STC. The SIR 40 standard contour has a transmission loss of 40 at 500 Hz. SIR standard contours have a slope of +3 dB per octave or +1 dB per one-third octave. Thus, the transmission

TABLE 6.5.1a   SHELL ISOLATION RATING CONTOUR: SIR 40

1/3 octave band	Frequency (Hz)	Contour level − SIR	Contour level (dB)	TL (dB)	Deficiency CL − TL (dB)
1	125	−6	34	22	12
2	160	−5	35	23	12
3	200	−4	36	28	8
4	250	−3	37	31	6
5	315	−2	38	34	4
6	400	−1	39	36	3
7	500	0	40	38	2
8	630	1	41	39	2
9	800	2	42	36	6
10	1000	3	43	41	2
11	1250	4	44	41	3
12	1600	5	45	43	2
13	2000	6	46	44	2
14	2500	7	47	45	2
15	3150	8	48	45	3
16	4000	9	49	47	2
			Sum of deficiencies (dB) =		71
			Pass = 1 Fail = 0		0

loss of a standard SIR contour at 125 Hz is 6 dB less than the value at 500 Hz. The SIR 40 standard contour is described by a line with a +1 dB per one-third octave slope where TL = 40 − 6 = 34 dB at 125 Hz. These relationships were incorporated into the spreadsheet program which generated Table 6.5.1a. It

TABLE 6.5.1b   SHELL ISOLATION RATING CONTOUR: SIR 37

1/3 octave band	Frequency (Hz)	Contour level − SIR	Contour level (dB)	TL (dB)	Deficiency CL − TL (dB)
1	125	−6	31	22	9
2	160	−5	32	23	9
3	200	−4	33	28	5
4	250	−3	34	31	3
5	315	−2	35	34	1
6	400	−1	36	36	0
7	500	0	37	38	0
8	630	1	38	39	0
9	800	2	39	36	3
10	1000	3	40	41	0
11	1250	4	41	41	0
12	1600	5	42	43	0
13	2000	6	43	44	0
14	2500	7	44	45	0
15	3150	8	45	45	0
16	4000	9	46	47	0
			Sum of deficiencies (dB) =		30
			Pass = 1 Fail = 0		1

shows the measured transmission loss of the wall for each one-third octave band, the transmission loss values for the SIR 40 contour, and the deficiencies.

It can be seen that total deficiencies for the SIR 40 contour exceed twice the number of measurements or 32 dB. Let us enter the second approximation: SIR 37. The spreadsheet is automatically recomputed as shown in Table 6.5.1b. In this case, total deficiencies total 30 dB. Thus, the wall transmission loss is equivalent to SIR 37. Figure 6.5.1 is a computer-generated plot showing the results.

The field incidence mass law,

$$TL = 20 \lg(fm) - 47 \text{ dB}$$

may be of some help in extrapolating data. Consider construction element 1 whose transmission loss is known for all frequencies of interest and a similar element 2 of different surface mass and unknown transmission loss. Then,

$$TL_2 = TL_1 + 20 \lg\left(\frac{m_2}{m_1}\right)$$

may be used to estimate the unknown transmission loss. If the relationship holds for all frequencies in the range of interest, then values of SIR are similarly related.

EXAMPLE PROBLEM: SIR EXTRAPOLATION

Four-inch-thick dense poured concrete with 50 lb/ft^2 surface mass has a rating of SIR 41. Estimate the SIR for (a) 6-in-thick dense poured concrete with 73 lb/ft^2 surface mass and (b) 8-in-thick dense poured concrete with 95 lb/ft^2 surface mass.

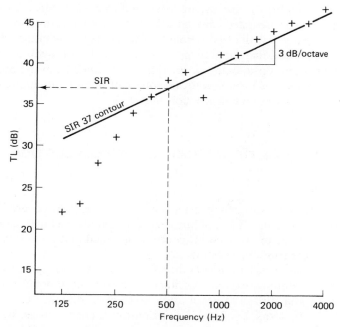

Figure 6.5.1 SIR determination.

Solution. Using the mass law relationship to extrapolate for the unknown SIR's we have

$$SIR_2 = SIR_1 + 20 \lg\left(\frac{m_2}{m_1}\right)$$

from which

$$\text{(a)} \quad SIR_{\text{6-in concrete}} = 41 + 20 \lg\left(\frac{73}{50}\right) = 44.3$$

and

$$\text{(b)} \quad SIR_{\text{8-in concrete}} = 41 + 20 \lg\left(\frac{95}{50}\right) = 46.6$$

Actual structural elements are more complicated than the mathematical model used to derive the mass law. Resonances, air leakage, and flanking paths contribute to sound transmission in practical members, limiting the validity of mass law extrapolations. The 6- and 8-in concrete walls are given SIR 43 and SIR 46 ratings, respectively, using data from the reference used to compute the SIR for the 4-in concrete wall.

Representative SIR Values for Construction Elements

Representative SIR values, compiled by the National Bureau of Standards (Pallett et al., 1978) from a number of sources, are listed in Table 6.6.1. SIR's for construction elements other than those listed may be calculated from transmission loss data, or estimated by comparison with listed elements. These data are included only to provide a sample of available building components. When specifying products for construction, it is recommended that up-to-date information be obtained from the manufacturers. The periodical *Sound and Vibration* is one source of names and addresses of manufacturers of acoustically rated construction materials.

6.6 PREDICTION AND CONTROL OF INTERIOR SOUND LEVELS DUE TO INTRUSIVE NOISE

Noise levels inside of a room can be determined if all noise sources are identified and the transmission loss values (TL's) of building components are known. Only intrusive noise will be considered in this section, since it is assumed that we may control sounds generated within the room in question.

Suppose it is necessary to predict intrusive noise levels in a proposed residential building. Before beginning, we must decide on the amount of detail necessary in the solution. Aircraft and surface transportation noise may impinge on the roof and exterior walls of the building. Each noise contribution is characterized by its level, fre-

TABLE 6.6.1 SHELL ISOLATION RATING

Description	Weight (lb/ft^2)	SIR rating
Dense poured concrete or solid block walls		
4 in thick	50	41
6 in thick	73	43
8 in thick	95	46
12 in thick	145	49
16 in thick	190	51
Hollow concrete block walls		
6 in thick	21	41
8 in thick	30	43
Brick veneered frame walls	—	48 to 53
Stuccoed frame walls	—	34 to 52
Frame walls with wood siding	—	33 to 40
Metal walls, curtain walls	—	25 to 39
Shingled wood roof with attic	10	40
Steel roofs	—	36 to 51
Fixed, single-glazed windows (the higher SIR values apply to windows with special mountings and laminated glass)	—	22 to 39
Fixed, double-glazed windows (the higher SIR values apply to windows with large spaces between the glass and special mountings)	—	22 to 48
Double-hung windows		
Single-glazed	—	20 to 24
Double-glazed	—	20 to 29
Casement windows, single-glazed	—	19 to 29
Horizontal sliding windows	—	16 to 24
Glass doors	2.6 to 3	24
Wood doors (the higher SIR values apply to weatherstripped doors)		
Hollow core	1.2 to 5	14 to 26
Solid core	4 to 5	16 to 30
Steel doors (the higher SIR values apply to acoustical doors)	4 to 23	21 to 50

Source: NBS (1978).

quency content, and time pattern. Transmission loss values for the roof, walls, and other building components are frequency dependent. Considering these variables as well as the spacial variables within the building, the problem appears to be overwhelming with regard to effort required in the solution and the amount of output data. Problems of this type are usually made tractable by using single-number descriptors for noise levels such as equivalent sound level (L_{eq}) or day–night sound level (L_{DN}) and single-number descriptors for structural noise attenuation such as sound transmission class (STC) or shell isolation rating (SIR). The SIR method will be used in examples in this section because of its particular application to transportation noise. If STC is preferred, a similar procedure may be used.

Noise Criteria

Noise level criteria should be established based on the intended use of each room. The Environmental Protection Agency (EPA) and Department of Housing and Urban Development (HUD) have published material that will aid in selecting criterion levels. The following levels of yearly equivalent sound level and day–night sound level are identified for protection of public health and welfare by the EPA (1978). However, in some areas, exterior noise levels are so high that no feasible design would satisfy the identified level based on indoor activity interference and annoyance. In such areas, particularly near airports and highways, other criteria would be selected.

EPA IDENTIFIED LEVELS

Effect	Level	Area
Hearing	$L_{eq24} \leq 70$ dBA	All areas (measured at the ear)
Indoor activity interference	$L_{DN} \leq 45$ dBA	Indoor residential areas
and annoyance	$L_{eq24} \leq 45$ dBA	Other indoor areas with human activities such as schools, and so on

Analysis and Design Strategies

In most cases, representative rooms will be selected for analysis instead of making detailed calculations for every room in a proposed building. Let us assume that the noise exposure is known at each exterior wall and the roof. Exposure data could be based on measurements or, if measurements are unavailable, exterior noise exposure can be calculated from the prediction methods given in chapters that follow. Usually analysis begins with the "worst case" rooms, those rooms with the greatest noise exposure and the most sensitive usage. Different strategies may be selected, the following suggested by NBS (Pallett et al., 1978).

Strategy 1   Analyze the "worst case" rooms. If the noise criteria are satisfied, no further action is necessary. If noise levels exceed the criteria, redesign the room until the criteria are met. Continue with the remaining rooms which now become "worst case."

Strategy 2   Repeat strategy 1. Then examine "best case" rooms, those with the lowest noise exposure and the least sensitive use. If noise levels are below the criteria, consider degrading these rooms, providing the changes result in significant cost savings and do not violate building codes.

Strategy 3   Analyze representative rooms. Improve "worst case" rooms until the average sound level of all rooms in the building satisfies the appropriate criterion, while no room exceeds the criterion by more than 5 dBA.

Strategy 1 will be the best choice in most circumstances. Strategy 2 could provide cost savings, for example, by using single-glazed instead of double-glazed windows on the sides of the building with the least roadway exposure. However, many such changes in the plans could result in negligible construction savings and poorer thermal insulation. Criterion 3, if applied to a multiple dwelling, could result in indoor activity interference and annoyance for some occupants.

Noise Reduction of a Composite Structure

A building may be subject to noise contributions from aircraft, highway, and railway noise. Noise may enter a "worst case" room through the roof, through the building facade, and through a flanking wall, where each of the walls may be made up of components with different noise control properties. If the data and the steps in the solution are tabulated, it is easier to identify critical components for changes if improved noise control is necessary. Recalculation of various noise control options along with a cost analysis is further expedited if an electronic spreadsheet program is used. Figure 6.6.1, which follows, is one possible format.

Calculation Procedure for Determination of Intrusive Noise Level

1. Custom design a worksheet for the proposed building. Use a separate worksheet for each room. Begin with a room that appears to be a "worst case" room. Identify the measurement units and enter the room data. Enter data for shell members (e.g., facade, roof, flanking wall). Enter data for shell member components (e.g., brick wall, windows). Enter component SIR's from the table of representative values, or values calculated from other source material.

2. It will be assumed that single-number descriptors like SIR and STC behave in the same way as transmission loss (TL) with regard to combining components. Then, the transmission coefficient (TC), the fraction of incident sound energy transmitted through the component, is given by

$$TC = 10^{-SIR/10} \qquad (6.6.1)$$

The member transmission coefficient is obtained by combining the element transmission coefficients as follows:

$$TC_{member} = \frac{\sum\limits_{i=1}^{n} (A\,TC)_i}{\sum\limits_{i=1}^{n} A_i} \qquad (6.6.2)$$

for n components of area A_1, A_2, and so on. For open areas and cracks, SIR = 0 and TC = 1. Applying equation 6.6.1 to the member and taking the base-ten logarithm of both sides, we have

$$SIR_{member} = 10 \lg\left(\frac{1}{TC_{member}}\right) \qquad (6.6.3)$$

Building description and location _____

Room description and location _____ w ___ l ___ h ___

Shell member								
Shell member area								
Shell member components								
Component SIR								
Component dimensions								
Component area								
Component fractional area								
Member SIR								
Air leakage								
Member area/floor area								
Geometry correction								
Absorption corrections								
Adjusted member SIR								
Room SIR								

Noise contributions: Highway _____ Aircraft _____ Railway _____

Combined _____

Indoor intrusive sound level _____

Criterion level _____   Exceeded? Yes ____ No ____

Figure 6.6.1 Noise reduction worksheet.

The above equations may be combined to compute member SIR in one step:

$$SIR_{member} = 10 \lg \left[\frac{\sum_{i=1}^{n} (A_i)}{\sum_{i=1}^{n} (A10^{-SIR/10})_i} \right] \qquad (6.6.4)$$

3. If air leakage was not considered in step 2, member SIR should now be adjusted, based on the quality of workmanship. Typical air leakage areas are given below, where

$$\frac{1 \text{ in}^2}{100 \text{ ft}^2} = \frac{1}{14,400} = 69.44 \times 10^{-6}$$

AIR OPENINGS (in^2/100 ft^2 of wall)

Workmanship	Excellent	Good	Average
Monolithic walls	0	0.75 to 1.5	1.5 to 3
Walls with fixed windows or other panels	0	1.5 to 3	3 to 4.5
Walls with weatherstripped operable windows	0	3 to 4.5	4.5 to 6
Walls with nonweatherstripped operable windows	0	4.5 to 6	6 to 7.5

Source: Pallett et al. (1978).

If the ratio of air opening area to member area is A_A, then the member SIR corrected for air leakage, SIR$_A$, may be calculated by rewriting the above equation as follows:

$$\text{SIR}_A = 10 \lg\{1/[A_A + (1 - A_A)10^{-\text{SIRmember}/10}]\}$$

$$= -10 \lg[A_A + (1 - A_A)10^{-\text{SIRmember}/10}] \qquad (6.6.5)$$

The significance of a small crack or air leak depends on the acoustic properties of the basic wall. For example, a wall rated SIR 60 would theoretically transmit only one-millionth of the transportation noise energy incident on it. Consider the same wall with air openings of 3 in^2/100 ft^2 of wall area ($A_A = 3/14,400$). The corrected SIR, as given by the above equation, is

$$\text{SIR}_A = -10 \lg[2.083 \times 10^{-4} + (1 - 2.083 \times 10^{-4})10^{-60/10}]$$

$$= 36.8$$

indicating the wall would transmit roughly one five-thousandth of the incident energy. In contrast, a wall rated SIR 25 is not significantly degraded by the same air openings. A similar calculation for the SIR 25 wall leads to SIR$_A$ = 24.7.

4. For a given room, a large exposed wall would transmit more sound energy than a similar wall of small area. It is suggested that the following corrections be applied to SIR$_A$:

ROOM GEOMETRY CORRECTION

Wall area/floor area	Correction
0.94 to 1	−2
0.67 to 0.93	−1
0.50 to 0.66	0
0.37 to 0.49	+1
0.28 to 0.36	+2
0.22 to 0.27	+3
0.17 to 0.21	+4
0.13 to 0.16	+5
0.10 to 0.12	+6
All roof areas	−2

Source: Pallett et al. (1978).

5. Actual sound levels within a room will depend on sound absorption within the room, which can be determined by measuring reverberation time. If we are predicting sound levels in a room in a proposed building, the effect of absorption may be estimated. The following corrections to SIR_A are suggested:

ABSORPTION CORRECTION

Room description	Correction
Carpeted room without acoustical ceiling and without heavy drapes	0
Acoustical ceiling or 50% or more of wall area covered with draperies	+2
No carpet, no acoustical ceiling, and no heavy draperies	−4

Source: Pallett (1978).

6. Member SIR's are calculated for each exposed wall and the roof as appropriate. Each member SIR is corrected for air leakage and then corrected for geometry and absorption to form $SIR_{adjusted}$. These values are then combined as were the component values. However, in this case, the area adjustments were already made. Thus, we find the room SIR as follows:

$$SIR_{room} = 10 \lg\left[1 \left/ \sum_{i=1}^{n} (10^{-SIRadjusted/10})_i \right.\right]$$

$$= -10 \lg\left[\sum_{i=1}^{n} (10^{-SIRadjusted/10})_i \right] \qquad (6.6.6)$$

7. Noise contributions from highway, aircraft, and railway traffic may be measured or predicted. Noise levels will be combined as follows:

$$L_{exterior} = 10 \lg(10^{L(highway)/10} + 10^{L(aircraft)/10} + 10^{L(railway)/10}) \qquad (6.6.7)$$

If the descriptor of choice is 24-hour equivalent sound level (L_{eq24}), then L_{eq24}'s for highway, aircraft, and railway noise may be substituted in equation 6.6.7 to produce combined exterior L_{eq24}.

The procedure is the same if day–night sound level (L_{DN}) is the descriptor of choice. In some cases, data may be available as hourly equivalent sound levels predicted for representative intervals during the day and night. Using equation 6.6.7, the transportation noise L_{eq} contributions are combined for the 7 A.M. to 10 P.M. daytime period to form L_{eqD}. Then, L_{eqN} is formed from the 10 P.M. to 7 A.M. nighttime contributions. Combined exterior L_{DN} is given by

$$L_{DNexterior} = 10 \lg\left[\frac{1}{24} (15 \times 10^{L_{eqD}/10} + 9 \times 10^{(L_{eqN}+10)/10}) \right] \qquad (6.6.8)$$

For statistical descriptors like L_{10}, a more detailed level-time pattern would be required. Fortunately, noise criteria in the form of statistical descriptors have largely been replaced by L_{eq} and L_{DN}. Noise-measuring equipment is available which can be programmed to produce L_{eq}, L_{DN}, L_{10}, or other descriptors. Of course, noise measurements during representative periods will produce the combined contributions directly.

8. Interior intrusive sound level is given by

$$L_{interior} = L_{exterior} - SIR_{room} \qquad (6.6.9)$$

In some cases, a flanking wall or roof will have a significantly different noise exposure than a building facade. When this occurs, the interior noise contribution at each member should be calculated based on the adjusted member SIR's. For this alternative case, interior intrusive sound level is given by

$$L_{interior} = 10 \lg \sum_{i=1}^{N} 10^{L_i/10} \qquad (6.6.10)$$

where L_1 is the level of interior noise transmitted through member 1, and so on.

9. Indoor intrusive sound level is compared with the criterion level. If the criterion is exceeded, redesign of critical components should be considered. These components will be identified on the worksheet by their low SIR's. Improvements in components with high SIR's are unlikely to produce any significant overall improvement.

EXAMPLE PROBLEM: PREDICTION OF INTERIOR SOUND LEVELS

A top-floor corner room in a proposed residential structure is to be constructed as follows:

Member 1, Facade Wall
Component 1: 7 m^2 (net) wall of $8 \times 8 \times 16$ in hollow concrete blocks with gypsum-board fastened on furring strips inside.

Component 2: 5 m^2 double-glazed window, 6-mm glass, 13.3-mm airspace, 8-mm glass, sealed unit.

Member 2, Flanking Wall
Similar to facade wall.

Component 1: 4 m^2 (net) wall.

Component 2: 2.6 m^2 double-glazed window.

Member 3, Steel Roof
3-in-thick roof with 20 gage steel roof decking.

The floor area of the room will be 13 m^2. The floor will be carpeted and an acoustical ceiling will be installed. Expected transportation activity near the site results in predicted day–night sound level contributions of 70, 67, and 61 for highway, aircraft, and railway sources, respectively.

(a) Estimate intrusive interior noise levels due to transportation noise, and evaluate the results.

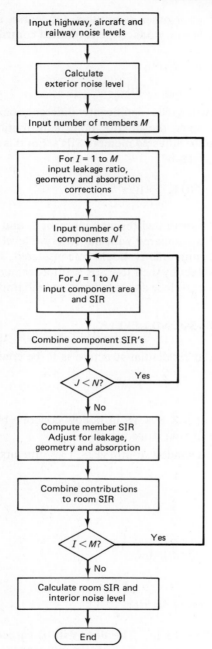

Figure 6.6.2 Flowchart for prediction of interior noise.

Solution. The noise reduction worksheet may be used to assemble data and solve the problem. If several rooms are to be evaluated, or if changes in construction are possible, a computer solution will save time and aid in selecting the best construction alternatives. One possible solution form is outlined in the flowchart for prediction of interior noise, Figure 6.6.2. The computer program should initialize variables as required. If a printer is available, input data and intermediate results can be printed as well as the solution. These items make it easier to evaluate critical construction elements. All calculations are based on equations given in this section. Note the nested loops, arranged so that each equation is coded only once. Although fractional dBA values are retained in the calculation, the accuracy of our data does not warrant their retention in the results. In fact, the margin of error in noise predictions often exceeds 1 dBA.

Input data and results for the proposed construction project are shown in Table 6.6.2. The three transportation sources produce a combined level of

$$L_{DN} = 72 \text{ dB}A$$

Based on the table of air openings, walls of average construction with fixed windows have air leakage areas of 3 to 4.5 in^2/ft^2 (2.08×10^{-4} to 3.13×10^{-4}). We will assume air openings of 3×10^{-4}. After we add net wall area and window area, the facade wall area is 12 m^2 and the flanking wall area 6.6 m^2. The wall area to floor area ratios are 0.92 for the facade wall and 0.51 for the flanking wall. Using these values in the room geometry correction table, the corrections are, respectively, -1 and 0. A room geometry correction of -2 is specified for all roof areas. Using the absorption correction table, we find the correction to be $+2$ for carpeted rooms with acoustical ceilings. The shell isolation rating table gives values of SIR 46 for the concrete block walls, SIR 32 for the double-glazed windows, and SIR 43 for the steel roof. After we combine component values and adjust for air leakage, geometry, and absorption, the corrected values are SIR 33 for the facade wall, SIR 34 for the flanking wall, and SIR 43 for the roof.

TABLE 6.6.2 INTERIOR NOISE PREDICTION

NOISE LEVELS IN DBA   HIGHWAY: 70   AIRCRAFT: 67   RAILWAY: 61
EXTERIOR NOISE LEVEL (DBA) =   72.11408
MEMBER   1
LEAKAGE RATIO=   .0003   GEOMETRY COR.= −1   ABSORPTION COR.= 2
COMPONENT   1   AREA=   7   SIR=   46
COMPONENT   2   AREA=   5   SIR=   32
MEMBER # 1   SIR =   35.56656   LEAKAGE CORRECTED SIR=   32.38472
         ADJUSTED SIR =   33.38472
MEMBER   2
LEAKAGE RATIO=   .0003   GEOMETRY COR.= 0   ABSORPTION COR.= 2
COMPONENT   1   AREA=   4   SIR=   46
COMPONENT   2   AREA=   2.6   SIR=   32
MEMBER # 2   SIR =   35.78754   LEAKAGE CORRECTED SIR=   32.4895
         ADJUSTED SIR =   34.4895
MEMBER   3
LEAKAGE RATIO=   .0003   GEOMETRY COR.= −2   ABSORPTION COR.= 2
COMPONENT   1   SIR=   43
MEMBER # 3   SIR =   43   LEAKAGE CORRECTED SIR=   34.55803
         ADJUSTED SIR =   34.55803
ROOM SIR =   29.3
INTERIOR NOISE LEVEL (DBA) =   42.8

The combined result is a room SIR of 29. Subtracting the room SIR from the exterior noise level, we obtain

$$L_{\text{DNinterior}} = L_{\text{DNexterior}} - \text{SIR}_{\text{room}} = 72 - 29 = 43 \text{ dB}A$$

If we use the $L_{\text{DN}} \leq 45$ dBA criterion, based on indoor activity interference and annoyance, the room is satisfactory.

(b) A proposed airport improvement will result in flightpath changes and increased air traffic. It is predicted that the L_{DN} contribution due to aircraft will increase to 74 dBA. Evaluate the impact of this change.

Solution. The contributions are combined as in part (a), resulting in a noise level of

$$L_{\text{DNexterior}} = 75.6 \text{ dB}A$$

If the building construction is unchanged, the interior noise level is

$$L_{\text{DNinterior}} = 46 \text{ dB}A$$

due to transportation noise. Predicted interior noise level exceeds the indoor activity interference and annoyance criterion.

(c) Suggest construction changes to counteract the effect of increased air traffic. Evaluate the result.

Solution. When we review the SIR's, the windows appear to be the weakest link in the system. A wider airspace between the panes of double-glazed windows and other improvements are suggested. By selecting windows with 6-mm glass, 100-mm airspace, and 6-mm glass with absorbing material in the frame channel, we obtain a rating of SIR 39. In addition, by ensuring good workmanship, particularly with regard to window installation and roof eaves, the air leakage ratio may be reduced to 1.5×10^{-4}. After we enter the new data into the program used to solve part (a), the adjusted SIR's are increased to 37.6, 38.7, and 37.0 for the facade wall, flanking wall, and roof, respectively. Combining these values, the room SIR is 32.9, resulting in an interior noise level of

$$L_{\text{DNinterior}} = 75.6 - 32.9 = 43 \text{ dB}A$$

The redesigned room is acceptable.

If the increased noise exposure in the above example had been higher, other measures might have been considered. For example, consider a building in the northern hemisphere with a major highway immediately to the south. A windowless solar wall (Trombe wall) might be specified for the southern facade. In making such a decision, it would be necessary to balance the advantages of reduced interior noise and potential energy savings against a lack of windows in the facade.

Figure 6.7.1 shows simultaneous indoor and outdoor noise readings made at a residential building in the vicinity of an international airport. The outdoor readings are plotted with dashes, indoor readings with dots, and the difference (apparent trans-

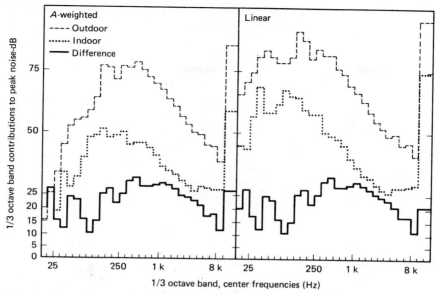

Figure 6.7.1 Simultaneous indoor and outdoor noise measurements.

mission loss) with a solid line. Both A-weighted and unweighted readings are plotted in one-third octave bands, with the last value representing the overall sound level. Although the differences are the same for each one-third octave, the apparent transmission loss is greater for overall A-weighted levels than for overall unweighted levels. The apparent transmission loss is a function of the building wall and window construction, room absorption, structural resonances, and room eigenfrequencies. The low-frequency dips in apparent transmission loss correspond to eigenfrequencies in the room. The difference between overall A-weighted outdoor and indoor sound levels is the measured room shell isolation rating (SIR).

6.7 CONTROL OF HOME APPLIANCE NOISE

Noise levels in dBA for typical household appliances and garden equipment are given in Table 6.7.1. The degree of annoyance and activity interference due to noise depends on noise level, frequency content, time of exposure, exposure duration, and other factors. One of the other significant variables is the control the exposed person can exert over the noise source. For example, dishwashers are inherently noisy (typically 54 to 85 dBA close to the appliance), partly because the contents tend to strike one another during the washing cycle. However, the user has the option of selecting a time of operation which causes minimal interference with other activities. By contrast, refrigerators must be made as quiet as practical (typically about 40 dBA) because they cycle on and off throughout the day and night. In multiple dwellings, individuals are exposed to many noise sources over which they have no control. Noise may reach annoying levels if the party walls have low transmission loss (TL) values.

TABLE 6.7.1 TYPICAL HOUSEHOLD NOISE SOURCES

Noise source	Sound level for operator (dBA)
Refrigerator	40
Floor fan	38 to 70
Clothes dryer	55
Washing machine	47 to 78
Dishwasher	54 to 85
Hair dryer	59 to 80
Vacuum cleaner	62 to 85
Sewing machine	64 to 74
Electric shaver	75
Food disposal (grinder)	67 to 93
Electric lawn edger	81
Home shop tools	85
Gasoline power mower	87 to 92
Gasoline riding mower	90 to 95
Chain saw	100
Stereo	Up to 120

Source: EPA (1971).

Noise Control at the Source

The possibility of noise control at the source should be considered first. The purchase of quiet appliances is an important step in quieting the home. Some appliances and garden equipment items are labeled for noise level at the operator. Although most consumers lack access to sound level meters, comparisons of apparent loudness may provide some help in selecting appliances that do not carry noise labeling.

Design Implications Prediction of noise levels that will be produced by a proposed product is difficult and far from exact. A clothes washer, for example, may consist of an electric motor, geared transmission, pumps, belts, pulleys, shafts, cams, bearings, switches, and valves. These components produce airborne noise directly, as well as structure-borne noise that radiates from the metal housing of the clothes washer. In addition there is the flow noise of the wash water. However, in spite of the complexity of some noise control problems, there are some general considerations that can aid in producing quieter appliances.

Each noise problem must be evaluated individually by considering the noise source and its setting. A procedure that is effective in one case may be useless, or even increase noise in another. The noise sources that make the greatest noise contributions should be considered first. Effectiveness of product modifications may be evaluated by noise measurement on prototypes before design changes in production models are incorporated. Many of the procedures discussed in Chapter 7 apply to household noise as well.

6.8 HEATING, VENTILATING, AND AIR CONDITIONING NOISE; PLUMBING NOISE

Heating, ventilating, and air conditioning (HVAC) noise is particularly troublesome in that it is usually generated within a building. Interior walls and doors commonly have poorer transmission loss (TL) values than exterior walls. In addition, piping and ducts are usually run through walls, floors and ceilings, with discharge and return grills in every room. Thus, plumbing and HVAC noise may be noticeable in every room in a building unless these systems are carefully designed for noise control.

HVAC Noise Sources Sources of noise and remedies are discussed by Berendt et al. (1978) and EPA (1971). The following contributions should be considered in attempts to control noise due to basement, attic, window, and closet HVAC installations.

1. High-speed motor-coupled blowers, common on small HVAC units, are a major noise source. This is due to the high tip speed of the blower, the high air velocity, and the lack of isolation between motor and blower. A dominant noise frequency, called "blade frequency," is given by

$$f_{\text{blade}} = n_B \frac{n}{60} \tag{6.8.1}$$

where f_{blade} = blade frequency (Hz)
$\quad n$ = blower speed (rpm)
$\quad n_B$ = number of blades

2. Bearings, brushes, and switches generate noise which may be carried through the ducts.

3. HVAC equipment is often rigidly mounted to the floor with ducts rigidly fastened to walls, ceiling, and floors. Vibration of the motor and other components and turbulence-induced vibration may be transmitted to the structure via the rigid mountings.

4. Condensing systems, consisting of a motor, compressor, and fan are usually the noisiest air conditioner components. The compressor operates cyclically throughout the day and night, often starting with a low-frequency "groan." On large units, the compressor is heavily loaded. On belt-driven units, the belt may slip, causing a high-frequency screech at startup. The condensing system, which discharges heat, is often mounted on the ground outside a dwelling, or on the roof of a commercial establishment. Outside mountings can cause objectionable noise levels in nearby dwellings, particularly at night. If buildings are close, reflections may contribute to the overall noise level.

5. Turbulence due to high velocity airflow contributes to duct vibration and airborne noise. This problem occurs at the blower discharge, and at obstacles including sharp corners, dampers, and grilles.

6. Short unlined return ducts used in some heating and air conditioning systems radiate turbulence-generated noise and noise from the motor. If individual rooms lack return ducts, the doors may be undercut by about 25 mm (1 in) to allow for return

air. These spaces allow free passage of noise to other rooms without significant attenuation.

7. Some units are installed in centrally located closets, with louvered doors and
large return grilles. Thus, noise is transmitted to nearby rooms without loss in intensity.

8. Window-mounted room air conditioners transmit compressor vibration to
the structure through the window frame. Because of their compact size, they employ
high-speed fans which generate turbulence noise.

HVAC Noise Control   Ideally, manufacturers should consider noise control in the
earliest equipment design stages, and consumers should consider noise levels before
purchasing. However, there are many noise control procedures that may be effective
when HVAC is in the prototype stage, or even fully installed. The following procedures
for avoiding noise problems and correcting noise problems may prove effective.

TABLE 6.8.1   OUTDOOR AIR REQUIREMENTS FOR VENTILATION
(ASHRAE, 1981)

Use	Smoking	Nonsmoking	Smoking	Nonsmoking
	(ft^3/min per person)		(l/s per person)	
Restaurant				
Dining rooms	35	7	17.5	3.5
Cafeterias	35	7	17.5	3.5
Offices:				
Office space	20	5	10	2.5
Meeting and waiting space	35	7	17.5	3.5
Retail stores	25	5	12.5	2.5
Classrooms	25	5	12.5	2.5
Hospitals:				
Patient rooms	35	7	17.5	3.5
Operating rooms	na	40	na	20
Industrial				
2.5 met[a,b]	35	20	17.5	10
2.0 met	35	10	17.5	5
1.5 met	35	7	17.5	3.5
	(ft^3/min per room)		(l/s per room)	
Hotel, motel				
Bedrooms	30	15	15	7.5
Private dwellings[b]				
Kitchen[c]		100		50
Baths, toilets[c]		50		25

na = not applicable.

[a] 1.0 met = sedentary activity level
       = 18.4 (Btu/hr)/ft^2 body surface
       = 58.2 W/m^2 body surface
  1.5 met = low activity level (laboratory work, light assembly)
  2.0 met = medium activity level (assembly line)
  2.5 met = high activity level (mining, foundry)

[b] Operable windows or mechanical ventilation shall be provided for contaminants or greater than usual
occupancy.

[c] Installed capacity for intermittent use.

1. Look for noise labeling. Compare equipment based on labeling, or noise measurements, or subjective loudness judgment. The difference in cost for quiet equipment is likely to be less than the cost of add-on noise control.

2. Consider centrifugal or squirrel-cage fans which are usually quieter than vane-axial propeller fans. Select large-diameter slow-speed blowers over small-diameter high-speed blowers. Use belt drives in preference to direct coupling to a motor.

3. Compute the heating and cooling requirements of the building and select equipment accordingly. If the equipment is underdesigned, it may be necessary to operate fans at high speed, producing excess noise. If the equipment has too large a capacity, the larger motor and/or compressor may be noisier, and it may be more disturbing due to on-and-off cycling. Capacity calculations are based on climate, occupancy, building construction, ventilation requirements, and other factors. ASHRAE (1981) specifies a ventilation requirement of 5 ft^3/min [about 2.5 liters per second (l/s)] per person of outdoor air to dilute the carbon dioxide produced by metabolism and expired by the lungs. Higher ventilation requirements apply when tobacco smoke and other contaminants are present, adding to the heating or cooling system load and increasing noise levels. Thus, HVAC equipment noise output can be reduced in buildings where smoking is prohibited. Ventilation requirements for various facilities are given in Table 6.8.1.

4. Locate the condensing system of an air conditioner as far as possible from any bedrooms. Select vibration isolation mounts based on system mass and operating speed. If the condenser unit is to be outdoors, install the unit on resilient mounts on

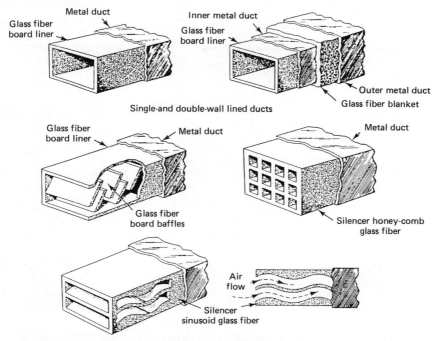

Figure 6.8.1 Various types of acoustical duct lining, baffles, and silencers. (*Source:* EPA (1978))

a heavy concrete slab at least 1 ft (300 mm) from any residence wall, avoiding locations near a bedroom window of a neighboring residence. Use rubber sleeves where piping goes through walls, so that piping vibrations are isolated from the structure. Tighten loose parts, align belt pulleys, and balance and lubricate the unit. Reduce blower speed if practical; clean grilles and protective screens to ensure adequate airflow. Install an enclosure around the condenser unit.

5. Install acoustical duct liners in supply and return ducts, or use prefabricated duct silencers. Replace rigid mountings with rubber isolator mounts (see Figures 6.8.1 and 6.8.2). If pressure changes cause the duct to expand and collapse noisily, install metal stiffeners at wide duct sections. "Crosstalk" is transmission of sound from room to room through a common duct when the grilles are close together. The duct may be separated by a metal splitter bulkhead to reduce crosstalk by lengthening the sound path. Acoustical duct lining in the section between the grilles will also reduce crosstalk.

6. Gas and oil furnaces sometimes ignite with a muffled explosion noise. High-velocity gas flow through the fuel nozzle or burner jets can also cause a high-frequency

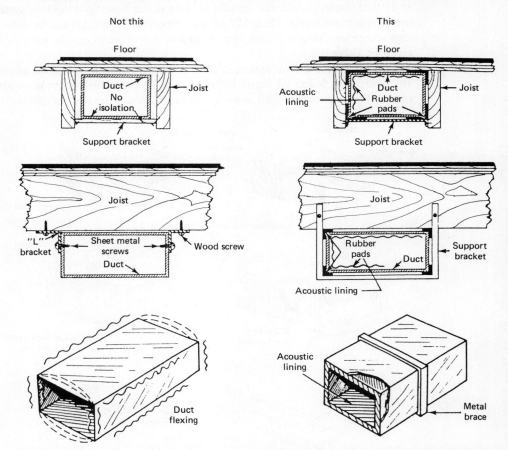

Figure 6.8.2 Methods of reducing noise due to airflow and vibration in duct systems. (*Source:* EPA (1978))

whistling sound. These noises may be reduced by installing nozzles designed for quiet flow, adjustment of fuel pressure, or changes in the ignition system. Some large unsupported sheetmetal furnace components are subject to internal pressures above and below atmospheric pressure, causing them to change shape with snap-through noise each time a blower cycles on and off. Stiffeners will prevent the snap-through noise.

7. Steam heating systems make hammering noises when condensate is trapped in the system. This problem can be corrected by improved system drainage, by replacement of faulty pressure relief valves, and by opening radiator valves completely to allow condensate to return. Steam pipes expand and contract at different rates from the building. The piping design must allow for the expansion, with the use of flexible supports. In addition, flexible heat-resistant material should be placed around the pipe at wall and floor penetrations to eliminate rubbing noises.

8. Hot water baseboard heater noise results from expansion and contraction, fluid flow, and pump and motor vibration. Heat-resistant resilient sleeves installed at pipe clamps, wall penetrations, and floor penetrations will isolate fluid noise and reduce noise due to relative motion. Fluid flow velocities can be reduced and pumps and motors can be mounted on vibration isolators.

9. Electric baseboard heater noise includes banging noises due to expansion and contraction, and electrical humming. Multiples of the electrical frequency will predominate in the humming noise (i.e., 60 and 120 Hz for 60-Hz electric service). Isolation of the heater from the building walls and floor by heat-resistant resilient sleeves, mounts, and spacers should reduce noise from both sources.

Duct Silencers

Duct silencers are devices designed to reduce noise transmission in air handling systems by introducing dissipative and reactive losses. Prefabricated silencers have an effect similar to duct lining, but cause more sound attenuation per unit length. Figure 6.8.3 shows a cross section through a typical dissipative duct silencer. Sound energy is dissipated in the absorbing material which is enclosed in perforated metal. Packless silencers containing no fibrous absorbing material and silencers in which the acoustic filler is contained in special envelopes are available for special clean room applications. Figure 6.8.4 shows typical silencer applications in a variety of HVAC systems.

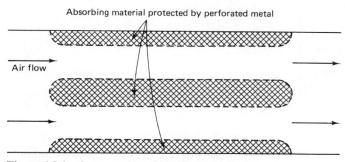

Absorbing material protected by perforated metal

Air flow

Figure 6.8.3 Cross section view of a duct silencer.

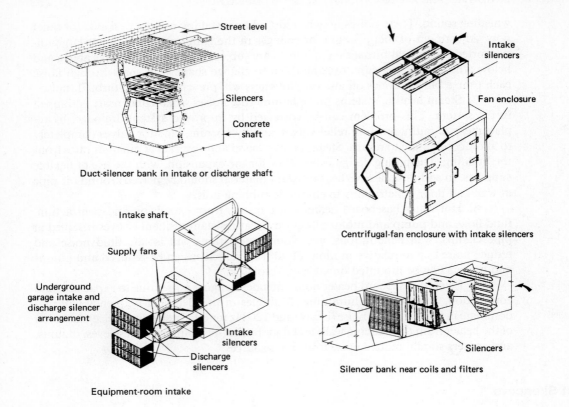

Duct-silencer bank in intake or discharge shaft

Centrifugal-fan enclosure with intake silencers

Underground garage intake and discharge silencer arrangement

Equipment-room intake

Silencer bank near coils and filters

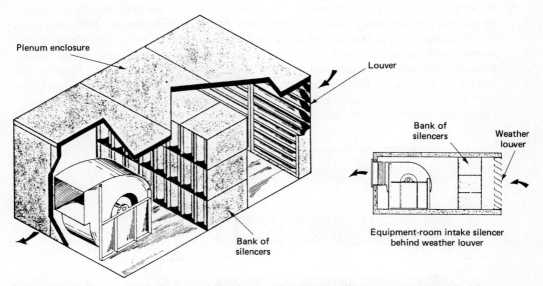

Equipment-room intake silencer behind weather louver

Figure 6.8.4 Some typical silencer application and installation diagrams. (*Source:* Industrial Acoustics Co.)

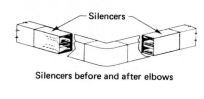

Silencers before and after elbows

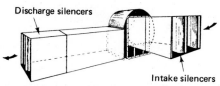

Intake and discharge silencers for
centrifugal fans

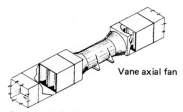

Intake and discharge silencers for
vane axial fans

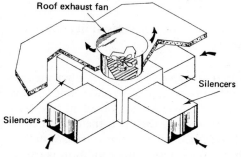

Roof exhaust silencer arrangement for
propeller fans

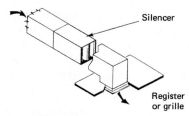

Silencer near air terminal

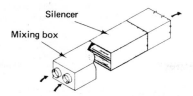

Discharge silencer attached to mixing box

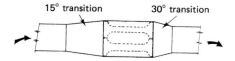

Silencer between upstream and downstream
transitions

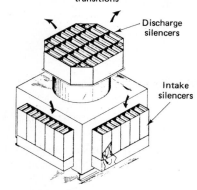

Silencers for cooling tower

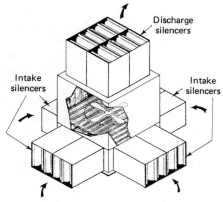

Silencers for air-cooled condenser

Figure 6.8.4   (*Continued*)

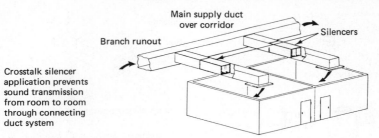

Crosstalk silencer
application prevents
sound transmission
from room to room
through connecting
duct system

Figure 6.8.4 (*Continued*)

Duct noise is generated by turbulence due to fans, duct elbows, and other obstructions. The sound power generated by airflow is very sensitive to velocity. In straight ducts, sound power is assumed to be proportional to air velocity to the fifth or seventh power. Thus, the relationship between sound intensity I and air velocity V is

$$\frac{I_2}{I_1} = \left(\frac{V_2}{V_1}\right)^N \tag{6.8.2}$$

where $5 \leq N \leq 7$, from which

$$L_2 - L_1 = 10 \lg\left(\frac{V_2}{V_1}\right)^N = 10N \lg\left(\frac{V_2}{V_1}\right) \tag{6.8.3}$$

Based on the relationship above, a doubling of air velocity could result in an increase of 15 to 21 dB in the flow-generated noise contribution.

Insertion Loss (IL) Let sound level be measured at a given location. A duct silencer is then installed between the noise source and the measuring point and sound level is again measured at the same point. The difference in sound levels is called the insertion loss (IL). If the measurement is made with air flowing in the duct, the difference in sound levels is called the dynamic insertion loss (DIL). When noise is transmitted in the direction of airflow, as in air conditioning supply ducts, this condition is called "forward flow." When noise transmission and airflow are in opposite directions, as in return ducts, the condition is called "reverse flow." The absolute velocity of sound transmission is given by the speed of sound in still air plus or minus the air speed for forward and reverse flow, respectively. For a typical duct silencer, reverse flow DIL is higher than forward flow DIL for frequencies up to about 1 kHz. Table 6.8.2a lists DIL ratings versus silencer length, air velocity, and frequency for one commercially available silencer type. Note that 1 ft = 0.3048 m and 1 ft/min = 0.00508 m/s.

Aerodynamic Performance Silencers are designed to produce maximum noise reduction with a minimum obstruction of airflow. However, the presence of silencers in a duct system does induce a loss in airflow energy which should be considered when designing or specifying the blower. Table 6.8.2b shows measured static pressure drop (inches of water) versus silencer length and air velocity in one commercially available silencer type. When the air handling system is completely specified, pressure drop can be related to power loss as follows:

$$P = 10^{-3} \, p_{\text{drop}} \frac{Q}{\text{eff}}$$ (6.8.4)

where P = power (kW)

p_{drop} = pressure drop (Pa)

Q = airflow through the silencer (m³/s)

eff = air handling system efficiency

Noting that 1 in of water (i.w.g.) = 249 Pa and 1 ft³/min = 4.719×10^{-4} m³/s (approximately), the above equation may be rewritten as

$$P = 1.175 \times 10^{-4} \, p'_{\text{drop}} \frac{Q'}{\text{eff}}$$ (6.8.5)

where p'_{drop} = pressure drop (i.w.g.)

Q' = airflow through the silencer (ft³/min)

Thus, energy conservation considerations should enter into silencer selection in large HVAC systems.

Self-Noise Silencers, like any other duct obstruction, generate noise which is called "self-noise." Of course, the noise reduction due to a well-designed silencer far exceeds the self-noise. However, tests of silencers without airflow produce unrealistically high ratings of performance. Hirschorn (1981) gives the following equation for self-noise power level L_W dB with reference to 1 pW (dBpW = dB re 10^{-12} W)

$$L_W = K + 10N \lg\left(\frac{V}{V_1}\right) + 10 \lg\left(\frac{A}{A_1}\right)$$ (6.8.6)

where K = base power level of a silencer of cross section area A_1 and velocity V_1 at specified frequency and flow mode

A = silencer cross section area

V = air velocity

N = power function of velocity in the range $4.7 \le N \le 8$ for forward flow $2.3 \le N \le 8.6$ for reverse flow

The power function is based on measured changes in self-noise (dB re 10^{-12} W) as air velocity is doubled. Typically, self-noise changes range from 14 to 24 dBpW per velocity doubling for forward flow, and 7 to 26 dBpW per velocity doubling for reverse flow.

The range of power function values is too great to allow precise prediction of self-noise, but the above equation may be of some value in estimating the noise consequences of design changes. Wherever possible, predictions should be verified by noise measurements on prototype systems. Table 6.8.2c gives self-noise measurements for the type of silencer considered in the above tables. Values of self-noise power level are given in dBpW for a 4-ft² face area silencer. Face area adjustments may be made using the 10 $\lg(A/A_1)$ term in the above equation or by using the face area adjustment factor table.

TABLE 6.8.2   SILENCERS[a]

(a) Dynamic Insertion Loss (DIL) Ratings: Forward (+)/Reverse (−) Flow

Octave bands (Hz)		1 63	2 125	3 250	4 500	5 1000	6 2000	7 4000	8 8000
Silencer and length (ft)	Silencer face velocity (ft/min)	Dynamic insertion loss (dB)							
3	−5000	7	9	11	16	25	18	13	7
	−2000	5	6	10	15	25	19	13	8
	+2000	4	5	9	14	23	24	14	10
	+5000	3	4	7	12	21	25	16	12
5	−5000	9	11	15	24	31	32	17	10
	−2000	7	8	14	23	31	33	17	11
	+2000	6	7	13	21	29	39	20	14
	+5000	5	6	11	19	27	39	20	15
7	−5000	11	17	20	31	43	40	24	14
	−2000	8	14	19	30	43	41	24	15
	+2000	8	13	18	28	40	47	26	18
	+5000	7	9	16	27	38	47	27	19
10	−5000	12	22	27	41	50	50	34	20
	−2000	10	19	26	40	49	50	34	21
	+2000	10	18	25	38	48	50	35	24
	+5000	10	14	23	38	47	50	37	25

(b) Aerodynamic Performance Data

Silencer face velocity (ft/min)	1000	1420	1750	2000	2250	2470	2840	3180	3500	3900	4500	5030
Length (ft)	Static pressure drop (i.w.g.)											
3	0.05	0.10	0.15	0.20	0.25	0.30	0.40	0.50	0.60	0.75	1.00	1.25
5	0.06	0.11	0.17	0.22	0.28	0.33	0.44	0.55	0.66	0.83	1.10	1.40
7	0.06	0.12	0.18	0.24	0.30	0.36	0.48	0.60	0.72	0.90	1.20	1.50
10	0.07	0.13	0.20	0.27	0.34	0.40	0.54	0.68	0.80	1.00	1.36	1.70

(c) Self-Noise Power Levels (dB re 10^{-12} W)

Octave bands (Hz)	1 63	2 125	3 250	4 500	5 1K	6 2K	7 4K	8 8K
Face velocity (ft/min)	Self-noise power levels (dB)							
−5000	74	67	67	73	65	67	73	78
−4000	69	63	63	68	63	64	68	69

Face velocity (ft/min)	Self-noise power levels (dB)							
−3000	64	59	58	62	60	62	62	58
−2000	55	52	52	53	56	56	53	43
−1000	41	41	41	38	49	48	38	<20
+1000	38	31	37	32	32	36	24	<20
+2000	57	51	51	49	47	50	44	35
+3000	68	63	59	60	56	58	56	50
+4000	76	71	65	66	62	64	64	59
+5000	82	77	70	72	67	69	71	67

(d) Face Area Adjustment Factors, Add or Subtract from PWL Values Above

Quiet-duct face area (ft²)	0.5	1	2	4	8	16	32	64	128
PWL adjustment factor (dB)	−9	−6	−3	0	+3	+6	+9	+12	+15

[a] For intermediate face areas, interpolate to nearest whole number.
Source: Industrial Acoustics Co.

Plumbing Noise

Plumbing noise is particularly troublesome because the use of plumbing facilities in one part of a building may result in noise throughout the building. Although pipes and fixtures have small noise radiating surfaces, these components are often rigidly fastened to walls and other radiating surfaces. Some of the following techniques have been found useful for design of quiet systems and control of noise in existing systems (Berendt et al., 1978).

Isolation Pipe hangers with resilient sleeves and flexible connectors can be used to isolate plumbing vibrations from the building structure to prevent noise radiation by walls, ceilings, and floors. Isolation is effective in the control of flow-generated noise and noise due to expansion and contraction due to temperature change. Since most of the piping system will be enclosed in the walls or will otherwise be inaccessible, isolation is most effective at the time of building construction.

Control of Flow-Generated Noise High velocities in plumbing systems cause turbulence, particularly at pipe bends and obstructions. Cavitation noise, associated with the formation and collapse of vapor bubbles, occurs at high velocity and low pressure. If the system is designed with adequate pipe sizes, keeping flow velocities to 2 m/s (6 ft/s) or less, turbulence-generated noise should be reduced.

Water Hammer, Vibration, and Chattering   Water hammer is the noise of shock waves caused by sudden flow interruption. Some problems are corrected if quick-acting valves are replaced by slower acting valves in clothes washers and dishwashers. The use of additional pipe supports and the isolation of piping with rubber-covered supports and flexible connectors prevent the transmission of water hammer noise to the structure. Chattering refers to flow-induced vibration of valves. Chattering noise is usually eliminated by correcting and replacing loose and defective parts. Vibration transmission to piping systems and structures can be corrected by isolating pumps and other sources by using flexible connectors.

Plumbing System Design and Specification   The best opportunity for noise control in plumbing systems is in the design stage. A simple layout with a minimum of fittings and bends should be quieter than a complicated system. Bedroom walls and other areas where quiet is important should be free of piping if possible. Noise levels should be a consideration in the selection of plumbing fixtures. Aeration devices can be specified for faucets to reduce noise. Nonsetting waterproof caulking should be used to seal pipe penetrations through walls and floors. Party walls between bathrooms should be completely finished on both sides to provide adequate transmission loss between apartments.

6.9 GENERAL CONSIDERATIONS FOR BUILDING NOISE CONTROL

The significance of the problem of noise generated within buildings is indicated by the exposure estimates given by EPA (1971). Table 6.9.1 lists order-of-magnitude exposure estimates for the United States in millions of person-hours per week. The figures do not actually represent hours of speech interference or lost sleep, since most equipment would not be used at times reserved for conversation or sleep. If the figures are projected to the year 2000, the hearing damage risk estimates may be multiplied by a factor of about 2.5, and exposure estimates in the sleep and speech interference range multiplied by 2.2. Note that noise contributions due to external sources (transportation, construction, industry, etc.) are excluded from the estimates. Also excluded are entertainment sounds (television, radio, phonographs, tape and disk players) which are usually unwanted noise to people other than the user.

Figure 6.9.1 shows estimates of building equipment noise levels to which people are exposed. Where appropriate, noise reduction due to intervening walls and roof structure, duct treatment, equipment enclosures, buffer zones, and vibration isolation are considered. Some of the noise sources are in use for only limited periods of time. Diesel engines would be for emergency use during power outages, and thus of little consequence in day-to-day noise control.

Noise Criteria Curves (NC)

Noise criteria (NC) curves were developed by Beranek (1957) as a single-number rating system to specify acceptable noise levels in buildings. The most common use

TABLE 6.9.1 ORDER OF MAGNITUDE ESTIMATES OF EXPOSURE TO HOME APPLIANCE AND BUILDING EQUIPMENT NOISE EXPRESSED IN MILLIONS OF PERSON-HOURS PER WEEK

Noise source	Speech interference		Sleep interference		Hearing damage risk	
	Moderate (45–60)	Severe (>60)	Slight (35–50)	Moderate (50–70)	Slight (70–80)	Moderate (80–90)
Group I: quiet major equipment and appliances						
Fans	1200		0		0	
Air conditioner	242		121		0	
Clothes dryer	94		10		0	
Humidifier	10		15		0	
Freezer	0		0		0	
Refrigerator	0		0		0	
Group II: quiet equipment and small appliances						
Plumbing (faucets, toilets)		535	267		0	
Dishwasher		461	4		0	
Vacuum cleaner		280	0.5		0	
Electric food mixer		222	1		0	
Clothes washer		215	0.5		0	
Electric knife		1	0.1		0	
Group III: noisy small appliances						
Sewing machine		19		0.5	9	
Electric shaver		6		1	5	
Food blender		2		0.2	0.5	
Electric lawn mower		1		1	0.3	
Food disposer		0.5		0.5	0.5	
Group IV: noisy electric tools						
Home shop tools		5		2		1
Electric yard care tools		1.5		0.1		0.4

Source: EPA.

of NC curves is specification of limits for HVAC noise levels. Figure 6.9.2 shows a set of NC curves. Recommended NC ratings for various environments are given in Table 6.9.2. If a set of octave-band sound level measurements falls on or below a given NC curve, then that NC rating applies. By an alternative procedure, the NC rating is met if the specified NC curve passes through the average of the levels of the three contiguous octave-band measurements highest relative to the curve, with no penetration more than 2 dB above the curve. NC-15 to NC-20 is acceptable for broadcasting and recording studios, whereas NC-35 to NC-45 is acceptable for general offices. Substantially higher NC ratings would be acceptable in heavy industrial settings. However, standards based on hearing conservation generally govern in such situations.

A revision of the NC curves, called the preferred noise criteria (PNC) curves, was proposed by Beranek et al. (1971). The PNC curves are 4 to 5 dB lower than the NC curves in the 63-Hz band, about 1 dB lower in the 125-, 250-, 500-, and 1000-Hz bands and 4 to 5 dB lower in the 2-, 4-, and 8-kHz bands.

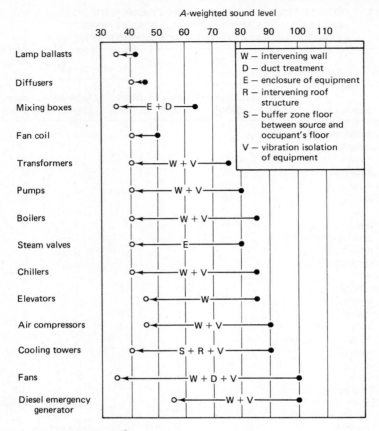

• Sound level at 3 ft from source
o Sound level at occupant's position

Figure 6.9.1 Range of building equipment noise levels to which people are exposed. (*Source:* EPA)

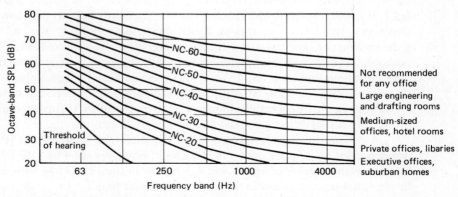

Figure 6.9.2 Noise rating curves (NR). (*Source:* Bruel & Kjaer Instrumentns, Inc.)

TABLE 6.9.2   RECOMMENDED NC VALUES FOR VARIOUS ENVIRONMENTS

Environment	Range of NC levels likely to be acceptable
Factories (heavy industry)	55 to 75
Factories (light industry)	45 to 65
Kitchens	40 to 50
Swimming pools and sports areas	35 to 50
Department stores and shops	35 to 45
Restaurants, bars, cafeterias, and canteens	35 to 45
Mechanized offices	40 to 50
General offices	35 to 45
Private offices, libraries, courtrooms, and schoolrooms	30 to 35
Homes, bedrooms	25 to 35
Hospital wards and operating theatres	25 to 35
Cinemas	30 to 35
Theatres, assembly halls, and churches	25 to 30
Concert and opera halls	20 to 25
Broadcasting and recording studios	15 to 20

Source: Bruel and Kjaer.

Noise Rating Curves (NR)

Noise rating (NR) curves, a set of curves similar to the NC curves but for more general application, were developed by a working group of the International Organization for Standardization (ISO). Figure 6.9.3 shows the family of NR curves. Recommended NR values are NR-10 to NR-20 for diagnostic clinics and audiometric rooms and NR-50 to NR-55 for mechanized offices. Other recommended NR values for various environments are given in Table 6.9.3. It is impossible to convert sound levels in dB*A* to precise NR ratings. However, the suggested relationship is that NR criteria be taken as 5 units lower than the corresponding criteria in dB*A*. The following corrections are also suggested:

Peak Factor   Adjust impulsive noise (e.g., hammering) by +5 dB*A*.

Spectrum Character   Adjust audible "pure" tone components (whine, whistle) by +5 dB*A*.

Duration   Duration adjustments may be made on an energy basis.

Additional Considerations in Building Noise Control

Many energy conservation measures are consistent with noise control procedures. As a result of poor design, HVAC systems run constantly in many buildings. In some buildings, the system is designed so poorly that occupants must use portable heaters to warm rooms which were made excessively cool by air conditioning. Design changes that can result in both noise reduction and energy conservation include the following:

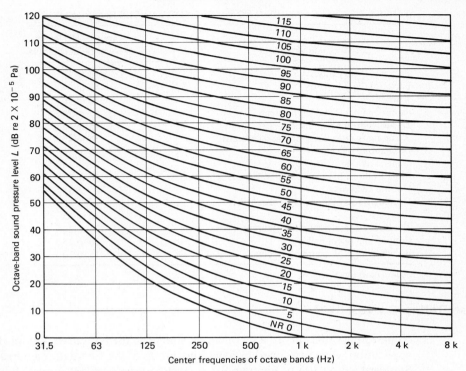

Figure 6.9.3 Noise rating curves (NR). (*Source:* Bruel & Kjaer Instruments, Inc.)

1. Provide zoned or room-by-room thermostat controls. The controls may be key operated in certain locations where irresponsible use is likely.
2. Allow a temperature range for which no heating or cooling is required.
3. Provide well-fitted operable windows where practical.
4. If possible, use low-speed settings on HVAC equipment. Figure 6.9.4 shows the one-third octave-band sound levels measured at 3 ft from one air conditioner with low-fan and high-fan settings.

TABLE 6.9.3 RECOMMENDED NR VALUES FOR VARIOUS ENVIRONMENTS

Environment	Range of NR levels likely to be acceptable
Workshops	60 to 70
Mechanized offices	50 to 55
Gymnasia, sports halls, swimming pools	40 to 50
Restaurants, bars, cafeterias	35 to 45
Private offices, libraries, courtrooms	30 to 40
Cinemas, hospitals, churches, small conference rooms	25 to 35
Class rooms, T.V. studios, large conference rooms	20 to 30
Concert halls, theatres	20 to 25
Diagnostic clinics, audiometric rooms	10 to 20

Source: Bruel and Kjaer.

Noise control should be considered early in building design, rather than considering it an add-on. For example, open-plan offices are sometimes designed without regard to possible speech interference problems. The sound of office machines and conversation in one area may interfere with communication and thinking in another area. If most of the sound energy arrives by a direct line-of-sight path, acoustical treatment of the walls, ceiling, and floor will have little effect.

When interior partitions end before the ceiling or extend only to a dropped ceiling, noise can travel over the partitions. Other building interior designs using light materials and poorly fitted doors allow flanking paths for noise. Consider a conversation in one office and an individual performing a task requiring concentration in an adjacent office. If the transmission loss between the offices is low, the conversation may be intelligibile in the second office. Thus, the conversation will lack privacy, and it will interfere with the concentration of the individual in the second office. In situations of this type, fans and air conditioners are sometimes used to mask intelligibility, since noise without speech content may be less disrupting to concentration. Masking by use of small air jets producing broadband noise, "acoustical perfume," is also used. In residential situations, classical music or other instrumental music may be used to mask intrusive conversation or television noise so that reading or study is possible. Speech intelligibility may be predicted by the use of transmission loss data (TL, discussed in this chapter) and articulation index (AI, defined in an earlier chapter). In-

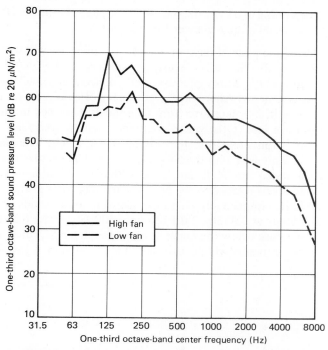

Figure 6.9.4 Sound pressure levels from air conditioner on two settings (measured at 3 ft). (*Source:* EPA)

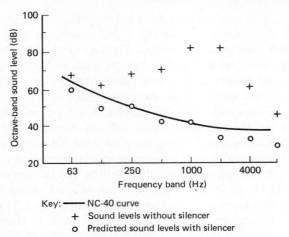

Key: —— NC-40 curve
+ Sound levels without silencer
o Predicted sound levels with silencer

Figure 6.9.5   Noise criteria and duct silencer selection.

tentional masking of intrusive noise by generating additional noise is generally a poorer solution than designing interior walls to provide adequate transmission loss.

EXAMPLE PROBLEM: NOISE CRITERIA AND DUCT SILENCER SELECTION

A large office air conditioning system produces the following sound levels in the eight 1/1 octave bands beginning at 63 Hz: 68, 63, 69, 71, 82, 82, 61, and 48 dB. The airflow rate is 4000 ft^3/min. Select a duct silencer for the system.

Solution.   Using the table of recommended NC values, we will select NC-40 for the office. Obviously, the noise levels are well above the NC-40 contour, as shown in Figure 6.9.5. Many prefabricated silencers are available which will satisfy the requirements. After some preliminary calculations, let us select a 7-ft long silencer with 2-ft^2 face area from the models described in the table giving dynamic insertion loss (DIL) versus frequency, length, and face velocity. The DIL values are subtracted from the original noise levels. The silenced sound levels are then compared with the NC-40 contour. The results are plotted in the figure and tabulated below. It can be seen that the highest three contiguous silenced sound levels relative to the NC-40 curve are 51, 43, and 42 dB at 250, 500, and 1000 Hz, respectively. With the silencer, sound levels are 1 dB above the NC-40 contour at 250 Hz, 2 dB below at 500 Hz, and 1 dB above at 1000 Hz. Sound levels are below the curve at other frequencies. Thus, it is predicted that NC-40 requirements will be satisfied after the silencer is installed.

DUCT SILENCER SELECTION

Frequency (Hz)	63	125	250	500	1000	2000	4000	8000
L without silencer (dB)	68	63	69	71	82	82	61	48
DIL (dB)	8	13	18	28	40	47	26	18
L with silencer (dB)	60	50	51	43	42	35	35	30
NC-40 (dB)	64	56	50	45	41	39	38	37
Difference (dB)	4	6	1[a]	2	1[a]	4	3	7

[a] Above NC-40 contour.

BIBLIOGRAPHY

American Society of Heating, Refrigeration and Air-Conditioning Engineers, Inc., Ventilation for acceptable indoor air quality, ASHRAE Standard 62-1981.

Beranek, L. L., "Revised criteria for noise in buildings," *Noise Control* **3**, 19–27, 1957.

Beranek, L. L., *Noise and Vibration Control,* pp. 566–568, McGraw-Hill, New York, 1971.

Beranek, L. L., W. Blazier, and J. Figwer, "Preferred noise criteria (PNC) curves and their applications," 81st meeting, Acoust. Soc. Am., April 20, 1971.

Berendt, R. D., E. Corliss, and M. Ojalvo, Quieting in the home (Reprinted from National Bureau of Standards Handbook 119, *Quieting: A Practical Guide to Noise Control*), EPA, Washington D.C., 1978.

Bruel & Kjaer, *Measurements in Building Acoustics,* p. 19, Naerum, Denmark, 1980.

Environmental Protection Agency, Noise from construction equipment and operations, building equipment, and home appliances, NTID300.1, December 31, 1971.

Environmental Protection Agency, Protective noise levels, 550/9-79-100, November 1978.

Ginn, K. B., *Architectural Acoustics,* 2nd ed., Bruel & Kjaer, Naerum, Denmark, 1978.

Hirschorn, M., *ASHRAE Trans.* **87,** Part 1, CH-81-6, No. 1, 625–647, 1981.

Pallett, D., R. Wehrli, R. Kilmer, and T. Quindry, Design guide for reducing transportation noise in and around buildings, National Bureau of Standards, April 1978.

Reynolds, D. D., *Engineering Principles of Acoustics,* Allyn and Bacon, Boston, 1981.

Sound and Vibration, Acoustical Publications, Inc., Bay Village, OH 44140 (monthly).

Ver, I. L., and C. I. Holmer, "Interaction of sound waves with solid structures," *Noise Control,* pp. 270–361, L. L. Beranek, Ed., McGraw-Hill, New York, 1971.

PROBLEMS

6.2.1. A 0.5-m^2 sample of building material is placed in a window between a receiving room and source room. There is no significant sound transmission except through the sample. Average sound levels in the 1-kHz octave band are 97 dB in the source room and 72 dB in the receiving room. The equivalent absorption area of the receiving room is 1.5 m^2. Find transmission loss (TL) and transmission coefficient (TC) for the sample at 1 kHz.

6.2.2. Repeat for a 0.75-m^2 sample, 89-dB sound level in the source room and 70 dB in the receiving room, with 3.0-m^2 equivalent absorption.

6.2.3. Repeat for a 6-ft^2 sample, 20-ft^2 equivalent absorption in the receiving room, 80-dB source room sound level, and 69-dB receiving room sound level.

6.2.4. An exposed wall consists of a 20-dB (TL at 500 Hz) wood door (23% of the exposed area), 2% airspace, and the remainder 51-dB TL solid wall. Estimate TL of the composite wall at 500 Hz.

6.2.5. Repeat, using a 35-dB TL acoustic door, with the same airspace.

6.2.6. Repeat, using the 35-dB door, and reducing the airspace to 0.1%.

6.2.7. Write an equation for transmission loss versus frequency for 3-mm-thick glass in the mass-controlled region. Assume a specific gravity of 2.6.

6.2.8. Repeat for 8-mm-thick glass.

6.2.9. Rewrite the field incidence mass law with English units.

6.2.10. Relate transmission loss to frequency for 1-in-thick white pine in the mass-controlled region. The density of white pine is about 27 lb/ft^3.

6.2.11. It is necessary to increase transmission loss of a panel in the mass-controlled region. Write an equation for finding percent transmission loss increase in terms of surface mass.

6.2.12. Transmission loss of a panel in the mass-controlled region is to be increased by 4 dB. Determine the required thickness change.

6.2.13. Calculate the transmission loss and transmission coefficient for 7-mm-thick glass at the critical frequency. Estimate a loss factor of 0.05.

6.2.14. Repeat for 12-mm-thick glass and a loss factor of 0.1.

6.2.15. A double-panel wall is constructed with an airspace h (mm). One panel has two-thirds the surface mass of the other and the sum of the surface masses is m_T kg/m^2. Plot resonant frequency versus the product of m_T and h.

6.2.16. Repeat for airspace h' (in) and total surface weight m'_T (lb/ft^2).

6.2.17. Estimate the resonant frequency of a double-panel partition made of 4 lb/ft^2 and 5 lb/ft^2 panels with a 5.5-in airspace.

6.4.1. Find the sound transmission class (STC) of a wall based on the following measured transmission loss values for the one-third octave bands beginning at 125 Hz: 25, 24, 31, 31, 38, 40, 40, 47, 48, 47, 49, 48, 46, 45, 46, and 43 dB.

6.4.2. Repeat with the same data except TL values in the four highest frequency bands are 40, 41, 39, and 38 dB.

6.5.1. Find shell isolation rating (SIR) for the wall described in Problem 6.4.1.

6.5.2. Find SIR for the wall described in Problem 6.4.2.

6.6.1. Write a program to predict interior noise levels from known transportation noise levels and proposed construction details.

6.6.2. Verify the results of parts b and c of the example problem: Prediction of interior sound levels.

For Problems 6.6.3 through 6.6.6, room dimensions are given in ft^2 in Problems 6.6.3 and 6.6.4, and in m^2 in Problems 6.6.5 and 6.6.6. Predicted contributions to day–night sound level L_{DN} are given in dBA for each source. In each problem, shell isolation ratings and other data are given for each member (facade, flanking wall, roof) and component (windows, solid wall, etc.).

(a) Predict intrusive L_{DN} for the room which is described.

(b) Evaluate the results in terms of residential use.

6.6.3. NOISE LEVELS IN DBA: HIGHWAY: 68   AIRCRAFT: 70
RAILWAY: 60

```
MEMBER   1
LEAKAGE RATIO=   .0003     GEOMETRY COR.= −1     ABSORPTION COR.=   0
COMPONENT   1     AREA=   70      SIR=   51
COMPONENT   2     AREA=   60      SIR=   30


MEMBER   2
LEAKAGE RATIO=   .0003     GEOMETRY COR.=   0     ABSORPTION COR.=   0
COMPONENT   1     AREA=   45      SIR=   50
COMPONENT   2     AREA=   30      SIR=   29
COMPONENT   3     AREA=   10      SIR=   25
```

MEMBER   3
LEAKAGE RATIO=   .0001   GEOMETRY COR.= −2   ABSORPTION COR.=   0
                 AREA=   200   SIR=   40

6.6.4. NOISE LEVELS IN DBA: HIGHWAY: 68   AIRCRAFT: 70
       RAILWAY: 60

MEMBER   1
LEAKAGE RATIO=   .0003   GEOMETRY COR.= −1   ABSORPTION COR.=   0
COMPONENT   1   AREA=   70   SIR=   51
COMPONENT   2   AREA=   58   SIR=   30
COMPONENT   3   AREA=   2   SIR=   0

MEMBER   2
LEAKAGE RATIO=   .0003   GEOMETRY COR.=   0   ABSORPTION COR.=   0
COMPONENT   1   AREA=   45   SIR=   50
COMPONENT   2   AREA=   30   SIR=   29
COMPONENT   3   AREA=   10   SIR=   25

MEMBER   3
LEAKAGE RATIO=   .0001   GEOMETRY COR.= −2   ABSORPTION COR.=   0
                 AREA=   200   SIR=   40

6.6.5. NOISE LEVELS IN DBA. HIGHWAY: 64   AIRCRAFT: 62
       RAILWAY: 71

MEMBER   1
LEAKAGE RATIO=   .0001   GEOMETRY COR.= −1   ABSORPTION COR.= −4
COMPONENT   1   AREA=   7   SIR=   50
COMPONENT   2   AREA=   5.5   SIR=   25

MEMBER   2
LEAKAGE RATIO=   .0001   GEOMETRY COR.= −1   ABSORPTION COR.= −4
COMPONENT   1   AREA=   6   SIR=   50
COMPONENT   2   AREA=   3.5   SIR=   27

MEMBER   3
LEAKAGE RATIO=   .0001   GEOMETRY COR.= −2   ABSORPTION COR.= −4
                 AREA=   16   SIR=   44

6.6.6. FACADE EXPOSURE IS DIFFERENT FROM FLANKING WALL AND ROOF
       EXPOSURE.

(a) NOISE LEVELS IN DBA HIGHWAY: 75   AIRCRAFT: 60   RAILWAY: 0
     AT FACADE
     MEMBER   1A (FACADE)
     LEAKAGE RATIO=   .0003   GEOMETRY COR.= −1   ABSORPTION COR.=   0
     COMPONENT   1   AREA=   8   SIR=   48
     COMPONENT   2   AREA=   4   SIR=   20

(b) NOISE LEVELS IN DBA HIGHWAY: 71   AIRCRAFT: 60   RAILWAY: 0
AT FLANKING WALL AND ROOF.
MEMBER   1B (FLANKING WALL)
LEAKAGE RATIO=   .0003   GEOMETRY COR.=   0   ABSORPTION COR.=   0
COMPONENT   1   AREA=   12   SIR=   48
COMPONENT   2   AREA=   5   SIR=   20

MEMBER   2 (ROOF)
LEAKAGE RATIO=   .0001   GEOMETRY COR.= −2   ABSORPTION COR.=   0
                 AREA=   22   SIR=   38

6.9.1. Refer to the example problem: Noise criteria and duct silencer selection.
   (a) Select a silencer to meet NC-45 criteria.
   (b) Show that the requirements are met.

6.9.2. Repeat, using the NR-50 curve and a flow rate of 1.5 m³/s.

Chapter 7

Industrial Noise Control

Millions of workers suffer psychological and physical stress as well as significant hearing loss due to industrial noise. In addition, industrial noise prevents communication within factories, sometimes causing accidents by making it impossible to hear warning signals. When industrial zones border on residential zones, the contribution of industrial noise may have adverse effects on the community in general.

The industrial machines and processes producing the highest noise levels include blowers, air nozzles for cleaning, riveters, chipping hammers, pneumatic chisels, diesel generators, dust collectors, pneumatic hammers, ball mills, rock crushers, die casting machines, drop hammers, metal presses and shears, and power saws. Typical operator-location noise levels range from 95 to 120 dBA for these machines. Principal noise source contributions from these machines and processes include hammer deceleration, workpiece distortion and vibration, ringing, supporting structure excitation, air ejection, blow-off valves, jet emission, and fans.

Exposure to industrial noise can be controlled at the source, or controlled by interruption of sound transmission paths, or exposure can be reduced by protecting the receiver. Source control may involve selection of quieter work processes, such as welding instead of riveting. It is often most effective to redesign machinery for minimum sound generation if effective noise control has not been incorporated in the initial design. Sound transmission paths may be interrupted by enclosing the machine, or providing an enclosure for the worker. If these methods of noise control are not feasible, the worker can use personal hearing protection devices (HPD's).

This chapter begins with a discussion of noise generation mechanisms applicable to industrial machinery, and methods of predicting noise levels due to these processes. Various types of noise sources including specific machines and components are considered. Where appropriate, noise prediction methods and noise control techniques are given for specific machines. That section is followed by general methods of noise control, which are not machine specific, and some case studies in industrial noise control.

7.1 ACCELERATION NOISE

The processes of noise generation by a machine are subject to many variables over which the manufacturer has little control. As a result, precise prediction of noise levels may never be possible for a machine in the design stage. However, the cost to society of noise-induced hearing loss makes industrial noise control an important goal. One useful noise control tool is the ability to develop relationships between noise levels and other machine characteristics.

Many industrial processes involve impact, where energy is built up (stored) over 1 s or so, and then used over a period of about 1 ms. Impact is present in the processes of stamping, forging, riveting, and sawing. Reciprocating engines, powered hammers, and gear meshing involve impact as well. Typical processes giving rise to impact noise include the following (Richards et al., 1979a):

1. A mass acting as an "energy container," for example, a hammer, punch, or saw tooth, decelerates or accelerates on impact, causing a pressure perturbation which radiates as a single pulse (acceleration noise).
2. A workpiece changes shape and causes a single pressure perturbation.
3. Excess energy in the initial energy container or workpiece energy container may cause it to vibrate (workpiece noise or ringing noise).
4. Some of the energy may be transmitted to the supporting structure or the floor, causing it to vibrate.
5. The above processes may be accompanied by air ejection noise.

Peak Acceleration Sound Due to Impact

If a moving solid body strikes a stationary solid body, the first body will undergo negative acceleration, and the second, positive acceleration. During the interval of contact, the signs of the acceleration will typically reverse, as illustrated in Figure 7.1.1. The first sound pressure pulses are acceleration noise, which is then followed by ringing. For metal-to-metal impacts, the impact duration is not long compared with the time taken for the sound to travel over the impacting bodies. Richards et al. (1979a) relate peak sound pressure to geometry and impact conditions by the following equations.

For a sphere:

$$\frac{P_{0max}r}{a\rho c v_0} = 1.207(4T_1^4 + 4)^{-1/2} \tag{7.1.1}$$

where

P_{0max} = the maximum bound of peak sound pressure P_0 (Pa)

In practice, $P_0 \le P_{0max}/2$.

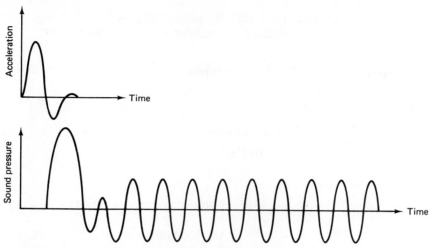

Figure 7.1.1 Acceleration and sound pressure due to impact of solid bodies.

r = radial distance from point of impact (m)
a = radius of sphere (m)
ρ = air density (kg/m^3)
c = propagation speed of sound (m/s)
v_0 = impact velocity (m/s)
$T_1 = ct_0/[\pi a]$ = dimensionless impact duration
t_0 = time for velocity to change from v_0 to zero (s)

For a general shape:

$$\frac{P_{0max}r}{\rho c v_0 V^{1/3}} = 1.5[(ct_0V^{-1/3})^4 + 4]^{-1/2} \tag{7.1.2}$$

where

V = volume of the impacting body (m^3)

EXAMPLE PROBLEM: PEAK SOUND PRESSURE DUE TO IMPACT

A metal forming process will utilize a 150-mm-diameter by 300-mm-long steel cylinder which will impact another steel body at a velocity of 60 m/s. The deceleration time is estimated to be 0.5 ms based on measurements of a similar process. Predict peak sound pressure due to the process at 1 m from the impact point for an air temperature of 20°C.

Solution. Using equations from Chapter 2, we find the speed of sound c at

$$T' = 20°C \quad \text{or} \quad T = 20 + 273.16 = 293.16 \text{ K}$$
$$c = 20.04T^{1/2} = 20.04 \times 293.16^{1/2} = 343 \text{ m/s}$$

For gas constant $R = 287$, the ratio of specific heats $\gamma = 1.4$, and $p_0 = 1.01325 \times 10^5$ Pa, one standard atmosphere, air density is given by

$$\rho = \frac{p_0}{RT} = 1.01325 \times \frac{10^5}{287 \times 293.16} = 1.204 \text{ kg/m}^3$$

Volume of the cylinder is

$$V = \pi \times \text{diameter}^2 \times \text{length}/4 = \pi \times 0.150^2 \times 0.300/4$$

$$= 0.0053 \text{ m}^3$$

Thus,

$$\rho c v_0 V^{1/3} = 1.204 \times 343 \times 60 \times 0.0053^{1/3} = 4321$$

$$c t_0 V^{-1/3} = 343 \times 0.0005 \times 0.0053^{-1/3} = 0.9836$$

The maximum bound of peak sound pressure is found from

$$\frac{P_{0\text{max}} r}{\rho c v_0 V^{1/3}} = 1.5[(c t_0 V^{-1/3})^4 + 4]^{-1/2}$$

$$P_{0\text{max}} \times 1/4321 = 1.5(0.9836^4 + 4)^{-1/2} = 0.675$$

$$P_{0\text{max}} = 2917 \text{ Pa}$$

which is equivalent to a peak sound pressure level of

$$L_{\text{peak(max)}} = 20 \lg\left(\frac{P_{0\text{max}}}{p_{\text{ref}}}\right) = 20 \lg\left(\frac{2917}{20 \times 10^{-6}}\right)$$

$$= 163 \text{ dB peak}$$

Empirical Data

Experimental verification of the peak sound pressure equation is given by Richards et al. (1979a). For values of normalized impact duration,

$$T^* = c t_0 V^{-1/3} = 1.0 \text{ (approximately)}$$

as in the above example, normalized peak pressure $P^* = P_0 r/[\rho c v_0 V^{1/3}]$ ranges from about 0.12 to 0.35. These experimental values, obtained from tests using 75-mm-, 100-mm-, and 150-mm-diameter cylinders, range from about 18 to 52% of the maximum bound found above.

Combining these results with the given data in the above example, we might expect peak sound pressures $P_0 = 525$ to 1517 Pa, corresponding to peak sound pressure levels $L_{\text{peak}} = 148$ to 158 dB peak. Note that even the lowest of these values is a dangerous level of exposure. The Occupational Safety and Health Act (1978, 1981) states that "Exposure to impulsive or impact noise should not exceed 140 dB peak sound pressure."

Richards et al. also fit an empirical upper limit to the impact test data:

$$P^* = 0.7 \quad \text{for} \quad T^* \leq 1.0$$

$$P^* = 0.7T^{*-2} \quad \text{for} \quad T^* > 1.0 \tag{7.1.3}$$

All of their experimental data for impacting cones and impacting cylinders fell within this bound.

Acceleration Noise Energy

Kinetic energy of a body in rectilinear motion is given by

$$\text{KE} = \frac{Mv^2}{2} = \frac{\rho_M V v^2}{2} \tag{7.1.4}$$

where M = mass (kg)
   V = volume (m^3)
   v = velocity (m/s)
   ρ_M = density of the body (kg/m^3)

It can be shown (Richards et al., 1979a) that the acceleration noise energy radiated due to decelerating a rigid sphere of radius a from velocity v_0 to zero velocity is approximated by

$$E_{\text{acc}} = \pi\rho a^3 v_0^2/3 = \rho v_0^2 V/4 \tag{7.1.5}$$

where ρ = air density kg/m^3, and it is assumed that the impact time is small. This value of E_{acc} is equivalent to half the kinetic energy of a volume of air traveling at velocity v_0. If we assume this relationship applies to impacting bodies of general shape, then the efficiency of acceleration noise radiation for one body is given by

$$\frac{E_{\text{acc}}}{\text{KE}} = \frac{0.5\rho}{\rho_M} \tag{7.1.6}$$

If the impact involves two bodies having the similar masses, then one would decelerate and the other accelerate, producing, roughly, twice the acceleration noise energy, from which

$$\frac{E_{\text{acc}}}{\text{KE}} = \frac{\rho}{\rho_M} \tag{7.1.7}$$

The density of steel is about

$$0.283 \text{ lb/in}^3 = 0.283 \times 2.768 \times 10^4 = 7833 \text{ kg/m}^3$$

As determined in the example problem above, the density of air at 20°C at one standard atmosphere is 1.204 kg/m^3. Thus, the efficiency of acceleration noise radiation is $E_{\text{acc}}/\text{KE} = \rho/\rho_M = 1.204/7833 = 1.5 \times 10^{-4}$ (approximately) for impacting steel bodies.

EXAMPLE PROBLEM: ACCELERATION NOISE ENERGY

(a) Predict acceleration noise energy, using the data from the previous example problem.

Solution. The mass of the cylinder in the example problem above is

$$m = 7833 \text{ kg/m}^3 \times 0.0053 \text{ m}^3 = 41.5 \text{ kg}$$

The kinetic energy of the impact is then

$$\text{KE} = \frac{mv_0^2}{2} = 41.5 \times \frac{60^2}{2} = 74,700 \text{ N} \cdot \text{m (joules)}$$

if the air volume in motion is neglected in this term. Assuming impact of a pair of bodies of similar mass, acceleration noise radiation would be about

$$E_{\text{acc}} = 1.5 \times 10^{-4} \text{ KE} = 1.5 \times 10^{-4} \times 74,700 = 11.2 \text{ N} \cdot \text{m}$$

(b) Compare the results of part (a) with the results of the previous example problem.

Solution. If, for simplicity, the shape of the impact noise pulse is assumed to approximate a rectangle, then the sound power during the impact time $t_0 = 0.5$ ms is

$$W = \frac{E_{\text{acc}}}{t_0} = \frac{11.2}{0.0005} = 22,400 \text{ W}$$

If sound is radiated in full space, the rectangular wave assumption corresponds to a sound intensity at $r = 1$ m of

$$I = \frac{W}{4\pi r^2} = \frac{22,400}{4\pi \times 1^2} = 1783 \text{ W/m}^2$$

Converting to sound intensity level,

$$L_I = 10 \lg\left(\frac{I}{I_{\text{ref}}}\right) = 10 \lg\left(\frac{1783}{10^{-12}}\right) = 153 \text{ dB (peak)}$$

If a triangular pulse shape is assumed, and if the impact occurs above a hard reflecting surface, maximum sound power is given by

$$W = \frac{2E_{\text{acc}}}{t_0} = 2 \times \frac{11.2}{0.0005} = 44,800 \text{ W}$$

For the triangular pulse assumption, with sound radiated into a half-space the corresponding sound intensity is

$$I = \frac{W}{2\pi r^2} = \frac{44,800}{2\pi 1^2} = 7130 \text{ W/m}^2$$

and the sound intensity level

$$L_I = 10 \lg\left(\frac{7130}{10^{-12}}\right) = 159 \text{ dB (peak)}$$

The predictions of acceleration noise in the first example problem resulted in a theoretical maximum peak sound pressure level of 163 dB. Peak sound pressure levels calculated from experimental results ranged from 148 to 158 dB. These values are reasonably consistent with the sound intensity levels calculated above. Recall that sound pressure level and sound intensity level are identical if sound pressure and particle velocity are in-phase and the product of the density of air and the propagation speed of sound,

$$\rho c = 400$$

In the example problem,

$$\rho c = 1.204 \times 343 = 413$$

and there is no significant difference between sound pressure level and (scalar) sound intensity level.

Ringing Noise Due to Impact

For impacting bodies that are fairly compact, ringing noise energy will usually be of the same order of magnitude as acceleration noise. If the shape of one of the bodies is such that flexural vibration modes are possible, then ringing noise energy is likely to be much greater than acceleration noise energy. Under steady-state conditions, vibrational energy input (watts) can be equated to radiated noise energy and energy absorbed by damping:

$$W_{\text{input}} = W_{\text{radiated}} + W_{\text{structural}} \tag{7.1.8}$$

where radiated noise energy

$$W_{\text{radiated}} = \rho c S \langle v_{\text{rms}}^2 \rangle \sigma_{\text{rad}} \tag{7.1.9}$$

Energy absorbed by damping,

$$W_{\text{structural}} = S \rho_s C_{\text{abs}} f \langle v_{\text{rms}}^2 \rangle \tag{7.1.10}$$

where
ρ = air density (kg/m^3)
c = propagation speed of sound in air (m/s)
$\langle v_{\text{rms}}^2 \rangle$ = space-averaged mean-square velocity of vibration (m^2/s^2)
σ_{rad} = radiation efficiency (adjusted for A-weighting if A-weighted energy is to be determined)
S = area of vibrating surface
ρ_s = surface density of vibrating surface (kg/m^2)
f = vibration frequency (Hz)
C_{abs} = fraction of vibrational energy absorbed per cycle by damping

Noise levels can be predicted if one knows the vibrational energy input and the fraction of input energy converted to noise radiation. As an alternative, the above equations may be used to predict noise radiated from a machine if the vibration levels, rates of decay, and radiation efficiency are known for each machine component. Data from earlier machines of similar design may be used to estimate vibration characteristics. Note that radiation efficiency and the fraction of sound energy absorbed per cycle are frequency dependent.

Radiation Efficiency At frequencies below the critical (wave coincidence) frequency, plates have a low radiation efficiency. At frequencies above the critical frequency, the radiation efficiency of plates and platelike structures may be estimated from

$$\sigma_{\text{rad}} = \left(1 - \frac{f^*}{f}\right)^{-1/2} \tag{7.1.11}$$

where $f > f^*$
$\quad\quad\quad f$ = forcing frequency
$\quad\quad\quad f^*$ = critical frequency
$\quad\quad\quad \sigma_{\text{rad}} \leq 5$ (approximately) at $f = f^*$ and f near f^*

Critical frequencies are given for plates of various materials as a function of thickness in Section 6.2. The plot for steel may be approximated by the expression

$$\lg f^*_{\text{steel}} = 4.1 - \lg t \tag{7.1.12}$$

where f^* = critical frequency (Hz)
$\quad\quad\quad t$ = plate thickness (mm)
$\quad\quad\quad \lg$ = base-ten logarithm

Radiation efficiencies are given for spheres, cylinders, plates, pipes, tubes, and beams by Richards et al. (1979b). Both theoretical and experimental values are given. It is observed that increasing the resilience between impacting members and increasing contact time will result in frequency reduction, and a reduction in A-weighted equivalent sound level. Thus, impact noise can be reduced by the use of soft impact surfaces, by packing bearing surfaces and gears with grease, by the use of plastics, and by lining materials-handling devices and bins with rubber. Vibration isolation and damping should be considered as well.

7.2 GEAR NOISE

Electric motors and internal combustion engines are ordinarily designed to operate at speeds of one-thousand to several thousand revolutions per minute. High-speed operation usually produces the greatest ratio of power to weight and the greatest ratio of power to initial cost. Geared transmissions and other speed reducers are used when the driven machinery has high torque and low speed requirements. The relation between mechanical power, shaft speed, and torque is given by

$$P_{\text{kW}} = 10^{-6} T\omega \tag{7.2.1}$$

where P_{kW} = transmitted power (kW)
$\quad\quad\quad T$ = torque (N · mm)
$\quad\quad\quad \omega = \pi n/30$ = angular velocity (rad/s)
$\quad\quad\quad n$ = shaft speed (rpm)

Using customary U.S. units, the equivalent relationship is

$$P_{hp} = \frac{Tn}{63,025}$$ (7.2.2)

where P_{hp} = transmitted power (hp)
T = torque (lb-in)
n = shaft speed (rpm)

Hand (1982) states that gear noise rises with speed at a rate of 6 to 8 dB per doubling of speed. He also notes that measurements have shown an increase in gear noise of 2.5 to 4 dB per doubling of load. A designer of machinery may not be free to make changes in gear speeds for the purpose of noise reduction alone. Furthermore, it can be seen from equations 7.2.1 and 7.2.2 that a reduction in speed requires an increase in torque, if transmitted power is to be maintained. The above relationships are useful, however, if we wish to use noise levels of an existing design to predict noise levels for a proposed gear train.

Noise produced by a gear train could be objectionable, even though only a minute fraction of the mechanical power transmitted by the gears is converted into sound energy. For example, consider a gear train transmitting 100 kW of mechanical power and producing a sound power level of

$$L_W = 94 \text{ dB re } 1 \text{ pW}$$

The sound power in this case is

$$W = 10^{(L_W - 120)/10} = 10^{(94 - 120)/10} = 2.5 \times 10^{-3} \text{ W (approximate)}$$

and the fraction of sound power to transmitted power is

$$2.5 \times 10^{-8} = \frac{1}{40,000,000}$$

Gear Tooth Meshing Frequencies

It is sometimes difficult to identify noise sources within industrial machines due to the many possible contributors. Some machine elements have distinct noise and vibration "signatures" or amplitude-frequency-time patterns which may be identified through the use of frequency analyzers. Some malfunctions and other problems can be identified by observing prominent frequencies alone.

Most gear tooth profiles are based on the involute curve. Force is transmitted from the driving gear to the driven gear along the line-of-action, which is fixed in space (except for planetary gear trains). Ideally, for rigid, perfect gears transmitting constant torque at constant speed, power will be transmitted smoothly without vibration or noise. Actual gears have tooth errors, both in tooth form and spacing, and in some cases, significant shaft eccentricity. Gear teeth are elastic, and bend slightly under load. As a result, the driving gear teeth that are not in contact are slightly ahead of their theoretical rigid-body positions. The driven teeth that are not in contact are slightly behind their theoretical positions. Thus, there is an abrupt transfer of force when each pair of teeth comes into contact, momentarily accelerating the driven gear and decelerating the driving gear. The resulting fundamental frequency of noise and vibration is given by

$$f_{(1)} = \frac{nN}{60} \qquad (7.2.3)$$

where $f_{(1)}$ = the fundamental tooth meshing frequency (Hz)
          n = rotational speed of one of the gears (rpm)
          N = the number of teeth in the same gear

Harmonics (noise and vibration at integer multiples of the tooth meshing frequency) are usually present as well. The first two or three harmonics,

$$f_{(2)} = 2f_{(1)}, \qquad f_{(3)} = 3f_{(1)}, \qquad \text{and so on} \qquad (7.2.4)$$

may make significant noise contributions. Figure 7.2.1 shows a typical gear noise spectrum.

Tooth Error

If a single tooth on a gear is poorly cut, chipped, or otherwise damaged, then it will generate a noise impulse once every shaft revolution. The fundamental frequency of noise or vibration due to tooth error is given by

$$f_{(1E)} = \frac{n}{60} \qquad (7.2.5)$$

where $f_{(1E)}$ = fundamental frequency due to tooth error (Hz)
          n = shaft speed

Harmonics of the tooth-error frequency may appear as well.

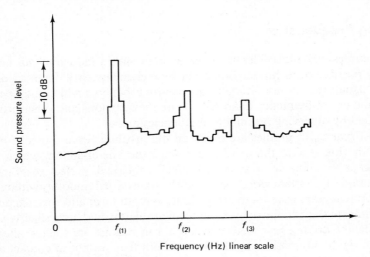

Figure 7.2.1 Gear noise.

If the shaft centerline is not straight, or if a gear or bearing is not concentric with the shaft centerline, noise and vibration at the tooth-error frequency may be observed. In addition, these causes may result in sideband frequencies of the tooth meshing frequencies. The sideband frequencies of the fundamental tooth meshing frequencies are given by

$$f_S = f_{(1)} \pm f_{(1E)} \tag{7.2.6}$$

Gear Trains

Consider a pair of nonplanetary gears in mesh. The absolute value of the speed ratio is given by the inverse of the ratio of numbers of teeth:

$$\frac{n_2}{n_1} = \frac{N_1}{N_2} \tag{7.2.7}$$

If both gears are external spur gears, the speed ratio is negative, that is, one will turn clockwise and the other counterclockwise. If one is an internal gear (ring gear), the speed ratio is positive, that is, both gears will turn in the same direction.

For a gear train with several gears, the output to input speed ratio is given by

$$\frac{n_{\text{output}}}{n_{\text{input}}} = \frac{\text{product of driving gear teeth}}{\text{product of driven gear teeth}} \tag{7.2.8}$$

An idler gear serves both as a driving gear and driven gear. Idler gears must be considered when determining the direction of rotation of shafts in a gear train.

EXAMPLE PROBLEM: GEAR TOOTH MESHING FREQUENCY AND TOOTH-ERROR FREQUENCY

In the reverted gear train of Figure 7.2.2, gear 1, on the input shaft, has 20 teeth and rotates at 3600 rpm. Gears 2, 3, and 4 have 45, 22, and 43 teeth, respectively. Narrow band spectral analysis of noise and vibration measurements shows discrete tones and vibration energy peaks at frequencies of 15, 29, 613, 1200, 1227, and 2400 Hz. Identify the probable contributors to the noise and vibration at these frequencies.

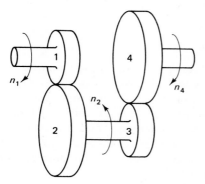

Figure 7.2.2 Reverted gear train.

Solution. Gear speeds are determined from

$$\frac{n_2}{n_1} = \frac{N_1}{N_2}$$

from which

$$n_2 = n_3 = 3600 \times \frac{20}{45} = 1600 \text{ rpm}$$

and

$$\frac{n_{\text{output}}}{n_{\text{input}}} = \frac{\text{product of driving gear teeth}}{\text{product of driven gear teeth}}$$

from which

$$n_4 = \frac{3600(20 \times 23)}{45 \times 42} = 876.19 \text{ rpm}$$

Fundamental tooth-error frequencies are given by

$$f_{(1E)} = \frac{n}{60}$$

$$= \frac{3600}{60} = 60 \text{ Hz for gear 1}$$

$$= \frac{1600}{60} = 26.67 \text{ Hz for gears 2 and 3}$$

$$= \frac{876.19}{60} = 14.60 \text{ Hz for gear 4}$$

Fundamental tooth meshing frequencies are given by

$$f_{(1)} = \frac{nN}{60}$$

$$= 3600 \times \frac{20}{60} = 1200 \text{ Hz for gears 1 and 2}$$

$$= 1600 \times \frac{23}{60} = 613.33 \text{ Hz for gears 3 and 4}$$

Comparing the calculated results with the spectral analysis, it appears that the 15- and 29-Hz discrete tones and vibration energy peaks correspond to the fundamental and one harmonic of the tooth-error frequency for gear 4. The teeth on gear 4 and shaft straightness should be examined. The discrete tones at 613 and 1227 Hz correspond to the fundamental and one harmonic of the tooth meshing frequency of gears 3 and 4. Discrete tones at 1200 and 2400 Hz correspond to the fundamental and one harmonic of the tooth meshing frequency of gears 1 and 2.

Noise Frequencies Generated by Planetary Gear Trains

Planetary (epicyclic) gear transmissions typically consist of a sun gear, several planet gears, a planet carrier, and a ring gear. Alternative designs may have two sun gears and no ring gear, or two ring gears and no sun gear. Most planetary trains are designed for balanced load sharing between the planet gears, which reduces tooth loads and eliminates bending loads on the input and output shafts. Planetary transmission designs are usually more suitable for speed ratio changing than nonplanetary designs. Determination of speed ratios and gear noise frequencies is complicated by the fact that the planet gears rotate about their own axes, which in turn rotate about the center of the planetary train.

Planetary train speed ratios can be determined as follows:

1. Designate two gears, x and y, and find their speed ratio with respect to the planet carrier:

$$r^* = \frac{n_y^*}{n_x^*}$$

(7.2.9)

where n^* = speed with respect to the carrier
  r^* = speed ratio determined with the planet carrier fixed (positive if gears x and y rotate in the same direction, negative otherwise)

2. Solve for the unknown quantity in the planetary train equation

$$r^* = \frac{n_y - n_c}{n_x - n_c}$$

(7.2.10)

where n_x and n_y = actual (absolute) speeds of gears x and y, respectively
  n_c = carrier speed

Since the above equations involve ratios, speeds can be expressed in rpm or rad/s as long as the designation is consistent. In this work, however, n will be expressed in rpm for use in later calculations.

Once the individual gear and carrier speeds are determined, the tooth-error and tooth meshing frequencies can be predicted. These frequencies depend on the absolute and relative gear speeds, tooth numbers, and the number of planet gears. Each configuration should be examined separately to predict noise and vibration frequencies.

Speed Ratios in a Simple Planetary Gear Train

In the planetary gear train of Figure 7.2.3 the sun gear, planet gears, and ring gear are designated by S, P, and R, respectively. Planet carrier C is not shown in the figure. The train is a balanced train if the four planets are equally spaced. It is possible to balance a train with this configuration if the tooth numbers are related by

$$\frac{N_S + N_R}{\text{number of planets}} = \text{an integer}$$

(7.2.11)

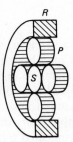

Figure 7.2.3 Planetary gear train.

In addition, the geometry of this train configuration requires that

$$N_R = N_S + 2N_P \qquad (7.2.12)$$

Let us arbitrarily replace gears x and y in the planetary train equations by the sun gear and ring gear, respectively. Treating the sun gear as the input gear and the ring gear as the output gear for now, the speed ratio relative to the carrier is given by

$$r^* = \frac{n_R^*}{n_S^*} = \frac{(\pm)(\text{product of driving gear teeth})}{\text{product of driven gear teeth}}$$

$$= -\frac{N_S N_P}{N_P N_R} = -\frac{N_S}{N_R}$$

The minus sign applies because the motion of the planet gears relative to the carrier is opposite the motion of the sun gear relative to the carrier, while the planet gears and ring gear rotate in the same direction relative to the carrier. The speed ratio relative to the carrier is also given by

$$r^* = \frac{n_R - n_C}{n_S - n_C}$$

which results in the speed ratio equation for the simple planetary train

$$\frac{n_R - n_C}{n_S - n_C} = -\frac{N_S}{N_R} \qquad (7.2.13)$$

The above equation applies regardless of which gears are the actual input and output gears. Note that the speed ratio is not dependent on the number of planet gears. If we wish to know the planet speeds, they can be found in a similar manner. The equation is

$$\frac{n_P - n_C}{n_S - n_C} = -\frac{N_S}{N_P} \qquad (7.2.14)$$

EXAMPLE PROBLEM: PLANETARY TRAIN SPEEDS AND VIBRATION AND NOISE FREQUENCIES

A simple, balanced planetary train of the type described above is to have a 36-tooth sun gear and four 32-tooth planet gears. The sun gear rotates at 4000 rpm clockwise and the ring gear is held stationary with a band brake. The sun gear is mounted on the input shaft and the planet carrier on the output shaft.

(a) Find the speeds of rotation.

Solution. Based on the geometry requirement of this simple planetary train, the number of teeth in the ring gear must be

$$N_R = N_S + 2N_P = 36 + 2 \times 32 = 100 \text{ teeth}$$

The condition for equal planet spacing, that is, 90° apart in this case, is met since

$$\frac{N_S + N_R}{\text{number of planets}} = \frac{36 + 100}{4}$$

$$= 34, \text{ an integer}$$

Using the given data in the speed ratio equation for the simple planetary train, we obtain

$$\frac{n_R - n_C}{n_S - n_C} = -\frac{N_S}{N_R}$$

$$\frac{0 - n_C}{4000 - n_C} = -\frac{36}{100}$$

from which the carrier speed is found to be

$$n_C = 4000 \times \frac{36}{136} = 1058.8 \text{ rpm clockwise}$$

Planet gear speeds are given by

$$\frac{n_P - n_C}{n_S - n_C} = -\frac{N_S}{N_P}$$

$$\frac{n_P - 1058.8}{4000 - 1058.8} = -\frac{36}{32}$$

which yields a planet speed of

$$n_P = -2250 = 2250 \text{ rpm counterclockwise}$$

The speed or a planet relative to the carrier is given by

$$n_P^* = n_P - n_c = -2250 - 1058.8 = -3308.8$$

$$= 3308.8 \text{ rpm counterclockwise}$$

(b) Predict noise and vibration frequencies which may result from operation of this planetary train.

Solution. Some noise or vibration may correspond to shaft speeds of the sun gear, the planet carrier, and the planet gears relative to the planet carrier. The corresponding frequencies are

$$\frac{n_S}{60} = \frac{4000}{60} = 66.67 \text{ Hz}$$

$$\frac{n_C}{60} = \frac{1058.8}{60} = 17.65 \text{ Hz}$$

$$\frac{n_P^*}{60} = \frac{3308.8}{60} = 55.15 \text{ Hz}$$

and harmonics (integer multiples of these values).

Tooth meshing frequencies depend on speeds relative to the carrier. The fundamental tooth meshing frequency is given by

$$f_{(1)} = \frac{n^* N}{60}$$

where n^* = rotational speed of one gear relative to the carrier
         N = number of teeth on the same gear

The speed of the sun gear relative to the carrier is given by

$$n_S^* = n_S - n_C = 4000 - 1058.8 = 2941.2 \text{ rpm}$$

from which

$$f_{(1)} = \frac{n_S^* N_S}{60} = 2941.2 \times \frac{36}{60} = 1764.7 \text{ Hz}$$

The result is the same if we consider a planet gear or the ring gear:

$$f_{(1)} = \frac{n_P^* N_P}{60} = \frac{n_R^* N_R}{60} = 1764.7 \text{ Hz}$$

Since each of the four planet gears meshes with both the sun gear and the ring gear, there are

$$8 \times 1764.7 = 14{,}118 \text{ tooth meshes/s}$$

Tooth-error frequencies depend on speeds relative to the carrier and the number of planet gears. If a single tooth on the sun or ring gear is poorly cut, chipped or otherwise damaged, the fundamental tooth-error frequency is given by

$$f_{(1E)} = \frac{n^* \#_P}{60} \tag{7.2.15}$$

where n^* = gear speed relative to the carrier
         $\#_P$ = number of planet gears

In the case of a damaged tooth on one planet gear, the tooth-error frequency is

$$f_{(1E)} = \frac{2n_P^*}{60} = \frac{n_P^*}{30} \qquad (7.2.16)$$

For the gear train considered above, a tooth error on the sun gear will result in a fundamental tooth-error frequency of

$$f_{(1E)} = \frac{n_S^* \#_P}{60} = (4000 - 1058.8) \times \frac{4}{60} = 196.1 \text{ Hz}$$

For a ring gear tooth error,

$$f_{(1E)} = \frac{n_R^* \#_P}{60} = (0 - 1058.8) \times \frac{4}{60} = 70.6 \text{ Hz}$$

(the minus sign is ignored). For a planet gear tooth error,

$$f_{(1E)} = \frac{n_P^*}{30} = \frac{-2250 - 1058.8}{30} = 110.3 \text{ Hz}$$

(again, the final minus sign is ignored). Harmonics of these frequencies are also likely to be present.

Contact Ratio (CR)

The contact ratio (CR) for a pair of gears is defined as the average number of pairs of teeth in contact. Of course, there must be contact between at least one tooth on the driving gear and one tooth on the driven gear at all times. Considering tooth error, wear, shaft deflection, and tolerances, a value of about CR = 1.2 is usually selected as a practical minimum. When the contact ratio is near the minimum value, contact begins at the tips of the driven teeth, and impact loads due to tooth meshing are high. If tooth meshing frequencies are prominent in the noise spectrum, an increase in contact ratio should be considered. A contact ratio of 2 or more usually results in better tooth-load sharing and quieter operation, since two or more pairs of teeth will be in contact at all times (neglecting deflection, tooth error, etc.).

Spur Gear Terminology   Gears are designed for specified power and speed ratio requirements. These requirements affect the selection of gear material, tooth width, module or diametral pitch, number of teeth, and other parameters. The following definitions are related to determination of contact ratio.

$$d = \text{pitch diameter (nominal diameter)}$$

$$r = \text{pitch radius} = \frac{d}{2}$$

$$c = \text{center distance} = r_1 + r_2 \text{ for a pair of gears in mesh}$$

where, for nonplanetary spur gears

$$\frac{r_1}{r_2} = \frac{n_2}{n_1}$$

the speed ratio, and

$$\phi = \text{pressure angle}$$

the angle of force transmission between gear teeth. Standard gears have pressure angles of 14.5° (an old standard), 20°, and 25°.

$$N = \text{number of teeth}$$

$$m = \frac{d}{N}, \text{ the module (standardized for metric units)}$$

$$P_d = \frac{N}{d}, \text{ the diametral pitch (standardized for customary U.S. units)}$$

$$a = \text{addendum, the extent of the gear tooth beyond the pitch radius}$$

For full depth gears with 14.5°, 20°, and 25° pressure angles, the standard addendum is $a = m = 1/P_d$. The standard addendum is $a = 0.8m = 0.8/P_d$ for 20° pressure angle stub teeth.

$$r_a = r + a = \text{radius of addendum circle}$$

$$p_c = \frac{\pi d}{N} = \pi m = \frac{\pi}{P_d} = \text{circular pitch}$$

$$b = \text{face width (thickness of gear blank)}$$

High torque requirements are satisfied by gears with large face width and large module (i.e., large circular pitch, small diametral pitch). A larger number of teeth improves the tooth form in terms of strength, as does a larger pressure angle. Stub teeth are stronger in terms of beam strength since the moment arm of force is reduced. However, some of these parameters affect contact ratio and noise as well.

Determination of Contact Ratio   The contact ratio for a pair of spur gears is given by

$$\text{CR} = [(r_{a1}^2 - r_1^2 \cos^2 \phi)^{1/2}$$
$$+ (r_{a2}^2 - r_2^2 \cos^2 \phi)^{1/2} - c \sin \phi]/(p_c \cos \phi) \qquad (7.2.17)$$

where subscripts 1 and 2 refer to the driver and driven gears. Pressure angle ϕ must be the same for both.

EXAMPLE PROBLEM: CONTACT RATIO

Shaft speed is to be reduced from 1800 to 900 rpm. The driving gear is to have 20 teeth and a diametral pitch of 5. The design calls for 20° pressure angle stub teeth.

(a) Find the contact ratio.

Solution. For nonplanetary gears, the speed ratio is given by

$$\frac{n_2}{n_1} = \frac{N_1}{N_2}$$

from which

$$N_2 = 20 \times \frac{1800}{900} = 40 \text{ teeth}$$

The diametral pitch

$$P_d = \frac{N}{d} = 5$$

must be common to a pair of spur gears, from which the pitch diameters and pitch radii are

$$d_1 = \frac{20}{5} = 4 \text{ in}, \qquad r_1 = 2 \text{ in}$$

$$d_2 = \frac{40}{5} = 8 \text{ in}, \qquad \text{and} \quad r_2 = 4 \text{ in}$$

The center distance is the sum of the pitch radii

$$c = r_1 + r_2 = 2 + 4 = 6 \text{ in}$$

For stub teeth, the addendum is

$$a_1 = a_2 = \frac{0.8}{P_d} = \frac{0.8}{5} = 0.16 \text{ in}$$

and the addendum circle radii

$$r_a = r + a$$

from which

$$r_{a1} = 2 + 0.16 = 2.16 \text{ in}$$

$$r_{a2} = 4 + 0.16 = 4.16 \text{ in}$$

Circular pitch, also common for a pair of spur gears is given by

$$p_c = \frac{\pi}{P_d} = \frac{\pi}{5} = 0.6283 \text{ in}$$

Using these values, contact ratio is given by

$$CR = [(2.16^2 - 2^2 \cos^2 20°)^{1/2}$$
$$+ (4.16^2 - 4^2 \cos^2 20°)^{1/2} - 6 \sin 20°]/(0.6283 \cos 20°)$$
$$= 1.347$$

(b) Suppose the noise spectrum of the gear train shows objectionable discrete tones at 600 and 1800 Hz. Suggest a design change.

Solution. The fundamental tooth meshing frequency is given by

$$f_{(1)} = \frac{nN}{60} = 1800 \times \frac{20}{60} = 600 \text{ Hz}$$

and the harmonics (integer multiples) are

$$2 \times 600 = 1200 \text{ Hz}, \qquad 3 \times 600 = 1800 \text{ Hz}, \qquad \text{and so on}$$

Thus, tooth meshing frequencies appear to be a problem. Let us increase the contact ratio in an attempt to reduce the noise problem. Since diametral pitch is based on required tooth strength, it will not be changed. The number of teeth in gear 1 will be increased to 30 while retaining the 20° pressure angle and selecting full depth tooth form. Full depth teeth are subject to greater bending stress than stub teeth if contact is assumed to occur at the tooth tip. However, depending on tooth accuracy, this effect should be mitigated by the increased contact ratio. The result is as follows:

$$N_2 = 30 \times \frac{1800}{60} = 60 \text{ teeth}$$

$$d_1 = \frac{30}{5} = 6 \text{ in}, \qquad r_1 = 3 \text{ in}$$

$$d_2 = \frac{60}{5} = 12 \text{ in}, \qquad r_2 = 6 \text{ in},$$

$$c = 3 + 6 = 9 \text{ in}$$

$$r_{a1} = 3 + 0.2 = 3.2 \text{ in}$$

$$r_{a2} = 6 + 0.2 = 6.2 \text{ in}$$

Contact ratio for the revised design is

$$\text{CR} = [(3.2^2 - 3^2 \cos^2 20°)^{1/2}$$
$$+ (6.2^2 - 6^2 \cos^2 20°)^{1/2} - 9 \sin 20°]/(0.6283 \cos 20°)$$
$$= 1.719$$

The fundamental tooth meshing frequency for the revised design is

$$f_{(1)} = 1800 \times \frac{30}{60} = 900 \text{ Hz}$$

Although the increase in CR may decrease noise levels, additional noise control procedures should be considered as well.

Helical Gears

When a pair of spur gear teeth begins contact, contact occurs simultaneously across the entire face width. Helical gear teeth come into contact gradually, with contact beginning at a point, and then extending across the tooth face. As a result the impact loads which appear as tooth meshing frequency noise and vibration are reduced. Thus, spur gear trains may be replaced by helical gears on parallel shafts to reduce noise. The actual number of pairs of teeth in contact will be increased by this substitution as well. For smooth, quiet operation, it is recommended that the thickness of the helical gear blank be 1.2 to 2 times the axial pitch. Axial pitch is the distance between corresponding points on two adjacent teeth measured parallel to the gear shaft. When helical gears are used to replace spur gears, thrust (axial) loads must be considered in the design of the shafts and bearings.

Other Considerations in the Control of Gear Noise

Gear production methods, including milling, die casting, drawing, extruding, stamping, and production from sintered metal, tend to produce gears with significant tooth error. Such gears are sometimes responsible for high noise levels. For most gears produced by milling cutters, the tooth form will only approximate the correct form. To produce a precise tooth form, a different milling cutter would be required for each diametral pitch or module, and for each tooth number. In practice, a different milling cutter is used for each diametral pitch; however, each cutter is used for a range of tooth numbers. Cast, drawn, and extruded gear inaccuracies result from shrinkage and other dimensional changes.

Noise due to tooth error can be reduced by using precision methods of generating gear teeth. These include the generating rack cutter, the generating gear shaper cutter, and the generating hob. Precision gears are often finished by grinding or shaving. Other finishing methods include burnishing, lapping, and honing.

Damping can be used to absorb vibration energy in large gears. Constrained layer damping, in which a layer of damping material is sandwiched between the gear web and a rigid steel plate, may be effective in reducing noise. Fiber, plastic, and fiber-reinforced plastic gears are sometimes used in applications where loads are low and temperatures are not excessive for the material. These materials have a low modulus of elasticity and high internal damping compared with steel. As a result, shock loads due to tooth meshing and tooth error are absorbed, reducing noise.

Housings or enclosures are also useful for controlling gear noise. The enclosure should be isolated to prevent vibration transmission, and adequate lubrication should be assured within the enclosure. If a bending frequency (resonance) of a housing corresponds to a tooth meshing frequency or other excitation frequency, then the housing may radiate substantial noise energy. This problem is solved by tuning the housing, that is, stiffening it to change its resonance. The stiffeners themselves should be designed for low radiation efficiency. Directivity patterns should be considered when orienting machinery. For example, noisy gearing may be positioned so that employee noise exposure and community noise exposure are minimized.

7.3 BEARINGS, BELTS, CHAINS, AND OTHER DRIVE TRAIN ELEMENTS

Journal Bearings

Hydrodynamic lubrication relies on shaft rotation to pump a film of lubricant between the shaft and bearing. If the product of lubricant viscosity and speed is adequate for the ratio of load to projected bearing area, then thick-film hydrodynamic lubrication exists. This condition ensures stable operation without metal-to-metal contact, and is likely to result in quiet operation. Starting, stopping, and direction changing may result in temporary rupture of the lubricant film and metal-to-metal contact. Hydrostatic lubrication utilizes fluid (oil, air, or water) introduced to the bearing surface at sufficient pressure to support the shaft, even when stationary. A change in the noise level produced by a journal bearing is likely to indicate a failure of the lubrication system.

Ball and Roller Bearings

In many applications, ball and roller bearings need to be replaced after a finite period of use. Failure usually begins with pitting or spalling of a ball or roller due to high contact stresses. Although 90% survival bearing life and average bearing life can be predicted, incipient bearing failure is often detected by noise and vibration measurements. Discrete tones in the noise spectrum measured near a ball or roller bearing may also indicate manufacturing defects in the bearing. Narrow band vibration spectra are also used to detect wear and defects.

The rotational speed of the elements of a ball or roller bearing may be determined by analogy to the speed ratio equations for a simple planetary train. For this application, tooth numbers of the sun, planet, and ring gears are replaced by bearing inner race, ball, or roller, and outer race diameters, respectively. The speed relationships are

$$\frac{n_O - n_C}{n_I - n_C} = -\frac{D_I}{D_O} \tag{7.3.1}$$

and

$$\frac{n_B - n_C}{n_I - n_C} = -\frac{D_I}{D_B} \tag{7.3.2}$$

where n = rotational speed (rpm)
 D = diameter (in or mm)

Race diameters are measured at the point of contact with the balls or rollers. Subscripts are as follows:

$$I = \text{inner race}$$

$$B = \text{ball or roller}$$

$$O = \text{outer race}$$

$$C = \text{ball cage or separator}$$

Ball and Roller Bearings with Stationary Outer Races

In most ball and roller bearing applications, the outer race is stationary. Using this information in the speed relationships, we have

$$\frac{0 - n_C}{n_I - n_C} = -\frac{D_I}{D_O}$$

from which we find separator speed

$$n_C = \frac{n_I D_I}{D_O + D_I} \tag{7.3.3}$$

and the speed of the balls with respect to the separator

$$n_B^* = n_B - n_C = -\frac{n_I^* D_I}{D_B} = \frac{(n_I - n_C)D_I}{D_B} \tag{7.3.4}$$

Vibration and noise frequencies will be related to the absolute speeds n, relative speeds $n^* = n - n_C$, and the number of balls or rollers $\#_B$. The following fundamental frequencies f(Hz) may appear if the outer race is stationary. Note that f is taken as a positive number regardless of rotation direction.

1. Shaft imbalance:

$$f = \frac{n_I}{60} \tag{7.3.5}$$

2. Outer race defect:

$$f = \frac{n_O^* \#_B}{60} = \frac{n_C \#_B}{60} \tag{7.3.6}$$

3. Inner race defect:

$$f = \frac{n_I^* \#_B}{60} = \frac{(n_I - n_C)\#_B}{60} \tag{7.3.7}$$

4. Damage to one ball or roller:

$$f = \frac{2n_B^*}{60} = \frac{n_B - n_C}{30} \tag{7.3.8}$$

5. Damage or imbalance in the separator:

$$f = \frac{n_C}{60} \tag{7.3.9}$$

Harmonics $2f$, $3f$, and so on are likely to appear for each of these frequencies.

**EXAMPLE PROBLEM: VIBRATION AND NOISE FREQUENCIES
DUE TO DEFECTS IN A BALL BEARING**

A ball bearing is constructed with eleven 7-mm-diameter balls. The inner and outer race diameters are $D_I = 25$ and $D_O = 39$ mm, measured at the point of ball contact. Obviously, $D_I + 2D_B = D_O$. The outer race is stationary, and the inner race rotation speed is $n_I = 4300$ rpm clockwise.

(a) Determine rotational speeds.

Solution. The separator speed is given by

$$n_C = \frac{n_I D_I}{D_O + D_I}$$

$$= 4300 \times \frac{25}{39 + 25} = 1679.7 \text{ rpm}$$

and the speed of the balls relative to the separator is

$$n_B^* = -(n_I - n_C)D_I/D_B = -(4300 - 1679.7) \times 25/7$$

$$= -9358.2 \ (9358.2 \text{ rpm counterclockwise})$$

(b) Determine the noise and vibration frequencies which may occur due to imbalance and defects.

Solution. The fundamental frequencies are as follows.
Shaft imbalance:

$$f = \frac{n_I}{60} = \frac{4300}{60} = 71.7 \text{ Hz}$$

Outer race defect:

$$f = \frac{n_C \#_B}{60} = 1679.7 \times \frac{11}{60} = 307.9 \text{ Hz}$$

Inner race defect:

$$f = (n_I - n_C)\frac{\#_B}{60} = (4300 - 1679.7) \times \frac{11}{60} = 480.4 \text{ Hz}$$

Damage to one ball:

$$f = \frac{n_B^*}{30} = -\frac{9358.2}{30} = 311.9 \text{ Hz}$$

(The sign is ignored in the answer.)
Imbalance in the separator:

$$f = \frac{n_C}{60} = \frac{1679.7}{60} = 28.0 \text{ Hz}$$

Harmonics (multiples of the fundamental frequencies) are also likely to appear.

Ball and Roller Bearings with Rotating Outer Races

In some applications, the shaft connected to the inner race of a bearing is stationary, and the outer race rotates. In this case the basic speed relationship equations become

$$\frac{n_O - n_C}{0 - n_C} = -\frac{D_I}{D_O}$$

from which carrier speed is given by

$$n_C = \frac{n_O D_O}{D_O + D_I} \tag{7.3.10}$$

and the speed of the balls with respect to the carrier

$$n_B^* = n_B - n_C = \frac{n_O^* D_O}{D_B} = \frac{(n_O - n_C) D_O}{D_B} \tag{7.3.11}$$

Vibration and noise frequencies that might result when the outer race rotates are as follows.

1. Imbalance of rotating members connected to the outer race:

$$f = \frac{n_O}{60} \tag{7.3.12}$$

2. Outer race defect:

$$f = n_O^* \frac{\#_B}{60} = (n_O - n_C) \frac{\#_B}{60} \tag{7.3.13}$$

3. Inner race defect:

$$f = n_I^* \frac{\#_B}{60} = n_C \frac{\#_B}{60} \tag{7.3.14}$$

4. Damage to one ball or roller:

$$f = \frac{n_B^*}{30} \tag{7.3.15}$$

5. Damage or imbalance in the separator:

$$f = \frac{n_C}{60} \tag{7.3.16}$$

Harmonics are likely to appear as well.

For a given bearing fault, the noise and vibration spectra measured at the bearing are likely to be essentially tonal. That is, much of the noise energy or vibration energy will be concentrated in the bands represented by the fundamental frequency and one or two harmonics. Thus, the spectra might resemble a typical gear noise spectrum (e.g., Figure 7.2.1).

Belt Drives

Machines are often designed with belt drives in preference to gear drives for reasons of cost and noise control. Because of the belt elasticity, shock loads at a driven machine are not transmitted back to the driver. Thus, solid-borne noise and vibration are reduced. Flat belts and V-belts operating on smooth pulleys transmit power through friction. Thus, there must be adequate belt tension to oppose centrifugal effects and prevent significant slipping. The wedging action of V-belts increases their power transmission capacity. In some cases, belts slip when suddenly loaded, causing a squeal-type noise. This can sometimes be corrected by increasing belt tension. When precise speed ratios are required, toothed belts on toothed pulleys can be used. Toothed belts maintain timing and phase relationships, but unlike gears, they isolate vibration and shock forces rather than transmitting them between driving and driven elements.

Chain Drives

Roller chain is made up of side plates and pin and bushing joints which mesh with toothed sprockets. Although chain flexibility limits transmission of shock and vibratory forces, initial contact between the chain and sprockets may be noisy at high speeds. For high-speed operation with high loads, inverted-tooth or "silent" chain is often preferred. Since inverted-tooth chain engages the sprockets with less impact force, it usually operates more quietly than roller chain.

Both inverted-tooth chain and roller chain are made up of links of finite length. As chain links engage a sprocket, the pitch line (the centerline of link pins) moves up and down due to chordal action. Let the center of a link pin be at a radius $R_{\max}$ from the center of the sprocket on which it rides. Then, $R_{\max}$ is the maximum distance of the pitch line from the sprocket center as shown in Figure 7.3.1. As the link is further engaged, the pitch line moves closer to the sprocket center, and both pins of the link become colinear with the pitch line. The new position is

$$R_{\min} = R_{\max} \cos\left(\frac{180°}{N_t}\right) \tag{7.3.17}$$

where N_t = number of sprocket teeth. Typically, roller chain sprockets have no less than 8 teeth, and inverted-tooth chain sprockets no less than 17 teeth.

If the drive sprocket rotates at constant speed n_1 rpm, then the pitch line velocity

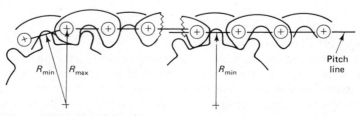

Figure 7.3.1 Chordal action.

of the chain will change in proportion to its distance from the sprocket center. The ratio of velocity change amplitude to mean velocity is given by

$$V^* = \frac{R_{max} - R_{mean}}{R_{mean}}$$

$$= \frac{1 - [1 + \cos(180°/N_t)]/2}{[1 + \cos(180°/N_t)]/2}$$

$$= \frac{1 - \cos(180°/N_t)}{1 + \cos(180°/N_t)} \tag{7.3.18}$$

where

$$V^* = \frac{\text{maximum} - \text{mean}}{\text{mean pitch line velocity}}$$

The speed ratio for a chain drive is given by

$$\frac{n_2}{n_1} = \frac{N_1}{N_2} \tag{7.3.19}$$

where n = sprocket speed, N = number of sprocket teeth, and subscripts 1 and 2 refer to driver and driven sprockets, respectively. The following fundamental frequencies of noise and vibration (Hz) may occur.

1. Imbalance in the driver or driven shaft, or damage to one sprocket tooth:

$$f = \frac{n_1}{60} \quad \text{or} \quad f = \frac{n_2}{60} \tag{7.3.20}$$

2. Damage to one chain link: For a chain with N_L links, a damaged link will strike each sprocket $n_1 N_1/N_L$ times per minute from which

$$f = \frac{n_1 N_1}{30 N_L} \tag{7.3.21}$$

3. Tooth engagement and chordal action:

$$f = \frac{n_1 N_1}{30} \tag{7.3.22}$$

These values will change if idler sprockets are used. Harmonics of these frequencies are also likely to be present. Noise levels and vibration amplitude due to chain meshing and chordal action depend on sprocket configuration, and speeds and masses of the sprockets and chain.

EXAMPLE PROBLEM: CHAIN DRIVE

An eight-tooth drive sprocket rotates at 3600 rpm. The driven sprocket has 18 teeth and the chain has 40 links.

(a) Find the ratio of velocity change amplitude to mean velocity.

Solution. The ratio is greatest at the smaller sprocket which is the driver. It is given by

$$V^* = \frac{1 - \cos(180/8)}{1 + \cos(180/8)} = 0.0396$$

That is, the velocity varies by about $\pm 4\%$ from the average.

(b) Determine possible vibration and noise frequencies due to the chain drive if there are no idler sprockets.

Solution. The speed of the output sprocket is given by

$$n_2 = n_1 \times \frac{N_1}{N_2} = 3600 \times \frac{8}{18} = 1600 \text{ rpm}$$

The following fundamental frequencies may be present:
Imbalance of either shaft or damage to one tooth.

$$f = \frac{n}{60} = \frac{3600}{60} = 60 \text{ Hz}$$

$$f = \frac{1600}{60} = 26.7 \text{ Hz}$$

Damage to one link:

$$f = \frac{n_1 N_1}{30 N_L} = 3600 \times \frac{8}{30 \times 40} = 24 \text{ Hz}$$

Tooth engagement and chordal action:

$$f = \frac{n_1 N_1}{30} = 3600 \times \frac{8}{30} = 960 \text{ Hz}$$

Harmonics of these frequencies should also be considered. The large velocity change determined in part (a) indicates that a redesign may be necessary. Possibly, the number of teeth in each pulley would be doubled.

Universal Joints

Sometimes the relative position of a driving element and driven element changes while a system is operating. The misalignment may be due to changes in loading or other causes. Flexible couplings, flexible shafts, and universal joints are used to transmit power between shafts that are misaligned. Flexible couplings are generally limited to shafts with slight misalignment. Flexible shafts can handle large amounts of misalignment, but are limited in torque capacity.

Universal joints may be designed for shaft misalignment angles of several degrees and large torque capacities. A Hooke-type universal joint is illustrated in Figure 7.3.2. Consider the position shown in the top figure, for shaft misalignment ϕ and the cross-

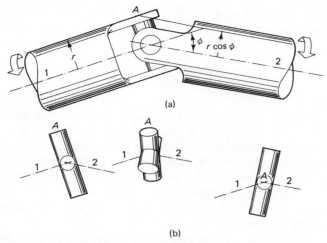

Figure 7.3.2 Hooke-type universal joint.

link plane perpendicular to the axis of shaft 1. At this instant, the speed ratio is given by

$$\frac{n_2}{n_1} = \frac{1}{\cos \phi} \qquad (7.3.23)$$

As the shafts rotate through 90°, the cross-link plane becomes perpendicular to the axis of shaft 2. Then the speed ratio is given by

$$\frac{n_2}{n_1} = \cos \phi \qquad (7.3.24)$$

The speed ratio changes from maximum to minimum to maximum twice per shaft revolution. Thus, the associated noise and vibration frequency (in hertz) is given by

$$f = \frac{n}{30} \qquad (7.3.25)$$

for shaft speed n (rpm).

One constant velocity universal joint is designed with balls held in intersecting ball grooves. The balls are restrained to lie in a plane which is oriented at an angle of $\phi/2$ from the centerline of either shaft. As a result the input and output shafts rotate at the same speed, eliminating a source of noise and vibration characteristic to the Hooke-type universal joint.

7.4 OTHER INDUSTRIAL NOISE SOURCES

Other sources of industrial noise include processes involving gas and liquid flow, electric motors and internal combustion engines, materials-handling equipment, and systems generating ultra- and infra-sound. Some of these industrial noise sources may be controlled by the same methods suggested for control of noise in residential buildings. The methods suggested for control of construction noise may be applicable to other industrial noise sources.

Noise Due to Gas Flow

As noted in Chapter 2, aerodynamic noise sources are often modeled as monopoles, dipoles, and quadrupoles. Pulsed jets of gas, including air periodically ejected through a nozzle and combustion noise, may be modeled as monopole sources. Internal combustion engine exhaust noise and the discharge from HVAC ducts may also have monopole sources characteristics. Fan and compressor noise where turbulent flow encounters rotor or stator blades, flow through grids, and vibrating beams may be modeled as dipole sources. The quadrupole model is applied to noise due to turbulent mixing in air jets where there is no interaction with adjacent surfaces.

An ideal monopole source has a directivity index $DI(\theta, \phi) = 0$ and directivity factor $Q(\theta, \phi) = 1$. Radiated sound power of a monopole is given by

$$W = K_1 \rho d^2 \frac{v^4}{c} \tag{2.1.14}$$

Consider a nozzle discharging air from a reservoir, approximating this source as a monopole. If flow is assumed to be isentropic, the following relationship may be derived from Euler's equation (Huang and Rivin, 1985)

$$\left(\frac{v}{c}\right)^2 = \frac{2(1 - P^{(1-\gamma)/\gamma})}{\gamma - 1} \tag{7.4.1}$$

where v = gas velocity
  c = speed of sound propagation in the gas
  γ = ratio of specific heats
  $P = p_i/p_a$ = pressure ratio
  p_i = inlet (absolute) pressure
  p_a = ambient pressure

Average sound intensity at a distance r due to discharge from a nozzle of diameter d may be approximated by

$$I = \frac{W}{4\pi r^2} = \frac{K_1 \rho c^3 d^2}{4\pi r^2} \left(\frac{v}{c}\right)^4$$

$$= \left[\frac{K_1 \rho c^3 d^2}{4\pi r^2}\right]\left[\frac{2}{\gamma - 1}(1 - P^{(1-\gamma)/\gamma})\right]^4 \tag{7.4.2}$$

If the gas is air, the ratio of specific heats is $\gamma = 1.4$. For nozzle diameter $d \le 30$ mm, the constant $K_1 = 0.3 \times 10^{-4}$, based on experimental results for air jets given by Lush (1971) and Olsen (1973). Using these values, sound intensity is given by

$$I = 1.492 \times 10^{-3} \rho c^3 \left(\frac{d}{r}\right)^2 (1 - P^{-0.2857})^4 \tag{7.4.3}$$

The resulting sound intensity level may be predicted from the following equation:

$$L_I = 10 \lg\left(\frac{I}{I_{ref}}\right) = 10 \lg\left(\frac{I}{10^{-12}}\right)$$

$$= 91.7 + 10 \lg(\rho c^3) + 20 \lg\left(\frac{d}{r}\right) + 40 \lg(1 - P^{-0.2857}) \qquad (7.4.4)$$

which should approximate the sound pressure level L_P at a distance r from the nozzle.

The noise spectrum of a nozzle usually has maxima in the 4-, 8-, and 16-kHz octave bands. Although A-weighted noise levels will generally be lower than unweighted noise levels predicted by the above equation, the noise level generated by a nozzle may be 90 to 100 dBA when measured at the operator's ear. Air jets from blow-off nozzles are used for ejecting, cleaning, and drying parts in industrial operations involving stamping, casting, assembly, and a number of other processes. Where air jets are used extensively, they contribute to high levels of equivalent sound level and potential hearing damage.

EXAMPLE PROBLEM: NOISE DUE TO AN AIR JET

(a) Write an equation for estimating sound pressure level due to a simple air jet nozzle operating at 20°C at typical atmospheric conditions.

Solution. The speed of sound is given by

$$c = 20.04(T' + 273.16)^{1/2}$$

$$= 20.04(20 + 273.16)^{1/2} = 343.1 \text{ m/s}$$

Air density is given by

$$\rho = \frac{p_a}{RT}$$

Using p_a = one standard atmosphere = 1.01325×10^5 Pa, gas constant $R = 287$ N·m/(kg·K), and absolute temperature $T = 20 + 273.16 = 293.16$ K, the air density is

$$\rho = \frac{1.01325 \times 10^5}{287 \times 293.16} = 1.204 \text{ kg/m}^3$$

Assuming the nozzle approaches a monopole source, we have

$$L_P = 91.7 + 10 \lg(\rho c^3) + 20 \lg\left(\frac{d}{r}\right) + 40 \lg(1 - P^{-0.2857})$$

$$= 91.7 + 10 \lg(1.204 \times 343.1^3) + 20 \lg\left(\frac{d}{r}\right) + 40 \lg(1 - P^{-0.2857})$$

$$= 168.6 + 20 \lg\left(\frac{d}{r}\right) + 40 \lg(1 - P^{-0.2857})$$

where $P = p_i/p_a = 1 + p'/p_a$ for inlet gauge pressure p'. If inlet gauge pressure p' is given in pascals, then

$$P = 1 + p'/(1.01325 \times 10^5)$$

If inlet gauge pressure p' is in psi,

$$P = 1 + p'/14.696$$

(b) Predict the sound pressure level at a distance of 3 ft from a simple $\frac{1}{4}$-in-diameter nozzle air jet if the inlet pressure is 60 psi (gauge) and air temperature 68°F.

Solution. The pressure ratio is given by

$$P = 1 + \frac{p'}{14.696} = 1 + \frac{60}{14.696} = 5.083$$

from which the predicted sound pressure level is

$$L_P = 168.6 + 20 \lg\left(\frac{d}{r}\right) + 40 \lg(1 - P^{-0.2857})$$

$$= 168.6 + 20 \lg\left(\frac{0.25}{36}\right) + 40 \lg(1 - 5.083^{-0.2857})$$

$$= 108 \text{ dB}$$

Tests of blow-off nozzles of various diameters and with various pressure ratios were conducted by Huang and Rivin (1985). In one test, which resembles the above example problem, a 6-mm-diameter nozzle was directed at a target disk 150 mm away. At an inlet gauge pressure of 60 psi, a sound level of about 105 dBA was recorded at a distance of one meter at 90° from the direction of air flow. At inlet gauge pressures of 20 and 40 psi, recorded sound levels were about 87 and 102 dBA, respectively.

Control of Noise Due to Gas Flow

As observed above, sound intensity is proportional to the fourth power of velocity in gas flows which may be modeled as aerodynamic monopoles. Sound intensity in dipole and quadrupole sources is proportional to the sixth and eighth powers, respectively. Thus, wherever practical, air velocity should be reduced to reduce noise levels. In blow-off nozzles used for parts ejection and cleaning, however, high air velocities are required to obtain adequate thrust.

Pressure and velocity fluctuations occur in the turbulent mixing region where the air jet meets the surrounding air, and when the air jet impinges on solid objects. Turbulence-related noise can be reduced by introducing an air stream of lower velocity between the high-velocity jet and the ambient air. Air jet silencers include multiple jets, restrictive diffusers, and air shrouds. The results of tests by Huang and Rivin (1985) indicate that multiple-jet and air-shroud-type nozzle silencers cause noise reductions of 3 to 10 dBA. These types require an increase of 0 to 50% in air consumption to maintain thrust. Restrictive diffuser-type nozzle silencers provided noise reductions of up to 20 dBA, but required a more than threefold increase in air consumption to maintain thrust.

Electric Motors and Transformers

In electric motors, electromagnetic forces between the armature and field magnet, or the rotor and stator, cause vibration. These vibratory forces may cause a noise problem by exciting large sheetmetal components into vibration. Transmission of vibratory forces may be limited by using vibration isolators at the base of the motor. The use of belt drives limits transmission of vibration between the motor and driven machinery. Airborne noise may be generated directly by interaction of the slots in the rotor and stator of an electric motor.

Magnetostriction is a change in the dimensions of a ferromagnetic material subject to a magnetic field. The changing magnetic field in a transformer causes deformation of the transformer core which occurs at the alternating current (AC) frequency and higher harmonics, particularly twice the AC frequency. This results in the characteristic transformer hum at 120 Hz, twice the AC frequency used in the United States. High frequencies are used in some industrial applications, and a frequency of 50 Hz is used in the United Kingdom and some other countries. When noise spectrum peaks are detected at the AC frequency or a harmonic of it, then electrical components may be the source.

Internal Combustion Engines

Most spark-ignition engines operate with a four-stroke cycle, that is, each thermo-dynamic cycle involves an intake stroke, compression stroke, combustion stroke, and exhaust stroke. Thus, there is one combustion noise peak per cylinder every two crankshaft rotations. Two-stroke-cycle engines combine these processes; the fuel–air mixture is ignited in each cylinder during each crankshaft rotation. As a result, two-stroke-cycle engines have a more favorable power-to-weight ratio. Most two-stroke-cycle engines are designed with intake and exhaust ports, while valves are utilized in four-stroke-cycle engines. The use of exhaust ports contributes to the higher noise levels typical of two-stroke-cycle engines.

Due to their high compression and rapid burning of fuel, diesel engines generate prominent impact noise. While underway, diesel trucks with refrigeration units utilize the diesel power to operate the refrigerator. The refrigeration unit can also be designed for operation from electric power lines. In order to reduce noise while trucks are loading or unloading or standing at a terminal, it should be required that the diesel engine be turned off and electrical service be connected.

Sources of internal combustion noise include the engine exhaust, engine surface radiation, the air intake, and auxiliaries such as the fan. The engine exhaust is typically the most prominent contribution. However, a well-designed exhaust muffler may reduce the exhaust noise contribution to below that of another engine source. Consideration can then be given to reducing engine surface radiation, possibly by using an enclosure. Air intake silencers should be considered. Cooling fans are ordinarily designed for continuous operation at fan speeds based on worst-case cooling loads. In order to reduce fan noise, the cooling fan may be thermostatically controlled so that it operates at high speed only when required.

The use of internal combustion engines is limited in factories due to problems with exhaust gases and noise. Most of the materials handling can be done with electrically driven belts and conveyors, vibratory conveyors, and battery-powered forklift trucks.

Ultrasound and Infrasound

Ultrasound and infrasound are sounds at frequencies generally considered outside of the audible range. Ultrasound frequencies are those above 20 kHz. Bass and Bolin (1985) studied industrial operations including impact, bending, grinding, drilling, laser etching, and high-velocity fluid and air sprays in the 0 to 1 MHz frequency range. The purpose of the study was to determine sources of ultrasonic noise in typical industrial environments in order to estimate the signal-to-noise ratio for robotic control applications. High-velocity fluid and air sprays were found to be the most prevalent sources of ultrasonic noise in the plants that were surveyed.

According to EPA (1973, 1974) there have been no observed adverse effects of ultrasound at levels below 105 dB. The effects of high-intensity ultrasound (levels > 105 dB) are also the effects observed during stress. However, the data are insufficient to assure the safety of ultrasound. In many cases, ultrasound is accompanied by broadband audible noise and by subharmonics, making experimental assessments of ultrasound effects difficult. Atmospheric attenuation of high-frequency ultrasonic waves is significant, increasing roughly as the frequency squared.

Sound at frequencies below 16 or 20 Hz is referred to as infrasound. Infrasound is produced by the wind, by jet aircraft, and by some industrial processes. According to EPA (1973, 1974) it does not appear that exposure to infrasound at levels below 130 dB poses a serious health hazard. The A-weighted relative response at sound frequencies of 10, 12.5, and 16 Hz is -70.4, -63.4, and -56.7 dB, respectively, as given in Chapter 1. Thus, a sound level of 130 dB in one of these one-third octave bands would correspond to 59.6 or 66.6 or 73.3 dBA, respectively. Complaints associated with high levels of infrasound resemble mild stress reactions and bizarre auditory sensations such as pulsating and fluttering. As with ultrasound, there is insufficient data to assess the health effects of low levels of infrasound.

7.5 PREDICTION OF INDUSTRIAL NOISE LEVELS

Indoor sound levels are influenced by direct sound (transmitted directly from source to observer) and by reverberant sound due to reflections. In the absence of prominent standing waves, the scalar sound intensity due to a single source is given by

$$I = W\left[\frac{Q(\theta, \phi)}{4\pi r^2} + \frac{4}{R}\right] \tag{2.5.12}$$

where
I = scalar sound intensity (W/m^2) including the reactive component
W = sound power (W)
$Q(\theta, \phi)$ = directivity

r = distance to the source (m), where $r > \lambda$

λ = wavelength (m)

$R = S_T \alpha_{mean}/(1 - \alpha_{mean})$ = room constant (m²)

S_T = total room surface area (m²)

α_{mean} = mean absorption coefficient. It is assumed that the distribution of absorptive material is fairly uniform throughout the room.

For common atmospheric conditions, sound pressure level and scalar sound intensity level are approximately equal, from which

$$L_P \approx L_I = L_W + 10 \lg\left[\frac{Q(\theta, \phi)}{4\pi r^2} + \frac{4}{R}\right] \qquad (7.5.1)$$

where L_W = sound power level of the source (dB re 1 pW). Directivity of a machine may vary as it performs different functions. Thus, if the floor is acoustically reflective, we may simplify the above equation, assuming uniform directivity in a half-space, to obtain

$$L_P \approx L_I = L_W + 10 \lg\left(\frac{1}{2\pi r^2} + \frac{4}{R}\right) \qquad (7.5.2)$$

Sound Level Due to Several Machines

In a typical factory setting, with n machines contributing to the noise exposure of a worker, we have

$$L_P \approx 10 \lg\left[\sum_{i=1}^{n} \frac{W_i[1/(2\pi r_i^2) + (4/R)]}{I_{ref}}\right]$$

$$= 10 \lg\left\{\sum_{i=1}^{n}\left[W_i\left(\frac{1}{2\pi r_i^2} + \frac{4}{R}\right)\right]\right\} + 120 \qquad (7.5.3)$$

where $I_{ref} = 10^{-12}$ W/m²

r_1 = distance to machine 1, etc.

While the direct contribution of the nearest machine is likely to predominate, all of the machines may make a significant reverberant sound contribution.

Absorption coefficient and room constant are frequency dependent. Thus, for a reasonably accurate estimate of sound pressure level, sound power levels and room constant values should be obtained in octave or one-third octave bands. Then the contributions to sound pressure level can be obtained in each frequency band and combined. If worker exposure is to be determined in dBA, the frequency band contributions can be A-weighted and combined.

Noise Contour Plotting

A large number of calculations are required to produce a contour plot of noise due to several sources. If a detailed contour plot is required, it is recommended that a computer program be written to determine the noise level at an array of grid points.

Consider a proposed industrial facility with six machines which are to be operated simultaneously. The room constant of the facility is calculated from construction specifications. The floor plan could be divided into a 50 by 50 point grid, with each grid point identified by its x and y coordinates in meters. The proposed location of each machine could be similarly identified along with its sound power. Thus, the first machine would be identified by sound power W_1 and location x_1, y_1, and so on. For a given grid point x, y the square of the distance to machine 1 is given by

$$r^2 = (x - x_1)^2 + (y - y_1)^2$$

The sound intensity contribution at grid point x, y is calculated for machine 1, using the above equations. If one of the grid points has the same coordinates as a machine, a nonzero value of r^2 can be assigned to avoid division by zero in the intensity equation. Then the intensity contribution at grid point x, y due to machine 2 located at coordinates x_2, y_2 is added. When the contributions of all six machines have been added to obtain I_T, then noise level L is calculated for the grid point. The noise level may be printed on the floor plan grid or stored for later use. The entire process is repeated for the next contour point until all sound levels have been determined (250 values of L, each based on six contributions to I_T in this case).

If the noise levels have been printed on a floor plan grid, equal values may be joined to form a noise contour map. If the noise levels have been stored, then the program may call a subroutine to form a contour plot. If the contour plot indicates that some personnel are exposed to excessive noise, the following courses of action may be considered:

1. The machinery specifications may be changed.
2. The layout may be rearranged.
3. Barriers or enclosures may be installed.
4. Administrative changes may be made, including personnel location changes.
5. Additional absorptive material may be installed to reduce reverberant sound.

EXAMPLE PROBLEM: NOISE CONTOURS DUE TO DIRECT AND REVERBERANT CONTRIBUTIONS FROM SEVERAL MACHINES

A planned industrial facility will include six machines. The room constant is estimated to be 900 m^2 for the range of frequencies the machines will produce. The proposed machine locations and estimated values of sound power are as follows:

Machine	Location x (m)	y (m)	Sound power (W, A-weighted)
1	5	10	0.015
2	9	2	0.005
3	9	15	0.004
4	14	6	0.003
5	15	16	0.002
6	18	3	0.006

Plot sound level contours with a 5-dBA interval.

Solution. The noise levels at each of 250 grid points were calculated with a FORTRAN program incorporating the equations given in this section. The array of levels was linked with a commercially available plotting routine for personal computers, producing the noise contour plot shown in Figure 7.5.1. Contours within about 1 m of a source may be inaccurate since they are likely to be closer to the source than a characteristic source dimension, or closer than one wavelength. High noise levels in much of the area indicate that noise reduction will be necessary.

Sound Generated by Vibrating Surfaces

Sound intensity in the direct field is given in Chapter 1 as

$$I = \frac{1}{T} \int_0^T pu \, dt = p_{rms}u_{rms} = \rho c u_{rms}^2 \tag{7.5.4}$$

where p = sound pressure = $\rho c u$
ρ = air density
c = propagation velocity
u = particle velocity

Thus, the sound power generated by a large surface vibrating normal to itself is given by

$$W = \rho c S \langle v_{rms}^2 \rangle \sigma_{rad} \tag{7.5.5}$$

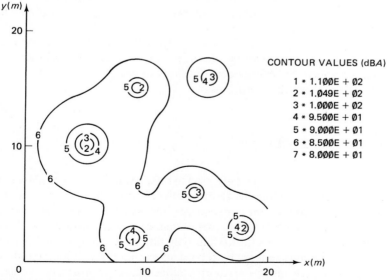

CONTOUR VALUES (dBA)

1 * 1.100E + 02
2 * 1.049E + 02
3 * 1.000E + 02
4 * 9.500E + 01
5 * 9.000E + 01
6 * 8.500E + 01
7 * 8.000E + 01

Figure 7.5.1 Predicted noise level contours due to direct and reverberant contributions from six machines.

where $\quad S$ = area of the vibrating surface

$\langle v_{\text{rms}}^2 \rangle$ = mean-square vibration velocity averaged across the surface

σ_{rad} = radiation efficiency

Sound pressure level due to a single radiating surface in half-space is given by

$$L_P = 10 \lg \left[\rho c S \langle v_{\text{rms}}^2 \rangle \frac{\sigma_{\text{rad}}(1/(2\pi r^2) + 4/R)}{I_{\text{ref}}} \right]$$

$$= 10 \lg S + 10 \lg \langle v_{\text{rms}}^2 \rangle + 10 \lg \sigma_{\text{rad}} + 10 \lg \left(\frac{1}{2\pi r^2} + \frac{4}{R} \right) + 146 \quad (7.5.6)$$

where it is assumed that $\rho c = 400$ and $r > \lambda$. If sound level is to be expressed in dBA, then σ_{rad} is adjusted for A-weighting. When several machines contribute to the sound pressure level, the result is

$$L_P = 10 \lg \left\{ \sum_{i=1}^{n} \left[\rho c S_i \langle v_{\text{rms}}^2 \rangle_i \frac{\sigma_{\text{rad}(i)}(1/(2\pi r_i^2) + 4/R)}{I_{\text{ref}}} \right] \right\}$$

$$= 10 \lg \left\{ \sum_{i=1}^{n} \left[S_i \langle v_{\text{rms}}^2 \rangle_i \sigma_{\text{rad}(i)} \left(\frac{1}{2\pi r_i^2} + \frac{4}{R} \right) \right] \right\} + 146 \quad (7.5.7)$$

The difficulties encountered in the use of the above equations for noise prediction include estimation of S, the radiating surface area, radiation efficiency σ_{rad}, and space average mean square velocity $\langle v_{\text{rms}}^2 \rangle$. Finite-element methods of analysis may be used to determine space average mean-square velocity, and all three quantities can be estimated from measurements taken on earlier versions of a proposed machine. Richards (1983) presents a basic theoretical framework for the study of machinery noise including radiation efficiency.

Many of the terms in the above equations are frequency dependent. Unless a typical noise frequency can be identified for the class of machines considered, it is necessary to solve for energy contributions in each octave band or one-third octave band, and combine the contributions.

7.6 MUFFLERS AND SILENCERS

The term "muffler" is commonly used to refer to an exhaust gas silencer on an internal combustion engine, while the term "silencer" commonly refers to a noise suppressor in a duct or air intake. For convenience, the words muffler and silencer will be used interchangeably, since the principles of operation are common. Mufflers and silencers are designed to allow gas flow while reducing noise energy. Dissipative mufflers and silencers reduce noise energy by the use of sound-absorbing materials which are flow resistive at frequencies in the audible range. Reactive mufflers and silencers employ destructive interference to reduce noise. For effectiveness over a wide frequency range, both reactive and dissipative properties may be combined in a single muffler or silencer.

Reactive Mufflers and Silencers

The simple expansion chamber, Figure 7.6.1, is a basic form of reactive muffler. Although sound waves are transmitted to the right in the inlet pipe, reflections occur in the expansion chamber, causing destructive interference under most conditions.

The analysis which follows is based on the work of Davis et al. (1984), and the following assumptions are made:

1. Sound pressures are small compared with absolute pressure in the expansion chamber.
2. There are no reflected waves in the tailpipe (outlet pipe).
3. The expansion chamber walls neither conduct nor transmit sound.
4. Only plane waves are present.
5. Viscosity effects are negligible.

Particle displacements of incident and reflected waves are written in complex form as follows:

$$\xi_I = A_I e^{j(\omega t - kx)}$$

and

$$\xi_R = A_R e^{j(\omega t + kx)} \tag{7.6.1}$$

where subscript I is used for incident waves, R for reflected waves, and A_I and A_R are, in general, complex. Differentiating with respect to time, we obtain particle velocities:

$$u_I = j\omega A_I e^{j(\omega t - kx)}$$

and

$$u_R = j\omega A_R e^{j(\omega t + kx)} \tag{7.6.2}$$

For a plane wave in the direct field, sound pressure is given by

$$p = \rho c u \tag{7.6.3}$$

from which

$$p_I = j\omega \rho c A_I e^{j(\omega t - kx)}$$

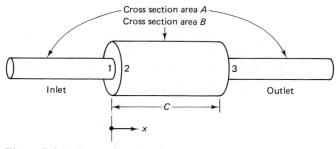

Figure 7.6.1 Expansion chamber.

and

$$p_R = j\omega\rho c A_R e^{j(\omega t + kx)} \tag{7.6.4}$$

Consider the junction of the inlet pipe and expansion chamber at $x = 0$. The condition of pressure continuity requires

$$(p_{I1} + p_{R1})_{x=0} = (p_{I2} + p_{R2})_{x=0}$$

from which

$$A_{I1} + A_{R1} = A_{I2} + A_{R2} \tag{7.6.5}$$

where subscript 1 refers to the left of the junction and 2 refers to the right. Continuity of flow volume requires

$$A(u_{I1} - u_{R1})_{x=0} = B(u_{I2} - u_{R2})_{x=0}$$

from which

$$A_{I1} - A_{R1} = m(A_{I2} - A_{R2}) \tag{7.6.6}$$

where $m = B/A$
A = the flow area of the inlet pipe and the outlet pipe
B = the flow area of the expansion chamber
C = the length of the expansion chamber

Similarly, at $x = C$, the junction of the expansion chamber and outlet pipe, pressure and flow volume continuity require

$$(p_{I2} + p_{R2})_{x=C} = p_3$$

from which

$$A_{I2}e^{-jkC} + A_{R2}e^{jkC} = A_3 \tag{7.6.7}$$

and

$$B(u_{I2} - u_{R2})_{x=C} = Au_3$$

from which

$$m(A_{I2}e^{-jkC} - A_{R2}e^{jkC}) = A_3 \tag{7.6.8}$$

Transmission Loss

For a given expansion chamber configuration and wave number, we now have four equations (7.6.5 through 7.6.8) and five unknowns, A_{I1}, A_{R1}, A_{I2}, A_{R2}, and A_3. The equations are solved simultaneously to relate conditions at the inlet and outlet of the expansion chamber, yielding the complex ratio

$$\frac{A_{I1}}{A_3} = \frac{(1 + m)(1 + 1/m)e^{jkC} + (m - 1)(1/m - 1)e^{-jkC}}{4}$$

$$= \cos(kC) + \frac{j}{2}\left(m + \frac{1}{m}\right)\sin(kC) \tag{7.6.9}$$

The ratio of incident sound intensity at the expansion chamber inlet to transmitted sound intensity at the outlet is given by

$$\frac{I_{I1}}{I_3} = \frac{p^2_{rms(I1)}}{p^2_{rms(3)}} = \left| \frac{A^2_{I1}}{A^2_3} \right|$$

$$= \cos^2(kC) + \frac{1}{4}\left(m + \frac{1}{m}\right)^2 \sin^2(kC)$$

$$= 1 + \frac{1}{4}\left(m - \frac{1}{m}\right)^2 \sin^2(kC) \tag{7.6.10}$$

Transmission loss of a muffler is a function of the ratio of power incident on the muffler to power transmitted:

$$TL \equiv 10 \lg\left(\frac{W_{incident}}{W_{transmitted}}\right) \tag{7.6.11}$$

If the inlet and outlet areas are equal, we have

$$TL = 10 \lg\left(\frac{W_{I1}}{W_3}\right) = 10 \lg\left(\frac{I_{I1}}{I_3}\right)$$

$$= 10 \lg\left[1 + \frac{1}{4}\left(m - \frac{1}{m}\right)^2 \sin^2(kC)\right] \tag{7.6.12}$$

where $k = 2\pi/\lambda$ = wave number
$\lambda = c/f$ = wavelength
c = sound propagation velocity
f = frequency

The equation is not valid if any lateral dimension of the expansion chamber exceeds about 0.8λ.

Theoretical transmission loss of an expansion chamber was plotted against C/λ for various area ratios with the aid of a personal computer (Figure 7.6.2). It can be seen that the above equation predicts a transmission loss of zero when the argument of the sine is 0, π, 2π, and so on, and a maximum transmission loss when the argument is $\pi/2$, $3\pi/2$, $5\pi/2$, and so on. Thus, the expansion chamber works best when length C is an odd number of quarter-wavelengths:

$$C = \frac{\lambda}{4}, \frac{3\lambda}{4}, \frac{5\lambda}{4}, \text{ and so on (for maximum TL)} \tag{7.6.13}$$

The expansion chamber is ineffective when length C is an integer number of half-wavelengths:

$$C = \frac{\lambda}{2}, \lambda, \frac{3\lambda}{2}, \text{ and so on (for minimum TL)} \tag{7.6.14}$$

For very low frequencies, C/λ approaches zero and the transmission loss approaches zero as well.

Theoretical transmission loss, a function of wavelength and muffler characteristics, is relatively easy to calculate. However, transmission loss measurement is difficult,

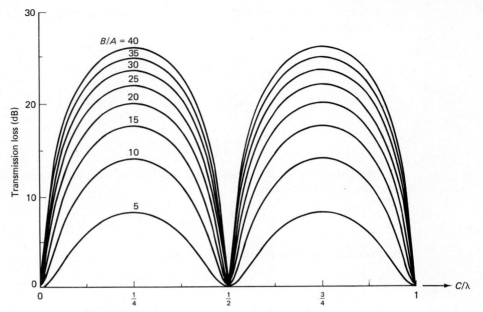

Figure 7.6.2 Transmission loss in an expansion chamber.

due to the presence of reflected waves which contribute to total sound pressure. Although vector sound intensity measurement systems can distinguish direct and reflected waves, standard sound intensity probes are not suitable for measurements inside typical mufflers.

EXAMPLE PROBLEM: REACTIVE MUFFLER

Design an expansion chamber to produce a transmission loss of 15 dB at 100 Hz. The inlet and outlet pipes are 50 mm in diameter and the average gas temperature is 90°C.

Solution. The speed of sound at 90°C is given by

$$c = 20.04(T' + 273.16)^{1/2}$$

$$= 20.04(90 + 273.16)^{1/2} = 381.9 \text{ m/s}$$

At 90°C, the wavelength of 100-Hz sound is $\lambda = c/f = 381.9/100 = 3.819$ m. For the shortest expansion chamber producing maximum transmission loss, the argument of the sine,

$$kC = \frac{2\pi C}{\lambda} = \frac{\pi}{2} \text{ rad}$$

from which the chamber length is

$$C = \frac{\lambda}{4} = \frac{3.819}{4} = 0.9547 \text{ m} = 954.7 \text{ mm}$$

The transmission loss is given by

$$TL = 10 \lg\left[1 + \frac{1}{4}\left(\frac{B}{A} - \frac{A}{B}\right)^2 \sin^2(kC)\right]$$

Substituting the known values,

$$TL = 10 \lg\left[1 + \frac{1}{4}\left(\frac{B}{A} - \frac{A}{B}\right)^2 \sin^2\left(\frac{2\pi 0.9547}{3.819}\right)\right]$$

$$\frac{TL}{10} = \lg\left[1 + \frac{1}{4}\left(\frac{B}{A} - \frac{A}{B}\right)^2\right]$$

which may be written as

$$\frac{B}{A} - \frac{A}{B} = a$$

or

$$\frac{A}{B}\left[\left(\frac{B}{A}\right)^2 - \frac{aB}{A} - 1\right] = 0$$

where $a = 2(10^{TL/10} - 1)^{1/2}$. The solution to the quadratic is

$$B/A = [a + (a^2 + 4)^{1/2}]/2$$

For a transmission loss of 15 dB,

$$a = 2(10^{15/10} - 1)^{1/2} = 11.068$$

and

$$B/A = [11.068 + (11.068^2 + 4)^{1/2}]/2 = 11.15$$

(the negative root has no significance). The cross-sectional areas of the inlet pipe and the outlet pipe are each

$$A = \frac{\pi 50^2}{4} = 1963.5 \text{ mm}^2$$

The expansion chamber cross-sectional area is

$$B = A \times \frac{B}{A} = 1963.5 \times 11.15 = 21{,}893 \text{ mm}^2$$

If the expansion chamber is to have a circular cross section,

$$B = \frac{\pi d^2}{4}$$

from which the inside diameter of the expansion chamber is

$$d = \left(\frac{4B}{\pi}\right)^{1/2} = \left(4 \times \frac{21{,}893}{\pi}\right)^{1/2} = 167 \text{ mm}$$

Area B is the theoretical minimum expansion chamber cross section required to produce 15-dB transmission loss. A larger chamber cross section could be used.

Insertion Loss

Let sound level be measured at a given point in free space or nonreflective space before and after a muffler is installed between that point and a noise source. The reduction in sound level due to the muffler is called the insertion loss. Comparing the definitions of insertion loss and transmission loss, we see that insertion loss involves two sound level measurements at the same point, while transmission loss involves determination of incident sound power at the muffler inlet and transmitted sound power at the outlet.

Consider an exhaust system made up of an exhaust pipe (inlet), a muffler, and a tailpipe (outlet) as in Figure 7.6.3a. Analysis of this system is based on the work of Prasad and Crocker (1981a). Upstream of the muffler, pressure and volume velocity are related by

$$\mathbf{V}_1 = \mathbf{V}_S - \frac{\mathbf{p}_1}{\mathbf{Z}_S} \tag{7.6.15}$$

where $\mathbf{V}$ = total acoustic volume velocity
  $\mathbf{p}$ = total acoustic pressure
  $\mathbf{Z}_S$ = source impedance

At the discharge end (termination)

$$\mathbf{V}_2 = \frac{\mathbf{p}_2}{\mathbf{Z}_R} \tag{7.6.16}$$

where $\mathbf{Z}_R$ = radiation impedance at the termination.

The state variables at the source end are related to those at the termination by

$$\mathbf{p}_1 = \mathbf{A}\mathbf{p}_2 + \frac{\mathbf{B}\mathbf{p}_2}{\mathbf{Z}_R} \tag{7.6.17}$$

$$\mathbf{V}_1 = \mathbf{C}\mathbf{p}_2 + \frac{\mathbf{D}\mathbf{p}_2}{\mathbf{Z}_R} \tag{7.6.18}$$

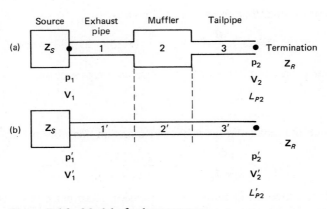

Figure 7.6.3 Model of exhaust system.

The system constants are related to the individual component constants by the matrix equation

$$\begin{bmatrix} A & B \\ C & D \end{bmatrix} = \begin{bmatrix} A_1 & B_1 \\ C_1 & D_1 \end{bmatrix}\begin{bmatrix} A_2 & B_2 \\ C_2 & D_2 \end{bmatrix}\begin{bmatrix} A_3 & B_3 \\ C_3 & D_3 \end{bmatrix} \tag{7.6.19}$$

where subscripts 1, 2, and 3 refer, respectively, to the exhaust pipe, muffler, and tailpipe.

Part (b) of the figure represents the same system except that the muffler is replaced by a straight pipe. Similar equations can be written, using the prime (') for this system. Insertion loss for the system is defined by

$$IL \equiv L'_{p2} - L_{p2} = 20 \text{ lg}\left|\frac{\mathbf{p}'_2}{\mathbf{p}_2}\right| \tag{7.6.20}$$

Simultaneous solution of the above equations yields

$$IL = 20 \text{ lg}\left|\frac{AZ_R + B + CZ_SZ_R + DZ_S}{A'Z_R + B' + C'Z_SZ_R + D'Z_S}\right| \tag{7.6.21}$$

It can be seen that insertion loss is difficult to predict since it depends on source and termination impedances as well as muffler characteristics. Other silencer and muffler performance descriptors in common use include *noise reduction* and *attenuation*. Noise reduction (NR) refers to the difference between sound pressure levels measured at the input of a muffler and its output. Attenuation (L_A) also refers to the decrease in sound pressure levels between two points. However, L_A is more commonly used for describing the acoustical properties of heating, ventilating, and air conditioning ducts lined with sound absorbing material. When applied to the acoustics of ducts, L_A can be reported in decibels per unit length of duct. Like IL, NR and L_A depend on source and/or termination impedances as well as the characteristics of the muffler or silencer itself. Since the performance of mufflers and silencers is frequency dependent, the descriptors TL, IL, NR, and L_A are reported as functions of frequency. Additional theoretical and experimental studies of exhaust system performance are reported by Prasad and Crocker (1981b, 1983a, 1983b).

Dissipative and Dissipative–Reactive Mufflers and Silencers

Dissipative silencers for use in heating, ventilation, and air conditioning ducts were discussed in Chapter 6. In some applications, simply lining ducts with absorptive material produces adequate noise attenuation. Many industrial applications, however, require a silencer that produces a high value of noise attenuation or insertion loss in a small space. When noise energy is concentrated in one or two narrow frequency bands, reactive silencers are often chosen. Reactive silencers are also preferred for applications involving gas flows with particles or other components that would contaminate absorptive materials. Dissipative silencers are effective over a wide frequency band and for silencing the noise of machinery which fluctuates in speed.

In order to obtain the greatest noise reduction over a wide frequency range the dissipative and reactive principles are often combined in a single silencer. Multichamber designs are also employed to provide greater noise reduction values and effectiveness over a wider frequency range. Figure 7.6.4 shows the internal configurations of a number of commercially available silencers. Table 7.6.1 gives the description and typical applications for the types of silencers shown in the cutaway drawings.

7.7 ENCLOSURES FOR INDUSTRIAL NOISE CONTROL

Some methods for controlling exposure to industrial noise are applicable to many different processes and situations. These include noise barriers, enclosures, adminis-

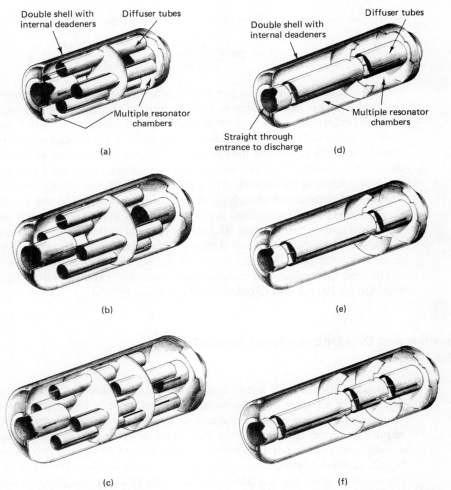

Figure 7.6.4 Internal configuration of various silencer models. (*Source:* Industrial Acoustics Co.)

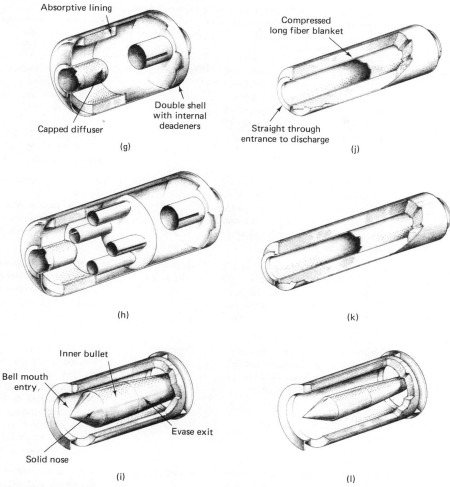

Figure 7.6.4 (*Continued*)

trative changes, changes in plant layout, and the application of sound absorption material and damping.

Noise Barriers

A noise barrier, as used in this section, refers to a partial enclosure. In a typical barrier installation, a noise reduction of 10 to 15 dBA can be achieved. Barrier effectiveness is limited by the sound energy which travels over or around the barrier as well as the sound energy transmitted through the barrier. Thus, high values of noise reduction cannot be obtained by simply increasing barrier thickness and mass.

If a machine requires only occasional attention, then a noise barrier may be a practical method for reducing employee noise exposure. Some noise barrier materials

TABLE 7.6.1   SILENCER DESCRIPTIONS AND TYPICAL APPLICATIONS

Silencer configuration	Description	Basic silencer design	Application
Refer to Figure 7.6.4 a, b, and c	Broadband silencing under the most adverse pulsating-flow conditions. Utilizes multiple resonator chambers interconnected by one or more offset tubes available in three degrees of noise control.	Reactive design	Recommended applications include intake and exhaust of diesel and gas engines; suction and discharge of rotary positive, spiral lobe and sliding vane blowers; suction of reciprocating and rotary positive compressors; discharge of reciprocating and rotary positive vacuum pumps, vents and blowdowns.
d, e, and f	Broadband silencing in high-velocity applications requiring both minimum size and low-pressure drop. Multiple, full-open, straight-through resonator design. Available in three degrees of noise control.	Reactive design	Specifically developed for the exhaust of 2- and 4-cycle turbocharged engines. May be used in other, selected applications needing broad-spectrum silencing and low-pressure drop.
g and h	Reactive–dissipative silencer. Single or multichamber design. Acoustic liner is positioned away from the direct flow path to avoid erosion of material. Available in two degrees of noise control.	Reactive and absorptive design	High-velocity vents and blowdowns to atmosphere, safety reliefs, switch valves and ejectors. Recommended for medium to high pressure applications.
j and k	High-frequency silencing at minimum flow restriction. Absorptive, straight-through design. Available in two degrees of noise control.	Absorptive design	Intake of turbocharged and centrifugally scavenged engines; suction of rotary positive, spiral lobe and sliding vane blowers; suction and discharge of centrifugal blowers; suction of rotary positive and centrifugal compressors; discharge of centrifugal compressors; discharge of centrifugal vacuum pumps, vents and blowdowns.
i and l	Broadband silencing, in a shorter-length unit than conventional straight-through absorptive silencers. Available in two degrees of silencing depending upon pressure drop and noise control requirement.	Absorptive design	Intake and exhaust of gas turbines and the suction and discharge of centrifugal blowers. Also for the intake of turbocharged and centrifugally scavenged engines; the suction of rotary positive spiral lobe, and sliding vane blowers; suction of rotary positive and centrifugal compressors; discharge of centrifugal vacuum pumps, vents and blowdowns.

Source: Industrial Acoustics Co.

are supplied as flexible curtains which may be suspended from a track system to partially surround a machine, while providing access for the operator.

The actual A-weighted noise reduction of a barrier depends on the barrier material and geometry and the noise frequency content. Tests of various materials and configurations, reported by Stahovic and Stone (1976), illustrate barrier and enclosure effectiveness in an industrial setting. The following materials were examined:

A: 2-in thick acoustical panels designed with 20 gauge steel outer face, acoustic fill wrapped in Mylar, and 22 gauge perforated steel inner face.

B: Similar to barrier A, but 4 in thick, with 16 gauge outer face.

C: 1 lb/ft² loaded vinyl.

D: 1 lb/ft² loaded vinyl with 1 in Mylar facing foam.

E: 1.5 lb/ft² quilted laminate consisting of two layers of medium-density fiberglass with 1 lb/ft² acoustical lead septum between the layers.

The following test data were reported:

TRANSMISSION LOSS VERSUS FREQUENCY

Barrier material	Octave-band center frequency (Hz)					
	125	250	500	1000	2000	4000
A	13	23	32	43	52	53
B	23	32	40	50	57	63
C	13	18	20	27	32	37
D	15	19	21	28	33	37
E	10	22	23	27	39	58

Each of the barrier materials was used to fabricate a 5-ft-wide by 9-ft-long by 8-ft-high barrier about a 45-ton automatic punch press. The barrier had a sliding access door, a small viewing window, and feed and discharge openings. Noise levels were measured (with and without the barrier) at operator location which was 3 ft from the die guard and 1 ft from the barrier wall. The noise level was 90 dBA without the barrier when the press was operating. The following values of noise reduction were reported by Stahovic and Stone (1976) for various barrier configurations.

Barrier configuration	Noise reduction (dBA)
Material A, no roof	10 to 12
Material A, with roof, ventilation, inlet, and exhaust silencers	15 to 25
Material B, no roof	12 to 14
Material B, with roof, ventilation, inlet, and exhaust silencers	20 to 30
Material C, with roof and acoustic ventilation package	6 to 9
Material D, no roof	10
Material E, no roof	10

The above study was initiated by a need to reduce operator noise exposure to 85 dBA or lower. Background factory noise level (without the press) at the operator location was 76 dBA. Thus, little could be gained by selecting an expensive noise control treatment which would result in a noise reduction of 20 to 30 dBA. Based on cost and noise considerations, the final choice for this application was material E with no roof.

If test data are not available for a particular barrier configuration, barrier effectiveness can be predicted from transmission loss data. First, the contributions of noise passing through the barrier may be estimated from the barrier transmission loss. Flanking and leakage should be considered as they were in Chapter 6. Then the contribution of noise passing around or over the barrier may be determined using Fresnel theory as described in Chapter 2. The contributions are then combined to produce operator noise exposure.

Noise Enclosures

Noise enclosures are sometimes used to enclose a noise source, and sometimes to enclose personnel in a noisy area of a factory. Three of the barrier configurations described in the above section could be considered enclosures. Portable employee shelters or shop offices are available for use where additional control of noise at the source is not practical. One type is made up of modular panels that consist of a sandwich of mineral fiber between two sheets of steel or aluminum. Usually one of the sheets is perforated to absorb sound energy. The shelters may be equipped with doors, windows, heating, lighting, ventilation, and air conditioning. The following transmission loss values are given for one type of high-performance personnel shelter.

ACOUSTICAL PERFORMANCE
OF A PERSONNEL SHELTER

Frequency (Hz)	Transmission loss (dB)
63	18
125	22
250	28
500	34
1000	40
2000	44
4000	46
8000	48

Source: Industrial Noise Control, Inc.

7.8 NOISE CONTROL CONSIDERATIONS IN DESIGN

The design of quiet machines and processes can be a most effective means to control noise levels in industry. Methods of noise control with possible application to industrial noise are listed in the following paragraphs. These procedures are based on suggestions of Berendt et al. (1978).

1. *Impact and impulsive forces.* Impact noise is produced when one part of a machine strikes forcefully against another part or strikes a workpiece. In addition, quick-acting automatic valves can cause impact noise. When liquid flow is suddenly interrupted by a quick-acting valve, the momentum of the liquid causes a sharp pressure rise. If this shock wave is reflected back and forth by a piping system, the resulting impulsive noise is called "water hammer."

Control of impact and impulsive noise. One or more of the following design changes that reduce or absorb impact energy may be effective.

(a) Reduce the impacting mass. Reduce the impact energy by reducing the height of fall of the mass or the elastic energy involved.

(b) Absorb impact energy by cushioning the impact with shock-absorbing material. Prevent solid-borne noise transmission by isolating an impacting part from the rest of the assembly.

(c) If two parts impact, design one of the parts of nonmetallic material.

(d) Consider using a small force over a longer time period to replace an operation utilizing a large force over a short interval.

(e) Reduce peak acceleration and peak angular acceleration. Reduce jerk (the derivative of acceleration with respect to time). Reduce the mass of accelerating parts.

(f) Reduce clearances, looseness, or play in cams, linkages, and other mechanisms. Consider spring-loaded restraints or guides.

(g) Belt drives may be substituted for gear drives. For light loads, gear drives may be replaced by friction drives utilizing one rubber-covered wheel and one metal wheel.

(h) Redesign quick-acting valves to reduce shock waves. Incorporate a shock-absorbing air chamber in the system.

2. *Noise related to machine speed, flow velocity, and fluid pressure.* Some of the following changes which reduce speed, flow velocity, or pressure may reduce noise levels.

(a) Reduce blade-tip velocity to the minimum practical value in fans, blowers, impellers, and other fluid moving devices.

(b) Replace small-diameter high-speed fans with large-diameter low-speed fans.

(c) Design for centrifugal squirrel-cage-type fans which are often quieter than vane-axial or propeller-type fans.

3. *Rotational imbalance.* Structural vibration due to rotational imbalance is a common cause of noise. The imbalance may be in a fan, flywheel, pulley, cam, shaft, rotating drum, or other part rotating at high speed. Force amplitude due to rotational imbalance is given by

$$F = m\omega^2 r \tag{7.8.1}$$

where F = force amplitude
   m = mass
   ω = angular velocity = $\pi n/30$
   n = rotational speed (rpm)
   r = eccentricity

It can be seen that force amplitude is most sensitive to rotational speed. By halving the rpm, force amplitude will be reduced to one-fourth its original value. The noise implications of changing speed depend on the natural frequencies of the system. A reduction in mass is sometimes helpful. Parts may be made of lighter materials or redesigned with less material where stresses are not critical. Usually dynamic balancing is the best solution to rotational imbalance. The part is rotated at high speed in a balancing machine to determine the angular location, axial location, and mass that must be added or removed to achieve dynamic balance.

4. *Frictional resistance.* Friction between rotating and sliding parts may result in rough operation, excessive wear, and excessive noise. Fluid friction can also generate noise. Some of the following measures may reduce noise generated by friction.

  (a) Provide lubrication for all rotating, sliding, and meshing surfaces. For some light-duty applications, nylon sleeve bearings or prelubricated sintered metal bearings may be used.
  (b) Align all rotating, sliding, and contacting parts correctly. Misalignment in pulleys, gear trains, couplings, and bearings results in excessive rubbing and poor force distribution, both of which may generate noise.
  (c) Specify a smooth surface finish for gears, bearings, cams, and followers and guides.
  (d) Noise is often generated by turbulent flow of water or air. Design fluid systems for laminar flow rather than turbulent flow. Avoid sharp transitions by using long radius turns and flared sections. Specify smooth interior pipe walls and remove or streamline obstructions in the flow path.

5. *Vibration isolation.* A vibrating machine component may transmit energy through a structure, causing large surfaces to vibrate and radiate sound. In some cases, it is more cost effective to isolate a vibrating part than to try to eliminate vibration at the primary site. The following methods of vibration isolation are in common use.

  (a) Support the vibrating component on a soft mounting connected to a rigid, massive part of the structure.
  (b) Use flexible couplings and nonrigid piping where practical to absorb vibration energy and limit solid-borne vibration paths.

6. *Radiating surfaces.* Large sheetmetal surfaces can, with a small excitation force, radiate considerable sound energy. Noise generation may be reduced by one of the following methods.

  (a) Isolate the surface by avoiding rigid connections with vibrating parts.
  (b) Apply a viscoelastic coating to the surface to damp vibration.
  (c) Make the surface more rigid by welding on stiffeners, or by forming it with stiffeners.
  (d) Perforate the surface so that sound pressure is partially equalized on either side of the surface. Thus, sound generation will be partially canceled.

7.9 INDUSTRIAL NOISE CONTROL CASE HISTORIES

Case histories involving industrial noise control can sometimes offer clues to solving similar problems in other industries. Much of the material in this section is based on problems and solutions reported by Jensen et al. (1978).

Gas Turbine Test Station

This problem involved hearing conservation and speech communications. A gas turbine test stand was surrounded by a 14-ft-high acoustically lined open top barrier. Sound levels of 90 to 95 dBA were measured in the workfloor area surrounding the barrier. Forty employees, including fabrication and assembly workers, spent varying periods in this area.

It would be impractical to roof over the barrier due to the need for crane accessibility. Therefore, various sound absorption treatments were considered. It was decided to use a 1-in-thick layer of sprayed-on cellulose-fiber-based material applied to the walls and ceiling of the room to reduce reverberation effects. This treatment reduced sound levels by 5 dBA in one area, while improving thermal insulation. The manned areas with sound levels above 90 dBA were eliminated.

Paper Mill

Sound levels were 92 to 94 dBA at the operator aisle of a paper machine, and over 100 dBA at one point closer to the machine where adjustments were periodically required. It was determined that noise reduction in the machine was not practical.

A personnel booth was constructed to house the operator and the controls needed during most of his shift. The booth was constructed of 2 by 4 in framing with $\frac{1}{2}$-in plywood walls inside and out, double-glazed windows, and a solid door. Light, heat, and air conditioning were provided and part of the interior was covered with acoustic tile. The operator was able to spend 5 hours per shift in the booth, where sound levels were reduced to 75 dBA from the previous exposure at 92 to 94 dB. The remaining time was spent in machine adjustments in the 100-dBA area (1 hour per shift) and in general observations in an area where noise levels were 92 dBA (2 hours per shift).

Occupational Safety and Health Administration (OSHA) regulations applied in this case. Using the information given in Chapter 4, we find allowable exposure times as follows:

$$T_1 = 2 \text{ hr at } 100 \text{ dB}A$$

$$T_2 = 6 \text{ hr at } 92 \text{ dB}A$$

Exposure at 75 dBA is not considered. Percent noise dose is given as follows in terms of actual exposure times C and allowable exposure times T:

$$D_\% = 100\left(\frac{C_1}{T_1} + \frac{C_2}{T_2}\right) = 100\left(\frac{1}{2} + \frac{2}{6}\right) = 83\%$$

Since the noise dose does not exceed 100%, it is acceptable. However, it would be prudent to require the use of hearing protectors during any noise exposure above 90 dBA.

Blanking Press

An 800-ton blanking press for producing automobile chassis sections generated noise levels of 120 dB on impact, 105 dBA quasipeak, and 94.5 dBA (slow scale) at operator location about 4 ft in front of the press. Quasipeak is defined as the maximum value of a continuously updated 600-ms average of peaks. Vibration data were recorded for the support foundation, the floor near the press, and for structural elements of the press and building.

On the basis of the vibration measurements, and the press weight and repetition rate, isolators were selected for the press feet. This resulted in a substantial reduction in horizontal and vertical vibration of the floor. It is assumed that vertical motion of the floor makes a significant contribution to radiation of airborne noise. A reduction of quasipeak noise to 98.5 dBA and operator location noise level to about 88 dBA resulted from installation of the isolators. More noise control effort is likely to be required in this case due to the contributions of other nearby presses. It must also be noted that noise level reduction due to vibration isolation is difficult to predict. Radiation efficiency is dependent on frequency and many other variables.

Pneumatic Scrap Handling

The scrap-disposal system on a cutting press used to produce folding cartons produced noise levels above 90 dBA at the operator location. Presses are equipped with automatic strippers for removal of waste material between the cartons. The disposal system uses a horizontal air vane conveyor to move scrap to the intake of a centrifugal fan which pushes the scrap to a bailer. Paper scrap striking the fan and ducts caused sound levels to reach 95 dBA at each stroke of the press, making the noise almost continuous.

Sheetmetal parts of the stripper, fan, and ducts were damped by gluing a layer of lead sheeting to the outside surfaces. Transmission loss was also improved by the lead sheet which was $\frac{1}{32}$ in thick and weighed about 2 lb/ft^2. Noise levels at the operator location were reduced to between 88 and 90 dBA.

Parts Conveyor Chute

The impact of small parts on a 14 gauge sheetmetal chute resulted in a noise level of 88 dBA at 3 feet to the side of the chute (Cudworth, 1959). Possible noise control measures include reducing the distance the parts must fall to the chute, and stiffening and damping the chute.

In this case, constrained layer damping was used. The chute was lined with 0.035-in cardboard which was covered with a 20 gauge galvanized steel wear plate. Rubber deflector plates were used to funnel the parts to the center section of the chute where the damping was applied. A 10-dBA noise reduction was achieved. Additional noise reduction could result from using commercially available constrained-layer damping materials, by treating a greater area of the chute or both sides of the chute, and by covering the conveyor top between the inlet and outlet sections.

Plastics Scrap Grinder

Sound level maxima of 125 dBA have been recorded during the initial grinding phase of plastics grinding machines, and levels of 100 dBA are common. The increased toughness of plastics in common use has increased noise problems with scrap grinders and plastic granulators. In one case, much of the noise due to a scrap grinder was radiated by the sheetmetal casing. Application of $\frac{1}{4}$-in-thick damping material to all of the sheetmetal surfaces resulted in a noise reduction of 10 to 12 dBA.

Spinning Frame Lint Removal System

A vacuum-cleaner-type lint removal system on a thread-making machine produced noise levels of 88 to 93 dBA at workstations. Air velocity was estimated at 115 ft/s through a 37-in^2 air discharge opening. Installation of a silencer was considered. It was decided instead to increase the discharge area by a factor of ten. The discharge vent was carefully modified so that leakage and vibration did not counteract the reduced air velocity at discharge. Noise levels at the work stations were reduced by about 7 dBA.

Gas flow past an obstruction is sometimes modeled as an aerodynamic dipole, and a turbulent jet at subsonic velocity as an aerodynamic quadrupole. In the discussion of aerodynamic dipoles and quadrupoles earlier in this chapter, we see that sound power is proportional to d^2v^6 for dipoles, and d^2v^8 for quadrupoles where d = diameter or another characteristic dimension, v = flow velocity, and it is assumed that air density and temperature are constant. To maintain a given flow rate, the product d^2v = a constant. For two dipoles with the same volumetric flow rate,

$$d_2^2 v_2 = d_1^2 v_1$$

and the relationship between velocity and sound power is given by

$$\frac{W_2}{W_1} = \frac{d_2^2 v_2^6}{d_1^2 v_1^6} = \left(\frac{v_2}{v_1}\right)^5$$

For two quadrupoles with the same volumetric flow rate,

$$\frac{W_2}{W_1} = \frac{d_2^2 v_2^8}{d_1^2 v_1^8} = \left(\frac{v_2}{v_1}\right)^7$$

In the free field, at a given distance, we would expect the ratio of intensities to have the same relationship, that is, for two dipoles with the same flow rate,

$$\frac{I_2}{I_1} = \frac{W_2}{W_1} = \left(\frac{v_2}{v_1}\right)^5$$

from which the difference in sound level is given by

$$L_2 - L_1 = 10 \lg\left(\frac{I_2}{I_1}\right) = 50 \lg\left(\frac{v_2}{v_1}\right)$$

For two quadrupoles with the same volumetric flow rate,

$$\frac{I_2}{I_1} = \frac{W_2}{W_1} = \left(\frac{v_2}{v_1}\right)^7$$

from which the difference in sound level is given by

$$L_2 - L_1 = 10 \lg\left(\frac{I_2}{I_1}\right) = 70 \lg\left(\frac{v_2}{v_1}\right)$$

The above relationships might approximate results which could be obtained in a laboratory. In practice, noise sources are often complex, and when a change is made to reduce a given source, another source may become dominant. If we were to use these equations to predict the noise reduction possible in the case study, it is seen that a tenfold increase in discharge area would result in a one-to-ten velocity ratio. Thus, the sound level would theoretically change by

$$L_2 - L_1 = 50 \lg\left(\frac{1}{10}\right) = -50 \text{ dB}$$

based on the dipole model or −70 dB based on the quadrupole model, instead of the 7 dB*A* measured noise reduction. In the actual factory situation, the fan and other machinery contributed to noise levels. The noise level achieved after the discharge vent modification was approximately equal to the background noise level.

Air Hammer

An air hammer (air-driven chisel) was used in a manufacturing plant for separating stacked folded cartons. Since available mufflers do not reduce air hammer noise to acceptable levels, the operator must use hearing protectors. It was necessary to protect other workers from noise due to the air hammer.

It was decided to construct a 6-ft-high by 10-ft-long wooden noise barrier between the hammer operator and the other workers. Barrier attenuation can be predicted from Fresnel theory as described in Chapter 2. In this case, predicted attenuation was 10 to 15 dB at the dominant frequencies of the air hammer. The measured attenuation was 7 to 12 dB*A* at the location of the protected workers. If the factory area was reverberant, that is, if there had been a low acoustically hard ceiling, or nearby hard walls, absorptive material would have been added to prevent reflected noise from canceling the effect of the barrier.

Surface Grinders

Operation of surface grinders caused sound levels of about 75 dB*A* in an office area located 7 m from the grinders. There was a 4-m gap over the 2-m-high office partition.

Grinder sounds interfered with meetings and telephone conversation in the office. When the grinders were not operating, the office noise level was 63 to 66 dBA.

Moving the office to another location was considered as was extension of the existing drywall partition to the ceiling. It was decided to extend the existing wall to the true ceiling by adding a lead-impregnated vinyl curtain, with lead sheeting used in the truss area. The noise reduction was 11 dBA in the office, and the office workers found the noise environment satisfactory.

Punch Press

Two 200-ton punch presses running at 250 strokes per minute were used to stamp out laminations for a motor. The presses were located in a metal-construction building. Frequent die changes were required. Sound levels in the plant were about 92 dBA, with the punch press operator exposure at 104 dBA.

The punch presses were totally enclosed, using panels constructed with one layer of absorbent polyurethane acoustical foam, one layer of $\frac{1}{64}$-in sheet lead, one layer of 3-in fiberglass, and one layer of fiberglass cloth. The enclosures include an access door for maintenance, a stock-feed opening, an exhaust fan, and silencer. Finished parts leave the enclosure by underfloor part-guides. The operator stays outside of the enclosure except to change dies and feed reels or make adjustments. After installation of the enclosures, the punch press operator was subject to sound levels of 83 dBA, and the general plant sound level was reduced to 87 dBA. Both measurements included contributions of other equipment.

Refrigeration Trucks

In this industrial noise/community noise problem, 12 refrigeration trucks were left at a loading dock overnight. A nearby resident was disturbed by noise as the refrigeration compressors ran intermittently during the night. As a result of complaints, notice was served on the owner to reduce sound levels to 44 dBA at the property line. The loading dock was fully enclosed with acoustic roll-up doors with a positive seal to ensure the necessary transmission loss. An air circulation system was installed on the roof to remove heat generated by the air conditioning units. The installation resulted in acceptable sound levels and was approved by state authorities.

In the above case, it is noted that other-than-acoustic aspects of community noise problems should be considered. Other possible solutions to the problem would have left the refrigeration trucks visible to the community, and may not have satisfied the complainant. In other cases involving refrigeration trucks, a wide variation in sound power due to refrigeration compressors was measured. In some, loose and poorly designed sheetmetal components radiated high levels of noise. One community noise problem was partly solved when the owner of the business agreed to dispose of the refrigeration trucks producing the highest noise levels. Another community noise problem involving refrigeration trucks was solved by requiring that parked units be connected to electric power at the loading dock. The use of the truck diesel engines for operation of refrigeration units was forbidden when the trucks were parked to await unloading.

Food-Processing Machinery

This industrial noise problem involves two filling machines used to fill glass jars with freeze-dried coffee. One operator responsible for maintaining a steady flow of bottles and for checking and adjusting the weight of filled bottles was exposed to noise levels of 94 to 96 dBA. An inspector and roving worker in the area were exposed to 92-dBA noise levels. High noise levels were partly due to the reverberant nature of the room. This is a result of the hard, easy-to-clean surfaces generally required in food-processing plants. The background noise level (with the filling machines stopped) was 74 dBA.

The possibility of rotating workers with workers in a quieter area was considered. We may compute the allowable exposure time at a given level using Occupational Safety and Health Administration standards (see Chapter 4). For a criterion level of 90 dBA and 5-dBA exchange rate, allowable exposure time is given by

$$T = \frac{8}{2^{(L-90)/5}} \tag{4.8.4}$$

At 96 dBA the allowable exposure time is

$$T = \frac{8}{2^{(96-90)/5}} = 3.48 \text{ hr}$$

Since a worker would receive 100% of the allowable noise dose in less than 3.5 hours at the 96-dBA exposure area near the filling machine, rotation was not feasible.

Octave-band spectrum measurements were made to determine the noise contributions of gear noise, jar-to-jar contact, and vibrations in the feed mechanism. The major noise contributions were found to be jar-to-jar and jar-to-machine impacts. An enclosure was designed for the feed and discharge parts of the machine, combined with a closure for the bottom of the machine. The enclosure included transparent removable covers to allow inspection and correction of jar feed problems. After the improvements, the measured noise level was 85 dBA at operator position with one machine operating. Assuming closely spaced identical machines, the noise level at operator location could not exceed $85 + 3 = 88$ dBA with both machines running.

Engine Test Cell

Fourteen vacuum pumps were used to extract exhaust gases from an engine test cell operated at low pressures. The pumps discharged into a common duct leading to three low-frequency mufflers located outside the test cell building. The pump had 12 vanes and rotated at 435 rpm.

The fundamental frequency due to the pump is

$$f = \frac{nN_v}{60}$$

where n = pump rotation speed (rpm)
        N_v = the number of vanes

from which

$$f = 435 \times \frac{12}{60} = 87 \text{ Hz}$$

A distinct tonal ("pure tone") noise was audible in the surrounding community during operation of the test cell. High levels of vibration were measured on the muffler shells and the duct. Frequency analysis of the noise and vibration identified the fundamental frequency of the pump and its harmonics up to about 1 kHz.

The mufflers and intake duct were enclosed with a staggered-double-stud wall with sound absorptive material on the interior. The design calls for an outer wall of 24-gauge corrugated steel siding bonded to $\frac{1}{2}$-in-thick gypsum-board supported on steel studs. A separately supported inner wall consists of $\frac{1}{2}$-in-thick gypsum-board with 4-in-thick 4 lb/ft^2 fiberglass board for sound absorption. A gasketed acoustical-type door is provided for access. When the enclosure was completed, the vacuum pump noise was nearly inaudible.

Pneumatic Motor

A materials-handling system used an air-operated motor hoist. The principal noise source was the exhaust air. An octave-band analysis of the noise showed a rising spectrum, characteristic of freely escaping high-pressure gas. The spectrum reached a maximum value above 110 dB at 4 kHz, and the overall A-weighted sound level was 115 dBA. After an off-the-shelf exhaust muffler was installed, all octave-band contributions were below 90 dB and the overall A-weighted sound level was reduced to 81 dBA.

In another case, the effect of an air exhaust muffler is shown for various modes of operation of a 1-ton air hoist. Sound levels are measured near floor level.

EFFECT OF AN EXHAUST MUFFLER
ON AN AIR HOIST

Direction	Load (lb)	Sound level (dBA)	
		Without muffler	With muffler
Up	0	98	85
Up	600	96	84
Down	0	102	88
Down	600	100	86

Induced Draft Fan for a Power Plant

Two oil-fired 600-MW electric generating units were constructed within 1500 ft of a suburban community. After operation began, many complaints and threats of legal action were received due to noise levels in the community. It was determined that the principal noise contributions were generated by induced draft fans and radiated from the top of the discharge stack and the fan discharge breeching. The fans involved are

12-blade centrifugal units, each delivering 800,000 ft^3/min at 19 in of water static pressure at a gas temperature of 300°F. They are driven by 5000-hp 900-rpm electric motors.

Octave-band measurements of late night and early morning noise showed that fan-generated noise far exceeded ambient levels. A parallel baffle absorptive muffler was designed and inserted in the fan discharge duct near the fan discharge. Design considerations included the insertion loss requirement to ensure that fan sounds would be nearly inaudible in the community, structural requirements, aerodynamic pressure loss, corrosion, erosion, clogging from contaminated gas, self-noise, and available space for inspection. As a result of the muffler installation, the power plant contribution to community noise was about equal to ambient community noise.

Gas Turbine Generator

Gas turbines are used to supply emergency reserve power and peaking power to electric utility systems. Three gas turbine units capable of generating 60 MW of electricity were installed in a rural/suburban area. Each generator was driven by four aircraft-type jet engines, and each pair of engines shared a common exhaust. Each generating unit was originally installed with two muffled exhaust stacks, 4 m in diameter and 15 m tall. Complaints of low-frequency noise were received from neighbors living at a distance of 300 m from the station. Measurements showed that low-frequency sounds exceeded ambient levels by 10 to 20 dB.

It was determined that the dominant radiant path of low-frequency noise was from the open top of the six exhaust stacks. After model tests on a number of configurations, a 5-m-diameter by 8-m-long muffler was installed in the lower section of the exhaust stack, and the original stack installed above the muffler. Octave-band measurements at the nearest residence, before and after installation of the new muffler, showed an insertion loss of 8 to 9 dB at 31.5 Hz and 7 to 11 dB at 63 Hz.

Process Plant Noise Control at the Plant Design Stage

A catalytic hydrodesulfurizing facility was in the design stage. As-purchased noise emission data were obtained for each of 78 proposed pieces of process equipment, mainly from the equipment vendors. A computer-generated plot of predicted sound level contours was made on the basis of these data. The predicted sound level plots were then compared with the design objectives of 85 dBA maximum at workstations and 87 dBA maximum in passageways and maintenance areas. Problem areas where these values were exceeded were identified to determine the principal equipment units contributing to the problem. Once problems were identified, some of the equipment was repositioned, and a second contour plot was constructed. Based on problem areas remaining as indicated by the second contour plot, standard off-the-shelf noise control treatments were considered for some machines. Sound power levels were adjusted accordingly, and a third noise contour plot was constructed.

The plant was subsequently built, using the final equipment arrangement plan and with the specified noise treatment. Noise contours based on measurements in the plant while operating were generally similar to the final predicted contours. Variations were traced to an unexpectedly noisy pump, two improperly insulated valves, and a noisy coupling. These remaining problems were easily corrected once the plant was operational.

BIBLIOGRAPHY

Bass, H. E., and L. N. Bolen, "Ultrasonic background noise in industrial environments," *J. Acoust. Soc. Am.* **78**(6), 2013–2016, 1985.

Berendt, R. D., E. Corliss, and M. Ojalvo, Quieting the home (Reprinted from NBS Handbook 119, *Quieting: A Practical Guide to Noise Control*), EPA, October 1978.

Cudworth, A. L., "Field and laboratory examples of industrial noise control," *Noise Control* **5**(1), 39, 1959.

Davis, D. D., G. M. Stokes, D. Moore, and G. L. Stevens, "Theoretical and experimental investigation of mufflers with comments on engine-exhaust muffler design" (Reprint, NACA report 1192, 1954), *Noise Control,* M. J. Crocker, Ed., Van Nostrand Reinhold, New York, 1984.

Eckel Industries, Inc., Materials for noise control, SES 84002, 1984.

Environmental Protection Agency, Public health and welfare criteria for noise, 550/9-73, July 27, 1973.

Environmental Protection Agency, Information on levels of environmental noise requisite to protect public health and welfare with an adequate margin of safety, 550/9-74-004, March 1974.

Fahy, F. J., *Sound and Structural Vibration: Radiation, Transmission and Response,* Academic Press, New York, 1985.

Faulkner, L. L. (Ed.), *Handbook of Industrial Noise Control,* Industrial Press, 1976.

Hand, R. F., "Accessory noise control," *Noise Control in Internal Combustion Engines,* pp. 437–477, D. E. Baxa, Ed., Wiley-Interscience, New York, 1982.

Huang, B., and E. I. Rivin, "Noise and air consumption of blow-off nozzles," *Sound and Vibration* **19**(7), 26–33, 1985.

Industrial Noise Control, Inc., *1983–1984 Catalog of Products for In-plant Noise Control,* p. 50, 1982.

Jensen, P., C. R. Jokel, and L. N. Miller, *Industrial Noise Control Manual,* rev. ed., NIOSH 79-119, 96-291, December 1978.

Lush, P. A., "Measurement of subsonic jet noise and comparison with theory," *J. Fluid Mech.* **46**, 477–550, 1971.

Olson, W. A., O. Gutierez, and R. Dorsch, The effect of nozzle inlet shape, lip thickness, and exit shape and size on subsonic jet noise, NASA Report TMX-68182, 1973.

Prasad, M. G., and M. J. Crocker, "Insertion loss studies on models of automotive exhaust systems," *J. Acoust. Soc. Am.* **70**(5), 1339–1344, 1981a.

Prasad, M. G., and M. J. Crocker, "A scheme to predict the sound pressure radiated from an automotive exhaust system," *J. Acoust. Soc. Am.* **70**(5), 1345–1352, 1981b.

Prasad, M. G., and M. J. Crocker, "Acoustical source characterization studies on a multi-cylinder engine exhaust system," *J. Sound Vibration* **90**(4), 479–490, 1983a.

Prasad, M. G., and M. J. Crocker, "Studies of acoustical performance of a multi-cylinder engine exhaust system, *J. Sound Vibration* **90**(4), 491–508, 1983b.

Richards, E. J., "On the prediction of impact noise, III: Energy accountancy in industrial machines," *J. Sound Vibration* **76**(2), 187–232, 1981.

Richards, E. J., "Vibration and noise relationships—some simple rules for the machinery design engineer," *Noise Control Eng. J.* **20**(2), 46–60, 1983.

Richards, E. J., M. E. Wescott, and R. K. Jeyapalan, "On the prediction of impact noise, I: Acceleration noise," *J. Sound Vibration* **62**(4), 547–575, 1979a.

Richards, E. J., M. E. Wescott, and R. K. Jeyapalan, "On the prediction of impact noise, II: Ringing noise," *J. Sound Vibration* **65**(3), 419–451, 1979b.

Stahovic, S. J., and E. W. Stone, "The use of absorber/barrier materials for noise control enclosures," *Sound and Vibration* **10**(9), 1976.

PROBLEMS

7.1.1. A steel body of 0.003-m^3 volume impacts another steel body at 40 m/s. Estimated deceleration time is 0.7 ms and the air temperature is 22°C. Predict the following at a distance of 2 m from the impact point:
(a) peak sound pressure
(b) peak sound level

7.1.2. Repeat for 75 m/s impact velocity.

7.1.3. Repeat for 80 m/s impact velocity and 0.4-ms deceleration time.

7.1.4. Using the data of Problem 7.1.1, and an acceleration noise radiation efficiency of 1.5 × 10^{-4}, predict:
(a) acceleration noise energy, and
(b) the corresponding peak sound level at a distance of 2 m.

7.1.5. Repeat, using Problem 7.1.2.

7.1.6. Repeat, using Problem 7.1.3.

7.1.7. Plot the critical frequency of steel plate versus thickness.

7.1.8. Plot radiation efficiency of a plate against the ratio of excitation frequency to critical frequency.

7.2.1. The space-average sound level is 95 dBA at a distance of 4 ft from a machine in full anechoic space. The machine requires 1.8-kW input power. Find the efficiency of the machine as a generator of A-weighted sound.

7.2.2. Repeat for a level of 92 dBA at 2 m and 3-kW input power.

7.2.3. The gears of a reverted gear train (see Figure 7.2.2) have the following numbers of teeth. Gear 1 (driver): 20; gear 2: 35; gear 3: 18; gear 4 (output): 37. The input shaft rotates at 1760 rpm.
(a) Find the other shaft speeds.
(b) Find each of the fundamental tooth-error (and shaft eccentricity) frequencies and their first two harmonics.
(c) Find each of the fundamental tooth meshing frequencies and their first two harmonics.
(d) Find the sideband frequencies.

7.2.4. The gears of a reverted gear train (see Figure 7.2.2) have the following numbers of teeth. Gear 1 (driver): 22; gear 2: 30; gear 3: 20; gear 4 (output): 32. The input shaft rotates at 900 rpm.

(a) Find the other shaft speeds.

(b) Find each of the fundamental tooth error (and shaft eccentricity) frequencies and their first two harmonics.

(c) Find each of the fundamental tooth meshing frequencies and their first two harmonics.

(d) Find the sideband frequencies.

7.2.5. The gears of a reverted gear train (see Figure 7.2.2) have the following numbers of teeth. Gear 1 (driver): 25; gear 2: 45; gear 3: 23; gear 4 (output): 47. The input shaft rotates at 3600 rpm.

(a) Find the other shaft speeds.

(b) Find each of the fundamental tooth-error (and shaft eccentricity) frequencies and their first two harmonics.

(c) Find each of the fundamental tooth meshing frequencies and their first two harmonics.

(d) Find the sideband frequencies.

7.2.6. A simple planetary gear train consists of a 20-tooth sun gear, four 18-tooth planet gears, a ring gear, and a planet carrier. The sun gear, which is the input gear, rotates at 4000 rpm clockwise. The ring gear is held stationary, and the planet carrier is the output.

(a) Find the number of teeth in the ring gear.

(b) Can this be a balanced gear train?

(c) Determine the speed of the planet carrier.

(d) Determine the speed of the planets.

(e) Find the frequencies of vibration and noise which correspond to shaft speeds.

(f) Find the fundamental tooth meshing frequency.

(g) Find each of the fundamental tooth-error frequencies.

7.2.7. A simple planetary gear train consists of a 24-tooth sun gear, four 20-tooth planet gears, a ring gear, and a planet carrier. The sun gear is the input gear, the ring gear is held stationary, and the planet carrier is the output. The output speed is 400 rpm clockwise.

(a) Find the number of teeth in the ring gear.

(b) Can this be a balanced gear train?

(c) Determine the speed of the sun gear.

(d) Determine the speed of the planets.

(e) Find the frequencies of vibration and noise which correspond to shaft speeds.

(f) Find each of the fundamental tooth meshing frequency.

(g) Find each of the fundamental tooth-error frequencies.

7.2.8. A simple planetary gear train consists of a 21-tooth sun gear, three 18-tooth planet gears, a ring gear, and a planet carrier. The sun gear is the input gear, the ring gear is held stationary, and the planet carrier is the output. The input speed is 1760 rpm counterclockwise.

(a) Find the number of teeth in the ring gear.

(b) Can this be a balanced gear train?

(c) Determine the speed of the planet carrier.

(d) Determine the speed of the planets.

(e) Find the frequencies of vibration and noise which correspond to shaft speeds.

(f) Find the fundamental tooth meshing frequency.

(g) Find each of the fundamental tooth-error frequencies.

7.2.9. A simple planetary gear train consists of a 25-tooth sun gear, three 20-tooth planet gears, a ring gear, and a planet carrier. The ring gear is the input gear, the sun gear is

held stationary, and the planet carrier is the output. The speed of the ring gear is 2400 rpm clockwise.
   (a) Find the number of teeth in the ring gear.
   (b) Can this be a balanced gear train?
   (c) Determine the speed of the planet carrier.
   (d) Determine the speed of the planets.
   (e) Find the frequencies of vibration and noise which correspond to shaft speeds.
   (f) Find the fundamental tooth meshing frequency.
   (g) Find each of the fundamental tooth-error frequencies.

7.2.10. A pair of spur gears is used to reduce shaft speed from 1800 to 1200 rpm. The driver has 18 teeth and a diametral pitch of 4. The design calls for 20° pressure angle stub teeth.
   (a) Calculate the fundamental tooth-error frequencies.
   (b) Calculate the fundamental tooth meshing frequency.
   (c) Determine the contact ratio, and evaluate the result in terms of noise.

7.2.11. A pair of spur gears is used to reduce shaft speed from 1800 to 600 rpm. The driver has 40 teeth and a diametral pitch of 6. The design calls for 20° pressure angle full depth teeth.
   (a) Calculate the fundamental tooth-error frequencies.
   (b) Calculate the fundamental tooth meshing frequency.
   (c) Determine the contact ratio, and evaluate the result in terms of noise.

7.2.12. A pair of spur gears is used to reduce shaft speed from 3000 to 1900 rpm. The driver has 19 teeth and a module of 5 mm. The design calls for 25° pressure angle full depth teeth.
   (a) Calculate the fundamental tooth-error frequencies.
   (b) Calculate the fundamental tooth meshing frequency.
   (c) Determine the contact ratio, and evaluate the result in terms of noise.

7.3.1. A ball bearing is constructed with nine 4-mm-diameter balls. The inner race diameter is 15 mm at the point of ball contact. The inner race rotates at 2000 rpm and the outer race is stationary. Determine:
   (a) rotational speed of the separator
   (b) the speed of the balls relative to the separator
   (c) shaft imbalance frequency
   (d) inner race defect frequency
   (e) outer race defect frequency
   (f) frequency due to damage to one ball
   (g) frequency due to imbalance in the separator

7.3.2. A ball bearing is constructed with twelve 15-mm-diameter balls. The inner race diameter is 50 mm at the point of ball contact. The inner race rotates at 1200 rpm and the outer race is stationary. Determine:
   (a) rotational speed of the separator
   (b) the speed of the balls relative to the separator
   (c) shaft imbalance frequency
   (d) inner race defect frequency
   (e) outer race defect frequency
   (f) frequency due to damage to one ball
   (g) frequency due to imbalance in the separator

7.3.3. The inner race of a roller bearing is stationary. The bearing is constructed with ten 8-mm diameter rollers. The inner race diameter is 30 mm. The outer race rotates at 750 rpm. Determine:
  (a) rotational speed of the separator
  (b) the speed of the rollers relative to the separator
  (c) vibration frequency due to imbalance of rotating members connected to the outer race
  (d) inner race defect frequency
  (e) outer race defect frequency
  (f) frequency due to damage to one roller
  (g) frequency due to imbalance in the separator

7.3.4. A roller bearing is constructed with ten 8-mm-diameter rollers. The inner race diameter is 30 mm. The inner race rotates at 4000 rpm and the outer race is stationary. Determine:
  (a) rotational speed of the separator
  (b) the speed of the rollers relative to the separator
  (c) shaft imbalance frequency
  (d) inner race defect frequency
  (e) outer race defect frequency
  (f) frequency due to damage to one roller
  (g) frequency due to imbalance in the separator

7.3.5. The 15-tooth input sprocket of a chain drive rotates at 2500 rpm. The chain has 90 links, and the output sprocket is to rotate at 1500 rpm.
  (a) How many teeth are required in the output sprocket?
  (b) Determine the range of output speed if input speed is constant.
  (c) Find the possible frequencies of noise and vibration due to imbalance of either shaft or damage to one tooth, **(d)** damage to one link, and **(e)** chordal action.

7.3.6. The output speed of a chain drive is to be one-half the input speed. The 12-tooth input sprocket rotates at 1200 rpm. The chain has 80 links.
  (a) How many teeth are required in the output sprocket?
  (b) Determine the range of output speed if input speed is constant.
  (c) Find the possible frequencies of noise and vibration due to imbalance of either shaft or damage to one tooth, **(d)** damage to one link, and **(e)** chordal action.

7.3.7. The 20-tooth input sprocket of a chain drive rotates at 1800 rpm. The chain has 110 links, and the output sprocket is to rotate at 1200 rpm.
  (a) How many teeth are required in the output sprocket?
  (b) Determine the range of output speed if input speed is constant.
  (c) Find the possible frequencies of noise and vibration due to imbalance of either shaft or damage to one tooth, **(d)** damage to one link, and **(e)** chordal action.

7.3.8. A Hooke-type universal joint is used on a shaft with a misalignment of 7°. The input shaft rotates at a constant speed of 850 rpm.
  (a) Find the speed range of the output shaft.
  (b) Find the resulting vibration or noise frequency.

7.3.9. A Hooke-type universal joint is used on a shaft with a misalignment of 12°. The input shaft rotates at a constant speed of 4200 rpm.
  (a) Find the speed range of the output shaft.
  (b) Find the resulting vibration or noise frequency.
  (c) Suggest a possible design change.

7.4.1. A simple $\frac{1}{2}$-in-diameter nozzle has an inlet pressure of 95 psi (gauge). Predict sound level at a distance of 4.5 ft for an air temperature of 75°F.

7.4.2. A simple 20-mm-diameter nozzle has an inlet pressure of 500,000 Pa (gauge). Predict sound level at a distance of 1.1 m for an air temperature of 25°C.

7.4.3. Plot sound level at 1 m versus gauge pressure (atmospheres) for a simple $\frac{1}{4}$-in-diameter nozzle air jet.

7.4.4. Plot sound level at 1 m versus gauge pressure (atmospheres) for a simple 20-mm-diameter nozzle air jet.

7.5.1. Several machines are to be installed in a planned industrial facility. The estimated room constant is 500 m² based on material properties for the frequency range of the machines. Machine locations and sound power levels are as follows.

Machine	x (m)	y (m)	Sound power (W, A-weighted)
1	5	8	0.010
2	10	8	0.005
3	15	8	0.005
4	3	16	0.006
5	8	15	0.009
6	13	15	0.004

Plot noise level contours at 5-dB*A* intervals.

7.5.2. Several machines are to be installed in a planned industrial facility. The estimated room constant is 800 m² based on material properties for the frequency range of the machines. Machine locations and sound power levels are as follows.

Machine	x (m)	y (m)	Sound power (W, A-weighted)
1	7	10	0.010
2	9	5	0.005
3	9	15	0.004
4	14	6	0.003
5	15	14	0.002
6	18	3	0.006

Plot noise level contours at 5-dB*A* intervals.

7.5.3. Three machines are to be installed in a planned industrial facility. Reverberant sound may be neglected. Machine locations and sound power levels are as follows.

Machine	x (m)	y (m)	Sound power (W, A-weighted)
1	0	0	0.001
2	10	10	0.010
3	20	0	0.001

Plot noise level contours at 5-dB*A* intervals.

7.5.4. Several machines are to be installed in a planned industrial facility. The estimated room constant is 1000 m^2 based on material properties for the frequency range of the machines. Machine locations and sound power levels are as follows.

Machine	Location		Sound power
	x (m)	y (m)	(W, A-weighted)
1	0	0	0.010
2	10	10	0.005
3	20	0	0.010
4	0	20	0.010
5	20	20	0.010

Plot noise level contours at 5-dBA intervals.

7.6.1. A transmission loss of 20 dB is required at 150 Hz. Design an expansion chamber with 1.5-in-diameter inlet and outlet pipes, based on an average gas temperature of 190°F.

7.6.2. A transmission loss of 12 dB is required at 75 Hz. Design an expansion chamber with 1.75-in-diameter inlet and outlet pipes, based on an average gas temperature of 190°F.

7.6.3. A transmission loss of 25 dB is required at 175 Hz. Design an expansion chamber with 60-mm-diameter inlet and outlet pipes, based on an average gas temperature of 90°C.

7.6.4. Plot transmission loss versus the ratio of chamber length to wavelength for expansion chambers with area ratios of 10 to 100.

Chapter 8

Highway and Other Surface Transportation Noise: Prediction and Control

Although automobiles outnumber trucks, trucks make a greater contribution to noise levels in the vicinity of highways. Motorcycles, which have characteristically high noise emission levels, cause intermittent high noise levels. A few vehicles with engine exhaust systems which are defective or modified intentionally to produce more noise can result in a significant noise impact. In the United States, only a small percentage of the total passenger miles of travel involves rail travel. The noise impact due to rail passenger and freight service is limited to narrow corridors.

Transportation noise control is a particularly difficult problem in that highway travel involves millions of individual decisions each day, and that the noise is produced by millions of vehicles in various states of repair. The control of highway noise is dependent on noise emission standards imposed at the vehicle design stage and at subsequent inspections, and on highway design and siting based on environmental impact statements. Thus, noise prediction is an important key to highway noise control.

8.1 SOURCES OF VEHICLE NOISE

Major contributors to motor vehicle noise include the engine exhaust and air intake, engine radiation, fans and auxiliary equipment, and tires. Other noise sources are the transmission, rear axle, and aerodynamic noise due to the vehicle body. The relative importance of each component depends on vehicle type and condition, vehicle load, speed, acceleration, and highway grade and surface condition.

Components Contributing to Truck Noise

One standard method of measuring exterior noise due to heavy trucks, truck tractors, and buses may be summarized as follows (SAE, 1973). A large open area is used, free of reflecting objects within 100 ft of the vehicle or microphone. A type one (precision) sound level meter is located 50 ft from the centerline of the vehicle passby. The vehicle approaches the acceleration point with the engine operating at about two-thirds of maximum rated or governed engine speed. At the acceleration point, the accelerator is fully depressed. Maximum rated or governed engine speed must be reached 10 to 50 ft beyond the microphone without exceeding 35 mi/hr. Several runs are performed in different directions, and *A*-weighted fast-response sound level measurements are made. The average of the two highest sound levels within 2 dB*A* of each other, taken on the noisiest side of the vehicle, are reported. Since vehicle speed does not exceed 35 mi/hr, tire noise is not as significant as it would be at higher speed. The test primarily indicates engine-related noise including the exhaust, cooling fan, transmission, air intake, and rear axle. Tests of 384 new diesel trucks produced in 1973 (Bender, 1974) indicated a mean noise level of 84.7 dB*A* and a standard deviation of 2.24 dB*A*. The actual distribution was bimodal, not normal, with many trucks producing noise levels of 82 and 86 dB*A*.

When the high levels of truck noise and the large number of miles driven per year are considered, a reduction in truck noise output is likely to produce the following benefits:

1. A reduction in overall noise levels and associated long-term impact on the exposed population.
2. Fewer activities disrupted by single-event truck passby noise.
3. A reduction in noise exposure of truck drivers.

The following ranges of source levels were measured in tests of medium and heavy diesel and gasoline trucks reported by the EPA (March 1976).

Source	Diesel trucks	Gasoline trucks
Engine	75 to 85 dB*A*	75 to 77 dB*A*
Fan	75 to 85 dB*A*	80 to 85 dB*A*
Exhaust	75 to 85 dB*A*	80 dB*A*

Various regulatory noise levels were considered. Then, component noise levels were selected so that the median overall truck noise level would be 2 to 3 dB*A* below the regulatory level. The 83-dB*A* regulatory level can be met with production (off-the-shelf) components. The table that follows shows combinations of component noise levels which will meet various regulatory levels.

POSSIBLE COMBINATIONS OF COMPONENT
SOURCE LEVELS TO MEET A GIVEN
REGULATORY LEVEL (dB*A*)

Regulatory level	83	80	78	75
Component level				
Engine	77	74	71	68
Fan	73	70	64	64
Exhaust	73	69	69	65
Air intake	72	69	65	65
All others	70	70	70	65
Total	80.6	77.9	75.6	72.6

The noise contributions of each component are uncorrelated. Thus, scalar sound intensities may be added, and the total noise level of the vehicle calculated from

$$L_{\text{total}} = 10 \lg\left(\sum_{i=1}^{n} 10^{L_i/10}\right) \tag{8.1.1}$$

where n = the number of components contributing to total noise level.

The 83-dBA regulatory level may be met by all but the noisiest diesel trucks by selecting well-designed, slow-speed fans with shrouds, best available mufflers, engine quieting kits, and in some cases, noise side-shields. The 83-dBA regulatory level may be met by most gasoline-fueled trucks by cooling fan modification and selection of best available mufflers, without engine treatment.

The 80-dBA regulatory level may require the above treatment plus thermostatically controlled fan clutches, advanced mufflers, and partial engine enclosures for diesel trucks. Most gasoline-fueled trucks can meet the 80-dBA regulatory level with fan modifications, engine side-shields, and advanced mufflers.

In order for diesel- and gasoline-fueled trucks to meet 78- or 75-dBA regulatory levels, it may be necessary to install large engine side-shields and underpans or engine enclosures; large low-speed thermostatically controlled fans with engine-mounted shrouding; and advanced mufflers and air-intake silencers. In addition, special engine mounts, manifold mufflers, muffler jackets, and double-wall exhaust piping may be required. In some cases, redesigned engines or quiet-kits will be necessary.

Engine Noise Control

A sudden increase in pressure occurs as fuel is burned in a cylinder of an internal combustion engine. This pressure rise excites the engine structure, causing vibration and sound radiation. In gasoline (spark-ignition) engines, a mixture of air and fuel is compressed, and then ignited by a spark plug. The last fraction of the mixture to be burned in the cylinder is further compressed by the fraction which has already burned. If the temperature of the unburned fraction reaches the autoignition temperature, spontaneous combustion may occur, resulting in an extremely rapid pressure rise. This effect produces a sharp knock or ping and is called engine knocking. The conditions under which knocking occur include a high compression ratio, a fuel with too low an octane rating, high engine load, and poor spark timing. Autoignition in spark-ignition engines ordinarily contributes only a small fraction of the noise generated by the engine. Other noise sources include the normal combustion process, noise due to inertia forces in the engine, impact of moving parts, and aerodynamic effects. Vibrations excited by these forces can be radiated by the engine structure.

Most automotive engines operate on the four-stroke-cycle principle. The strokes, each representing one-half engine revolution, are intake, compression, combustion-expansion, and exhaust. The intake and exhaust processes are controlled by cam-operated valves, where the camshaft rotates at precisely one-half of engine speed. In most cases, there are four, six, or eight cylinders, and the operations in each cylinder are ordered for optimum balancing of forces.

The intake process in naturally aspirated engines operates at approximately atmospheric pressure. In turbocharged engines, a greater mass of fuel and air can be burned in the same cylinder volume. Thus, a turbocharged engine can be made with a smaller total piston displacement than a naturally aspirated engine with the same power. Alternatively, comparing two engines of the same displacement, the turbo-charged engine can produce the same power at a lower speed than the naturally as-pirated engine. In many instances, turbocharging has resulted in reduced engine noise due to improved combustion characteristics, due to reduced surface radiation (if op-erating speed is lower or a smaller engine is used), and due to reduced exhaust noise.

Two-stroke-cycle engines have a combustion–expansion stroke (i.e., power stroke) every crankshaft revolution. Instead of valving, these engines are designed with intake and exhaust ports which are uncovered by the piston. Thus, for equal power capacity, two-stroke-cycle engines can be made smaller and lighter than four-stroke-cycle engines. This advantage in power to weight, power to cost, and power to size ratio has caused two-stroke-cycle engines to be selected for powering motorcycles, outboard motors, snowmobiles, dirt-bikes, and other off-road vehicles (ORV's). However, two-stroke-cycle engines have a poorer combustion process which produces polluting products of combustion and unburned hydrocarbons, and high noise levels. While the motor-cycle has increased in popularity as a means of transportation, the percentage of two-stroke-cycle engines has diminished due to emission standards.

Motorcycle noise can be reduced by selection of an effective exhaust muffler, by engine balancing to reduce radiated sound, and by other measures. Unfortunately, many motorcycle and ORV operators equate noise with power and replace or modify the exhaust system to produce more noise. ORV's which are used in previously quiet natural areas are a particular problem in that emission standards may not apply. The most effective control for ORV-generated noise may be restriction of ORV's to very limited areas.

Diesel (compression-ignition) engines compress a charge of air, and then inject fuel into the cylinder. The compression ratio is higher than in spark-ignition engines so that autoignition will occur. As a result, a knocking or pinging sound is characteristic of diesel engines. Diesel engines are typically noisier than gasoline engines, partly due to greater combustion forces producing vibration in the mid to high frequencies which correspond to resonant structural modes in the engine.

When much of the fuel charge is injected into a cylinder of a diesel engine before ignition occurs, this situation is called ignition lag. The result is a rapid burning and a sharp pressure rise, producing higher than normal noise levels. The fuel qualities and other factors which cause knocking in a spark-ignition engine tend to suppress knocking in a compression-ignition engine. The ignition quality of a diesel fuel is rated by its cetane number, with higher cetane numbers tending to produce lower noise levels. The following relationships between cetane number (CN) and the change in diesel engine noise level (ΔL) at full load are given by Wu and Case (1982).

$$\Delta L = -2 \text{ dB}A/10 \text{ CN increase for naturally aspirated engines} \quad (8.1.2)$$

$$\Delta L = -0.7 \text{ dB}A/10 \text{ CN increase for turbocharged engines} \quad (8.1.3)$$

The effects of turbocharging, thermostatically controlled and shrouded fans, and engine enclosures are noted above. Other possible noise reduction measures include improved fuel injection control, combustion chamber redesign, balancing, closer tolerances to reduce piston slapping, and changes in the engine structure and engine mounts in order to reduce structural response to engine forces.

Cooling Fan Noise Control

Small, high-speed fans tend to produce high noise levels. As noted above, the use of large, low-speed fans with shrouding, and the use of thermostatically controlled clutch-operated fans is likely to reduce noise levels. Some noise reduction is possible through redesign of the radiator for low airflow requirements, thus permitting a reduction in fan speed. On some trucks, thermostatically controlled shutters are used to regulate airflow and prevent cold water from overcooling the engine. When the shutters are closed, the fans generate more noise. Noise reduction is possible if the shutters are replaced by thermostats and bypass tubing. These systems operate on demand, disengaging the fan when forward motion of the vehicle provides sufficient ram-air. Tests have shown fan on-time to be 3% or less with a system of this type.

Air Intake Noise Control

With each intake stroke, each cylinder draws in a volume of air equal to the cylinder volume times the volumetric efficiency. Noise is generated by this large unsteady airflow. Although turbochargers tend to smooth airflow and reduce flow-generated noise, Rootes-blower-type superchargers generate pure tones associated with the lobe passage frequency. A well-designed air cleaner can act as a reactive-dissipative muffler as well. Other control measures include the use of air intake ducts and installation of air intake silencers.

Exhaust Noise Control

Most automobile and truck mufflers combine the dissipative and reactive principles. In order to reduce noise energy in a wide range of frequencies, the muffler geometry may be equivalent to several expansion chambers with perforated metal dissipative elements providing additional noise energy reduction. Unmuffled diesel engine noise levels can be over 100 dBA at a distance of 50 ft, with two-stroke-cycle engines producing higher noise levels than four-stroke-cycle engines.

When the noise energy at the outlet of the exhaust system is substantially reduced, then other noise contributions, including muffler shell noise, become more prominent. Shell-radiated noise consists of noise energy transmitted to the external surface of the muffler and exhaust pipes from the gases inside, and from engine vibration. Shell noise is reduced by double-wall construction of mufflers and exhaust pipes if the two walls are isolated from one another. Other noise control measures include sealing of exhaust leaks, and vibration isolation of exhaust systems to limit transmission of vibration to other radiating surfaces on the vehicle.

8.2 CONTROL OF HIGHWAY NOISE IMPACT

In the United States alone, more than 100 million vehicles contribute to noise near highways and other roads. Transportation noise control involves reduction of noise emission of individual sources and control of the noise impact on human activities. The adverse impact of highway noise is a major concern to land-use planners, regulatory agencies, and individuals who are or will be exposed to highway noise at their residence or workplace.

Generally, agencies that fund highway construction and reconstruction can impose restrictions to control noise impact. For certain types of projects, the Federal Highway Administration (FHWA, May 1976) requires that expected traffic noise impacts be determined and analyzed. Overall benefits that can be achieved by noise abatement measures are to be determined, giving weight to adverse social, economic, and environmental effects.

Design Noise Levels

Design noise levels are given in Table 8.2.1. These levels represent a balancing of noise levels which may be desirable and those which may be achievable. Consequently,

TABLE 8.2.1   DESIGN NOISE LEVEL/ACTIVITY RELATIONSHIPS

Activity category	Design noise levels (dBA)[a]		Description of activity category
	L_{eq}	L_{10}	
A[b]	57 (Exterior)	60 (Exterior)	Tracts of land in which serenity and quiet are of extraordinary significance and serve an important public need and where the preservation of those qualities is essential if the area is to continue to serve its intended purpose. Such areas could include amphitheaters, particular parks or portions of parks, open spaces, or historic districts which are dedicated or recognized by appropriate local officials for activities requiring special qualities of serenity and quiet.
B[b]	67 (Exterior)	70 (Exterior)	Picnic areas, recreation areas, playgrounds, active sports areas, and parks which are not included in category A and residences, motels, hotels, public meeting rooms, schools, churches, libraries, and hospitals.
C	72 (Exterior)	75 (Exterior)	Developed lands, properties or activities not included in categories A or B above.
D	—	—	Undeveloped lands
E	52 (Interior)	55 (Interior)	Residences, motels, hotels, public meeting rooms, schools, churches, libraries, hospitals, and auditoriums.

[a] Either L_{10} or L_{eq} (but not both) design noise levels may be used on a project.

[b] Parks in categories A and B include all such lands (public or private) which are actually used as parks as well as those public lands officially set aside or designated by a governmental agency as parks on the date of public knowledge of the proposed highway project.

Source: FHWA (May 1976).

noise impacts may occur even when the design noise levels are not exceeded. Design noise levels for categories A, B, C, and E should be viewed as maximum values, recognizing that achievement of lower noise levels could result in greater benefits to the community. Every reasonable effort should be made to achieve substantial noise reductions when predicted noise levels exceed the design levels. Design noise levels apply to:

1. Undeveloped lands for which development is planned, designed, and programmed on the date of public knowledge of the highway project.
2. Existing activities and land uses.
3. Areas which have regular human use and in which a lowered noise level would be of benefit. Such areas would not ordinarily include junkyards, industrial areas, service stations, parking lots, and storage areas.

Interior design levels in category E apply to:

1. Indoor activities for those parcels where no exterior noise sensitive activity is identified, and
2. Those situations where exterior activities are remote from the highway, or shielded from noise, so that outdoor activities will not be significantly affected by noise, while indoor activities will.

Traffic Noise Analysis

The traffic noise analysis required by FHWA (May 1976) is to be conducted in the following manner:

1. Identify existing land uses or activities which may be affected by noise from the proposed highway.

2. Predict traffic noise levels for each highway design or routing alternative under detailed study. Include predictions based on the "do-nothing" or "no-build" alternative. Predictions are usually made for the year following completion of construction and for the *design year*. The design year is the future year used to estimate the probable traffic volume which becomes a basis for design. A highway may reach its design traffic volume 10 or 20 years after the start of construction. The predictions in this section identify an impact zone within which developed land uses and activities are adversely affected by highway noise. For developed areas outside of the impact zone, the next four steps in the traffic noise analysis are not required.

3. Measure noise levels for existing activities or existing land uses. Measurements may not be necessary if existing levels are predominantly from the highway being improved, and can be estimated using prediction methods. These measurements or predictions provide a base for assessing the impact of noise level increases. The descriptors for existing noise (L_{eq} or L_{10}) shall be consistent with the descriptors used for predicted noise levels and the design noise levels (Table 8.2.1).

4. Compare the predicted traffic noise levels for each alternative under detailed study with existing noise levels and with design noise levels. The comparison should

include predicted traffic noise levels for the no-build alternative in the design year. This information is used primarily to describe the noise impact of proposed highway improvements in contrast with noise levels likely to be reached in the same area if no highway improvement is undertaken. Noise impacts can be expected when predicted traffic noise levels (for the design year) approach or exceed the design noise levels given in the table, or when predicted traffic noise levels are substantially higher than existing noise levels.

5. Examine and evaluate alternative measures for reducing noise impact. Include consideration of the following:

(a) Traffic management, for example, prohibition of certain vehicle types, time-use restrictions for certain vehicle types, modified speed limits, exclusive lane designations, and traffic control devices.
(b) Changes in vertical and horizontal highway alignment.
(c) Acquisition of property rights for installation of noise abatement barriers. Installation of noise barriers, including landscaping for aesthetic purposes, whether inside or outside the highway right-of-way.
(d) Acquisition of property to serve as a buffer zone to preempt development which would be adversely impacted by traffic noise. Acquisitions would be predominantly unimproved property, although improved parcels could be included for uniformity. Buffer zone acquisition should be performed in conjunction with local zoning and land-use controls exercised in accordance with a comprehensive plan.

6. Identify noise abatement measures which are likely to be incorporated into the project plans. Identify those noise impacts where noise abatement measures appear impracticable or not prudent, or for which no apparent solution is available.

8.3 PREDICTION OF HIGHWAY NOISE—THE FEDERAL HIGHWAY ADMINISTRATION MODEL

Noise levels in the vicinity of highways can be predicted on the basis of vehicle noise emission levels, vehicle volume and speed, observer distance, shielding, and other considerations. Reagan (1978) gives a procedure for measuring the noise emission levels for automobiles, trucks, buses, and motorcycles. The required equipment includes a type 1 or 2 sound level meter with windscreen, calibrator and tripod, a windspeed indicator, and a radar vehicle-speed-indication unit. Two or three people are required to carry out measurements and record data. It is not practical to automate this procedure, since vehicle identification and speed determination are required as well as noise measurement.

Test Conditions for Determination of Reference Energy
Mean Emission Levels

The suggested test site is similar to that described in an earlier section for measurement of truck noise (SAE, 1973), but other conditions are different. The recommended procedure is as follows:

1. Select a level open space free of large reflecting surfaces within 30 m (100 ft) of the vehicle path or microphone. A 150° clear line-of-sight arc is required from the microphone position.
2. The microphone is located 15 m (50 ft) from the centerline of the near traffic lane.
3. The surface of the ground must be free of snow and may be hard or soft. The roadway should be relatively level, smooth, dry concrete or asphalt, free of gravel.
4. Background sound level from all sources except the vehicle in question (including other vehicles and wind effects) should be 10 dB*A* lower than the level of the vehicle in question.
5. The vehicle in question should be traveling at constant speed without acceleration or deceleration.
6. The microphone is mounted 1.5 m (5 ft) above the roadway surface, and not less than 1 m (3.5 ft) above the surface on which the microphone stands, and oriented according to the manufacturer's specifications.
7. The highest *A*-weighted fast-response sound level is observed as a vehicle passes the microphone. The vehicle type and speed is recorded along with the sound level. Measurements are continued until sufficient samples are obtained to calculate representative sound levels for each class of vehicle.

Calculation of Reference Energy Mean Emission Levels

Vehicles are grouped into three classes as follows:

1. Automobiles (A)—All vehicles with two axles and four wheels, including automobiles designed for transportation of nine or fewer passengers, and light trucks. Generally, the gross vehicle weight (GVW) is less than 4500 kg (10,000 lb).
2. Medium trucks (MT)—All vehicles having two axles and six wheels. Generally, 4500 kg $\leq$ GVW $<$ 12,000 kg (10,000 lb $\leq$ GVW $<$ 26,000 lb).
3. Heavy trucks (HT)—All vehicles having three or more axles, including three-axle buses and three-axle tractors with and without trailers. Generally GVW $\geq$ 12,000 kg (GVW $\geq$ 26,000 lb).

Measurements are made by vehicle type for each selected speed $\pm$ 5 km/h ($\pm$3 mi/hr). For a given class of vehicles at a given speed, the reference energy mean emission level is given by

$$L_0 = L_{0\text{mean}} + 0.115 L_{0\text{SD}}^2 \qquad (8.3.1)$$

where L_{0mean} = arithmetic average emission level for that class and speed
   L_{0SD} = standard deviation of the emission level for that class and speed

As an alternative, data may be collected over a wide range of speeds for a given vehicle class, and fit to the equation

$$L_{0mean} = A + B \lg S \qquad (8.3.2)$$

where S = vehicle speed, and A and B are computed by regression analysis of data for the given vehicle class. Standard deviation is also computed by regression analysis of the data for the given vehicle class. Reference energy mean emission level for that class of vehicles is given by

$$L_0 = A + B \lg S + 0.115L_{0SD}^2 \qquad (8.3.3)$$

National Reference Energy Mean Emission Levels

The following relationships have been standardized by the Federal Highway Administration (Barry and Reagan, 1978).

ENERGY MEAN EMISSION LEVELS (dBA)
VERSUS SPEED S (km/h) AT 15-m
REFERENCE DISTANCE

Automobiles:	
$L_{0A} = 38.1 \lg S - 2.4$	$S \geq 50$ km/h
$= 62$	$S < 50$ km/h
Medium trucks:	
$L_{0MT} = 33.9 \lg S + 16.4$	$S \geq 50$ km/h
$= 74$	$S < 50$ km/h
Heavy trucks:	
$L_{0HT} = 24.6 \lg S + 38.5$	$S \geq 50$ km/h
$= 87$	$S < 50$ km/h

The energy mean emission levels for automobiles and medium trucks traveling at low speeds ($S < 50$ km/h) are assumed to be equal to the levels computed for $S = 50$ km/h. However, it was found that typical heavy truck noise levels increase at low speeds because these vehicles cannot operate in the cruise mode for $S < 50$ km/h.

EXAMPLE PROBLEM: EMISSION LEVELS

(a) Convert the National Energy Mean Emission Levels equations so that speed may be expressed in mile-per-hour units.

Solution. Noting that 1 mile = 1.609344 km, 50 km/h = 31 mi/hr and speed S' is given in mi/hr, then

$$\lg S = \lg(1.609344 S') = \lg 1.609344 + \lg S'$$

$$= 0.20665 + \lg S'$$

Thus, the above table may be changed to the following:

ENERGY MEAN EMISSION LEVELS (dBA)
VERSUS SPEED S (mi/hr) AT A REFERENCE
DISTANCE OF 49 ft

Automobiles:
$L_{0A} = 38.1 \lg S' + 5.5$ $S' \geq 31$ mi/hr
   $= 62$ $S' < 31$ mi/hr

Medium trucks:
$L_{0MT} = 33.9 \lg S' + 23.4$ $S' \geq 31$ mi/hr
   $= 74$ $S' < 31$ mi/hr

Heavy trucks:
$L_{0HT} = 24.6 \lg S' + 43.6$ $S' \geq 31$ mi/hr
   $= 87$ $S' < 31$ mi/hr

(b) Compute the energy mean emission level for a heavy truck at 55 mi/hr.

Solution. Using the above results,

$$L_{0HT} = 24.6 \lg S' + 43.6 = 24.6 \lg 55 + 43.6 = 86.4 \text{ dBA}$$

Equivalent Sound Level

Equivalent sound level is an energy average. In Chapter 1, equivalent sound level was defined as follows:

$$L_{eq} = 10 \lg\left(\frac{1}{T} \int_{t=0}^{T} 10^{L/10} \, dt\right) \tag{8.3.4}$$

where L = instantaneous sound level (dBA)
    L_{eq} = equivalent sound level (dBA)
    T = the time interval to which it applies

Writing the above equation in terms of sound intensity, we have

$$L_{eq} = 10 \lg\left(\frac{1}{T} \int_{t=0}^{T} \frac{I}{I_{ref}} \, dt\right) \tag{8.3.5}$$

since sound level is defined by

$$L = 10 \lg\left(\frac{I}{I_{ref}}\right) \tag{8.3.6}$$

where I = instantaneous (scalar) sound intensity (W/m^2)
    $I_{ref} = 10^{-12}$ W/m^2

Vehicle Speed

As indicated in the above tables, the energy mean emission level for each vehicle class is a function of speed. For speeds greater than 50 km/h, energy mean emission level increases with speed. Vehicle speed has an additional effect in that it determines the length of time a vehicle will contribute significantly to equivalent sound level at a given location. The higher the speed, the shorter the time to pass the general area of the observer. For speeds $S > 50$ km/h, the first effect has a greater influence on L_{eq} than the second, causing L_{eq} to increase with speed, while the opposite is true for $S < 50$ km/h.

Consider a single vehicle traveling at constant speed S on an infinitely long, straight roadway. The energy contribution at a distance D_0 from the center of the roadway is given by

$$\int I \, dt = I_0 \int \frac{D_0^2}{r^2} \, dt \tag{8.3.7}$$

where the vehicle is approximated as a point source, $I_0 = I_{ref} \, 10^{L_0/10} =$ the sound intensity corresponding to L_0, the energy mean emission level for the vehicle, and $r =$ the instantaneous distance to the observer. Referring to Figure 8.3.1, we see that

$$r^2 = D_0^2 + (S`t)^2 \tag{8.3.8}$$

where the units must be consistent, that is, $S` =$ vehicle speed (m/h) if D_0 and r are in meters, $t =$ time (hr), and $t = 0$ at the instant the vehicle passes closest to the observer.

Substituting the last equation into the preceding one, the energy contribution is found for observer distance D_0 from the roadway if the vehicle travels an infinite distance along the roadway from the point closest to the observer. The result is

$$\int_{t=0}^{\infty} I \, dt = I_0 \int_{t=0}^{\infty} \frac{D_0^2}{D_0^2 + (S`t)^2} \, dt$$

$$= I_0 \frac{D_0}{S`} \int_{S`t=0}^{\infty} \frac{D_0}{D_0^2 + (S`t)^2} \, d(S`t)$$

$$= I_0 \frac{D_0}{S`} \frac{\pi}{2} \tag{8.3.9}$$

where the equation is rewritten to put it into a familiar form and evaluated with the aid of a table of definite integrals.

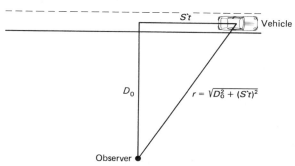

Figure 8.3.1 Vehicle speed correction.

The above result is doubled to account for a roadway extending infinitely in both directions. Combining the contributions of V vehicles/hr of the same class, we obtain the contribution of that vehicle class to hourly equivalent sound level:

$$L_{eqH} = 10 \lg\left(\frac{1}{T} \int_{t=0}^{T} \frac{I}{I_{ref}}\, dt\right)$$

$$= 10 \lg\left(\frac{I_0}{I_{ref}} \frac{\pi D_0 V}{S`}\right)$$

$$= L_0 + 10 \lg\left(\frac{\pi D_0 V}{S`}\right)$$

$$= L_0 + 10 \lg\left(\frac{D_0 V}{S}\right) - 25 \qquad (8.3.10)$$

where

L_{eqH} = hourly equivalent sound level contribution (dBA)
L_0 = energy mean emission level (dBA)
V = vehicle volume (vehicles/hr)
S = vehicle speed (km/h)
$S`$ = vehicle speed (m/h) = $1000\, S$
   all for one class of vehicle
D_0 = 15 m, the reference distance
$10 \lg \pi/1000 = -25$

Observer Distance

The sound intensity due to an ideal point source is inversely proportional to the distance squared, while intensity due to a line source is inversely proportional to the distance from the source. Field studies have shown that when the intervening ground between the highway and observer is acoustically soft, then the effect of distance falls between the line and point source models. When the space between the highway and the point in question is acoustically soft or covered with vegetation, or when the view of the roadway is interrupted by isolated buildings, scattered trees or clumps of bushes, the distance adjustment may be taken as

$$A_D = 15 \lg\left(\frac{D_0}{D}\right) \qquad (8.3.11a)$$

where A_D = distance adjustment (dBA)
D_0 = 15 m, the reference distance
D = distance from the traffic lane to the point in question

If there is a clear line-of-sight averaging more than 3 m above the ground, or if there is a clear line-of-sight and the ground is acoustically hard, then the distance adjustment is given by

$$A_D = 10 \lg\left(\frac{D_0}{D}\right) \qquad (8.3.11b)$$

The first of the above equations, for distance adjustment over soft ground, represents a decrease in noise level of approximately 4.5 dBA per doubling of distance from the roadway. The second, for acoustically hard sites, represents a decrease of approximately 3 dBA per doubling of distance.

Buildings

A row of buildings which lies between the source and the observer may further reduce noise exposure. The adjustment for buildings depends on the percent coverage, that is, the portion of the row occupied by buildings. The following adjustments are suggested:

ADJUSTMENTS FOR BUILDINGS

Row	Coverage (%)	Adjustment A_s (dBA)
First	<40	0
First	40 to 65	−3
First	65 to 90	−5
First	100	Use Fresnel theory
Additional rows		−1.5/row
Limit of total adjustment for coverage < 100%		−10

Source: Barry (1978).

Highway Grade

Heavy trucks tend to produce higher noise levels when ascending hills. The following adjustments are suggested (Gordon et al., 1971).

GRADE ADJUSTMENT

Grade (%)	A_G (dBA)
≤2	0
3 to 4	+2
5 to 6	+3
>7	+5

As an alternative, grade adjustment may be calculated from the following equation (NCHRP, 1976) which produces different adjustment values:

$$A_G = 6.6 - 3.3 \lg S' + G \qquad (8.3.12)$$

where A_G = grade adjustment (dBA)
   S' = truck speed (mi/hr)
   G = grade (%)

Grade adjustment A_G, however determined, is applied only to heavy trucks on an upgrade.

Finite Highway Segments

The basic traffic noise prediction model applies to a straight highway subtending an angle of approximately 180° as viewed by an observer. If the roadway is curved, or if conditions vary along its length, then it is analyzed in segments. Figure 8.3.2 shows a finite highway segment, where angle ϕ is positive to the right of the perpendicular and negative to the left. For acoustically hard sites, the finite segment adjustment is given by

$$A_F = 10 \lg\left(\frac{\phi_2 - \phi_1}{180°}\right) \tag{8.3.13}$$

where A_F = finite segment adjustment (dBA)
         $\phi_2 - \phi_1$ = the total angle subtended by the segment as seen by the observer (degrees)

For acoustically soft sites, the adjustment is given by

$$A_F = 10 \lg\left(\frac{\psi}{180°}\right) \tag{8.3.14}$$

where

$$\psi = \int_{\phi_1}^{\phi_2} (\cos \phi)^{1/2} \, d\phi \tag{8.3.15}$$

The integration may be performed numerically, using a computer or calculator. Some scientific calculators have a preprogrammed integration routine (e.g., one based on Simpson's rule) which can be used to compute this function.

Combined Contributions

At this point we may determine the noise contributions of each class of vehicle on each roadway element which will affect a given location. Each contribution, which

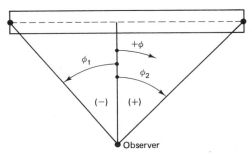

Figure 8.3.2 Finite roadway segment.

depends on the energy mean emission level and the appropriate adjustments, may be written in the following form:

$$L_{eqH} = L_0 + 10 \lg\left(\frac{D_0 V}{S}\right) + A_B + A_D + A_F + A_G + A_S - 25 \qquad (8.3.16)$$

where L_{eqH} = the contribution of a given vehicle class and roadway segment to hourly equivalent sound level (dBA)

L_0 = energy mean emission level of the vehicle class (dBA)

D_0 = 15 m

V = volume of the vehicle class (vehicles/hr)

S = speed of the vehicle class (km/h)

A_B = barrier adjustment

A_D = distance adjustment

A_F = finite segment adjustment

A_G = grade adjustment

A_S = shielding adjustment for buildings

The adjustments apply to the particular vehicle class and roadway segment, and are expressed in dBA.

It is assumed that the first calculations of highway noise impact will be performed without considering a noise barrier, unless one is already in place. If these calculations indicate the need for noise reduction, then a barrier may be considered. Typical barrier adjustments A_B range to -10 dBA, with adjustments of -15 to -20 dBA possible, but difficult to attain. Noise barrier construction and analysis are discussed in the next section. The predictions are reasonably accurate for observer to highway lane distances of 15 m or more. The model is less accurate for locations within 15 m of the highway. Obviously, any prediction model is affected by the underlying assumptions and the accuracy of input data.

Since noise contributions from different classes of vehicles and highway segments are uncorrelated noise, they may be combined by addition of sound intensities, which is equivalent to the expression

$$L_{eqH(combined)} = 10 \lg \sum_{i=1}^{n} 10^{L_{eqHi}/10} \qquad (8.3.17)$$

where $L_{eqH(combined)}$ = hourly equivalent sound level at a point due to all highway contributions

L_{eqHi} = the contributions from autos, medium trucks, and heavy trucks on each highway segment and lane

For a simple two-lane highway, $n = 6$, that is, there are three vehicle classes in each of the two lanes. A flowchart outlining the calculations for a single lane of traffic is shown in Figure 8.3.3.

EXAMPLE PROBLEM: HIGHWAY NOISE PREDICTION

An observer is located 40 m from the center of a proposed two-lane highway. The intervening land is acoustically soft, and there is a row of buildings with about 50%

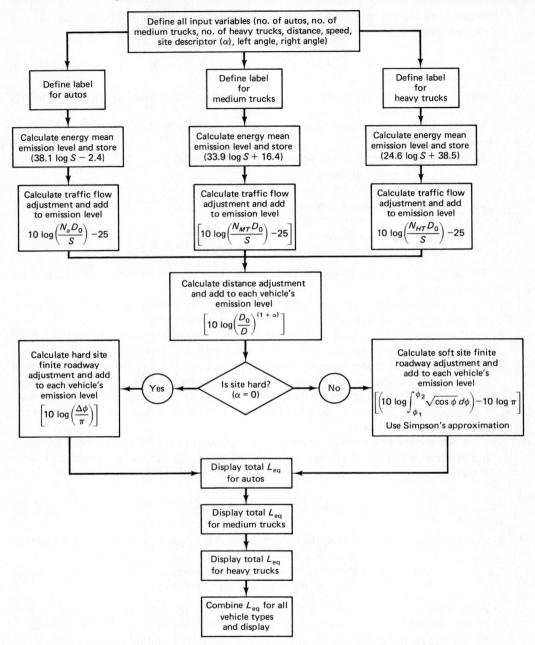

Figure 8.3.3 Flowchart for highway noise prediction. (*Source:* FHWA (Barry, 1978))

coverage between the proposed highway and observer. The highway segment in question will subtend an angle of 40° to the right and 60° to the left. The centers of the lanes of travel will be located 2 m from the highway center. Predicted "worst hour" vehicle speed (km/h) and volume (vehicles/hr) are as follows for each vehicle class and lane:

Vehicle class	Lane	Speed	Volume
Autos	Near	87	300
Autos	Far	87	190
Medium trucks	Near	80	35
Medium trucks	Far	87	21
Heavy trucks	Near	70	33
Heavy trucks	Far	82	19

There will be a 4% upgrade in the near lane. Predict equivalent sound level for "worst hour" conditions.

Solution. The data were entered into a computer worksheet (electronic spreadsheet) program. The spreadsheet is reproduced in Table 8.3.1. The finite segment adjustment for soft sites is given by

$$A_F = 10 \lg\left(\frac{\psi}{180°}\right)$$

TABLE 8.3.1 NOISE PREDICTION SPREADSHEET

	A	B	C	D	E	F	G	H
1	Highway noise prediction model without barrier attenuation.							
2								
3	Application: Distance ≥ 15 m and speed ≥ 50 km/hr.							
4	Site identification: Map 1		Location		A			
5	Distance: observer to highway centerline (m).						40.0	
6	Site: hard = 0 soft = 0.5						.5	
7	Building shielding adjustment (dBA).						−3.0	
8	Segment angle (degrees)						92.7	
9	Finite segment adjustment (dBA)						−2.9	
10								
11	Lane				near		far	
12	Distance to highway center (m)					−2.0		2.0
13	Distance adjustment (dBA)					−6.1		−6.7
14								
15	Vehicle class		Autos		Medium trucks		Heavy trucks	
16	Lane		near	far	near	far	near	far
17	Speed (km/hr)		87.0	87.0	80.0	87.0	70.0	82.0
18	Volume (veh/hr)		300.0	190.0	35.0	21.0	33.0	19.0
19	Grade adj. (dBA)		na	na	na	na	2.0	0.0
20	Emission							
21	level (dBA)		71.5	71.5	80.9	82.1	83.9	85.6
22	Volume/speed							
23	adj (dBA)		17.1	15.2	8.2	5.6	8.5	5.4
24	Hourly							
25	Leq (dBA)		51.7	49.1	52.1	50.1	57.4	53.4
26	I/Iref		1.5E+05	8.1E+04	1.6E+05	1.0E+05	5.6E+05	2.2E+05
27	Observer location.							
28	I/Iref		1.3E+06					
29	Hourly equivalent sound level at observer (dBA)						61.0	

where

$$\psi = \int_{\phi_1}^{\phi_2} (\cos \phi)^{1/2} \, d\phi = \int_{-60°}^{40°} (\cos \phi)^{1/2} \, d\phi = 92.67°$$

The integration may be performed by an integration routine preprogrammed as a "macro," a sequence of commands stored in the worksheet, or performed separately, using a computer or scientific calculator.

It can be seen that the largest contribution to hourly equivalent sound level, 57.4 dBA, is made by heavy trucks on the near-lane upgrade. The predicted "worst hour" combined noise level for all vehicle classes in both lanes is 61 dBA. The form of the solution permits examination of points at other distances from the highway, and examination for other times of the day and night, without additional programming effort. The worksheet format also makes "what if" analysis convenient. For example, what if heavy trucks were banned from the roadway, or what if the alignment and grade were changed? What would be the noise impact at various locations as a result of these changes?

8.4 NOISE BARRIERS

Highway noise barriers are commonly constructed in the form of earth berms, or walls of concrete, masonry, steel, or wood. If a noise barrier is continuous, free of cracks and holes, and fairly dense, then the noise energy transmitted through the barrier is likely to be insignificant when compared to the noise energy that reaches the other side of the barrier by diffraction. Barrier attenuation of noise from a point source was discussed in Chapter 2. Highway barrier analysis is similar in that barrier attenuation is predicted as a function of Fresnel number defined as follows:

$$N = 2(A + B - C)/\lambda \tag{2.6.1}$$

where N = Fresnel number
$A + B$ = path length over the barrier (see Figure 2.6.1)
C = path length through the barrier
λ = wavelength of the sound

Eleven examples of highway noise spectra were compiled by Pallett et al. (1978). They are shown in Figure 8.4.1, normalized so that the overall A-weighted level is zero for each. That is, the overall A-weighted sound level was subtracted from each one-third octave-band sound pressure level before plotting. It is possible to compute Fresnel number and barrier attenuation for each frequency band. However, to save time, an effective radiating frequency of $f = 550$ Hz is used for all vehicles to approximate the effect of a barrier in reducing A-weighted noise from a typical vehicle. At $T' = 20°C$, the speed of sound is given by

$$c = 20.04(T' + 273.16)^{1/2} = 20.04(20 + 273.16)^{1/2} = 343 \text{ m/s}$$

and the wavelength of sound at $f = 550$ Hz is

$$\lambda = \frac{c}{f} = \frac{343}{550} = 0.624 \text{ m}$$

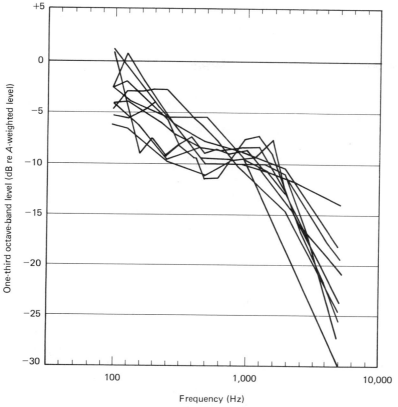

Figure 8.4.1 Eleven highway spectra normalized to equivalent *A*-weighted sound pressure levels. (*Source:* NBS (Pallett et al., 1978)

Thus, for $f = 550$ Hz, we have

$$N = 2(A + B - C)/0.624 = 3.21D_P \tag{8.4.1}$$

where N = Fresnel number (dimensionless) for the effective radiating frequency
$D_P = A + B - C$, the path difference (m), for a path that lies in a plane perpendicular to the barrier

The *shadow zone* is defined as those locations in which the direct path between source and observer goes through the barrier, as in the figure. Fresnel number N is positive in the shadow zone. The *bright zone* is defined as the region where line-of-sight noise transmission takes place, and N is negative in that zone. For highway noise, it may be assumed that the noise source is located:

1. At the road surface for automobiles.
2. 0.7 m above the roadway for medium trucks.
3. 2.44 m above the roadway for heavy trucks.

Barrier Attenuation

Consider a noise barrier that is parallel to a highway and between the highway and an observer. The instantaneous value of barrier adjustment depends on vehicle location with respect to the barrier and observer. The following values for various ranges of Fresnel number are based on diffraction theory and field measurements (Barry, 1978).

$$A(\phi) = 0 \quad \text{for} \quad N \cos \phi \le -0.1916 - 0.0635b* \tag{8.4.2a}$$

$$A(\phi) = -5(1 + 0.6b*) - 20 \lg\left[\frac{(-2\pi N \cos \phi)^{1/2}}{\tan(-2\pi N \cos \phi)^{1/2}}\right]$$

$$\text{for} \quad -0.1916 - 0.0635b* < N \cos \phi \le 0 \tag{8.4.2b}$$

$$A(\phi) = -5(1 + 0.6b*) - 20 \lg\left[\frac{(2\pi N \cos \phi)^{1/2}}{\tanh(2\pi N \cos \phi)^{1/2}}\right]$$

$$\text{for} \quad 0 < N \cos \phi < 5.03 \tag{8.4.2c}$$

$$A(\phi) = -20(1 + b*) \quad \text{for} \quad N \cos \phi \ge 5.03 \tag{8.4.2d}$$

where $A(\phi)$ = barrier adjustment for a point source (dBA)
ϕ = angular position of the source from a perpendicular drawn from the observer to the highway
$b*$ = 0 for a freestanding wall
$b*$ = 1 for an earth berm
N = Fresnel number when the source-to-observer path is perpendicular to the barrier

The barrier adjustment for a class of vehicles is found by integrating the energy loss due to the barrier over the barrier length. It is given by

$$A_B = 10 \lg\left(\frac{1}{\phi_2 - \phi_1} \int_{\phi_1}^{\phi_2} 10^{A(\phi)/10} d\phi\right) \tag{8.4.3}$$

where A_B = barrier adjustment for a given class of vehicles (dBA), and angles are defined as they were for finite roadway segments. For an infinite barrier, $\phi_1 = -90°$ and $\phi_2 = 90°$.

For freestanding barriers, where the Fresnel number is positive, the barrier adjustment is given by

$$A_B = 10 \lg\left\{\frac{[1/(\phi_2 - \phi_1)]\int_{\phi_1}^{\phi_2} \tanh^2(2\pi N \cos \phi)^{1/2}}{2 \times 10^{1/2}\pi N \cos \phi}\right\} \quad \text{for} \quad 0 \le N \le 5.03 \quad \text{and}$$

$$A_B = 20 \quad \text{for} \quad N > 5.03 \tag{8.4.4}$$

The integration may be carried out using an integration routine such as Simpson's approximation or the trapezoidal approximation programmed on a computer or scientific calculator. Angles should be expressed in radians for this calculation. Figure 8.4.2 shows a flowchart for barrier attenuation calculation.

Tables showing barrier adjustment versus Fresnel number and barrier angles (Barry, 1978) may be used as an alternative. If a barrier subtends an angle of less than

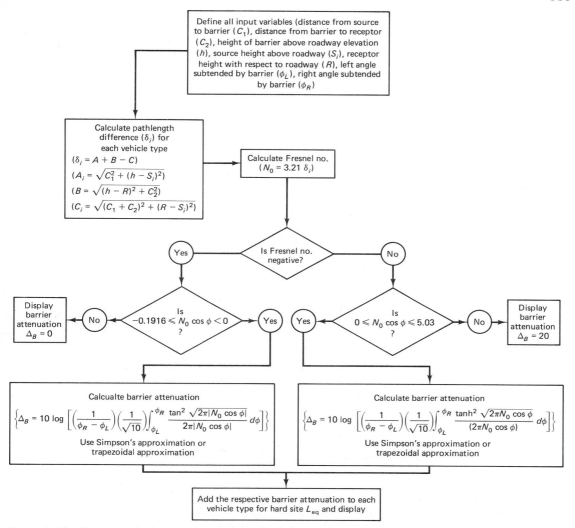

Define all input variables (distance from source to barrier (C_1), distance from barrier to receptor (C_2), height of barrier above roadway elevation (h), source height above roadway (S_i), receptor height with respect to roadway (R), left angle subtended by barrier (ϕ_L), right angle subtended by barrier (ϕ_R)

Calculate pathlength difference (δ_i) for each vehicle type
($\delta_i = A + B - C$)
($A_i = \sqrt{C_1^2 + (h - S_i)^2}$)
($B = \sqrt{(h - R)^2 + C_2^2}$)
($C_i = \sqrt{(C_1 + C_2)^2 + (R - S_i)^2}$)

Calculate Fresnel no.
($N_0 = 3.21\,\delta_i$)

Is Fresnel no. negative?

Yes

No

Is $-0.1916 \leqslant N_0 \cos \phi < 0$?

No

Yes

Yes

Is $0 \leqslant N_0 \cos \phi \leqslant 5.03$?

No

Display barrier attenuation $\Delta_B = 0$

Display barrier attenuation $\Delta_B = 20$

Calcualte barrier attenuation
$$\left\{ \Delta_B = 10 \log \left[\left(\frac{1}{\phi_R - \phi_L} \right) \left(\frac{1}{\sqrt{10}} \right) \int_{\phi_L}^{\phi_R} \frac{\tan^2 \sqrt{2\pi |N_0 \cos \phi|}}{2\pi |N_0 \cos \phi|} \, d\phi \right] \right\}$$
Use Simpson's approximation or trapezoidal approximation

Calculate barrier attenuation
$$\left\{ \Delta_B = 10 \log \left[\left(\frac{1}{\phi_R - \phi_L} \right) \left(\frac{1}{\sqrt{10}} \right) \int_{\phi_L}^{\phi_R} \frac{\tanh^2 \sqrt{2\pi N_0 \cos \phi}}{(2\pi N_0 \cos \phi)} \, d\phi \right] \right\}$$
Use Simpson's approximation or trapezoidal approximation

Add the respective barrier attenuation to each vehicle type for hard site L_{eq} and display

Figure 8.4.2 Flowchart for barrier attenuation calculations. (*Source:* FHWA (Barry, 1978))

180°, and if highway segments extend beyond the ends of the barrier, then the noise contributions from these highway segments must be combined with contributions from behind the barrier. Figure 8.4.3 (Simpson, 1976) shows barrier adjustments for infinite barriers (approximately 180° subtended angle). The Transportation Systems Center model, National Cooperative Highway Research Program model, and *Federal Highway Administration Barrier Handbook* model are compared. The curves are essentially the same except for high Fresnel numbers, where authors have made adjustments to account for field measurements. The *Noise Barrier Design Handbook* (Simpson, 1976) provides design evaluation and selection procedures with evaluations of acoustical characteristics, cost, durability, safety, and community acceptance.

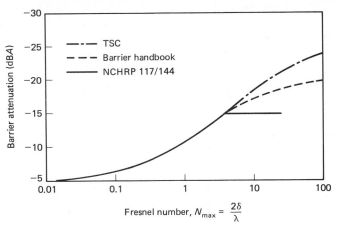

Figure 8.4.3 Comparison of approved barrier attenuation curves for incoherent line source. (*Source:* FHWA (Simpson, 1976))

EXAMPLE PROBLEM: HIGHWAY NOISE BARRIERS

An observer is located 1.5 m above, and 20 m horizontal distance from the center of a proposed two-lane highway. The intervening land is acoustically soft, and there are no buildings between the proposed highway and observer. The highway segment in question will subtend an angle of 180°. The centers of the lanes of travel will be located 2 m from the highway center. A 4-m-high barrier will be constructed along the entire length of the proposed highway, 10 m from the observer. Predicted "worst hour" vehicle speed (km/h) and volume (vehicles/hr) are as follows for each vehicle class and lane:

Vehicle class	Lane	Speed	Volume
Autos	Near	85	350
Autos	Far	88	295
Medium trucks	Near	80	75
Medium trucks	Far	88	70
Heavy trucks	Near	75	52
Heavy trucks	Far	83	48

There will be a 3% upgrade in the near lane. Predict equivalent sound level for "worst hour" conditions.

Solution. The data were entered into a computer worksheet. The results are shown in Table 8.4.1. The barrier results in Fresnel numbers ranging from 1.2 for heavy trucks in the far lane to 3.8 for autos in the near lane. The corresponding barrier adjustments range from −10.7 dBA to −14 dBA. It can be seen that the largest contribution to hourly equivalent sound level, 58.3 dBA, is made by heavy trucks on the near-lane upgrade. The predicted "worst hour" combined noise level for all vehicle classes in both lanes is 61.6 dBA. The second part of the table shows results based on the same data with the barrier eliminated from the plans. Without the barrier, the predicted combined noise level at the observer

TABLE 8.4.1   HIGHWAY NOISE PREDICTION WITH AND WITHOUT A BARRIER

(a) With barrier

Application: Distance ≥ 15 m and speed ≥ 50 km/hr.
Site identification: Map 1   Location   E

Distance: observer to highway centerline (m).				20.0	
Site: hard = 0 soft = 0.5				.5	
Building shielding adjustment (dBA).				0.0	
Segment angle (degrees)				137.3	
Finite segment adjustment (dBA)				−1.2	
Barrier ht, obs dist, ht (m)		4.0	10.0	1.5	
Lane			near		far
Distance to highway center (m)			−2.0		2.0
Distance adjustment (dBA)			−1.2		−2.5

Vehicle class	Autos		Medium trucks		Heavy trucks	
Lane	near	far	near	far	near	far
Speed (km/hr)	85.0	88.0	80.0	88.0	75.0	83.0
Volume (veh/hr)	350.0	295.0	75.0	70.0	52.0	48.0
Grade adj. (dBA)	na	na	na	na	2.0	0.0
Emission level (dBA)	71.1	71.7	80.9	82.3	84.6	85.7
Volume/speed adj (dBA)	17.9	17.0	11.5	10.8	10.2	9.4
Noise path geometry (m)						
A	8.9	12.6	8.7	12.4	8.2	12.1
B	10.3	10.3	10.3	10.3	10.3	10.3
C	18.1	22.1	18.0	22.0	18.0	22.0
Fresnel No. N	3.8	2.9	3.0	2.4	1.4	1.2
Barrier adj (dBA)	−14.0	−13.4	−13.6	−12.8	−11.1	−10.7
Hourly Leq (dBA)	47.7	46.6	51.4	51.6	58.3	55.7
I/Iref	5.8E+04	4.6E+04	1.4E+05	1.5E+05	6.8E+05	3.7E+05
Observer location.						
I/Iref		1.4E+06				
Hourly equivalent sound level at observer (dBA)					61.6	

(b) Without barrier

Barrier adj (dBA)	0.0	0.0	0.0	0.0	0.0	0.0
Hourly Leq (dBA)	61.7	60.0	65.0	64.4	69.4	66.4
I/Iref	1.5E+06	1.0E+06	3.2E+06	2.8E+06	8.8E+06	4.4E+06
Observer location.						
I/Iref		2.2E+07				
Hourly equivalent sound level at observer (dBA)					73.3	

is 73.3 dB*A*. Thus, the overall predicted effect of the barrier is a noise level reduction of 11.7 dB*A*.

8.5   PREDICTION OF HIGHWAY NOISE—THE NATIONAL COOPERATIVE HIGHWAY RESEARCH PROGRAM MODEL

The National Cooperative Highway Research Program (NCHRP) model is described by Gordon et al. (1971). This model is based on the statistical descriptors L_{50} and L_{10}.

Predictions are based on only two vehicle types, autos (A) defined as vehicles with gross weights under 10,000 lb, and trucks (T) with gross weights of 10,000 lb or more. For field identification, four-wheeled vehicles are considered automobiles, and vehicles with six or more wheels are considered trucks.

The contributions to median sound level on an infinite, level roadway are predicted as follows:

Autos:

$$L_{50(A)} = 10 \lg V - 15 \lg D + 20 \lg S$$
$$+ 10 \lg\left[\tanh\left(1.19 \times 10^{-3} V \frac{D}{S}\right)\right] + 29 \tag{8.5.1}$$

Trucks:

$$L_{50(T)} = 10 \lg V - 15 \lg D - 10 \lg S$$
$$+ 10 \lg\left[\tanh\left(1.19 \times 10^{-3} V \frac{D}{S}\right)\right] + 95 \tag{8.5.2}$$

where L_{50} = median sound level due to a single lane of autos or trucks (dBA)
   V = volume (vehicles/hr)
   D = distance from observer to roadway centerline (ft)
   S = speed (mi/hr)

The 10% exceeded levels for each vehicle class are determined by applying the following adjustment:

$$L_{10} - L_{50} = 10 \lg\left\{\frac{\cosh(1.19 \times 10^{-3} \, VD/S)}{\cosh(1.19 \times 10^{-3} \, VD/S) - 0.951}\right\} \tag{8.5.3}$$

where $L_{10} - L_{50}$ = the adjustment to be added to median sound level for each vehicle class to obtain the 10% exceeded level (dBA). The above adjustment is sometimes inconsistent with field data, particularly for low traffic volume. When measurements of L_{10} and L_{50} are possible, the measured difference may be used to adjust predicted L_{50} values based on projected highway traffic for future years.

The contributions are combined to produce predicted noise level at the observer as follows:

$$L_{\text{combined}} = 10 \lg\left(\sum_{i=1}^{n} 10^{L_i/10}\right) \tag{8.5.4}$$

where, for example, $L_{\text{combined}} = L_{10\text{combined}}$ for the combined contributions on a two-lane roadway (dBA)
   $n = 4$, the number of contributions
   L_i = the individual L_{10} contributions from autos and trucks in the near and far lanes

Where applicable, corrections are made for barriers, intervening structures, finite roadway elements, trucks on an upgrade, road surface, and interrupted traffic flow.

The NCHRP model may be of use when updating older noise impact statements.

However, the FHWA model will usually be found more accurate, partly due to the use of three vehicle classes, since the medium truck–heavy truck mix in cities tends to differ from that on interstate highways. An important feature of the FHWA model is the use of equivalent sound level as a descriptor. L_{eq} may be readily extended to a 24-hour period. In addition, day–night sound level may be obtained from the FHWA model. Thus, the results obtained from the FHWA model are essentially consistent with descriptors used by the Environmental Protection Agency.

8.6 NONHIGHWAY SURFACE TRANSPORTATION

Nonhighway surface transportation includes railroad and rapid transit line operations, railroad yard operations, watercraft and recreational vehicles. Of these, the noise impact of railroad and rapid transit line operations have been of greatest interest.

Railroad Yards, Recreational Watercraft, and Off-Road Vehicles

The noise impact of these sources is difficult to predict because they lack a definite pattern of operation. However, some noise control can be effected by regulation of sound power at the source, and by controlling the location of these activities. For railroad yards located near residential areas, certain operations might be restricted to daytime hours to reduce noise impact. Recreational watercraft noise can be controlled by restrictions on the horsepower of motors and requirements for adequate mufflers. Small bodies of water can be limited to nonpowered boats. As noted in Chapter 5, one model ordinance gives the following limits for recreational vehicles operating off public rights of way: motorcycles, 84 dB*A;* other vehicles, 80 dB*A*. These values are maximum permissible sound levels at or across real property lines, when the vehicles are operated on private property. The above values are applied at a distance of 50 ft (15 m) from the path of a vehicle operating in a public space. In many jurisdictions, an outright ban on the use of off-road vehicles on public lands is the most effective way of dealing with recreational vehicle noise.

Railroad and Rapid Transit Line Operations

Noise impact due to railroad and rapid transit line operations has been studied in some detail. There are four general types of vehicles involved: locomotives, passenger cars, freight cars, and rapid transit vehicles. These vehicles produce a variety of frequency spectra and noise levels. Figure 8.6.1 (Pallett et al., 1978) shows 11 railway noise spectra, normalized so that the overall *A*-weighted level is zero for each. That is, the overall *A*-weighted sound level was subtracted from each one-third octave-band sound pressure level before plotting.

Most locomotives are diesel–electric, utilizing a diesel engine to drive an alternator or generator which, in turn, drives electric traction motors on the wheels. Some locomotives are all-electric, obtaining power from an overhead line or "third rail," and a few are gas turbine driven. A freight train is usually made up of one or more diesel–

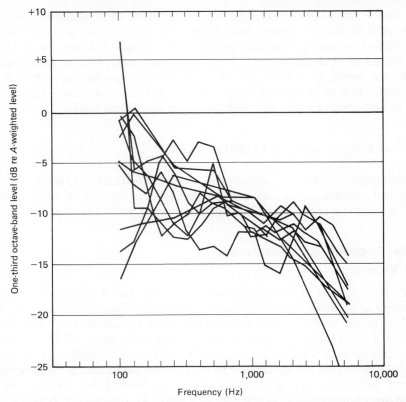

Figure 8.6.1   Eleven railway noise spectra. (*Source:* NBS (Pallett et al., 1978))

electric locomotives pulling a number of freight cars. A passenger train may be made up of one or more diesel–electric or all-electric locomotives pulling a number of passenger cars. Many railway lines serving cities and using long tunnels are electrified. Rapid transit trains are made up of a number of cars, usually with electric motors on the axles of each car, and no separate locomotive.

Principal diesel–electric locomotive noise sources include the engine casing and exhaust, and rail/wheel interaction. Other noise sources include the air intake, cooling fans, compressors, and vibration transmitted to structures including parts of the locomotive and steel bridge structures. Exhaust noise is usually the dominant source in diesel–electric locomotives, particularly when accelerating, or pulling a heavy load up a grade. Rail/wheel interaction is the principal noise source of railway passenger and freight cars, all-electric locomotives, and rapid transit cars.

Railway Noise Prediction: National Bureau of Standards Model

The National Bureau of Standards (NBS) model for prediction of railway noise is described by Pallett et al. (1978). The model is based on a single infinite straight track at grade level, and three train classes, freight, conventional passenger, and rapid transit. A diesel–electric train is modeled as two distinct sources, the locomotive and the cars. Rapid transit trains and all-electric passenger railway trains are considered to generate noise primarily by wheel/track interaction. It is assumed that equivalent sound level decreases by about 5 dBA per doubling of distance from a diesel–electric locomotive. For freight and passenger cars, all-electric locomotives, and rapid transit cars, the equivalent sound level is assumed to decrease by about 6 dBA per doubling of distance. These empirically derived assumptions are valid for distances of 150 ft or more from the railway.

Swing and Pies (1973) determined reference noise levels versus speed for diesel–electric locomotives and attenuation versus distance relationships for diesel–electric locomotives and railway cars. Using their data, we may write the following approximate relationship for diesel–electric locomotive noise level:

$$L_{\text{loc}} = 105 - \frac{S}{12} \tag{8.6.1}$$

where L_{loc} = reference noise level for diesel–electric locomotives (dBA at 100 ft)
S = speed (mi/hr) for $10 \leq S \leq 100$

The distance adjustment data for diesel–electric locomotives may be related to the base-ten logarithm of distance as follows:

$$A_{DL} = 33.7 - 16.4 \lg D \tag{8.6.2}$$

where A_{DL} = distance adjustment for diesel–electric locomotives (dBA)
D = distance (ft) for $D \geq 150$

For railway cars, the following equation gives a reasonable fit to available data:

$$A_{DC} = 39.3 - 19 \lg D \tag{8.6.3}$$

where A_{DC} = distance adjustment for railway cars (dBA), which may be used for rapid transit cars as well.

Using data from Bender et al. (1974), noise levels may be related to speed for railway cars and rapid transit vehicles. The relationship for railway cars is

$$L_C = 32 + 31 \lg S \tag{8.6.4}$$

where L_C = reference noise level for railway cars (dBA at 100 ft)
S = speed (mi/hr) for $10 \leq S \leq 100$

The noise level versus speed relationship for rapid transit vehicles is

$$L_{\text{RT}} = 23.5 + 31 \lg S \tag{8.6.5}$$

where L_{RT} = reference noise level for rapid transit vehicles (dBA at 100 ft).

The following corrections are made for track characteristics (Pallett et al., 1978; Swing and Pies, 1973). This adjustment is applied if the track variation occurs within a distance of $2D$ on either side of the track from the point closest to the observer, where D is the distance from the observer to the track.

Track characteristics	Adjustment A_{track} (dBA)
Straight machine-welded track	0
Straight jointed track	4
Presence of switches or grade crossing	4
Tight radius curve	
Radius < 600 ft	4
$600 \leq$ radius < 900 ft	1
900 ft $\leq$ radius	0
Presence of bridge	
Concrete	0
Steel girder with concrete deck	5
Steel girder with open tie deck	5
Steel girder with steel plate deck	14

Additional adjustments are required for the number of passbys during a specified time interval, for the duration of a passby, and for shielding by buildings and barriers. The following corrections are suggested.

Barriers   Path difference is calculated for barriers as in the previous section. It is assumed that the noise source location for diesel–electric locomotives in the exhaust outlet, about 15 ft above the rails. The noise source location for railway cars, all-electric locomotives, and rapid transit vehicles is assumed to be at the level of the rails. Fresnel number is given by

$$N = \frac{2D_P}{\lambda} \tag{8.6.6}$$

where N = Fresnel number
            D_P = path difference
            $\lambda = c/f$ = the wavelength of sound
            c = 343 m/s = 1125 ft/s = the speed of sound propagation at 20°C (68°F)

and it is assumed that the actual frequency spectra of the sources can be represented by sounds at the following frequencies:

f = 125 Hz for diesel locomotives

f = 500 Hz for railway cars, all-electric locomotives, and rapid transit vehicles

The adjustment for barriers $A_{barrier}$ may be calculated as in the previous section, except that $A_{barrier} = 0$ for $N \leq 0$ (the bright zone), and $A_{barrier} \leq 12$ dBA for $N > 0$ (the shadow zone). Barrier adjustment data given by Pallett et al. (1978) results, in general, in a somewhat different correction. This alternative relationship may be fit to the equations which follow.

1. Railway cars, all-electric locomotives, and rapid transit vehicles:

$$A_{barrier} = 0 \qquad \text{for} \quad D'_P \leq 0.075 \text{ ft}$$

$$= -8.4 - 7.5 \lg D'_P \qquad \text{for} \quad 0.075 < D'_P < 3 \text{ ft}$$

$$= -12 \qquad \text{for} \quad D'_P \geq 3 \text{ ft} \tag{8.6.7}$$

where $A_{barrier}$ = barrier adjustment (dBA)

D'_P = path difference (ft)

2. Diesel–electric locomotives:

$$A_{barrier} = 0 \qquad \text{for} \quad D'_P \leq 0.3 \text{ ft}$$

$$= -3.9 - 7.5D'_P \qquad \text{for} \quad 0.3 < D'_P < 12 \text{ ft}$$

$$= -12 \qquad \text{for} \quad D'_P \geq 12 \text{ ft} \qquad (8.6.8)$$

These barrier adjustments may be used for determining the effect of freestanding walls, earth barriers, and railway cuts on noise levels at 150 ft or more from the source. These calculations do not treat reflections due to barriers or noise levels in railway cars and subway tunnels.

Buildings For railway cars, all-electric locomotives, and rapid transit vehicles, the effect of shielding due to buildings is about the same as for highway noise. Due to the source location for diesel–electric locomotives, it will be assumed that shielding correction $A_S = 0$ for low buildings in the presence of diesel–electric locomotive noise. Even for rows of buildings which interrupt line-of-sight noise transmission from diesel–electric locomotives, attenuation will be limited due to the energy content in the low-frequency bands. This is a result of greater diffraction of sound with long wavelengths. If field measurements are unavailable, the following estimates may be used for rows of buildings which interrupt line-of-sight noise transmission.

ADJUSTMENTS FOR BUILDINGS IN THE PATH OF RAILWAY NOISE

Row	Coverage (%)	Adjustment A_s (dBA)	
		Diesel–electric locomotives	Railroad cars, electric locomotives
First	<40	0	0
First	40 to 65	0	−1 to −3
First	66 to 90	−1 to −2	−4 to −5
First	100	Treat as barrier	Treat as barrier
Additional rows		−1/row	−1.5/row
Limit of total adjustment for <100% coverage		−5	−10

Passbys Noise energy is proportional to the number of contributions of each type (diesel–electric locomotives, trains of railway cars, etc.). The passby adjustment is given by

$$A_{passby} = 10 \lg N_P \qquad (8.6.9)$$

where A_{passby} = passby adjustment (dBA)

N_P = number of trains, or number of diesel–electric locomotives passing during the interval used to calculate equivalent sound level L_{eq}

When calculating day–night sound level L_{DN}, the number of passbys during the night-time period (10 P.M. to 7 A.M.) is multiplied by 10 and added to the number of daytime (7 A.M. to 10 P.M.) passbys to obtain N_P.

Passby Duration   Noise energy is also a function of the time it takes a train to pass a given point, which is, in turn, proportional to train length divided by speed. Using data reported by Pallett et al. (1978), the adjustment can be written as

$$A_{dur} = -1.8 + 10 \lg\left(\frac{T_L}{S}\right) \tag{8.6.10}$$

where A_{dur} = passby duration adjustment (dBA)
   S = speed (mi/hr)
   T_L = train length (ft)

If train length is unknown, it may be estimated by assuming that the average freight car is 55 ft long and the average passenger car and rapid transit vehicle 75 ft long. All-electric locomotives may be treated as passenger cars and added to train length.

Time Interval   The reference noise levels are based on a 1-s contribution to equivalent sound level. The time interval correction is given by

$$A_{int} = -10 \lg t = -10 \lg(3600\ T) \tag{8.6.11}$$

where A_{int} = time interval adjustment (dBA)
   t = time (s)
   T = time (hr)

Thus, the correction is

$$A_{int} = -35.6 \text{ for } L_{eqH}, \text{ the hourly equivalent sound level}$$

$$= -44.6 \text{ for } L_{eq8}, \text{ the 8-hr equivalent sound level}$$

$$= -49.4 \text{ for } L_{eq24}, \text{ 24-hr equivalent sound level}$$

$$= -49.4 \text{ for } L_{DN}, \text{ day–night sound level}$$

Prediction of Equivalent Sound Level and Day–Night Sound Level Due to Railway and Rapid Transit Noise

Suppose it is necessary to predict the noise impact which will occur if a proposed railway or rapid transit is constructed or improved. The following steps are suggested:

   1. One or more of the following descriptors is selected:
      (a) L_{eqH}, hourly equivalent sound level for the hour of greatest railway service.
      (b) L_{eqT}, equivalent sound level for some interval T (hours) representing a school-day or some other interval of interest.

      (c) L_{eq24}, equivalent sound level for a typical 24-hour day.
      (d) L_{DN}, day–night sound level for a typical 24-hour day.
  2. Relevant sources of railway and rapid transit noise are identified, including estimated speeds, train lengths, proposed service schedules, and estimated freight movements.
  3. Maps and plans including elevations are obtained.
  4. Nearby sensitive noise receptors including residences, schools, and hospitals are identified.
  5. The contribution of each source type to noise at a particular location is calculated.
  6. The contributions are combined, and the result is compared with acceptable levels given by the Environmental Protection Agency, or the Department of Transportation, or Department of Housing and Urban Development, or with other relevant codes or standards.

The sound level contribution due to a given source type is given by

$$L = L_{ref} + A_D + A_{track} + A_{barrier} + A_{passby} + A_S + A_{dur} + A_{int} \qquad (8.6.12)$$

where L = the sound level contribution due to a given source type (diesel–electric locomotives, railway cars, or rapid transit vehicles) (dBA)
    L_{ref} = the reference level for that source type (dBA)
    $A_{(\ )}$ = the adjustments for distance, track condition, barriers, number of passbys, building shielding, passby duration, and time interval (dBA)

Combined sound level at the selected observer point is given by

$$L_{eq} = 10 \lg \sum_{i=1}^{n} 10^{L/10} \qquad (8.6.13)$$

where L_{eq} = combined sound level L_{eqH} or L_{eq24} or L_{DN} (dBA), depending on the time period and weighting of nighttime passbys used to obtain the adjustments above
    n = the number of source types which affect sound level at the observer

    A different model for predicting the impact of railway noise is given by the U.S. Department of Housing and Urban Development (HUD, 1983). The HUD model uses data on types of service and schedules, with adjustments similar to the NBS model, to predict day–night sound level and categorize the location as acceptable or unacceptable with regard to railway noise impact. The propagation of railway noise in residential areas is also investigated by Gill (1975). Measured peak sound levels due to railway operations are reported for locations inside and outside of residential buildings. Measurements are expressed in one-third octave-band levels and in dBA. A prediction model is also given.

    Some reduction in railway noise may be expected with improved maintenance and when new equipment is phased in. The following regulations were promulgated by EPA (1975, 1976) in response to section 17 of the Noise Control Act of 1972.

NOISE STANDARDS FOR LOCOMOTIVES AND RAIL CARS,
SOUND LEVEL (dB*A*) MEASURED AT 100 ft

Locomotives	Best maintenance	Newly manufactured
At idle	73	70
All other throttle settings	93	87
Moving at any speed	96	90

Rail cars	Speed ≤ 45 mi/hr	Speed > 45 mi/hr
	88	93

EXAMPLE PROBLEM: PREDICTION OF NOISE LEVELS DUE TO RAILWAYS AND RAPID TRANSIT SYSTEMS

A proposed improvement project will increase the level of service on a railway line and a rapid transit system. Location A is 160 ft from the rapid transit line and 2400 ft from the railway. The expected level of service will be as follows:

	Diesel–electric locomotives	Railway cars	Rapid transit vehicles
Worst hour	20	11	9
Day (7 A.M.–10 P.M.)	150	90	55
Night (10 P.M.–7 A.M.)	16	8	5

The average speed will be 65 mi/hr on the railway and 55 mi/hr on the rapid transit system. Average train lengths will be 3100 ft for railway passenger and freight trains (excluding diesel–electric locomotives) and 450 ft for rapid transit trains. The railway has a straight jointed track and the rapid transit system a straight welded track. There is a barrier between the railway and location A, producing 4-dB*A* attenuation for railway cars and zero attenuation for diesel–electric locomotives. A row of low buildings with about 50% coverage lies between the railroad and location A.

(a) Determine day–night equivalent sound level at location A.

Solution. Since different locations and other descriptors and conditions may be considered, it may be most efficient to employ a computer worksheet or write a computer program to obtain the solution. Table 8.6.1 shows a solution where intermediate steps and adjustments are displayed so that the effect of changes can be evaluated. To obtain L_{DN}, the number of nighttime passbys is multiplied by ten and added to the daytime passbys. The reference levels and adjustments are calculated according to the equations and tables in this section. An adjustment of +4 dB*A* is used for jointed rails on the railroad. The effect of the low buildings between the observer and railway is estimated to produce an adjustment of −2 dB*A* for railway cars only. Since L_{DN} refers to a 24-hour period, an interval correction of −49.4 dB*A* is applied. The predicted combined noise level will be $L_{DN} = 59.2$ dB*A*, with diesel–electric locomotives producing the greatest contribution (57.4 dB*A*).

TABLE 8.6.1 RAILWAY AND RAPID TRANSIT SYSTEM NOISE PREDICTION

Site: Location A, map 1 Descriptor: L_{DN} Source:	Diesel–electric locomotive	Railway cars	Rapid transit vehicles
Observer distance (ft)	2400	2400	160
Speed (mi/hr)	65	65	55
Train length (ft)	n.a.	3100	450
Passbys (night weighted if applicable)	310	170	105
Reference level (dBA)	99.6	88.2	77.5
Adjustments (dBA) for:			
Distance (D $\geq$ 150 ft)	−21.7	−24.9	−2.6
Track condition	4.0	4.0	0.0
Barriers	0.0	−4.0	0.0
Buildings	0.0	−2.0	0.0
Passbys	24.9	22.3	20.2
Duration	n.a.	15.0	7.3
Interval	−49.4	−49.4	−49.4
Noise contribution (dBA)	57.4	49.2	53.0
I/I_{ref}	5.45E+05	8.25E+04	2.00E+05
Combined noise level (dBA)	59.2		

(b) Determine 24-hour equivalent sound level at the same location.

Solution. This descriptor is used when sleep interference is not an issue. Daytime and nighttime railway operations are added without nighttime weighting. The duration correction is again −49.4 dBA. The predicted combined noise level is L_{eq24} = 56.6 dBA, with diesel–electric locomotives again producing the greatest contribution (54.6 dBA) followed by rapid transit vehicles (50.6 dBA) and railway cars (46.8 dBA).

(c) Determine hourly equivalent sound level for maximum or worst hour service.

Solution. This descriptor evaluates noise when service conditions produce the highest noise level, or when noise would produce the greatest activity interference. The duration correction for 1 hour is −35.6 dBA. The noise level contributions at worst hour service conditions are diesel–electric locomotives, 59.3 dBA, railway cars, 51.1 dBA, and rapid transit vehicles, 56.1 dBA. The contributions are combined to produce a noise level of L_{eqH} = 61.4 at location A.

8.7 ENVIRONMENTAL IMPACT STATEMENTS

Environmental impact statements (EIS's) are required by many agencies as a condition for funding of new construction projects, and projects involving changes that may have a substantial effect on the environment. The noise section of an EIS for a transportation project will describe how changes in transportation noise will affect nearby residential and other land uses. If a highway project is proposed, Federal Highway Administration design noise level/activity relationships, Table 8.2.1, may be used. In addition, current noise levels and future year projected noise levels computed for the no-build alternative are compared with predicted noise levels for various construction alternatives. The benefits of possible noise abatement procedures are evaluated in the EIS as well. EIS's are also required for some major construction projects that do not involve construction of highways or other transportation facilities. In such cases it would be necessary to analyze the noise impact due to increased roadway traffic generated by the proposed project.

TABLE 8.7.1 TRAFFIC VOLUME AND NOISE LEVELS AT
VARIOUS LEVELS OF SERVICE
(a) Noise Level Versus Level of Service ($T = 0\%$)

Level of service	Capacity (vehicles/hr) A	T	Speed (km/h)	L_{eqHi} A	T	L_{eqH} (dBA)
A	700		100	69.0		69.0
B	1000		90	69.3		69.3
C	1500		80	69.6		69.6
D	1800		65	67.9		67.9
E	2000		50	65.1		65.1
F	—	—	—	—	—	—

(b) Noise Level Versus Level of Service ($T = 2\%$)

Level of service	Capacity (vehicles/hr) A	T	Speed (km/h)	L_{eqHi} A	T	L_{eqH} (dBA)
A	672	14	100	68.8	65.9	70.7
B	960	20	90	69.1	66.8	71.1
C	1440	30	80	69.4	67.8	71.7
D	1728	36	65	67.7	67.3	70.5
E	1920	40	50	64.9	66.1	68.6
F	—	—	—	—	—	—

(c) Noise Level Versus Level of Service ($T = 4\%$)

Level of service	Capacity (vehicles/hr) A	T	Speed (km/h)	L_{eqHi} A	T	L_{eqH} (dBA)
A	644	28	100	68.6	68.9	71.8
B	920	40	90	68.9	69.8	72.4
C	1380	60	80	69.2	70.8	73.1
D	1656	72	65	67.5	70.3	72.1
E	1840	80	50	64.8	69.1	70.5
F	—	—	—	—	—	—

Source: FHWA (Barry, 1978).

Highway Capacity

The data necessary to construct an EIS for a proposed highway include the predicted volume of automobiles and trucks. If these values are not otherwise available, then the values in Tables 8.7.1a through 8.7.1c based on data compiled by the Highway Research Board (Barry, 1978; HRB, 1965) may be used to estimate traffic volume. These tables assume freeway conditions, a level roadway, and an average highway (design) speed of 113 km/h (1 mile = 1.6093 km). Highway capacity (vehicles/hr) and hourly equivalent sound level (dBA) are based on a single lane of traffic. Sound levels are based on an acoustically hard site and an observer located 15 m from the highway lane.

The percent of heavy trucks, T, is varied from zero to 4% in the tables, and each heavy truck is assumed to reduce automobile capacity by two automobiles. As the traffic volume is increased above level-of-service A, the average speed is reduced. In each table, it can be seen that level-of-service C represents a combination of volume and speed which produces the highest noise levels. Thus an EIS for a proposed highway will ordinarily include noise predictions for the year in which traffic volume reaches level-of-service C. Note that at truck percentage $T = 2\%$, truck noise is dominant at level-of-service E, and at $T = 4\%$, truck noise is dominant for all levels of service.

Highway capacity volumes are also given in Figure 8.7.1 (Gordon et al., 1971; HRB, 1965) for various design speeds and vehicle speeds in miles per hour. These capacities are given in vehicles per hour for uninterrupted flow on a single lane of a six-lane freeway.

The percentages of medium and heavy trucks used for future year predictions in an EIS may be based on current local experience on the roadways from which a proposed highway will draw traffic. Volume variation with time of day may be estimated in the same way, taking into account the schedules of local industries and other activities. As an alternative, Figure 8.7.2 can be used to estimate hourly highway volume variation as a percentage of average daily traffic. This figure, based on traffic counts on rural and urban highways, shows a range of values typical for each hour of the

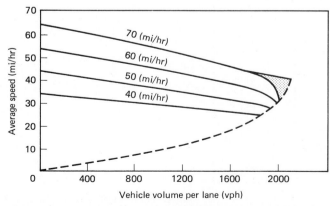

Figure 8.7.1 Relationship between traffic volume per lane and average speed of vehicle travel for uninterrupted flow. (*Source:* NCHRP (Gordon, 1971))

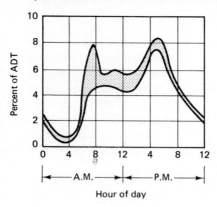

Figure 8.7.2 Average traffic volume varia-tion with time of day. (*Source:* NCHRP (Gordon, 1971))

day. Typical truck mix as a percentage hourly traffic is given by Figure 8.7.3. This figure is based on counts of commercial vehicles on urban highways. Average truck mix as a percentage of average daily traffic is estimated in Figure 8.7.4. On major interstate highways, almost all of the trucks will be in the heavy truck class, with three or more axles, having gross vehicle weights (GVW) of 12,000 kg (26,000 lb) or more. The fraction of medium trucks, with two axles and six wheels, and GVW's between 4500 and 12,000 kg (10,000 lb ≤ GVW < 26,000 lb) is likely to be more significant on highways serving cities. Typical values taken from these figures and tables, sup-plemented by local information when available, can be used to predict worst hour equivalent sound level and day–night equivalent sound level.

Elements of an Environmental Impact Statement

The length of an EIS and the amount of detail depend on the scope of the project and the number of individuals likely to be impacted. More detailed analysis would be

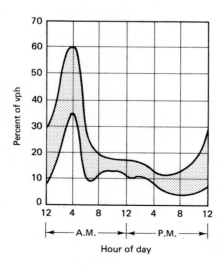

Figure 8.7.3 Truck traffic as a percent of total vehicles per hour versus time of day. (*Source:* NCHRP (Gordon, 1971))

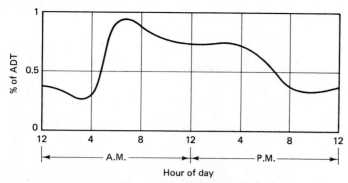

Figure 8.7.4 Typical hourly truck volume as a percentage of average daily traffic.

required for a noise impact study of a proposed highway in a residential area than for one in a sparsely populated area. If the agency requesting the EIS does not specify the format, the following components might be included in the noise report of an EIS for a proposed highway improvement.

Executive Summary   A few paragraphs are used to describe the proposed project, the noise descriptors used, and the method of noise measurement and analysis. The noise impacts due to each construction alternative are compared with the noise impact in future years for the no-build alternative.

Introduction   The objectives of the project and of the noise study are stated, including information on why the study was initiated. The project area is defined and described in terms of sensitive receptors. The impact assessment methodology is outlined.

Project Description   The project is divided into sections and each design alternative is described for that section. For example, one highway design alternative may call for a six-lane expressway throughout, another alternative may require no improvements in some sections, and a four-lane expressway in others.

Noise Prediction Methodology   Noise sources are identified along with other input data required to determine noise impact. The prediction model is described including the effect of traffic volume, truck mix, and shielding due to buildings, barriers, and depressed roadways. The method of assessing impact is described in detail. For a highway project, impact zones within which exterior equivalent sound level $L_{eq} \geq 67$ dBA for the peak travel hour could be defined. Land-use categories are identified, and design-noise-level/activity-relationships are stated. In addition, the following impact categories can be defined in terms of noise level increases due to the proposed project:

Category	Increase (dBA)	Effect
I	<5	None to minor
II	5 to 10	Moderate
III	>10	Significant to severe

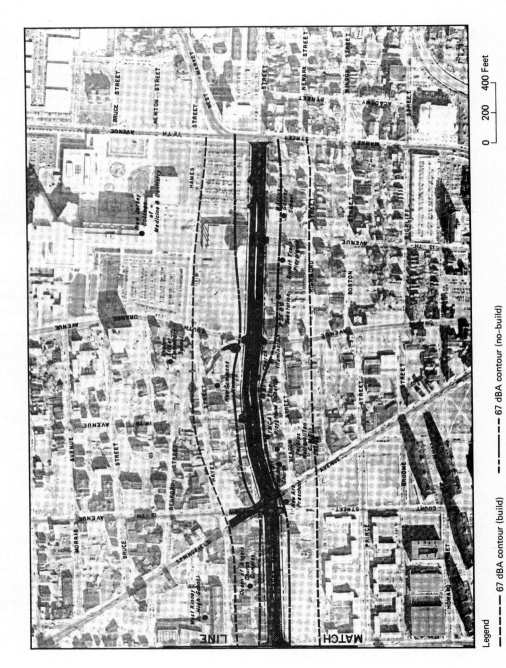

Legend

————— 67 dBA contour (build)

– – – – – 67 dBA contour (no-build)

Figure 8.7.5 Noise contour map.

0   200   400 Feet

The calibration of the prediction model based on measurements is described, and the prediction error is stated.

Results Noise contour maps or impact zone maps are plotted for noise levels based on future year predictions for each design alternative. Figure 8.7.5 shows an example of a worst hour $L_{eq} = 67$ dBA impact zone for one highway design alternative. This map was constructed by drawing the noise contour on a transparent overlay over an aerial photograph of the impact area. Other overlays are drawn for other design alternatives and other future years. The year after completion of construction, and the year in which predicted traffic volume will reach level-of-service C are of particular interest. The worst hour $L_{eq} = 72$ dBA contour may be drawn also, if noise impact on commercial areas is to be identified. Day–night noise level may be used as an alternative descriptor for some projects, using different criterion levels. The noise impact may be described at a list of facilities identified as sensitive receptors, and compared with the no-build alternative. In addition, the number of individuals, dwelling units, parks, schools, churches, hospitals, and libraries impacted, and the degree of impact may be presented in tabular form.

Conclusions Noise impacts are summarized for individuals, residences, and various facilities. Impacts due to each construction alternative are compared with the no-build alternative for the same future year.

Recommendations and Ranking of Construction Schemes in Terms of Noise Impact
The construction alternatives are ranked from least impact to greatest impact on number of individuals, number of dwelling units, and on other facilities. Recommendations for mitigating impacts are discussed. This information is to be combined with information from other studies including cost, traffic patterns, residential and business dislocation, and air quality predictions.

BIBLIOGRAPHY

Barry, T. M., and J. A. Reagan, FHWA highway traffic noise prediction model, FHWA-RD-77-108, December 1978.

Bender, E. K., W. Patterson, and G. Fax, The technology and cost of quieting medium and heavy trucks, BBN Report 2710, Oct. 30, 1974.

Environmental Protection Agency, Regulations governing interstate rail carriers, EPA 550/9-76-005, December 31, 1975.

Environmental Protection Agency, Background document for medium and heavy truck noise emission regulations, EPA-550/9-76-008, March 1976.

Environmental Protection Agency, EPA Noise control program, progress to date, May 1976.

Federal Highway Administration, Procedures for abatement of highway traffic noise and construction noise, FHPM 7-7-3, May 14, 1976.

Gill, H. S., The propagation of railway noise in residential areas, ISVR Technical Report No. 73, Institute of Sound and Vibration Research, February 1975.

Gordon, C. G., W. J. Galloway, B. A. Kugler, and D. L. Nelson, Highway noise: A design guide for highway engineers, Highway Research Board, NCHRP 117, 1971.

Highway Research Board, *Highway Capacity Manual,* HRB Special Report 87, National Academy of Sciences, 1965.

National Cooperative Highway Research Program, Highway noise, a field evaluation of traffic noise reduction measures, NCHRP Report 144, 1973.

National Cooperative Highway Research Program, Highway noise, a design guide for prediction and control, NCHRP Report 174, 1976.

Pallett, D. S., et al., Design guide for reducing noise in and around buildings, BSS 844, NBS, April 1978.

Reagan, J. A., Determination of reference energy mean emission levels, FHWA-OEP/HEV-78-1, July 1978.

Simpson, M. A., *Noise Barrier Design Handbook,* FHWA-RD-76-58, February 1976.

Society of Automotive Engineers, Exterior sound level for heavy trucks and buses, SAE Standard J366b, 1973.

Swing, J. W., and D. B. Pies, Assessment of noise environments around railroad operations, Wyle Laboratories Rept., WCR73-5, El Segundo, CA, July 1973.

U.S. Department of Housing and Urban Development, Noise assessment guidelines, 14–31, 1983.

Wu, T., and J. I. Case, "Effect of operating perameters on bare engine and engine contributing noise levels," Chapter 2, *Noise Control in Internal Combustion Engines,* D. E. Baxa, Ed., Wiley-Interscience, New York, 1982.

PROBLEMS

8.1.1. Verify the combined noise levels given in the table of "Possible combinations of component source levels to meet a given regulatory level."

8.1.2. Using the table of "Possible combinations of component noise source levels to meet a given regulatory requirement" determine the effect on each combined noise level if
(a) the greatest contributor is quieted by 3 dBA
(b) the least contributor is quieted by 3 dBA

8.3.1. Express the adjustments to the equation for adjusted energy mean emission level L_{eqH} in terms of feet and miles per hour where applicable.

8.3.2. Write a computer program to compute the adjustment for finite highway segments at acoustically soft sites.

8.3.3. Compute the adjustment for finite highway segments at soft sites subtended by various angles. Plot or tabulate the results. If a computer is not used, a scientific calculator with a preprogrammed integration routine can be used.

8.3.4. An observer is located 18 m from the center of a proposed two-lane highway. The intervening land is acoustically soft, and there are no buildings between the proposed highway and observer. The highway segment in question will subtend an angle of about 90° to the right and 90° to the left. The centers of the lanes of travel will be located 2 m from the highway center. Predicted "worst hour" vehicle speed (km/h) and volume (vehicles/hr) are as follows for each vehicle class and lane:

Vehicle class	Lane	Speed	Volume
Autos	Near	87	300
Autos	Far	87	190
Medium trucks	Near	80	35
Medium trucks	Far	87	21
Heavy trucks	Near	70	33
Heavy trucks	Far	82	19

There will be a 4% upgrade in the near lane. Predict equivalent sound level for "worst hour" conditions.

8.3.5. An observer is located 20 m from the center of a proposed two-lane highway. The intervening land is acoustically soft, and there are no buildings between the proposed highway and observer. The highway segment in question will subtend an angle of about 90° to the right and 90° to the left. The centers of the lanes of travel will be located 2 m from the highway center. Predicted "worst hour" vehicle speed (km/hr) and volume (vehicles/hr) are as follows for each vehicle class and lane:

Vehicle class	Lane	Speed	Volume
Autos	Near	85	310
Autos	Far	87	120
Medium trucks	Near	80	55
Medium trucks	Far	85	18
Heavy trucks	Near	65	41
Heavy trucks	Far	82	22

There will be a 5% upgrade in the near lane. Predict equivalent sound level for "worst hour" conditions.

8.3.6. An observer is located 65 m from the center of a proposed two-lane highway. The intervening land is acoustically soft, and there is a row of buildings with about 55% coverage between the proposed highway and observer. The highway segment in question will subtend an angle of 0° to the right and 90° to the left. The centers of the lanes of travel will be located 2 m from the highway center. Predicted "worst hour" vehicle speed (km/hr) and volume (vehicles/hr) are as follows:

Vehicle class	Lane	Speed	Volume
Autos	Near	88	335
Autos	Far	88	295
Medium trucks	Near	88	75
Medium trucks	Far	88	70
Heavy trucks	Near	83	52
Heavy trucks	Far	83	48

There will be a 1% upgrade in the near lane. Predict equivalent sound level for "worst hour" conditions.

8.3.7. Note: The following problem is solved by using charts and nomographs in "FHWA highway noise prediction model" (Barry and Reagan, 1978). An observer is located 61.8 m from the center of a proposed two-lane highway. The intervening land is acoustically hard to the observer's left, and soft to the observer's right. There are no buildings between the proposed highway and observer. The total highway segment in question will subtend an angle of about 90° to the right and 90° to the left. The centers of the lanes of travel will be located 1.8 m from the highway center. Predicted "worst hour" vehicle speed (km/hr) and volume (vehicles/hr) are as follows for each vehicle class and lane:

Vehicle class	Lane	Speed	Volume
Autos	Near	75	317
Autos	Far	75	281
Medium trucks	Near	75	24
Medium trucks	Far	75	12
Heavy trucks	Near	75	22
Heavy trucks	Far	75	25

There will be a 1% upgrade in the near lane. Predict equivalent sound level contributions for "worst hour" conditions for the highway segment to the right of the observer, and the segment to the left. Combine the results.

8.4.1. An observer is located 2 m below, and 20 m horizontal distance from the center of a proposed two-lane highway. The intervening land is acoustically soft, and there are no buildings between the proposed highway and observer. The highway segment in question will subtend an angle of 180°. The centers of the lanes of travel will be located 2 m from the highway center. A 4.5-m-high barrier will be constructed along the entire length of the proposed highway, 8 m from the observer. Predicted "worst hour" vehicle speed (km/hr) and volume (vehicles/hr) are as follows for each vehicle class and lane:

Vehicle class	Lane	Speed	Volume
Autos	Near	85	350
Autos	Far	88	295
Medium trucks	Near	80	75
Medium trucks	Far	88	70
Heavy trucks	Near	75	52
Heavy trucks	Far	83	48

There will be a 3% upgrade in the near lane. Predict equivalent sound level for "worst hour" conditions.

8.4.2. Repeat the above problem for an observer location 3 m above, and 40 m horizontal distance from the roadway. Assume the traffic volume has doubled.

8.4.3. An observer is located 0.5 m above, and 16 m horizontal distance from the center of a proposed two-lane highway. The intervening land is acoustically soft, and there is a row of buildings with 80% coverage between the proposed highway and observer. The highway segment in question will subtend an angle of 180°. The centers of the lanes of travel will be located 2 m from the highway center. A 5.5-m-high barrier will be constructed along the entire length of the proposed highway, 8 m from the observer. Predicted "worst hour" vehicle speed (km/hr) and volume (vehicles/hr) are as follows for each vehicle class and lane:

Vehicle class	Lane	Speed	Volume
Autos	Near	80	550
Autos	Far	80	480
Medium trucks	Near	75	81
Medium trucks	Far	80	77
Heavy trucks	Near	70	68
Heavy trucks	Far	78	65

There will be a 5.5% upgrade in the near lane. Predict equivalent sound level for "worst hour" conditions.

8.5.1. Predict L_{50} and L_{10} for the following conditions. An observer is located 110 ft from the center of a proposed two-lane highway. There are no buildings between the proposed highway and observer. The highway segment in question will subtend an angle of about 90° to the right and 90° to the left. The centers of the lanes of travel will be located 2 m from the highway center. Predicted "worst hour" vehicle speed (mi/hr) and volume (vehicles/hr) are as follows for each vehicle class and lane:

Vehicle class	Lane	Speed	Volume
Autos	Near	55	400
Autos	Far	55	390
Heavy trucks[a]	Near	40	50
Heavy trucks	Far	55	48

[a] MGW > 10,000 lb.

There will be a 4% upgrade in the near lane.

8.6.1. Write a computer program or computer worksheet program for prediction of railway and rapid transit noise.

8.6.2. A proposed improvement project will increase the level of service on a railway line and a rapid transit system. Location A is 3000 ft from the rapid transit line and 510 ft from the railway. The expected level of service will be as follows:

	Diesel–electric locomotives	Trains of railway cars	Rapid transit vehicles
Day (7 A.M.–10 P.M.)	200	100	30
Night (10 P.M.–7 A.M.)	45	25	8

The average speed will be 45 mi/hr on the railway and 55 mi/hr on the rapid transit system. Average train lengths will be 4500 ft for railway passenger and freight trains (excluding diesel–electric locomotives) and 300 ft for rapid transit trains. The railway has a straight jointed track and the rapid transit system a straight welded track. There is a barrier which results in 6 dBA attenuation for railway cars and rapid transit vehicles, and zero attenuation for diesel–electric locomotives. A row of buildings with about 50% coverage lies between both lines and location A.
(a) Determine day–night equivalent sound level at location A.
(b) Determine 24-hour equivalent sound level at the same location.

8.6.3. Determine worst hour L_{eqH} based on the above data if maximum hourly passbys are 25 for diesel–electric locomotives, 14 for trains of railway cars, and 5 for rapid transit vehicles.

8.6.4. A proposed improvement project will increase the level of service on a railway line and a rapid transit system. Location B is 250 ft from the rapid transit line and 165 ft from the railway. The expected level of service will be as follows:

	Diesel–electric locomotives	Trains of railway cars	Rapid transit vehicles
Worst hour	30	14	11
Day (7 A.M.–10 P.M.)	250	115	100
Night (10 P.M.–7 A.M.)	30	15	9

The average speed will be 62 mi/hr on the railway and 59 mi/hr on the rapid transit system. Average train lengths will be 4200 ft for railway passenger and freight trains (excluding diesel–electric locomotives) and 375 ft for rapid transit trains. The railway has a straight jointed track and the rapid transit system a straight welded track. There is a barrier between the railway and location B, producing 3.5-dBA attenuation for railway cars and zero attenuation for diesel–electric locomotives. A row of low buildings with about 65% coverage lies between the rapid transit line and location B.

(a) Determine day–night equivalent sound level at location B.

(b) Determine 24-hour equivalent sound level at the same location.

(c) Determine hourly equivalent sound level for maximum or worst hour service.

8.6.5. Consider the proposed railway and rapid transit system described above. Determine hourly equivalent sound level for maximum or worst hour service, for a location 265 ft from the railroad, and 150 ft from the rapid transit line.

8.7.1. An observer is located 1 m below, and 16 m horizontal distance from the center of a proposed two-lane highway. The intervening land is acoustically soft, and there is a row of buildings with 50% coverage between the proposed highway and observer. The highway segment in question will subtend an angle of 180°. The centers of the lanes of travel will be located 2 m from the highway center. A 3.6-m-high barrier will be constructed along the entire length of the proposed highway, 8 m from the observer. Predicted "worst hour" vehicle speed (km/hr) and volume (vehicles/hr) are to be based on level-of-service C with 4% trucks (almost all heavy trucks). There will be a 5.5% upgrade in the near lane. Predict equivalent sound level for "worst hour" conditions.

Chapter 9

Aircraft Noise

Airlines transport the vast majority of common-carrier intercity passengers in the United States, and an increasing amount of freight. During peak traffic hours, takeoffs at major airports may occur every 60 to 90 s. As a result, aircraft operations are one of the major causes of noise complaints. The introduction of turbojet-powered aircraft on commercial routes in the 1950s, along with increased service, caused an increase in the portion of the population exposed to high levels of aircraft noise. Some factors that decrease noise impact, or at least prevent an increase in noise impact with increases in aircraft operations, include the introduction of high-bypass-ratio turbofan engines, retrofitting and redesign for quieter operation, restriction of nighttime flights, flight path changes, and land use planning.

9.1 AIRCRAFT NOISE SOURCES, AND HUMAN RESPONSE TO AIRCRAFT NOISE

Jet aircraft thrust is dependent on a large mass flow of air. Mixing of this air at the jet discharge results in turbulence and noise. Aerodynamic monopoles, dipoles, and quadrupoles were discussed in Chapters 2 and 7. Turbulent jets at subsonic velocity behave approximately as quadrupoles (Lighthill, 1952) with sound power given by

$$W = K_1 \rho d^2 v^8 / c^5 \qquad (9.1.1)$$

where W = approximate sound power (W)
$K_1 = 3 \times 10^{-5}$ (approximately)
ρ = air density (kg/m^3)
d = jet diameter (m)
v = jet velocity (m/s)
c = speed of sound propagation (m/s)

Laboratory studies by Olson et al. (1973) and Lush (1971) show an increase of about 24 dB in sound power level of an air jet with each doubling of discharge velocity (after adjusting data for nozzle diameter and ambient conditions). This result verifies the eighth power relationship for velocity, since

$$10 \log[2^8] = 24 \text{ approximately}$$

Initial turbulence can greatly increase the constant K_1 in the above equation, while design changes to reduce velocity gradients in the mixing region can reduce K_1.

Modeling the noise production mechanism of jet aircraft is more complicated than modeling simple jets, but the above equation does provide some guidance. Noting that sound power has a strong velocity dependence, attempts have been made to reduce aircraft noise by reducing discharge velocity, and by reducing the velocity gradient in the region surrounding the discharge. Of course, thrust must be maintained, and initial turbulence avoided. The physical mechanisms of various noise sources are discussed by von Gierke (1984).

Turbojet Engines

Major turbojet engine components are the compressor, the burner, the gas-driven turbine which drives the compressor, the afterburner, and the nozzle. Figure 9.1.1 is a simplified schematic, showing the major components of a turbojet engine. Turbulence due to interaction of high-velocity exhaust gas with the surrounding air results in broadband noise. The multibladed compressor may produce a pure-tone component. Note that a "pure tone" refers to a discernible frequency or a spike or narrow peak in a frequency spectrum. High levels of broadband noise are produced in all flight modes, particularly during takeoff, when high thrust is required.

Figure 9.1.2 shows five aircraft noise spectra, all adjusted to an overall A-weighted sound level of 0 dBA. The frequency spectra of noise generated by aircraft have more sound energy at high frequencies than these spectra, which were measured thousands of feet from the source. As noise travels large distances, air absorption has a greater effect in reducing high-frequency noise than low-frequency noise.

Turbofan Engines

The turbofan engine design introduces a multibladed turbine-driven fan before the compressor section. The other major components of a turbofan engine are roughly

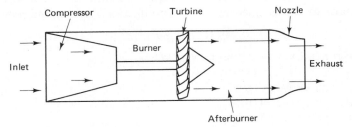

Figure 9.1.1 Turbojet engine schematic.

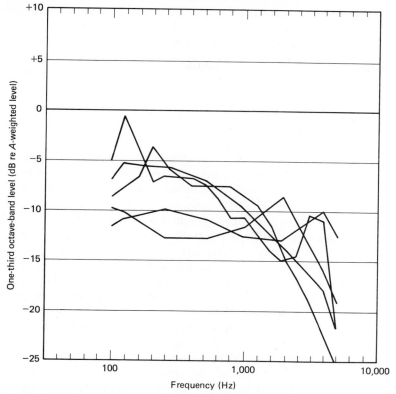

Figure 9.1.2 Five aircraft spectra normalized to equivalent *A*-weighted sound pressure levels. (*Source:* NBS (Pallett et al., 1978))

similar to a turbojet engine. The fan, as shown in the simplified schematic, Figure 9.1.3, discharges air forward of the primary jet exhaust nozzle. In high-bypass-ratio jet engines, a large mass flow rate of air is discharged by the fan at a lower velocity than the primary jet exhaust. As a result, typical noise levels are lower, while thrust is maintained by the increased mass flow. High-bypass-ratio turbofan engines also have better fuel economy. As a result, they have largely replaced turbojet engines in commercial airline fleets. In turbojet and turbofan engines, much of the jet noise is

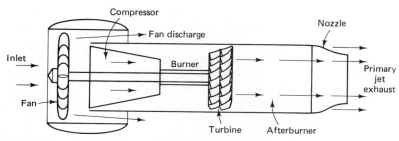

Figure 9.1.3 Simplified turbofan engine schematic.

produced in the region where high-velocity gas exhausts into the stationary atmosphere. In the turbofan engine, the air discharged by the fan shrouds the primary jet exhaust, reducing the velocity gradient, and thus reducing turbulence-induced noise. The multibladed fan in a turbofan engine introduces a high-frequency pure tone (whine) which is particularly noticeable on approach. At takeoff, the broadband turbulent jet noise is usually dominant.

Helicopters and Propeller Aircraft

A major source of helicopter noise, blade-slap, appears to occur as the helicopter blade interacts with a vortex formed by the blade preceding it. Since both blades and vortices are moving, blade-slap frequencies cannot be predicted precisely. Dwyer (1985) observed an 82-ms period or 12-Hz fundamental blade-slap frequency from in-air data for a two-blade main rotor operating at 300 to 350 rpm. Although 12-Hz sound is generally considered outside of the audible range, this frequency represents the repetition rate of impulse noise with audible components. Other noise sources include the engine exhaust, compressor noise (in gas turbine engines), the tail rotor, the gear box, and the airframe. Since blade-vortex interaction noise has a large energy content in the low-frequency range, it travels over large distances with little energy loss due to air absorption. The location of heliports in cities causes an additional problem due to the proximity of residences and businesses. In some cases, triple glazing is used on nearby buildings to reduce intrusive noise.

Propeller-driven aircraft are common for general aviation use, which includes corporate and private (mostly recreational) operations, but little used by commercial airlines. Propeller aircraft in current use are generally small, with low horsepower ratings. However, the large number of general aviation airports and the low-altitude flight paths of general aviation aircraft result in noise impact on otherwise quiet communities. Monitoring noise at airports and enforcement of noise regulations may have some effect in limiting noise impact. Many airports operate at a loss, which is made up from tax revenue or other sources such as other operations of port authorities. Any policies which subsidize general aviation should be reviewed by communities that experience an aircraft noise problem.

Supersonic Aircraft and Sonic Boom

Typical commercial airliners fly at a speed of about Mach 0.84, where Mach 1 is the speed of sound propagation at the flight altitude. Some military aircraft and a few commercial aircraft fly at supersonic speeds, that is, at speeds greater than Mach 1. In addition to the noise sources present in other jet aircraft, supersonic aircraft produce shock waves or pressure pulses called N-waves or sonic booms. During high-altitude supersonic diving maneuvers of military aircraft, a shock wave forms on the bow, and then detaches itself and travels to earth. Supersonic aircraft in steady flight produce a shock wave which propagates to a wide area under the flight path. The shock waves that reach the ground are called N-waves due to their form, a sharp rise above atmospheric pressure, a drop below atmospheric pressure, and a return to atmospheric pressure. Typical pressure changes due to supersonic overflights are in the 50- to 100-Pa range with sonic boom durations of 50 to 400 ms, and much of the sound energy at frequencies under 100 Hz.

EXAMPLE PROBLEM: JET NOISE

The velocity of a jet is to be reduced by 30% while thrust is to be maintained.
   (a) Estimate the effect on sound power.

Solution. Thrust is proportional to change in momentum, which is related to mass flow rate from the jet. We will assume that the forward motion of the nozzle is small compared to the jet velocity, corresponding to takeoff conditions, when the greatest thrust is required. To maintain thrust, the jet discharge cross section must be adjusted to satisfy the following relationship:

$$(vA\rho)_1 = (vA\rho)_2 \qquad (9.1.2)$$

where v = jet discharge velocity
     $A = \pi d^2/4$ = cross-sectional area for a circular discharge
     ρ = mass density of the fluid (principally air)

and subscripts 1 and 2 refer to the initial and final designs, respectively.
   If fluid density is essentially unchanged, we have

$$(vd^2)_2 = (vd^2)_1 \qquad (9.1.3)$$

Using the equation for sound power from a quadrupole,

$$W = K_1 \rho d^2 v^8/c^5 \qquad \mathbf{(9.1.1)}$$

and again assuming that temperatures and other conditions are essentially constant, that is, ρ, K_1, and c are unchanged, we have

$$\frac{W_2}{W_1} = \frac{(d^2 v^8)_2}{(d^2 v^8)_1} \qquad (9.1.4)$$

Substituting equation 9.1.3 in the last equation, the result is

$$\frac{W_2}{W_1} = \left(\frac{v_2}{v_1}\right)^7 = 0.7^7 = 0.0824$$

(b) Estimate the change in sound power level.

Solution. Sound power level is given by

$$L_W = 10 \lg\left(\frac{W}{W_{ref}}\right) \qquad (9.1.5)$$

where $W_{ref} = 10^{-12}$ W. The change in sound power level is given by

$$L_{W2} - L_{W1} = 10 \lg\left(\frac{W_2}{W_1}\right)$$

$$= 10 \lg(0.7^7) = -10.8 \text{ dB}$$

The actual change would depend on the applicability of the model. If the new configuration was designed to produce a smooth velocity transition, the improvement could be greater than predicted. However, other noise sources could become prominent, limiting the effect of a reduction in jet noise.

Human Response to Aircraft Noise and Noise-Induced Vibration

At one time, interest in aircraft noise centered around concerns for pilot hearing conservation and attempts at quieting military aircraft to avoid detection. Current interest is centered around community noise impact. The Environmental Protection Agency (1978) estimated that 16 million people live in urban areas of the United States where outdoor day–night sound levels (L_{DN}) exceed 60 dBA due to aircraft operations alone. A substantially larger population is exposed to aircraft noise which exceeds the protective level ($L_{DN} \leq 55$ dBA) identified by EPA on the basis of activity interference and annoyance. This estimate must, of course, be adjusted for increases in air traffic and changes in equipment and flight patterns since the date of the report.

The significance of aircraft noise is illustrated by a survey of reasons people gave for wanting to move from a given location (HMSO, 1963; EPA, 1974). For $L_{DN} > 68$ dBA, aircraft noise was the reason given by the highest percentage in the survey, exceeding the percentage of respondents giving as reasons: climate; better living accommodations; smoke/dirt/smells; and distance from work.

Descriptors L_{DN} and L_{eq}, based on A-weighting, correlate well with annoyance and other effects of noise in most cases. For example, the correlation between percent of individuals disturbed and L_{DN} is shown in Figure 5.5.1. However, humans are more likely to react adversely to helicopter noise and supersonic aircraft noise than to noise from other sources which produces the same L_{DN}. These exceptions may be explained by the time pattern and frequency content of the noise.

Noise-Induced Vibration and Rattle   Building vibration results when a noise spectrum contains significant energy at frequencies corresponding to structural resonances, usually below 250 Hz, which is called the rattle boundary. The rattle threshold is the acceleration corresponding to an inertia force which will cause an object to slide or jump. This could be a vertical inertia force amplitude equal to the weight of an object or horizontal amplitude equal to the force of friction.

Response to Helicopter Noise   One-third octave-band helicopter noise spectra, based on flyover data from Raney and Cawthorn (1979), are shown in Figure 9.1.4. Sound pressure levels at $t = -4$ s are given by the solid line and levels at $t = 0$ by the dashed line, where $t = 0$ is the instant the helicopter passed directly overhead. Both spectra are normalized to the overall flat (unweighted) sound pressure level at $t = -4$ s. A blade-slap component is prominent in the one-third octave band with 12.5-Hz center frequency, consistent with the study by Dwyer (1985). It is presumed that this low-frequency noise component induces structural vibration and rattle.

Schomer and Neathammer (1987) determined that A-weighted descriptors are generally adequate to assess community response to helicopter noise when no per-

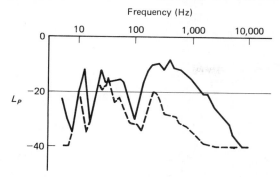

Figure 9.1.4 Helicopter noise spectra based on data of Raney and Cawthorn (1979).

ceptible vibration or rattle is induced by the noise. However, they found that neither *A*- nor *C*-weighting properly assesses human response to noise-induced vibration and rattle of windows, building components, and objects in a room. Using sound exposure level (SEL) as a basis, with a control signal in the 500-Hz octave-band, the following offsets were determined for helicopter noise:

RATTLE CORRECTION

	Vibration or rattle perceived as:		
	"None"	"A little"	"A lot"
Offset (dB*A*) Indoors	0	12	20 or more
Outdoors	0	0	4 or less

The results indicate, for example, that helicopter noise with a little noise-induced vibration or rattle is as bothersome or annoying as the control signal at a level 12 dB*A* higher. However, if the vibration level is below the level of human perception, no offset is applied.

Supersonic Aircraft—Noise and Vibration Spectra Human response to supersonic aircraft overflights is influenced by their characteristic high noise levels, sonic boom, and noise-induced vibration and rattle. Wesler (1975, 1978) reported on U.S. Department of Transportation-sponsored tests and scheduled operations of the Concorde supersonic transport (SST). The following root-mean-square (rms) accelerations (dB re 10^{-6} *g*) were measured in a motel building near the flight path: 115 at the center of a window, and 106 at the center of an exterior wall. Comparable measurements during flights of a subsonic jetliner were 101.5 dB on the window and 88.5 dB on the wall.

Figure 9.1.5a shows one-third octave-band sound pressure levels near the takeoff path for the SST (solid line) and for a subsonic turbofan-powered Boeing 707 (dashed line) under comparable conditions. It can be seen that the SST spectrum is uniformly higher up to about 4 kHz, which is presumed to be the compressor-whine frequency of the turbofan engine. For this event, peak sound levels for the SST were 121 dB*A* and 126 dB flat (unweighted overall). Corresponding values for the turbofan aircraft

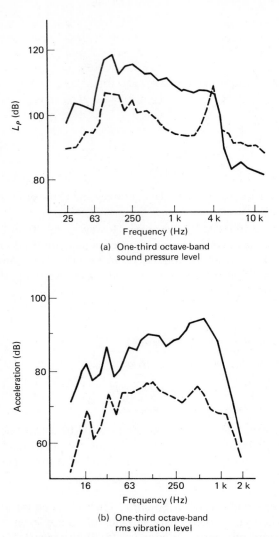

(a) One-third octave-band
sound pressure level

(b) One-third octave-band
rms vibration level

Figure 9.1.5 Sound and vibration spectra for aircraft flyovers. (*Source:* Wesler (1975))
Key: SST—solid line
    Subsonic airliner—dashed line

were 109.5 dBA and 116 dB. Part (b) of the figure shows vibrations (one-third octave-band rms acceleration, dB re 10^{-6} g) measured on a building wall for the same events. Vibration levels due to the SST were higher for all frequencies of interest. Complaints relating to SST operations at subsonic speeds included perceived danger, excessive noise, rattling of dishes, and vibration of windows.

Sonic Boom Large aircraft in supersonic flight may produce an audible boom "carpet" 80 to 100 km (50 to 60 miles) wide. As noted above, overpressures of about 50 to 100

Pa are typical (peak sound pressures over 130 dB). Annoyance factors due to sonic boom include shaking of buildings, startle, sleep interruption, rest interruption, and communication interference. In addition, there is evidence of damage to building elements such as glass and plaster. It was estimated that 50 million people would be subject to 10 to 15 sonic booms per day if commercial supersonic flights were permitted over the United States. At the time of this writing, civilian operations are not permitted to produce sonic booms over the United States.

Much of the energy in a sonic boom is concentrated at the low-frequency end of the spectrum (from below the audible range to about 100 Hz). As noted above, low-frequency noise excites building resonances. In addition, transmission loss characteristics of barriers and buildings are typically poor at low frequencies. Thus, sonic booms tend to be more intrusive than other sounds, whereas people expect more acoustical privacy indoors than out. When assessing community response to high-energy impulsive noise including sonic booms, *A*-weighted descriptors are generally inadequate. As noted by Schomer (1986), impulsive noise is commonly hidden in other neighborhood sources when using *A*-weighting, but rarely when using *C*-weighting.

9.2 AIRCRAFT CERTIFICATION

U.S. Federal Aviation Administration (FAR 36, 1985a) type-certification requires feasible use of aircraft noise control technology, sets standards for acquisition of noise levels, and provides a method of predicting noise impact on airport neighborhood communities. The original standard, promulgated in 1969, was the first type-certification for aircraft noise prescribed by any nation. Subsequent amendments have recognized advances in noise control technology, advances in noise measurement, and the significance of community noise impact. Some provisions of the standard are outlined below.

Aircraft Noise Certification Measurements

FAR 36 standards are based principally on the noise descriptor *effective perceived noise level* (EPNL) measured in decibel units identified as EPNdB. Calculation of EPNL begins with determination of sound levels in the 24 one-third-octave bands with center frequencies from 50 Hz to 10 kHz. Measurements are made during a standard takeoff profile described in Figure 9.2.1, where the position and angle parameters are functions of aircraft performance and weight, and the atmospheric conditions of temperature, pressure, and wind velocity and direction. Position K is the takeoff measuring station. The aircraft position is recorded for the entire interval during which measured aircraft noise level is within 10 dB of the maximum tone-corrected perceived noise level PNLTM. A typical approach profile is also specified, with the noise measuring station located 6562 ft from the runway threshold.

Tests consist of a series of takeoffs and approaches during which simultaneous noise measurements are taken at the measuring stations below the flight line and at a minimum of four sideline stations. Certain atmospheric conditions, limitations on

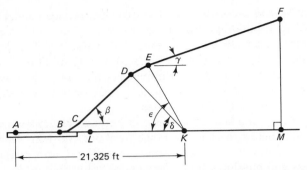

Figure 9.2.1 Measured takeoff profile. The aircraft begins the takeoff roll at point *A*, lifts off at point *B*, and initiates the first constant climb at point *C* at an angle *β*. The noise-abatement thrust cutback is started at point *D* and completed at point *E* where the second constant climb is defined by the angle *γ* (usually expressed in terms of the gradient in percent). The end of the noise certification takeoff flight path is represented by aircraft position *F* whose vertical projection on the flight track (extended centerline of the runway) is point *M*. (*Source:* FAA (FAR36))

background noise, and aircraft loading requirements must be met for the tests to proceed. Specifications and calibration requirements are given for the acoustical measurement system. During the takeoffs and approaches, air speed, flight path, and engine performance data are sampled and recorded.

Test data are corrected for deviation from the following standard conditions:

1. Sea level pressure of 2116 lb/ft^2 (1.013 × 10^5 Pa).
2. 77°F (25°C) ambient temperature.
3. 70% relative humidity.
4. Zero wind velocity.
5. Specified aircraft position and performance conditions.

The corrected measurements form an array of one-third octave-band sound pressure levels. Array elements have the form SPL(*i*, *k*) where *i* = 1 to 24 for the one-third octave center frequencies from 50 Hz to 10 kHz, and *k* is the time increment index. Half-second time intervals are usually used.

Effective Perceived Noise Level

The calculation of effective perceived noise level proceeds as follows:

Step 1 Each element SPL(*i*, *k*) in the array of one-third octave-band sound pressure levels is converted to perceived noisiness as follows, using Table 9.2.1:

Case 1. $f < 400$ Hz or $f > 6300$ Hz, (a) SPL(b) ≤ SPL ≤ SPL(a).

$$n = 10^{M(b)[SPL-SPL(b)]} \qquad (9.2.1)$$

(b) SPL > SPL(a).

$$n = 10^{M(c)[SPL-SPL(c)]} \qquad (9.2.2)$$

TABLE 9.2.1 CONSTANTS FOR MATHEMATICALLY FORMULATED NOY VALUES

Band, i	f (Hz)	M (b)	SPL (b) (dB)	SPL (a) (dB)	M (c)	SPL (c) (dB)
1	50	0.043478	64	91.0	0.030103	52
2	63	0.040570	60	85.9	0.030103	51
3	80	0.036831	56	87.3	0.030103	49
4	100	0.036831	53	79.9	0.030103	47
5	125	0.035336	51	79.8	0.030103	46
6	160	0.033333	48	76.0	0.030103	45
7	200	0.033333	46	74.0	0.030103	43
8	250	0.032051	44	74.9	0.030103	42
9	315	0.030675	42	94.6	0.030103	41
10	400	—	—	—	0.030103	40
11	500	—	—	—	0.030103	40
12	630	—	—	—	0.030103	40
13	800	—	—	—	0.030103	40
14	1,000	—	—	—	0.030103	40
15	1,250	—	—	—	0.030103	38
16	1,600	—	—	—	0.029960	34
17	2,000	—	—	—	0.029960	32
18	2,500	—	—	—	0.029960	30
19	3,150	—	—	—	0.029960	29
20	4,000	—	—	—	0.029960	29
21	5,000	—	—	—	0.029960	30
22	6,300	—	—	—	0.029960	31
23	8,000	0.042285	37	44.3	0.029960	34
24	10,000	0.042285	41	50.7	0.029960	37

Source: FAA (1985a).

Case 2. 400 Hz $\leq f \leq$ 6300 Hz and SPL $\geq$ SPL(c).

$$n = 10^{M(c)[SPL-SPL(c)]} \qquad (9.2.3)$$

where n = perceived noisiness (noys) at an instant in time for a given one-third octave frequency band

SPL = SPL(i, k), the corrected one-third octave band sound pressure level (dB)

and M(b), SPL(b), and so on, are constants for the given frequency, listed in Table 9.2.1. If sound pressure levels fall outside of the ranges indicated, a table of perceived noisiness versus frequency and sound pressure level, such as found in FAR 36 (FAA, 1985, pp. 26–28) may be used.

Step 2 The perceived noisiness values are combined according to the formula

$$N(k) = n(k) + 0.15\left\{\left[\sum_{i=1}^{24} n(i, k)\right] - n(k)\right\}$$

$$= 0.85n(k) + 0.15\sum_{i=1}^{24} n(i, k) \qquad (9.2.4)$$

where $N(k)$ = total perceived noisiness (noys) at the kth instant in time, combined for all frequency bands

$n(i, k)$ = perceived noisiness (noys) determined in step 1 for the ith octave band at the kth instant in time

$n(k)$ = the maximum value among the 24 values of $n(i, k)$ at the kth instant in time

Step 3 Compute perceived noise level

$$\text{PNL}(k) = 40 + 33.22 \lg N(k) \tag{9.2.5}$$

where PNL(k) is perceived noise level (PNdB) at the kth instant in time, where the unit PNdB distinguishes PNL from measured sound levels in decibels.

Step 4 If there are prominent spectrum irregularities including discrete frequency components or tones, a correction term is added to PNL(k) to obtain tone-corrected perceived noise level PNLT(k). The tone-correction procedure, which accounts for subjective response to pure tones, is described in FAR 36. The maximum value of PNLT(k) is identified as PNLTM, the maximum tone-corrected perceived noise level (PNdB). If there are no pronounced spectrum irregularities, then PNLT(k) = PNL(k) and PNLTM is given by the maximum value of PNL(k).

Step 5 Effective perceived noise level EPNL is determined by an energy average of the PNLT(k) time series over a specified time period which includes the time PNLTM is reached. In integral form the relationship is

$$\text{EPNL} = 10 \lg\left(\frac{1}{T} \int_{t(1)}^{t(2)} 10^{\text{PNLT}/10} \, dt\right) \tag{9.2.6}$$

where   EPNL = effective perceived noise level (EPNdB)

T = 10 s

and $t(1)$ and $t(2)$ are the limits of the significant noise-time history. Using discrete values of PNLT(k) taken at 0.5-s intervals to calculate EPNL, we have the summation form

$$\text{EPNL} = 10 \lg\left[\frac{1}{T} \sum_{k=0}^{d/\Delta t} (\Delta t \, 10^{\text{PNLT}(k)/10})\right]$$

$$= 10 \lg\left(\sum_{k=0}^{2d} 10^{\text{PNLT}(k)/10}\right) - 13 \tag{9.2.7}$$

where Δt = 0.5 s

$d = t(2) - t(1)$ = the interval (s) defined by the points at which PNLT(k) is 10 PNdB less than PNLTM

This interval could be called the 10-dB down interval. If there is more than one peak value of PNLT(k), the limits are chosen to yield the largest possible duration.

Noise Certification Standards for Jet Aircraft

Depending on the aircraft configuration and the date of application for certification, aircraft are required to meet stage 1, 2, or 3 standards (FAA, 1985a). Stage 1 and 2 requirements generally refer to older aircraft designs. However, some newly produced aircraft are based on older type designs. During the lifetime of a particular aircraft design, the manufacturer may attempt to increase capacity and range. As a result, there may be an increase in gross weight and a decrease in climbing performance. This will lead to a demand for increased thrust, which may lead to increased noise levels. The regulations attempt to address this problem by limiting increases in noise level due to design changes.

The requirements of FAR 36 (FAA, 1985a) include exacting test procedures and repeated tests to ensure statistical significance of results. In addition, the regulation provides for trade-offs, where noise levels exceeded at one or two measuring points are offset by measurements at other points. Noise measurement points are located as follows:

> Takeoff: 21,325 ft (6500 m) from the start of the takeoff roll on the extended centerline of the runway.
>
> Approach: 6562 ft (2000 m) from the threshold on the extended centerline of the runway.
>
> Sideline: On a line parallel to and 1476 ft (450 m) from the extended centerline of the runway where the noise after lift-off is greatest. For an airplane powered by more than three turbojet engines, the distance is 0.35 nautical miles to show compliance with stage 1 or 2 limits as applicable.

Some of the stage 2 and 3 noise level limits are indicated below to illustrate the effect of aircraft weight, configuration, and design stage. Values are limits of effective perceived noise level (EPNdB).

Stage 2

Takeoff: 108 EPNdB for maximum weights of 600,000 lb or more, reduced by 5 EPNdB per halving of weight down to 93 EPNdB for 75,000 lb or less.

Sideline and approach: 108 EPNdB for maximum weights of 600,000 lb or more, reduced by 2 EPNdB per halving of weight down to 102 EPNdB for 75,000 lb or less.

Stage 3

Takeoff: Airplanes with more than three engines: 106 EPNdB for maximum weights of 850,000 lb or more, reduced by 4 EPNdB per halving of weight down to 89 EPNdB for 44,673 lb or less. Three engines: 104 EPNdB for maximum weights of 850,000 lb or more, reduced by 4 EPNdB per halving of weight down to 89 EPNdB for 63,177 lb or less. One or two engines: 101 EPNdB for maximum weights of 850,000 lb or more, reduced by 4 EPNdB per halving of weight down to 89 EPNdB for 106,250 lb or less.

Sideline, regardless of number of engines: 103 EPNdB for maximum weights of 882,000 lb or more, reduced by 2.56 EPNdB per halving of weight down to 94 EPNdB for 77,200 lb or less.

Approach, regardless of number of engines: 105 EPNdB for maximum weights of 617,300 lb or more reduced by 2.33 EPNdB per halving of weight down to 98 EPNdB for 77,200 lb.

Propeller-driven Small Airplanes

Certification of small propeller-driven aircraft is based on recordings of the noise produced by six level flights at 1000- (±30) ft altitude over the recording station. Flyovers are made with the airplane in cruise configuration at the highest power in the normal operating range. The following performance correction is added algebraically to the measured value:

$$C_{\text{performance}} = 60 - 20 \lg[(11{,}430 - D_{50})R_C/V_Y + 50] \qquad (9.2.8)$$

where $C_{\text{performance}}$ = the performance correction (dBA), limited to 5 dBA
D_{50} = takeoff distance (ft) to 50 ft at maximum certified weight
R_C = certified best rate of climb (ft/min)
V_Y = speed for best rate of climb (ft/min)

FAR 36 (FAA, 1985a) limits A-weighted sound for recent-design small propeller aircraft to 68 dBA for aircraft weight ≤ 1320 lb (600 kg), increasing at a rate of 1 dBA/165 lb (1 dBA/75 kg) for weights above 1320 lb, but not exceeding 80 dBA for weights between 3300 and 12,500 lb inclusive.

Supersonic Aircraft

In order to operate in the United States, civil supersonic transports (SST's), except Concordes with flight time before 1980, are required to comply with the same FAR 36 stage 2 noise limits which apply to subsonic aircraft. The following restrictions apply to U.S. operations of the excepted British-French Concorde SST's:

1. They may not be modified in any way which increases their noise.
2. Scheduled operations at U.S. airports are prohibited between 10 P.M. and 7 A.M.
3. SST's, whether inside or outside the United States, are prohibited from causing sonic booms in the United States when flying to or from U.S. airports.

Certification tests of the Concorde at Fairbanks, Alaska are reported by Wesler (1975). In the following table, noise levels of the Concorde are compared with reported noise levels of the Russian Tupolev TU-144 SST and FAR 36 limits which would apply to subsonic aircraft of the same weight, certified at that time.

EFFECTIVE PERCEIVED NOISE LEVELS (EPNdB)
AT FAR 36 CERTIFICATION POINTS

	Takeoff	Approach	Sideline
Concorde	118	115	114
TU-144	110	110	114
FAR 36	104	106	106

9.3 AIRPORT NOISE COMPATIBILITY PLANNING

Ideally, noise should be reduced at the source whenever activity interference or annoyance occurs. Aircraft certification procedures, which were discussed in Section 9.2, are one attempt at source noise reduction which may be combined with a program of retrofitting current aircraft with quieter engine nacelles. Other strategies to reduce noise impact include:

1. Acquisition of land.
2. Acquisition of air rights, easements, and development rights to ensure that land uses are compatible with airport operations.
3. Barrier construction to reduce noise transmission from ground operations.
4. Soundproofing of public buildings.
5. Implementation of a preferential runway system.
6. Changes in flight paths to reduce exposure of noise-sensitive areas.
7. Denial of airport use to aircraft which do not meet certain noise standards.
8. Airport capacity limitations based on noise levels of different aircraft types.
9. A noise allotment plan, giving each airline a noise budget (to encourage use of quieter aircraft by airlines wishing to schedule more flights).
10. Use of noise-abatement takeoff and approach procedures.
11. Implementation of landing fees based on noise emission levels and on time of arrival.
12. Curfews (e.g., prohibiting jet aircraft takeoffs or landings between 11 P.M. and 6:30 A.M.).
13. Land use controls.

The last of the above items, land use controls, puts the burden of noise impact control on the community surrounding an airport, rather than on the airport or airport users. However, governmental policy and court decisions have required a weighting and balancing of air transportation and air commerce objectives against the social, community, and other real interests affected by aircraft noise. The U.S. Federal Aviation Administration (FAR 150, 1985b) has identified compatible land uses based on day–night sound level L_{DN}. These land uses, given in Table 9.3.1, may be compared with predicted or measured yearly average L_{DN}. Note that these levels may differ from other community noise standards. For example, the EPA (1974, 1978) identifies $L_{DN} \leq 55$ dBA as the protective level for activity interference and annoyance outdoors in residential areas and farms and other outdoor areas where people spend widely

TABLE 9.3.1 LAND USE COMPATIBILITY[a] WITH YEARLY DAY–NIGHT AVERAGE SOUND LEVELS

Land use	Yearly day–night average sound level (L_{DN}) (dB)					
	Below 65	65 to 70	70 to 75	75 to 80	80 to 85	Over 85
Residential						
Residential, other than mobile homes and transient lodgings	Y	N[b]	N[b]	N	N	N
Mobile home parks	Y	N	N	N	N	N
Transient lodgings	Y	N[b]	N[b]	N[b]	N	N
Public use						
Schools	Y	N[b]	N[b]	N	N	N
Hospitals and nursing homes	Y	25	30	N	N	N
Churches, auditoriums, and concert halls	Y	25	30	N	N	N
Governmental services	Y	Y	25	30	Y[e]	Y[e]
Transportation	Y	Y	Y[c]	Y[d]	Y[e]	N
Parking	Y	Y	Y[c]	Y[d]	Y[e]	N
Commercial use						
Offices, business and professional	Y	Y	25	30	N	N
Wholesale and retail—building materials, hardware, and farm equipment	Y	Y	Y[c]	Y[d]	Y[e]	N
Retail trade—general	Y	Y	25	30	N	N
Utilities	Y	Y	Y[c]	Y[d]	Y[e]	N
Communication	Y	Y	25	30	N	N
Manufacturing and production						
Manufacturing, general	Y	Y	Y[c]	Y[d]	Y[e]	N
Photographic and optical	Y	Y	25	30	N	N
Agriculture (except livestock) and forestry	Y	Y[g]	Y[h]	Y[i]	Y[i]	Y[i]
Livestock farming and breeding	Y	Y[g]	Y[h]	N	N	N
Mining and fishing, resource production, and extraction	Y	Y	Y	Y	Y	Y

Recreational

Outdoor sports arenas and spectator sports	Y	Yᶠ	N	N	N
Outdoor music shells, amphitheaters	Y	N	N	N	N
Nature exhibits and zoos	Y	Y	N	N	N
Amusements, parks, resorts, and camps	Y	Y	N	N	N
Golf courses, riding stables, and water recreation	Y	Y	25	30	N

Y (Yes) Land use and related structures compatible without restrictions.

N (No) Land use and related structures are not compatible and should be prohibited.

NLR Noise level reduction (outdoor to indoor) to be achieved through incorporation of noise attenuation into the design and construction of the structure.

25, 30, or 35 Land used and related structures generally compatible: measures to achieve NLR of 25, 30, or 35 dB must be incorporated into design and construction of structure.

[a] The designations contained in this table do not constitute a federal determination that any use of land covered by the program is acceptable or unacceptable under federal, state, or local law. The responsibility for determining the acceptable and permissible land uses and the relationship between specific properties and specific noise contours rests with the local authorities. FAA determinations under part 150 are not intended to substitute federally determined land uses for those determined to be appropriate by local authorities in response to locally determined needs and values in achieving noise compatible land uses.

[b] Where the community determines that residential or school uses must be allowed, measures to achieve outdoor to indoor Noise Level Reduction (NLR) of at least 25 dB and 30 dB should be incorporated into building codes and be considered in individual approvals. Normal residential construction can be expected to provide an NLR of 20 dB, thus, the reduction requirements are often stated as 5, 10 or 15 dB over standard construction and normally assume mechanical ventilation and closed windows year round. However, the use of NLR criteria will not eliminate outdoor noise problems.

[c] Measures to achieve NLR of 25 dB must be incorporated into the design and construction of portions of these buildings where the public is received, office areas, noise sensitive areas, or where the normal noise level is low.

[d] Measures to achieve NLR of 30 dB must be incorporated into the design and construction of portions of these buildings where the public is received, office areas, noise sensitive areas, or where the normal noise level is low.

[e] Measures to achieve NLR of 35 dB must be incorporated into the design and construction of portions of these buildings where the public is received, office areas, noise sensitive areas, or where the normal noise level is low.

[f] Land use compatible provided special sound reinforcement systems are installed.

[g] Residential buildings require an NLR of 25.

[h] Residential buildings require an NLR of 30.

[i] Residential buildings not permitted.

Source: FAA (1985b).

varying amounts of time and other places in which quiet is a basis for use. By contrast, FAR 150 lists $L_{DN} < 65$ dBA as compatible with residential use, and other uses listed in Table 9.3.1 are considered compatible with noise levels varying from $L_{DN} < 65$ dBA to $L_{DN} > 85$ dBA.

The Federal Aviation Administration states that it is not the intent of the agency, through FAR 150, to encourage one noise abatement alternative over another, but to provide a planning and implementation approach to ensure that maximum noise abatement benefits are derived in a manner that does not place an undue burden on air commerce, is not discriminatory, and does not adversely affect the safe and efficient use of airspace.

Noise Exposure Maps

In order to foster compatible land use, airport operators may submit the following:

1. Noise exposure maps based on data as of the date of submission.
2. Noise exposure maps based on forecast aircraft operations five years after submission (based on assumptions concerning future type and frequency of aircraft operations, number of nighttime operations, flight patterns, planned airport development, planned land use changes, and demographic changes in the surrounding area).
3. An indication of the nature and extent forecast operations will affect compatibility of land uses.

To determine the extent of noise impact around an airport, the noise exposure maps are to indicate the following:

1. Continuous contours for annual average L_{DN} = 65, 70, and 75 dBA, and other contours where appropriate.
2. Runways, flight paths, and airport boundaries.
3. Noncompatible land uses within the contours including the L_{DN} = 65 contour (land is not identified as noncompatible if self-generated noise, and noise due to nonaircraft and nonairport sources is equal to or greater than noise from airport and aircraft sources).
4. The location of schools, hospitals, and other noise-sensitive public buildings.
5. Locations of aircraft monitoring sites.
6. Estimates of the number of people residing within the L_{DN} = 65, 70, and 75 dBA contours.

Figure 9.3.1 shows a noise contour map typical of a major international airport. Predictions are based on adoption of quiet-engine jet aircraft. Flight paths have been adjusted so that much of the area within the L_{DN} = 65 and 75 dBA contours consists of water, unoccupied swamp, and land protected against development by conservation regulations. The irregular contour lines represent the boundaries of various 1-mi^2 tracts of land in the impact area. These tracts were examined in order to determine the number of individuals, the land area, the number of buildings, and the value of property within the 65- and 75-dBA contours.

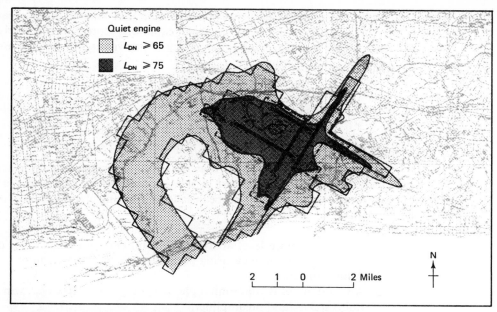

Figure 9.3.1 A noise contour map typical of a large international airport.

Noise Measurements

Noise contours for current conditions may be based on measurements. Day–night sound levels based on measured values are defined by

$$L_{DN} = 10 \lg\left[\frac{1}{86400}\left(\int_{7\text{A.M.}}^{10\text{P.M.}} 10^{L/10}dt + \int_{10\text{P.M.}}^{7\text{A.M.}} 10^{(L+10)/10}dt\right)\right] \quad (9.3.1)$$

where L_{DN} = day–night sound level (dBA) based on measurements for one 24-hour (86,400-s) day

   L = instantaneous A-weighted, slow response sound level (dBA)

   t = time (s)

Equivalent sound levels may be determined for the daytime and nighttime periods and combined, yielding an alternative expression for day–night sound level:

$$L_{DN} = 10 \lg\left[\frac{1}{24}\left(15 \times 10^{L_{eqD}/10} + 9 \times 10^{(L_{eqN}+10)/10}\right)\right] \quad (9.3.2)$$

where L_{DN} = day–night sound level for one 24-hour day

$$L_{eqD} = 10 \lg\left[\frac{1}{54,000}\left(\int_{7\text{A.M.}}^{10\text{P.M.}} 10^{L/10}dt\right)\right] \quad (9.3.3)$$

$$L_{eqN} = 10 \lg\left[\frac{1}{32,400}\left(\int_{10\text{P.M.}}^{7\text{A.M.}} 10^{(L+10)/10}dt\right)\right] \quad (9.3.4)$$

   L = instantaneous sound level (dBA)

   t = time (s)

If the selected 24-hour measuring period is typical of any day in the year, the value of L_{DN} obtained from either of the above equations represents the yearly day–night average sound level. If there is significant day-to-day variation in airport use, the yearly average is computed from

$$L_{DN} = 10 \lg\left(\frac{1}{365} \sum_{i=1}^{365} 10^{L_{DNi}/10}\right) \qquad (9.3.5)$$

where L_{DN} = yearly average day–night sound level (dBA)
         L_{DNi} = day–night sound level (dBA) for one 24-hour day

Recordings of airport noise may be obtained using portable instrumentation tape recorders, and then analyzed in a laboratory. As an alternative, a permanent outdoor measurement system may be installed, consisting of some or all of the following components:

1. A portable noise level analyzer for computation of L_{eq}, L_{DN}, or other descriptors based on measuring periods up to 24 hours or more.
2. A built-in printer.
3. An outdoor all-weather microphone system with rain cover, windscreen, antibird spikes, and preamplifier.
4. A weatherproof housing, amplifier, calibration oscillator, dehumidifier, and power supply.

9.4 AIRCRAFT NOISE PREDICTION

A computer prediction model, the integrated noise model (INM), is available for airport operators to use in developing noise contours. The INM is available to the public to provide interested parties the opportunity to substantiate results. The following input information must be obtained to use the INM or an equivalent model:

1. A map of the airport and environs indicating runways, landing thresholds, takeoff start-of-roll points, airport boundaries, and flight tracks out to at least 30,000 ft from the end of each runway.
2. Daytime and nighttime airport activity levels and operational data, including aircraft by type using each flight track.
3. Approach profiles and engine power levels.
4. Takeoff profiles and engine power levels. Use of noise-abatement departure procedures, and takeoff weight if applicable.
5. Topographical and airspace restrictions.
6. Government-furnished aircraft noise characteristics data. (This data may already be part of the computer program's data base.)
7. Airport elevation and average temperature.

Noise contour maps are available for most major civil and military airports. Noise levels may be interpolated for locations between contours. Since these maps are based on aircraft operations only, it is necessary to combine noise levels from surface transportation sources or other significant contributors to evaluate total noise level at a site. Many of the older maps use noise exposure forecast (NEF), composite noise rating (CNR), or community noise equivalent level (CNEL) as descriptors. There is no precise relationship between these descriptors and day–night sound level (L_{DN}), since measurement and prediction methods differ. However, approximate relationships can be developed.

Composite Noise Rating (CNR)

At one time, CNR was widely used to evaluate land use around airports (EPA, March 1974). It is based on single-event perceived noise level (PNL) without time duration correction or tone correction. To determine PNL, we acquire a time-frequency array of one-third octave-band sound pressure levels at a given location, and apply equations 9.2.1 through 9.2.5. This procedure yields the series PNL(k), the perceived noise level (PNdB) at the kth instant in time. CNR is then given by

$$\text{CNR} = \text{PNLM} + 10 \lg(N_D + 16.7 N_N) - 12 \tag{9.4.1}$$

where   CNR = composite noise rating (PNdB)
     PNLM = the maximum value of PNL(k) (PNdB)
     N_D = number of flyovers between 7 A.M. and 10 P.M.
     N_N = number of flyovers between 10 P.M. and 7 A.M.

If the location in question is subject to noise from several types of aircraft operating from more than runway, or using various flight paths, then the combined composite noise rating is given by

$$\text{CNR}_{\text{combined}} = 10 \lg\left(\sum_{i=1}^{m} \sum_{j=1}^{n} 10^{\text{CNR}ij/10}\right) \tag{9.4.2}$$

where $\text{CNR}_{\text{combined}}$ = composite noise rating (PNdB) for all aircraft operations near the site
     m = the number of aircraft types
     n = the number of flight paths affecting the site
     CNR_{ij} = composite noise rating (PNdB) for the ith aircraft type on the jth flight path

These values may be measured at the site or calculated from aircraft noise certification data. To obtain a rough approximation for day–night sound level, we may use

$$L_{DN} = \text{CNR}_{\text{combined}} - 35 \tag{9.4.3}$$

where L_{DN} = day–night sound level at the site (dBA ± about 3 dBA).

Noise Exposure Forecast (NEF)

NEF has been the most widely used descriptor for aircraft noise prediction. It is based on effective perceived noise level (EPNL), which is given by equations 9.2.1 through 9.2.7, or estimated by the following equation:

$$\text{EPNL} = \text{PNLM} + \lg\left[\frac{t(2) - t(1)}{20}\right] + F \tag{9.4.4}$$

where EPNL = approximate effective perceived noise level (EPNdB)

PNLM = maximum perceived noise level (PNdB) during a flyover, as defined above

$t(2) - t(1)$ = the interval (seconds) of significant noise-time history during the flyover, that is, the interval between the 10-dB down points

F = the tone or spectral irregularity correction (dB)

$F = 0$ if there are no prominent tones or spectral irregularities in the noise. For typical aircraft noise, $0 \leq F \leq 3$ dB.

The noise exposure forecast contribution of a single aircraft type on one flight path is given by

$$\text{NEF}_{ij} = \text{EPNL}_{ij} + 10 \lg\left(\frac{N_{Dij}}{20} + \frac{N_{Nij}}{1.2}\right) - 75 \qquad (9.4.5)$$

where NEF_{ij} = the contribution of the ith aircraft type on the jth flight path

EPNL_{ij} = effective perceived noise level for that aircraft (EPNdB)

N_{Dij} and N_{Nij} = the number of the ith aircraft type on the jth flight path during a typical day (7 A.M. to 10 P.M.) or night (10 P.M. to 7 A.M.), respectively

The noise exposure forecast at a particular location is given by

$$\text{NEF} = 10 \lg\left(\sum_{i=1}^{m} \sum_{j=1}^{n} 10^{\text{NEF}_{ij}/10}\right) \qquad (9.4.6)$$

where NEF = noise exposure forecast for all aircraft operations (in dB units, but expressed as NEF 20, NEF 25, etc.)

m = the number of aircraft types

n = the number of flight paths affecting the site

If the site in question is exposed to noise from only one runway noise exposure forecast may be approximated by

$$\text{NEF} = \text{EPNL}_{\text{mean}} + 10 \lg(N_D + 16.7N_N) - 88 \qquad (9.4.7)$$

where $\text{EPNL}_{\text{mean}}$ = energy average EPNL (EPNdB), that is, EPNL for one typical flyover

N_D and N_N = the total number of flyovers during the day (7 A.M. to 10 P.M.) and night (10 P.M. to 7 A.M.), respectively

NEF may be converted to approximate day–night sound level by the following equation:

$$L_{DN} = \text{NEF} + 35 \qquad (9.4.8)$$

where L_{DN} = day–night sound level at the site (dBA ± about 3 dBA).

Community Noise Equivalent Level (CNEL)

Community noise equivalent level is based on single-event noise exposure level, which is approximated by

$$\text{SENEL} = L_{\text{max}} + 10 \lg\{[t(2) - t(1)]/2\} \qquad (9.4.9)$$

where   SENEL = single-event noise exposure level (dB*A*)
L_{max} = maximum *A*-weighted sound level during a flyover
$t(2) - t(1)$ = the effective event duration (s) given by the interval between the 10-dB*A* down points

Community noise equivalent level is given by

$$CNEL = SENEL_{mean} + 10 \lg(N_d + 3N_e + 10N_n) - 49.4 \qquad (9.4.10)$$

where   CNEL = community noise equivalent level (dB*A*)
$SENEL_{mean}$ = energy average SENEL (dB*A*), that is, SENEL for one typical flyover
N_d = number of flyovers between 7 A.M. and 7 P.M.
N_e = flyovers 7 P.M. to 10 P.M.
N_n = flyovers 10 P.M. to 7 A.M.

If it is necessary to convert forecasts in terms of CNEL to L_{DN} the approximate relationship is

$$L_{DN} = CNEL \pm 3 \text{ dB}A \qquad (9.4.11)$$

Equivalent Sound Level (L_{eq}) and Day–Night Sound Level (L_{DN})

Wherever practical, equivalent sound level should be measured with an integrating sound level meter or noise level analyzer, or determined from representative measurements according to equations 9.3.1 through 9.3.5. If single events strongly dominate the total noise exposure, the following estimate may be used for day–night sound level:

$$L_{DN} = SENEL_{mean} + 10 \lg(N_D + 10N_N) - 49.4 \qquad (9.4.12)$$

where L_{DN} = the contribution of these events (flyovers) to total noise (dB*A*)
N_D = number of flyovers between 7 A.M. and 10 P.M.
N_N = flyovers 10 P.M. to 7 A.M.

Mapping Predicted Noise Contours

Current noise contour maps and future noise contour maps are unavailable for some airports. Although airport operators must base noise contour determinations on FAA approved methods, this amount of detail may be unnecessary in some other instances. The procedure that follows may be used to estimate jet aircraft noise for determination of site acceptability.

   1. Obtain a map or site plan of the airport and a map of the surrounding area.
   2. Determine the current number of daytime and nighttime jet aircraft operations on each runway, and the major flight path patterns.
   3. Determine expected changes in aircraft volume and flight paths, and proposed runway construction for the future years that are of interest.
   4. Calculate the effective number of jets using a given runway:

$$N = N_D + 10N_N \qquad (9.4.13)$$

where N = effective number of jet operations on that runway
         N_D = the number of jet operations (takeoffs and landings) on that runway between 7 A.M. and 10 P.M. on a typical day
         N_N = 10 P.M. to 7 A.M. operations

5. Determine approximate L_{DN} contour distances based on the effective number of flights. Charts for estimating L_{DN} contour locations for aircraft operations are given by HUD (1983). Referring to Figure 9.4.1, these distances give the extent of each noise contour beyond the runway, and to the sides of the runway. The approximate contour distances can also be expressed in equation form as follows:

$$A = WN^x \tag{9.4.14}$$

$$B = YN^z \tag{9.4.15}$$

where A and B are lateral and longitudinal distances (ft) from a given runway, respectively, and W, X, Y, and Z are constants given by the following table:

	Contour location constants			
L_{DN} contour	W	X	Y	Z
65	510	0.401	1460	0.567
70	426	0.356	668	0.606
75	296	0.340	292	0.658

6. After determining contour distances A and B, each L_{DN} contour is plotted as in the figure. If the airport has more than one runway, the process is repeated for each runway.

7. For locations between the contours, L_{DN} exposure levels may be estimated by interpolation. For locations beyond the L_{DN} = 65 dBA contour, exposure levels may be estimated from the inverse-square law as follows:

$$\Delta L = 20 \lg\left(\frac{D_2}{D_1}\right) \tag{9.4.16}$$

where D_2 = the distance from the runway or flight path to the point in question
         D_1 = the distance from the runway or flight path to the L_{DN} = 65 dBA contour

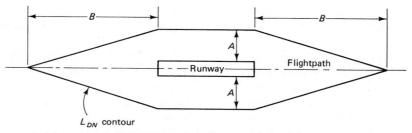

Figure 9.4.1 Approximate day–night sound level contour.

ΔL = the value (dBA) to be subtracted from the contour value, that is, the exposure (dBA) at location D_2 is given by

$$L_{DN} = 65 - \Delta L \qquad (9.4.17)$$

8. In order to estimate the location of contours outside of the L_{DN} = 75, 70, and 65 contours, equation 9.4.16 may be rewritten in the form

$$\frac{D_2}{D_1} = 10^{\Delta L/20} \qquad (9.4.18)$$

9. For locations that are close to two runways, the contours should be adjusted to account for combined contributions from both runways. Consider a location near the intersection of the L_{DN} = 65 dBA contours of two runways. The L_{DN} = 62 dBA contours may be estimated in that region by using the above equation, where

$$\Delta L = 3 \text{ dB}A$$

The result is

$$\frac{D_2}{D_1} = 10^{3/20} = 1.41$$

At the intersection of the two L_{DN} = 62 dBA contours, the combined day–night sound level is L_{DN} = 65 dBA, and the 65-dBA contour is adjusted to go through that point.

Note that the procedure outlined above neglects noise level differences due to aircraft types and due to variations in landing and takeoff procedures. Thus, the results might be considered a first approximation. This first approximation could be used to decide if more precise studies were called for (e.g., use of the FAA integrated noise model).

EXAMPLE PROBLEM: AIRPORT NOISE CONTOURS

A proposed airport improvement will result in the following air traffic volume. On a typical 24-hour day there will be 80 daytime (7 A.M. to 10 P.M.) jet aircraft operations

TABLE 9.4.1 APPROXIMATE DAY–NIGHT SOUND
LEVEL CONTOUR DISTANCES

Jet aircraft operations				
Runway 1 day: 80		night: 6	$N_{(effective)}$: 140	
Runway 2 day: 55		night: 4	$N_{(effective)}$: 95	

Distance LDN contour	A1	B1	A2	B2
75	1,588	7,543	1,392	5,844
70	2,474	13,345	2,155	10,551
65	3,700	24,055	3,167	19,307
62	5,226	33,979	4,473	27,272
60	6,579	42,777	5,632	34,334
57	9,293	60,424	7,955	48,498
55	11,700	76,069	10,015	61,055
52	16,526	107,450	14,146	86,243

on runway 4-22 and 6 jet operations at night (10 P.M. to 7 A.M.). Runway 13-31 will have 55 daytime and 4 nighttime jet operations. Each runway will be 12,000 ft long, and 1000 ft wide. The southernmost point on runway 4-22 will be 2000 ft due east of the southernmost point on runway 13-31. Plot approximate noise contours.

Solution. The runway configuration is shown in Figure 9.4.2. Runway designations apply to orientation in tens of degrees. Thus, runway 4-22 is oriented at 40° (roughly northeast), or 220° when approached from the other end. The effective number of jet operations on runway 4-22 is given by

$$N = N_D + 10N_N = 80 + 10 \times 6 = 140$$

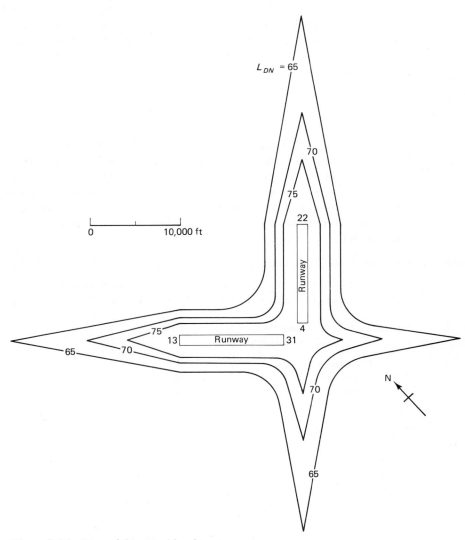

Figure 9.4.2 Day–night sound level contours.

Using the above equations and table, we find that the $L_{DN} = 65$ dBA contour is located a distance

$$A = WN^x = 510 \times 140^{0.401} = 3700 \text{ ft}$$

to each side of runway 4-22, and

$$B = YN^z = 1460 \times 140^{0.567} = 24,055 \text{ ft}$$

beyond each end of the runway.

The $L_{DN} = 70$ and 75 dBA are similarly located, with the results given in Table 9.4.1, where $A1$ and $B1$ refer to runway 4-22, and $A2$ and $B2$ to runway 13-31. The L_{DN} contours are plotted in Figure 9.4.2. Distances for contours outside of the $L_{DN} = 65$ dBA contour are located by the equation

$$D_2 = D_1 10^{(65-L_2)/20}$$

where D_2 = the distance to the $L_{DN} = L_2$ contour
  D_1 = the distance to the $L_{DN} = 65$ contour

Contours at large distances are of doubtful validity, since air attenuation and noise from other sources were not considered.

BIBLIOGRAPHY

Dwyer, R. F., "Extraction of helicopter-radiated noise by frequency domain processing," *J. Acoust. Soc. Am.* **78**(1), 95–99, 1985.

Environmental Protection Agency, Information on levels of environmental noise requisite to protect public health and welfare with an adequate margin of safety, EPA 550/9-74-004, March 1974.

Environmental Protection Agency, Protective noise levels, EPA 550/9-79-100, November 1978.

Federal Aviation Administration, Federal aviation regulations part 36, Noise standards: aircraft type and airworthiness certification, August 12, 1985a.

Federal Aviation Administration, Federal aviation regulations part 150, Airport noise compatibility planning, January 18, 1985b.

HMSO, Noise—final report, Cmnd. 2056, London, July 1963.

Lighthill, M. J., *Proc. Royal Soc. (London)* **A211,** 564–587, 1952.

Lush, P. A., "Measurement of subsonic jet noise and comparison with theory," *J. Fluid Mechanics* **46,** 477–550, 1971.

Olson, W. A., O. Gutierez, and R. Dorsch, "The effect of nozzle inlet shape, lip thickness, and exit shape and size on subsonic jet noise," NASA Report TMX-68182, 1973.

Pallett, D., R. Wehrli, R. Kilmer, and T. Quindry, Design guide for reducing transportation noise in and around buildings, National Bureau of Standards, April 1978.

Raney, J. R., and J. M. Cawthorn, "Aircraft noise," *Handbook of Noise Control,* 2nd ed., 34-1 to 34-18, C. M. Harris, Ed, McGraw–Hill, New York, 1979.

Schomer, P. D., "High-energy impulsive noise assessment," *J. Acoust. Soc. Am.* **79**(1), 182–185, 1986.

Schomer, P. D., and R. D. Neathammer, "The role of helicopter noise-induced vibration and rattle in human response," *J. Acoust. Soc. Am.* **81**(4), 966–975, 1987.

U.S. Department of Housing and Urban Development, Noise assessment guidelines, 4–5, August 1983.

von Gierke, H. E., "Physical characteristics of aircraft noise sources" (reprinted from *J. Acoust. Soc. Am.* **25**, 367–378, 1953), *Noise Control,* M. J. Crocker, Ed, Van Nostrand Reinhold, New York, 1984.

Wesler, J. E., "Noise and induced vibration levels from Concorde and subsonic aircraft," *Sound and Vibration* **9**(10), 18–23, 1975.

Wesler, J. E., "Aircraft noise and structural vibration," *Sound and Vibration* **12**(2), 24–28, 1978.

PROBLEMS

9.1.1. The velocity of a jet is to be reduced by 50% while thrust is to be maintained.
  (a) Estimate the effect on sound power.
  (b) Find the resulting change in sound power level.

9.1.2. The velocity of a jet is to be reduced by 20% while thrust is to be maintained.
  (a) Estimate the effect on sound power.
  (b) Find the resulting change in sound power level.

9.1.3. The velocity of a jet is to be decreased by 10%.
  (a) Estimate the effect on sound power if the jet diameter is unchanged.
  (b) Find the resulting change in sound power level.

9.1.4. The velocity of a jet is to be increased by 33%.
  (a) Estimate the effect on sound power if the jet diameter is unchanged.
  (b) Find the resulting change in sound power level.

9.2.1. At one instant in time the following sound levels (dB) were recorded in the 24 one-third octave bands from 50 to 10,000 Hz.
  64, 62, 60, 63, 61, 58, 59, 65, 62, 61, 68, 69, 63, 70, 68, 67, 60, 59, 55, 53, 52, 50, 48, 44.
  (a) Compute perceived noisiness (noys).
  (b) Compute perceived noise level (PNdB).

9.2.2. At one instant in time the following sound levels (dB) were recorded in the 24 one-third octave bands from 50 to 10,000 Hz.
  70, 65, 60, 57, 61, 58, 59, 65, 62, 61, 68, 69, 63, 70, 71, 60, 59, 55, 53, 52, 50, 48, 47, 42.
  (a) Compute perceived noisiness (noys).
  (b) Compute perceived noise level (PNdB).

9.3.1. There are 310 daytime (7 A.M. to 10 P.M.) operations and 17 nighttime (10 P.M. to 7 A.M.) operations during a typical 24-hour day at a general aviation airport. At a nearby site, a typical operation produces an energy average sound level of 62 dB*A* for 50 s. Daytime background noise levels average 52 dB*A*, and nighttime background noise levels 45 dB*A*. Compute day–night sound level at the site:
  (a) based on aircraft operations alone
  (b) based on all contributions

9.3.2. There are 155 daytime (7 A.M. to 10 P.M.) operations and 30 nighttime (10 P.M. to 7 A.M.) operations during a typical 24-hour day at a general aviation airport. At a nearby site, a typical operation produces an energy average sound level of 84 dB*A* for 90 s.

Daytime background noise levels average 50 dB*A*, and nighttime background noise levels 40 dB*A*. Compute day–night sound level at the site:

(a) based on aircraft operations alone

(b) based on all contributions

9.4.1. At the instant that sound levels were a maximum during a typical event, the following sound levels (dB) were recorded in the 24 one-third octave bands from 50 to 10,000 Hz. 65, 63, 61, 58, 59, 65, 62, 61, 68, 69, 63, 70, 68, 67, 60, 59, 55, 53, 52, 50, 48, 44, 43, 44.

(a) Compute (maximum) perceived noise level for this event.

(b) There were 150 such events between 7 A.M. and 10 P.M. and 22 between 10 P.M. and 7 A.M. Compute composite noise rating for these events.

(c) Estimate day–night sound level.

9.4.2. The interval between the 10-dB down points, $t(2) - t(1) = 20$ s for the typical event (flyover) described above.

(a) Compute noise exposure forecast based on the given number of flyovers.

(b) Estimate day–night sound level from the computed value of noise exposure forecast.

9.4.3. An airport improvement is proposed which will result in an average of 45 daytime (7 A.M. to 10 P.M.) jet aircraft operations and 4 nighttime (10 P.M. to 7 A.M.) operations on runway 2-20. Runway 11-29 will have 35 daytime and 2 nighttime operations. Each runway is 11,000 ft long and 1000 ft wide. The eastern end of runway 11-29 is 2000 ft west of the southern end of runway 2-20. Plot approximate day–night sound level contours.

9.4.4. An airport improvement is proposed which will result in an average of 200 daytime (7 A.M. to 10 P.M.) jet aircraft operations and 22 nighttime (10 P.M. to 7 A.M.) operations on runway 1-19. Runway 11-29 will have 185 daytime and 15 nighttime operations. Each runway will be 12,000 ft long and 1000 ft wide. The eastern end of runway 11-29 will be 2000 ft west of the southern end of runway 1-19. Determine the approximate location of the 65-, 70-, and 75-dB*A* day–night sound level contours.

9.4.5. An airport improvement is proposed which will result in an average of 112 daytime (7 A.M. to 10 P.M.) jet aircraft operations and no nighttime (10 P.M. to 7 A.M.) operations on one runway. Another runway will have 60 daytime and 6 nighttime operations. Each runway is 11,000 ft long and 1000 ft wide. The runways are perpendicular, and intersect to form an "L." Determine the approximate location of the 65-, 70-, and 75-dB*A* day–night sound level contours.

9.4.6. A north–south and an east–west runway are planned for an airport improvement which will result in an average of 30 daytime (7 A.M. to 10 P.M.) jet aircraft operations and 2 nighttime (10 P.M. to 7 A.M.) operations on the north–south runway. The east–west runway will have 19 daytime and 1 nighttime operations. Each runway is 10,000 ft long and 1000 ft wide. The eastern end of one runway is adjacent to the northern end of the other. Determine the approximate location of the 65-, 70-, and 75-dB*A* day–night sound level contours.

9.4.7. An airport improvement is proposed which will result in an average of 500 daytime (7 A.M. to 10 P.M.) jet aircraft operations and 85 nighttime (10 P.M. to 7 A.M.) operations on runway 2-20. Runway 11-29 will have 200 daytime and 40 nighttime operations. Each runway is 13,000 ft long and 1500 ft wide. The eastern end of runway 11-29 is 2000 ft west of the southern end of runway 2-20. Determine the approximate location of the 65-, 70-, and 75-dB*A* day–night sound level contours.

Chapter 10

Vibration Analysis and Control

Noise problems often result from vibration of large surfaces. If the vibration results from imbalance, it may be possible to correct the imbalance. In other cases, isolation of the source of the vibration energy from surfaces that would act as radiators of sound is a more effective solution. In many systems, additional vibration damping helps to reduce vibration-induced noise. However, incorrect analysis may lead one to add damping in a manner that increases vibration transmission and worsens a noise problem.

10.1 BASIC ONE-DEGREE-OF-FREEDOM SYSTEMS

A basic one-degree-of-freedom system is modeled as a mass, a spring, and a damper (Figure 10.1.1). The mass is constrained to motion in only the x-direction, and the variables and system components are as follows:

Item	Symbol	Units	
External force	$F(t)$	lb	N
Displacement	$x(t)$	in	m
Mass	M	lb-s^2/in	kg
Damper (viscous damping coefficient)	C	lb-s/in	N·s/m
Spring (spring rate)	K	lb/in	N/m

Consider all of the forces acting on the mass including the inertia effect (reverse effective force) when the system is in motion. Equilibrium of forces yields the equation

$$M \frac{d^2x}{dt^2} + C \frac{dx}{dt} + Kx = F(t) \qquad (10.1.1)$$

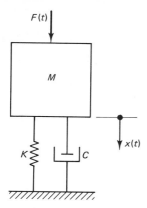

Figure 10.1.1 Basic one-degree-of-freedom model.

where t = time (s), and if English units are used
$M = W/g$
W = supported weight (lb)
g = 386 in/s^2 (approx.) the acceleration of gravity at sea level

Free, Damped Vibration

Damping represents the energy dissipation due to hysteresis, air friction, sliding friction, and other causes. The damping force may be proportional to velocity, or to velocity squared, or to some other power of velocity. Sliding friction is sometimes represented by a constant force magnitude in a direction opposite the velocity. Viscous damping, proportional to and opposing velocity, is a reasonable model in many cases. Another reason for the selection of viscous damping as a model is that it results in equations that are easy to treat mathematically. The equation describing the free, viscously damped, one-degree-of-freedom system is

$$M \frac{d^2x}{dt^2} + C \frac{dx}{dt} + Kx = 0 \tag{10.1.2}$$

For lightly damped and moderately damped systems, the above equation is satisfied by a displacement function in the form of exponentially decaying harmonic motion:

$$x = e^{-Ct/(2M)} \left[X_0 \cos(\omega_d t) + \left(\frac{V_0}{\omega_d} + \frac{CX_0}{2M\omega_d} \right) \sin(\omega_d t) \right] \tag{10.1.3}$$

where e = the base of natural logarithms
$\omega_d = [K/M - C^2/(2M)^2]^{1/2}$ = the damped natural angular frequency of vibration (rad/s)

As observed in Chapter 1, the natural frequency of a one-degree-of-freedom system without damping is $\omega_n = (K/M)^{1/2}$.

Critical Damping

Inspection of the frequency term in the above equation shows that the decaying harmonic form is not valid for highly damped systems, that is, for

$$\frac{C^2}{(2M)^2} \geq \frac{K}{M}$$

Such systems are called critically damped and overdamped systems. The value of the damping coefficient, for which

$$\frac{C^2}{(2M)^2} = \frac{K}{M}$$

is called the critical damping coefficient. Thus,

$$C_c = 2(KM)^{1/2} \tag{10.1.4}$$

where C_c = the critical damping coefficient (lb-s/in or N·s/m). The displacement-time relationship for critically damped systems is given by

$$x = e^{-C_c t/(2M)}\left[X_0 + \left(V_0 + C_c \frac{X_0}{2M}\right)t\right] \tag{10.1.5}$$

After reaching its greatest positive or negative displacement from the equilibrium position, the mass in a critically damped system returns toward the equilibrium position, without oscillation. The solution form for overdamped systems (which are of little interest in noise control) consists of decaying exponentials without harmonic components. Systems with less-than-critical damping ($C < C_c$) are called underdamped. The damping ratio is defined as the ratio of the damping coefficient to the critical damping coefficient

$$r_d = \frac{C}{C_c} \tag{10.1.6}$$

where r_d = the damping ratio for viscous damping.

Logarithmic Decrement

It is possible to estimate the damping coefficient by observing the change in displacement amplitude with time, in free vibration of underdamped systems. Suppose displacement amplitude is found to be $X(T)$, measured at time T, and $X(T + \tau_d)$ one vibrational period later, where $\tau_d = 2\pi/\omega_d$ = the period of damped vibration (s). Referring to equation 10.1.3 for damped free vibration, we see that the harmonic component of the displacement is identical at times $t = T$ and $t = T + \tau_d$. The ratio of displacement amplitudes is given by

$$\frac{X(T)}{X(T + \tau_d)} = \frac{e^{-CT/(2M)}}{e^{-C(T + \tau_d)/(2M)}}$$

$$= e^{C\tau_d/(2M)} = e^Z \tag{10.1.7}$$

where Z = the logarithmic decrement. Taking the natural logarithm of both sides of the above equation, we have

$$Z = \ln\left[\frac{X(T)}{X(T + \tau_d)}\right]$$

$$= \frac{C\tau_d}{2M} = \frac{C\pi}{M\omega_d} \qquad (10.1.8)$$

EXAMPLE PROBLEM: FREE, DAMPED VIBRATION

A 20-lb body is supported on mounts with an effective spring rate of 50 lb/in. The mass is struck to excite it into vibration. Instrumentation attached to the mass indicates the following amplitude ratios:

$$\frac{X(T)}{X(T + 4\tau_d)} = 1.28$$

$$\frac{X(T)}{X(T + 8\tau_d)} = 1.65$$

(a) Find undamped natural frequency.

Solution. If there were no damping, the system would oscillate at

$$f_n = \frac{(K/M)^{1/2}}{2\pi} = \frac{(Kg/W)^{1/2}}{2\pi}$$

$$= \frac{(50 \times 386/20)^{1/2}}{2\pi} = 4.9441 \text{ Hz}$$

(b) Find the logarithmic decrement.

Solution. Measurements were made over several periods to increase accuracy. For viscous damping, the logarithmic decrement is a constant. Since logarithmic decrement is based on two successive cycles, we must divide by the number of periods considered. Thus,

$$Z = \frac{1}{n_P} \ln\left[\frac{X(T)}{X(T + n_P\tau_d)}\right] \qquad (10.1.9)$$

where n_P = the number of periods between amplitude measurements. Based on eight periods, we have

$$Z = \frac{1}{8} \ln 1.65 = 0.0626$$

(c) Is the assumption of viscous damping valid?

Solution. One test is the determination of whether Z is actually a constant. Using the data for four periods, we have

$$Z = \frac{1}{4} \ln 1.28 = 0.0617$$

Thus, the assumption of viscous damping is reasonable, based on available data. Viscous damping is only a model used to approximate actual systems. It is not a precise description of actual system response. Observe, for example, that a system would theoretically vibrate forever at an ever-decreasing amplitude based on the model.

(d) Determine the damping coefficient.

Solution. Using

$$Z = \frac{C\pi}{M\omega_d}$$

$$\omega_d = \left[\frac{K}{M} - \frac{C^2}{(2M)^2} \right]^{1/2}$$

we have

$$\frac{C\pi}{Z} = M \left[\frac{K}{M} - \frac{C^2}{(2M)^2} \right]^{1/2}$$

from which

$$C = \left(\frac{KM}{\pi^2/Z^2 + 1/4} \right)^{1/2} \tag{10.1.10}$$

Using the average value of Z based on eight periods, we obtain

$$C = \left[\frac{50 \times (20/386)}{\pi^2/0.0626^2 + 1/4} \right]^{1/2}$$

$$= 0.0321 \text{ lb-s/in}$$

(e) Determine the critical damping coefficient and the damping ratio.

Solution. The critical damping coefficient is given by

$$C_c = 2(KM)^{1/2} = 2 \left(50 \times \frac{20}{386} \right)^{1/2} = 3.219 \text{ lb-s/in}$$

and the damping ratio by

$$r_d = \frac{C}{C_c} = \frac{0.0321}{3.219} = 9.96 \times 10^{-3}$$

(f) Determine the damped natural frequency.

Solution. The damped natural frequency is given by

$$f_n = \left(\frac{1}{2\pi}\right)\omega_d = \left(\frac{1}{2\pi}\right)\left[\frac{K}{M} - \frac{C^2}{(2M)^2}\right]^{1/2}$$

$$= \left(\frac{1}{2\pi}\right)\left[\frac{50 \times 386}{20} - \frac{0.0321^2}{(2 \times 20/386)^2}\right]^{1/2}$$

$$= 4.9438 \text{ Hz}$$

Note that, in lightly damped systems, the damping has little effect on the frequency of vibration. As a result, it would be difficult to estimate the damping coefficient by measuring natural frequency.

10.2 FORCED, DAMPED VIBRATION

As observed in the above section, the frequency of free vibration depends on the system parameters, and the amplitude depends on system parameters and initial conditions. Free vibration can be considered a transient response to a single initial displacement or impulse. The total response of a system in forced vibration is given by the transient solution and the particular solution. Although the transient solution may be of importance in ensuring that components are not subjected to high stress, the particular solution is of most interest in noise control. Thus, when examining forced vibration, we usually ignore the transient component, which dies out after several cycles of vibration, and consider the steady-state response of the system. The particular solution to the differential equation of the damped one-degree-of-freedom system,

$$M\frac{d^2x}{dt^2} + C\frac{dx}{dt} + Kx = F(t) \qquad \textbf{(10.1.1)}$$

depends on the form of the forcing function $F(t)$.

Forcing functions due to machine imbalance can usually be represented by one or more sinusoidal or complex exponential functions. The following form may be used:

$$M\frac{d^2x}{dt^2} + C\frac{dx}{dt} + Kx = Ae^{j\omega t} \qquad (10.2.1)$$

where A = forcing function amplitude (lb or N)
                  ω = forcing function angular frequency (rad/s)
                  $j = (-1)^{1/2}$
           $e^{j\omega t} = \cos(\omega t) + j\sin(\omega t)$

The motion is, of course, a real function of time. The complex exponential representation is only used for computational convenience. Observing the form of the differential equation, we assume a response in the form $x = Be^{j\omega t}$ where $B = B(j\omega)$. Substituting the response form in the differential equation, the result is

$$(-M\omega^2 + jC\omega + K)Be^{j\omega t} = Ae^{j\omega t}$$

Dividing both sides of the equation by $e^{j\omega t}$ and rearranging, we have

$$\frac{B}{A/K} = \frac{1}{1 - \omega^2 M/K + j\omega C/K}$$

$$= \frac{1}{1 - r_f^2 + j2r_d r_f}$$

where $r_f = \dfrac{\omega}{\omega_n} = \dfrac{f}{f_n} = \dfrac{\omega}{(K/M)^{1/2}}$

$r_d = \dfrac{C}{C_c} = \dfrac{C}{2(KM)^{1/2}}$

f = forcing function frequency (Hz)

The normalized response amplitude of the mass is given by the absolute value of the above complex expression:

$$\frac{X}{A/K} = \left|\frac{B}{A/K}\right|$$

$$= \frac{1}{[(1 - r_f^2)^2 + (2r_d r_f)^2]^{1/2}} \tag{10.2.2}$$

where X = displacement amplitude (in or m) of the mass
A = amplitude of a harmonic forcing function (lb or N)
K = spring rate (lb/in or N/m)
A/K = the displacement (in or m) due to a static load A, that is, the system response as $\omega \to 0$

For nonzero damping, the displacement lags the forcing function by a phase angle which depends on damping ratio r_d and frequency ratio r_f as follows:

$$\phi = \arctan\left(\frac{2r_d r_f}{1 - r_f^2}\right) \tag{10.2.3}$$

where ϕ = phase angle, which lies between zero and 180°. The damping coefficient can be determined experimentally by measuring phase lag between the forcing function and response. Otherwise, the phase angle is not usually of interest in the study of forced vibration.

Resonance

Systems in free vibration vibrate at the natural frequency if undamped; if underdamped they vibrate at the natural damped frequency. The steady-state response of a system with a harmonic forcing function occurs at the forcing frequency. Resonance occurs when the forcing frequency corresponds to the natural frequency. Multidegree-of-freedom systems have a natural frequency which corresponds with each degree of freedom, and continuous systems have, theoretically, an infinite number of natural frequencies. Forcing function frequencies should be compared with all of the natural frequencies of multidegree-of-freedom systems and with the lower natural frequencies of continuous systems.

It can be seen by reference to equation 10.2.2 that the response amplitude of an undamped system becomes infinite when the frequency ratio $r_f = 1$. Although undamped systems exist only in textbooks, this result gives us some insight into the behavior of very lightly damped systems at resonance. Each cycle of the forcing function puts additional energy into the system, increasing displacement amplitude until some limit is reached (e.g., a snubber or stop) or until the mountings fail.

At $r_f = 1$, the normalized response of a one-degree-of-freedom system is given by

$$\left[\frac{X}{A/K}\right]_{r_f=1} = \frac{1}{2r_d} \tag{10.2.4}$$

For lightly damped systems, this value is very near to the maximum response. For moderate damping, the maximum response occurs at a frequency ratio below 1.0.

Transmissibility

Referring to Figure 10.1.1 it can be seen that both spring and damper transmit force to the frame or support. Spring force Kx opposes the displacement, and damping force $C\,dx/dt$ opposes the velocity. The complex ratio of transmitted force to the forcing function is

$$\frac{K + j\omega C}{-M\omega^2 + j\omega C + K}$$

and the ratio of amplitudes is

$$\frac{F_{tr}}{A} = \left[\frac{1 + (2r_d r_f)^2}{(1 - r_f^2)^2 + (2r_d r_f)^2}\right]^{1/2} \tag{10.2.5}$$

where F_{tr} = transmitted force amplitude (lb or N)
             A = forcing function amplitude (lb or N)
       F_{tr}/A = transmissibility

Figure 10.2.1 shows the transmissibility for one-degree-of-freedom systems with damping ratios $r_d = C/C_c = 0.1$ to 0.5 and frequency ratios $r_f = f/f_n = 0$ to 3. For lightly damped systems, maximum transmissibility occurs at approximately $r_f = 1$ and is given approximately by the following equation

$$\frac{F_{tr(max)}}{A} = \frac{1}{2r_d} \qquad \text{(approximate, for } r_d \ll 1\text{)} \tag{10.2.6}$$

where $F_{tr(max)}$ = approximate maximum transmitted force amplitude.

Isolation

Isolation refers to a transmissibility of less than unity. Referring to equation 10.2.5 or Figure 10.2.1, we see that

$$\frac{F_{\text{tr}}}{A} < 1 \quad \text{for} \quad r_f > 2^{1/2} \tag{10.2.7}$$

for all values of r_d.

For $r_f > 1$, isolation improves, that is, transmissibility decreases monotonically with increasing r_f. If the forcing function results from an unbalanced machine running at constant speed, then an isolator may be designed to produce a high value of frequency ratio r_f. The only variables at our disposal are the damping coefficient and spring constant of the mounts we select. Isolation is achieved by specifying soft enough mountings so that the system has a low natural frequency.

It can be seen from the transmissibility curves that damping reduces transmissibility in the force amplification region $0 < r_f < 2^{1/2}$. In the isolation region ($2^{1/2} < r_f$) the influence of damping is unfavorable; damping increases transmissibility in the isolation region. For high-frequency ratios ($r_f \gg 2^{1/2}$) transmissibility is roughly proportional to damping ratio, and inversely proportional to frequency as follows

$$\frac{F_{\text{tr}}}{A} = \frac{2r_d}{r_f} \quad \text{(approximate, for } r_f \gg 2^{1/2}) \tag{10.2.8}$$

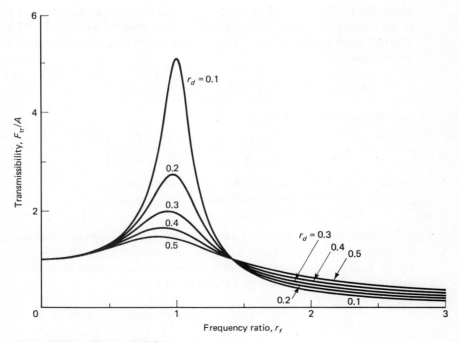

Figure 10.2.1 Transmissibility.

In an attempt to obtain the best response in both regions, a mounting system may be designed with snubbers which damp large amplitude vibrations, while providing little damping if the amplitude is small.

Note that the above results are based on a one-degree-of-freedom system with a harmonic forcing function in the form $Ae^{j\omega t}$. While this model will give reasonable results in many cases, the performance of some systems is dependent on the mechanical source impedance of a machine. Crede and Ruzicka (1961) discuss problems of this type in greater detail.

EXAMPLE PROBLEM: ISOLATION

A 1200-lb machine is rigidly mounted to the floor of a factory. It transmits an objectionable 40-Hz sinusoidal vibration to the floor, which excites vibration in other items, resulting in a noise problem as well. Specify a mounting system which will reduce transmitted force by a factor of 10 at operating speed. Maximum transmissibility must be less than 3 at any speed, including machine startup.

Solution. The transmissibility curves, Figure 10.2.1, show that a damping ratio $r_d = 0.2$ will produce a maximum transmissibility of less than 3. Using this ratio in equation 10.2.5, and setting the transmissibility at 0.1, we have

$$0.1 = \left[\frac{1 + (2 \times 0.2 r_f)^2}{(1 - r_f^2)^2 + (2 \times 0.2 r_f)^2} \right]^{1/2}$$

which is satisfied by $r_f = 4.7205$. This value is verified by Figure 10.2.2 which shows plots of transmissibility for a wider range of frequency ratios. By definition,

$$r_f = \frac{f}{f_n} = \frac{2\pi f}{(Kg/W)^{1/2}}$$

Using the given data, we have

$$4.7205 = 2\pi \times \frac{40}{386K/1200}$$

from which the combined spring rate of the mountings will be

$$K = 165.5 \text{ lb/in}$$

The damping ratio is defined by

$$r_d = \frac{C}{C_c} = \frac{C}{2(KM)^{1/2}} = \frac{C}{2(KW/g)^{1/2}}$$

Using the given data, we obtain

$$0.2 = \frac{C}{2(165.5 \times 1200/386)^{1/2}}$$

from which the required combined damping coefficient is

$$C = 9.07 \text{ lb-s/in}$$

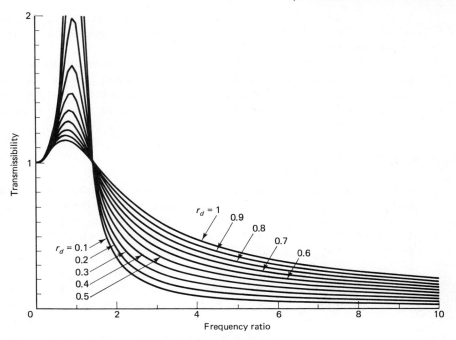

Figure 10.2.2 Transmissibility plot for example problem.

Fourier Series Representation of General Periodic Forcing Functions

The above analysis is based on a sinusoidal forcing function which can be described in the form $F(t) = a \cos(\omega t) + b \sin(\omega t)$, where the amplitude of the forcing function is $A = (a^2 + b^2)^{1/2}$. General periodic forcing functions can be described by a Fourier series in the form

$$F(t) = A_0 + A_1 \cos(\omega t) + A_2 \cos(2\omega t) + \cdots + B_1 \sin(\omega t) + B_2 \sin(2\omega t) + \cdots$$

$$= A_0 + \sum_{i=1}^{\infty} [A_i \cos(i\omega t) + B_i \sin(i\omega t)] \tag{10.2.9}$$

where $\omega = 2\pi/T$ = fundamental (lowest) forcing function angular frequency (rad/s)

T = fundamental period of forcing function (s) and the coefficients are given by

$$A_0 = \frac{1}{T} \int_0^T F(t)\,dt$$

$$A_i = \frac{2}{T} \int_0^T F(t) \cos(i\omega t)\,dt \left.\vphantom{\int_0^T}\right\} \tag{10.2.10}$$

$$B_i = \frac{2}{T} \int_0^T F(t) \sin(i\omega t)\,dt$$

The differential equation of motion of a one-degree-of-freedom system subject to a general periodic forcing function may be written as follows:

$$M\frac{d^2x}{dt^2} + C\frac{dx}{dt} + Kx = F(t) = A_0 + \sum_{i=1}^{\infty}[A_i\cos(i\omega t) + B_i\sin(i\omega t)] \quad (10.2.11)$$

Once the coefficients are determined, the response to the forcing function may be obtained as in the above sections.

Fourier Series in Exponential Form   As an alternative, a periodic forcing function can be described in complex exponential form as follows:

$$F(t) = \sum_{i=-\infty}^{\infty} C_i e^{ji\omega t} \quad (10.2.12)$$

The complex coefficients are given by

$$C_i = \frac{1}{T}\int_{-T/2}^{T/2} F(t)e^{-ji\omega t}\,dt \quad (10.2.13)$$

EXAMPLE PROBLEM: FOURIER EXPANSION OF A PERIODIC FORCING FUNCTION

A spring-mass-damper system is acted on by a forcing function which is described by the positive portion of a sine wave, that is,

$$F(t) = F_1\sin(\omega t) \quad \text{for} \quad 0 \le \omega t \le \pi,\, 2\pi \le \omega t \le 3\pi,$$

and so on, and

$$F(t) = 0 \quad \text{for} \quad \pi < \omega t < 2\pi,\, 3\pi < \omega t < 4\pi,$$

and so on where F_1 and ω are given constants.

(a) Construct the Fourier expansion of the forcing function in sine-cosine form.

Solution.   The angular frequency of the forcing function is ω (rad/s), and the period $T = 2\pi/\omega$ (s). A table of integrals is helpful when evaluating the coefficients. The constant term is given by

$$A_0 = \frac{1}{T}\int_0^{T/2} F(t)dt = \frac{1}{T}F_1\int_0^{\pi/\omega}\sin(\omega t)dt$$

$$= \frac{F_1}{T}\left[\frac{-\cos(\omega t)}{\omega}\right]_0^{\pi/\omega} = \frac{F_1}{\pi}$$

The cosine coefficients are

$$A_i = \frac{2}{T}\int_0^{T/2} F(t)\cos(i\omega t)dt$$

$$= \frac{2}{T}F_1\int_0^{\pi/\omega}\sin(\omega t)\cos(i\omega t)dt$$

$$= \left(\frac{2F_1}{T}\right)\left\{\frac{-[\cos(\omega t + i\omega t)]_0^{\pi/\omega}}{2\omega(1 + i)} - \frac{[\cos(\omega t - i\omega t)]_0^{\pi/\omega}}{2\omega(1 - i)}\right\}$$

$$= \frac{F_1 \omega}{\pi}\left[\frac{-\cos(\pi + i\pi) + 1}{2\omega(1 + i)} + \frac{-\cos(\pi - i\pi) + 1}{2\omega(1 - i)}\right]$$

$$= \frac{F_1}{(2\pi)}\left[\frac{\cos(i\pi) + 1}{1 + i} + \frac{\cos(i\pi) + 1}{1 - i}\right]$$

$$= F_1 \frac{\cos(i\pi) + 1}{\pi(1 - i^2)} \quad \text{for} \quad i > 1$$

$$A_1 = \frac{2}{T}F_1 \int_0^{T/2} \sin(\omega t) \cos(\omega t)dt = 0$$

The sine coefficients are

$$B_i = \frac{2}{T}\int_0^{T/2} F(t) \sin(i\omega t)dt$$

$$= \frac{2F_1}{T}\int_0^{\pi/\omega} \sin(\omega t) \sin(i\omega t)dt$$

$$= 0 \quad \text{for} \quad i > 1$$

$$B_1 = \frac{2}{T}F_1 \int_0^{T/2} \sin^2(\omega t)dt$$

$$= \frac{F_1 \omega}{\pi}\frac{\pi}{2\omega} = \frac{F_1}{2}$$

Evaluating the first seven nonzero terms, the Fourier expansion becomes

$$F(t) = F_1\left\{\frac{1}{\pi} + \frac{\sin(\omega t)}{2}\right.$$

$$\left. - \frac{2}{\pi}\left[\frac{\cos(2\omega t)}{3} + \frac{\cos(4\omega t)}{15} + \frac{\cos(6\omega t)}{35} + \frac{\cos(8\omega t)}{63} + \frac{\cos(10\omega t)}{99} + \cdots\right]\right\}$$

The first term on the right, F_1/π, has the effect of a constant force, simply changing the equilibrium position. Since the terms that follow decrease in magnitude, usually only the first few terms are considered.

(b) Construct the Fourier expansion in complex exponential form.

Solution. Using the Euler formula to convert the sinusoidal forcing function to complex exponential form, we have

$$F(t) = \begin{cases} 0 & \text{for} \quad -T/2 \leq t \leq 0 \\ & \text{and} \\ F_1(e^{j\omega t} - e^{-j\omega t})/(j2) & \text{for} \quad 0 \leq t \leq T/2 \end{cases}$$

The general form of the coefficient is given by

$$C_i = \frac{1}{T} \int_{-T/2}^{T/2} F(t)e^{-ji\omega t}\, dt$$

$$= \frac{\omega F_1}{(2\pi)} \int_{0}^{\pi/\omega} [e^{j(1-i)\omega t} + e^{-j(1+i)\omega t}]\, dt$$

$$= \frac{F_1}{4\pi}\left(\frac{1 - e^{j(1-i)\pi}}{1 - i} + \frac{1 - e^{-j(1+i)\pi}}{1 + i}\right)$$

from which

$$C_{-2} = -\frac{F_1}{3\pi}$$

$$C_{-1} = \frac{jF_1}{4}$$

$$C_0 = \frac{F_1}{\pi}$$

$$C_1 = -\frac{jF_1}{4}$$

$$C_2 = -\frac{F_1}{3\pi}$$

Thus, we have

$$F(t) = F_1\left(-\frac{e^{-j2\omega t}}{3\pi} + \frac{je^{-j\omega t}}{4} + \frac{1}{\pi} - \frac{je^{j\omega t}}{4} - \frac{e^{j2\omega t}}{3\pi} + \cdots\right)$$

By combining terms, and using the Euler sine and cosine formulas, it can be seen that the above result duplicates the first three terms found in part (a).

Reciprocating Engines and Compressors

The slider-crank linkage is a basic component of reciprocating engines, pumps, and compressors. Inertia forces in the linkage can result in vibration. Figure 10.2.3 shows a sketch of an in-line slider-crank linkage. A skeleton diagram representation for kinematic and dynamic analysis is also shown. The following notation is used:

O_1 = crankshaft center

P = crankpin

Q = wristpin

D = mounts permitting motion in the vertical direction only

E = fixed support

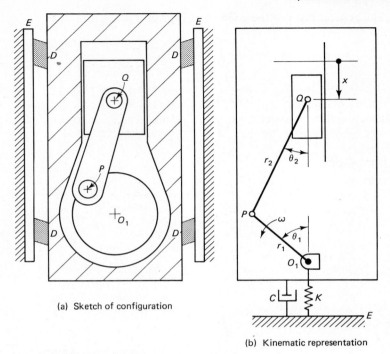

(a) Sketch of configuration

(b) Kinematic representation

Figure 10.2.3 Reciprocating engine or pump.

$r_1 = O_1P$ = crank length

$r_2 = PQ$ = connecting rod length

ω = angular velocity of the crank (rad/s)

θ_1 = crank position

θ_2 = connecting rod position

x = piston position measured from extreme position of wristpin

K = effective spring rate of mounts

C = effective damping coefficient of mounts

It can be seen that the piston position is given by

$$x = r_1(1 - \cos \theta_1) + r_2(1 - \cos \theta_2) \tag{10.2.14}$$

and that the angles are related by

$$r_1 \sin \theta_1 = r_2 \sin \theta_2$$

Using the above equation and the identity

$$\cos \theta_2 = (1 - \sin^2 \theta_2)^{1/2}$$

we have the equation for piston position in terms of crank position only:

$$x = r_1(1 - \cos\theta_1) + r_2\left\{1 - \left[1 - \left(\frac{r_1}{r_2}\right)^2 \sin^2\theta_1\right]^{1/2}\right\} \qquad (10.2.15)$$

If sufficient data are available, including component masses and mass moments of inertia, exact relationships may be used to determine velocities, accelerations, angular velocities, angular accelerations, inertia forces, and inertia torques. In many cases, however, approximate relationships are adequate for a first approximation. If the first approximation indicates that further study is necessary, then the exact relationships are used. Two terms of a binomial expansion may be used to obtain the approximate relationship:

$$\left[1 - \left(\frac{r_1}{r_2}\right)^2 \sin^2\theta_1\right]^{1/2} = 1 - \left(\frac{1}{2}\right)\left(\frac{r_1}{r_2}\right)^2 \sin^2\theta_1$$

Substituting the above approximation in equation 10.2.15, the result is

$$x = r_1\left[1 - \cos\theta_1 + \left(\frac{1}{2}\right)\left(\frac{r_1}{r_2}\right)\sin^2\theta_1\right] \qquad (10.2.16)$$

where x = approximate piston displacement.

The above equation is differentiated with respect to time to obtain piston velocity

$$v = r_1\omega\left[\sin\theta_1 + \left(\frac{r_1}{r_2}\right)\sin\theta_1\cos\theta_1\right]$$

$$= r_1\omega\left[\sin\theta_1 + \left(\frac{1}{2}\right)\left(\frac{r_1}{r_2}\right)\sin 2\theta_1\right] \qquad (10.2.17)$$

where $v = dx/dt$ = approximate piston velocity
$\omega = d\theta_1/dt$ = crank angular velocity

Differentiating once more to obtain piston acceleration, where the angular velocity of the crank is assumed to be a constant,

$$a = r_1\omega^2\left[\cos\theta_1 + \left(\frac{r_1}{r_2}\right)\cos(2\theta_1)\right] \qquad (10.2.18)$$

where a = approximate piston acceleration
ω = crank angular velocity (constant)

Dynamic analysis of a system may be simplified by approximating the actual system elements as concentrated masses. Referring to Figure 10.2.3, the piston and wristpin mass and part of the connecting rod mass may be considered a concentrated mass M_Q located at the wristpin, point Q. The remaining connecting rod mass and other unbalanced masses may be considered a concentrated mass M_P located at the crankpin, point P. The crank may be balanced about the crankshaft axis, point O_1, so that it does not affect inertia forces when the angular velocity of the crank is constant.

We are interested in the forcing function $F(t)$, which is approximated by the inertia forces due to accelerations of the concentrated masses M_P and M_Q. Angular velocity of the crank will be assumed constant. The reverse-effective-force (inertia effect) at mass M_Q is given by

$$F_Q = -aM_Q = -M_Q r_1 \omega^2 \left[\cos \theta_1 + \left(\frac{r_1}{r_2} \right) \cos(2\theta_1) \right] \qquad (10.2.19)$$

For constant angular velocity ω, the acceleration of point P is given by

$$a_P = \omega^2 r_1 \qquad (10.2.20)$$

which is parallel to the crank (PO_1) and directed toward O_1. The reverse effective force at M_P is given by

$$a_P M_P = M_P \omega^2 r_1$$

parallel to the crank and directed away from O_1. The vertical component of this force is

$$F_P = -M_P \omega^2 r_1 \cos \theta_1 \qquad (10.2.21)$$

Combining the vertical forces, and letting $\theta_1 = \omega t$, the differential equation of motion of the system as a whole becomes:

$$M \frac{d^2 x}{dt^2} + C \frac{dx}{dt} + Kx = F(t) = F_P + F_Q$$

$$= -\omega^2 r_1 \left[(M_P + M_Q) \cos(\omega t) + M_Q \left(\frac{r_1}{r_2} \right) \cos(2\omega t) \right] \qquad (10.2.22)$$

where M = total supported system mass including the engine block and the moving parts, and units are as follows: angular velocity: rad/s; mass: kg or lb-s^2/in; distances: m or in; forces: N or lb; damping coefficient: N·s/m or lb-s/in; spring rate: N/m or lb/in; time: s.

EXAMPLE PROBLEM: TRANSMISSIBILITY AND ISOLATION OF A SINGLE CYLINDER COMPRESSOR

A motor-driven single cylinder compressor has a balanced crankshaft. The following data apply:

$$\text{total supported weight } W = 40 \text{ lb}$$

$$\text{effective weight at wristpin } W_Q = 2.5 \text{ lb}$$

$$\text{effective weight at crankpin } W_P = 4.0 \text{ lb}$$

$$\text{crank length } r_1 = 2 \text{ in}$$

$$\text{connecting rod length } r_2 = 6 \text{ in}$$

$$\text{crankshaft speed } n = 880 \text{ rpm (constant)}$$

$$\text{combined spring rate of mounts (initial design) } K = 2300 \text{ lb/in}$$

$$\text{damping ratio } r_d = 0.02$$

(a) Find the steady-state force transmitted to the supporting structure.

Solution. The natural frequency of the system is given by

$$\omega_n = \left(\frac{K}{M}\right)^{1/2} = \left(\frac{Kg}{W}\right)^{1/2} = \left(2300 \times \frac{386}{40}\right) = 149 \text{ rad/s}$$

The angular velocity of the crank is

$$\omega = \frac{n\pi}{30} = \frac{880\pi}{30} = 92.15 \text{ rad/s}$$

The forcing function is approximated by

$$F(t) = -\omega^2 r_1[(M_P + M_Q) \cos(\omega t) + M_Q(r_1/r_2) \cos(2\omega t)]$$

$$= -92.15^2 \times 2[(4 + 2.5) \cos(92.15t) + 2.5(2/6) \cos(184.31t)]/386$$

$$= -268 \cos(92.15t) - 36.67 \cos(184.31t)$$

Steady-state transmitted force is made up of one sinusoid at a frequency corresponding to crankshaft speed, and a second corresponding to twice the crankshaft speed. The frequency ratios are

$$r_f = \frac{\omega}{\omega_n} = \frac{92.15}{149} = 0.6185$$

$$\frac{2\omega}{\omega_n} = \frac{184.31}{149} = 1.237$$

respectively. The transmissibility is

$$\frac{F_{\text{tr}}}{A} = \left[\frac{1 + (2r_d r_f)^2}{(1 - r_f^2)^2 + (2r_d r_f)^2}\right]^{1/2}$$

$$= \left[\frac{1 + (2 \times 0.02 \times 0.6185)^2}{(1 - 0.6185^2)^2 + (2 \times 0.02 \times 0.6185)^2}\right]^{1/2}$$

$$= 1.62 \text{ for the lower frequency ratio}$$

$$\frac{F_{\text{tr}}}{A} = \left[\frac{1 + (2 \times 0.02 \times 1.237)^2}{(1 - 1.237^2)^2 + (2 \times 0.02 \times 1.237)^2}\right]^{1/2}$$

$$= 1.88 \text{ for the higher frequency ratio}$$

For lightly damped systems, displacement and transmitted force are approximately in-phase with the forcing function for forcing frequencies below the resonant frequency. Displacement and transmitted force are approximately 180° out-of-phase with the forcing function for lightly damped systems when the forcing frequency is above resonance. Considering the phase relationship, and multiplying the transmissibilities by the respective forcing function amplitudes, we obtain the approximate relationship for transmitted force

$$F_{tr} = -286 \times 1.62 \cos(\omega t) - 36.67 \times 1.88 \cos(2\omega t)$$

$$= -463 \cos(\omega t) - 69 \cos(2\omega t)$$

where F_{tr} = approximate transmitted force (lb, positive downward)
  ω = 92.15 rad/s = crank angular velocity

At $\omega t = \pi, 3\pi, 5\pi$, and so on, the approximate transmitted force is

$$F_{tr} = 463 - 69 = 394 \text{ lb downward}$$

At $\omega t = 0, 2\pi, 4\pi$, and so on,

$$F_{tr} = -463 - 69 = -532 \text{ (532 lb upward)}$$

(b) Give mounting specifications to reduce transmitted force amplitude to less than 500 lb at resonance, and less than 30 lb at operating speed.

Solution.   Try softer springs such that $r_f = 4$ at the operating speed. Then

$$K = (W/g)(\omega/r_f)^2 = 55 \text{ lb/in}$$

and

$$C = 2r_d(KW/g)^{1/2} = 0.095 \text{ lb-s/in}$$

Using the same equations, the result is

$$F_{tr} = 20 \text{ lb upward and 19 lb downward at operating speed.}$$

The new resonant frequency is

$$\omega_n = 23 \text{ rad/s}$$

At resonance, the transmitted force is less than 500 lb.

Motion of a Supporting Structure

It is sometimes necessary to protect delicate instruments and critical operations from vibration due to motion of a supporting structure. For the one-degree-of-freedom damped system shown schematically in Figure 10.2.4, force is transmitted from the moving support to the mass through the spring and damper. If the support moves harmonically, with support displacement in the form $y = Y \cos(\omega t)$, then the steady-state motion of mass M will also be harmonic, with displacement in the form $x = X \cos(\omega t - \phi)$, where ϕ is a phase angle. The steady-state response ratio is

$$\frac{X}{Y} = \left[\frac{1 + (2r_d r_f)^2}{(1 - r_f^2)^2 + (2r_d r_f)^2} \right]^{1/2} \tag{10.2.23}$$

where X = steady-state response amplitude of the mass
  Y = the amplitude of harmonic vibration of the support

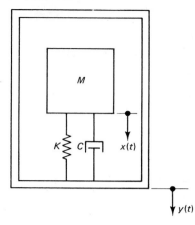

Figure 10.2.4 Motion of a supporting structure.

X/Y = motion transmissibility
r_f = frequency ratio
r_d = damping ratio

It can be seen that the right side of the above equation is identical to the right side of the force-transmissibility equation. Thus, the force-transmissibility curves can be used to identify the regions of amplification and isolation where motion transmissibility is of interest.

Eccentricity

The normalized response amplitude of a mass to a harmonic forcing function of amplitude A is given by

$$X/(A/K) = 1/[(1 - r_f^2)^2 + (2r_d r_f)^2]^{1/2} \tag{10.2.2}$$

Figure 10.2.5 shows a system in which an eccentric rotating mass results in vibration. Replacing the forcing function amplitude A by the inertia effect, we have $A = M_E \omega^2 y_E$.

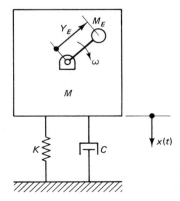

Figure 10.2.5 Eccentricity.

Noting that the frequency ratio is given by $r_f = \omega/\omega_n$, from which $r_f^2 = \omega^2 M/K$, the normalized response/input relationship becomes

$$MX/[M_E \, y_E] = r_f^2/[(1 - r_f^2)^2 + (2r_d r_f)^2]^{1/2}$$

where M = total mass including the eccentric mass
M_E = eccentric mass
X = amplitude of response
y_E = eccentricity

10.3 VIBRATION AND SHOCK MOUNTS—DESIGN CONSIDERATIONS

Vibration and shock mounts are available in a number of forms including helical compression springs, torsion bars, elastomeric compression pads, elastomeric shear mounts, pneumatic mounts, wire mesh mounts, leaf springs, and conical washer springs. They are used to limit steady-state vibration amplitude and transmissibility, and to absorb shock loading by storing and dissipating energy.

Helical Compression Springs

The spring rate of a helical compression spring is given by

$$K = \frac{GD^4}{64N_a R^3} = \frac{GD}{8N_a C_I^3} \tag{10.3.1}$$

where K = spring rate (lb/in or N/mm)
G = shear modulus (psi or MPa)
D = wire diameter (in or mm)
N_a = number of active coils
R = mean coil radius (in or mm)
$C_I = 2R/D$ = the spring index

Note that the value of K (N/mm) as found above is multiplied by 1000 to obtain K (N/m) as used in the natural frequency equations:

$$\omega_n = \left(\frac{K}{M}\right)^{1/2} \quad \text{and} \quad f_n = \frac{(K/M)^{1/2}}{2\pi}$$

where M = mass (kg)
ω_n = natural angular frequency (rad/s)
f_n = natural frequency (Hz)

The number of active coils N_a is about two coils less than the total number of coils N_t if the spring has squared and ground ends, or if the spring rests in a stamping which conforms with the end turns. Mean coil radius R is given by $R = (OD - D)/2$, where OD = the outside diameter of the spring coil.

When a spring is compressed to its solid height

$$h_{\text{solid}} = N_t D \qquad (10.3.2)$$

then it is protected against failure due to additional loading since it cannot deflect further. The free or unloaded height of a spring is given by

$$h_{\text{free}} = h_{\text{solid}} + (1 + r_c)P_{\text{working}}/K \qquad (10.3.3)$$

where h_{free} = free height
P_{working} = maximum expected load
K = spring rate
r_c = clash allowance

A clash allowance of 0.20 to 0.25 is reasonable in that it allows a 20 to 25% overload before clashing. Too large a clash allowance will fail to protect the spring against overload. When a spring is compressed to its solid height, it cannot perform its primary function, for example, protecting equipment against vibration or shock. Thus, a mounting system will be unsatisfactory if the clash allowance is inadequate.

Springs used in vibration mounts are subject to both static and varying stresses. Spring design for fatigue loading takes into account the mean and range stresses and the yield point and endurance limit properties of the spring material.

EXAMPLE PROBLEM: COMPRESSION SPRING MOUNTING

A machine is isolated satisfactorily by a set of compression springs which produces a frequency ratio $r_f = 4$ with a damping ratio $r_d = 0.1$. A new machine of the same design is to be installed on similar mounts, except that the new mounts are available with a wire diameter of 10 mm, whereas the mounts on the first machine had a wire diameter of 5 mm. The material, mean coil radius, and number of coils are unchanged. Will the new mounts be satisfactory?

Solution.   The mounts on the original machine would produce a transmissibility of

$$\frac{F_{\text{tr}}}{A} = \left[\frac{1 + (2r_d r_f)^2}{(1 - r_f^2)^2 + (2r_d r_f)^2} \right]^{1/2}$$

$$= \left[\frac{1 + (2 \times 0.1 \times 4)^2}{(1 - 4^2)^2 + (2 \times 0.1 \times 4)^2} \right]^{1/2}$$

$$= 0.085$$

Spring rate is given by

$$K = \frac{GD^4}{64 N_a R^3}$$

Since only wire diameter has been changed, the ratio of spring rates for the two mounts is

$$\frac{K_{\text{new}}}{K_{\text{old}}} = \left(\frac{D_{\text{new}}}{D_{\text{old}}} \right)^4 = \left(\frac{10}{5} \right)^4 = 16$$

Natural frequency is given by

$$\omega_n = \left(\frac{K}{M}\right)^{1/2}$$

Since machine mass is unchanged,

$$\frac{\omega_{n(\text{new})}}{\omega_{n(\text{old})}} = \left(\frac{K_{\text{new}}}{K_{\text{old}}}\right)^{1/2} = 16^{1/2} = 4$$

The frequency ratio is $r_f = \omega/\omega_n = 1$ for the machine with the new mounts. By doubling the wire diameter, the natural frequency is increased by a factor of 4, and the system will be in resonance. Damping ratio is given by

$$r_d = C/C_c = \frac{C}{2(KM)^{1/2}}$$

If C and M are unchanged,

$$\frac{r_{d(\text{new})}}{r_{d(\text{old})}} = \left(\frac{K_{\text{old}}}{K_{\text{new}}}\right)^{1/2} = \left(\frac{1}{16}\right)^{1/2} = \frac{1}{4}$$

$$r_{d(\text{new})} = \frac{0.1}{4} = 0.025$$

The transmissibility at resonance becomes

$$\frac{F_{\text{tr}}}{A} = \frac{(1 + 4r_d^2)^{1/2}}{2r_d}$$

$$= \frac{(1 + 4 \times 0.025^2)^{1/2}}{2 \times 0.025} = 20.05$$

The new mounts will obviously be unsatisfactory.

Torsion Bars

Torsion bars are rods that are subject to twisting (see Figure 10.3.1). They can be used in suspension systems to isolate against shock loading. Torsion bars are selected for some automotive applications where space is a consideration. Angular deflection is given by

$$\phi = \frac{LPR}{GJ} \tag{10.3.4}$$

where ϕ = relative rotation of the ends (rad)
L = length (in or mm)
PR = torque
P = load (lb or N)
R = moment arm (in or mm)
G = shear modulus (psi or MPa)

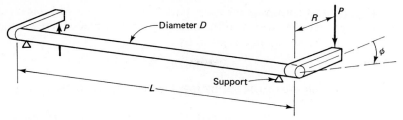

Figure 10.3.1 Torsion bar.

J = moment of inertia (in^4 or mm^4)
$J = \pi D^4/32$ for a solid circular bar
$J = \pi(D^4 - D_I^4)/32$ for a hollow circular bar
D = (outside) bar diameter
D_I = inside diameter

For small deflections due to a load applied with a moment arm R, the spring rate of a torsion bar is

$$K = \frac{GJ}{LR^2} \tag{10.3.5}$$

where K = spring rate (lb/in or N/mm) for a load perpendicular to the moment arm.

Leaf Springs

Leaf springs usually take the form of cantilevers, simply supported single beams, and multiple leaves. For a cantilever spring of uniform cross section, Figure 10.3.2, the spring rate is

$$K = 0.25bh^3E/L^3 \tag{10.3.6}$$

where K = spring rate (lb/in or N/mm) based on loading at the end
b = width, h = thickness, and L = length (all in or mm)
E = modulus of elasticity = 30×10^6 psi (207,000 MPa) for steel

For a single simply supported leaf, Figure 10.3.3,

$$K = 4bh^3E/L^3 \tag{10.3.7}$$

where K = spring rate based on loading at the center.

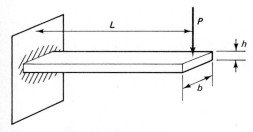

Figure 10.3.2 Cantilever spring.

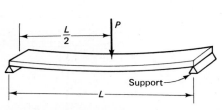

Figure 10.3.3 Simply supported leaf spring.

Multiple leaf springs (see Figure 10.3.4) are designed with leaves of graduated lengths to produce the desired stiffness (spring rate) with adequate strength and minimum weight. The spring rate is given by

$$K = 2.67 b_{\text{total}} h^3 E / L^3 \qquad (10.3.8)$$

where K = approximate spring rate for the loading shown
$\quad b_{\text{total}} = b N_{\text{leaves}}$
$\qquad b$ = width of a single leaf
$\quad N_{\text{leaves}}$ = number of leaves
$\qquad h$ = thickness of a single leaf

Elastomers

Many commercially available vibration mounts utilize natural or synthetic rubber acting in compression or shear. The relatively high inherent damping of elastomers reduces noise transmission through the mounts, and limits force transmissibility at resonance.

The spring rate of the compression mount shown in Figure 10.3.5 is given by

$$K = \frac{A_c E}{h} \qquad (10.3.9)$$

where K = spring rate (lb/in or N/mm)
$\quad A_c$ = cross section area (in^2 or mm^2) measured in a horizontal plane = πa^2
$\qquad$ for a circular cross section
$\quad E$ = elastic modulus (psi or MPa) which depends on the composition of the elastomer

The elastomer may have a high value of Poisson's ratio (near 0.5). As a result, the mount will tend to expand laterally when compressed. Since the expansion is partly restrained, the load-deflection relationship is not constant, and spring rate depends somewhat on load.

The shear mount in Figure 10.3.6 has a spring rate of

$$K = \frac{A_c G}{h} \qquad (10.3.10)$$

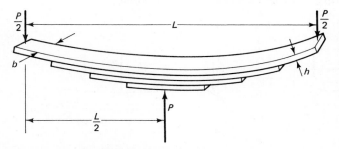

Figure 10.3.4 Multiple leaf spring.

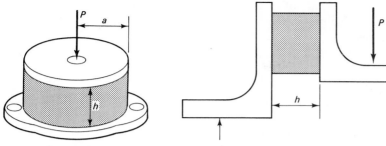

Figure 10.3.5 Compression mount.

Figure 10.3.6 Shear mount.

where A_c = cross section area measured in a plane perpendicular to dimension h

G = shear modulus (psi or MPa)

For the cylindrical shear mount, Figure 10.3.7, shear stress depends on radius as follows, $\tau = P/[2\pi hr]$, and deflection is given by

$$y = \int_a^b \left(\frac{\tau}{G}\right) dr = \left(\frac{P}{2\pi Gh}\right) \int_a^b \left(\frac{1}{r}\right) dr$$

$$= \frac{P \ln(b/a)}{2\pi Gh}$$

from which we find the spring rate

$$K = \frac{P}{y} = \frac{2\pi Gh}{\ln(b/a)} \tag{10.3.11}$$

where τ = average shear stress in the elastomer at radius r

y = deflection due to load P

a and b = the inner and outer radii and h the vertical dimension of the elastomer

ln = the natural logarithm

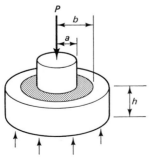

Figure 10.3.7 Cylindrical shear mount.

More efficient use is made of material if the vertical dimension h is inversely proportional to radius, resulting in the constant shear stress mount, Figure 10.3.8. In this mount, shear stress

$$\tau = \frac{P}{2\pi hr} = \frac{P}{2\pi bh_1}$$

and deflection is given by

$$y = \frac{\tau(b - a)}{G} = \frac{P(b - a)}{2\pi bGh_1}$$

The spring rate is

$$K = \frac{P}{y} = \frac{2\pi bGh_1}{b - a} \qquad\qquad (10.3.12)$$

where $h = h_1 b/r$.

Pneumatic Mounts

Pneumatic mounts (air springs) are suitable for applications requiring very high vibration isolation. Figure 10.3.9 shows a pneumatic mount system with a reservoir. Unlike most other vibration mounts, the natural frequency of high-pressure pneumatic mounts with reservoirs is practically independent of the supported mass. Utilizing the gas law to describe the system,

$$pV^n = \text{a constant} = p_o V_o^n = p(V_o - A_c y)^n \quad \text{and}$$

$$p = p_o V_o(v_o - A_c y)^{-n} \qquad\qquad (10.3.13)$$

where
p = absolute pressure (psi or Pa)
V = volume of the reservoir and bellows (in^3 or m^3), subscript o refers to initial conditions
A_c = effective cross section area of bellows (in^2 or m^2)
y = deflection of mount (in or m)

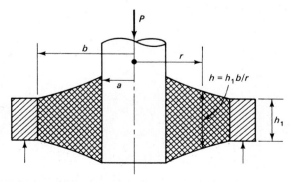

Figure 10.3.8 Constant stress shear mount.

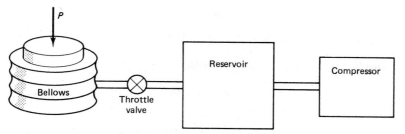

Figure 10.3.9 Pneumatic mount with reservoir.

n = the gas constant = 1.0 for a constant temperature process and 1.4 for air in an adiabatic process

For typical operating conditions, n will fall between these values.
Spring rate is given by

$$K = \frac{dP}{dy} = A_c \frac{dp}{dy} = A_c^2 n p_o V_o^n (V_o - A_c y)^{-n-1}$$

where P = supported load (lb or N). For systems with a large reservoir or for small deflections of mounts without a reservoir, $A_c y \ll V_o$, and the spring rate is approximated by

$$K = A_c^2 n p_o / V_o \qquad (10.3.14)$$

For a supported mass

$$M = \frac{P}{g} = \frac{A_c p_o'}{g} \text{ (lb-s}^2\text{/in or kg)}$$

the natural frequency of the mount is given by

$$\omega_n = \left(\frac{K}{M}\right)^{1/2} = \left(\frac{A_c g n p_o}{V_o p_o'}\right)^{1/2}$$

$$= \left[\frac{A_c g n (p_o' + p_a)}{V_o p_o'}\right]^{1/2} \qquad (10.3.15)$$

and

$$f_n = \frac{[A_c g n (p_o' + p_a)/(V_o p_o')]^{1/2}}{2\pi} \qquad (10.3.16)$$

where
ω_n = approximate natural angular frequency (rad/s)
g = acceleration of gravity = 386 in/s^2 or 9.8 m/s^2
p_o' = P/A_c = Mg/A_c = gauge pressure (psi or Pa) at equilibrium conditions due to supported load
p_a = atmospheric pressure = 14.7 psi or 1.013×10^5 Pa
f_n = approximate natural frequency (Hz)

For high pressures ($p_o' \gg p_a$), natural frequency is practically independent of p_o' and supported mass.

EXAMPLE PROBLEM: PNEUMATIC MOUNTS

A 6000-lb machine is to be supported by four equally loaded pneumatic mounts. The effective bellows cross section area is $A_c = 23$ in^2, and the air volume is 172 in^3. Find the system natural frequency.

Solution. Since each mount supports one-quarter of the machine, the gauge pressure due to the load is

$$p'_o = \frac{P}{A_c} = \frac{6000/4}{23} = 65.2 \text{ psi}$$

Using $n = 1.4$, the natural angular frequency is

$$\omega_n = \left[\frac{A_c gn(p'_o + p_a)}{V_o p'_o}\right]^{1/2}$$

$$= \left[\frac{23 \times 386 \times 1.4(65.2 + 14.7)}{172 \times 65.2}\right]^{1/2}$$

$$= 9.41 \text{ rad/s}$$

and the natural frequency

$$f_n = \frac{\omega_n}{2\pi} = 1.50 \text{ Hz}$$

Vibration Mount Configurations

In most applications, vibration mounts are arranged so that forces are divided roughly equally between the mounts, as in the above example. In this arrangement, the springs and dampers are said to be in parallel. Figure 10.3.10a shows a mass on four mounts, each mount with a spring rate K and damping coefficient C. Part (b) of the figure shows a symbolic representation. We may divide the mass among the four mounts, and solve the problem as above. Or, we may add the spring rates to obtain $K_{eq} = 4K$ and add the damping coefficients to obtain $C_{eq} = 4C$. The natural frequency of the system is given by

$$f_n = \frac{(K_{eq}/M)^{1/2}}{2\pi} \qquad (10.3.17)$$

where f_n = natural frequency (Hz). The damping ratio is

$$c_d = \frac{C_{eq}}{C_c} = \frac{C_{eq}}{2(K_{eq}M)^{1/2}} \qquad (10.3.18)$$

In part (c) of the figure, the change in length of each spring and the velocity across each damper is the same as that of the mass. This is also a parallel system, and the equivalent system parameters are

$$K_{eq} = 2K_1 + 2K_2 \quad \text{and} \quad C_{eq} = 2C_1 + 2C_2$$

Natural frequency and damping ratio are obtained from equations 10.3.17 and 10.3.18. It can be seen that the stiffer elements in a parallel system are most significant to

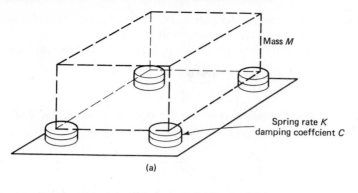

(a)

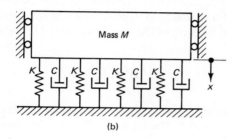

(b)

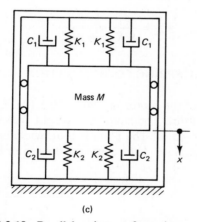

(c)

Figure 10.3.10 Parallel spring configurations.

system characteristics (i.e., the larger values of K and C tend to govern natural frequency and system response characteristics).

Mounts are sometimes arranged in series (tandem) to reduce effective stiffness. In series arrangements, the force is the same in all springs, and the total of the changes in spring length equals mass displacement. Equivalent spring rate for springs in series is given by

$$K_{eq} = \frac{1}{1/K_1 + 1/K_2 + 1/K_3 + \cdots} \qquad (10.3.19)$$

The softer springs in a series system are most significant to system characteristics, that is, smaller values of K tend to govern system response.

For the two mounts in series shown in Figure 10.3.11 (a and b),

$$K_{eq} = \frac{1}{1/K + 1/K} = \frac{K}{2}$$

For a pair of identical mounts in series, the equivalent damping coefficient is given by

$$C_{eq} = \frac{1}{1/C + 1/C} = \frac{C}{2}$$

For the general case, however, equivalent damping depends on the relationship of the damping to the springs. If a machine is supported by several pairs of mounts, and each pair supports an equal fraction of the machine mass, M', then natural frequency of the system is given by

$$f_n = \frac{(K_{eq}/M')^{1/2}}{2\pi}$$

Series-parallel spring configurations like that shown in Figure 10.3.12 may be treated as follows. The four mounts that act in parallel are combined as in the previous example for parallel springs to obtain $K_{eq1} = 4K_1$. This result is combined with the stiffness of the cantilever plate, and the overall equivalent stiffness is given by

$$K_{eq} = \frac{1}{1/K_{eq1} + 1/K_2}$$

EXAMPLE PROBLEM: SERIES-PARALLEL SPRING CONFIGURATION

Find the natural frequency of the motor in Figure 10.3.12a. Each motor mount has a spring constant $K_1 = 60$ lb/in. The supported weight including the motor and a portion of the beam is $W = 45$ lb. The plate is 6 in. wide, and made of $\frac{1}{2}$-in-thick aluminum. The length of the plate to the center of the motor is 24 in.

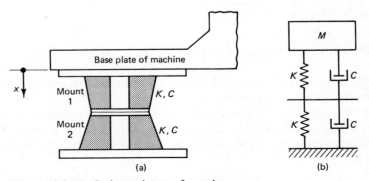

Figure 10.3.11   Series spring configuration.

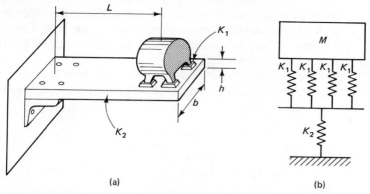

(a)   (b)

Figure 10.3.12 Series-parallel spring configuration.

Solution. For the motor mounts, $K_{eq1} = 4K_1 = 4 \times 60 = 240$ lb/in. The elastic modulus for aluminum is about $E = 10 \times 10^6$ psi, and the spring rate for the cantilever plate is

$$K_2 = 0.25bh^3 \frac{E}{L^3} = 0.25 \times 6 \times 0.5^3 \times 10 \times \frac{10^6}{24^3}$$

$$= 135.6 \text{ lb/in}$$

The system may be treated as a series-parallel combination, shown symbolically in part (b) of the figure. Combining the stiffnesses,

$$K_{eq} = \frac{1}{1/K_{eq1} + 1/K_2} = \frac{1}{1/240 + 1/135.6}$$

$$= 86.65 \text{ lb/in}$$

The natural frequency of the system is

$$f_n = \frac{(K_{eq}g/W)^{1/2}}{2\pi} = \frac{(86.65 \times 386/45)^{1/2}}{2\pi}$$

$$= 4.34 \text{ Hz}$$

Q-Factor and Isolation Efficiency

Some types of mounts have nonlinear properties, in that the equation

$$M\frac{d^2x}{dt^2} + C\frac{dx}{dt} + Kx = F(t) \qquad (10.1.1)$$

does not apply. In some cases, the above equation can be used to describe the motion of a mass on nonlinear mounts for a limited range of displacement amplitude. Helical steel compression springs are fairly linear, that is, spring rate K is essentially constant over the entire range of practical operation. Springs with varying pitch (varying center-to-center coil spacing) or varying coil diameter are nonlinear. In these springs, the number of active coils is reduced, and spring rate K increases when the closest coils clash, or when the largest diameter coils come to rest on the base. Elastomer mounts, mounts with snubbers, and mounts employing isolators made of knitted steel pads typically have nonlinear properties.

Q-factor (quality-factor) is sometimes used to describe the response of a vibrating system. It is the maximum value of normalized displacement response to a harmonic forcing function, that is,

$$Q = \left(\frac{X}{A/K}\right)_{max} \tag{10.3.20}$$

where X = displacement amplitude (in or m) of the mass in a one-degree-of-freedom system
  A = harmonic forcing function amplitude (lb or N)
  K = spring rate (lb/in or N/m)

Q-factor may be determined by measurement, or by calculation from known system parameters. For linear systems,

$$X/(A/K) = 1/[(1 - r_f^2)^2 + (2r_d r_f)^2]^{1/2} \tag{10.2.2}$$

and for lightly damped linear systems ($r_d \ll 1$), we have the approximate relationship

$$Q = \frac{1}{2r_d} \tag{10.3.21}$$

where Q = approximate quality factor for $r_d \ll 1$.

Isolation efficiency is another term used to describe mounting system performance. It is given by

$$E_I = 100\left(1 - \frac{F_{tr}}{A}\right) \tag{10.3.22}$$

where E_I = isolation efficiency (%)
  F_{tr}/A = transmissibility

Isolation efficiency has meaning only in the isolation region ($r_f > 2^{1/2}$ for linear systems). The following table is a guide to isolation efficiencies which are generally acceptable for motors in industrial applications. Greater isolation would be required for machines producing significant vibration, and for critical locations.

RECOMMENDED ISOLATION EFFICIENCY
FOR INDUSTRIAL LOCATIONS

Driving motor (kW)	Basement or ground floor (%)	Upper floor heavy construction (%)	Upper floor light construction (%)
Up to 4	—	50	90
4 to 10	50	75	93
10 to 30	80	90	95
30 to 75	90	95	97.5
75 to 225	95	97	98.5

Source: Stock Drive Products.

Commercially Available Shock and Vibration Mounts

Hundreds of different shock and vibration mount designs are available. A few representative types are described below, with typical application data. Natural frequencies, where given, are based on the average mass which would be supported by an individual mount. Maximum transmissibility and Q-factor are an indication of the effective damping at typical operating conditions. Given data apply to a particular model only.

EXAMPLES OF VIBRATION AND SHOCK MOUNT DESIGNS

Type	Isolator construction	Notes
Cup-mount	Natural rubber	See Figure 10.3.13. Note the nonlinear load-deflection relationship
Cylindrical mounting	Natural rubber	See Figure 10.3.14. May be loaded in shear or compression
Mesh base mount	Stainless steel mesh	See Figure 10.3.15. Applications include marine fans, instrument consoles, punch presses, etc.
Spring and mesh base mount	Stainless steel spring and mesh	See Figure 10.3.16. Aircraft, marine, mobile, and rotary machine application.
Parallel spring mount	Steel springs, stainless steel mesh	See Figure 10.3.17. Used for heavy loads including compressors, pumps and grain vibrators. $f_n = 4$ to 4.5 Hz and $r_d = 0.15$ to 0.2.
Pneumatic mount	Neoprene	See Figure 10.3.18. Isolation for precision machines, high-speed punch presses, vibrators, and compressors.

10.4 MULTIDEGREE-OF-FREEDOM SYSTEMS

The systems described above were modeled as a single mass which could move in one axis only. This one-degree-of-freedom idealization is reasonable when the mass is fairly rigid, the elastic elements in the system are low in mass, and only one axis of motion is of interest. Systems with more than one mass, and systems in which a mass has significant translation or rotation in more than one direction are treated as multidegree-of-freedom systems.

Two-Degree-of-Freedom Systems

Consider the idealized system of Figure 10.4.1 in which the masses are constrained to motion in the x-direction. Equilibrium of all forces acting on mass 1 including inertia effects yields the following equation:

$$M_1 \frac{d^2x_1}{dt^2} + C_1 \frac{dx_1}{dt} + C_2\left(\frac{dx_1}{dt} - \frac{dx_2}{dt}\right) + K_1x_1 + K_2(x_1 - x_2) = F_1(t) \qquad (10.4.1)$$

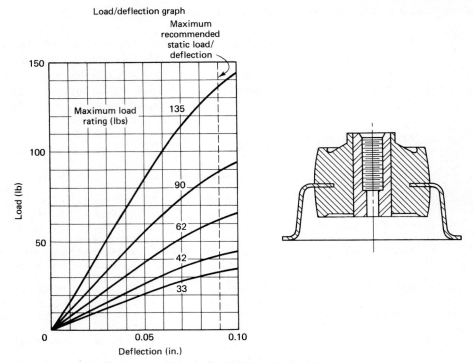

Figure 10.3.13 Cupmount. (*Source:* Stock Drive Products)

The corresponding equation for mass 2 is

$$M_2 \frac{d^2 x_2}{dt^2} + C_3 \frac{dx_2}{dt} + C_2\left(\frac{dx_2}{dt} - \frac{dx_1}{dt}\right) + K_3 x_2 + K_2(x_2 - x_1) = F_2(t) \qquad (10.4.2)$$

where M, C, and K = system parameters
        x = displacement
        $F(t)$ = forcing function and subscripts are as indicated in the figure

The two above equations can be written as one matrix equation as follows:

$$\mathbf{Ma} + \mathbf{Cv} + \mathbf{Kx} = \mathbf{F} \qquad (10.4.3)$$

where $\mathbf{M} = \begin{bmatrix} M_1 & 0 \\ 0 & M_2 \end{bmatrix}$, the mass matrix

$\mathbf{C} = \begin{bmatrix} C_1 + C_2 & -C_2 \\ -C_2 & C_2 + C_3 \end{bmatrix}$, the damping matrix

$\mathbf{K} = \begin{bmatrix} K_1 + K_2 & -K_2 \\ -K_2 & K_2 + K_3 \end{bmatrix}$, the stiffness matrix

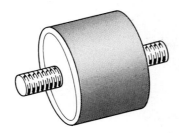

Load deflection graphs

Deflections below the X - - -X are considered safe
practice for static loads; data above that line are useful
for calculating deflections under dynamic loads.

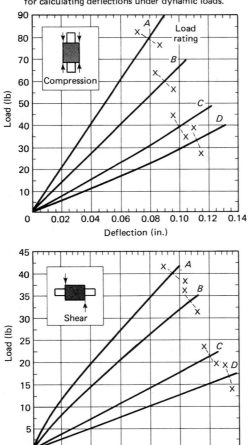

Figure 10.3.14 Cylindrical mounting. (*Source:* Stock Drive Products)

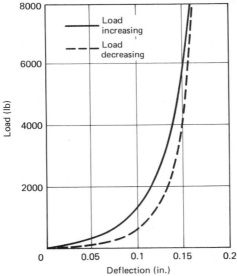

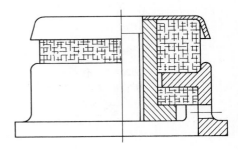

Figure 10.3.15 Elliptic leaf spring. (*Source:* Stock Drive Products)

$$\mathbf{a} = \begin{bmatrix} d^2x_1/dt^2 \\ d^2x_2/dt^2 \end{bmatrix}, \text{ the acceleration vector}$$

$$\mathbf{v} = \begin{bmatrix} dx_1/dt \\ dx_2/dt \end{bmatrix}, \text{ the velocity vector}$$

$$\mathbf{x} = \begin{bmatrix} x_1 \\ x_2 \end{bmatrix}, \text{ the displacement vector}$$

$$\mathbf{F} = \begin{bmatrix} F_1(t) \\ F_2(t) \end{bmatrix}, \text{ the force vector}$$

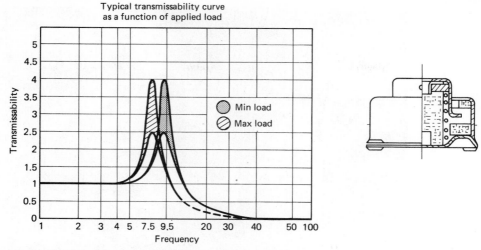

Typical transmissability curve
as a function of applied load

Figure 10.3.16 Base mounting. (*Source:* Stock Drive Products)

The term "vector," as used above, refers to a state vector or column matrix; in this context, it does not represent a magnitude and direction in space.

Free Vibration

Matrix equations describing forced, damped systems with two or more degrees-of-freedom can be manipulated by computer to obtain response characteristics. Analytical solutions are quite involved. However, some insight can be gained by an analytical solution of the two-degree-of-freedom free undamped case. For this problem, the matrix equation is reduced to

$$\mathbf{Ma} + \mathbf{Kx} = 0$$

or

$$\begin{bmatrix} M_1 & 0 \\ 0 & M_2 \end{bmatrix} \begin{bmatrix} d^2x_1/dt^2 \\ d^2x_2/dt^2 \end{bmatrix} + \begin{bmatrix} K_1 + K_2 & -K_2 \\ -K_2 & K_2 + K_3 \end{bmatrix} \begin{bmatrix} x_1 \\ x_2 \end{bmatrix} = 0 \qquad (10.4.4)$$

Assuming harmonic motion of both masses in the form $x = X \cos(\omega_n t)$, then acceleration has the form $d^2x/dt^2 = -X\omega_n^2 \cos(\omega_n t)$ and equation 10.4.4 becomes

$$\mathbf{KX} - \omega_n^2 \mathbf{MX} = 0$$

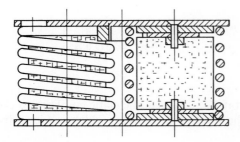

Figure 10.3.17 Damped spring mounting. (*Source:* Stock Drive Products)

Figure 10.3.18   Pneumatic mount. (*Source:* Vlier Engineering)

or

$$\begin{bmatrix} K_1 + K_2 - \omega_n^2 M_1 & -K_2 \\ -K_2 & K_2 + K_3 - \omega_n^2 M_2 \end{bmatrix} \begin{bmatrix} X_1 \\ X_2 \end{bmatrix} = 0 \qquad (10.4.5)$$

Natural Frequencies

The above equation is satisfied if $X_1 = X_2 = 0$, the static equilibrium condition. We are, of course, interested in the nontrivial solution, which is found by setting the

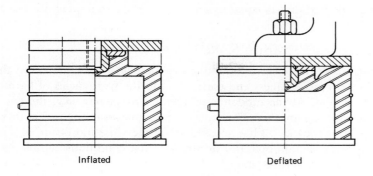

Inflated   Deflated

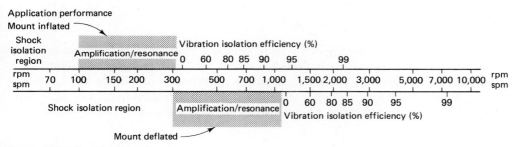

Figure 10.3.18 (*Continued*)

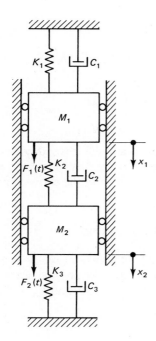

Figure 10.4.1 Two-degree-of-freedom system.

determinant of the first matrix equal to zero. This results in a quadratic equation in ω_n^2:

$$M_1 M_2 \omega_n^4 - [(K_2 + K_3)M_1 + (K_1 + K_2)M_2]\omega_n^2 + K_1 K_2 + K_2 K_3 + K_1 K_3 = 0 \quad (10.4.6)$$

The two roots, ω_{n1}^2 = the lower root, and ω_{n2}^2 = the higher root, are called the characteristic values (or eigenvalues) and correspond to the frequencies of harmonic vibration of the system. At the fundamental angular frequency, ω_{n1}, the two masses move in phase with one another. The motion of the masses is opposed at the second-mode angular frequency ω_{n2}. First and second mode vibration occur as a result of certain sets of initial conditions. For arbitrary initial conditions, simple harmonic motion will, in general, not occur.

Mode Shapes

The mode shape of a continuous system, such as a beam or plate in vibration, refers to the actual shape of the deflected body. When used to describe motion of a multidegree-of-freedom system, mode shape refers to the amplitude ratio. When a two-degree-of-freedom system is vibrating at the fundamental frequency, $\omega_n = \omega_{n1}$, then, using the first equation represented by the matrix equation 10.4.5, we have

$$(K_1 + K_2 - \omega_{n1}^2 M_1)X_1 - K_2 X_2 = 0$$

and using the second,

$$-K_2 X_1 + (K_2 + K_3 - \omega_{n1}^2 M_2)X_2 = 0$$

The first or fundamental mode shape, that is, the first mode amplitude ratio, given by either of the above equations is

$$(X_1/X_2)_1 = K_2/(K_1 + K_2 - \omega_{n1}^2 M_1)$$
$$= (K_2 + K_3 - \omega_{n1}^2 M_2)/K_2 \quad (10.4.7)$$

Similarly, the second mode shape, for $\omega_n = \omega_{n2}$ is

$$(X_1/X_2)_2 = K_2/(K_1 + K_2 - \omega_{n2}^2 M_1)$$
$$= (K_2 + K_3 - \omega_{n2}^2 M_2)/K_2 \quad (10.4.8)$$

The system will vibrate in simple harmonic motion at the first (fundamental) or second mode frequency if initial conditions correspond to the first or second mode shape, respectively. The actual amplitudes cannot be found from the above equations, since they depend on initial conditions.

EXAMPLE PROBLEM: NATURAL FREQUENCIES AND MODE SHAPES

Find the natural frequencies and mode shapes for the two-degree-of-freedom system represented by Figure 10.4.1 if the supported weights in pounds are $W_1 = 40$ and $W_2 = 65$, and the spring rates in lb/in are $K_1 = 90$, $K_2 = 110$, and $K_3 = 25$. The system is undamped, in free vibration.

Solution. Masses (lb-s^2/in) are given by

$$M = \frac{W}{g}$$

where $g = 386$ in/s^2. The system parameters are substituted in equation 10.4.6, and the two roots (ω_n^2's) are found, from which the fundamental frequency is

$$\omega_{n1} = 18.97 \text{ rad/s} \quad \text{and} \quad f_{n1} = \frac{\omega_{n1}}{2\pi} = 3.02 \text{ Hz}$$

The second natural frequency is

$$\omega_{n2} = 48.70 \text{ rad/s} \quad \text{and} \quad f_{n2} = 7.75 \text{ Hz}$$

Using the lower root in equation 10.4.7, the first mode shape (amplitude ratio) is found to be

$$\left(\frac{X_1}{X_2}\right)_1 = 0.676$$

The second mode shape is found by using the higher root. Using equation 10.4.8,

$$\left(\frac{X_1}{X_2}\right)^2 = -2.403$$

Two-Degree-of-Freedom Systems Under Forced Vibration

Consider the system in Figure 10.4.1 except that $K_3 = 0$ and damping is neglected. Equation 10.4.3 reduces to

$$\mathbf{Ma} + \mathbf{Kx} = \mathbf{F}$$

or

$$\begin{bmatrix} M_1 & 0 \\ 0 & M_2 \end{bmatrix} \begin{bmatrix} d^2x_1/dt^2 \\ d^2x_2/dt^2 \end{bmatrix} + \begin{bmatrix} K_1 + K_2 & -K_2 \\ -K_2 & K_2 \end{bmatrix} \begin{bmatrix} x_1 \\ x_2 \end{bmatrix} = \begin{bmatrix} F_1(t) \\ F_2(t) \end{bmatrix} \qquad (10.4.9)$$

If we have a sinusoidal forcing function on mass 1 in the form

$$F_1(t) = F_0 \cos(\omega t) \quad \text{and} \quad F_2(t) = 0$$

then the steady-state solution to equation 10.4.9 is

$$\frac{X_1}{F_0/K_1} = \frac{1 - r_2^2}{(1 - r_1^2 + k_2/k_1)(1 - r_2^2) - k_2/k_1} \qquad (10.4.10)$$

$$\frac{X_2}{F_0/K_1} = \frac{1}{(1 - r_1^2 + k_2/k_1)(1 - r_2^2) - k_2/k_1} \qquad (10.4.11)$$

where X_1 and X_2 = the steady-state vibration amplitudes of mass 1 and 2, respectively
$$r_1 = \omega/(k_1/m_1)^{1/2}$$
$$r_2 = \omega/(k_2/m_2)^{1/2}$$

The derivation is suggested as an exercise.

The Dynamic Vibration Absorber

When noise and/or vibration problems occur in a one-degree-of-freedom lightly damped system, possible solutions include reducing the excitation force (e.g., balancing a rotor), addition of damping, a change in stiffness, or a change in mass. Examination of equations 10.4.10 and 10.4.11 leads to another possible solution, the dynamic vibration absorber.

Consider the system modeled by Figure 10.4.2a, where $F_1(t) = F_0 \cos(\omega t)$ and the system is in resonance, that is, $\omega = (K_1/M_1)^{1/2}$. If another mass and spring are added as in part (b) of the figure, where the auxiliary system is designed so that $(K_2/$

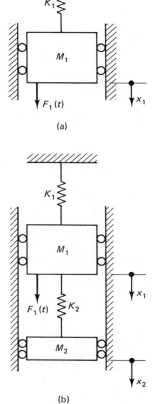

(a)

(b)   **Figure 10.4.2** Dynamic vibration absorber.

$M_2)^{1/2} = \omega$, then, we have constructed a dynamic vibration absorber. According to equations 10.4.10 and 10.4.11, the vibration amplitudes are $X_1 = 0$ and $X_2 = -F_0/K_2$. Theoretically, the main mass is stationary and no vibration force is transmitted to the support. Force in spring K_2 balances the forcing function.

Dynamic vibration absorbers have been used in both torsional and rectilinear systems where the forcing function was generated by a constant speed machine. In an actual system, there is always some damping, causing some motion of M_1, the main mass, and some force transmitted to its support. Since the system now has two degrees-of-freedom, there are two natural frequencies. A change in forcing-function frequency could excite the modified system at one of these frequencies, making the absorber useless.

EXAMPLE PROBLEM: LOW-FREQUENCY RESONANCE IN A DOUBLE-PANEL PARTITION

A partition is made of two gypsum-board panels separated by a 0.0889-m airspace. One panel has a surface mass of 14.65 kg/m², and the other 19.53 kg/m². Estimate the low-frequency resonance of the partition.

Solution. The wall will be modeled as a spring-mass system. The spring rate due to air compressibility is given by

$$K' = \frac{\gamma p}{h} = 1.4 \times 1.013 \times \frac{10^5}{0.0889} = 1,595,000 \text{ N/m}^3$$

where γ = the ratio of specific heats for air
p = atmospheric pressure (Pa)
h = panel separation (m)

Considering 1 m² of the partition, the masses are

$$M_1 = 14.65 \text{ kg} \quad \text{and} \quad M_2 = 19.53 \text{ kg}$$

The spring rates are taken as

$$K_1 = K_3 = 0 \quad \text{and} \quad K_2 = K' = 1,595,000 \text{ N/m}$$

Using these values in equation 10.4.6, and solving for the roots, we find the low-frequency double-panel resonance:

$$\omega_{n2} = 436.5 \text{ rad/s} \quad \text{or} \quad f_{n2} = 69.5 \text{ Hz}$$

The other root, $\omega_{n1} = 0$, is meaningless in this problem since it represents translation of the wall. A similar result was obtained in a somewhat different manner when this problem was solved in Chapter 6.

The Rayleigh Method for Multidegree-of-Freedom Systems

The Rayleigh method is an energy method which may be used to estimate the fundamental frequency of a multimass system. Since the method is based on conservation of energy, it is theoretically valid only for undamped systems. However, the Rayleigh method should give reasonable results for lightly damped systems.

Consider a vibrating system consisting of several masses M_1, M_2, and so on, mounted on a beam or shaft as in Figure 10.4.3. Let the amplitude at the masses be y_1, y_2, and so on, when vibration occurs at the fundamental frequency. Thus, the set of vibration amplitudes y_1, y_2, . . . , defines the first mode shape. The first mode shape will be approximated by the static deflection curve, except that overhung masses will be treated as upward loads as is M_4 in the figure. When the system reaches its maximum displacement, the strain energy is equal to the work done by the weights:

$$\text{PE}_{\text{max}} = \frac{1}{2} \sum_{k=1}^{n} (W_k y_k) \qquad (10.4.12)$$

where PE_{max} = maximum potential energy (strain energy) (in lb or N · m)
   n = the number of masses
   W_k = weight (lb), or force $W_k = M_k g$ (N) for the kth mass
   y_k = displacement of the kth mass (in or m) for the (approximate) first mode shape
   g = acceleration of gravity = 386 in/s^2 or 9.8 m/s^2 at sea level

The actual vibration is assumed to occur about the static equilibrium position. Thus, y is measured from the static equilibrium position, and PE refers to strain energy change, from the amount of strain energy at the static equilibrium position.

Assuming harmonic vibration, the velocity amplitude of the kth mass is $v_k = \omega_n y_k$ and its maximum kinetic energy is given by $\text{KE}_k = M_k v_k^2 / 2 = W_k \omega_n^2 y_k^2 / 2g$. The maximum kinetic energy of the system is given by

$$\text{KE}_{\text{max}} = \frac{\omega_n^2}{2g} \sum_{k=1}^{n} (W_k y_k^2) \qquad (10.4.13)$$

If we approximate a lightly damped system as a conservative system, the total energy, KE + PE, is constant. Since displacement is zero at maximum velocity and velocity

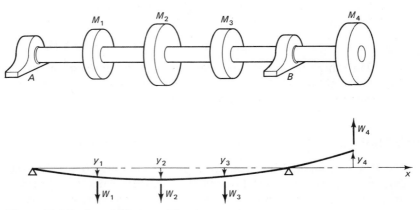

Figure 10.4.3   A multidegree-of-freedom system.

is zero at maximum displacement, we have $KE_{max} = PE_{max}$. This relationship allows us to estimate the natural frequency

$$\omega_n = \sqrt{\frac{g \sum\limits_{k=1}^{n} (W_k\, y_k)}{\sum\limits_{k=1}^{n} (W_k\, y_k^2)}} \tag{10.4.14}$$

where ω_n = the approximate fundamental frequency of shaft or beam vibration (rad/s). For a rotating shaft, ω_n is the critical rotation speed (rad/s), where

$$f_n = \frac{\omega_n}{2\pi} \tag{10.4.15}$$

and

$$n_c = \frac{30\omega_n}{\pi} \tag{10.4.16}$$

where f_n = natural frequency (Hz) or critical speed (rev/s)
n_c = critical speed (rpm)

Severe vibration may occur if a lightly damped shaft rotates at its critical speed.

10.5 TORSIONAL VIBRATION

Torsional vibration sometimes occurs in machine systems. Consider the torques and reverse effective (inertia) torques acting on the basic one-degree-of-freedom torsional system of Figure 10.5.1a. The equilibrium equation is

$$J_M \frac{d^2\phi}{dt^2} + C_T \frac{d\phi}{dt} + K_T\phi = T(t) \tag{10.5.1}$$

where J_M = mass moment of inertia ($kg \cdot m^2$ or $lb \cdot s^2 \cdot in$),
C_T = torsional damping coefficient ($N \cdot m \cdot s$ or $lb \cdot in \cdot s$),
K_T = torsional stiffness ($N \cdot m$ or $lb \cdot in$)
ϕ = angular displacement (rad)
t = time (s)

The mass moment of inertia of a body is given by

$$J_M = Mr_G^2 \tag{10.5.2}$$

where $M = W/g$ = mass (kg or $lb \cdot s^2/in$)
r_G = radius of gyration (m or in)
W = weight (lb)
$g = 386\ in/s^2$ = acceleration of gravity at sea level

For a circular disk of diameter D, $J_M = MD^2/8$.

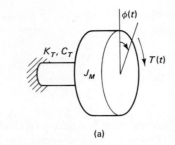

(a)

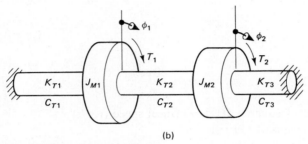

(b)

Figure 10.5.1   Torsional system.

The torsional stiffness of a circular shaft is given by

$$K_T = \frac{\pi d^4 G}{32L} \tag{10.5.3}$$

where d = shaft diameter (m or in)
        L = length (m or in)
        G = shear modulus (Pa or psi)

For steel, $G = 79 \times 10^9$ Pa or 11.5×10^6 psi (approximate).

Free Vibration

For an undamped system without a forcing torque, the equilibrium equation is satisfied by

$$\phi = \phi_0 \cos(\omega_n t) + \frac{\phi_0'}{\omega_n} \sin(\omega_n t) \tag{10.5.4}$$

where $\phi_0 = \phi(0)$ = initial displacement (rad)
        $\phi_0' = d\phi/dt(0)$ = initial angular velocity
        $\omega_n = (K_T/J_M)^{1/2}$ = natural angular frequency of vibration (rad/s)
        $f_n = \omega_n/(2\pi)$ = natural frequency (Hz)

Forced Vibration

It can be seen that the equilibrium equation has the same form as that for rectilinear vibration. Thus, if a harmonic forcing torque is applied to the mass, the transmissibility will have the same form as for rectilinear vibration. This applies to motion transmissibility as well. The relationship for torsional systems is

$$\frac{\phi_x}{\phi_y} = \frac{T_{tr}}{T_{in}}$$

$$= \left[\frac{1 + (2r_d r_f)^2}{(1 - r_f^2)^2 + (2r_d r_f)^2}\right]^{1/2} \quad\quad (10.5.5)$$

where ϕ_x = steady-state vibration amplitude of the mass (rad)
   ϕ_y = amplitude of harmonic rotation of the other end of the shaft (rad)
   T_{tr} = steady-state torque amplitude transmitted to the structure
   T_{in} = amplitude of harmonic torque applied to the mass
   $r_f = \omega/\omega_n$ = frequency ratio
   $r_d = C_T/C_{cT}$ = damping ratio
   $C_{cT} = 2(K_T J_M)^{1/2}$ (N·m·s or in·lb·s)

The vibration amplitude response to a harmonic torque applied to the mass is given by

$$\frac{\phi_x}{T_{in}/K_T} = \frac{1}{[(1 - r_f^2)^2 + (2r_d r_f)^2]^{1/2}} \quad\quad (10.5.6)$$

Two-Degree-of-Freedom Torsional Systems

Multimass torsional systems can be described in the following matrix form by analogy to multimass rectilinear systems:

$$\mathbf{J}_M\boldsymbol{\phi}'' + \mathbf{C}_T\boldsymbol{\phi}' + \mathbf{K}_T\boldsymbol{\phi} = \mathbf{T} \quad\quad (10.5.7)$$

For the two-degree-of-freedom system sketched in Figure 10.5.1b, the matrices are

$$\mathbf{J}_M = \begin{bmatrix} J_{M1} & 0 \\ 0 & J_{M2} \end{bmatrix}, \text{ the mass matrix}$$

$$\mathbf{C}_T = \begin{bmatrix} C_{T1} + C_{T2} & -C_{T2} \\ -C_{T2} & C_{T2} + C_{T3} \end{bmatrix}, \text{ the damping matrix}$$

$$\mathbf{K}_T = \begin{bmatrix} K_{T1} + K_{T2} & -K_{T2} \\ -K_{T2} & K_{T2} + K_{T3} \end{bmatrix}, \text{ the stiffness matrix}$$

$$\boldsymbol{\phi}'' = \begin{bmatrix} d^2\phi_1/dt^2 \\ d^2\phi_2/dt^2 \end{bmatrix}, \text{ the acceleration vector}$$

$$\boldsymbol{\phi}' = \begin{bmatrix} d\phi_1/dt \\ d\phi_2/dt \end{bmatrix}, \text{ the velocity vector}$$

$$\boldsymbol{\phi} = \begin{bmatrix} \phi_1 \\ \phi_2 \end{bmatrix}, \text{ the displacement vector}$$

$$\mathbf{T} = \begin{bmatrix} T_1(t) \\ T_2(t) \end{bmatrix}, \text{ the torque vector}$$

The natural frequencies of free vibration are given by the roots of the following quadratic equation in ω_n^2:

$$J_{M1} J_{M2} \omega_n^4 - [(K_{T2} + K_{T3})J_{M1} + (K_{T1} + K_{T2})J_{M2}]\omega_n^2$$
$$+ K_{T1}K_{T2} + K_{T2}K_{T3} + K_{T1}K_{T3} = 0 \qquad (10.5.8)$$

EXAMPLE PROBLEM: TORSIONAL VIBRATION

Two solid disks are joined by a 15-in-long stepped steel shaft. The disk weights are $W_1 = 40$ lb and $W_2 = 55$ lb, and diameters are $D_1 = 8$ in and $D_2 = 9$ in. The shaft diameter is 1.0 in for 3 in of its length, 1.125 in for the next 10 in, and 1.0 in for the remaining 2 in. Find the natural frequency of the system.

Solution.   Mass moments of inertia are

$$J_M = \frac{MD^2}{8} = \frac{WD^2}{8g}$$

$$J_{M1} = \frac{40 \times 8^2}{8 \times 386} = 0.829$$

$$J_{M2} = 1.443 \text{ lb} \cdot \text{s}^2 \cdot \text{in}$$

Torsional stiffnesses are

$$K_T = \frac{\pi d^4 G}{32L}$$

For the first section,

$$K_{TA} = \pi 1.0^4 \times 11.5 \times \frac{10^6}{32 \times 3} = 376{,}300$$

and for the others,

$$K_{TB} = 180{,}800 \quad \text{and} \quad K_{TC} = 564{,}500 \text{ in} \cdot \text{lb}$$

The shaft sections behave as springs in series. The combined torsional stiffness is given by

$$K_{T2} = \frac{1}{1/K_{TA} + 1/K_{TB} + 1/K_{TC}}$$

$$= \frac{1}{1/376{,}300 + 1/180{,}800 + 1/564{,}500} = 100{,}400 \text{ in} \cdot \text{lb}$$

Setting the other two stiffnesses equal to zero in the equation for natural frequency, the equation reduces to

$$J_{M1} J_{M2} \omega_n^4 - K_{T2}(J_{M1} + J_{M2})\omega_n^2 = 0$$

The roots are $\omega_{n1}^2 = 0$, representing rigid body rotation, and

$$\omega_{n2}^2 = \frac{K_{T2}(J_{M1} + J_{M2})}{J_{M1} J_{M2}}$$

or

$$\omega_{n2} = \left[\frac{K_{T2}(J_{M1} + J_{M2})}{J_{M1}J_{M2}}\right]^{1/2}$$ (10.5.9)

for the two masses moving in opposition to one another. Using the values computed above,

$$\omega_{n2} = \left[\frac{100,400(0.829 + 1.443)}{0.829 \times 1.443}\right]^{1/2}$$

$$= 436.7 \text{ rad/s}$$

$$f_{n2} = \frac{\omega_{n2}}{2\pi} = 69.5 \text{ Hz}$$

10.6 CONTINUOUS SYSTEMS

Vibration of continuous systems was discussed in earlier chapters including the wave equation for sound in air, and longitudinal vibration of a slender rod. Wave coincidence in partitions was also examined. Vibrating systems already treated in this chapter, however, were modeled as discrete or lumped-parameter systems. For the case of a heavy rigid body supported on spring mounts, a discrete system model is quite valid. For the case of a beam or plate, a better representation is obtained by considering the mass and stiffness as distributed through the body. In some instances, even the distributed mass of a spring must be considered.

Surging of Helical Compression Springs

In most applications, springs are uniformly compressed and extended, and may be modeled by their stiffness alone. In certain high-speed applications, wave motion, called surging, occurs within the spring. Surging may cause fatigue failure of the springs. In control applications, surging may cause the system to oscillate. In valve springs, for example, surging may prevent the valves from opening and closing with precision.

Considering the forces and inertia forces acting on an element of spring coil, the motion may be described by a partial differential equation in time and space. Assuming harmonic motion, the spring may be described by the total differential equation

$$\frac{d^2u}{dN^2} + p^2u = 0$$ (10.6.1)

where $u = u(N)$ = vibration amplitude (in or m) at any axial location
   N = coil number from 0 to N_a
   N_a = number of active coils
   $p = (4\pi\omega R^2/D)(2\rho/G)^{1/2}$
   ρ = mass density (lb-s^2/in^4 or kg/m^3)
   R = mean coil radius (in or m)
   ω = surging frequency (rad/s)

D = wire diameter (in or m)
G = shear modulus (psi or Pa)

The differential equation is satisfied by

$$u = A \cos(pN) + B \sin(pN) \tag{10.6.2}$$

where A and B are arbitrary constants, depending on the end restraints of the spring.

Fixed-Free Case If one end of the spring, coil zero, is fixed, then

$$u(0) = A = 0$$

If the other end, $N = N_a$, is free, then

$$\frac{du}{dN}(N_a) = Bp \cos(pN_a) = 0$$

Since $B = 0$ or $p = 0$ would be trivial solutions, we have $\cos(pN_a) = 0$ from which

$$pN_a = \frac{n\pi}{2} \quad \text{where} \quad n = 1, 3, 5, \ldots$$

and the surging frequencies are

$$\omega_{(n)} = \frac{nD}{8N_a R^2}\left(\frac{G}{2\rho}\right)^{1/2} \tag{10.6.3a}$$

or

$$f_{(n)} = \frac{nD}{16\pi N_a R^2}\left(\frac{G}{2\rho}\right)^{1/2} \tag{10.6.3b}$$

where ω_n = natural angular frequency of surging (rad/s)
           f_n = surging frequency (Hz)
           $n = 1, 3, 5, \ldots$

Fixed-Fixed Case If both ends of the spring are fixed, then the boundary conditions result in $\sin(pN_a) = 0$, and the above natural frequency equations apply except that $n = 2, 4, 6, \ldots$.

Flexural Vibration of Beams

If a uniform beam is subject to a distributed load $q(x)$, then deflection $y(x)$ is related to loading by

$$\frac{d^4y}{dx^4} - \frac{q}{EI} = 0 \tag{10.6.4}$$

where y = deflection (in or m)
           x = axial location (in or m)
           q = distributed load (lb/in or N/m)

E = elastic modulus (psi or Pa)

I = moment of inertia about the neutral axis in bending (in^4 or m^4)

For a vibrating beam,

$$q = q(x, t) \quad \text{and} \quad y = y(x, t)$$

functions of both location and time. Assuming harmonic vibration in the form

$$y(x, t) = Y(x) \cos(\omega t)$$

the inertia loading is

$$q(x) = -\frac{\rho A \partial^2 y}{\partial t^2} = \omega^2 \rho A Y \cos(\omega t)$$

where ρ = mass density (kg/m^3 or lb $\cdot$ s^2/in^4)

A = cross section area (in^2 or m^2)

The deflection equation becomes

$$\frac{d^4 Y}{dx^4} - p^4 Y = 0 \tag{10.6.5}$$

where $Y = Y(x)$ = deflection amplitude (in or m) due to flexural vibration

$p = [\omega^2 \rho A / (EI)]^{1/4}$

The deflection equation is satisfied by functions in the form

$$Y = C_1 \cos(px) + C_2 \sin(px) + C_3 \cosh(px) + C_4 \sinh(px) \tag{10.6.6}$$

where the C's are arbitrary constants that depend on the boundary conditions, that is, the deflection, slope, moment, and shear force constraints on the beam. For free vibration of a beam, one of the arbitrary constants will be unknown if the initial conditions are unspecified. The following boundary conditions apply.

1. Simply supported end:

$$Y = 0 \quad \text{and} \quad \frac{d^2 Y}{dx^2} = 0$$

2. Clamped end:

$$Y = 0 \quad \text{and} \quad \frac{dY}{dx} = 0$$

3. Free end:

$$\frac{d^2 Y}{dx^2} = 0 \quad \text{and} \quad \frac{d^3 Y}{dx^3} = 0$$

EXAMPLE PROBLEM: FLEXURAL VIBRATION OF A BEAM

A uniform beam of length L is simply supported at both ends.

(a) Find the natural frequencies of vibration.

Solution.   As given above, the general solution is $Y = C_1 \cos(px) + C_2 \sin(px) + C_3 \cosh(px) + C_4 \sinh(px)$. Differentiating, we have

$$\frac{dY}{dx} = p[-C_1 \sin(px) + C_2 \cos(px) + C_3 \sinh(px) + C_4 \cosh(px)]$$

and

$$\frac{d^2Y}{dx^2} = p^2[-C_1 \cos(px) - C_2 \sin(px) + C_3 \cosh(px) + C_4 \sinh(px)]$$

The boundary conditions for a simply supported beam are

$$Y(0) = \frac{d^2Y}{dx^2}(0) = Y(L) = \frac{d^2Y}{dx^2}(L) = 0$$

Using the first,

$$Y(0) = C_1 + C_3 = 0$$

and from the second,

$$d^2Y/dx^2(0) = -C_1 + C_3 = 0$$

Solving the two simultaneous equations from the first two boundary conditions, the result is

$$C_1 = C_3 = 0$$

reducing the deflection equation to

$$Y = C_2 \sin(px) + C_4 \sinh(px)$$

Using the remaining two boundary conditions,

$$C_2 \sin(pL) + C_4 \sinh(pL) = 0$$

and

$$-C_2 \sin(pL) + C_4 \sinh(pL) = 0$$

By adding these equations, we have

$$2C_4 \sinh(pL) = 0$$

and by subtracting,

$$2C_2 \sin(pL) = 0$$

Solutions include the trivial solutions in which there is no motion or the physical constants are not finite, and the following valid solution:

$$C_4 = 0 \quad \text{and} \quad \sin(pL) = 0$$

This is satisfied by

$$pL = n\pi \quad \text{or} \quad p = \frac{n\pi}{L}$$

from which

$$\omega_{(n)} = \frac{n^2\pi^2}{L^2}\left(\frac{EI}{\rho A}\right)^{1/2}$$ (10.6.7)

where $\omega_{(n)}$ = the nth natural frequency (rad/s) of flexural vibration of a uniform simply supported beam

$f_{(n)} = \omega_{(n)}/2\pi$ = natural frequency (Hz)

$n = 1, 2, 3, \dots$

When the beam is vibrating at the nth natural frequency the deflection amplitude shape has the form

$$Y = C_2 \sin(px) = C_2 \sin\left(\frac{n\pi x}{L}\right)$$

that is, the first mode shape is a half-sine, the second a full sine, and so on. For a rotating shaft, the critical speed is the shaft speed corresponding to the first mode of vibration,

$$n_c = \frac{30\pi}{L^2}\left(\frac{EI}{\rho A}\right)^{1/2}$$ (10.6.8)

where n_c = critical speed (rpm) for a uniform, simply supported shaft, without added masses

L = length (between bearings)

$I = \pi(D^4 - D_I^4)/64$ = moment of inertia

D = shaft diameter

D_I = inside diameter if the shaft is hollow

ρ = mass density

A = cross section area

(b) A machine brace is to be made of a $1/4 \times 3/8 \times 30$ in aluminum strip (see Figure 10.6.1). Assume the ends are simply supported. There is some concern that it may be excited into vibration by the vibration frequencies of the machine. Find the natural frequencies of the brace.

Solution. Typical properties for aluminum are elastic modulus $E = 10.3 \times 10^6$ psi and

$$\text{weight density} = 0.097 \text{ lb/in}^3$$

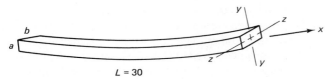

$L = 30$

Figure 10.6.1 Flexural vibration.

from which

$$\text{mass density } \rho = \frac{0.097}{386} = 2.513 \times 10^{-4} \text{ lb-s}^2/\text{in}^4$$

For thickness $a = \frac{1}{4}$ and width $b = \frac{3}{8}$, cross section area $A = (\frac{1}{4})(\frac{3}{8}) = 0.09375$, and moments of inertia are

$$I_{zz} = \frac{ba^3}{12} = 0.375 \times \frac{0.25^3}{12} = 4.8828 \times 10^{-4}$$

$$I_{yy} = \frac{ab^3}{12} = 0.25 \times \frac{0.375^3}{12} = 1.0986 \times 10^{-3}$$

Natural frequencies are given by

$$f_{(n)} = \left(\frac{n^2\pi}{2L^2}\right)\left(\frac{EI}{\rho A}\right)^{1/2}$$

$$= \frac{n^2\pi}{2 \times 30^2}\left(\frac{10.3 \times 10^6 I}{2.513 \times 10^{-4} \times 0.09375}\right)^{1/2}$$

$$= 1154 n^2 I^{1/2}$$

For flexural vibration about the zz-axis,

$$f_1 = 25.50 \text{ Hz}, \qquad f_2 = 102.0 \text{ Hz}, \qquad f_3 = 229.5 \text{ Hz, etc.}$$

For flexural vibration about the yy-axis,

$$f_1 = 38.25 \text{ Hz} \qquad f_2 = 153.0 \text{ Hz}, \qquad f_3 = 344.3 \text{ Hz, etc.}$$

10.7 FINITE-ELEMENT ANALYSIS

Vibration analysis of plates, shells, and other continuous systems can require a large number of calculations. Practical options for solution include:

1. Simplifying the mathematical model of the system to one that can be easily solved analytically.
2. Experimental modal analysis.
3. Finite-element analysis.

Each option has advantages and drawbacks. The simplified mathematical model is probably quickest and easiest, but may result in solutions that miss important natural frequencies and mode shapes. Experimental modal analysis is often the most credible method, since it is based on response of the actual structure or a physical model or prototype. However, experimental modal analysis requires specialized test equipment. Furthermore, it may be desirable to predict the vibration response of a structure before construction of a physical model or prototype of the structure. Finite-element analysis permits the actual problem to be represented with some detail. However, adequate computer facilities must be available, since the finite-element model is limited by the size of matrix that can be handled by the computer. Experimental modal analysis and finite-element analysis are often used in combination.

Finite-element analysis (FEA) can be used for static and dynamic analysis of beams, plates, shells, trusses, and other solid bodies. FEA has also been applied to problems involving fluids, including airborne noise problems. Many different finite-element programs have vibration analysis capabilities, including general purpose codes such as NASTRAN (a code developed by the National Aeronautics and Space Administration which is in the public domain), MSC-NASTRAN (a proprietary code developed from NASTRAN, available from MacNeal-Schwendler Corp.), and ANSYS (a proprietary code available from Swanson Analysis Systems Inc.).

The structure to be analyzed is modeled using various types of finite elements from the finite-element library. The library may include more than 100 element types including beam elements, triangular and rectangular plate and shell elements, conical shell elements, and mass, damping, and stiffness elements. The programs are developed for efficient solution to matrix problems involving large numbers of finite elements.

The preprocessing step in FEA involves generation of a finite-element mesh to represent the structure to be analyzed. The elements may be automatically sized by proportional spacing so that the mesh is denser in areas of greatest interest. Constraints and forcing functions are applied. Usually, the final mesh is plotted to verify that it actually represents the problem being modeled. The input data are converted to matrix form by the FEA code. The form of the matrix equation is

$$\mathbf{Ma} + \mathbf{Cv} + \mathbf{Kx} = \mathbf{F} \qquad (10.7.1)$$

where $\mathbf{M, C,}$ and $\mathbf{K}$ = the mass, damping, and stiffness matrices, respectively, for the finite-element representation of the problem

$\mathbf{a, v,}$ and $\mathbf{x}$ = the acceleration, velocity and displacement vectors, respectively

$\mathbf{F}$ = the forcing function vector

In the solution step, the matrices are manipulated to determine natural frequencies, mode shapes, and response amplitudes, and/or dynamic stresses due to harmonic, random, or transient forcing functions. In the postprocessor step, the FEA program arranges the output data in a convenient form for interpretation. Usually, the deformed structure is portrayed graphically as an overlay over the undeformed mesh diagram. Mode shapes or displacement amplitudes are exaggerated in the display. Even if an efficient program is used, many hours of engineering effort may be required to define a vibration problem, to model it, and to generate a satisfactory mesh. However, once a solution is obtained, redesign to improve vibration characteristics can be done very efficiently, by altering stored data. Design sensitivity analysis may be available, permitting the identification of critical elements in the problem. Design optimization is also a feature of some FEA codes. FEA software is available for personal computers. However, minicomputers and mainframe computers are used for involved problems requiring large matrices.

General references on the finite-element method include Grandin (1986), Huebner and Thornton (1982), and Hughes (1987). Blakely et al. (1985) and Brooks (1986)

discuss stress and vibration analysis using finite-element analysis programs designed for a personal computer. The relationship between finite-element analysis and modal analysis is discussed by Rieger (1986).

10.8 RANDOM VIBRATION

In deterministic vibration problems, the forcing function can be described as a function of time. Vibration due to imbalance of a rotor operating at known speed is a deterministic problem. Random vibration problems involve excitation which can only be described statistically. Structural excitation of an aircraft due to jet engine noise or turbulent flow is considered a random process. Both frequency and amplitude vary, following no known deterministic pattern.

Probability Density

Since the amplitude or acceleration of random vibration is not known as a function of time, it is described in terms of its probability density. One possible model is the Gaussian or normal probability density curve given as follows in normalized form:

$$p(x) = \frac{1}{\text{SD}(2\pi)^{1/2}} e^{-0.5x^2/\text{SD}^2} \qquad (10.8.1)$$

and the probability of the value of x falling between a and b is

$$P(a < x < b) = \int_a^b p(x)dx \qquad (10.8.2)$$

where $p(x)$ = the probability density of the function
$\qquad\quad x$ = the amount by which the function differs from the mean
$\qquad$ SD = the standard deviation
$\qquad\quad e$ = the base of natural logarithms
$\qquad\quad P$ = the probability of x falling in a particular range

It is certain that x must fall between $-\infty$ and $+\infty$. This is verified by the total area under the probability density function curve:

$$P(-\infty < x < \infty) = \int_{-\infty}^{\infty} p(x)dx = 1 \qquad (10.8.3)$$

Mean-Square Value and Autocorrelation

The temporal mean square of a function is given by

$$x_{\text{rms}}^2 = \lim_{T \to \infty} \left(\frac{1}{T} \int_0^T x^2(t)dt \right) \qquad (10.8.4)$$

where x_{rms} = the root mean square
$\qquad x_{\text{rms}}^2$ = the mean square, that is related to energy
$\qquad\quad T$ = the time interval

The temporal autocorrelation function describes (on the average) how the instantaneous value of a function depends on previous values. It is given by

$$R(\tau) = \lim_{T \to \infty} \left(\frac{1}{T} \int_0^T x(t)x(t + \tau)dt \right) \qquad (10.8.5)$$

where $R(\tau)$ = autocorrelation function
         τ = the time interval between measurements
         t = time

Stationary and Ergodic Processes

A general function may vary in such a way that there is no time interval in which the function is typical, and that, in an ensemble of tests, no test is typical of all other tests in the ensemble. However, if the probability distributions of a function are independent of the time interval during which they were measured, for sufficiently long averaging times, then the function represents a stationary process. That is, for a stationary process, the mean-square value measured during one interval is essentially equal to the mean-square value measured during a later interval. The autocorrelation function is likewise unaffected by a time shift. If mean-square values and autocorrelation functions of a number of ensembles of data are equal to the temporal values, then the process is ergodic as well as stationary. In vibration studies, it is usual to assume that processes are ergodic, which implies that they are stationary as well.

Spectral Density

The mean-square spectral density, also called the power spectral density, can be obtained from the autocorrelation function as follows:

$$S(\omega) = \frac{\int_{-\infty}^{\infty} R(\tau)e^{-j\omega\tau}\, d\tau}{2\pi} \qquad (10.8.6)$$

where

$S(\omega)$ = mean-square spectral density $[g^2/(\text{rad/s})$ or $\text{in}^2/(\text{rad/s})$ or $(\text{m/s}^2)^2/(\text{rad/s})$, etc.]

    ω = circular frequency (rad/s)

This equation is sometimes used in analytical studies. The inverse relationship is

$$R(\tau) = \int_{-\infty}^{\infty} S(\omega)e^{j\omega\tau}\, d\omega \qquad (10.8.7)$$

Vibration measurements obtained from a fast Fourier transform (FFT) analyzer or other instrumentation may be expressed in dB re 1 g or dB re 1 m/s, and so on, within each frequency band. These may be converted to mean-square spectral density $W(f)$ (g^2/Hz or other convenient engineering units), where $S(\omega)$ and $W(f)$ are related by

$$W(f) = 4\pi S(\omega) \qquad (10.8.8)$$

where $W(f)$ = spectral density (units^2/Hz), defined for positive frequencies only
   f = frequency (Hz)
   $S(\omega)$ = spectral density [units^2/(rad/s)] defined for positive and negative frequencies (a mathematical artifice)

If the vibration measurements are representative, and the process is stationary, then the mean-square value is given by

$$x_{rms}^2 = \lim_{T \to \infty} \left(\frac{1}{T} \int_0^T x^2(t)dt \right) = \int_0^\infty W(f)df = R(0) \qquad (10.8.9)$$

where x_{rms}^2 = mean-square value [g^2 or (in/s^2)^2, etc.], and
   $R(0)$ = the autocorrelation function for $\tau = 0$

White Noise

White noise is a random signal having a constant mean-square spectral density for all frequencies from zero to infinity. That is,

$$W_{white}(f) = W_0, \qquad 0 < f < \infty$$

This idealization is not physically realizable since it would require infinite power. However, it is useful in analytical investigations.

Band-limited white noise is a random signal with constant spectral density over a specified frequency range:

$$W_{BLW}(f) = W_0, \qquad f_1 < f < f_2$$

White noise generators are designed produce a signal with random variation in amplitude and frequency, with relatively constant spectral density over various frequency ranges.

Complex Frequency Response—The Fourier Transform and Fourier Integral

For harmonic vibration excitation represented by the real part of

$$x = Ae^{j\omega t} \qquad (10.8.10)$$

the response of a linear system can be written in the form

$$y = B(\omega)e^{j\omega t} \qquad (10.8.11)$$

where $B(\omega)$ is the complex frequency response, having the dimensions of y/x. This relationship was used earlier for periodic functions. When the excitation function $x(t)$ is not periodic, but has a Fourier transform

$$X(\omega) = \int_{-\infty}^\infty x(t)e^{-j\omega t}\, dt \qquad (10.8.12)$$

where $X(\omega)$ is the Fourier transform or frequency domain representation of $x(t)$, then for each frequency component

$$Y(\omega) = B(\omega)X(\omega) \qquad (10.8.13)$$

where

$$Y(\omega) = \int_{-\infty}^{\infty} y(t)e^{-j\omega t}\, dt \qquad (10.8.14)$$

is the Fourier transform of the response.

The response is given by the inverse transform

$$y(t) = \frac{\int_{-\infty}^{\infty} Y(\omega)e^{j\omega t}\, d\omega}{2\pi} \qquad (10.8.15)$$

where $y(t)$ is the Fourier integral of $Y(\omega)$. Combining the above relationships, we obtain

$$y(t) = \frac{1}{2\pi} \int_{-\infty}^{\infty} B(\omega)e^{j\omega t}\, d\omega \int_{-\infty}^{\infty} x(t)e^{-j\omega t}\, dt \qquad (10.8.16)$$

If the input-response relationships are written in terms of spectral densities, they become

$$S_Y(\omega) = |B(\omega)|^2 S_X(\omega) \qquad (10.8.17)$$

where S_X and S_Y are, respectively, input and output function spectral densities [units^2/(rad/s)], and

$$W_Y(f) = |B(f)|^2 W_X(f) \qquad (10.8.18)$$

where W_X and W_Y are, respectively, input and output function spectral densities (units^2/Hz). The validity and limitations of this procedure are discussed by Broch (1972), Crandall and Mark (1963), and Robson (1964).

EXAMPLE PROBLEM: RANDOM VIBRATION

The mass in a one-degree-of-freedom damped system is subject to a forcing function in the form of white noise with a mean-square spectral density of W_0 lb^2/Hz. Determine the displacement response.

Solution. The complex frequency response for this system has already been determined in an earlier section. Changing the notation for this problem, the function becomes

$$B(\omega) = B(f) = 1/[K(1 - r_f^2 + j2r_d r_f)]$$

and the mean-square response spectrum is

$$W_Y(f) = |B(f)|^2 W_X(f)$$
$$= W_0/\{K^2[(1 - r_f^2)^2 + (2r_d r_f)^2]\}$$

where $W_Y(f)$ = displacement spectral density (in^2/Hz). Using mathematical instead of engineering units, the spectral density of the input white noise is

$$S(\omega) = S_0 = \frac{W(f)}{4\pi} = \frac{W_0}{4\pi} \text{ (lb}^2\text{-s/rad)}$$

over the frequency range $-\infty < \omega < \infty$. The complex frequency response spectrum is given by

$$B(\omega) = \frac{1}{K(1 - r_f^2 + j2r_d r_f)}$$

$$= \frac{\omega_n^2/K}{\omega_n^2 - \omega^2 + j2r_f \omega_n \omega}$$

$$= \frac{1/M}{\omega_n^2 - \omega^2 + j2r_d \omega_n \omega}$$

and the response spectral density by

$$S_Y(\omega) = |B(\omega)|^2 S_0$$

The mean-square response is

$$Y' = S_0 \int_{-\infty}^{\infty} |B(\omega)|^2 \, d\omega$$

For functions in the form

$$B(\omega) = \frac{a + j\omega b}{c - \omega^2 d + j\omega g}$$

the mean square is given by

$$\int_{-\infty}^{\infty} |B(\omega)|^2 \, d\omega = \frac{\pi[b^2 + a^2 d/c]}{gd}$$

Making the indicated substitutions, we have

$$Y' = \frac{\pi S_0}{2M^2 r_d \omega_n^3} = \frac{W_0}{8M^2 r_d \omega_n^3}$$

$$= \frac{W_0}{64\pi^3 M^2 r_d f_n^3} \text{ (in}^2\text{)}$$

10.9 NONLINEAR VIBRATION

The mathematical model of linear vibration, which employs springs with a constant spring rate and viscous (velocity proportional) damping, is easily handled mathematically, and gives reasonable results for most problems. If a mass is supported on helical compression springs, for example, the spring rate is a function of only the shear modulus of the spring material and the spring geometry. The spring rate of a helical steel compression spring is essentially constant over a wide range of displacements. The linearity assumption allows us to develop generalized input–output relationships such as the transmissibility curves.

Elastomer mounts tend to be displacement dependent in their properties. Wire mesh dampers are sometimes incorporated in helical spring mounts. These dampers are designed to provide a combination of hysteresis losses and friction losses at large vibration amplitudes (near resonance), but have little effect at small amplitudes (the isolation region). The wire mesh may also add significantly to the spring rate at large vibration amplitudes. When displacement limiters or snubbers are employed, they also make the system properties displacement-dependent. These nonlinear effects are sometimes great enough to make the linear model invalid.

The force displacement relationship of a hardening spring is illustrated in Figure 10.9.1. The slope of the curve increases with increased displacement magnitude $|x|$. For a softening spring, the slope of the force displacement curve decreases with increased displacement magnitude. For a nonlinear spring, spring rate is not constant; spring force is given by $F_s = F_s(x)$, not Kx. Similarly, damping force may be a function of displacement and/or velocity, given by $F_d = F_d(x, v)$, not necessarily Cv. In one damping model, constant or Coulomb damping, the damping force is constant in magnitude but, like viscous damping force, it opposes velocity.

The response of a nonlinear system with a hardening spring is shown in Figure 10.9.2. For a given system, the shape of the curve depends on the magnitude of the forcing function F. In the region of frequencies between f_1 and f_2, the system is not stable, and the vibration amplitude X may jump from one level to another.

Natural Frequency

For a nonlinear one-degree-of-freedom system, the equilibrium equation may take the form

$$M \frac{d^2x}{dt^2} + F_d(x, v) + F_s(x) = F(t) \tag{10.9.1}$$

where F_d and F_s = damping and spring forces, respectively.

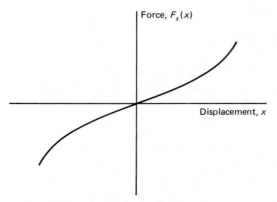

Figure 10.9.1 Hardening spring.

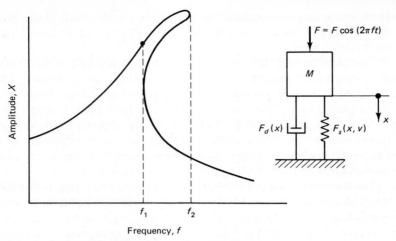

Figure 10.9.2 Response of a nonlinear system.

For a free undamped system, we may write

$$M \frac{d^2x}{dt^2} = M \frac{dv}{dt} = M \frac{dv}{dx}\frac{dx}{dt} = Mv \frac{dv}{dx} = -F_s(x) \qquad (10.9.2)$$

where $v = dx/dt$ = velocity of the mass. Multiplying both sides of the last equation by dx and integrating, the result is

$$\int_0^v Mv\, dv = M \frac{v^2}{2} = \int_{X_{max}}^x - F_s\, dx \qquad (10.9.3)$$

where X_{max} = maximum displacement, at which time the velocity $v = 0$. The velocity is given by

$$v = \frac{dx}{dt} = \left[\frac{2}{M}\left(\int_{X_{max}}^x - F_s\, dx \right) \right]^{1/2} \qquad (10.9.4)$$

Solving for dt and integrating again,

$$t = \left(\frac{M}{2} \right)^{1/2} \int_{X_{max}}^x \left(\int_{X_{max}}^x - F_s\, dx \right)^{-1/2} dx \qquad (10.9.5)$$

where t = the time during which mass displacement changed from X_{max} to x.

If the mass vibrates equally to either side of the $x = 0$ position, and the spring force is antisymmetric, that is,

$$F_s(-x) = -F_s(x)$$

then the period of vibration is given by four times the time for the displacement to change from X_{max} to zero. Thus,

$$\tau_n = 4\left(\frac{M}{2} \right)^{1/2} \int_{X_{max}}^0 \left(\int_{X_{max}}^x - F_s\, dx \right)^{-1/2} dx \qquad (10.9.6)$$

where τ_m = the period of natural vibration (s) the natural frequency is given by $f_n = 1/\tau_n$ (Hz)

Nonlinear systems are considered in more detail by Macduff and Curreri (1958).

10.10 SHOCK AND IMPACT LOADING

Shock and impact loading involve forces applied suddenly to a machine or other body. They induce vibration, and when large radiating surfaces are present, they may result in a noise problem. In addition, damage may be caused at the point of impact, or malfunction or damage may be caused elsewhere if large amplitude vibrations result from the impact.

Unit Impulse—The Dirac Delta Function

Consider a function in the form

$$x(t) = \delta(t - \tau) \tag{10.10.1}$$

the Dirac delta function or Dirac delta distribution, which has the following properties

$$\delta(t - \tau) = 0 \quad \text{for} \quad t \neq \tau$$

$$= \infty \quad \text{at} \quad t = \tau$$

$\delta(t - \tau)$ encloses a unit area in the $x(t)$ versus t plane. If $x(t)$ represents force, then $\delta(t - \tau)$ is a unit impulse equivalent to a unit change in momentum in a conservative system. However, the Dirac delta function may be used to represent other quantities as well, such as acceleration.

Impulse Response—The Convolution Integral

Suppose system response to the Dirac delta function is given by the impulse response function

$$y(t) = h(t - \tau) \tag{10.10.2}$$

where $h(t - \tau)$ = the impulse response function, which depends on system parameters. Then, for a linear system, we use the convolution or superposition interval to obtain the response to all input excitation $x(t)$

$$y(t) = \int_{-\infty}^{t} x(\tau)h(t - \tau)d\tau$$

$$= \int_{-\infty}^{\infty} x(\tau)h(t - \tau)d\tau \tag{10.10.3}$$

where $y(t)$ = system response to all excitation up to time t. The upper limit of integration was changed for mathematical convenience. This does not change the value of the integral since

$$h(t - \tau) = 0 \quad \text{for} \quad \tau > t$$

that is, there is no response before the impulse is applied. The units of h depend on the units which have been selected for x and y.

The equation of motion for free vibration of a one-degree-of-freedom undamped linear system is

$$M \frac{d^2x}{dt^2} + Kx = 0 \qquad \text{(from 10.1.2)}$$

which is satisfied by

$$x = X_0 \cos(\omega_n t) + \left(\frac{V_0}{\omega_n}\right) \sin(\omega_n t) \qquad \text{(from 10.1.3)}$$

where X_0 and V_0 = initial displacement and velocity, respectively.

Using the impulse-momentum relationship,

$$\int_{t_1}^{t_2} F(t)dt = M(v_2 - v_1) \qquad (10.10.4)$$

where $F(t) = \delta(t)$, and $\delta(t)$ = the Dirac delta function representing a unit force impulse at $t = 0$; we have by definition

$$\int_{t_1}^{t_2} \delta(t)dt = 1 = MV_0$$

from which $V_0 = 1/M$. The result is that the unit force impulse $\delta(t)$ causes an instantaneous unit change in momentum and the velocity goes from zero to $V_0 = 1/M$ instantaneously. The unit force impulse $\delta(t)$ is, of course, an idealization since a finite instantaneous change in momentum is impossible.

Assuming the system is at rest the instant before the impulse, letting $t = 0$ the instant after the impulse, we substitute the initial conditions $X_0 = 0$ and $V_0 = 1/M$ in the solution to the equation of motion, yielding

$$x = h(t) = \frac{1}{M\omega_n} \sin(\omega_n t) \qquad (10.10.5)$$

where $h(t)$ = system response to a unit force impulse occurring at $t = 0$.

The relationship between the impulse response function and the complex frequency response of a system is given by the Fourier transform pair

$$H(\omega) = \int_{-\infty}^{\infty} h(t)e^{-j\omega t} dt \qquad (10.10.6)$$

$$h(t) = \frac{1}{2\pi} \int_{-\infty}^{\infty} H(\omega)e^{j\omega t} d\omega \qquad (10.10.7)$$

For a one-degree-of-freedom damped linear system,

$$H(\omega) = B(\omega) = 1/[K(1 - r_f^2 + j2r_dr_f)] \qquad (10.10.8)$$

where $B(\omega)$ = the complex frequency response relating force input to displacement response as determined in an earlier section

$r_d = C/C_c$ = the damping ratio

$r_f = \omega/\omega_n$ = the frequency ratio

EXAMPLE PROBLEM: IMPULSE LOADING

Find the displacement response of an undamped one-degree-of-freedom system after a rectangular impulse is applied to the mass. The impulse is described by $F(t) = A$ for $0 \leq t \leq T$, and $F(t) = 0$ for $t < 0$ and $t > T$.

Solution.   Using the system response function obtained above in the convolution integral, we have

$$y = \int_{-\infty}^{\infty} x(\tau)h(t - \tau)d\tau$$

$$= \int_0^T A[1/(M\omega_n)] \sin[\omega_n(t - \tau)]d\tau$$

$$= A/(M\omega_n^2)\{-\cos[\omega_n(t - \tau)]\}_0^T$$

$$= (-A/K)\{\cos[\omega_n(t - T)] - \cos(\omega_n t)\} \quad \text{for} \quad t \geq T$$

where y = displacement (in or m)

A = force (lb or N)

K = spring rate (lb/in or N/m)

$\omega_n = (K/M)^{1/2}$ = natural frequency (rad/s)

M = mass (lb-s^2/in or kg)

t and T = time (s)

Control of Shock and Impact Loading

Some of the following methods may be useful in certain circumstances. A thorough analysis of each individual problem is required before selecting one or more control methods for shock and impact loading, since arbitrary changes may increase impact problems and noise emission.

1. Reduce impact energy by replacing quick-acting solenoid operated valves and other impact sources with other systems.
2. Design metal-forming and shearing dies and punches so that the process occurs more gradually.
3. Install shock and vibration mounts selected for the particular machine, considering machine mass and rate of operation.

4. To reduce displacement response, increase the mass of the machine which is to be struck.
5. Use damping to dissipate energy of an impact.

Crede (1965) considers analytical problems in shock control, and discusses engineering design implications.

10.11 VIBRATION AND SHOCK MEASUREMENTS

It is possible to measure vibration displacement and vibration velocity, but the most common measurements of vibration involve acceleration. The basic vibration and shock transducer is the accelerometer. Many of the other components in vibration measurement systems are similar to those used to measure airborne sound. Some instruments, including fast Fourier transform (FFT) analyzers, are designed for both acoustic and vibration applications.

Accelerometers

Accelerometers are usually mounted on a vibrating body, using a threaded stud, or adhesive, or wax. Some accelerometers are mounted in a probe, which is held against the vibrating body. A typical accelerometer consists of a small housing containing one or more piezoelectric sensing elements on which rest a mass that is preloaded by a stiff spring. The principle of operation is based on the piezoelectric effect: the surfaces of some crystals become charged when loaded mechanically.

When the accelerometer is subject to acceleration, the mass exerts a force on the piezoelectric element proportional to the acceleration. The charge, in turn, is proportional to the force. The accelerometer may be designed so that the piezoelectric element is stressed in compression or in shear. Commonly used piezoelectric elements include quartz crystals and specially processed ceramic materials.

Charge and Voltage Sensitivity of Accelerometers

The sensitivity of an electromechanical transducer is the ratio of electrical output to mechanical input. Accelerometer system sensitivities are given in terms of charge per unit acceleration or voltage per unit acceleration. Typical units are picocoulombs per meter-per-second-square ($pC \cdot s^2/m$), picocoulombs per g (pC/g), and millivolts per g (mV/g), where g = the acceleration of gravity. If the readout instrument is calibrated to read in root-mean-square (rms) units, then a sensitivity in mV/g is interpreted to mean mV_{rms}/g_{rms}. If it is calibrated to read in peak units, then the sensitivity is interpreted as mV_{peak}/g_{peak}. The relationship between charge and voltage sensitivity is given by

$$CS \ (pC/g) = VS \ (mV/g) \times C \ (pF)/1000 \qquad (10.11.1)$$

where   CS = charge sensitivity
VS = voltage sensitivity
C = capacitance of accelerometer and connecting cable (pF)

Charge sensitivity is not affected by cable length. If the accelerometer cable length is changed after calibration, it may be necessary to adjust voltage sensitivity as follows:

$$\text{system sensitivity} = \text{calibration sensitivity} \times \frac{C_S + C_{cc}}{C_S + C_c} \qquad (10.11.2)$$

where C_S = capacitance of sensor
C_{cc} = capacitance of cable used during calibration
C_c = capacitance of cable currently used

Cable capacitance is about 30 pF/ft and the capacitance of an accelerometer is given on its calibration chart. It can be seen from the above equation that a high-capacitance accelerometer is not greatly affected by a change in cable length.

Accelerometer Frequency Response

For frequencies of vibration ranging from near DC to about one-third of the resonant frequency of an accelerometer, the charge produced by the piezoelectric element is essentially proportional to the acceleration of the accelerometer as a whole. At 22% of the mounted resonance frequency, typical error is less than 5%, and at 30% of the mounted resonance frequency, typical error is less than 10%. At higher frequencies, accuracy is reduced by vibration within the mass-spring system of the accelerometer itself. The region of valid measurements is reduced if the accelerometer is not rigidly mounted to the surface where vibration is to be measured.

Typical lower frequency limits for accelerometers are 0.1 to 1.0 Hz. Some accelerometers have upper frequency limits as high as 25 to 50 kHz, but sensitivities of only a fraction of 1 pC·s^2/m. Typical upper frequency limits are 4 to 15 kHz for accelerometers with sensitivities ranging from about 1 pC·s^2/m to 32 pC·s^2/m, where both upper and lower frequency limits are based on 10% error.

Preamplifiers and Integration Networks

The high-impedance output of an accelerometer is usually fed through a preamplifier or charge amplifier to convert it to a form suitable for input to measuring and analyzing equipment. Filters and other signal conditioning equipment may be included in the preamplifier. Integration networks are used to convert acceleration-proportional signals to velocity- and/or displacement-proportional signals.

Frequency Analysis

An acceleration-time record produced by an accelerometer mounted on a machine is difficult to interpret, since the machine may vibrate in a complex manner, with no clear harmonics visible in the record. Thus, instrumentation is used to generate an amplitude versus frequency spectrum, which may indicate high acceleration values at a frequency corresponding to a certain process. For example, peaks in the spectrum may indicate an unbalance in a rotating body, or a problem with a gear mesh, or incipient bearing failure. Table 10.11.1 indicates some possible sources of vibration which may be detected in a frequency analysis. Note that speeds and frequencies are

TABLE 10.11.1 MACHINERY VIBRATION DIAGNOSTIC GUIDE

Probable source	Disturbing frequency (cpm)	Dominant plane	Phase angle relationship	Amplitude	Envelope characteristics	Comments
Unbalance						
(1) Mass imbalance	1× rotor speed	Radial (axial is higher on overhung rotors)	1. Force in-phase 2. Couple out-of-phase	Steady	Narrow band	Rotor looseness or bow due to thermal stresses may change the amplitude and phase with time.
(2) Bent shaft	1× rpm (2× rpm if bent at the coupling)	Axial	180° out-of-phase axially	Steady	Narrow band	Run-out at rotor mass appears as unbalance. Run-out at coupling appears as misalignment.
(3) Eccentric motor rotor	1× rpm, 1× and 2× line frequency	Radial	N/A	Steady (see comment)	Narrow band	Will fluctuate (beat) in amplitude and phase if an electrical problem also exists (see electrically induced)
Misalignment						
(1) Parallel	1×, 2× rpm	Radial	Radial—180° out-of-phase	Steady		Most misalignments will be a combination. Errors are most common in the vertical plane. On long coupling spans, 1× will be higher.
(2) Angular	1×, 2× rpm	Axial	Axials—180° out-of-phase	Steady	Narrow band	
(3) Both parallel and angular	1×, 2× rpm	Radial and axial	Both radial and axials will be 180° out-of-phase.			
Electrically induced						
All electrically caused problems	2× slip frequency sidebands around	Radial	N/A	Steady		Will fluctuate in amplitude and phase

can be isolated, i.e. eliminated by cutting the current to motor.	1× rpm, 1× and 2× line frequency.					if mechanical problems (imbalance) also exist.
(1) Eccentric rotor						
(2) Loose stator laminations	2× line frequency and high frequency (60K CPM) sidebands of 2× line frequency	Radial	N/A	High, steady	Narrow band sidebands of 2× line frequency	Not usually destructive
(3) Broken rotor bar	Running speed with 2× slip frequency sidebands.	Radial	N/A	Steady	Narrow spike with sidebands	Replace rotor bar
(4) Unbalanced coil or phase resistance	2× line frequency	Radial	N/A	Low, steady	Narrow band	
(5) Stator problems (heating, shorts)	2× line frequency	Radial (can cause axial)	N/A	Steady	Narrow band	Vibration will increase as motor heats up.
(6) Loose iron	2× line frequency	Radial	N/A	High, steady	Narrow band	
Defective bearings						
(1) Antifriction	Early stages—30K–60K cpm depending on size and speed. Late stages—high 1× and multiple harmonics	Radial, except higher axial on thrust bearing	N/A	Increases as bearing degrades; may disappear just before failure	Bandwidth broadens as bearing degrades. Baseline may increase across entire spectrum	
(2) Sleeve	Early stages—subharmonics (may only be noticeable on shaft). Late stages—will appear as mechanical looseness (see below)	Radial	Shaft proximity probe orbits will indicate shaft position and dynamic changes.	Increases as bearing degrades	High baseline energies below 1×, 2×, and 3× rpm	Monitoring of rotor position (thrust) via proximity probes can provide reliable protection against thrust bearing failure.

TABLE 10.11.1 (Continued)

Probable source	Disturbing frequency (cpm)	Dominant plane	Phase angle relationship	Amplitude	Envelope characteristics	Comments
Mechanical looseness						
(1) Bearings, pedestals, etc. (nonrotating)	1×, 2×, and 3× predominant: may be up to 10× at lower amplitude	Radial	Varies with type of looseness	Steady	May extend up to 10× shaft speed	Variance of amplitude or phase may be caused by center of gravity shifts.
(2) Impellers, etc. (rotating)	1× predominant, but may have harmonics up to 10× at low levels	Radial	Will vary from start-up to start-up	Steady while running, but will vary from start-up to start-up	May extend up to 10× shaft speed	
Operation (process-related)						
(1) Blade/vane pass	No. of blades/vane × rpm	Radial predominant in the direction of discharge piping	N/A	Fluctuating	Broadband	More than one (1) discharge volute will produce harmonics of blade passing frequency.
(2) Cavitation or starvation	Random—broadband	Radial	N/A	Fluctuating	Broadband up to 2000+ Hz	Vane pass frequencies may be superimposed.
Drive belts						
(1) Mismatched, worn or stretched—also applies to adjustable sheave applications	Many multiples of belt frequency but 2× belt frequency usually dominant	Radial, especially high in line with belts	N/A	May be unsteady and beating if a belt freq. is close to driver or driven speed	N/A	Belt frequency = 3.14 cpm × $\dfrac{\text{pitch diameter}}{\text{belt length}}$
(2) Eccentric and/or unbalanced sheaves	1× shaft speed	Radial	In-phase	Steady	N/A	Balancing is possible with washers applied to taper lock bolts.
(3) Drive belt or sheave face misalignment	1× driver shaft	Axial	In-phase	Steady	N/A	Confirm with a straight edge.
(4) Drive belt resonance	Belt resonance with no relationship to rotational speeds	Radial	N/A	May be unsteady	±20% resonant frequency depending upon damping	Confirm with strobe light and belt excitation techniques. Change belt tension or belt length to eliminate the problem.

	function to excite its natural frequencies		rotor resonance will display 180° out-of-phase bearing relationships. A component within a structure will display phase relationships dependent upon the bending mode excited.	baseline energy fluctuations depend on force and damping	base; width depends upon damping	independent of speed changes.
Instability						
(1) Oil whirl	40 to 46% of running speed	Radial	N/A	Steady	Discrete peaks	Considered excessive when amplitudes reach 50% of normal bearing clearances
(2) Oil whip	Subrotational and equal to shaft resonance	Radial	N/A	Steady	Discrete peaks	
(3) Rotor rub	50% of running speed and half harmonics	Radial	N/A	Steady	Discrete peaks	Rub increases the resonant frequency to the next highest fraction of running speed.
Gears						
(1) Transmission error (poorly finished tooth face)	Gear mesh frequency (gear rpm × no. of teeth) and harmonics	Radial for spur gears, axial for helical or herringbone gears	N/A	Depends on loading, speed and total transmission error	Usually single peak, but sometimes low sidebands	
(2) Pitch line runout, mass unbalance, misalignment or faulty tooth	1× rpm and gear mesh frequency with ± gear rpm sidebands	Radial for spur gears; axial for helical or herringbone gears	N/A	1× rpm and mesh frequency sidebands depend on fault severity	Discrete peaks	May excite lateral or torsional resonances at various frequencies. Machining errors during hobbing can cause high 2× or 3× gear rpm vibration.

Note 1: This guide is based on casing measurements unless otherwise noted.

Note 2: Vibration symptoms are based upon the observation of amplitude on a logarithmic scale.

Source: Rockland Scientific Corp., Rockleigh, NJ.

given in the table as revolutions per minute and cycles per minute, where n (rpm) = f' (cpm) = 60 f (Hz). A frequency spectrum may be produced by swept frequency analysis, using a tunable filter, if the signal does not vary significantly with time. However, microprocessor-based signal analyzers are more convenient to use, particularly with time-varying signals.

Vibration Analyzers

Portable microprocessor-based signal analyzers are used to examine vibration patterns in the time and frequency domains. Most are based on fast Fourier transform (FFT) processors. The process of converting a vibration signal from a transducer to a meaningful display may involve the following components in a typical vibration analyzer:

1. Low-pass filter—to filter out spurious frequency components, while retaining those of interest.
2. Sampler—to sample the analog signal. The number of samples or individual values stored in a record may be fixed by the FFT processor configuration. A high rate of sampling is used to examine high-frequency signals. To avoid aliasing, the sampled signal should not contain significant components at frequencies above half the sampling rate. That is, the minimum sampling rate should be twice the Nyquist frequency f_N where f_N is the highest frequency component in the signal.
3. Analog-to-digital (A/D) converter—to digitize the analog signal.
4. Digital mixing signal—to facilitate production of a high-resolution display in a selected frequency range (zoom analysis).
5. Digital filter—filters spurious frequency components.
6. Time record buffer—stores digital data.
7. FFT processor—converts the time-domain record to the frequency domain, that is, generates the frequency spectrum.
8. Display screen—displays the time record or frequency spectrum, along with annotated coordinates of the plot, and amplitude values at selected cursor locations.
9. Interface—permits transfer of data between the analyzer and a computer for hard-copy recording and plotting, data storage, and automated testing.

Other features which are available on some vibration analyzers include:

1. Built in preamplifier.
2. Integrator to produce velocity and displacement records.
3. Nonvolatile memory to store spectra within the analyzer.
4. Constant-percent bandwidth capability, for example, generation of one-third- and one-tenth-octave spectra. The basic FFT output is a constant-bandwidth spectrum.
5. Mathematics capability for adding and subtracting spectra and other simple calculations.
6. Trigger facilities to permit calculations to begin when an event causes a predetermined vibration level.

7. Selectable annotated display units such as dB, g, m/s^2, in/s, and so on.
8. Dual-channel capability permitting input-response determinations, or comparison of vibration data taken at two points simultaneously.

Coherence, Cross Correlation, and Autocorrelation Measurements

As observed earlier, dual-channel fast Fourier transform (FFT) analyzers are used for measurement of vector sound intensity. Available functions on some general purpose dual-channel FFT analyzers include auto- and cross power spectra, transfer function, and coherence in the frequency domain, as well as auto- and cross correlation, time record, and impulse function in the time domain.

The coherence function can confirm a suspected source of vibration or noise. For example, one accelerometer could be mounted on a piece of machinery and another on a building wall. A high value of coherence indicates that the two signals are likely to be related. Once the source is identified, corrective action can be taken.

Cross correlation of signals makes it possible to determine which of two alternate paths a signal has traveled between two points. For example, consider two structural paths of vibration which are of different length. The cross correlation function indicates a time delay between accelerometer signals at the two points. Knowledge of propagation speed permits identification of the actual structural path.

The autocorrelation function, discussed in the random vibration section in this chapter, can be used to detect harmonic signals which are buried in random noise. For ideal white noise, the autocorrelation function is

$$R(\tau) = 2\pi S_0\, \delta(\tau) \qquad (10.11.3)$$

and, for band limited white noise,

$$R(\tau) = 2S_0[\sin(\omega_2\tau) - \sin(\omega_1\tau)]/\tau \qquad (10.11.4)$$

where S_0 = spectral density which could be expressed in $g^2/(rad/s)$
    $\delta(\tau)$ = the Dirac delta function

For a sinusoid $x(t) = X_0 \sin(\omega t)$, the autocorrelation function is

$$R(\tau) = \left(\frac{X_0^2}{2}\right) \cos(\omega\tau) \qquad (10.11.5)$$

where X_0 = amplitude of the sinusoid which could be expressed in g's. Consider a vibration measurement in which random noise appears dominant. A harmonic signal might be detected in the autocorrelation function, possibly indicating imbalance in some machine component.

Cepstrum Analysis

Cepstrum analysis was developed to aid in detection of "echos" in seismographic records (Bogert et al., 1963). It has also been applied to machine vibration problems, such as blade failure detection in turbines, and to room acoustics and impedance measurement. Cepstrum analysis can aid in detection of certain harmonic patterns in machine vibration spectra which might remain obscure in the time domain and the frequency domain. Cepstrum analysis can also be used to detect and separate families of sidebands in a spectrum, an aid to detecting faults in gearboxes.

The terminology of cepstrum analysis includes letter transpositions such as spectrum to cepstrum and frequency to quefrency. Some authors even transpose phase to saphe, filter to lifter, and analysis to alanysis. The cepstrum concept and other frequency analysis techniques are discussed in detail by Randall (1977).

The Power Cepstrum   Consider a time function $x(t)$ which has a Fourier transform

$$X(f) = \mathcal{F}\{x(t)\} \tag{10.11.6}$$

where $\mathcal{F}$ = the Fourier transform
t = time
f = frequency

The power spectrum is given by

$$W(f) = |X(f)|^2 \tag{10.11.7}$$

where $W(f)$ = spectral density. The power cepstrum is defined by "the power spectrum of the natural logarithm of the power spectrum":

$$C_P(\tau) = |\mathcal{F}\{\ln[W(f)]\}|^2 \tag{10.11.8}$$

where $C_P(\tau)$ = the power cepstrum
τ = the quefrency (s)

If an inverse Fourier transform is used for the second transform, or if the common logarithm is used, the results will differ by a scaling factor. Some authors suggest use of the amplitude spectrum instead of the power spectrum in the second transform.

The Complex Cepstrum   The complex cepstrum of a signal is a real-valued function obtained from the complex spectrum without loss of phase information. It is given by "the inverse Fourier transform of the natural logarithm of the Fourier transform of the signal." Let the Fourier transform of a time function be expressed in complex form as follows:

$$X(f) = A(f)e^{j\phi(f)} \tag{10.11.9}$$

where $A(f)$ = the amplitude of the Fourier transform
$\phi(f)$ = the phase, which must be made continuous (not the principal value)

Then

$$C_c(\tau) = \mathcal{F}^{-1}\{\ln A(f) + j\phi(f)\} \tag{10.11.10}$$

where $C_c(\tau)$ = the complex cepstrum
τ = time delays in the quefrency domain

Holographic Interferometry

Holographic interferometry allows vibration displacement measurements to be made over an entire surface, without contacting the vibrating body. Figure 10.11.1a shows

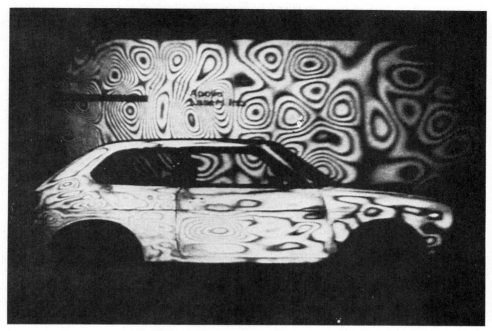

a

Pulsed Interferogram of an engine head.

b

Figure 10.11.1 Holograms. (*Source:* Apollo Lasers)

a hologram of an automobile body. Two exposures were made with a pulsed ruby laser system, during which the displacement of the vibrating surface changed. When the hologram is reconstructed, the images from the two exposures interfere with one another, producing an interference pattern that characterizes the displacement field of the deformed body. The actual displacement of a point can be calculated from the number of fringes on the interferogram. An interferogram of an engine head is shown in part (b) of the figure.

Holography is most sensitive to out-of-plane motion. Microscopic displacements may be measured; typical capabilities are from 0.5 to 100 μm. The range of strain measurement capability is typically from 1×10^{-6} to 500×10^{-6}, and the range of surface velocity measurement capability from 0.004 m/s to 100 m/s.

A laser synchronization system is available so that the laser is synchronized with the vibrating object, permitting a pair of laser pulses to be generated at any desired phase in the vibration cycle. This system requires that an accelerometer be mounted somewhere on the vibrating body.

Noise Control Implications

Product noise control may require both noise and vibration measurements. A measurement and redesign program for reduction of noise and vibration involves considerable engineering analysis and judgment. Some hints may be obtained from the flowchart for product noise reduction problems, Figure 10.11.2.

10.12 MODAL ANALYSIS

Modal analysis, combining dynamic testing and finite-element analysis (FEA) computer simulation, is an important design tool. It provides for system parameters to be determined experimentally, from prototype testing, and inserted into the FEA model. Proposed design alterations may be evaluated within the FEA model, and the results of this "what if" analysis incorporated into the design. For example, what if a stiffener is added at a particular location? A stiffener is incorporated into the FEA model and the results evaluated within the computer simulation. After evaluating a few different stiffener locations and stiffener designs, the best design is incorporated into the actual prototype and the results are verified by dynamic testing.

Figure 10.12.1a shows a modal analysis display on a unit with a dedicated structural dynamics keyboard. Part (b) of the figure shows first and second mode shapes based on tests and FEA simulations of a chain saw. The predicted effect of adding a stiffening link to a structure is shown in part (c). Note the change in mode shape and the increase in first-mode natural frequency.

Modal Analysis Procedure

The following steps may be part of a modal analysis:

   1. Setup
   (a) Select or construct a prototype structure.
   (b) Mount the structure if necessary. Obviously, a large structure or vehicle will

be tested in place. A smaller mass, for example, an engine block, might be hung from bungee cords (elastic shock cords).

(c) Mark test points on the structure.

(d) Select and calibrate the excitation and measurement system. An instrumented impact hammer or a shaker will usually be used to excite the structure. Measurements will ordinarily be made with accelerometers and a two-channel FFT analyzer. Data are processed in a computer. A microprocessor-based

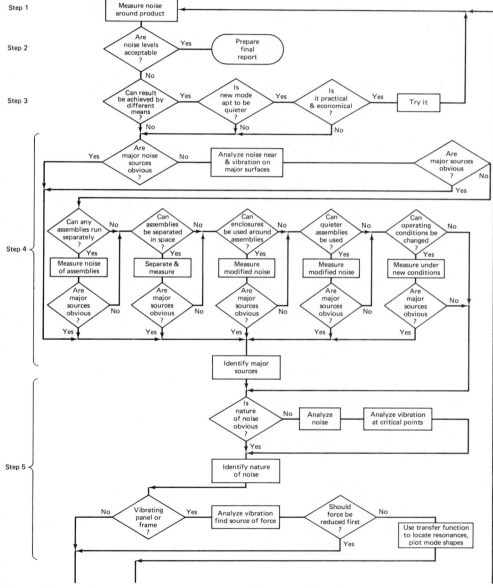

Figure 10.11.2 Simplified flowchart for product-noise reduction problems. (*Source:* GenRad)

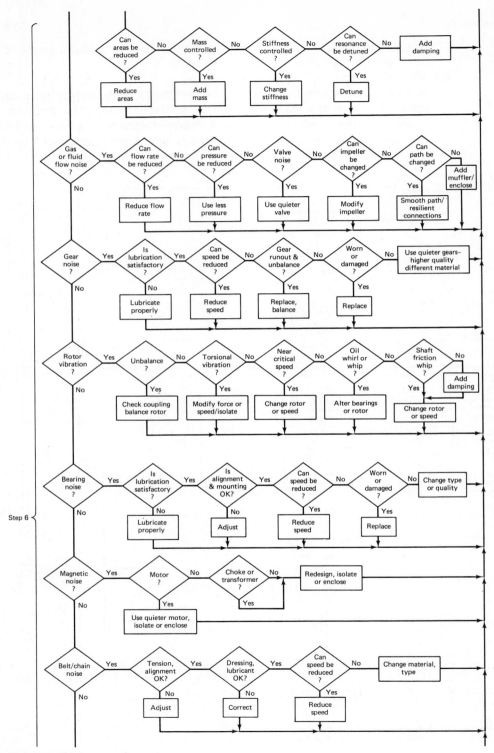

Figure 10.11.2 (*Continued*)

520

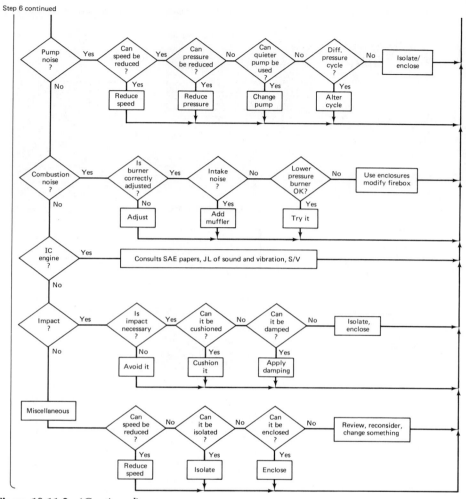

Figure 10.11.2 (*Continued*)

measurement system with a display screen and dedicated keyboard may be used. If a computer is not available at the test site, FFT-processed data may be stored, using a digital cassette recorder.

2. *Measurements*
(a) Make trial measurements. Select new test points if the results so indicate.
(b) Measure the frequency response function for all test points.
(c) Enter the frequency response data into the computer. The transfer of measurement data may be automatic.

3. *Parameter Estimation*
(a) Identify the modal frequencies.
(b) Curve-fit the measurements. Software is available for parameter estimation

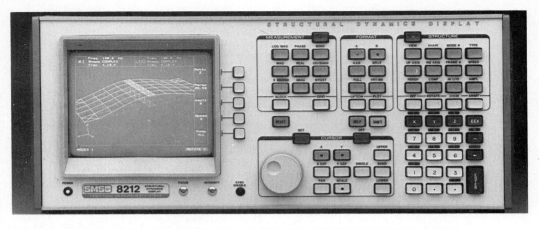

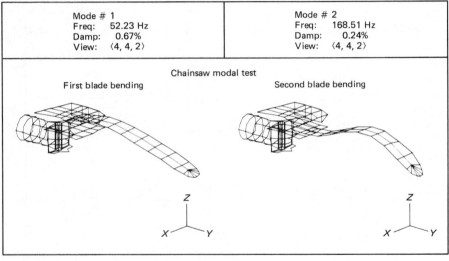

Mode # 1	Mode # 2
Freq: 52.23 Hz	Freq: 168.51 Hz
Damp: 0.67%	Damp: 0.24%
View: ⟨4, 4, 2⟩	View: ⟨4, 4, 2⟩

Chainsaw modal test

First blade bending

Second blade bending

(b)

Figure 10.12.1 Modal analysis. (*Source:* Structural Measurement Systems, Inc.)

by curve fitting. The operator uses cursors to identify the range of data to be considered and selects the type of fit. The degree of coupling indicates whether the resonance response of a system resembles a one- or multidegree-of-freedom system. Where measurement data indicate that the vibration modes are uncoupled or lightly coupled, one-degree-of-freedom curve fitting methods are used. Multidegree-of-freedom methods are used for closely spaced resonances and heavily coupled modes.

4. Defining a Geometric Model
(a) Define the structural coordinates and constraints for the geometric model.
(b) Select the output display form.

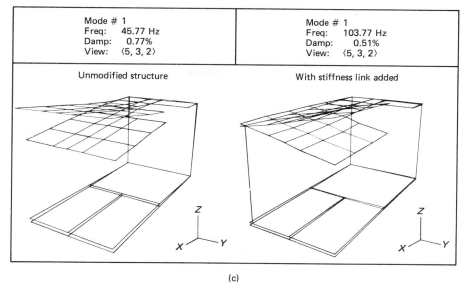

Mode # 1	Mode # 1
Freq: 45.77 Hz	Freq: 103.77 Hz
Damp: 0.77%	Damp: 0.51%
View: ⟨5, 3, 2⟩	View: ⟨5, 3, 2⟩
Unmodified structure	With stiffness link added

(c)

Figure 10.12.1 (*Continued*)

5. *Generation of Mode Shapes*

(a) Sort the modal fit data.

(b) Generate and display mode shapes. Rotate the views to determine the best viewing locations. The display may be stationary or animated.

(c) Print the required data. Make hard-copy plots of mode shapes from selected viewing locations. A mode shape plot of an engine block is shown in Figure 10.12.2, with the deformed shape shown superposed over the undeformed shape.

Excitation of the Structure

Structural vibration may be excited by several different methods including impact hammers and vibration exciters or shakers. One object of our investigation is usually the obtaining of a transfer function relating input excitation to output response. This makes it necessary to measure the input force function. An instrumented impact hammer used with a dual-channel FFT analyzer is often the most convenient method of obtaining a transfer function.

Impact Hammers

A typical impact hammer consists of a striking head, in which is mounted a quartz force sensor, an isolation amplifier, and a cable that extends through the handle and connects to a power unit. The striking head has a threaded hole to accept a variety of impact tips, which transfer impact force to the sensor. The hammer is designed to produce a nearly constant force over a broadband of excitation frequencies, exciting

| Mode #1
Freq: 446.75 Hz | Damp: 0.40%
View: ⟨−5, 3, 2⟩ |

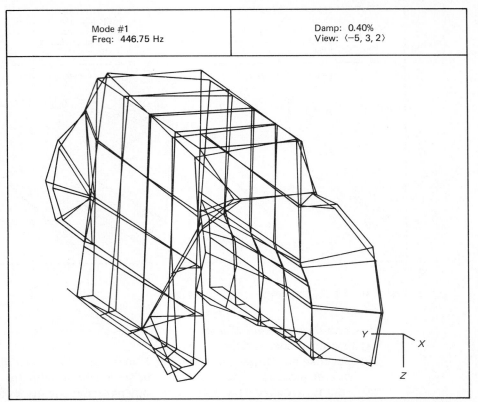

Figure 10.12.2 Mode shape plot of an engine block. (*Source:* Bruel & Kjaer Instruments, Inc.)

a structure in a large number of vibration modes. The impact pulse width and the frequency content of the force depend on the stiffness of the impact tip.

The usual application is as follows. An accelerometer is located at one point on a structure and the structure is struck at (near) that point and at other points of interest. The signal from the impact hammer sensor and from the accelerometer are simultaneously fed into the dual-channel FFT analyzer. The response spectrum (response/input versus frequency) is obtained. If the structure behaves as a linear system, then it is not important to strike each point with the same force, since we are interested only in the response/input ratio. Usually, a number of accelerometer locations are used, to obtain as much information about the structure as possible. The acceleration response may be integrated to obtain displacement or velocity response. Using velocity response, we may obtain the impedance

$$Z_{AB}(f) = \frac{F_A}{v_B} \qquad (10.12.1)$$

where Z_{AB} = impedance = the complex ratio of force at point A to velocity at
         point B

$$F = \text{force (lb or N)}$$
$$v = \text{velocity (in/s or m/s)}$$

Mobility is given by

$$M_{AB}(f) = \frac{v_A}{F_B} \tag{10.12.2}$$

where M_{AB} = mobility = the complex ratio of velocity at point A to force at point B.

The following articles provide additional information on modal analysis including practical applications in vibration and noise control:

> Allemang and Brown (1987): modal analysis from 1967 to 1987 with predictions for future developments.
>
> Halvorsen and Brown (1977): the impulse technique for structural frequency response testing.
>
> Ibrahim (1985): a comparison of modal identification techniques.
>
> Ramsey (1983): experimental troubleshooting of noise and vibration problems by modal analysis methods.
>
> Blakey et al. (1986): modal analysis and finite element analysis in the test laboratory.
>
> Schmidtberg and Pal (1986): the relative advantages of analytical modeling and modal testing.
>
> Dossing (1985): use of modal analysis to verify the dynamic design of a rail car prototype, including determination of sensitivity of the first bending mode to excitation.
>
> Talmadge and Banaszak (1985): a digital data acquisition system for modal testing.
>
> Stroud (1984): a modal survey of the Galileo spacecraft.
>
> Vold and Williams (1987): sinusoidal modal analysis.

10.13 VIBRATION QUALIFICATION TESTING

Most vibration testing falls into the following general classes:

1. Experimental modal analysis.
2. Shock, bump, and drop testing.
3. Frequency sweep tests.
4. Wideband random vibration tests.

These principles are often combined, as for example in sweep-random tests.

As observed above, experimental modal analysis produces the parameters necessary to form a finite-element simulation of a structure. Structural response to actual service loads can then be predicted from the simulation. This permits evaluation of aircraft and spacecraft structures without actually putting them into service.

Shock, bump, and drop tests are sometimes required as qualification for delicate and sensitive assemblies. These are sometimes destructive tests. In the case of sensitive mechanical and electronic equipment, the qualification requirement may be that the equipment perform satisfactorily during the test. In shock tests of instrumentation and control equipment, the equipment could be required to maintain calibration.

Vibration Exciters

Electrodynamic shakers are most widely used for frequency sweep and random vibration testing. They operate, typically, at frequencies ranging from about 10 Hz to 10 kHz. Hydraulic shakers are used for testing requiring large vibration amplitudes. See Figure 10.13.1. They operate in a frequency range from less than 1 Hz to about 1 kHz.

Hydraulic Shakers

A hydraulic shaker system accepts a low level drive signal, and processes it to drive a servo valve which controls the flow of high-pressure oil to an actuator. The actuator provides the mechanical force to drive the vibration table on which the test specimen is mounted. The system is mounted on a large reaction mass to provide inertia to work against. Dual-axis systems can either move vertically, driving a vibration table, or move horizontally, driving a slip table.

At the lower frequencies, displacement restrictions limit actuator motion, at intermediate frequencies, velocity limitations govern, and at higher frequencies, acceleration limitations govern. Actuators with strokes up to 12 in (6-in vibration amplitude) are available. Large-capacity systems produce sinusoidal forces up to 100,000 lb. However, equipment should be selected with the shortest stroke and the lowest load capacity consistent with test requirements in order to maximize performance at higher frequencies.

Electromagnetic Shakers

Electromagnetic shakers resemble a loudspeaker in their construction. They consist of a magnet producing a constant magnetic field, a coil mounted on the moving element, and a suspension system and constraints to limit the motion. The coil is fed an alternating current signal which causes it (and the vibration table and test specimen) to oscillate. Shaker force capacity is limited by the maximum current, the number of coil turns, shaker design, and cooling capacity. Most electromagnetic shakers are limited to 100 lb to a few hundred pounds of sinusoidal force amplitude and 1-in stroke or less (0.5-in vibration amplitude or less), although 30,000-lb force capacity electromagnetic shakers have been developed.

Frequency Sweep Testing

The frequency sweep test is normally run at constant vibration table amplitude and with slowly changing frequency. The power requirement for the test is related to the

Figure 10.13.1 Hydraulic shaker. (*Source:* Team Corp.)

parameters of the shaker and test specimen as well as to vibration table amplitude and frequency. An accelerometer is mounted on the vibration table to send a signal back to the shaker control panel so that constant amplitude is maintained. The control system in the feedback circuit should take frequency sweep speed and sharpness of resonance (*Q*-factor) into account. Some test specifications for sensitive equipment call for dwelling at resonant frequencies.

Random Vibration Testing

Wideband random testing is sometimes selected because it is a reasonable representation of the vibration exposure of actual systems. The random spectrum excites all resonances simultaneously, introducing possible interactions which could occur in actual service.

The effect of system loading may be significant. Consider a wideband random noise signal (voltage) produced by a white noise generator, and transmitted through a power amplifier to a shaker with a test specimen. Although the initial signal has a constant mean-square spectral density, the acceleration of the vibration table will vary with frequency due to the influence of resonances. This effect may be corrected by incorporating an equalizer into the system so the input signal is adjusted in each frequency band to produce a flat (constant) acceleration spectral density.

Comprehensive test programs may combine many types of excitation. Stroud (1984) describes a testing program to identify significant vibration modes of the Galileo spacecraft, and verify its analytical model. Vibration excitation methods included:

> Tuned multiexciter sinusoidal dwell
>
> Single-exciter sinusoidal sweeps
>
> Tuned multiexciter sinusoidal sweeps
>
> Chirps (fast sinusoidal sweeps)
>
> Single-exciter random vibration
>
> Multiexciter random vibration

10.14 MACHINERY CONDITION MONITORING AND VIBRATION SIGNATURE

Continuous monitoring of many variables, including temperature, pressure, and flow, is practiced at nuclear and fossil-fuel power plants to ensure safety and reliable service. Vibration is also a warning of machine deterioration and possible failure. Changes in vibration levels are likely to provide an earlier warning of machine failure than temperature monitoring.

Vibration Level Monitors

One type of vibration monitor continuously displays vibration level on an illuminated bar graph. The monitor has an alarm point and a machine shutdown point which may be set in terms of vibration velocity amplitude or vibration displacement amplitude. It monitors the signal from a vibration transducer mounted at a critical point such as a bearing housing. Proximity transducers may also be used.

Vibration Signature

The vibration spectrum obtained at a particular point on a given machine may be considered the vibration signature of the machine. Vibration spectra may be used for preventive-maintenance condition monitoring and as a product quality indicator. The spectra are acquired by mounting an accelerometer at a critical point on a machine, and processing the data with a vibration analyzer. The source of prominent resonances can usually be identified in a vibration spectrum. Sources of resonances include conditions such as rotor imbalance, electrically induced vibration, bearing noise, and misalignment.

Table 10.11.1 may be used to interpret the vibration spectrum. Once acceptable spectral levels are determined, a significant change from those levels is used as a warning of possible machine malfunction or failure. If the spectra are used for product quality assurance purposes, an instrumented test stand may be used for vibration measurements. Products that have vibration levels exceeding predetermined standards can be reworked or scrapped, with feedback to the production process to correct the manufacturing defect.

Figure 10.14.1a shows a three-dimensional vibration signature acquired from acceleration measurements on a machine, and processed with an FFT analyzer, computer, and special software. Three-dimensional vibration signatures are useful for time-varying processes. Part (b) of the figure is a waterfall plot made during machine runup.

10.15 BALANCING

Unbalanced rotating members are a major source of vibration and noise, and contribute to machine failure as well. Consider a single disk on a shaft. If the center of mass (center of gravity) of the disk does not lie on the centerline of the shaft, then the system will be in static imbalance. Significant static imbalance can be detected in a static test, simply by supporting the shaft between bearings and allowing it to seek its equilibrium position. When the shaft rotates, the system will generate an inertia force of

$$F_I = eM\omega^2 \qquad (10.15.1)$$

where F_I = inertia force (lb or N)
   e = eccentricity of the disk (in or m) measured from the shaft centerline to the disk center of mass, assuming the shaft is balanced
   $M = W/g$ = disk mass (lb-s^2/in or kg)
   W = disk weight (lb)
   $g = 386$ in/s^2 = the acceleration of gravity
   ω = angular velocity (rad/s)

Note that the speed-squared dependence causes imbalance to be a severe problem at high speeds. Some turbochargers, for example, rotate at 100,000 rpm, at which speed only slight imbalance can be tolerated.

As a second example, consider two unbalanced disks on a rotating shaft. In general, the system will be statically unbalanced and dynamically unbalanced. However, if the product of mass and eccentricity is the same for both disks, that is

$$e_1 M_1 = e_2 M_2$$

and the imbalances differ in orientation by 180°, then the system will be in static balance. It will be in static equilibrium at any position. But, the system will still be

(a)

Machine: RUNUP Z Testpoint: 1 Time: 09:36:47 Date: 22-JUL-1985
MAG −1

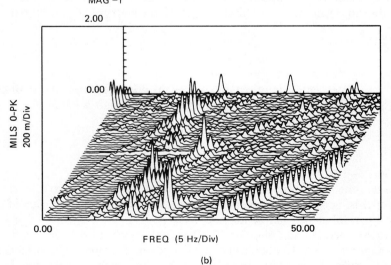

(b)

Figure 10.14.1 Three-dimensional vibration signature. (*Source:* Structural Measurement Systems, Inc.)

dynamically unbalanced. When it rotates, a shaking couple will cause vibration of the supporting structure.

Dynamic balancing involves selecting a point on the shaft centerline, and adding or removing mass in a plane perpendicular to the shaft through that point. Mass is added or removed until the inertia moments balance about the selected point. Dynamic balancing is completed by selecting a second point, and repeating the same process. It is assumed that the system is sufficiently rigid, so that elastic deflections do not contribute to imbalance.

The balancing procedure is aided by the use of balancing machines and instrumentation for measuring imbalance and vibration angle. Figure 10.15.1 shows a balancing machine and a crankshaft which is about to be balanced.

10.16 HUMAN RESPONSE TO VIBRATION

Exposure to high levels of vibration can cause damage to the lungs, joints, circulatory system, and other organs. Long-term exposure to whole-body vibration or to hand–arm vibration can cause disabling injury. Short-term vibration exposure can cause loss of tactile sensitivity, or loss of visual acuity, either of which may contribute to accidents.

It is difficult to obtain consistent, reliable data on human vibration response because the desired parameters vary with body position, and there is wide variation among individuals. Furthermore, some of the experiments that might produce the desired data would be hazardous to humans. The results of animal experiments are difficult to apply to humans since resonances of body parts measured in small animals may be several times higher than the corresponding resonances in humans. Thus, modeling of the human body is based on limited and approximate data. The following table lists the approximate properties of human soft tissue and compact bone.

Figure 10.15.1 Balancing machine and crankshaft. (*Source:* Bruel & Kjaer Instruments, Inc.)

PROPERTIES OF SOFT TISSUE AND BONE

	Soft tissue	Bone
Density (g/cm^3)	1.1	1.95
Elastic modulus (dyne/cm^2)	7.5×10^4	2.3×10^{11}
Volume compressibility (dyne/cm^2)	2.6×10^{10}	1.3×10^{11}
Speed of sound (m/s)	1500	3400

The human body appears to act as a single mass at frequencies below 2 Hz. Between about 2 and 100 Hz, the dynamic response of the human body may be modeled as a multidegree-of-freedom spring-mass-damper system which depends on whether the person is sitting or standing. Some vibrational modes are sufficiently uncoupled as to be treated as individual subsystem responses. At frequencies between 100 Hz and 100 kHz, the body may act as a distributed system.

Human Body Resonances

The following ranges of resonant frequencies have been reported in various studies.

HUMAN BODY VIBRATION RESPONSE

Component	Resonant frequency (Hz)
Whole body	4 to 6 and 10 to 14
Head–shoulder	20 to 30
Eyeball and intraocular structure	30 to 90
Lower arm	16 to 30
Spinal column (axial mode)	10 to 12
Hand grip	50 to 200
Thorax–abdomen system	3 to 4
Abdominal mass	4 to 8
Body below shoulder (subject standing)	3 to 6

Since vibration exposure conditions vary widely, the above values are only a rough guide as to what frequencies might pose problems. For example, high-amplitude vibration at frequencies between 20 and 90 Hz would be likely to cause head–shoulder resonances and eyeball and intraocular structure resonances, which could interfere with vision.

Hand–Arm Vibration

Hand–arm vibration is of particular interest because of occupational disease attributed to the use of hand-held power tools. Long-term users of chain saws, pneumatic and electric hammers, rock drills, and bolt guns are subject to large-amplitude vibration of the hand and arm. Some users are subject to diseases affecting the blood vessels, joints, bones, nerves, muscles, or connective tissue of the hand and arm. Short-term use of these tools frequently leads to a temporary loss of tactile sensitivity which may be a precursor to vibration syndrome (vibration-white-finger or Reynaud's disease), a disabling disease of the hand and fingers.

The National Institute of Occupational Safety and Health (NIOSH) has completed a comprehensive study which demonstrates the seriousness of vibration syndrome in workers. The following table summarizes the results of a study of workers exposed to hand–arm vibration from pneumatic chipping hammers and grinders at two foundaries and a shipyard (NIOSH, 1983).

PREVALENCE OF VIBRATION SYNDROME—PERCENT OF WORKERS
IN EACH GROUP WITH SYMPTOMS

| | | Exposed workers | |
Condition	Controls	Foundaries	Shipyard
Advanced vibration syndrome	0	47	19
Neurological symptoms alone	0	36	45
Total symptoms	0	83	65

NIOSH recommends that jobs be redesigned to minimize the use of vibrating handtools and that powered handtools be redesigned to minimize vibration. Where jobs cannot be redesigned to eliminate vibrating tools such as pneumatic hammers, gasoline chains saws, and other powered handtools, it is recommended that engineering controls, work practices, and administrative controls be employed to minimize exposure.

BIBLIOGRAPHY

Allemang, R. J., and D. L. Brown, "Modal analysis: twenty years back—twenty years ahead," *Sound and Vibration* **21**(1), 10–16, 1987.

Blakely, K., W. Ho, B. Lahey, B. Johnson, and P. Ibanez, "Finite element analysis in the test lab," *Sound and Vibration* **20**(4), 14–19, 1986.

Blakely, K., B. Lahey, and D. McLean, "Finite element analysis on your PC," *Sound and Vibration* **19**(1), 26–32, 1985.

Bogert, B., M. Healy, and J. Tukey, "The quefrency alanysis of time series for echos: cepstrum, pseudo-autocovariance, cross-cepstrum and saphe cracking," *Proceedings of the Symposium on Time Series Analysis,* pp. 209–243, M. Rosenblatt, Ed., Wiley, New York, 1963.

Broch, J. T., *Mechanical Vibration and Shock Measurements,* Bruel & Kjaer, Naerum, Denmark, 1972.

Brooks, P., "Solving vibration problems on a PC," *Sound and Vibration* **20**(11), 26–32, 1986.

Crandall, S. H., and W. D. Mark, *Random Vibration in Mechanical Systems,* Academic Press, New York, 1963.

Crede, C. E., *Shock and Vibration Concepts in Engineering Design,* Prentice-Hall, Englewood Cliffs, NJ, 1965.

Crede, C. E., and J. E. Ruzicka, "Theory of vibration isolation," *Shock and Vibration Handbook,* Vol. 2, 30-1 to 30-57, C. M. Harris and C. E. Crede, Eds., McGraw-Hill, New York, 1961.

Dossing, O., "Dynamic design verification of a rapid transit rail car," *Sound and Vibration* **19**(1), 16–21, 1985.

Grandin, H., *Fundamentals of the Finite Element Method,* Macmillan, New York, 1986.

Halvorsen, W. G., and D. L. Brown, "Impulse technique for structural frequency response testing," *Sound and Vibration* **11**(11), 8–21, 1977.

Huebner, K. H., and E. A. Thornton, *The Finite Element Method for Engineers,* 2nd ed., Wiley-Interscience, New York, 1982.

Hughes, T. J. R., *The Finite Element Method—Linear Static and Dynamic Finite Element Analysis,* Prentice-Hall, Englewood Cliffs, NJ, 1987.

Ibrahim, S. R., "Modal identification techniques assessment and comparison," *Sound and Vibration* **19**(8), 10–15, 1985.

Macduff, J. N., and J. R. Curreri, *Vibration Control,* McGraw-Hill, New York, 1958.

Meirovich, L., *Analytical Methods in Vibrations,* Macmillan, New York, 1967.

National Institute of Occupational Safety and Health, Current intelligence bulletin #38, DHSS (NIOSH) No. 83-10, March 29, 1983.

Ramsey, K. A., "Experimental modal analysis, structural modifications and FEM analysis on a desktop computer," *Sound and Vibration* **17**(2), 1983.

Randall, R. B., *Application of B&K Equipment to Frequency Analysis,* Bruel & Kjaer, Naerum, Denmark, 1977.

Rieger, N. F., "The relationship between finite element analysis and modal analysis," *Sound and Vibration* **20**(1), 16–31, 1986.

Robson, J. D., *Random Vibration,* Edinburgh Univ. Press/Elsevier, New York, 1964.

Schmidtberg, R., and T. Pal, "Solving vibration problems using modal analysis," *Sound and Vibration* **20**(3), 16–21, 1986.

Stroud, R. C., "The modal survey of the Galileo Spacecraft," *Sound and Vibration* **18**(4), 28–34, 1984.

Talmadge, R. D., and D. L. Banaszak, "Digital data acquisition system for modal testing," *Sound and Vibration* **19**(11), 12–16, 1985.

Vold, H., and R. Williams, "Multiphase-step-sine method for experimental modal analysis," *Sound and Vibration* **21**(6), 14–20, 1987.

Yang, T. Y., *Finite Element Structural Analysis,* Prentice-Hall, Englewood Cliffs, NJ, 1986.

PROBLEMS

10.1.1. A 40-lb weight is supported by a set of mounts with an effective spring rate of 110 lb/in and damping coefficient of 0.1 lb-s/in.
  (a) Find undamped natural frequency.
  (b) Determine the critical damping ratio.
  (c) Find the damped natural frequency.
  (d) Find displacement as a function of time if the mass is given an initial displacement of 0.5 in, and an initial velocity of 150 in/s.

10.1.2. A 65-lb weight is supported by a set of mounts with an effective spring rate of 80 lb/in and damping coefficient of 0.3 lb-s/in.
  (a) Find undamped natural frequency.
  (b) Determine the critical damping ratio.
  (c) Find the damped natural frequency.
  (d) Find displacement as a function of time if the mass is given an initial displacement of 1.0 in, and an initial velocity of 50 in/s.

10.1.3. A 20-kg mass is supported by a set of mounts with an effective spring rate of 7500 N/m and damping coefficient of 15 N·s/m.
  (a) Find undamped natural frequency.
  (b) Determine the critical damping ratio.
  (c) Find the damped natural frequency.
  (d) Find displacement as a function of time if the mass is given an initial displacement of 15 mm and an initial velocity of 5 m/s.

10.1.4. A 35-lb body is supported on mounts with an effective spring rate of 80 lb/in. The mass is struck to excite it into vibration. Measured vibration amplitude is 0.25 in at one instant, and 0.125 in three cycles later.
  (a) Find the undamped natural frequency.
  (b) Find the logarithmic decrement.
  (c) Find the damping coefficient.
  (d) Find the critical damping coefficient and the damping ratio.

10.1.5. A 16-kg body is supported on mounts with an effective spring rate of 1200 kg(force)/m. The mass is struck to excite it into vibration. Measured vibration amplitude is 5 mm at one instant, and 2 mm two cycles later.
  (a) Find the undamped natural frequency.
  (b) Find the logarithmic decrement.
  (c) Find the damping coefficient.
  (d) Find the critical damping coefficient and the damping ratio.

10.1.6. Plot the motion of the mass in Problem 10.1.4. Assume viscous damping.

10.1.7. Plot the motion of the mass in Problem 10.1.5. Assume viscous damping.

10.1.8. Plot the decay rate (amplitude ratio) in free vibration versus damping ratio
  (a) for two successive amplitudes
  (b) for amplitudes separated in time by 2, 5, 10, and 20 periods

10.2.1. A mass in a one-degree-of-freedom system is subject to a harmonic forcing function of amplitude A. Plot $X/(A/K)$ versus frequency ratio, where X = displacement amplitude and K = spring rate. Let frequency ratio range from zero to 3.
  (a) Let the damping ratio = 0.25.
  (b) Plot curves for damping ratio = 1/3, 2/3, and 1.0.

10.2.2. A mass in a one-degree-of-freedom system is subject to a harmonic forcing function of amplitude A. Plot $X/(A/K)$ on a logarithmic scale versus frequency ratio on a linear scale, where X = displacement amplitude and K = spring rate. Let frequency ratio range from zero to 3.
  (a) Let the damping ratio = 0.025.
  (b) Plot curves for damping ratio = 0.01, 0.05, 0.1, and 1.0.

10.2.3. Plot transmissibility versus frequency ratio for the range of frequency ratios between 0.8 and 1.2.
  (a) Let damping ratio = 0.2.
  (b) Let damping ratio = 0.4, 0.6, and 0.8.

10.2.4. Plot transmissibility versus frequency ratio for the range of frequency ratios between 0 and 2.
  (a) Let damping ratio = 0.2.
  (b) Let damping ratio = 0.4, 0.6, 0.8, and 1.0.

10.2.5. Find the frequency ratio at which maximum transmissibility occurs.

10.2.6. A spring-mass-damper system is acted on by a forcing function which is approximated by a square wave. Construct the Fourier expansion of the forcing function.

10.2.7. A single-cylinder engine has a balanced crankshaft. The total supported weight is 30 lb, and effective weights at the wristpin and crankpin are 3 and 1 lb, respectively. The length of the crank is 1.5 in and the connecting rod 4 in. Crankshaft speed is 1200 rpm (constant), the combined spring rate of the mounts is 2700 lb/in in the initial design, and the damping ratio 0.03.
   (a) Find the steady-state force amplitude transmitted to the supporting structure.
   (b) Give mounting specifications to reduce transmitted force to less than 400 lb at resonance, and less than 20 lb at operating speed.

10.2.8. A single-cylinder engine has a balanced crankshaft. The total supported weight is 25 lb, and effective weights at the wristpin and crankpin are 3 and 1 lb, respectively. The length of the crank is 1.5 in and the connecting rod 4 in. Crankshaft speed is 1800 rpm (constant), the combined spring rate of the mounts is 3000 lb/in in the initial design, and the damping ratio 0.05.
   (a) Find the steady-state force amplitude transmitted to the supporting structure.
   (b) Give mounting specifications to reduce transmitted force to less than 300 lb at resonance, and less than 30 lb at operating speed.

10.2.9. A one-degree-of-freedom system is mounted on a harmonically moving supporting structure. Plot the ratio of amplitude of the supported mass to amplitude of the supporting structure for frequency ratios from zero to three
   (a) for damping ratio = 0.5
   (b) for damping ratio = 0.6 to 1.0

10.3.1. A machine was originally mounted on four helical compression springs. The mounting system is changed to use eight springs, all in parallel, and each having only half the number of active coils as the original mounts. How is the natural frequency of the system changed?

10.3.2. A machine was originally mounted on four helical compression springs. The mounting system is changed to use six springs, all in parallel, and each having 1.5 times the mean coil diameter of the original mounts. Wire diameter and other parameters are unchanged. How is the natural frequency of the system changed?

10.3.3. Write an equation for the undamped natural frequency of a one-degree-of-freedom system in terms of static deflection of the mounting system, where static deflection is the compression of the mounts as they support the mass at rest.

10.3.4. Find the natural frequency of a 1-lb weight supported at the end of a 0.0625-in-thick by 0.5-in-wide by 6-in-long steel cantilever.

10.3.5. Find the natural frequency of a 2-kg mass supported at the end of a 2-mm-thick by 8-mm-wide by 100-mm-long steel cantilever.

10.3.6. A 4000-lb machine is to be supported by four equally loaded pneumatic mounts. The effective bellows cross section area is 20 in^2 and the air volume is 150 in^3. Find the system natural frequency.

10.3.7. A 2000-kg machine is to be supported by four equally loaded pneumatic mounts. The effective bellows cross section area is 0.02 m^2 and the air volume is 0.0025 m^3. Find the system natural frequency.

10.4.1. Write a computer program to find natural frequencies and mode shapes for a two-degree-of-freedom undamped system. Use English units.

10.4.2. Consider the two-degree-of-freedom system shown in Figure 10.4.1. Let $W_1 = 200$, $W_2 = 50$, $K_1 = 400$, $K_2 = 100$, and $K_3 = 0$, where weights are in pounds and spring rates in lb/in.

(a) Find the undamped natural frequencies of the system.

(b) Find the mode shapes.

10.4.3. Consider the two-degree-of-freedom system shown in Figure 10.4.1. Let $W_1 = 250$, $W_2 = 150$, $K_1 = 600$, $K_2 = 60$, and $K_3 = 300$, where weights are in pounds and spring rates in lb/in.

(a) Find the undamped natural frequencies of the system.

(b) Find the mode shapes.

10.4.4. Consider the two-degree-of-freedom system shown in Figure 10.4.1. Let $W_1 = 4$, $W_2 = 2.5$, $K_1 = 8$, $K_2 = 6$, and $K_3 = 1$, where weights are in pounds and spring rates in lb/in.

(a) Find the undamped natural frequencies of the system.

(b) Find the mode shapes.

10.4.5. Consider the two-degree-of-freedom system shown in Figure 10.4.1. Let $W_1 = W_2 = W$, and $K_1 = K_2 = K_3 = K$, where weights are in pounds and spring rates in lb/in.

(a) Find the undamped natural frequencies of the system in terms of K and W.

(b) Find the mode shapes.

10.4.6. Write a computer program to find natural frequencies and mode shapes for a two-degree-of-freedom undamped system. Use metric units.

10.4.7. Consider the two-degree-of-freedom system shown in Figure 10.4.1. Let $M_1 = 20$, $M_2 = 15$, $K_1 = 10^6$, $K_2 = 0.5 \times 10^6$, and $K_3 = 0$, where masses are in kilograms and spring rates in N/m.

(a) Find the undamped natural frequencies of the system.

(b) Find the mode shapes.

10.4.8. Find the low-frequency resonance for a double-panel partition made of two 15 kg/m² panels separated by an 0.1-m airspace.

10.4.9. Find the low-frequency resonance for two 3 lb/ft² panels separated by a 5.5-in airspace.

10.4.10. Estimate the lowest critical speed of a shaft with three masses of 20, 25, and 15 lb mounted between bearings if their static deflections are calculated to be 0.010, 0.025, and 0.015 in, respectively.

10.4.11. Estimate the critical speed of a shaft with four masses of 4, 3.5, 3.5, and 2 kg mounted between bearings if their calculated static deflections are 10, 20, 25, and 10 μm, respectively.

10.4.12. Derive equations 10.4.10 and 10.4.11.

10.5.1. Referring to Figure 10.5.1, let $J_{m1} = 0.5$, $J_{m2} = 0.2$, $K_{T1} = 200,000$, $K_{T2} = 50,000$, and $K_{T3} = 1000$, where mass moments of inertia are in kg·m² and torsional spring rates in N·m. Find the natural frequencies and mode shapes of the system.

10.6.1. A helical steel compression spring has 12 active coils of 0.125-in-diameter wire and a mean coil radius of 0.8 in. The shear modulus of steel is about 11.5×10^6 psi and the weight density about 0.28 lb/in³. Find the first three surging frequencies

(a) for the fixed-free case

(b) for the fixed-fixed case

10.6.2. A helical steel compression spring has 10 active coils of 0.25-in-diameter wire and a mean coil radius of 0.75 in. The shear modulus of steel is about 11.5×10^6 psi and the weight density about 0.283 lb/in³. Find the first three surging frequencies

(a) for the fixed-free case

(b) for the fixed-fixed case

10.6.3. Find the natural frequencies of a 0.125-in-thick by 0.25-in-wide by 15-in-long simply supported aluminum beam for vibration
   (a) about the cross section axis of least stiffness
   (b) about the other axis

10.6.4. Find the natural frequencies of a 0.125-in-thick by 0.25-in-wide by 15-in-long simply supported steel beam for vibration
   (a) about the cross section axis of least stiffness
   (b) about the other axis
   Use an elastic modulus of 30×10^6 psi and weight density of 0.283 lb/in^3.

10.6.5. Replace the equation for first natural frequency in Rayleigh's method by an integral form. Estimate the first natural frequency of a 0.125-in-thick by 0.25-in-wide by 15-in-long simply supported steel beam for vibration
   (a) about the cross section axis of least stiffness
   (b) about the other axis
   Use an elastic modulus of 30×10^6 psi and weight density of 0.283 lb/in^3. The static deflection of a simply supported beam is given by

$$y = w[L^3x - 2Lx^3 + x^4]/[24EI]$$

where w = weight per unit length, and L = length.

10.6.6. Repeat Problem 10.6.5 for an aluminum beam.

10.6.7. Derive the equation for natural frequencies of free vibration of a uniformly loaded cantilever beam.

10.8.1. An ideal white noise forcing function with a mean-square value of 5 N^2/Hz is applied to a 10-kg mass supported by mounts with a 10,000 N/m spring rate and damping ratio of 0.1. Find
   (a) the response spectrum
   (b) the mean-square response

10.8.2. An ideal white noise forcing function with a mean-square value of 0.5 lb^2/Hz is applied to a 20-lb mass supported by mounts with a 50 lb/in spring rate and damping ratio of 0.1. Find
   (a) the response spectrum
   (b) the mean-square response

10.8.3. The motion of a supporting structure is described by white noise with a mean-square acceleration of 0.1 g^2/Hz. The system consists of a 10-kg mass supported by mounts with a 10,000 N/m spring rate and damping ratio of 0.1. Find the response spectrum.

10.9.1. Find the natural frequency of a 7-lb mass mounted on a hardening spring with a spring rate $K = 0.5x^2$ opposing displacement, where x = displacement (in), and K = spring rate (lb/in).

10.9.2. Find the natural frequency of an 800-lb mass mounted on a hardening spring with a spring rate $K = 400$ lb/in for $|x| \le 1$ and 1000 lb/in for $|x| > 1$ opposing displacement, where x = displacement (in).

10.10.1. Find the displacement response of an undamped one-degree-of-freedom system after a half-sine impulse is applied to the mass. The impulse is described by $F(t) = A \sin(\omega t)$ for $0 \le t \le \pi/\omega$ and $F(t) = 0$ for $t > \pi/\omega$.

10.10.2. Find the displacement response of an undamped one-degree-of-freedom system after a single full-cycle sine impulse is applied to the mass. The impulse is described by $F(t) = A \sin(\omega t)$ for $0 \le t \le 2\pi/\omega$ and $F(t) = 0$ for $t > 2\pi/\omega$.

A-weighted sound level   The ear does not respond equally to all frequencies, but is less sensitive at low and high frequencies than it is at medium or speech range frequencies. Thus, to obtain a single number representing the sound level of a noise containing a wide range of frequencies in a manner representative of the ear's response, it is necessary to reduce the effects of the low and high frequencies with respect to the medium frequencies. The resultant sound level is said to be A-weighted, and the units are dBA. The A-weighted sound level is also called the noise level.

Absorption   Absorption is a property of materials that reduces the amount of sound energy reflected. Thus, the introduction of an "absorbent" into the surfaces of a room will reduce the sound pressure level in that room by virtue of the fact that sound energy striking the room surfaces will not be totally reflected. This is an entirely different process from that of transmission loss through a material, which determines how much sound gets into the room via the walls, ceiling, and floor. The effect of absorption merely reduces the resultant sound level in the room produced by energy that has already entered the room.

Absorption coefficient   A measure of sound-absorbing ability of a surface. This coefficient is defined as the fraction of incident sound energy absorbed or otherwise not reflected by the surface. The values of sound-absorption coefficient usually range from about 0.01 for smooth marble to almost 1.0 for long absorbing wedges such as are used in anechoic chambers.

Accelerometer (acceleration pickup)   An electroacoustic transducer that responds to the acceleration of the surface to which the transducer is attached, and delivers essentially equivalent electric waves.

* Based principally on definitions given by the U.S. Environmental Protection Agency.

Acoustics   (1) The science of sound, including the generation, transmission, and effects of sound waves, both audible and inaudible. (2) The physical qualities of a room or other enclosure (such as size, shape, amount of noise) that determine the audibility and perception of speech and music.

Aerodynamic monopoles, dipoles, and quadrupoles   Idealizations of noise due to gas flow. A monopole can be represented as a pulsating sphere, producing a spherical wave front. A dipole corresponds to two closely spaced out-of-phase monopoles, and a quadrupole to four closely spaced monopoles with adjacent monopoles out-of-phase.

Airborne sound   Sound that reaches the point of interest by propagation through air.

Analysis   The analysis of a noise generally refers to the examination of the composition of noise in its various frequency bands, such as octaves or third-octave bands.

Anechoic room   An anechoic room is one whose boundaries have been designed (with acoustically absorbent materials) to absorb nearly all the sound incident on its boundaries, thereby affording a test room essentially free from reflected sound.

Articulation index (AI)   A numerically calculated measure of the intelligibility of transmitted or processed speech. It takes into account the limitations of the transmission path and the background noise. The articulation index can range in magnitude between 0 and 1.0. If the AI is less than 0.1, speech intelligibility is generally low. If it is above 0.6, speech intelligibility is generally high.

Audiogram   A graph showing hearing loss as a function of frequency.

Audiometer   An instrument for measuring hearing sensitivity or hearing loss.

Aural   Of or pertaining to the ear or hearing.

Background noise   The total of all noise in a system or situation, independent of the presence of the desired signal. In acoustical measurements, the term "background noise" is also used with the same meaning as "residual noise."

Band   A segment of the frequency spectrum.

Band center frequency   The designated (geometric) mean frequency of a band of noise or other signal. For example, 1000 Hz is the band center frequency for the octave band that extends from 707 to 1414 Hz, or for the third-octave band that extends from 891 to 1123 Hz.

Boom carpet   The area on the ground underneath an aircraft flying at supersonic speeds which is hit by a sonic boom of specified magnitude.

Broadband noise   Noise components over a wide range of frequencies.

C-weighted sound level (dBC)   A quantity, in decibels, read from a standard sound level meter that is switched to the weighting network labeled "C". The C-weighting network weights the frequencies between 70 and 4000 Hz uniformly, but below and above these limits, frequencies are slightly discriminated against.

Coincidence effect   The coincidence effect occurs when the wavelength of the bending wave in a panel coincides with the length of an incident sound wave at the angle at which it strikes the panel. At any particular frequency, this effect can occur only if the wave in air is traveling at a particular angle with respect to the surface of the panel. Under this condition, a high degree of coupling is achieved between the bending wave in the panel and the sound in the air. When the coincidence effect occurs, the transmission loss for the panel is greatly reduced. See also critical frequency.

Community noise equivalent level   Community noise equivalent level (CNEL) is a scale that takes account of all the A-weighted acoustic energy received at a point, from all noise events causing noise levels above some prescribed value. Weighting factors are included that place greater importance upon noise events occurring during the evening hours (7:00 P.M. to 10:00 P.M.) and even greater importance upon noise events at night (10:00 P.M. to 6:00 A.M.).

Composite noise rating   Composite noise rating (CNR) is a scale that takes account of the totality of all aircraft operations at an airport in quantifying the total aircraft noise environment. It was the earliest method for evaluating compatible land use around airports. Basically, to calculate a CNR value, one begins with a measure of the maximum noise magnitude from each aircraft flyby and adds weighting factors that sum the cumulative effect of all flights.

Continuous sound spectrum   A continuous sound spectrum is composed of components that are continuously distributed over a frequency region.

Correlated sounds   Correlated sounds are pure-tone sound waves with precise time and frequency relationships. Most noise control situations involve uncorrelated sounds generated by sources that are essentially independent of one another.

Crest factor   The ratio of the instantaneous peak sound pressure to the root-mean-square sound pressure.

Critical damping   The degree of viscous damping (energy dissipation) in a structure just sufficient to prevent free oscillation. When disturbed, the mass in a critically damped or overdamped system returns toward the equilibrium position without oscillating about that position.

Critical frequency   The critical frequency is the lowest frequency at which the coincidence effect can occur. At this frequency, the coincidence angle is 90°, that is, the sound wave is traveling parallel to the surface of the panel. Below this frequency, the wavelength in air is greater than the bending wavelength in the panel.

Critical speed   The rotational speed of a shaft or other system corresponding to its natural frequency of vibration.

Damping   The dissipation of energy with time or distance. The term is generally applied to the attenuation of sound or vibration in a structure owing to the internal sound-dissipative properties of the structure or owing to the addition of sound-dissipative materials.

Day–night sound level   Equivalent sound level computed from A-weighted sound levels measured over a 24-hour period, with a 10-dBA penalty for sound contributions between 10 P.M. and 7 A.M.

Decibel The decibel (abbreviated "dB") is a measure, on a logarithmic scale, of the magnitude of a particular quantity (such as sound pressure level or sound power level) with respect to a standard reference value.

Degrees-of-freedom The number of independent coordinates needed to specify the motion of a vibrating system.

Diffuse sound field The presence of many reflected waves (echoes) in a room (or auditorium) having a very small amount of sound absorption, arising from repeated reflections of sound in various directions. In an ideal diffuse field, the sound pressure level, averaged over time, is everywhere the same and the flow of sound energy is equally probable in all directions.

Directivity index In a given direction from a sound source, the difference in decibels between (a) the sound pressure level produced by the source in that direction, and (b) the space-average sound pressure level of that source, measured at the same distance.

Directivity pattern The directivity pattern of a source of sound is the hypothetical surface in space over which the sound pressure levels produced by the source are constant. See also directivity index.

Dosimeter A special purpose integrating sound level meter carried by an industrial worker to measure accumulated noise exposure.

Effective perceived noise level (EPNL) A physical measure designed to estimate the effective "noisiness" of a single noise event, usually an aircraft flyover: it is derived from instantaneous perceived noise level (PNL) values by applying corrections for pure tones and for the duration of the noise.

Equivalent sound level (L_{eq}) The energy average sound level. Averaging time, commonly 1 hour, 24 hours, or one year should be indicated.

Exchange rate The increase in noise level (typically a 3- to 5-dBA increase) which results in a halving of allowable exposure time.

Far field Consider a sound source in free space. At a sufficient distance from the source, the sound pressure level obeys the inverse-square law (the sound pressure decreases 6 dB with each doubling of distance from the source). Also, the sound particle velocity is in phase with the sound pressure. This region is called the far field of the sound source. Regions closer to the source, where these two conditions do not hold, constitute the near field. In an enclosure, as opposed to free space, there can also sometimes be a far field region if there is not so much reflected sound that the near field and the reverberant field merge. See also reverberant field.

Fast Fourier transform (FFT) analyzer A digital frequency analyzer based on the fast Fourier transform algorithm. FFT analyzers convert data in the form of time series into information in the frequency domain.

Filter A device that transmits certain frequency components of the signal (sound or electrical) incident upon it, and rejects other frequency components of the incident signal.

Footprint (noise)   The shape and size of the geographical pattern of noise impact that aircraft make on the areas near an airport while landing or taking off.

Free field   A sound field in which the effects of obstacles or boundaries on sound propagated in that field are negligible.

Frequency   The number of times per second that the sine wave of sound repeats itself, or that the sine wave of a vibrating object repeats itself. Now expressed in Hertz (Hz), formerly in cycles per sound (cps).

Fundamental frequency   The lowest frequency component of a periodic function, sometimes called the first harmonic.

Harmonic   A sinusoidal (pure-tone) component whose frequency is a whole-number multiple of the fundamental frequency of the wave. If a component has a frequency twice that of the fundamental it is called the second harmonic.

Harmonic motion   Periodic motion which is symmetric about an equilibrium position and which can be represented by sine and cosine functions.

Hearing handicap   The disadvantage imposed by a hearing impairment sufficient to affect one's efficiency in the situation of everyday living.

Hearing loss   At a specified frequency, an amount, in decibels, by which the threshold of audibility for that ear exceeds a certain specified audiometric threshold, that is to say, the amount by which a person's hearing is worse than some selected norm. The norm may be the threshold established at some earlier time for that ear, or the average threshold for some large population, or the threshold selected by some standards body for audiometric measurements.

Hertz   Unit of measurement of frequency, numerically equal to cycles per second.

Impact   (1) An impact is a single collision of one mass in motion with a second mass that may be either in motion or at rest. (2) Impact is a word used to express the extent or severity of an environmental problem; for example, the number of persons exposed to a given noise environment.

Impulse noise   Sound with a rapid increase in sound pressure level such as produced by a punch press.

Infrasonic   Referring to sound frequencies below the audible range.

Integrating sound level meter   An instrument designed to measure energy average sound levels for periods up to several minutes or several hours.

Inverse-square law   The inverse-square law describes that acoustic situation where the mean-square pressure changes in inverse proportion to the square of the distance from the source.

Jet noise   Noise produced by the exhaust of a jet into its surrounding atmosphere. It is generally associated with the turbulence generated along the interface between the jet stream and the atmosphere.

L_{10} level   The sound level exceeded 10% of the time. Corresponds to peaks of noise in the time history of environmental noise in a particular setting.

L_{50} level   The sound level exceeded 50% of the time. Corresponds to the median average level of noise in a particular setting, over time.

L_{90} level   The sound level exceeded 90% of the time. Corresponds to the residual noise level.

Level   The value of a quantity in decibels. The level of an acoustical quantity (sound pressure or sound power), in decibels, is 10 times the logarithm (base 10) of the ratio of the quantity to a reference quantity of the same physical kind.

Line spectrum   The spectrum of a sound whose components occur at a number of discrete frequencies.

Live room   One characterized by an unusually small amount of sound absorption.

Loudness   The judgment of intensity of a sound by a human being. Loudness depends primarily upon the sound pressure of the stimulus. Over much of the loudness range it takes about a threefold increase in sound pressure (approximately 10 dB) to produce a doubling of loudness.

Mach number   The ratio of a speed of a moving element to the speed of sound in the surrounding medium.

Masking   The action of bringing one sound (audible when heard alone) to inaudibility or to unintelligibility by the introduction of another sound.

Masking noise   A noise that is intense enough to render inaudible or unintelligible another sound that is simultaneously present.

Mean free path   The average distance sound travels between successive reflections in a room.

Medium   A substance carrying a sound wave.

Microphone   An electroacoustic transducer that responds to sound waves and delivers essentially equivalent electric waves.

Modal analysis   Dynamic testing and finite-element analysis (FEA) computer simulation combined to determine the dynamic response of a structure.

Noise   Any sound that is undesirable because it interferes with speech and hearing, or is intense enough to damage hearing, or is otherwise annoying.

Noise criterion (NC) curves   Criteria used for rating the acceptability of continuous indoor noise levels, such as produced by air-handling systems.

Noise exposure forecast   Noise exposure forecast (NEF) is a scale that has been used by the federal government in land use planning guides for use in connection with airports. In the NEF scale, the basic measure of magnitude for individual noise events is the effective perceived noise level (EPNL), in units of EPNdB.

Nyquist frequency   A digital frequency analyzer samples a signal, forming a time series which is then represented in the frequency domain. In order to avoid erroneous interpretation (aliasing), the sampling rate should be at least twice the highest frequency component of the signal. One-half the sampling rate is called the Nyquist frequency. Thus, the presence of frequency components above the Nyquist frequency can cause aliasing.

Octave   An octave is the interval between two sounds having a basic frequency ratio of two. For example, there are 8 octaves on the keyboard of a standard piano.

Octave band   All of the components, in a sound spectrum, whose frequencies are between two sine wave components separated by an octave.

Octave-band sound pressure level   The integrated sound pressure level of only those sine wave components in a specified octave band, for a noise or sound having a wide spectrum.

Oscillation   The variation with time, alternately increasing and decreasing, (a) of some feature of an audible sound, such as the sound pressure, or (b) of some feature of a vibrating solid object, such as the displacement of its surface.

Peak sound pressure   The maximum instantaneous sound pressure (a) for a transient or impulsive sound of short duration, or (b) in a specified time interval for a sound of long duration.

Period   The duration of time it takes for a periodic waveform (like a sine wave) to repeat itself.

Pink noise   Noise where level decreases with increasing frequency to yield constant energy per octave of bandwidth.

Pistonphone   A sound level calibrator in which a pair of pistons produces a sound pressure proportional to the ratio of piston displacement to coupler cavity volume.

Pitch   A listener's perception of the frequency of a pure tone; the higher the frequency, the higher the pitch.

Plane wave   A wave whose wave fronts are perpendicular to the direction in which the wave is traveling.

Point source   An ideal nondirectional sound source obeying the inverse-square law.

Presbycusis   The decline in hearing acuity that occurs as a person grows older. Although the term presbycusis is intended to exclude hearing loss resulting from high levels of industrial noise, other noise typical of modern society may make important contributions.

Pure tone   A sound wave whose waveform is that of a sine wave.

Random incidence　If an object is in a diffuse sound field, the sound waves that comprise the sound field are said to strike the object from all angles of incidence at random.

Random noise　An oscillation (sound pressure or vibration) whose instantaneous magnitude and frequency are not specified for any given instant of time. It can be described in a statistical sense by probability distribution functions giving the fraction of the total time that the magnitude lies within a specified range.

Rate of decay　Rate of decay is the time rate at which the sound pressure level (or other stated characteristic, such as a vibration level) decreases at a given point and at a given time after the source is turned off. The commonly used unit is decibels per second.

Refraction　The bending of a sound wave from its original path, either because it is passing from one medium to another or because (in air) of a temperature or wind gradient in the medium.

Residual noise level　The term "residual noise" has been adopted to mean the noise that exists at a point as a result of the combination of many distant sources, individually indistinguishable.

Resonance　The relatively large amplitude of vibration produced when the frequency of some source of sound or vibration "matches" or synchronizes with the natural frequency of vibration of some object, component, or system.

Retrofit　The retroactive modification of an existing building or machine. In current usage, the most common application of the word "retrofit" is to the question of modification of existing jet aircraft engines for noise-abatement purposes.

Reverberant field　The region in a room where the reflected sound dominates, as opposed to the region close to the noise source where the direct sound dominates.

Reverberation　The persistence of sound in an enclosed space, as a result of multiple reflections, after the sound source has stopped.

Reverberation room　A room having a long reverberation time, especially designed to make the sound field inside it as diffuse (homogeneous) as possible. Also called a live room.

Reverberation time (T_{60})　The reverberation time of a room is the time taken for the sound intensity to decrease to one-millionth of its steady-state value when the source of sound energy is suddenly interrupted. The corresponding decrease in sound pressure level is 60 dB. It is a measure of the amount of acoustical absorption present inside the room.

Room constant　The room constant is equal to (a) the product of the average absorption coefficient of the room and the total internal area of the room, divided by (b) the quantity 1 minus the average absorption coefficient.

Root mean square (rms)　The root-mean-square value of a quantity that is varying as a function of time is obtained by squaring the function at each instant, obtaining the average of the squared values over the interval of interest, and taking the square root of this average. For a sine wave, multiply the rms value by the square root of 2 to get the peak value of the wave. The rms value, also called the effective value of the sound pressure, is the best measure of ordinary continuous sound, but the peak value is necessary for assessment of impulse noises.

Shell isolation rating (SIR)   A descriptor for rating the characteristics of buildings with regard to transportation noise.

Shielding   The attenuation of a sound by placing walls, buildings, or other barriers between a sound source and the receiver.

Sone   A unit of measurement for loudness.

Sonic boom   The pressure transient produced at an observing point by a vehicle that is moving past (or over) it faster than the speed of sound.

Sound insulation   (1) The use of structures and materials designed to reduce the transmission of sound from one room or area to another or from the exterior to the interior of a building. (2) The degree by which sound transmission is reduced by means of sound insulating structures and materials.

Sound level (noise level)   The weighted sound pressure level obtained by use of a sound level meter having a standard frequency filter for attenuating part of the sound spectrum.

Sound level meter   An instrument, comprising a microphone, an amplifier, an output meter, and frequency-weighting networks, which is used for the measurement of noise.

Sound power   The total amount of energy radiated into the atmospheric air per unit time by a source of sound.

Sound power level   The level of sound power expressed in terms of dB re 10^{-12} W.

Sound pressure   (1) The minute fluctuations in atmospheric pressure that accompany the passage of a sound wave; the pressure fluctuations on the tympanic membrane are transmitted to the inner ear and give rise to the sensation of audible sound. (2) For a steady sound, the value of the sound pressure averaged over a period of time. Sound pressure is usually measured in newtons per square meter (N/m^2) where $1 \ N/m^2 = 1$ Pa.

Sound pressure level   The root-mean-square value of the pressure fluctuations above and below atmospheric pressure due to a sound wave; expressed in decibels re a reference pressure (2×10^{-5} Pa).

Sound shadow   The acoustical equivalent of a light shadow. A sound shadow is often partial because of diffraction effects.

Sound transmission class (STC)   A single-figure rating system designed to give an estimate of the sound insulation properties of a partition or a rank ordering of a series of partitions. It is intended for use primarily when speech and office noise constitute the principal noise problem.

Sound transmission loss [transmission loss (TL)]   A measure of sound insulation provided by a structural configuration.

Spectrum   The description a sound resolved into components, each of different frequency.

Speech interference level (SIL)   A calculated quantity providing a guide to the interfering effect of a noise on reception of speech communication. The speech interference level is the arithmetic average of the octave-band sound pressure levels of the interfering noise in the most important part of the speech frequency range. The levels in the three octave-frequency bands centered at 500, 1000, and 2000 Hz are commonly averaged to determine the speech interference level.

Speed (propagation velocity) of sound in air   The speed of sound in air is about 344 m/s or 1128 ft/s at 70°F.

Spherical divergence   Spherical divergence is the condition of propagation of spherical waves that relates to the regular decrease in intensity of a spherical sound wave at progressively greater distances from the source. Under this condition the sound pressure level decreases 6 dB with each doubling of distance from the source.

Spherical wave   A sound wave in which the surfaces of constant phase are concentric spheres. A small (point) source radiating into an open space produces a free sound field of spherical waves.

Standing wave   A periodic sound wave having a fixed distribution in space, the result of interference of traveling sound waves of the same frequency and kind.

Steady-state sounds   Sounds whose average characteristics remain constant in time. An example of a steady-state sound is an air conditioning unit.

Structure-borne sound   Sound that reaches the point of interest, over at least part of its path, by vibration of a solid structure.

Tapping machine   A device that produces a standard impulsive noise by letting weights drop a fixed distance onto the floor. Used in tests measuring the isolation from impact noise provided by various floor–ceiling constructions.

Temporary threshold shift (TTS)   A temporary impairment of hearing capability as indicated by an increase in the threshold of audibility. By definition, the ear apparently recovers after a given period of time. Sufficient exposures to noise of sufficient intensity, from which the ear never completely recovers, will lead to a permanent threshold shift (PTS), which constitutes hearing loss.

Third-octave band   A frequency band whose cutoff frequencies have a ratio of 2 to the one-third power, which is approximately 1.26. The cutoff frequencies of 891 and 1112 Hz define the 1-kHz third-octave band.

Threshold of audibility (threshold of detectability)   The minimum sound pressure level at which a person can hear a specified sound for a specified fraction of trials.

Threshold shift   An increase in a hearing threshold level (i.e., hearing loss) at a given audiometric frequency.

Tone   A sound of given pitch. A pure tone has a sinusoidal waveform.

Transducer   A device capable of being actuated by waves from one or more transmission systems or media and supplying related waves to one or more other transmission systems or media. Examples are microphones, accelerometers, and loudspeakers.

Transmissibility   The frequency-dependent ratio of transmitted force amplitude to forcing function amplitude in a vibrating system.

Ultrasonic   Pertaining to sound frequencies above the audible sound spectrum (in general, higher than 20,000 Hz).

Vector sound intensity   The net rate of flow of acoustic energy. Vector sound intensity may be determined with a dual-microphone sound intensity probe and two-channel FFT analyzer system.

Vibration isolator   A resilient support for machinery and other equipment that might be a source of vibration, designed to reduce the amount of vibration transmitted to the building structure.

Waveform   A presentation of some feature of a sound wave, for example, the sound pressure, as a graph showing the moment-by-moment variation of sound pressure with time.

Wave front   An imaginary surface of a sound wave on its way through the atmosphere. At all points on the wave front, the wave is of equal amplitude and phase.

Wavelength   For a periodic wave (such as sound in air), the perpendicular distance between analogous points on any two successive waves.

White noise   Noise or vibration whose energy is uniform over a wide range of frequencies, being analogous in spectrum characteristics to white light. White noise has a "hissing" sound.

Window   Noise analysis is often based on a finite number of data samples used to represent a continuous process. The data or time window represents the time frame of the measurements. Various weightings are used to minimize the effects of discontinuities.

Windscreen   A porous microphone cover used to reduce the spurious signals caused by wind passing the microphone.

Partial Answers to Selected Problems

CHAPTER 1

1.1.2 (a) $f_n = 3.546$ Hz; (b) Period $= 0.282$ s

1.1.4 (a) $c = 202,500$ in/s; (b) Wavelength $= 450$ in; (c) $k = 0.55$ rad/m

1.2.2 Suggestion: Derivation may utilize equations 1.2.6 and 1.2.8.

1.3.2 $c = 342$ m/s, $k = 294$, wavelength $= 21$ mm

1.4.2

p_{rms} (Pa)	L_P (dB)
10^{-2}	54
10^{-1}	74
1	94

The plot is linear on semilog coordinates.

1.4.4 (a) 0.37 to 366; (b) 0.92 to 275; (c) 1.83 to 82

1.5.2 (a) $\phi_1 - \phi_2 = 1.885$ rad; (b) $p_{rms1} = 0.632$ Pa; (c) $L_P = 91.9$ dB

1.5.4 $L_P = L_{P1} + 10 \lg n$

1.5.6 (a) $p_{rms} = 0.3216$ Pa; (b) $f_{beat} = 35$ Hz; (c) $p = 0.283 \cos(785t) + 0.356 \cos(1005t)$

1.6.2 The program may be based on the following equation: $L_P = 10 \lg \sum_{i=1}^{n} 10^{Li/10}$

1.7.1 The program may be based on the following equation after each sound level is adjusted for A-weighting: $L_P = 10 \lg \sum_{i=1}^{n} 10^{Li/10}$

1.8.2 $L_{eq} = 85.2$

1.8.4 The sound levels during the first 45 minutes contribute less than 1/40,000th of the total energy, with the 100 dBA level contributing the rest.

1.8.6 $L_{eq} = 83.3$ dBA

1.9.2 L_{DN} = 63.3 dBA

1.10.2 Suggestion: Express p and **u** in complex form and use the form

$$\text{Re } z = [1/2][z + z^*]$$

1.11.2 Using zero dB for the threshold of hearing and 120 dB for the threshold of feeling, the ratio is 10^{12}.

1.12.2 The larger source contributes about 91% of the sound power.

CHAPTER 2

2.1.2 p_{rms} (6 m) = 1.4 Pa

2.1.4 I (2.5 m) = 1.29×10^{-4} w/m^2 A-weighted

2.1.6 $L(r)$ = 10 lg[20/r] + 80 dB

2.1.8 **(a)** L = 83.4 dBA; **(b)** L = 83.3 dBA

2.2.2 **(a)** Q_{max} = 6.31; **(b)** L_{max} = 68 dBA

2.3.2

Mode			Eigenfrequency
1	0	0	14.3
0	1	0	17.2
1	1	0	22.3

2.3.4 $f_E = [c/2][(n_x/A)^2 + (n_y/B)^2 + (n_z/C)^2]^{1/2}$. The n's can be incremented in three nested loops.

2.3.6

Mode			Eigenfrequency
1	0	1	18.7
0	1	0	22.5
1	1	0	29.2

2.3.6 The wavelength of the 3 3 2 mode is 7.88 ft.

2.4.1 In this case, source dimensions and background noise govern. The approximate region is defined by 1 m < r < 5 m.

2.5.2, 4, 6, and **8** Reverberation time:

Formula:	Sabine	Eyring	Millington-Sette
Problem			
2.5.2(a)	.96	.86	.70
2.5.2(b)	.81	.71	.58
2.5.4	5.85	5.75	5.69
2.5.6	.63	.55	.46
2.5.8	.76	.68	.55

2.5.10 α = 0.33

2.5.12 α = 0.76

2.6.2 A' = 20 dB

2.6.4 The flowchart is similar to figure 2.6.5 except that the slope is given by $f'(x_1) = df/dx$ evaluated at x_1.

2.6.6 The root of $F(x) = 0$ is 2.23.

2.6.8 The root of $F(x) = 0$ is 3.43.

2.7.2 A computer program was used to generate ratios. A few values include the following:

Level change	Ratio
0	1
1	.794
2	.631
3	.501
10	.1

2.7.4 The program includes input of source power and coordinates, printing of a grid, calculation of radius and sound intensity contribution of each source at each grid point, combining of contributions, and printing of sound levels at each grid point.

2.7.6 Suggestion: Use the program developed in Problem 2.7.4

CHAPTER 3

3.1.2 (a) $L = 71$ dB; (b) $L = 93$ dB

3.1.4 (a) Yes; (b) Not in general

3.2.2 (a) $L_{10} = 86$ dBA; $L_{50} = 84$ dBA; (b) $85 < L_{10} < 87$ dBA

3.5.1 and 2 A few of the values are as follows:

Difference (dB)	Background correction (dB)
3	−3
3.5	−2.6
4	−2.2
4.5	−1.9
12	−.3

3.5.4 The procedure depends on available equipment. A greater error may occur in the presence of time-varying background noise.

3.6.2 $L_{eq} = 10 \lg[(1/N) \sum 10^{Li/10}]$. The result may be expected to fall between L_{50} and L_{10}.

3.6.4 SEL $= 103$ dBA

3.7.1 If the dosimeter is programmed for a 90 dBA criterion level and 5 dBA exchange rate, 2 hrs at 100 dBA corresponds to 100% dose.

3.8.2 L (overall unweighted) $= 95$ dBA

3.8.4 $L_{pT} = 95$ dB

3.8.6 Results depend on engine and fan type. The engine at low speed is likely to produce prominent low frequency components. The fan may show significant high frequency components.

3.9.1 The suggested descriptor is day-night sound level.

3.10.2 A sampling interval of less than $1/16{,}000$ s should be used.

3.10.4 $T = 20$ s/band

3.10.6 e_{ms} = about 8%

3.12.2 A grid can be defined over imaginary surfaces enclosing the sources. Sound intensity can be measured by sweeping the probe over each grid element. Sound intensity at unsafe locations must be estimated on the basis of nearby measurements.

3.13.2 (a) $L_w = 59.8$ dB re 1 pW; (b) $L_w = 58.2$ dB re 1 pW

3.13.4 (a) $L = 87.8$ dB overall; (b) $I = 6.02 \times 10^{-4}$ W/m² A-weighted; (c) $L_w = 101.8$ dB re 1 pW unweighted; (d) $W = 0.015$ W A-weighted

3.13.6 $Q_{max} = 1.78$

3.13.8 $W = 3.8 \times 10^{-3}$ W at 1 kHz

CHAPTER 4

4.1.2 Some approximate ranges in octaves are as follows:

Frog	8
Human	10
Cricket	6
Bat	14

4.1.4 Values include the following:

Sound pressure level (dB)	Intensity (W/m²)	Sound pressure (Pa)	Loudness (Sones @ 1kHz)
0	10^{-12}	.00002	.0625
40	10^{-8}	.002	1
80	.0001	.2	16
120	1	20	256

4.4.2 Impairment = 2.1%

4.5.1 Impairment = 70% in left and 37% in right ear

4.7.2 $L_{NR} = 28.8$ dBA

4.8.2 (a) Noise dose = 194%; (b) TWA = 95 dBA

4.8.4 (a) Noise dose = 100%; (b) TWA = 90 dBA

4.9.2 Noise dose = 433%

4.9.4 Noise dose = 212%

4.9.6 $T_{daily} = 111 \times 10^6 \times 10^{-L/10}$ hours

4.9.8 (a) $L_{eq24} = 86.7$ dBA; (b) $L_{eq(yearly\ average)} = 85.1$ dBA; (c) 15.1 dBA

4.10.2 (a) NRR = 22; (b) 97.5 dBA; (c) 101 dBC

CHAPTER 5

5.1.2 (a) L_{eq} = 72.1 dBA; (b) L_{DN} = 72.2 dBA

5.1.4 (a) L_{eq} = 70 dBA; (b) L_{DN} = 70.5 dBA

5.1.6 T = 7.2 minutes

5.4.2 Articulation index = .520

5.4.4 (a) 4.5 m with normal male voice effort; (b) 2.5 m with normal female voice effort

5.4.6 (a) 4 m with normal male voice effort; (b) 2.3 m with normal female voice effort

5.5.2 Typical impact at this level: Keeps 46% of residents from going to sleep, or wakes 64%.

5.6.2 L_{DN} = 69 dBA

5.6.4 L_{DN} = 58 dBA

5.7.2 L_{eq} (workday) = 79 dBA; L_{eq24} = 74 dBA. The noise level at the property line exceeds the level identified for protection against outdoor activity interference and annoyance.

5.7.4 L_{eq} (workday) = 80 dBA; L_{eq24} = 75 dBA. The level identified for protection against outdoor activity interference and annoyance is exceeded.

5.8.2 The response depends on the community selected. The outline should include most of the elements of a community noise ordinance identified in section 5.8.

5.9.2 L (total) = 79 dBA

5.9.4 L (total) = 79.5 dBA

CHAPTER 6

6.2.2 TL = 13 dB at 1 kHz; TC = 0.050

6.2.4 $TL_{combined}$ = 16.5 dB at 500 Hz

6.2.6 $TL_{combined}$ = 29.7 dB at 500 Hz. The airspace is critical.

6.2.8 TL = 20 lg f − 21; TL_0 = 20 lg f − 16

6.2.10 TL = 20 lg f − 26

6.2.12 m_2/m_1 = 1.585

6.2.14 Transmission coefficient = 1.5×10^{-3}

6.2.16 f_N = 347.8$[m'_T h']^{-1/2}$

6.4.2 STC 41 is satisfied.

6.5.2 The wall corresponds to SIR 36.

6.6.2 L_{DN} (interior) = 42.7 dBA

6.6.4 L_{DN} (interior) = 56 dBA

6.6.6 L_{DN} (interior) = 53 dBA. The acceptable value for interior activity interference and annoyance is exceeded.

6.9.2 A 7-ft-long silencer with a 5000 fpm face velocity may be used. The required face area is 0.64 ft^2 or greater.

CHAPTER 7

7.1.2 **(a)** $p_{0max} = 973$ Pa A-weighted; **(b)** $L_{peak} = 148$

7.1.4 **(a)** $E_{ACC} = 2.82$ N · m; **(b)** $L_P = 145$ dB peak

7.1.6 **(a)** $E_{ACC} = 11.3$ N · m; **(b)** $L_P \approx 154$ dB peak

7.1.8 $\sigma_{RAD} = [1 - f^*/f]^{-1/2}$ where $\sigma_{RAD} \leq 5$

7.2.2 Efficiency $= 2.66 \times 10^{-3}\%$

7.2.4 **(a)** $n_4 = 412.5$ rpm; **(b)** 6.88 Hz (fundamental); **(c)** 330 and 220 Hz (fundamental); **(d)** Sidebands: 330 ± 15, 330 ± 11, 220 ± 11, and 220 ± 6.9 Hz

7.2.6 **(a)** $N_R = 56$ teeth; **(b)** balanced; **(c)** $n_c = 1052.6$ rpm CW; **(d)** $n_P = 2222.2$ rpm CC; **(e)** $n_{p^*} = -3278.4$; **(f)** Fundamental noise and vibration frequencies may include: 66.7, 17.5, 37 and 54.6 Hz; **(f)** $f_{(1)} = 982.5$ Hz

7.2.8 **(a)** $N_R = 57$; **(b)** balanced with equally spaced planets; **(c)** $n_c = 473.8$ rpm CC; **(d)** $n_p = 1026.7$ rpm CW; **(e)** Fundamental noise and vibration frequencies may include the following: 29.3, 7.9, 17.1 and 25 Hz.

7.2.10 **(a)** $f_{(1E)} = 30$ Hz for the driver and 20 Hz for the driven; **(b)** $f_{(1)} = 540$ Hz; **(c)** CR = 1.3; A contact ratio this low may result in noisy operation.

7.2.12 **(a)** $f_{(1E)} = 50$ Hz for the driver and 31.7 for the driven; **(b)** $f_{(1)} = 950$ Hz; **(c)** CR = 1.44

7.3.2 **(a)** $n_c = 461.5$ rpm; **(b)** $n_{B^*} = -2462$ rpm; **(c)** $f = 20$ Hz; **(d)** $f = 148$ Hz; **(e)** $f = 92$ Hz; **(f)** $f = 82$ Hz; **(g)** $f = 7.7$ Hz

7.3.4 **(a)** $n_c = 1579$ rpm; **(b)** $n_{B^*} = -9079$ rpm; **(c)** $f = 66.7$ Hz; **(d)** $f = 403.5$ Hz; **(e)** $f = 263$ Hz; **(f)** $f = 303$ Hz; **(g)** $f = 26.3$ Hz

7.3.6 **(a)** $N_2 = 24$ teeth; **(b)** 589.6 to 610.4 rpm; **(c)** 10 and 20 Hz; **(d)** 6 Hz; **(e)** 480 Hz

7.3.8 **(a)** $n_2 = 843.7$ to 856.4 rpm; **(b)** $f = 28.3$ rpm

7.4.2 $L_p = 118$ dB

7.4.4 $L_p \approx 134.6 + 40 \lg[1 - (1 + p'/p_a)^{-0.2857}]$

7.5.2 and 4 The plot may be based on equation 7.5.3. Contours closer than one typical source dimension or closer than one typical wavelength may be invalid.

7.6.2 The expansion chamber cross section area must be at least 19 in^2.

7.6.4 For $B/A = 100$, $TL_{max} \approx 34$ dB. Compare results with Figure 7.6.2 for B/A ratios between 10 and 40.

CHAPTER 8

8.1.2 The results are given for regulatory levels 83, 80, 78 and 75 respectively; **(a)** 79.6, 76.9, 74.8 and 71.8 dBA; **(b)** 80.5, 77.6, 75.4 and 72.3 dBA.

8.3.2 Suggestion: Write a computer program to numerically integrate equation 8.3.15, and use the result in equation 8.3.14.

8.3.4 $L_{eqH} = 71$ dBA

8.3.6 $L_{eqH} = 60$ dBA

8.4.2 $L_{eqH} = 65$ dBA

8.5.1 $L_{10} = 74$ dBA

8.6.2 L_{DN} = 73.5 dBA; L_{eq24} = 69 dBA
8.6.4 (a) L_{DN} = 81 dBA; (b) L_{eq24} = 78 dBA; (c) Worst hour L_{eq} = 82 dBA
8.7.1 Worst hour L_{eq} = 57 dBA

CHAPTER 9

9.1.2 (a) W_2/W_1 = .21; (b) $L_2 - L_1$ = −6.8 dB
9.1.4 (a) W_2/W_1 = 9.8; (b) $L_2 - L_1$ = 10 dB
9.2.2 (a) N = 75.7 noys; (b) PNL = 102.5 PNdB
9.3.2 (a) L_{DN} = 80.8 dBA; (b) L_{DN} is essentially unchanged by the background noise contribution.
9.4.1 (a) N = 75 noys; PNL = 102 PNdB; (b) CNR = 117; (c) L_{DN} = 82 (± about 3) dBA
9.4.2 Let F = 2. (a) NEF ≈ 43; (b) L_{DN} ≈ 82 dBA
9.4.4 The L_{DN} = 75 dBA contour is defined by A = 2308 and B = 15,540 ft.
9.4.6 The L_{DN} = 75 dBA contour is defined by A = 1120 and B = 3830 ft.

CHAPTER 10

10.1.2 (a) f_n = 3.5 Hz; (b) C_c = 7.3 lb·s/in; (c) f_d = 3.5 Hz
10.1.4 (a) f_n = 4.7 Hz; (b) Z = 0.23; (c) C = 0.2; (d) C_c = 5.4; r_d = 0.037
10.1.6 Suggestion: Use equation 10.1.3 and the values found in problem 10.1.4. Let t = 0 at the instant that x = 0.25 and v = 0.
10.1.8 Amplitude ratio $X_n/X_0 = e^{-nz}$ where $z = 2\pi r_d[1 - r_d^2]^{-1/2}$
10.2.2 $X/(A/K) = [(1 - r_f^2)^2 + (2r_d r_f)^2]^{-1/2}$
10.2.4 Use equation 10.2.5.
10.2.6 $A(i)$ = 0 for all i.

i	$B(i)$
1	1.273
3	0.424
5	0.255

$B(i)$ = 0 for i even.

10.2.8 Try softer springs. Let r_f = 5. Then K = 92. The result is as follows:

θ	F_{tr} (resonance)	F_{tr} (operating speed)
0	−224	−27.9
π	220	23.5

10.3.2 f_n (new)/f_n (old) = 0.667
10.3.4 f_n = 6.4 Hz
10.3.6 f_n = 1.5 Hz

10.4.2 **(a)** f_n = 3.45 and 5.66 Hz; **(b)** X_1/X_2 = 0.39 and $-.64$

10.4.4 **(a)** f_n = 3.5 and 7.0 Hz; **(b)** X_1/X_2 = 0.66 and -0.95

10.4.6 Suggestion: Use Equations 10.4.6, 7 and 8.

10.4.8 f_n = 69 Hz

10.4.10 The approximate critical speed is n_c = 1327 rpm.

10.4.12 Suggestion: Assume a steady-state solution in the form of a cosine function.

10.5.1 The natural frequencies are f_{n1} = 67.05 Hz and f_{n2} = 120.95 Hz. Normal mode shapes are ϕ_1/ϕ_2 = 0.31 and -1.29.

10.6.2 Surging frequencies are as follows:

n	$f(n)$
1	78 Hz
2	157
3	235
4	313

Odd values of n correspond to the fixed-free case; even values to the fixed-fixed case.

10.6.4 Frequencies of lateral vibration: **(a)** f_{n1} = 51 Hz; f_{n2} = 204 Hz; **(b)** f_{n1} = 102 Hz; f_{n2} = 408 Hz

10.6.6 Rayleigh's method: **(a)** 51 Hz; **(b)** 102 Hz

10.8.2 Response to white noise:

(a)

r_f	W_r
0	2×10^{-4}
0.5	3.5×10^{-4}
1.0	0.005

(b) Y' = 0.008

10.9.2 Nonlinear spring. f_n = 2.6 Hz for an amplitude of 1.5 in; f_n = 2.2 Hz for vibration amplitude $\leq$ 1 in.

10.10.2 Suggestion: Use the convolution integral. Note that $\sin u \cdot \sin v = [1/2][\cos(u - v) - \cos(u + v)]$

Index

ISBN 0-06-047155-7

90000

9 780060 471552